Arduino Measurements in Science

Advanced Techniques and Data Projects

Richard J. Smythe

Apress®

Arduino Measurements in Science: Advanced Techniques and Data Projects

Richard J. Smythe
Wainfleet, ON, Canada

ISBN-13 (pbk): 978-1-4842-6780-6   ISBN-13 (electronic): 978-1-4842-6781-3
https://doi.org/10.1007/978-1-4842-6781-3

Managing Director, Apress Media LLC: Welmoed Spahr
Acquisitions Editor: Natalie Pao
Development Editor: James Markham
Coordinating Editor: Jessica Vakili

Distributed to the book trade worldwide by Springer Science+Business Media New York, 1 NY Plaza, New York, NY 10014. Phone 1-800-SPRINGER, fax (201) 348-4505, e-mail orders-ny@springer-sbm.com, or visit www.springeronline.com. Apress Media, LLC is a California LLC and the sole member (owner) is Springer Science + Business Media Finance Inc (SSBM Finance Inc). SSBM Finance Inc is a **Delaware** corporation.

For information on translations, please e-mail booktranslations@springernature.com; for reprint, paperback, or audio rights, please e-mail bookpermissions@springernature.com.

Apress titles may be purchased in bulk for academic, corporate, or promotional use. eBook versions and licenses are also available for most titles. For more information, reference our Print and eBook Bulk Sales web page at http://www.apress.com/bulk-sales.

Any source code or other supplementary material referenced by the author in this book is available to readers on GitHub via the book's product page, located at www.apress.com/978-1-4842-6780-6. For more detailed information, please visit http://www.apress.com/source-code.

Printed on acid-free paper

Table of Contents

About the Author

Richard J. Smythe attended Brock University in Ontario and graduated with a four-year honors degree in chemistry with minors in mathematics and physics. He attended the University of Waterloo for a master's degree in analytical chemistry and computing science and a doctorate in analytical chemistry.

After a post-doctoral fellowship at the State University of New York at Buffalo in electro-analytical chemistry, Richard went into business in 1974 as Peninsula Chemical Analysis Ltd.

Richard is fluent in several computer languages and scripting codes. His professional career includes being a consulting analytical chemist, a civil forensic scientist at PCA Ltd., a full partner at Walters Forensic Engineering in Toronto, Ontario, and a senior scientist for Contrast Engineering in Halifax, Nova Scotia.

A large portion of Richard's professional career consists of devising methods for finding problem solutions that involve making fundamental measurements using equipment on hand or readily available off-the-shelf/out-of-the-box products.

About the Technical Reviewer

 **Roland Meisel** holds a Bachelor of Science in physics from the University of Windsor, a Bachelor of Education in physics and mathematics from Queen's University, and a Master of Science in physics from the University of Waterloo. He worked at Chalk River Nuclear Laboratories before entering the world of education. He spent 28 years teaching physics, mathematics, and computer science in the Ontario secondary school system. After retiring from teaching as the Head of Mathematics at Ridgeway Crystal Beach High School, he entered publishing, contributing to mathematics and physics texts from pre-algebra to calculus in various roles. He remains active in several organizations, including the Ontario Association of Physics Teachers, the Ontario Association of Mathematics Educators, the Canadian Owners and Pilots Association, and the Wainfleet Historical Society.

He has always had a strong interest in technology, mail-ordering his first personal computer, an Apple II with a 1 MHz CPU and 16 kB of memory, from California in 1979. He can be found piloting small airplanes, riding his bicycle or motorcycle, woodworking, and reading or playing the piano, among other instruments.

Acknowledgements

Acknowledgements begin with the author's late parents, Richard H. Smythe and Margaret M. Smythe (nee Earle), who emigrated from the remains of London England after the war with their small family of three and eventually raised four children in Canada. Our parents instilled in us the need to be educated as much as possible in order for each of us to be self-sufficient and independent. That independence has led to the comfortable retirement of the middle two, the youngest continuing in her chosen occupation for close to a decade past retirement, and the oldest still actively engaged in the business of chemical analysis consulting and the practice of civil forensic science.

Along the way, numerous individuals have served as an inspiration while teaching and mentoring this author, imparting knowledge, the art of rational thinking, tenacity, and in most cases valuable wisdom: From Merritton High School in St. Catharines Ontario, Mrs. E. Glyn-Jones, mathematics, Mr. J. A. Smith, principal, and Mr. E. Umbrico, physics. From Brock University in St. Catharines Ontario, Prof. E. A. Cherniak, Prof. R. H. Hiatt, Prof. F. Koffyberg, and Prof. J. M. Miller. From the University of Waterloo in Waterloo Ontario, Prof. G. Atkinson. From The State University of New York at Buffalo, Prof. S. Bruckenstein.

It may also be said that the seeds for the growth and development of this work began when as a parent the author made sure that both his daughters—Wendy and Christie—could read at a very early age and devised graphic teaching aids for them to learn and understand binary digital arithmetic.

Acknowledgements would not be complete without recognizing the person who has allowed me the time required to write, in spite of life's every day chaos in the country, my spouse Linda. She has suffered through many years of papers, notes, books, breadboards, wires, electronic components, and desktop experiments scattered everywhere in our home and when she wasn't looking, on the kitchen table! Thank You my love.

Although the author's career consists of solving essentially chemistry-based problems and writing reports explaining how the problem came into existence, how to correct its effects or avoid its recurrence, the author has never written a book. This work would not be possible without the help and guidance of editors at Apress—Ms. Natalie Pao, Ms. Jessica Vakili, and Mark Powers.

The Author's Preface to Arduino Measurements in Science

Arduino Measurements in Science introduces implementing the basic techniques that have been developed to engage in making experimental scientific measurements. I hope that this book can assist students—those new to or with limited backgrounds in electromechanical techniques or the physical sciences—to devise and conduct the experiments they need to further their research or education. I also hope that the book is useful where there are limited financial resources available to create and develop scientific programs based on experimental science.

Migrating or foraging animals and insects use daylight, near-infrared light, polarized light, celestial indicators, chemical traces in water, the earth's magnetic field, and other aids to navigate over the earth's surface in search of food or to return home to their breeding grounds.

Alphabetical classifications, such as astronomy, biology, chemistry, geology/ geography, mathematics, and physics through zoology, are human concepts and classifications entirely unknown to travelers of the animal world. There are parallels between the animal kingdom's classless usage of physiochemical parameters and current scientific investigations.

A significant amount of new scientific knowledge is being revealed by investigators educated in one classifiable discipline using the unfamiliar experimental techniques from another. Although written by an analytical chemist, this book is a compilation of basic introductory techniques applicable to any scientific discipline that requires the experimental measurements of basic physiochemical parameters.

I am an analytical chemist who has worked with vacuum tubes, transistors, integrated circuits, mainframe, minicomputers, microcomputers, and microcontrollers. Computing technology transitioned from BASIC, Fortran, variations of C then into iterations of the open source systems such as Python, Processing (the basis of the Arduino microcontroller *integrated development environment* (IDE) language), and Linux operating systems used in the Raspberry Pi. New and revised open source versions of languages, IDEs, and operating systems are available free of charge from the Internet.

This book could be considered virtually obsolete as it is being written, but as with the science and technology that it describes, it is a starting point in an ever-changing subject. For the researcher and practicing scientist, the fundamentals of science are relatively constant and reasonably well understood, so a great deal of caution must be used when deciding that a concept or technique is "obsolete."

The SCADA concept and its development significantly pre-date the PC. Some of the transistor and CMOS ICs and the 7400 series of integrated circuitry in heavy use today are from the 1970s. Chemical analysis and medical and physical measurement techniques taught and in use today date from the middle ages.

SCADA is the acronym for *supervisory control and data acquisition*. SCADA software allows a computer to supervise an electromechanical process by acquiring data from sensors monitoring the process being controlled. Many of the measurement techniques to be discussed can be considered as single element components that are not only a component of a SCADA system but may also be part of the developing technology being called the Internet of things (IoT).

HMI is the acronym for *human-machine interface*. The HMI can be an electronic device or construct that provides an interface between a computer, an experiment setup, and a human operator. (A graphical user interface (GUI) may serve as an HMI).

USB is the acronym for Universal Serial Bus, a written standard of specifications to which electromechanical hardware systems are expected to conform. The USB is a subsystem that lets a personal computer communicate with devices that are plugged into the universal serial bus. As this book was written, the USB was in its third iteration.

When a personal computer runs supervisory control and data acquisition software with a human-machine interface connected via the universal serial bus system, then investigative science experiments or other processes, experimental apparatus or equipment setups, either "in the field" miles away or "on the bench" next to the computer/workstation or laptop, can be monitored and controlled in real time.

Laptop, stand-alone desktop, cabled or wireless networked workstations together with internet connections now allow unprecedented flexibility in laboratory or "in-field" monitoring of investigative science experiments.

The options available to the experimenters for implementing SCADA systems can essentially be divided into three categories based upon the amount of development work required to achieve a fully functional system.

Complete, finished, working software systems that can measure and control virtually any electro-optical-mechanical system are available from manufacturers such as National Instruments and Foxboro. Commercially available fully functional, basic, software-only systems can be expected to cost in the range of several thousands of dollars.

I chose to develop this book on three lower-cost options for SCADA implementation on experiment setups.

A moderately cost implementation strategy involving the following resources was used to develop the exercises in this book. These resources should also be adequate for further experimental development of new applications.

- A PC with SCADA software. Numerous systems are available. DAQFactory Express and the base-level DAQFactory version from AzeoTech are both used in this book. DAQFactory's base-level software costs approximately $250 CDN.

  There are freeware versions of SCADA systems available for those who can adapt the software and may require extended flexibility. AzeoTech provides an excellent scaled-down but fully workable version of DAQFactory called Express with a fully functioning plotting facility with limited paging and scripting capabilities.

- A USB HMI. Many devices are available from many manufacturers, and the device chosen for this book is the model U12 from the LabJack Corporation. (U12 costs approximately $120. U3 was added later; it costs approximately $110 USD.)

  The LabJack devices are provided with software in the form of a working version of the DAQFactory program called Express. The LabJack software is excellent for its graphical display capabilities, and for many applications in investigative sciences is more than adequate.

  The DAQFactory Express is limited to ten lines of script code, five script sequences, and two display pages. The extensive capabilities of DAQFactory's commercial version may be required for some of the project exercises in this book. If the software is to be purchased, the reader should start with the most basic program available and add upgrades as required.

- The third option is the newest and lowest cost approach to implementing a SCADA system that consists of the Raspberry Pi (RPi), its Linux operating system, the Python programming language with its Matplotlib library, and the Tkinter graphical user interface.

  The Linux operating system, Python, and its modules are all open source projects and free for download from the Internet.

  The Raspberry Pi project has made available the Raspberry Pi single-board computer (SBC) that can be purchased from many large electronics supply houses such as Digi-Key or Newark Element 14, to name only two, for $35. The Raspberry Pi board requires an HDMI compatible TV or computer monitor, mouse, and keyboard to form a full function computing system. The Linux operating system software, the Python programming language, and its modules are open source software available for free downloading from the Internet.

  In addition to the virtually no-cost software, the Raspberry Pi board contains its own general-purpose input/output (GPIO) bus in addition to its USB input/output connection. It contains its own HMI requiring no additional circuitry or expense to interface to external electronics or experimental setups. The Raspberry Pi board is manufactured with an Ethernet connection and is thus network capable. Numerous libraries are available online and free of charge from the Raspberry Pi Foundation that can interface the RPi to sensors, robots, devices, and instruments resident in the real world.

In 2008, an open source project called Arduino made available a series of USB-connected microcontroller boards that allowed designers, artists, hobbyists, and non-electronics specialists to interface optical-electro-mechanical devices to a computer.

A basic Arduino Uno Rev 3 board can be purchased from any major electronics supply house for approximately $20. The software to program the microcontroller board is another open source project and is freeware that can be downloaded from the Internet. The Arduino board can be used with Windows or Linux-based operating systems. It is fully supported with an online forum, many tutorials, and an extensive range of example programs and applications. An Arduino can function as a smart interface for virtually any computing system.

Experiments using SCADA-type implementations can take the form of a complete commercially available package, useable as received with no required development time. A lesser cost system requiring a moderate amount of programming using the DAQFactory program and commercial HMI devices such as the LabJack series of interfaces is also possible. Finally an Arduino, or an assemblage of low-cost hardware and open source software freely available for download on the Internet can be used with added development time to form a working system.

In addition to the software and hardware required to implement the monitoring and controlling system, additional ancillary equipment may be required in the form of the following list.

- A solderless breadboard system, appropriate power sources such as battery or electronic regulated supplies, and access to various IC and passive electronic components are required.

- A multimeter is required for troubleshooting. A stand-alone oscilloscope or an oscilloscope program for a PC may be required for more advanced work.

I presumed that you are not entirely new to this technology and can work through any of the measurement procedures with the aid of reference texts, online tutorials, and component manufacturer's datasheets. If additional aid is required, academic course outlines with exercises can be located online to help you understand the base knowledge to implement a specific measurement technique. All science is empirical, and this book is no different than real-life scientific work.

You must progress from the simple to the more complicated facets of a measurement project, verifying and validating each intermediate step in any multiple-stage measurement process.

As the title states, this book deals with monitoring and measuring physical-chemical parameters with integrated circuitry and physical computational systems. Inexpensive off-the-shelf components are used to monitor and control experimental setups that can measure data in the form of basic physiochemical parameters in many classified sciences—in some cases, with astounding sensitivity, flexibility, accuracy, and precision.

Disclaimer

- 110-volt electricity can be lethal and will start fires.

- Soldering irons are hot enough to cause serious burns.

- This book is only for educational purposes and presents concepts demonstrated through experimental formats. These setups have not been tested for robustness and are not designed or intended for any form of implementation in field service.

  These concepts are the basis for education only. They are intended as being starting points for further R&D into instrumental methods of monitoring experimental scientific apparatus to gather data or make physical measurements.

- The concept for this book came to me in the mid-1960s. In the interim years, various portions were developed with the technology available.

  Although the formal assembly of this book began in 2008 using the integrated circuitry, physical computing, and Internet information resources available at that time, the document continued to develop as it was written using new integrated circuits, physical computing software, and online information sources. The continued availability of software or electromechanical hardware is never assured, and hence the practitioners of this or any science must learn the art of the "workaround."

Foreword for the Book's Exercises

Introduction

This work is not intended to be an introduction to data collection. Although motivated or enthusiastic investigators can plunge right in and try to pick up needed knowledge and skills on the fly, this guide is aimed at those who have at least some experience in working with electronic hardware and computer software. A basic familiarity with simple electronics and elementary programming in a structured language such as Python or C++ will shorten the time required to implement any of the measurement techniques presented.

The manufacturer's literature for most of the data collection hardware referred to in this guide provides guidance and elementary activities to familiarize a new user with its implementation. Online sources can also provide numerous practical applications using the hardware at hand.

This work is devoted to making experimental physio-chemical measurements with equipment assembled from readily available components and physical computing systems. This book offers written methodologies by which experimenters can make fundamental measurements with electronics, electro-optical, and simple mechanical systems. A series of experimental measurement procedures for the basic units of parameters such as temperature, distance, light intensity, sound frequency, relative humidity, and other fundamental measurements are described together with the methods for powering and controlling the experimental mechanisms.

The determinations or measurements of individual basic units of interest are unit operations that can be combined to measure or control more complex experimental investigations. The following techniques represent the unit operations that can be assembled in experiment setups to measure the fundamental parameters monitored in virtually any scientific discipline.

Project Management

The following is a suggested general procedure for developing a supervisory control and data acquisition/monitoring project.

1. In preparation for creating an experimental development project, whether for conducting one of the exercises in this book or for a new concept, you should review available up-to-date information. Collect published work relevant to your project if it adds to your depth of knowledge and helps you avoid unnecessary duplication of effort. Rough notes and drawings should be collected in a notebook (either on paper or in an electronic format).

2. Arrange the ideas into a logical sequence of development in a flow chart or process diagram. Common spreadsheet software and word processing programs contain flowcharting capabilities. In a flow chart, keep the main process flow downward in the middle of the sheet with forward branches to the left or right and the backward branches to the opposite side.

3. Revise the flow chart/process diagram until a final iteration is achieved.

4. Begin assembling the hardware/electronics and corresponding software from the project's simplest unit operations, debugging the individual modules and verifying operational status until the entire project functions as designed.

In all scientific reports, the documentation must be complete to the point at which any other researchers can duplicate the original experimental work and confirm the reported observations. Software code must be liberally commented for those attempting to duplicate the work being described and for the investigator to modify the code for more efficient operation or changes made to the electro-mechanical system under development.

To duplicate the work of another, clear definitions of units must exist. Caution is required in reading schematic diagrams and attempting to duplicate assembly. Discrete components and integrated circuitry are constantly decreasing in physical size or replaced with newer technology. The decrease in size means that identification markings on components are getting smaller also.

Resistor and capacitor markings may appear in several formats as combinations of numbers and letters, with the magnitude symbol sometimes replacing the decimal point. Surface mount technologies have a three-digit code in which the first two digits are the component value, and the third is the power of 10 of the value multiplier.

- Resistance is measured in units called ohms (Ω).

- A megohm ($M\Omega$) is 10^6 or 1,000,000 ohms; typical identifications may be, for example, 1.5M or 1M5.

- A kilohm ($k\Omega$) is 10^3 or 1,000 ohms; and typical identifications may be, for example, 1.2K or 1K2.

- R is 10^0 or 1 or 1 unit ohm; for example, 100 R or 100 since there is no decimal point to replace.

- A milliohm (m) is 1/1000 or 10^{-3} ohms; for example, 0.052 Ω is written as 52 mΩ.

Capacitor units in older works were mainly limited to microfarad and picofarad designations. Most current capacitor notation usage seems to adhere to the three main fractional designations listed next but has recently been expanded to include the farad to avoid using thousands and millions in the micro term when describing ultra and supercapacitor devices.

- Capacitance is measured in units called farads (F).

- A microfarad (μ) is one millionth (10^{-6}) of a farad.

- A nanofarad (nF) is one billionth (10^{-9}) of a farad.

- A picofarad (pF) is one micro micro farad or (10^{-12}) of a farad.

When selecting the components required to assemble an experimental setup, a certain amount of caution must be exercised to ensure that the finished construct is suitable for the desired measurement. A case in point can be found in the creation of something as simple as a linearly changing voltage value. Modern electronics technology presents two simple methods for the creation of a voltage ramp in which the value of a voltage varies linearly with time between a lower and upper voltage value. In a linear system, the electrical potential can be deemed to "ramp up" or "ramp-down."

If a 4-bit digital to analog converter is used, the values from 0 to 2^4 (0 to 15 or 16 digital values) can be created as incremental voltages. A 16 V signal applied to the digital to analog converter (DAC) can thus provide a series of discreet steps between the values of 0 V and 15 V in approximately 1 V increments. The one-volt steps may be adequate for positioning a robot or mirror in any one of 16 possible positions but may not be used in an electrochemical application.

In chemical reactions in which several metals are deposited from a solution at several different impressed non-integer voltage levels, it might be necessary to have a smooth voltage waveform whose voltage value continuously ramps between the desired levels. The smooth transition of continuously varying voltage values is an analog waveform. It must be generated by special methods, one of which uses a constant current source to charge a capacitor to produce a linear voltage change across the capacitor plates.

Although calculus demonstrates that by selecting a sufficiently large number of tiny steps, we can mimic an analog signal with a digital signal, a digital signal may not have the desired value for the application at hand. A continuously variable constant current–based capacitor charging methodology may be necessary. The selection of which variation technique to use for a problem depends on the voltage resolution needed and the availability of the required electronic components.

When working with electrical signals from a sensor or experimental apparatus, ensure that the output voltage level does not exceed the input voltage capability of the electronic components processing the signal. Most discrete integrated circuitry is limited to 5 V. Some op-amps operate at up to 18 V. Most surface mount technology operates at a nominal 3.3 V.

As with all scientific endeavors, a logical progression should be made from the simplest to the more complex. When developing software for a project, you should begin with the code required to connect the apparatus to the computing and display circuitry.

The simplest form of electrical signal transmission uses a series connection for both analog and digital signals.

Analog voltage signals are often connected directly to the input pins of integrated circuits that provide some form of signal processing. Digital signals are connected to pins that sense whether the signal is high or low. A large portion of sensor outputs are voltage based, but current sensing is also used in some sensor measurements.

Computational circuitry usually accesses external data through a serial port. The serial port is often a specific addressable location in the computer memory that accepts incoming digital data according to specific encoding, called a *protocol*. The protocol specifies the meaning of the high-to-low or low-to-high transitions that make up the digital signal for timing, data values, and signal processing control parameters. There are numerous scientific and industrial serial transmission protocols designed and optimized for specific applications.

Most of the exercises are confined to systems and breakout boards. The serial communication protocol is already embedded in the component firmware and is ready to use as received.

The measurement techniques use the DAQFactory scripting language, Python, and the variant of C used in Arduino programming. All three programming languages have reserved keywords that cannot be used as variable names. Follow the variable naming rule suggestions in the appropriate documentation for the language in use.

Create meaningful names by following traditional C styles such as MySignificantName, MySgnfcntNme, or My_Significant_Name. Do not use proper words, such as *temperature* or *Temperature*, or any other word that may be a proper word used within the Python, DAQFactory scripting, C, or C++ programming code. Scripts that contain proper words as variable names or channels for "clarity" by the author but fail to operate and produce baffling output suddenly perform flawlessly when the proper words are rekeyed with unique mixed uppercase and lowercase characters. Follow the proper formal methodology built into the software.

In the DAQFactory software, creating channels allows you to populate an intelligent listing of channels, variables, and constants to reduce error-prone typing. The primary step in all troubleshooting procedures involving written coded systems that do not work is to check all spelling. Names are case sensitive.

Keep detailed notes of what is being done, write down calculations, sketch schematics, and rough mechanical drawings. This is science, after all. The drawing conventions for mechanical systems and electronic circuits can be found in several reference works.[1] You are encouraged to follow these conventions.

As a measurement system is assembled from software control of the HMI to wiring of the circuitry on the breadboarding, test each segment of the process. Work neatly; lay out the wiring parallel to the lines and rows of pins on the breadboard socket. Cross

---

[1] 1) *Building Scientific Apparatus* 4th Ed., Cambridge University Press. *The Art of Electronics* 2nd Ed. Cambridge University Press. *Practical Electronics for Inventors* 3rd Ed. McGraw Hill.

wires at right angles and only bend small copper wires to right angles with your fingers to achieve a relatively large radius of curvature. Recall that copper, although ductile, "work hardens," so use new wire where possible or make sure that a wire is re-bent to a large radius and gentle curvatures, no more than a half dozen times.

A basic logical approach to activating an inoperative multicomponent measurement system is not always obvious. A unit operation testing philosophy can often make an apparently intractable problem manageable.

You should set up or configure the DAQFactory software to activate a channel. The channel can be assigned a hard-wired connection to or software configured to the appropriate input. When the sensor is activated, time-stamped data should appear in the channel table. The first step in our testing procedure is to verify the appearance of the time-stamped data in the DAQFactory program. If no data is streaming into the channel table, the source of the error must be in one of the three components of the system: the sensor, the DAQFactory configuration, or the transmission protocol.

Each component of the system must be examined, and its operation progressively validated from the basic power supply to the output signal. The output signal path must be followed, validated, and its conveyance to the next stage of the process confirmed. It is assumed that the entire process will work if all the component parts of the system work. Remember that this assumption is just that!

Isolation

A USB is essentially a communications standard and, as such, has a limited ability to supply power. The HMI used in this book is the LabJack, which draws its power from the computer's main supply. The LabJack can source up to 450 mA. It is good practice for an external power supply to power our experimental devices. In this book, we are working on a bench or desktop and with a self-contained power supply as encountered in any field or laboratory setup. Some setups draw more than a half amp, and some control line voltages and currents. Remote setup from SCADA software over networks or from laptops may not be able to supply current to the experimental equipment. In many situations, it is advisable to power sensors independently and controls the power through a "buffer" circuit consisting of a CD4050 CMOS IC chip. A CD4050 chip is a six-membered, voltage-sensitive, solid-state switch that turns low-current sensor power on and off. Remote control of higher currents with 5-volt (5 V) logic can be achieved with numerous devices and techniques, as described in several chapters.

An independent battery or highly regulated power supply is often required for measuring low-level analog signals. Investigators using the 5 V supply of the USB often find that the sensitivity of low-level analog signals is defined by the digital clock noise of the bus.

The systems being monitored and controlled in most real-world applications are self-powered and, in fact, may be linked to the computer and the SCADA software through a wireless link. When the USB is used for power, it is good practice not to load the computer power supply and hence draw only the minimum required current from the bus.

Some of the experimental measurement setups draw amps of current, and hence cannot be driven by the computer power supply, so some techniques must be self-powered. In some of the highly sensitive measurement techniques presented using the Arduino, USB noise limits the technique's sensitivity, and hence, battery power should be used. (USB 1 and 2 can supply 500 mA and USB 3 900 mA.)

Software Scripting

Every script written should be fully documented. The name of the sequence or code, the purpose of the sequence, and possibly the date the code was written should all be placed at the head of the actual code in accordance with the software language's naming and commenting conventions. The heading should outline what the code does, describe the algorithm, and define the variables used. Recall also that a variable must be declared in a scripted sequence, plus the sequence must be running for the variable to exist and be useable. DAQFactory has an autostart option for a sequence, which starts the sequence when the page is loaded. If necessary, the autostart option can automatically start a sequence that declares a set of variables for use in configuring a control screen or sequence.

The RPi and Arduino autostart their operating systems and defined software variables.

Integrated Circuitry and Surface Mount Technology (SMT)

Traditionally experimenters bought components for mounting on breadboards during testing and project development. The successful breadboard circuit could then be transformed into printed circuit boards with single- or double-sided etched patterns. The double-sided boards often used drilled holes to connect both sides of the board. However, as integrated circuits became significantly smaller, drawing less current, became faster, significantly more sensitive, and are now at the point at which many of these miniature ICs can neither be handled manually nor electrically connected to circuits by the average researcher.

Smaller IC size has given rise to smaller component areas and surface mount technology (SMT), which in turn has made circuit boards smaller, easier to manufacture, and less expensive. The decrease in physical size and the development of SMT has added a layer of complexity for experimenters. Using the advantages gained by physically decreasing the size of the integrated circuits requires adapters to convert SMT components into compatible breadboarding formats.

SMT can be used in development projects through printed circuit board adapters created from the datasheets by the IC manufacturer. Adapters, often called *breakout boards*, are available from several commercial suppliers. One of the more extensive selections is available from Proto-Advantage. In addition to a large collection of adapters, the company offers an assembly service and uses SMT techniques to mount an IC on your breakout board adapter.

SMT-to-breadboard transitions are affected by mounting a microchip on a small, printed, circuit adapter board that connects the IC to a series of header pins. The square or round header pins are then used with wire wrap or sockets to provide an electrical connection for power and I/O requirements between the IC and the experiment under development.

Many SMT components are available in several different mounting patterns that are usually defined and described in detailed drawings at the end of product datasheets. The following are some of the acronyms used in describing SMT devices.

SMT capacitors are specified by their four-digit size code for length and width in one-tenth of an inch (1210 is 0.12 long by 0.10 wide).

- CQFP: Ceramic multilayer QFP

- LCC: Leadless Chip Carrier (packages that are soldered directly onto circuit boards and have no leads)

- PLCC: Plastic Leaded Chip Carriers

- PQFP: Plastic Quad Flat Pack

- QFP: Quad Flat Package (a rectangular IC with leads on all four sides)

Resistors follow the convention of capacitors.

- SOIC: Small Outline Integrated Circuit (Often followed by the number of pins on the package and sometimes is even further abbreviated to SO-8, for example.)

- SOP: Small Outline Package (Has variations: Plastic Small Outline Package (PSOP), Thin Small Outline Package (TSOP), and Thin-Shrink Small Outline Package (TSSOP))

- TQFP: Thin QFP

More detailed dimensions are always found in a product's datasheet. They should be reviewed carefully before deciding upon a component and the breakout board required for a given prototype or project. SMT is a rapidly changing field, and new production methods make obsolescence a frequently encountered problem for investigators. However, equivalent, more powerful integrated circuits in newer and smaller packages are being brought to market virtually daily. You must research the literature for the present form of the circuitry required for a given prototype.

Prototyping breadboards, jumper wires or cables, and integrated circuits are usually the formats used to develop and test or "validate" a working measurement system. In several of the exercises and measurement techniques encountered in later portions of this book, you, the investigator/experimenter, will find that the use of a printed circuit board is required to enclose a working breadboard circuit in a shielded metal enclosure.

Prepared printed circuit boards, such as those depicted in Figure RE-1, are available for assembling circuitry into a fixed, secure, and compact format. The two boards to the extreme right are, in fact, the top and bottom of prototyping boards that mount directly onto the Arduino microprocessor boards to hold either test or permanently wired circuitry within the microcontroller footprint. All the I/O and power pins are carried through from the microcontroller board underneath to the circuit board above. These boards are often referred to as *shields* and are available from several manufacturers.

The etched universal boards displayed are available from electronics supply stores and online. The copper traces are 0.1 inch (2.45 mm) spacing that matches standard dual inline package pin spacing.

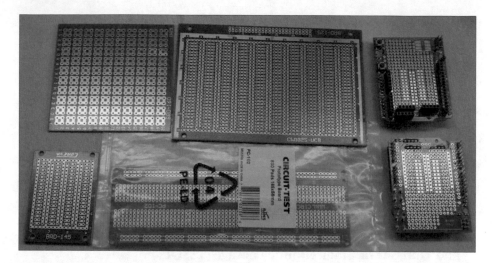

Figure RE-1. *Prototyping circuit boards*

Several circuit board manufacturers provide or can use standardized circuit board design software to manufacture a small or large number of complex circuit boards. Multiple layer boards and multi-leaded SMT components are best produced by commercial manufacturers. Occasionally, it may be necessary for you to design and make one or perhaps two simple printed circuit boards for a special application, such as the mounting of special components. Figure RE-2 depicts a pair of small 1 in × 1½ in (2.45 cm × 4 cm) hand-drawn PCBs to mount a pair of 30 kΩ thermistors and 33 kΩ resistors for the measurement of the hot and cold sides of a thermoelectric cooling plate test cell.

Figure RE-2. *Hand-drawn PCB for mounting and wiring Ssensors*

The basic board size and a simple outline of the copper traces required to hold the components essentially define the size of the board to be fabricated. In the PCB illustrated in Figure RE-2, a pair of boards were needed—one for each side of the test cell—and a single board with two copper tracings was etched, drilled, and then cut in half (see Figure 3-35 in Chapter 3) to facilitate handling during etching and drilling. A small, brass, round-head mounting screw holds the PCB wiring. Its mounted thermistor sensor is on the outside surface of the two chamber test cell walls.

A closer inspection of the copper tracing indicates coarseness in both the shape and surface texture of the etched copper patterns. The roughness reflects the hand drawing and the very thin nature of the marker pen ink forming the etchant "resist" layer. A more even and dense copper pattern can be obtained using either several coats of marker ink or using a much denser resist such as a colored, cosmetic nail polish. A colored nail polish is easier to see and can be removed after etching with nail polish remover or acetone.

There are several formulations available for etching the excess copper off the epoxy clad blank on which the desired pattern is drawn, and the author has had consistent success with ferric chloride solution.

Caution Concentrated ferric chloride solution is corrosive! Wear eye protection and chemical-proof gloves when working with any etchant that can remove copper from circuit boards.

Commercial ferric chloride etchant in 250 ml bottles is adequate for the small boards created, and one-half to one hour are the etch times at ambient room temperatures. The boards must be clean before etching as finger prints can resist if not removed. Soap and water or a mild kitchen abrasive such as Vim can to prepare the board before applying the resist and etching. A shallow pool of etchant in a plastic dish can be used as an etching tank. Warming the etchant solution decreases the time required to etch the board.

PCBs that require drilling should be center punched. The fine drills used to make holes compatible with electrical or electronic connections should be mounted in a high-speed rotary tool, such as a Dremel, for drilling the copper foil or epoxy board.

After preparing a PCB for a project test the continuity of all traces on the new board.

There are kits available that use a laser printer to create complex circuit boards from photos. A laser-printed pattern must be hot-pressed or ironed onto the board blank to transfer a plastic resist pattern and are a more complex process that you can use, if necessary.

Measuring Physical Parameters

Introduction

Various chemical and physical parameters can be monitored by measuring or observing changes in material properties. The laws or relationships honoring Ohm, Faraday, Ampere, Newton, Biot-Savard, Tesla, and Gauss, to name just a few, are used to determine material properties, forces, chemical quantities, and a host of other data needed for experimental work.

Researchers have divided nature into disciplines with names spanning the alphabet from astronomy to zoology. As our knowledge of mathematics, science, and technology advances, distinctions between the various scientific disciplines become less well defined. I used the chemical engineering concept of *unit operations* to select nine fundamental measurements and two experimental operations as the basis for assembling experimental investigations into scientific problems. For a host of reasons (budget, single-use only needs, or the limited capabilities of an "off the shelf" instrument), you may find it necessary to set up experiments using one or more of the measurement categories.

Precautions for High Sensitivity Measurements

The presentations on current, resistance, and voltage contain discussions on monitoring very low levels of these parameters using relatively inexpensive and readily available integrated circuitry or techniques. Current and voltage measuring systems using op-amps with high input impedances are presented. High resistance instruments are often referred to as *electrometers*. These devices require a great deal of care in assembly and application to produce accurate results.

The following list of generalized suggestions, precautions, and naturally occurring restrictions is an aid for creating experimental measurement systems that maximize the signal to noise ratio while implementing nominal measurement strategies.

- Temperature affects many physical parameters, and often experimental apparatus may need to be insulated, isolated, or even thermostated to minimize temperature variation.

- Use battery power whenever possible as the line or mains power, USB, and line-driven regulated supplies are very noisy for highly sensitive work.

- All wiring lines carrying signals of interest should be twisted and shielded against electromagnetic interference with grounded metal shielding.

- Physical contact between triboelectric active materials can cause static electrical accumulations that interfere with high sensitivity measurements. Static accumulations vary with room humidity, which can vary with the seasons in some climactic regions. Wood is an often-used construction material. When used in a measurement system, it may be influenced by static electrical accumulations, so it should be left unfinished.

- Prototype boards come in a variety of forms. In Figure 4-15, a small blue breadboard is affixed to the side of a colorimeter case. In Figure 4-19, a small whiteboard is seen. In Figures 4-28 and 4-29, a half-size prototyping board with power rails is identified as item 4.

A full-sized 6¼ in ×2 in (15.9 cm × 5.1 cm) board with 62 columns of ten tie-points and two power rails is seen in Figure 10-7. Each of these prototyping breadboards has internal rows of metal spring strips that accept the leads of components mounted on the board during prototype assemblies. However, the metal strips inside these boards can act as radio receivers and pick-up electromagnetic radiation. All the boards can test circuits, but for high-sensitivity measurements, hard-wired or printed circuit boards should be used and encased in grounded metal cases.

- As most scale expansions simultaneously increase both signal and noise, it is often necessary to use digital signal processing (DSP) to improve the signal to noise ratio. However, signal averaging improves the signal to noise ratio in proportion to the square root of the number of averages taken and slows the sensor response time.

- Resistors create electrical noise in proportion to the magnitude of the resistance and the resistor's temperature. Wire wound resistors are the least noisy, and metal films are less noisy than carbon-based devices.

- Visible, UV, and IR light can affect solid-state devices such as diodes and transistors.

- Air currents can cause variation in temperature, pressure, moisture, and dust movement or deposition.

- In trace quantity chemical analysis, greater sensitivity can be achieved by collecting and processing a bigger sample. When measuring very low values of variables such as resistance and capacitance if discrete units are available, consider measuring several units in series or parallel as required. For conductivity, a larger contact area can create a larger signal across the sample cell plates.

- Measurements can often be divided into two classifications: relative or absolute. Absolute measurements require calibration of the measurement apparatus with known or defined standards. Relative measurements monitor the change in the parameter being monitored. If an experiment can be devised to create a relative measurement rather than an absolute, a better measurement will result.

In addition to the chapters on conducting measurements of physical parameters, sections on data collection and energy provision have been added to aid you with using experimental devices or apparatus that are in a remote location from your lab.

CHAPTER 1

Capacitance and Charge

Separating two electrically conductive plates with an insulator forms a device called a *capacitor*. Among the many traditional uses of capacitors in experimental science are the storage or collection of charges, the blocking of DC currents, filtering electronic signals, and the generation of voltage ramps and timing. Devices with very large capacitance values are often used to store electrical power as memory backup or provide rapidly delivered high-voltage power pulses for "photo flash" bright-light production during photographic recordings.

Capacitance, measured in units called *farads* and represented by the symbol C, can be written in terms of charge Q and voltage V, written as

$$C = Q/V \text{ -- } (1)$$

The insulator is called a *dielectric*. The capacitance of the device is determined by several parameters: the chemical nature of the insulator dielectric ε_r, the permittivity of free space ε_0, the area of the capacitor plates, and the thickness of the dielectric or the distance between the plates.

$$C = \varepsilon_0 \times \varepsilon_r \times A / d \text{ farads -- } (2)$$

The permittivity of free space is 8.84×10^{-12} farads per meter. Capacitor value calculations made with air or a vacuum as a dielectric are usually quoted in microfarads (μF).

Dielectric constants tables are available in references such as the *CRC Handbook of Chemistry and Physics,* 84th edition by David Lide (CRC Press, 2003). Materials such as paper have dielectric constants that vary from 2.5 to 3.5. Glass has dielectric constants ranging from 3 to 10. Minerals such as mica range from 5 to 7. Wood ranges from 3 to 8. Metal oxide powders range from 6 to 20. Various types of dielectrics can create different types of capacitor devices. Chemical solutions are used in some capacitors to create large surface areas of high capacitance in relatively compact devices.

© Richard J. Smythe 2022
R. J. Smythe, *Arduino Measurements in Science,* https://doi.org/10.1007/978-1-4842-6781-3_1

No dielectric is a perfect insulator. Hence, all capacitors have a leakage current across the plates and a limitation on the voltage that the dielectric can withstand before breaking down under the voltage of the stored charge. Exceeding the safe working voltage of a capacitor may destroy the device through arcing between the plates.

If you consider Q the charge stored by the capacitor and recall that current is the rate of charge flow, you can write the following.

$$C = i \times t / V - \text{where } i \text{ is the current and } t \text{ is time} -- (3)$$

If the charging current is constant, as time progresses, the product of the current and time generates a linearly increasing Q on the capacitor. To keep C constant, the value of V, the voltage, must increase linearly. By charging or discharging the capacitor with a constant current, a linear voltage ramp is seen across the capacitor plates.

Capacitors charged from constant voltage sources display exponential voltage changes across the capacitor plates. Figure 1-1 shows that closing the switch allows the voltage source to force current through the resistance and into the capacitor. The DC current does not cross the insulating medium of the capacitor. Hence, the charge on the top plate becomes electron deficient or positively charged while the bottom becomes negative.

For circuits containing resistance and a capacitor in series, an important numerical value is the RC product, often specifically denoted by T (tau). The RC product of the circuit is known as the *time constant* and is the time required for the voltage on the capacitor to rise to approximately two-thirds of its final value or to decay to one-third of its initial value. These points are familiar to you as the charge and discharge voltage values in 555 timer, astable oscillation applications.

A capacitor is fully charged or discharged after the passage of five time constants.

Because electrons cannot move freely across the dielectric, the accumulating static charges on each plate require increasing energy to change values as the size of the charge grows. It can be shown that the rate of change displays an exponential form as the voltage on the capacitor approaches its final value, as seen in Figure 1-1.

Because of the inversion of the type of charge accumulating on one plate being mirrored in magnitude on the other, a varying electrical signal is inverted but passes through the capacitance.

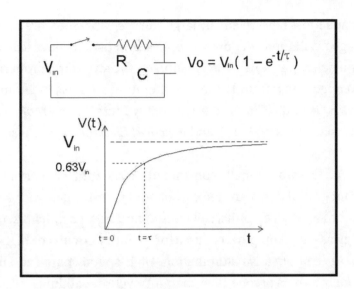

Figure 1-1. *Capacitor voltage vs. time with ז*

A circuit time constant ז is the product of the resistance in ohms and the capacitance in farads expressed as seconds.

$$ז = R \times C \text{ (sec.)} \text{-- (4)}$$

Tau represents a measurable point in the charging and discharging of capacitors. In a fully discharged capacitor, the voltage rises to $0.632V_{in}$ in ז seconds. Conversely, a fully charged capacitor discharges to $0.368V_{out}$ in ז seconds. In mathematical terms, establishing the relationship between the three measurable quantities enables the measurement of any one in terms of the remaining two.

A capacitor is an energy storage device in DC systems and constitutes frequency sensitive resistance in AC circuits. The basic unit of capacitance is the farad, which is the storage capacity able to hold a coulomb of charge at one volt. A coulomb of charge is equal to one ampere of current flowing for one second. A farad was at one time considered a large unit.

Capacitor storage capability depends on the plates' area, the nature of the dielectric material, and the distance between the plates. The construction materials used to make the capacitor determine its capabilities and deficiencies. If capacitors are used for timing in circuits, the dielectric should be selected for minimum charge leakage. Plastic film capacitors are best for low-leakage applications.

3

Electrolytic capacitors have relatively large storage capacities, are best for filtering or damping voltage oscillations in power supplies, and usually have leakage rates proportional to device capacitance. Information on the structure, properties, and best usage of various capacitors is found in several literature sources, including *Building Scientific Apparatus*, 4th Ed., (Cambridge University Press), *The Art of Electronics*, 2nd Ed. (Cambridge University Press), and *Practical Electronics for Inventors*, 3rd Ed., (McGraw Hill).

Although a farad was traditionally considered a large unit, capacitors are manufactured from granulated activated carbon and metallic gels with storage capacities measured in farads. Farad-sized units, called *ultra* and *super capacitors*, quickly store and release energy as a backup power source for memory circuits or high-discharge rate applications, such as camera flash illumination. High-speed charge and discharge rates, together with huge numbers of repetitive charging cycle capabilities, plus lightweight materials of construction for devices, offer numerous advantages for "super" capacitors over rechargeable batteries.

Capacitors are available in a wide range of charge storage abilities that roughly correspond to a device's physical size, as depicted in Figure 1-2.

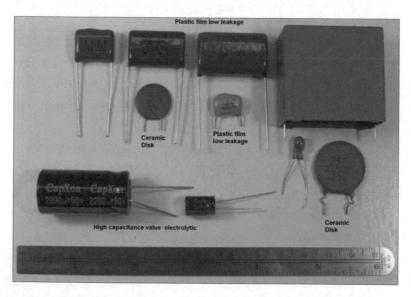

Figure 1-2. *Various capacitor types*

In summary, the three brown, rectangular devices in the upper left-hand field of view are metalized plastic film, low-leakage types of capacitors with capacitance values of 1.2 µF, 2.7 µF, and 5.6 µF, respectively. The large blue rectangular device in the upper right field of view is a low leakage 15 µF plastic film capacitor. The devices in the top row generally increase in dollar values from single to double digits in proportion to the increasing physical and capacitance value size.

The plastic film devices all have component leads of the same size and are non-polarized. The green drop-shaped and black cylindrical capacitors have electrical connection leads of different lengths and are polarized. The polarized devices have large capacitance values compared to the non-polarized ones because the green drop is a tantalum-based device of 22 µF while the large blue film capacitor is 15 µF. Polarized capacitors must be placed in service with the long lead at a more positive potential than the short lead. Polarized capacitors generally have much higher inter-plate leakage currents than non-polarized devices. The small black cylinder is a 1 µF 400 V unit, while the large cylinder is a 2200 µF 50 V device.

Ceramic disk capacitors are relatively inexpensive, stable units with metal oxide dielectrics generally rated in microfarad and picofarad ranges. An oxide dielectric can be produced in a small package, withstands higher voltages, and remains at a constant capacitance value with changing temperatures, voltages, and signal frequency.

A span of several orders of magnitude in capacitance range is not easily evaluated with a single measuring technique. Hence, several methods are examined for the determination of device capacitance values.

A substantial number of electronic circuits use capacitors in series with a resistance to form a circuit characteristic called the *time constant*. A time constant, often symbolized by τ, is the product of the capacitance and resistance expressed in seconds that are often used to adjust an electronic circuit's performance characteristics.

Figure 1-3 is an expanded nomograph depicting the theoretical relationship between the resistance-capacitance time constant value and the output oscillating frequency of an astable configured 555 timer IC chip.

In the astable configuration, the timer IC outputs a square wave with a frequency defined by the RC time constant in its timing component network. If a well-defined resistance value is used in the time constant network with a capacitance device as the second time-constant component, the value of the output signal's frequency is proportional to the capacitance.

When an IC device such as a 555 timer is to be used as a transducer to convert capacitor values into square waves of variable frequency for measurement, you should attempt to keep the range of frequencies measured within a readout device's capabilities. For a graphical screen display of the actual charging or discharging process generated by the code of Listing 1-1, a relatively low rate of data collection and display is required because of the large software overhead required for plotter displays.

If a numerical value output display is used, the frequency data can be collected by faster hardware counters, such as those available with the LabJack and Arduino devices that can stream the real-time data to a numerical counter display.

The higher frequencies generally encountered in radio frequency work and are best visualized with oscilloscope type displays.

This capacitor measurement/monitoring exercise is divided into four sections. Three sections use the graphical user interface in DAQFactory to display capacitance as a rotating analog gauge–type meter, a digital VOM type numerical readout, or a continuous display strip chart recording.

Splitting the measurement and display of capacitance values into these arbitrary divisions is created by the limitations of the recording and display systems to accommodate the large dynamic range available in capacitance devices.

The fourth capacitance measurement technique uses an Arduino microcontroller and its serial port readout as an autoranging capacitance meter in the microfarad to picofarad range. Two programs are available to use the microcontroller as a higher-resolution continuous-capacitance measuring meter.

The primary continuous display program in Listing 1-2 requires virtually no wiring. It uses stray input capacitance calibration and Arduino microcontroller board's internal "pull-up" input resistance to generate a stream of reasonably accurate capacitance values of a device under test (DUT).

The secondary continuous readout program, requiring some external components and wiring for accurate and continuous measurement of a capacitance DUT, is presented in Chapter 10.

The secondary program uses accurately measured time periods and known resistance values to determine capacitance values for the DUT. Significant timing accuracy is achieved using internal, microcontroller chip comparators, crystal-based timers, and operating system interrupt sequences to achieve accurate and reproducible time values.

Using a microcontroller such as the Arduino to measure a DUT's capacitance has the advantage of permitting the experimenter to build into the measurement system some digital signal processing such as a moving average to improve the system's signal to noise ratio.

There are numerous exercises in online forums that demonstrate common uses for a capacitive phenomenon in the assembly of a touchpad for activating an LED with an Arduino microcontroller.

Charges in a capacitor are determined using basic formulas describing the capacitance and voltage relationship. Non-capacitive static charges are discussed in Chapter 8.

Capacitor Characteristics

Capacitors are available in various charge storage sizes and dielectric properties. Capacitor properties are largely determined by the dielectric materials that fill the space between a device's conducting plates. Typically, high charge storage capacity devices have larger leakage currents that render these devices unsuitable for timing applications.

Leakage Currents

In theory, a capacitor is an electric charge storage device. With a highly polarizable insulating dielectric between its conducting plates, the device can store more energy or be made smaller for a given storage capacity. However, when charged, the voltage across the plates causes a current to flow through the dielectric, causing the capacitor to eventually discharge. The leakage current in the capacitor is largely determined by the chemical composition of the dielectric.

Electrolytic capacitors use an insulating layer of metal oxide as the device's dielectric. Aluminum and tantalum oxides form thin films with high dielectric constants, but the electrolytic devices also exhibit higher leakage currents.

Leakage currents are measured with the transimpedance amplifier (TIA) based current electrometer described in Figure 2-2 in Chapter 2. The TIA configuration is also applied to leakage current measurement described in Figure 7-4 in Chapter 7. Only low or line voltage–compatible capacitors are examined because high-voltage and high-current systems are beyond the introductory nature of this book.

The op-amp TIA electrometers' high input impedance can measure very low levels of current flow. The capacitor leakage current can be measured directly from the stable battery excitation voltage of the measurement circuit.

Care must be taken when measuring very small leakage currents in a discharged capacitor. The measurement can only be taken when the device has reached a steady-state equilibrium at the full battery-supplied test voltage.

Measurements of very small currents require special techniques and instrumentation, as explained in Chapter 2.

Typical leakage currents measured on various capacitors are shown in Table 2-4 in Chapter 2.

Leakage currents are sometimes considered detrimental to capacitor timing applications. In a timing circuit, leakage should be minimal to ensure reproducibility in timing operations. Capacitors using plastic films as dielectrics such as polyethylene, Mylar (polyethylene terephthalate film), and polystyrene have minimal leakage currents because of the high resistance or low conductivity of the plastic film dielectric. Most plastic films cannot store a significant charge, however. This non-polarizable nature of their molecular structure limits the capacitance values fabricated in reasonably sized devices. The large blue block seen in the upper-right corner of Figure 1-2 is a 15 µF polystyrene capacitor.

Leakage currents in capacitors used in filtering out the ripple in rectified AC power are orders of magnitude less than the current smoothed by the capacitor and have virtually no effect on the smoothing operation.

Ceramic capacitors are relatively lower leakage devices and are usually available in fractional µF and nF values.

Experiment A: Continuous Display of Lower Capacitance Values (< 10 µF)

Circuit: A Simple 555 Timer-Based Capacitance Meter

In most applications, a 555 timer generates a rectangular wave output of a fixed or varying duty cycle. A varying duty cycle can be obtained by substituting a variable resistance or potentiometer for one of the two fixed value resistors used in the astable mode of operation. If the two charging resistor values are fixed in a ten to one ratio then the output signal is an approximately 50% duty cycle square wave whose frequency f is determined solely by the value of the capacitor.

$$f = 1.44 / (Ra + 2Rb) * C -- (5)$$
$$C = 1.44 / (Ra + 2Rb) * f -- (6)$$

A capacitance value can be determined by measuring the frequency or counting the square wave pulses produced in a second.

An astable oscillator assembled from a traditional bipolar transistor 555 timer integrated circuit is limited to oscillation frequencies in the low hundreds or thousands of kilocycles. Timer ICs fabricated from CMOS technologies can oscillate in the megacycle range. The maximum frequency output of three common devices is listed in Table 1-1.

Table 1-1. *555 Timer High-Frequency Limits*

Manufacturer	Device Number	Maximum Oscillating Frequency
Intersil	IMC7555	1 MHz
Texas Instruments	TLC555	2 MHz
TI (National)	LMC555	3 MHz

Figure 1-3 is similar to Figure 1-4 in the IMC 7555 datasheets from Intersil, depicting the timer output frequency for various timing network RC component combinations. The plots for the various combinations of the two timing resistors indicate that if $(R_a + 2R_b)$ is 1 kΩ, by measuring the oscillator output frequency between 1/10 Hz and 3 MHz, the capacitance values between 1 pf and 10 mF (10,000 µF or 1/1000 F) should be measurable. The measurements should be made from the linear portions of the capacitance frequency data that follow the preceding formulas, which are reproducible and predictable. Low capacitance values below 100 pf may require a separate calibration with a 1 MΩ resistor network to ensure reasonable accuracy.

Resistor sums of 1 kΩ, 10 kΩ, 100 kΩ, and 1 MΩ should cover the range of capacitors encountered in regular circuitry. (Note: Some of the 555 variations will not oscillate with less than 1 kΩ in the RC network.)

Since a 10:1 resistance ratio is desired to keep the output reasonably symmetrical, you may write $(R_a + 2R_b) = 1K = (R_b/10 + 2R_b)$ and solve for R_b as 500 Ω, making R_a 50 Ω. For practical implementation standard sizes of, 47 Ω and 470 Ω or 56 Ω and 560 Ω could be used but since less than a kilohm in total resistance must be tested with the type of 555 timer selected for use.

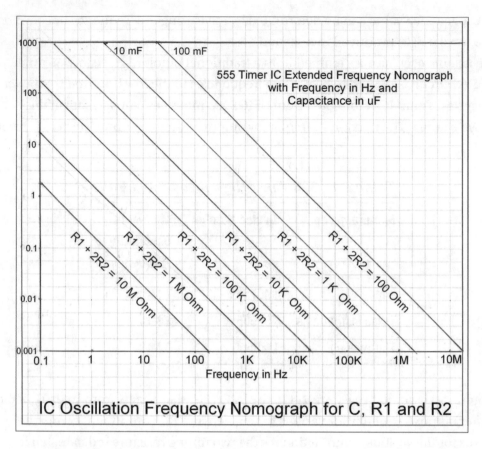

Figure 1-3. *Graphic 14 from the Intersil datasheets*

The plots in Figure 1-3 form a somewhat intuitive concept in which small capacitors that charge very quickly are associated with high oscillator frequencies. Large current-restricting resistors with large capacitances that charge slowly are associated with lower oscillation frequencies.

A review of the counter documentation for the LabJack indicates the counter registers a single event when it detects a falling edge followed by a rising edge. Each cycle of the rectangular output wave has one falling edge/rising edge pair. If the resistors' values are accurately known, the capacitor values can be calculated from the frequency measured.

Circuit Schematic

The timer circuit shown in Figure 1-4 can be powered from 5 V drawn from the LabJack supply. Resistance values are not shown in the schematic, as different sizes are used for different measurement ranges, as tabulated in Table 1-2. (Recall that the symbol for capacitance units is F for farads; µF or 10^{-6} F for microfarads; nF or 10^{-9} F for nanofarads; and pF or 10^{-12} F for picofarads).

Table 1-2 is a guideline for design. Any components can be used with the ranges listed. Recall that care must be given to the low-frequency counting capability of the counter and the increasing power dissipation required for low timing resistance values.

Table 1-2. *RC Constant Ranges for 555 Timer Oscillator Frequencies*

Capacitor Value Range	Resistor Values (Ohms) R1-R2	555 Frequency
1 mF to 10 µF	0.1 kΩ to 1 kΩ	< 6.86 Hz
10 µF to 0.01 µF	1 kΩ to 10 kΩ	6.86 Hz to 6860 Hz
10 nF to 1000 pF	10 kΩ to 100 kΩ	686 Hz to 6860 Hz
1000 pF to 10 pF	100 kΩ to 1 MΩ	686 Hz to 686K Hz

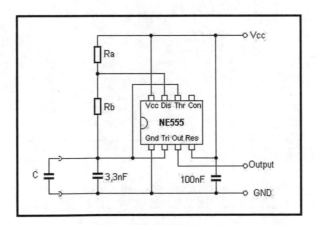

Figure 1-4. *555 IC capacitance measurement circuit*

Software

Initially, a two-dimensional graph and two-variable value components from DAQFactory developed the capacitance measurement screen. In conjunction with the 555 timer circuit in Figure 1-4, the LabJack counter determined the output frequency monitored in DAQFactory with the counter channel labeled FreqCnt.

The formula in the Y-Expression box in Figure 1-5 was used in both the graphical and variable value displays to convert from frequency to the capacitor's measured value. The numerical display of "Counts/sec:" or the frequency and capacitor values were used during development for debugging.

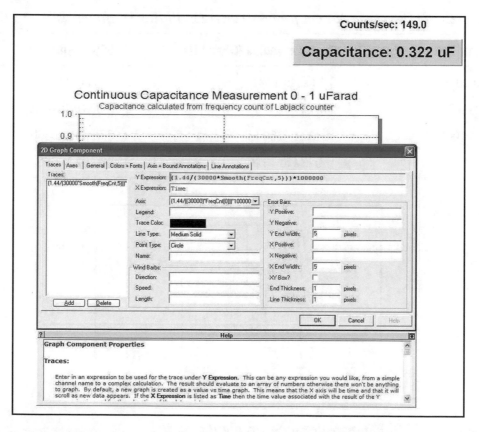

Figure 1-5. *DAQFactory 2D graph component display configuration window*

Capacitance measurements made with a traditional bipolar 555 timer's RC timing network are restricted by the chip's preference for RC network resistors no smaller than 1 kΩ and no larger than 1 MΩ. The measurement range could be extended marginally by using resistors slightly outside the preferred range (47 Ω and 470 Ω for a 100 μF range). Different timing chips such as the CMOS devices can provide wider testing range measurements.

The full-screen strip chart recording output was used to develop the measurement process. An analog dial with digital readouts and a miniature continuous recorder readout was later assembled to provide a visual image of the reading's tendency to drift.

The dial type meter and drift recorder are depicted in Figure 1-6.

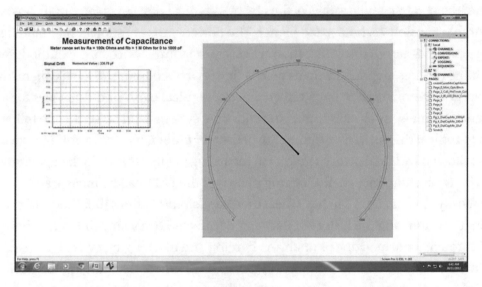

Figure 1-6. *DAQFactory meter and mini-SCR display*

If you need a capacitance measurement instrument, the circuit could be assembled on a perf board mounted in a utility box equipped with a range switch and test leads, and used with a laptop, tablet, or desktop.

Small capacitors must be charged through large resistances to keep the 555 oscillation frequency within the hardware's and software's capabilities. Testing large capacitors with a 555 timer requires small resistances and much larger current draws that eventually exceed the LabJack or USB supplied capabilities. To test the larger capacitor values that result from using liquid electrolytic systems as the dielectric medium, external power supplies in the form of batteries or regulated supplies are usually required. As the current supply increases, you must watch the power rating on much smaller resistors in the 555 timing network.

Experiment B: Measurement of Higher Capacitance Values (> 1000 µF or mF)

Generally, capacitors with values less than 10 µF are solid-state devices, whereas those greater than 10 µF are electrochemical. The significant differences between the lower valued solid-state devices and the electrochemical capacitors are "leakage current" or device resistance.

The larger capacitance values of the electrochemical devices create time constants measurable in minutes, hours, and higher. The devices are also subject to much higher leakage currents across the plates. In some cases, the same device may exhibit differing capacitance values, depending on its recent "in service" charging/discharging history.

Charge accumulation in large valued electrochemical capacitance devices for a given constant current is much slower than in solid-state systems and can easily be followed with a graphical display. The cyclic ability of the 555 timer generates a voltage waveform that is followed by DAQFactory's graphical recording display from which capacitance values for both charging and discharging phases of the DUT can be measured.

Electrolytic capacitors can have measured capacitance values that their history may influence. Minimizing the history's effect can be affected by cycling the device being tested through a normalizing or uniform charging and discharging cycle. If an astable 555 timer circuit is assembled with a constant current mirror for charging the device, followed by a discharge through a known fixed resistor, the device's performance in both phases of its functions can be monitored.

Circuit

In Figure 1-7, the oscillator circuit is essentially a 555 timer IC in an astable oscillator configuration but with different charging and discharging voltage waveforms.

A current mirror circuit supplies a constant current to the capacitance DUT. Once the capacitor charges to two-third of V_{cc}, the 555 changes state, and the charged capacitor discharges through a 1% metal film resistor. The constant current generates a linear voltage ramp on the capacitor while the discharge forms the exponential decay curve, both of which create the cyclic but asymmetric waveform output.

Since electrochemical charge storage devices can be influenced by their history, cycling through a device's charging and discharging functions should re-establish the electrolytic layers. This creates a reproducible device whose capacitance can be measured. Reproducible charge and discharge recorder tracing can establish and validate a device's electrolytic film restoration.

To generate an asymmetric oscillator waveform with a reasonable signal periodicity, high charging currents but at low voltage are necessary. Batteries or a regulated power supply can generate the current required to create a graphical display with a reasonable rate of change of voltage (slope) across the DUT plates. You must also ensure that $2/3\ V_{cc}$, the 555 IC peak voltage during oscillation, is less than the DUT's dielectric breakdown maximum voltage limit. For example, tantalum capacitors have low working voltage ranges.

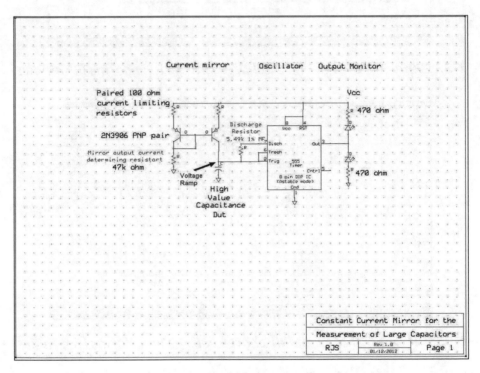

Figure 1-7. *Constant current charging circuit for large capacitors*

Software

A change in the methodology to determine large capacitance values is necessitated by the current flow required to compensate for the large size of the RC time constant generated when the capacitor value rises into the ranges above 10 µF. Capacitor charging times can become very large, as illustrated by the black traces in Figures 1-8 and 1-9. The red discharge voltage traces require up to a minute to complete, as seen in the trace recorded at 9:20 in Figure 1-9.

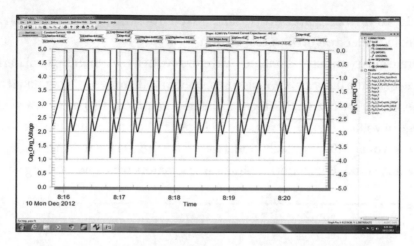

Figure 1-8. *Capacitor charge and discharge voltage waveforms (1 min tics)*

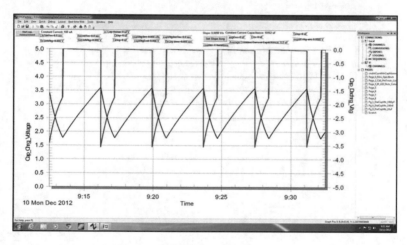

Figure 1-9. *Capacitor charge and discharge voltage waveforms (5 min tics)*

The waveforms (in black) in Figure 1-8 and 1-9 are obtained with the circuitry shown in Figure 1-7. A flow chart outlining the logic to be developed into DAQFactory scripting code to follow the voltage waveform and calculate the charging and discharging capacitance average is depicted in Figure 1-10.

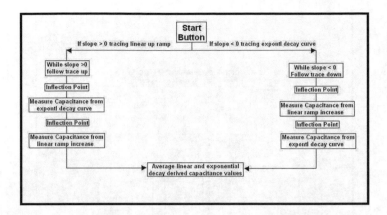

Figure 1-10. *Software flow sheet*

The code for large capacitor device measurements is provided in Listing 1-1 at the end of this chapter.

A DAQFactory control screen can be configured with a graphical display, a Start button, and variable value readouts, as illustrated in Figure 1-11.

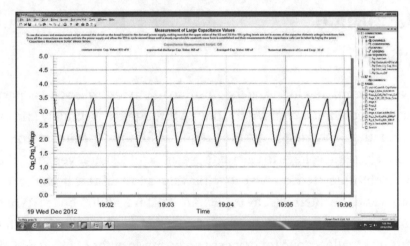

Figure 1-11. *DAQFactory large capacitor measurement*

Observations

Figure 1-12 depicts the response of the 555 timer chip capacitance measurement screen to the nominal capacitor values tested.

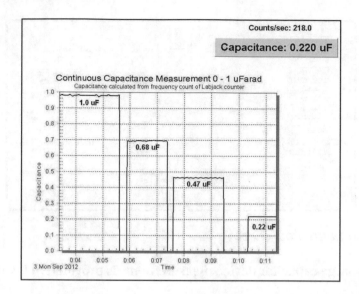

Figure 1-12. *Nominal vs. measured capacitor values*

Experiment C: Autoranging Measurements for Capacitance

Introduction

There are several techniques for using the Arduino microcontroller as a capacitance meter. The earlier techniques charged the device through an accurately known external charging resistor, then determined the time required for the capacitor charge to reach 66⅔% of the 5 V charging voltage to calculate the value of C. Later versions of the measurement technique used known capacitor values to calibrate both the internal pull-up resistors and the internal stray capacitance of an Arduino board. When using the internal stray resistance/capacitance values, reasonably accurate capacitance measurements on smaller capacitor devices can be made without using any external components. Newer versions of the original code modified for this book are at `https://wordpress.codewrite.co.uk/pic/2014/01/21/cap-meter-with-arduino-uno/` and `https://wordpress.codewrite.co.uk/pic/2014/01/25/capacitance-meter-mk-ii/`.

Software Code for Arduino Uno

Listing 1-2 was modified from the original programs published on the mk-ii version to run in my Windows 7 system.

18

Device calibration is required to achieve reasonable accuracy because each Arduino Uno board is different, with both the internal stray capacitance and actual "pull-up" resistance varying slightly. System calibration requires capacitors with accurately known values to evaluate the stray capacitance and the internal "pull-up" resistor values. Figure 1-13 shows the capacitor charging circuit's representative circuit schematic. The mathematics describing the voltage on the DUT, and reasonable assumptions for stray electrical effects can be found on the webpages referenced earlier.

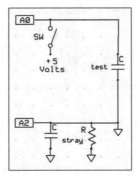

Figure 1-13. *Arduino internal components capacitance measuring circuit*

Known capacitance value, low-leakage dielectric devices like Mylar, polyester, or polystyrene units should calibrate the system. The calibration experiments can begin when the program code for the continuous, autoranging capacitance measurement runs satisfactorily on the Arduino and capacitance values appear on the serial monitor with the low-leakage test capacitor inserted into A0 and A2.

Listing 1-2 allows for the variation of stray capacitance and stray resistance. I had success using the stray resistance adjustment and found values between 35.9 and 37.0 brought most experimental setups into a reasonable degree of accuracy. You can begin the calibration process with the default values in Listing 1-2 and add or decrease the value a small amount and see what effect the change has on the value measured for the known standard. I only made three or four adjustments to bring the system to a reasonable degree of accuracy.

The system should be calibrated in a range as close to the desired point of actual operation as possible.

Take care if electrolytic capacitors are the only units available to calibrate in your desired operation range.

Observations

Measurement of a collection of capacitors of various nominal values produced the results tabulated in Table 1-3.

Table 1-3. *Capacitor Measurement Error*

Capacitor Value	Measured Value
10 pF	10.5 pF
1 nF	0.69 nF
1 µF	0.989 µF
22 µF	25.6 µF/2-3 sec
470 µF	475.4 µF/3 sec

The data for the 22 µF and 470 µF devices were slow to display on the serial monitor, probably due to the long charge times required for the voltage to reach the two-thirds point of the measurement.

Discussion

Measurement of capacitance from pF to F is a dynamic range of twelve orders of magnitude. Measurements spanning 12 orders of magnitude in the range are probably best measured, in experimental work, with several different techniques aptly suited to narrower ranges of interest.

The pF to nF range is well suited to the Arduino autoranging program in which the capacitor charge times can be realized in the "under a second" time frame. Capacitance values above 1 µF exhibit longer charging times during measurement and may be more accurately determined by larger charging currents and calculations made from graphical recordings of the data.

Capacitance devices such as those used in circuit boards are roughly divisible into the two categories of solid state and liquid electrolytic dielectric devices. Tantalum, aluminum, and carbon are the predominant liquid-electrochemical, charge storage devices. The current available from the USB bus or the LabJack type devices is insufficient to charge large capacitance devices in a reasonable time. However, as the capacitance value increases, the voltage that can be impressed across the dielectric decreases. Together with the limited voltage that can be impressed across their ionic layer and the large storage capacities available with electrolytic dielectric systems, you must be cautious with the voltage level of the source of power used, the power dissipation of the resistors to control the charging current, and the leakage current or resistance of the device.

Calibration of Capacitance Measurements

If precision resistors are used in the timing network of the 555 timer then the capacitance values measured can be expected to be proportionally or reasonably close to the values predicted by the mathematical model of the oscillator system. If precision components are not available, the system may have to be calibrated with known capacitance values to establish a level of accuracy.

Measured capacitance values can be displayed in various forms. A numerical visual display and the appropriate measurement units can be read directly from the Arduino serial output monitor to determine the capacitance of a device or component. However, for any form of digital signal processing or graphical display recording requiring transmission over a serial bus, the measurement software's output must be in a format amenable to the serial protocol.

Capacitance Measurement with the Raspberry Pi

Accurate timing with the RPi GPIO array is only possible using the PIGPIO library and its C language interface daemon. An alternate method to achieve a more accurate capacitance measurement is to transfer the timekeeping responsibility to the crystal-controlled clock of a microprocessor acting as a "smart sensor" for the RPi. The autoranging capacitance measuring program running on the Arduino is a robust and well-developed facility that can stream data out to the Python implementation on the RPi for display.

Arduino formatted capacitance data arriving at the Python serial port needs to be converted into a numerical format for either a Python console numerical value or a monitor screen graphical display.

Listing 1-3 in the code listings for this exercise contains the Python code to read the value of a capacitor connected between the A0 and A2 inputs of the Arduino ADC.

Experiment

To continuously measure capacitance with the Arduino board, the program for capacitance measurement (see Listing 1-2) is loaded onto the IDE's microcontroller and the Python program (see Listing 1-3) to receive the data from the serial port is loaded into the RPi.

The capacitor to be tested is then mounted in the A0 and A2 input header ports of the Arduino ADC. The values being streamed to the serial port are validated on the Arduino serial port monitor. The port monitor is closed before launching the Python program on the RPi.

Observations

In Figures 1-14 and 1-15, the character string, string length, and capacitor numerical value output from the serial port reading program were streamed out on the Python interactive terminal or console for recording before termination (Ctrl+C), which causes the system output in red.

Figure 1-14. *Console output for a 330 pF unit*

Figure 1-15. *Console output for a 1μF standard*

Discussion

The calibration of any measurement system with several orders of magnitude of variation in the value being determined should be done carefully and the values measured examined critically. The data streamed out for the 1 μF capacitor is the polystyrene standard on which the stray leakage estimates were made. The nominal 330 pF unit data in Figure 1-14 is measured at 323 pF.

A Siglent Technologies 5.5 digit bench meter measured the 330 pF unit as having a capacitance value of 0.364 nF.

The Arduino–RPi combination delivers very good data for such an inexpensive and readily available system.

Absolute accuracy in any measurement is difficult when very small or very large quantities are involved. Absolute accuracy depends on standards that are often unavailable. If possible, the absolute measurement requirement should be reformulated into a differential measurement problem that can often eliminate the need for an absolute standard.

The Arduino's continuous smaller capacitance monitor provides useful and sensitive differential capacitance measurement capabilities.

Measurement of Large Capacitance Values with Python and Raspberry Pi

The continuous capacitance measurement program running on the Arduino can measure capacitance values over a microfarad but begins to slow down as the capacitor's size increases. Timekeeping concerns involving the RPi, GPIO array, and the corresponding Python library become minor when the time spans involve minutes or longer time frames and the constant current, linear voltage ramp monitoring technique is used to measure capacitance values.

Larger charging currents and higher voltage power supplies can offset some of the problems caused by increased RC time constants. Higher power charging sources for large capacitors must be isolated from the low voltage, low current circuitry of the RPi GPIO array and the MCP3008 ADC.

A visual recording of the liquid dielectric medium's controlled preconditioning in large electrolytic devices before measuring the capacitor value can help get more consistent reproducible data. Listing 1-4 provides a method for establishing the visual validation of large electrolytic capacitor charging reproducibility.

Experiment

A traditional method for creating a linear voltage ramp is to charge a capacitor with a constant current supply. Current mirrors can provide a constant current power supply that, combined with a 555 timing IC can create an alternating charging/discharging cyclic reconditioning of the dielectric layer in a large capacitance DUT.

Two 2N3906 transistors wired into a current mirror configuration and an LM555 timer IC and 6 V battery pack (4 - 12,000 mA alkaline D cells) can be used with the RPi and the gpiozero library reading an MCP3008 ADC to record and display the charging history and capacitance values of large electrolytic capacitors (see Figure 1-7). The code for a cyclic reconditioning program is in Listing 1-4.

To use the Python RPi, premeasurement conditioning and data display or recording programs, the MCP3008 serial peripheral interface (SPI) protocol must be invoked on the RPi from the main menu selections, as seen in Figures 1-16 and 1-17.

Figure 1-16. *Performance menu submenu selections*

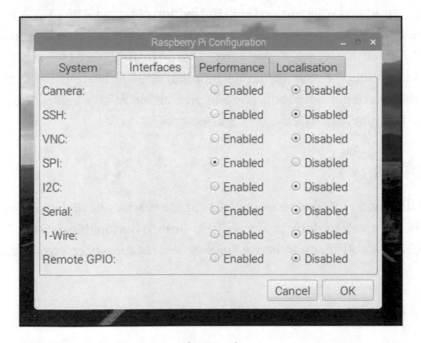

Figure 1-17. *SPI selection from Interfaces tab*

Figure 1-18 is a connection diagram that provides the transfer of power, control, and data between the RPi GPIO array and the MCP3008 ADC. Vin is the voltage ramp measurement being made at the point indicated by the arrow in Figure 1-7.

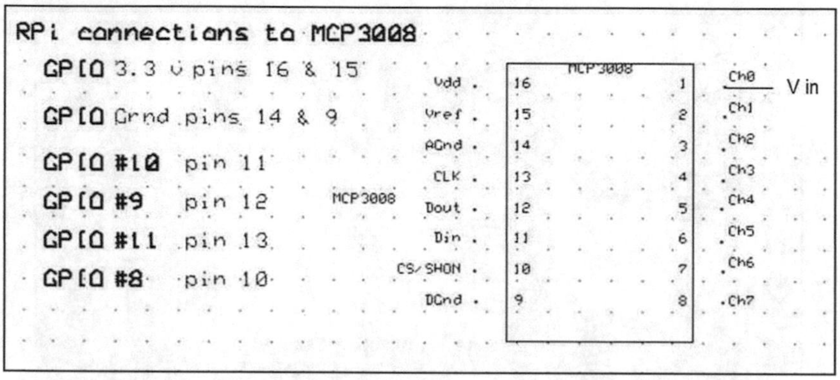

```
RPi connections to MCP3008
  GPIO 3.3 v pins 16 & 15                        MCP3008
                             Vdd .  | 16               1 |    Ch0   V in
  GPIO Grnd pins 14 & 9      Vref.  | 15               2 | .Ch1
                             AGnd.  | 14               3 | .Ch2
  GPIO #10  pin 11            CLK.  | 13               4 | .Ch3
  GPIO #9   pin 12   MCP3008  Dout. | 12               5 | .Ch4
  GPIO #11  pin 13            Din.  | 11               6 | .Ch5
  GPIO #8   pin 10       CS/SHDN.   | 10               7 | .Ch6
                             DGnd.  | 9                8 | .Ch7
```

Figure 1-18. *Connection diagram for MCP3008 10-bit ADC and RPi GPIO*

For simplicity and ease of implementation, two programs can be used for the large capacitor measurement: the first to precondition the electrolytic layer on the DUT and the second to measure the device's capacitance. With the current mirror, 555 timer IC, and RPi configured and programmed with the Python code in Listing 1-5, a repeating series of linear increasing voltage ramps from a constant current charging, followed by exponential voltage decay discharging curves should be produced (see Figure 1-19).

After conditioning the electrolytic dielectric with the hardware-based cyclic charging and discharging to obtain a reproducible and predictable voltage behavior pattern, the software can be launched to follow the timer-controlled cycling.

Observations

Figure 1-19 depicts a typical large electrolytic capacitor six-cycle dielectric conditioning program. The relatively uniform peak heights indicate a reasonable degree of reproducibility suitable for quantitative measurement of the device's capacitance.

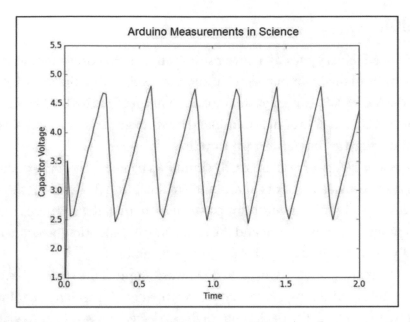

Figure 1-19. *Trace recording of voltage cycling for electrolytic capacitor dielectric conditioning*

Figure 1-19 shows a typical cycling pattern that conditioned the liquid dielectric on a nominal 470 µF electrolytic capacitor. Figure 1-20 illustrates the data output from a typical four-cycle measurement.

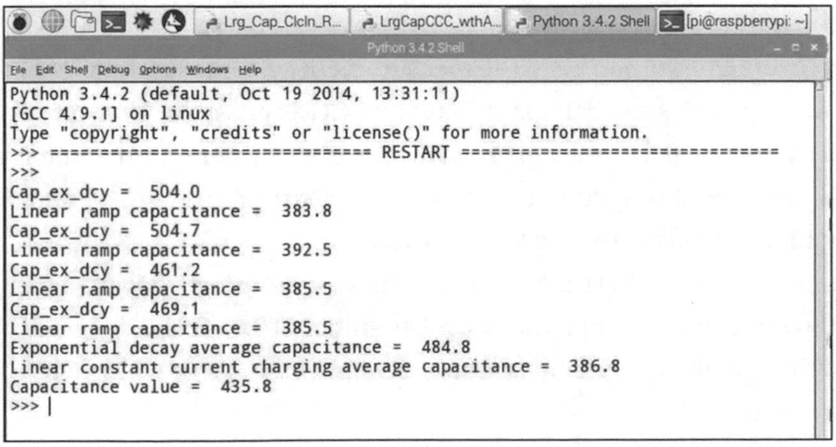

```
Python 3.4.2 (default, Oct 19 2014, 13:31:11)
[GCC 4.9.1] on linux
Type "copyright", "credits" or "license()" for more information.
>>> ============================== RESTART ==============================
>>>
Cap_ex_dcy =  504.0
Linear ramp capacitance =  383.8
Cap_ex_dcy =  504.7
Linear ramp capacitance =  392.5
Cap_ex_dcy =  461.2
Linear ramp capacitance =  385.5
Cap_ex_dcy =  469.1
Linear ramp capacitance =  385.5
Exponential decay average capacitance =  484.8
Linear constant current charging average capacitance =  386.8
Capacitance value =  435.8
>>> |
```

Figure 1-20. *Console output from large electrolytic capacitor constant current charging technique*

Discussion

With the 6 V D-cell battery pack as a power supply, the LM555 timer should cycle at one-third or two-thirds of the V_{cc} or between 2 V and 4 V—well within the electrical limits of the RPi and the MCP3008. The gpiozero implementation of the MCP3008 is a normalized output of 0 to 1.0. The ADC output is multiplied by six to generate the actual voltage on the capacitor during the charge/discharge cycling.

Large capacitor measurement is greatly simplified by using a visual graphic recording of the pre-measurement conditioning of the liquid dielectric in the DUT. When a series of uniform linear ramps and exponential decay curves are recorded, the graphics program can be closed and the capacitance evaluation program launched to numerically measure the device charge storage capability.

Careful examination of the right-hand downward slope of the sawtooth wave resulting from the conditioning of the electrolytic capacitor, especially near the lower portions of the trace, reveal the beginnings of the expected curvature or deviation from linearity.

My original program used a dual entry point algorithm to start on the up or downward sloping trace. However, numerical errors such as negative values, loss of synchronization between the hardware and software programs, and larger spreads in the observed individual data points led to the adoption of a code that only starts a capacitance measurement on the linear upward constant current charging (CCC) portion of the trace.

The best overall performance of the measurement system was obtained by launching the program at a point as close to the start of the CCC as possible. The starting point was determined by watching the red and green diodes in the timer output circuitry with the red diode illuminated during the exponential decay portion of the cycle and the green diode being illuminated during the CCC portion.

With the known RPi GPIO timing irregularities, better precision and accuracy is to be expected with longer timing sequences. A nominal 470 µF device typically required a 56 second time period to generate a result, as depicted in Figure 1-20, while a 1000 µF required 1.75 minutes.

Five electrolytic capacitors from a box of assorted capacitors were found to have measured values from 423 to 430 for a nominal label value of 470 µF (Siglent Technologies 5.5 digit bench meter). Six repetitive RPi measurements were made on a nominal 470 µF unit. The data produced is tabulated in Table 1-4.

An additional series of meter measurements made on five nominal 1000 μF units varied from 955 to 961. A series of five repetitive RPi measurements on the 1000 μF unit produced the large values in the tabulation.

Table 1-4. *Measured Capacitor Values for 470 and 1000 μF Devices*

Measurement	Value
1	429 – 936
2	443 – 940
3	431 – 940
4	427 – 937
5	436 – 940
6	425

Table 1-5 is a tabular comparison.

Table 1-5. *Data Comparison Siglent Bench Meter and Raspberry Pi*

Measurement type	Nominal value	Observed spread in values		Approximate difference
Siglent Meter @	470 μF	423 - 430	ΔC of 7 μF	43 μF
RPi @	470 μF	425 - 443	ΔC of 18 μF	36 μF
Siglent Meter @	1000 μF	955 - 961	ΔC of 6 μF	43 μF
RPi @	1000 μF	937 - 940	ΔC of 3 μF	62 μF

Comparing the individual numerical values generated by the RPi and those generated with the bench meter shows a remarkable correlation in accuracy and precision when the close to two orders of magnitude difference in costs between the two measurement systems are considered.

For experimental work with larger capacitors, the current regulating resistor of the current mirror can be reduced to produce a larger charging current. The 2N3906 can handle 200 mA as a continuous collector emitter current. If a smaller current programming resistor is used to increase the constant current charging value, the computing code current definition and the discharge resistor on the 555 timer must be changed. The conditioning program graphical display can adjust the timer discharge resistor to preserve the computing program's symmetry to track the changing capacitor voltage. You should also adequately adjust the power ratings on both current mirror, and discharge circuitry for any increases in current flow to measure larger capacitance devices.

Code Listings for Capacitance Measurement

Listing 1-1. DAQFactory Sequence Code

```
// Determination of Large Capacitor Values  Wed. 10-17,11-14 and 12 1 to 15/2012
// An astable 555 timer circuit uses a constant current derived from a
// current mirror to charge the cap dut(Capacitance device under test.) and
// a metal film 1% resistor connected between the Cap dut and pin 7 of the
// IC to discharge the charged device. The 555 cycles the output through a
// linear voltage ramp followed by an exponential decay.
//
// Started with a descriptive text component or a screen button "if else"
// code determines where the waveform is in its cycle by looking at the
// immediate slope of the capacitor voltage trace. The rising or falling
// trace is followed to an inflection point. At the inflection point code
// then calculates the capacitance first from the appropriate linear or
// exponential formula followed by the complementary exponential or linear
// formula after the next inflection point.
// The two calculated linear and exponential values are averaged and displayed.
//
// The nominal value of the exponential decay resistor is used as an
// initial approximation for the decay based calculation but when in the
// discharge cycle the resistor is in parallel with the resistance to
// ground through the current mirror. The value used for calculation of the
// decay based capacitance will have to be adjusted downward until the
// average of the charging/discharging values agree with known capacitance
// standards within experimental error.
//
```

```
// The value of the screen trace slope is declared global and calculated
// from the values of the capacitor voltage in the channel event monitoring
// the capacitor voltage.
// The current variable required to determine the accumulated capacitor
// charge is Icc for constant current charging. The slope and Icc values
// are calculated in the event tab of the channels monitoring the voltage
// drop across the programming resistor in the current mirror circuit and
// the capacitor under test.
//
global Flag = 0
//
//
global linStrtTm        // linear ramp start time
global linStrtVltg      // linear ramp start voltage
global linEndTm         // linear ramp end time
global linEndVltg       // linear ramp end voltage
global Ccc              // capacitance from constant current charging
//
global expVltgStrt      // initial cap vltg at start of exp dischrg
global expVltgStrtTm    // time of initial vltg msrmnt
global expVltgEnd       // final valu cap vltg at end of exp dischrg
global expVltgEndTm     // time of finl vltg vlu msrmnt
global Cexp             // capacitance from exp dischrg msrmnt
global Cavrg            // the lin charg expl dischrg capacitance average
//
// When start button is keyed Flag is set to 1 to indicate the program is
// measuring a large capacitance value
Flag = 1
//
//
if (slope < 0)      // the astable circuit is in the exponential discharging
                    portion of the cycle
// ----------------------------------------------------------------------
// ----------------------------------------------------------------------
```

```
// dual capacitance calculation starts here with exponential decay
// following the down slope to the inflection point then starts dual
// calculations on the constant current linear up slope.
//
// ------------ FINISH  DOWN-SLOPE ----------------------------------------
   while (slope < 0)
      delay(.25)     // wait for inflection point
      endwhile
    // ------- CALCULATE LINEAR UP-SLOPE CAPACITANCE -------------------
    // change of slope from decay to start of linear constant current ramp
    //
    linStrtTm = cnstntCurntCap.Time[0]    // record ramp start time
    linStrtVltg = cnstntCurntCap[0]       // record ramp start voltage
    while (slope > 0)                     // follow linear charging ramp up
        delay(.25) // wait for inflection point
        endwhile
        // change of slope from linear ramp to exponential decaying discharge
        //
        //
        linEndTm = cnstntCurntCap.Time[0] // record ramp end time
        linEndVltg = cnstntCurntCap[0]    // record ramp end voltage
        Ccc = Icc * ((linEndTm - linStrtTm)/(linEndVltg - linStrtVltg))
        //
        //------SLOPE CHANGE TO EXPONENTIAL DECAY DISCHARGE --------------
        //
        //
      expVltgStrt = cnstntCurntCap[0]
      expVltgStrtTm = cnstntCurntCap.Time[0]
      while (slope < 0)           // follow exponential decay down
        delay(.25)
        endwhile
       // change of slope from exponential decay to linear constant
          current charging for a linear voltage ramp
      expVltgEnd = cnstntCurntCap[0]
      expVltgEndTm = cnstntCurntCap.Time[0]
```

```
    //
        Cexp = (-(expVltgEndTm - expVltgStrtTm)/ 3400 * (ln(expVltgEnd/
        expVltgStrt))) * 1000000
        //
    // --- CALCULATE AVERAGE CAPACITANCE from constnt currnt charge and
        exp discharge traces ----
    //
        Cavrg = (Ccc + Cexp)/2
        //
// an averaged capacitor value from a single charge - discharge cycle is
    complete and Flag is reset to 0
//
Flag = 0
//
else

// the astable circuit is in the linear portion of the wave form
// ---------------------------------------------------------------------------
// ---------------------------------------------------------------------------
// dual capacitance calculation starts with the linear up slope being
// followed to the inflection point then first calculating the capacitance
// value from the exp discharge trace then using the linear trace to
// complete the dual measurement..
//
// -------------FINISH UP-SLOPE -----------------------------------------------
while (slope > 0)
    delay (.25)  // wait for inflection point
    endwhile
    // ----------CALCULATE EXPONENTIAL DECAY CAPACITANCE -------------------
    // change of slope from linear increase to exponential decay
    //
    expVltgStrt = cnstntCurntCap[0]
        expVltgStrtTm = cnstntCurntCap.Time[0]
        while (slope < 0)            // follow exponential decay down
          delay(.25)
          endwhile
```

```
    // change of slope from exponential decay to linear constant
    // current charging for a linear voltage ramp
    //
  expVltgEnd = cnstntCurntCap[0]
  expVltgEndTm = cnstntCurntCap.Time[0]
//
    Cexp = (-(expVltgEndTm - expVltgStrtTm)/ 3400 * (ln(expVltgEnd/
    expVltgStrt))) * 1000000
    //

    //
    //-------- SLOPE CHANGE TO LINEAR UP RAMP CALCULATION ------------
  // change of slope from decay to start of linear constant current ramp
  //
linStrtTm = cnstntCurntCap.Time[0]    // record ramp start time
linStrtVltg = cnstntCurntCap[0]       // record ramp start voltage
while (slope > 0)                     // follow linear charging ramp up
    delay(.25) // wait for inflection point
    endwhile
    // change of slope from linear ramp to exponential decaying discharge
    //
    linEndTm = cnstntCurntCap.Time[0] // record ramp end time
    linEndVltg = cnstntCurntCap[0]     // record ramp end voltage
    Ccc = Icc * ((linEndTm - linStrtTm)/(linEndVltg - linStrtVltg))
    //-------------------CALCULATE UP and DOWN SLOPE Average --------
    //
    // a single charge - discharge cycle complete and Flag is reset to 0
    //
    Cavrg = (Ccc + Cexp)/2
    //
    Flag = 0
    //
    //
Endif
```

Listing 1-2. Arduino Code for Continuous Capacitance Measurement

```
//CAPACITANCE METER PROGRAM
//Program requires calibration with known capacitors to evaluate internal
resistance
const int OUT_PIN = A2;
const int IN_PIN = A0;

//Capacitance DUT between IN_PIN and Ground
//Stray capacitance value will vary from board to board.
//Calibrate this value using known capacitor.
const float IN_STRAY_CAP_TO_GND = 24.48;
const float IN_CAP_TO_GND = IN_STRAY_CAP_TO_GND;
//Pull up resistance will vary depending on board
//Calibrate this with known capacitor.
const float R_PULLUP = 37.0;   //has been found to vary from 35.9 to 37.0 in
                               K ohms
const int MAX_ADC_VALUE = 1023;

void setup()
{
  pinMode(OUT_PIN, OUTPUT);
  //digitalWrite(OUT_PIN, LOW; //This is the default state for outputs
  pinMode(IN_PIN, OUTPUT);
  //digitalWrite(IN_PIN, LOW);

  Serial.begin(9600);
}

void loop()
{
  //Capacitor under test between OUT_PIN and IN_PIN
  // Rising edge on OUT_PIN
  pinMode(IN_PIN, INPUT);
  digitalWrite(OUT_PIN, HIGH);
  int val = analogRead(IN_PIN);
  digitalWrite(OUT_PIN, LOW);
```

```
  if (val < 1000)
{
  //Low value capacitor
  //Clear everything for the next measurement
  pinMode(IN_PIN, OUTPUT);

  //Calculate and print result

  float capacitance = (float)val * IN_CAP_TO_GND / (float) (MAX_ADC_VALUE - val);
 // Serial.print("Capacitance Value = ");
  Serial.print(capacitance, 1);
  Serial.println(" pF ");
  //Serial.print(val);          // optional for calibration
 // Serial.println("()");       // optional for calibration
}
else
{
  //Big capacitor - so use RCX charging method

  // discharge the capacitor (from low capacitance test)
  pinMode(IN_PIN, OUTPUT);
  delay(1);

  // Start charging the capacitor with the internal pullup
  pinMode(OUT_PIN, INPUT_PULLUP);
  unsigned long u1 = micros();
  unsigned long t;
  int digVal;

  //Charge to arbitrary level mid-way between 0 and 5 v
  //Best not to use analogRead() here because it's not really quick enough
  do
  {
    digVal = digitalRead(OUT_PIN);
    unsigned long u2 = micros();
    t = u2 > u1 ? u2 - u1 : u1 - u2;
  } while ((digVal < 1) && (t < 400000L));
```

```
  pinMode(OUT_PIN, INPUT);    //Stop charging
  //Now we can read the level the capacitor has charged up to
  val = analogRead(OUT_PIN);

  //Discharge capacitor for next measurement
  digitalWrite(IN_PIN, HIGH);
  int dischargeTime = (int) (t / 1000L) * 5;
  delay(dischargeTime);  //discharge slowly to begin with
  pinMode(OUT_PIN, OUTPUT);  //discharge remainder quickly
  digitalWrite(OUT_PIN, LOW);
  digitalWrite(IN_PIN, LOW);
 // calculate and print result
float capacitance = -(float)t / R_PULLUP / log(1.0 - (float)val / (float)
MAX_ADC_VALUE);

//Serial.print("Capacitance Value = ");  // optional print out on serial monitor
if (capacitance > 1000.0)
{
  Serial.print(capacitance / 1000.0, 2);
  Serial.println(" uF");
}
else
{
  Serial.print(capacitance, 2);
  Serial.println(" nF");
}

//Serial.print(" (");
//Serial.print(digVal == 1 ? "Normal" : "HighVal");
//Serial.print(", t= ");
//Serial.print(t);
//Serial.print(" us, ADC= ");
//Serial.print(val);
Serial.println(")");
}
while (millis() % 250 != 0);
}
```

Listing 1-3. Raspberry Pi – Python Serial Reading of Arduino Capacitance Data

```python
# Program to read serial port
# when the length of the input string appearing on the port varies
# with varying numerical values the max and min possible lengths of
# the string must be determined and a slicing operation set up to
# accommodate each of the possible input string lengths.
# If possible the line of string data sent by the Arduino should
# have the same character string before and after the digits of the
# varying numerical data so as the slice operation need only take a
# fixed number of characters off the front and back of the string to
# leave the numerical data as a remainder.
#
import serial
#
while True:
    ser = serial.Serial('/dev/ttyACM0')             # open serial port
    inPutln = ser.readline()                        # read complete line of
                                                    #  string input

    print('input string line  = ', inPutln)         # display input string
    str_len = len(inPutln)                          # determine input string
                                                    #  length

    print("string length =", str_len)              # print length
    dta_valu = str(inPutln)[slice(2, -8)]           # make list, slice digit
                                                    #  string

    cap_units = str(inPutln)[slice(-8, -5)]
    #
    print('dta_valu = ', dta_valu, "cap_units = ", cap_units)
```

Listing 1-4. Conditioning of Large Electrolytic Capacitor Dielectrics

```python
# SCR Plotting of Normalized Potentiometer Voltage Value from an MCP3008
# gpiozero used to configure MCP3008 and attributes for plotting
#
import matplotlib
import numpy as np
from matplotlib.lines import Line2D
```

```python
import matplotlib.pyplot as plt
import matplotlib.animation as animation
import time
from gpiozero import MCP3008
#
pot = MCP3008(0)
#
#
class Scope:
    def __init__(self, ax, maxt=4, dt=0.02):
        """maxt time width of display"""
        self.ax = ax
        self.dt = dt
        self.maxt = maxt
        self.tdata = [0]
        self.ydata = [0]
        self.line = Line2D(self.tdata, self.ydata)
        self.ax.add_line(self.line)
        self.ax.set_ylim(1.0,6.0)  # y axis scale
        self.ax.set_xlim(0, self.maxt)

    def update(self, y):
        lastt = self.tdata[-1]
        if lastt > self.tdata[0] + self.maxt: # reset the arrays
            self.tdata = [self.tdata[-1]]
            self.ydata = [self.ydata[-1]]
            self.ax.set_xlim(self.tdata[0], self.tdata[0] + self.maxt)
            self.ax.figure.canvas.draw()

        t = self.tdata[-1] + self.dt
        self.tdata.append(t)
        self.ydata.append(y)
        self.line.set_data(self.tdata, self.ydata)
        return self.line,
#
#
```

```
def rd_data():
    while True:
        inPutln = pot.value
        #print("inPutln = ", inPutln)
        line = (inPutln) * 6
        #print(line)
        yield (line)

fig = plt.figure()
fig.suptitle("The Scientyst's Ayde", fontsize = 12)
ax = fig.add_subplot(111)
ax.set_xlabel("Time")
ax.set_ylabel("Capacitor DUT Voltage")
scope = Scope(ax)

# uses rd_data() as a generator to produce data for the update func, the MCP3008
# value is read by the plotting code in 40 minute windows for the animated
# screen display. Software overhead limits response speed of display.
ani = animation.FuncAnimation(fig, scope.update, rd_data, interval=50,
blit=False)

plt.show()
```

Listing 1-5. Measurement of Large Electrolytic Capacitor Values

```
# Large Capacitor Measurement
# gpiozero MCP3008 ADC normalizes 0-5 v in to 0-1 output, time reqd for
# delay and tick count math required for log functions.
#
from gpiozero import MCP3008
import time
import math
#
adc = MCP3008(0)        # create an instance of ADC reading channel 0
icc = 5.365/47100       # voltage across the current mirror programming
                        resistor value
#
```

```
def calc_slope():      # calcs slope current mirror chrg/dschrg trace
    cap_vlu = (adc.value) * 6
    #print("Cap voltage = ", cap_vlu)
    frst_vltg = cap_vlu
    strt_tm = time.time()
    time.sleep(0.25)
    cap_vlu = (adc.value) * 6
    scnd_vlu = cap_vlu
    stp_tm = time.time()
    #
    slope = (scnd_vlu - frst_vltg) / (stp_tm - strt_tm)
    #print("slope = ", slope)
    return slope
#
trnd = calc_slope()                # determine position in cycle
#print("trnd = ", trnd)            # diagnostic print statement
#
if (trnd > 0):                          # trace in linear up constant current
                                               charging phase

    while(calc_slope() > 0):
        exp_dec_strt_tcks = time.time() # follow trace up to inflection
                                                    point where exp
        exp_dec_vlts = (adc.value) * 6  # dcy curve starts
        #print("expntl_dec_strt_ticks = ", expntl_dec_strt_tcks)
        # print out for diagnostics and error checking (PODEC)
        #print("expntl_dec_vlts = ", expntl_dec_vlts)          # PODEC
        #
        ExpDecayCap_ttl = 0
        LinCCC_Cap_ttl = 0
#
    for i in range(1 , 5):          # collect four sets of data
        #
        while(calc_slope() < 0):
            lnr_ccc_strt_tcks = time.time()      # track exp decay slope
                                                        down to inflection point
```

```
            lnr_ccc_strt_vlts = (adc.value) * 6  # and up date the end
                                                    inflection point variables
        #print("lnr_ccc_strt_tcks = ", lnr_ccc_strt_tcks)      # PODEC
        #print("lnr_ccc_strt_vlts = ", lnr_ccc_strt_vlts)      # PODEC
    cap_ex_dcy = (-(lnr_ccc_strt_tcks - exp_dec_strt_tcks) / 3400 *
    (math.log(lnr_ccc_strt_vlts / exp_dec_vlts))) * 1000000
    print("Cap_ex_dcy = ", round(cap_ex_dcy, 1))
    ExpDecayCap_ttl = ExpDecayCap_ttl + cap_ex_dcy
    lnr_ccc_strt_tcks = time.time()              # record start time of
                                                    linear ramp
    lnr_ccc_strt_vlts = (adc.value) * 6          # record start voltage of
                                                    linear ramp
#

    while(calc_slope() > 0):                     # follow linear ramp up
        lnr_ccc_fnl_tcks = time.time()           # track final ramp value
                                                    time ticks

        lnr_ccc_fnl_vlts = (adc.value) * 6       # and voltage value
    cap_lnr_vrmp = (icc * ((lnr_ccc_fnl_tcks - lnr_ccc_strt_tcks) /
    (lnr_ccc_fnl_vlts - lnr_ccc_strt_vlts)) * 1000000)
    print("Linear ramp capacitance = ", round(cap_lnr_vrmp, 1))
    LinCCC_Cap_ttl = LinCCC_Cap_ttl + cap_lnr_vrmp
    exp_dec_strt_tcks = lnr_ccc_fnl_tcks    # reset start ticks variable
                                                for exp dcy calcn
    exp_dec_vlts = lnr_ccc_fnl_vlts         # reset start voltage
                                                variable for exp dcy calcn
ExpDecayCap_avr = ExpDecayCap_ttl / 4
print("Exponential decay average capacitance = ", round(ExpDecay
Cap_avr, 1))
LinCCC_Cap_avr = LinCCC_Cap_ttl / 4
print("Linear constant current charging average capacitance = ",
round(LinCCC_Cap_avr, 1))
CapValue = (ExpDecayCap_avr + LinCCC_Cap_avr) / 2
print ("Capacitance value = ", round(CapValue, 1))
```

```
#
elif (trnd < 0):                                # trace in expntl decay
                                                capacitor discharging phase
    print("Not on constant current charging portion of the cycle, re-start
    measurement.")
else:
    print("Program started on an inflection point, re-start measurement.")
```

Summary

The mathematical theory of capacitor structure, charge storage, and the associated electron flow with constant current or constant voltage charging was presented.

Capacitance measurement techniques were presented for static and continuous determinations with commercial SCADA software and less-expensive systems assembled from single-board computing platforms using discrete IC components or microprocessors.

Some of the methods for determining large and small current flows are explored and evaluated in Chapter 2.

CHAPTER 2

Current

Electrical energy has two dynamic components: voltage and current. Resistance is an inherent property of the materials through which energy stored as voltage causes the current to move.

Electric current is the term applied to the flow of an electric charge, usually in the form of electrons but possibly also moving ions in a liquid, gas, or plasma. Current is measured in units known as *amperes*, which are the number of coulombs of charge passing through a circuit reference point in one second of time. (A coulomb of charge is 6.24×10^{18} electrons, and each electron carries an electric charge of 1.602×10^{-19} coulombs.)

In 1820, Oersted discovered that a current passing through a wire created a magnetic field around the conductor. Researchers soon developed instruments that could quantify the current flow in wires by measuring the deflection of compass needles caused by the magnetic field created around the conductors. Current measuring instruments based upon magnetic field deviations are called *galvanometers* in honor of Luigi Galvani, who discovered that electric current caused biological muscle tissues of frogs' legs to contract. Sensitive current measuring galvanometers were developed by passing unknown currents through coils, suspended in the fields created by fixed in position, permanent magnets. Numerous improvements, especially those developed by d'Arsonval and Weston, resulted in a reasonably robust device that became the mainstay of the volt-ohm-meter (VOM) in use from the late 1800s until the development of the solid-state systems in the late twentieth century. Devices with fixed permanent magnets surrounding a suspended wire coil and mounted on spiral springs are known as *d'Arsonval/Weston galvanometers*, which measure microamperes of current.

Current measurements are made with the galvanometer connected in series with the circuit under test. Current to be measured flows through a fine wire coil suspended by spiral springs in a stationary magnetic field created by permanent magnets. Magnetic fields created in the suspended coil interact with the stationary field of the permanent magnets and turn the suspended coil in proportion to the magnitude of the current

© Richard J. Smythe 2022
R. J. Smythe, *Arduino Measurements in Science*, https://doi.org/10.1007/978-1-4842-6781-3_2

flowing through it. Pointers attached to the spring-mounted coils move over numerical scales in galvanometer-based instruments to provide quantitative current flow measurements.

The dynamic range of galvanometers was extended by using parallel "shunt resistors" of low resistance to carry the bulk of the current flow for higher value measurements to make a current–measuring device known as an *ammeter*. Ideally, the ammeter should not affect the circuit and current being measured. But connecting wires, the moving coil, and shunt resistors all have measurable resistance, and thus, meters required calibration.

A portion of the current passing through the ammeter causes a voltage to develop in the device. The voltage developed in the ammeter is known as the *burden voltage*. For large current values, losses caused through the development of a small burden voltage are usually small enough not to influence the observed magnitude of the large current being measured. A burden voltage can cause significant error in the measurement of small currents.

Current measurement by a moving coil galvanometer was the basis of the analog VOM that was able, through Ohm's law, to measure both resistance and voltage by determining the current flow through precision resistors and from known voltage sources. Modern current measuring instruments are voltage based, solid-state devices that use Ohm's law and analog to digital converters to measure the voltage drop across accurately known resistance values.

The physical properties of the construction materials are the limiting factors that determine the way a current measurement can be made. Very large currents passing through small resistance values cause heat to develop. Tiny currents are virtually lost to the circuit when minute resistances are present in the measuring system.

In virtually all experiments, the measurement process should minimize the disturbance to the phenomenon observed. In terms of current measurement there should not be any voltage burden created by the measurement meter.

Low current measurements are discussed in Keithley Instruments' "Low-Level Measurements Handbook" at `www.tek.com/document/handbook/low-level-measurements-handbook`. This document explains the real problems present in making current measurements in the micro (10^{-6}), nano (10^{-9}), pico (10^{-12}), or femto (10^{-15}) ampere ranges. Current measurements made below the microampere levels require the use of electrometers and picoammeters that are reviewed in terms of these commercially available instruments.

Currents in the microampere range and lower are encountered in digital photography, physiology, electrochemical reactions, and spectroscopic and chromatographic analysis systems. The small current flows generated by photon-gathering charge-coupled devices, nerve tissues, trace quantities of moving ions in solution, ionized combustion products in flame ionization detectors, or photoelectrons released by light impinging on a PN junction photodiode are unable to power or "drive" normal resistive loads to develop measurable signals. To quantify or measure these small current flows, special instruments and techniques are required to minimize the effects of "loading" caused by attempting to measure these minuscule current flows.

Operational amplifiers have various means of current control. They can also be used in current measurement applications.

Operational amplifiers (op-amps) are integrated circuits based on the idealized concept of the perfect, theoretical DC amplifier. An ideal op-amp has infinite open-loop gain, infinite input impedance, zero output impedance, infinite bandwidth, and zero output voltage with no voltage across the input terminals. The ideal op-amp has a pair of differential inputs termed the inverting and non-inverting inputs that invert or reproduce the voltage of the respective inputs at the device output.

Modern-day operational amplifiers are the descendants of analog computers that performed mathematical operations in many linear, non-linear, and frequency-dependent circuits. Integrated circuits such as the general-purpose µA709 introduced in 1965 and the µA741 first produced in 1968, and still in production today, are reasonable approximations of an ideal DC amplifier.

Figure 2-1 illustrates a small or low-level current measurement technique that uses a high-quality op-amp in a *feedback ammeter* or transimpedance amplifier (TIA) configuration. The schematic converts a small current into a larger measurable voltage in proportion to the resistance in the feedback circuit.

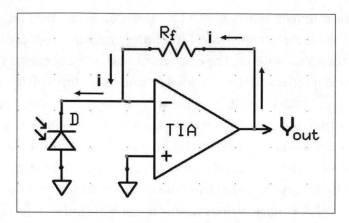

Figure 2-1. *A transimpedance amplifier*

Op-amps are often used as analog computers. In this case, a high-quality, high-input impedance integrated circuit such as the AD 8628 or LMC6081 can be configured for measuring small sources of current that are prone to distortion from loading caused by the measurement instrumentation.

Theoretical "op-amps" are DC-coupled, high-gain, electronic voltage amplifiers whose output is controlled by the negative feedback of the output to the input. Negative feedback is the process of coupling output back in such a way as to cancel some of the input. Op-amps are essentially differential amplifiers that amplify the difference between their inverting and non-inverting input terminals indicated on the triangular amplifier schematic by + and – signs. The application of a conditioned portion of the output, back to the inverting input, can change the op-amp circuit's characteristics by reducing its gain, altering its input and output impedances, changing its bandwidth, and lessening the effects of manufacturing variations and temperature drifting.

Traditionally, op-amps are DC-coupled amplifiers in which the output voltage is determined by the difference between the inverting and non-inverting inputs multiplied by the amplifier gain. In Figure 2-2, the non-inverting input is maintained at a fixed voltage by a voltage divider.

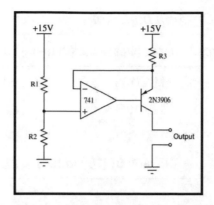

Figure 2-2. *An op-amp constant current configuration*

In the op-amp constant current configuration for current control, the base emitter junction is in the negative feedback loop. It is driven by the op-amp's output to maintain the same voltage on the inverting input as is present on the non-inverting input. The voltage on the non-inverting input is defined by the voltage divider created by R1 and R2, and variation of the voltage divider ratio adjusts the current through the transistor.

In the TIA configuration, the non-inverting input is grounded. The op-amp output is fed back to the inverting input through a gain resistor. The op-amp voltage requirement that the inverting and non-inverting inputs must be the same potential makes the current source see the non-inverting input as a short circuit to ground. The deceptively simple circuit achieves non-interference with the signal being measured. A transimpedance amplifier can be difficult to implement and requires high-quality op-amps for measuring low current values below the microampere and nanoampere levels.

Prior to the development of solid-state electronics, ammeters based upon the d'Arsonval/Weston galvanometer electro-mechanical movements were the most readily available instruments for measuring low-level currents. The development of solid-state electronics and integrated circuitry made possible op-amp chips, such as the LM741 and the field-effect transistor (FET) high-impedance input LF 411. Both are used in TIA configuration to replace ammeters as current-measuring devices. In current-to-voltage conversion mode, op-amp TIA configurations measure current at milliamp and lower ranges through variation of the feedback resistor's value.

Sensitivity in measuring low levels of current flow with op-amp IC chips depends on the input impedance that a chip presents to the current source being tested. In Table 2-1, some op-amp input impedances are tabulated for comparison.

Table 2-1. *Op-Amp Impedance and Costs*

Integrated Circuit	Input Impedance (Ohms)	Costs ($ CDN)
LM741	2 MΩ (10^6)	< $1
LF411	1 TΩ (10^{12})	$1 to $2
LMC6081	10 TΩ (10^{13})	$4 to $5
OPA129	10T to 100T (10^{13} to 10^{15})	$12

Integrated circuit operational amplifier costs rise significantly as the input impedances increase in the 10^{13} ohms to 10^{15} ohms range.

High current measurements significantly greater than the microamp and milliamp range of experimentally derived measurement signal processing are encountered when motors or heat transferring operations are invoked. In order to minimize the hazards to health and the possibility of fire ignition, there are numerous codes written for the safe implementation of high-voltage, high-current electrical systems. When applications require high-voltage, high-current electrical energy, appropriate experts and applicable electrical codes should be consulted. The higher currents monitored and discussed in the following sections are of a low-voltage nature.

Solid-state electronics systems operate in the 3 V to 30 V range. Hence, the higher currents needed to energize common stepper motors, cooling fans, thermoelectric heat transfer systems, and electrochemical operations rarely exceed these ranges.

Most hand-and-bench electronics metering instruments measure up to 10 A when the meters are connected in series with the current source and the load. However, low-voltage, high-current experiments involving electrolysis, electro-deposition, or solid-state thermoelectric heat transfers often use low voltage currents over 10 A while 12 V lead-acid batteries (as used in automotive starter applications) can supply 500 A on demand.

Recalling that two resistors placed in parallel divide the total current flow between them in proportion to their resistance, you can visualize the means to modify a fixed-scale ammeter to measure higher currents. When traditional ammeters such as those based upon the d'Arsonval/Weston galvanometer movements with their low internal resistance were required to measure higher currents, a known value "shunt" resistor was placed across the meter input terminals to form a pair of parallel resistors. The shunt resistor was of a much lower resistance value than that displayed by the meter's internal components, and thus a known larger proportion of the circuit current flowed through the shunt.

Commercial shunt resistors are available in several values, precisions, physical formats, and costs from surface mount devices to discrete flat board mounted units with screw or bolt type electrical connections. Shunt fabrication is described later in this exercise and the methods to determine current magnitudes.

Ampere's law relates current flow and magnetic fields, making it possible to measure conductor current in a non-contact methodology by measuring the strength of the magnetic field around the conductor joining the current source and the load (see Chapter 5). Magnetic field current determinations are termed indirect. The measuring sensors are isolated from the energized conductor.

Direct sensing is dependent on Ohm's law. For a direct measurement, the shunt resistor is placed in series with the current source, the load, or ground. If the shunt is between the current source and load, the measurement is considered on the "high side." If it is between the load and the ground, it is on the "low side."

The concern with high and low side positioning of the current shunt influences the technique to measure a small voltage drop across a low resistance current shunt.

Experiment

In Figure 2-3, two schematic diagrams for circuits measure low levels of electrical energy. The two electrometer circuits emphasize several important similarities common to the measurement of low-level electrical signals. In both cases, the measuring circuits must minimize the interference or distortion caused by the signal being tested by the measurement instrumentation.

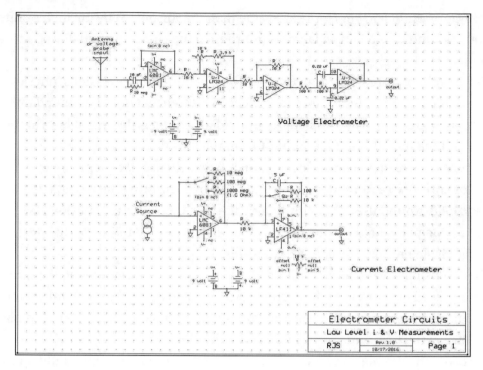

Figure 2-3. *Op-amp-based electrometers*

Hardware

Each of the circuits in Figure 2-3 uses a high-input impedance operational amplifier in the appropriate configuration. A voltage follower measures voltage and a transimpedance amplifier measures current. The circuits should be assembled on circuit boards, in metal enclosures, and follow the manufacturer's suggestions for "air insulated" input circuitry.[1] In both cases, the electrometers' readout is processed and displayed by a LabJack U-3 HV with a DAQFactory strip chart recorder display. The full-scale display (FSD) can be adjusted to suit the readings being monitored. With a +/– 9 V power supply, the display readout is limited to the +/– 7 V to 8 V swing allowed by the various IC amplifiers.

The voltage electrometer is calibrated by connecting a special battery of a precisely known voltage to the system's inputs and adjusting the variable trim resistor until the meter reads the correct voltage.

---

[1]National Semiconductor LMC6081 Data Sheet, Printed-Circuit-Board layout for high impedance work and fig. 29 "Air Wiring"

Two pins on the LM411 op-amp are marked as "offset null" and are connected to either end of a 10 kΩ variable resistor whose wiper is wired to the negative supply voltage. The offset null adjustment ensures that when both inputs have the same voltage and zero differential input, the amplifier's output is also zero. When assembling the circuit on a board and installing the board into a metal case, you should ensure that the inputs to the LF411 can be temporarily shorted to a common voltage or ground and that the trim can be adjusted on the null offset to achieve zero output with no input.

A low ohm value resistor called a *shunt resistor* converts current fluctuations to voltage variations to measure large currents. The voltage variations across low value resistors produce millivolt and lower signal levels that may require a high input impedance voltage measuring electrometer as depicted in Figure 2-3 to accurately measure larger currents and fluctuations.

A transimpedance amplifier (see Figure 2-1) converts a current into a voltage as per for in accordance with the following relationship.

$$V_{out} = -i_{in} * R_{fb} \ \text{----}(1)$$

If two TIAs are cascaded, as depicted in Figure 2-3, the current through the 10 kΩ resistor connecting the two stages is found using Ohm's law by dividing the resistance value by the output voltage of the first amplifier, as follows.

$$V_{out1} / R_{fb1} = -i_{in2} \ \text{----}(2)$$

In Eq. (1), the gain for the second amplifier is

$$V_{out2} = -i_{in2} * R_{fb2}$$

In Eq. (2),

$$V_{out2} = - (V_{out1} / 10k) * R_{fb2}$$

$$\text{since } V_{out1} = -i_{in1} * R_{fb1}$$

$$V_{out2} = - ((-I_{in1} * R_{fb1}) / 10k) * R_{fb2}$$

This can be rearranged to measure the input current in terms of the observed output voltage and the appropriate resistance values.

$$i_{in1} = V_{out2} * (10k / R_{fb1} * R_{fb2})$$

Inspection of the values of the feedback resistors in Figure 2-3 indicates that currents down to the 10^{-12} A range are measurable with the dual TIA configuration.

The measurement of higher currents with direct and indirect techniques involves shunts and magnetic field strength determinations.

Current Shunts

Passing a large current through a resistor causes the resistor to heat up in accordance with the following power expression.

$$P = i * V \text{ or } P = i^2 * R$$

A larger resistor can dissipate more heat. To keep the shunt resistor to a reasonable size, the resistance that it exhibits to the current flow must be small. Many shunt resistors are in the milliohm range (10^{-3} ohm) and can be purchased for several to tens of dollars (CDN) from electronics suppliers.

Experiments can use a measured length of readily available copper house or magnet wire whose resistance is measured in ohms per thousand feet. The resistance values can be obtained from reference books or online databases, such as at www. engineeringtoolbox.com or www.arrl.org.

Table 2-2 lists copper wire properties, including common American wire gauge size, diameter in millimeters (mm) (1/1000 in), and resistance per thousand feet at 77°F (25°C). (1000 mls/in, 1 inch = 25.400051 mm, 1 ft = 304.8 mm exactly or 0.3048 m).

Table 2-2. *Copper Wire Properties*

AWG	Dia. (mm)	Dia. (in)	R/1000 ft	Max. Current (A)
12	2.05	0.081	1.62	41
14	1.63	0.064	2.58	32
16	1.29	0.051	4.09	22
18	1.02	0.040	6.51	16

As an example of shunt usage, you can calculate the resistance required to measure a DC current in the 10 A to 20 A range as sourced from a large automotive-type lead-acid battery. An electrochemical plating or a robotics motor with a load resistance of from 1.2 Ω to 0.5 Ω could have a shunt resistor added to the circuit, as shown in Figure 2-4.

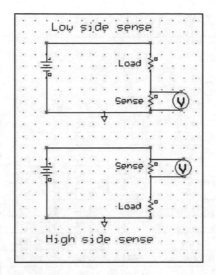

Figure 2-4. *The placement of current sensing shunts*

In terms of resistance and wattage, the shunt resistor's size determines the voltage developed across the shunt and the power that the device can safely dissipate. The choice of proximity to ground (either the high or low side of the circuit load) is determined by the technique used to measure the voltage developed across the sensing resistor.

The lower the sensing resistor's value, the less heat dissipated by the shunt and the lower the disturbance to the current flow in the operating circuit as the shunt resistor heats up. However, the lower the shunt resistance, the lower the voltage developed across the shunt with current variation and the more sensitive the voltage measurement requirement.

Numerous op-amp configurations and other specialty integrated circuits monitor the shunt voltage. Several of these circuits are best used in one of the two positions available for current monitoring, as detailed in Figure 2-4. Differential amplifiers in the form of op-amps, fabricated into special ICs known as *current shunt monitors* (CSM) or *instrumentation amplifiers*, monitor any voltage developed across the shunt resistor caused by current fluctuations.

A simple calculation indicates that a one-foot length of any of the wires listed in Table 2-2 produces an experimental shunt resistance element of from 1.62 mΩ to 6.51 mΩ. With a load resistance varying from 1.2 Ω to 0.4 Ω, the circuit current variation of approximately 10 A to 30 A results in the tabulated voltage differences shown in Table 2-3.

Table 2-3. *AWG Shunt Voltages*

		Shunt Resistance in mΩ			
Voltage =	12				
Load R$_{max}$ =	1.2				
Load R$_{min}$ =	0.6				
Δ Load R	Current	0.00162	0.00258	0.00409	0.00651
1.2	10	0.016	0.026	0.041	0.065
1.1	11	0.018	0.028	0.045	0.071
1	12	0.019	0.031	0.049	0.078
0.9	13	0.022	0.034	0.055	0.087
0.8	15	0.024	0.039	0.061	0.098
0.7	17	0.028	0.044	0.070	0.112
0.6	20	0.032	0.052	0.082	0.130
0.5	24	0.039	0.062	0.098	0.156
0.4	30	0.049	0.077	0.123	0.195

Table 2-3 shows the voltages developed across a one-foot-long shunt resistor made from the nominal copper AWG and the corresponding circuit current. The small additional resistance of the shunt has not been added to the varying total circuit resistance for simplicity of calculation.

The millivolt ranges predicted for the shunts with foot-length wire resistances vary from 16 mV to 195 mV across the lower right-hand quarter of the table for the 10 A to 30 A circuit currents. For more exacting work, the true resistance of the individual shunts should be calibrated with the technique described in the low-ohm measurement technique described in Chapter 7.

Observations

Very low-level leakage currents are often encountered when working with capacitors used in timing circuits where large or reproducible time constants are required. Leakage currents can be measured with the current electrometer circuit of Figure 2-3 configured as the circuit depicted in Figure 7-4 in Chapter 7. The device under test (DUT) is replaced by the capacitor to be tested. The configuration is simple to understand if you recall that a transimpedance amplifier appears as a "short circuit" to ground to any current source connected to its inverting input.

Figure 2-5 is the recorder trace generated by the leakage current induced in a 1 μF tantalum capacitor by a 4.72 V excitation voltage from a LiMH battery pack. The 10 tera (T) ohm input impedance, TIA current electrometer of Figure 2-3 is at its maximum sensitivity with the 1 giga (G) ohm feedback resistor in the feedback-gain loop.

Comparison of Figure 2-5 through Figure 2-7 demonstrate the capabilities available with the DAQFactory display. The top figure shows the recording of the experimental data without any data processing, and the second figure invokes a times 25 averaging of the data. Figure 2-7 demonstrates the scale expansion capabilities available with the graphical leakage display.

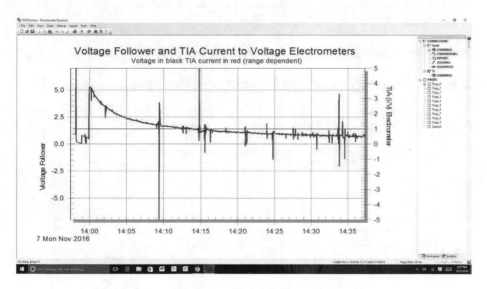

Figure 2-5. *Leakage current 1 μF tantalum capacitor*

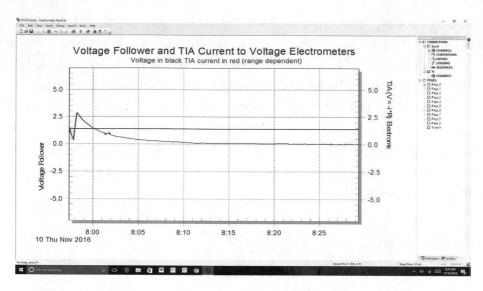

Figure 2-6. *Leakage current of two 1 μF polystyrene capacitors in parallel*

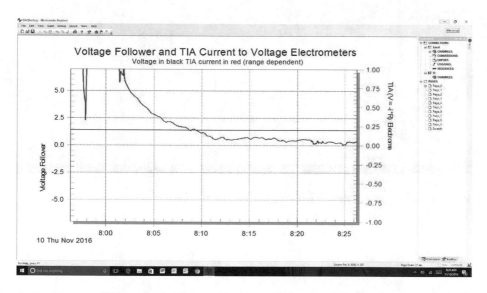

Figure 2-7. *Expanded scale leakage current of two1 μF polystyrene capacitors in parallel*

Initial attempts to measure the leakage current of a typical 1 μf polystyrene capacitor were unsuccessful. The noise in the electrometer's voltage tracing at high-scale expansion was high enough to hide any difference between the trace's averaged value and the zero line in the display. To increase the measurement's signal-to-noise ratio, two 1 μF capacitors were placed in parallel and the pair were connected to the test circuit, producing the tracings in Figures 2-6 and 2-7.

Table 2-4 tabulates the measured leakage currents of four different types of capacitors.

Table 2-4. *Measured Capacitor Dielectric Leakage Currents and Calculated Resistance*

Capacitor Type	Measured Leakage Current	Calculated Resistance
Electrolytic	1.5×10^{-6} A	$3.1 \times 10^{6}\ \Omega$
Tantalum	2.5×10^{-10} A	$1.9 \times 10^{10}\ \Omega$
Polystyrene	2.5×10^{-11} A	$1.9 \times 10^{11}\ \Omega$
Traditional HV tubular	6×10^{-10} A	$7.8 \times 10^{9}\ \Omega$

Discussion

Current flow determines the power available from electrical energy. High current flows, even at low voltages, must be channeled through carefully designed and tested circuitry able to safely dissipate the heat generated by the current passage. All materials at ambient temperatures possess some electrical resistance that opposes current flow and develops heat in the conductor (see Chapter 7).

Electrical energy flow causes magnetic fields around the conductors carrying the current with field strengths directly proportional to the current flow. Before initiating a large current passage, the resulting magnetic fields' effects on the areas around the circuitry should be evaluated.

An apparatus designed with an electromechanical ammeter can be upgraded using a TIA, a suitable feedback resistor, and a convenient readout to record or display measured currents.

An IC op-amp attempts to keep both its inputs at the same voltage level. When the non-inverting input is connected directly to ground, current sources connected to the non-inverting input see the op-amp as a "virtual" direct short to ground. An op-amp with a grounded non-inverting input with its output fed back to the inverting input through a fixed, known-value resistor is called a *transimpedance amplifier* (TIA). A TIA converts an input current to a negative output voltage. As can be seen in Figure 2-3, a cascaded pair of high-input impedance transimpedance amplifiers can be used to measure low current levels.

Current Measurements with Raspberry Pi and Python

Traditional current measurement techniques that measure the voltage drop across a known resistance require a voltage monitoring system for the Raspberry Pi (RPi). The RPi communicates with external peripherals through its general-purpose input/output (GPIO) pin array described in several texts and references, including the following.

- *Raspberry Pi User Guide* by Eben Upton and Gareth Halfacree (John Wiley and Sons, 2016)

- *Practical Raspberry Pi* by Brendan Horan (Apress, 2013)

- *Learn Raspberry Pi* with Linux by Peter Membrey and David Hows (Apress, 2012)

Voltages from sensors can be measured with the RPi by either external ADC chips or with a USB connection to an Arduino microcontroller board equipped with its 10-bit ADC. A relatively simple voltage measurement facility can be made with the GPIOZERO Python library and Microchip Technology Inc.'s MCP3008 ADC chip.

The MCP3008 is an eight-input channel device that can monitor up to eight single voltage points in a circuit or perform four differential voltage measurements. The IC chip costs approximately $5 (CDN) and is a 10-bit successive approximation register (SAR) device. A 10-bit resolution used in the LabJack, Arduino, and MCP3008 divides the input voltage into 1024 units for quantification. The 16-pin, dual inline package, plastic (PDIP), IC is connected to the RPi GPIO pins (see Figure 2-8) and uses the Python serial peripheral interface (SPI) protocol to transfer control commands and data. Ensure that the correct serial protocol has been invoked for the RPi in accordance with the actions depicted in Figures 1-16 and 1-17 in Chapter 1.

Experiment: Typical and Lower Electronic Circuit Currents

Figure 2-8 is a graphical depiction of the connections made from the RPi GPIO array to the MCP3008 and a schematic drawing of four channels that measure the current flow through the colored diodes with the accurately measured current limiting resistors.

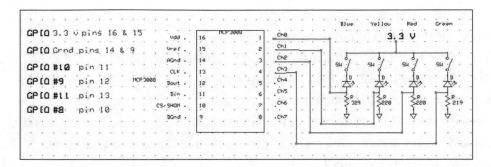

Figure 2-8. *RPi circuitry for a power monitor of LED currents*

To simplify Figure 2-8, the connecting wires between the GPIO pins and those on the MCP3008 have not been drawn in. The RPi's 3.3 V supply on the upper-left pin of the GPIO array is connected to pins 16 and 15 on the IC. The remainder of the connections are specified and connected in the same manner.

The Python code for strobing (activating) the ADC chip to conduct a conversion, then reading and displaying the 10-bit voltage value is provided in Listing 2-1 at the end of the chapter.

All complex experiment systems begin with testing each component and validating performance as a stand-alone entity. A complex system is assembled by adding a single component and, if possible, testing the assembly as each increment is made until a complete operational apparatus is built.

The early models of the RPi are reported to have been designed to provide an output current of 3 mA at the 3.3 V logic level, and hence the entire power draw available was 17 pins × 3 mA = 51 mA total. Tiny 3 mm indicator LEDs are limited to a maximum current draw of 20 mA and should be operated in the 16 mA to 18 mA range. 5 mm and 10 mm LEDs draw currents in the 20 mA to 40 mA range, and for longer service lives should be operated at 15% to 20% below their maximum short-term current handling capability.

LED emissions are directly proportional to the current flowing through the diodes. The current recommendations in a datasheet are given for a device operating at or near its maximum brightness, which is not always required for experimental work. LED currents of 5 mA to 10 mA often produce ample brightness and prevent overloading the RPi power connections on the GPIO pins.

To accommodate the limited current available from the RPi GPIO pins, the circuit in Figure 2-8 can be assembled with readily available 5 mm LEDs, suitable known value resistance CLRs, and individual manual-power control switches—all set in the open position during assembly. An array of open switches is the configuration used in the initial testing of the power monitoring exercise.

Each of the four LEDs in the array should be tested independently. Confirm their illumination when power is applied from the supply. (See the gpiozero tutorial at `https://gpiozero.readthedocs.io/en/stable/` for the command-line terminal method for manual LED activation or testing.) Once the LED diodes are successfully illuminated, with the power off, connect the diode junction and its CLR to the appropriate ADC input channel.

With the ADC correctly wired to the LED array, the connections between the MCP3008 and the RPI GPIO pins can be made, and the Python program can be run. The initial output from the system should indicate no output current for any channel or the sum. The simplicity of the system requires a manual operating mode to see the data from the power loading and distribution of the LED lighting system. As each LED is manually switched on and illuminated, the power monitor program should be run to calculate and display the individual currents drawn and their sum.

By keeping the currents through the LEDs in the 12 mA to 16 mA range, the RPi should fully illuminate three of the LEDs and illuminate the fourth diode for short periods of time while the power monitoring program collects and displays higher power consumption data. For experiments using more power than is available from the GPIO pins, an auxiliary supply, and several CMOS 4050 buffer chips could be used.

Observations

One of the objectives of this exercise is to impart a method to work safely around the limitations of a system using RPi GPIO pins to provide power to your experimental setup.

Figure 2-9 depicts a typical output in a Python console or shell from a power monitoring program.

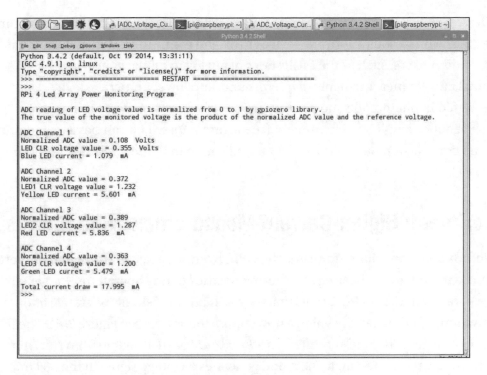

Figure 2-9. *RPi display of power monitor output program*

Figure 2-8 reveals that the voltage drop across the measured resistance of the current limiting resistor (CLR) is caused by the current flow through the diode/resistor combination. The MPC3008 channels directly measure the voltage drop across a grounded resistor to indirectly measure the current that is constant throughout the circuit.

Discussion

As an educational computer, the Raspberry Pi functions in an information processing mode and as a physical computing platform. However, when used in a physical computing mode, the limitations of the compact, inexpensive system must be recognized. The RPi operating system is process-driven and may not immediately respond to an event on a GPIO pin if a higher-priority process runs in the processor core. Graphics processing is a large consumer of computing resources. Hence, the RPI should use the most utilitarian or minimal screen displays possible in a physical computing mode.

The Raspberry Pi Foundation offers several Python libraries that allow the computer to interface with various hardware devices to extend communication with external devices and sensors, such as the MCP series of analog to digital converters.

Small current measurements of micro, nano, and lower amperage levels, as encountered in photodiode and phototransistor currents, are monitored with a transimpedance amplifier electrometer (see Figure 2-3), which can be read and printed to an RPi console or plotted with a slight modification to Python (see Listing 1-4 in Chapter 1).

Experiment: Higher Current Measurement with Shunts

Less information is available for using the GPIO array to measure the higher amperage currents encountered in heating and thermoelectric cooling operations. Larger currents can be measured with an INA219 IC that uses a "high side" shunt resistance and sensitive amplifier to read the voltage drop across the shunt (see Figure 2-4). The INA219 is a special current shunt IC mounted on a *breakout board* available from Adafruit Industries. It can measure up to 3.2 A and generates a voltage signal in the 300 millivolt range, which can be read directly by the MCP3008 ADC.

Experiment

A wide range of currents can be monitored with the RPi and the commercially available breakout board containing the surface mount technology (SMT) Texas Instruments INA219 current sensor. The board is available from Adafruit Industries ($10 CDN) and has a 0.1 Ω 1% shunt resistor in addition to the INA219 IC. The board can be fitted with header pins to allow the sensor to be mounted onto a prototyping board for development work in current monitoring.

The board has two-screw terminal connections for wiring the sensor in series with the current source to be monitored. For demonstration purposes, the sensor can be used with the RPi–Arduino IDE and the previously assembled current mirror circuit in Figure 1-7 used to charge the large capacitors in Chapter 1.

The current from the capacitor charging transistor's collector is rerouted through the INA219 sensor board's screw terminals and into and out of the capacitor.

A ground and 5 V board power are supplied by connecting the nominal pins and sockets on the Arduino and the breakout board. Communication between the RPi

Arduino IDE and the breakout board is established by connecting the SCL of the sensor board to the A5 analog input (or SCL) connection on the microcontroller and connecting the sensor board SCA to the A4 Arduino input (or SCA).

The manufacturer provides a complete Arduino library for reading the sensor. It is available for download.

Once the connections between the microcontroller and the sensor board are all secure, power can be applied to the current mirror to cycle the capacitor under test through the charge and discharge cycles, as indicated by the red and green LEDs on the 555 timer output.

The Adafruit_INA219 Arduino library has a (get current) "get_current" method or function option that displays data on the Arduino's serial monitor.

Observations

In Figure 2-9, the current cycling, as monitored by the Arduino on the SPI serial bus, is validated. Figure 2-10 shows the discharge cycle.

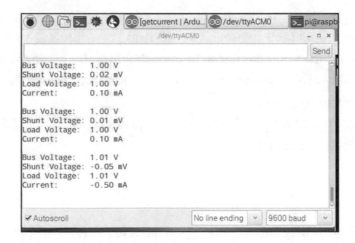

Figure 2-10. *INA219 serial port data output from current mirror*

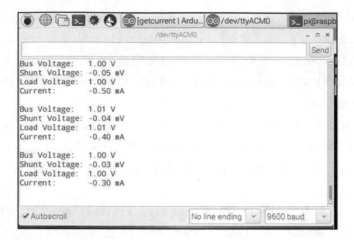

Figure 2-11. *INA219 data output from current mirror discharge cycle*

With a 2000 µF electrolytic capacitor connected to the current mirror powered by 5.95 V C cell batteries and a 47 kΩ discharge resistor, the cycle charged for 36 seconds and discharged for 9 seconds. From Ohm's law, the theoretical mirror current is calculated to be 5.95 / (47000 + 100) or 0.126 mA.

The current sense board indicates a charging current of 0.10 mA.

The 555 timer should cycle between one-third and two-thirds (2 V or 4 V) of the 6 V supply. Hence at 4 V, the timer connects the capacitor and discharge resistor to ground. Both the mirror current and the charge on the capacitor flow through the current sensor and discharge resistor to ground.

The discharge current recorded in Figure 2-10 peaks at –.50 mA and decays in subsequent readings from the sensor.

Discussion

Newer Arduino boards may have SCA and SCL input headers adjacent to the reference (ref) voltage header for the communication connections. Older microcontrollers use A5 and A4 analog inputs.

The default serial baud rate in the Arduino executable "get_current" (get current) code function call is set to 115200, resulting in a random hash output on the serial port if the serial port window is not configured to accept the breakout board rate. A normal readout can often be obtained by resetting the Arduino program serial baud rate to 9600.

Although the breakout board and library are not set up for rapidly varying current flows, a satisfactory bidirectional current flow can be followed for slowly varying signals, as evident in Figures 2-9 and 2-10.

The Texas Instruments (TI) INA219 is a current sense monitor (CSM) IC with a programmable gain amplifier (PGA) to read the shunt voltage. The PGA output is converted to a digital format by an onboard ADC and sent to the Arduino-RPi on an I2C, or a SMBus-compatible serial transmission format on an Arduino serial port display. The library default output reports bus voltage from 0 to 26 V, the current, shunt voltage, and load voltage. With a 0.01 Ω shunt able to produce a +/– 320 mV signal, the system can monitor up to 3.2 A.

If a project requires the recording and displaying high or low current measurements, the Python serial port's data capture code and the Matplotlib plotter code (see Listings 1-3 and 1-4 in Chapter 1) can be adapted as required. Listing 2-2 is a supplementary and completely documented version of the plotter code.

Code Listings

Listing 2-1. Python Code for the Raspberry Pi: Monitoring the Power Draw of a 4 LED Array

```
print("RPi 4 Led Array Power Monitoring Program")
print() # a blank line for output screen spacing
print("ADC reading of LED voltage value is normalized from 0 to 1 by
gpiozero library.")
print("The true value of the monitored voltage is the product of the
normalized ADC value and the reference voltage.")
print()
# a single normalized value is printed each time the module is run

from gpiozero import MCP3008
# create an object representing the device and assign the input channels
ADC_vlu = MCP3008(0)    # the number in brackets is the channel on the device
ADC_vlu1 = MCP3008(1)
ADC_vlu2 = MCP3008(2)
ADC_vlu3 = MCP3008(3)
```

```
#
print("ADC Channel 1")
print('Normalized ADC value = %.3f'%ADC_vlu.value,' Volts')
# the blue LED in the author's circuit
#
# convert object, value into a numerical parameter
ledVltg = float(ADC_vlu.value) * 3.3
print('LED CLR voltage value = %.3f'%ledVltg, ' Volts')
# calculate the LED current from Ohms law
blue = (float((ADC_vlu.value) *3.3) / 329) * 1000
print('Blue LED current = %.3f'%blue,' mA')
#
print()
#
print("ADC Channel 2")
print('Normalized ADC value = %.3f'%ADC_vlu1.value)
# the yellow LED in the author's circuit
#
# convert object, value into a numerical parameter
led1Vltg = float(ADC_vlu1.value) * 3.3
print('LED1 CLR voltage value = %.3f'%led1Vltg)
# calculate the LED1 current from Ohms law
yellow = (float((ADC_vlu1.value) *3.3) / 220) * 1000
print('Yellow LED current = %.3f'%yellow,' mA')
#
print()
#
print("ADC Channel 3")
print('Normalized ADC value = %.3f'%ADC_vlu2.value)
# the red LED in the author's circuit
#
# convert object, value into a numerical parameter
led2Vltg = float(ADC_vlu2.value) * 3.3
print('LED2 CLR voltage value = %.3f'%led2Vltg)
```

```
# calculate the LED2 current from Ohms law
red = (float((ADC_vlu2.value) *3.3) / 220) * 1000
print('Red LED current = %.3f'%red,' mA')
#
print()
#
print("ADC Channel 4")
print('Normalized ADC value = %.3f'%ADC_vlu3.value)
# the green LED in the author's circuit
#
# convert object, value into a numerical parameter
led3Vltg = float(ADC_vlu3.value) * 3.3
print('LED3 CLR voltage value = %.3f'%led3Vltg)
# calculate the LED3 current from Ohms law
green = (float((ADC_vlu3.value) *3.3) / 219) * 1000
print('Green LED curret = %.3f'%green,' mA')
#
print()
#
ttl_Currnt_drw = blue + yellow + red + green
print('Total current draw = %.3f'%ttl_Currnt_drw, ' mA')
```

Listing 2-2. Python Strip Chart Recorder Plotting Code

```
# SCR Plotting of Normalized Potentiometer Voltage Value from an MCP3008 ADC.
# gpiozero library used to configure MCP3008 and generate the ADC instance
# attributes for plotting. SCR emulation is implemented as a series of
# sequential time windows controlled by the maxt variable in Line 19.
# The default value from the Matplotlib code is 40 min. Set as required for
# the desired trace resolution. The y axis is determined by the bracketed
# values in line 29. Positive and negative values can be for a normal
# display while a display about zero can be created by using the desired
# amplitudes above and below the zero axis by indicating the desired
# sign of the values to graph.
```

```python
# Data is generated in the rd_data() function with the pot.value attribute
  of the MCP3008(0) instance, pot created in line 21.
# The x and y axes labels are created in lines 63 and 64 respectively.
#
import matplotlib
import numpy as np
from matplotlib.lines import Line2D
import matplotlib.pyplot as plt
import matplotlib.animation as animation
import time
from gpiozero import MCP3008
#
pot = MCP3008(0)
#
#
class Scope:
    def __init__(self, ax, maxt=4, dt=0.02):
        """maxt time width of display"""
        self.ax = ax
        self.dt = dt
        self.maxt = maxt
        self.tdata = [0]
        self.ydata = [0]
        self.line = Line2D(self.tdata, self.ydata)
        self.ax.add_line(self.line)
        self.ax.set_ylim(-1.0,1.0)  # y axis scale
        self.ax.set_xlim(0, self.maxt)

    def update(self, y):
        lastt = self.tdata[-1]
        if lastt > self.tdata[0] + self.maxt: # reset the arrays
            self.tdata = [self.tdata[-1]]
            self.ydata = [self.ydata[-1]]
            self.ax.set_xlim(self.tdata[0], self.tdata[0] + self.maxt)
            self.ax.figure.canvas.draw()
```

```python
        t = self.tdata[-1] + self.dt
        self.tdata.append(t)
        self.ydata.append(y)
        self.line.set_data(self.tdata, self.ydata)
        return self.line,
#
#
def rd_data():
    while True:
        inPutln = pot.value
        #print("inPutln = ", inPutln)  # print out for code development or
                                        error checking
        line = inPutln
        # print(line)                  # print out for code development or
                                        error checking
        yield (line)

fig = plt.figure()
fig.suptitle("The Scientyst's Ayde", fontsize = 12)
ax = fig.add_subplot(111)
ax.set_xlabel("Time")
ax.set_ylabel("Potentiometer Voltage")
scope = Scope(ax)

# uses rd_data() as a generator to produce data for the update func, the
# MCP3008 value is read by the plotting code in timed width windows
# (default minutes)for the animated screen display. Software overhead
# limits response speed of display.
ani = animation.FuncAnimation(fig, scope.update, rd_data, interval=50,
blit=False)

plt.show()
```

Summary

Prior to the development of solid-state systems, measuring voltage drops across known resistance for current measurements were made by evaluating the magnetic fields generated by moving currents.

Higher amperage current flows are often measured by determining the voltage drop across shunt resistors.

Very low current flows are measured with electrometers configured from high input impedance, integrated-circuit, transimpedance amplifiers.

Static and continuous measurements of current values that may span over six orders of magnitude need to be made with different techniques and software able to accommodate the corresponding orders of magnitude extremes found in the devices under test.

In many experimental setups, electrical current develops heat to change temperatures that are measured by the methods and techniques outlined in Chapter 3.

CHAPTER 3

Heat and Temperature

Temperature and heat measurements play significant roles in virtually every scientific, engineering, medical and technological discipline.

Heat is a form of energy attributable to molecular or atomic vibration and motion. Heat is transferred from hot objects to cooler by radiation, conduction, and convection. Heat transfer between masses is measured by observing the change in temperature of the masses exchanging energy and "specific heat" is the value relating heat difference per unit of mass to the observed temperature change.

Solid-state devices can move heat into and out of substrates solely by the application of electrical current.

Chemical reactions and phase changes involve heat liberation or up-take hence the progress of the phenomenon under study can be followed by monitoring temperature differences. (See Figure 3-47 for a graphic demonstration of latent heat.) Medical imaging, equipment overheating and physical heat loss through infrared scanning, thermometric (Enthalpimetric) titrations, differential scanning calorimetry and thermogravimetric analysis are some of the many measurement techniques reliant on heat and temperature measurements.

Usually experiments involving heat energy must follow the temperature. A review of temperature determination methods should precede the measurements of heat, solid-state heat transfer and the creation of high temperature, high heat systems.

Temperature Measurement

Life in our world has evolved in and from liquid water that, when boiled or frozen, defined two points on our temperature measurement system. Currently, superconductor research at cryogenic temperatures and fusion research deal with a greatly expanded temperature range than that defined by the phase changes of water.

© Richard J. Smythe 2022
R. J. Smythe, *Arduino Measurements in Science*, https://doi.org/10.1007/978-1-4842-6781-3_3

In keeping with the introductory nature of this book, dealing with basic experimental sciences, we measure the more moderate temperature ranges accessible with relatively inexpensive sensors and readout systems that theoretically range between –200°C and 1250°C. Temperature scales for science are Celsius or Kelvin in which the freezing point of water is the zero point for the Celsius scale, and absolute zero, the point at which all molecular motion ceases, is the zero point for the Kelvin scale. The zero for the Celsius scale is 273.15°K on the Kelvin scale. A third temperature measurement system commonly in use in North America is the Fahrenheit scale in which the freezing point of water is 32°F and the boiling point of water is 212°F. (To convert °F to °C, subtract 32 from the Fahrenheit number, then multiply by 5 and divide by 9. To convert °C to °F, multiply the Celsius value by 9, divide the product by 5, and add 32 to the quotient.)

$$(\text{Deg. C} \times 9/5) + 32 = \text{Deg. F}$$
$$(\text{Deg. F} - 32) \times 5/9 = \text{Deg. C}$$

Cryogenic temperatures in the Fahrenheit scale are degrees Rankine in which absolute zero, or 0°R, is –459.67°F.

Temperatures change the physical and chemical properties of materials and these effects must be considered when choosing a temperature measuring system for a specific application. In addition to the loss of structural strength imposed by the melting points of materials, more subtle effects such as in K-type thermocouples with chromel-alumel alloys with a discontinuity at 350°C due to a Curie point change in the nickel of the alloy's metals must be accommodated. Small compensation is required for the Curie point of nickel that at 358°C transitions from being ferromagnetic to paramagnetic, thus disturbing the voltage-temperature linearity (see NIST tables for corrections). Metals also exhibit increasing resistance with temperature, a phenomenon that is the basis for accurate temperature determinations using resistance temperature devices (RTD) fabricated from platinum thin films and wire.

Simplistically, heat is energy in the form of atomic or molecular vibration. Temperature is a measure of the amplitude of that vibration for each degree of freedom. If a temperature sensor is to monitor the temperature of a mass, then some of the heat in the mass must be transferred to the sensor to bring its temperature up to that of the mass. Recalling that heat is transferred by radiation, conduction, or convection, the experimenter must ensure unimpeded heat flow to the sensor. Total immersion, heat transfer fluids or pastes, agitation, and mechanical fasteners can ensure adequate heat transfer between mass and sensor. Optical temperature measurement may be required for small mass samples since any transfer of heat to the sensor disturbs the temperature being measured.

During the design of experimental setups, you must be careful in the use of materials such a polyvinyl chloride (PVC), polyethylene (PE) or Teflon and other plastics that insulate electrical conductors at room temperatures but soften and melt at temperatures above the boiling point of water and become increasingly brittle at temperatures below the freezing point. Glass, ceramics, and metals all have upper temperature limits at which they lose their mechanical strength and melt. Some of these materials withstand large and rapid temperature changes while others do not.

Increased temperatures increase the rates of chemical reactions. Metal materials of construction such as irons and steels that are moderately stable at room temperature, in dry conditions, oxidize as the temperature increases in the presence of oxygen. Elevated temperatures greatly increase corrosion rates at dissimilar metal points of contact. Screw connections on terminal blocks, threaded fasteners joining copper wires with steel bolts or screws must be configured, positioned, or protected to minimize heat exposure or air exposure.

Traditional temperature measurements have been standardized primarily around the boiling and freezing points of water. Thermometers using an expanding or contracting column of mercury encased in a graduated glass capillary are one of the more common traditional and current laboratory instruments in use for measuring temperatures. Mercury-in-glass thermometers are fragile and the temperature range available wide because of the $-38°C$ to $350°C$ liquid state of the metal. Mercury vapor is highly toxic, so great care must be taken to ensure the mercury remains encapsulated by the glass capillary and is completely cleaned up or re-encapsulated in the event of an accident.

Significantly more robust temperature measurements can be made electronically by several methods.

Thermocouples formed at the junction of dissimilar metals generate a small, relatively linear current over a wide range of temperatures. *Thermistors* (or *thermal resistors*) exhibit a non-linear resistance change over a limited range of temperatures, and special solid-state integrated circuits are made to measure essentially ambient environmental temperatures. Infrared sensors are available for non-contact measurements over an intermediate range of temperature. Resistance temperature devices (RTD) manufactured from thin films or platinum wires can be used for sensitive temperature measurements over a substantial range of degrees. The general properties of various sensors are summarized in Table 3-1.

Table 3-1. *Temperature Sensors*

Sensor	Range deg. C	Resolution deg. C	Sensitivity	Sensor Output Signal
IC (TI LM35)	-50 to 150	1/4 to 3/4	10mv/deg C	temperature proportional analog voltage
Infra-red	-70 to 380	0.5	0.01	SMBuss serial digital output
RTD	-200 to 800	0.15	0.00385 ohm/ohm/deg	linear temperature dependent resistance
Therrmistor (TMO)	-55 to 300	0.01 with dsp	4-5% dec./deg C.	exponential temperature dependant resistance
Therrmistor (SiC)	-200 to 500 deg. C	0.01 with dsp	8-9% dec./deg C	exponential temperature dependant resistance
Thermometer (Hg)	-35 to 350	1 deg grad	estimate 1/4 deg	liquid column expansion for visual observation
Thermocouple	-200 to 2350	1	approx 20 to 41 uV/deg C	temperature dependent microvolt generation
Sensor	Response time	Degree of robustness	Sensor Size and form	Cost
IC (TI LM35)	fast	good encapsulated IC	TO-49 and cct bd mt	1 to 2$
Infra-red	fast	complex metal crystal structure	TO-39	20 to 50$
RTD	slow 1 - 10 sec	metal film on ceramic plate	cylndrcl probe/flat tabs	$20 and up
Therrmistor (TMO)	1 sec.	good epoxy or glass coated	micro beads 2-3 mm dia.	2 - 10$
Therrmistor (SiC)	1 sec.	metal can or epoxy coated	TO-46 (6 mm dia.)	approx. 15$
Thermometer (Hg)	seconds	fragile borosilicate glass	bulky	approx. 75$
Thermocouple	1 sec.	robust welded metal wire	fine thin wire	base metals 15 - 20$

Platinum-based RTDs are generally more expensive than the conventional devices considered in this book. However, if the experiment requires precise measurement of temperatures not obtainable with the conventional techniques in the following exercises, the appropriate RTD needs to be used. There are excellent application notes and descriptions of RTDs available at www.omega.com, www.digikey.com, and www.littlefuse.com.

RTDs are available in thin film forms and as wire wound elements. The temperature range to be monitored and the experimental setup constraints determine which form must be used for the desired temperature resolution required. The complexities of specialty RTD applications are described in the literature available from the supplier noted earlier. A complete system for interfacing Pt-RTDs to microprocessors to obtain 0.5°C resolution over the –200°C to 800°C range is available in the MAX31865 SMT chip. US Sensor, 100 Ω thin-film platinum RTD devices p/n PPG101A are available from distributor DigiKey for $20.

Many traditional laboratory and clinical methods for temperature measurement still use mercury-in-glass thermometers in numerous physical forms for general and specialized measurements. Calibrated mercury-in-glass thermometers are theoretically available for measurements between –38.37°C to 356.73°C, the element's liquid range. Sets of liquid metals in glass or quartz thermometers are available capable of 0.1°C temperature resolution. (Mercury-in-glass thermometer sales are restricted in the EU). Temperatures above and below that measurable with mercury/liquid metals expansion can be made with thermocouples. Bimetallic junctions designated as J- and K-types have reproducible, specific voltage-temperature relationships that have been established between –200°C to 750°C and 1250°C, respectively.

In keeping with the intended nature of this book, the exercises and discussion to follow deal with the base metal thermocouple temperature sensors rather than the more expensive platinum-based devices. There are experimental conditions in which the platinum metals group is the only sensor type available. You should then consult the appropriate references in the literature.

Thermocouples produce microvolt signals that must be amplified to power any form of display. The thermistors, RTDs, and infrared sensors require power supplies for excitation or biasing to create electronic signals proportional to temperatures.

Thermistors are manufactured in microbead formats from solid-state mixtures of transition metal oxides for temperature sensing over a –100°C to 200°C range. Silicon carbide (SiC) thermistors are available for temperature measurements from –20°C up to 450°C. Thermistors are available with protective glass, epoxy, and metal coatings or sheaths. The silicon carbide sensors are available in metal TO-46 "Top Hat" cases with short electrical leads and epoxy-coated bead formats. The higher temperature capability of the SiC thermistor metal devices create some electrical connection problems. The higher end of the device's temperature measurement range is above the melting point of tin-lead solder. Electrically sound connections must be made mechanically to use the TO-46 devices.

Connecting a temperature sensor to a monitoring device creates a time delay between temperature changes in the mass being monitored and the alteration of the output of the monitoring device. The time difference is the *response time*. For simple experiments measuring the temperature at which an event occurs or recording data over time to detect multiple thermal events, the time lag in display response is usually of secondary importance to the numerical temperature value being measured. If the thermal data controls a process, such as keeping a furnace at a constant temperature or adding a reagent to a chemical system, then the system response time becomes of primary importance and sensor response, heat transfer, and data processing times must all be minimal.

As in virtually all forms of experimental measurements, a method must be available for verification or validation of the values being produced by the measurement system in use. The International Temperature Scale (1990) defines the boiling point and freezing points of various elemental standards that can verify temperatures ranging from close to absolute zero to 1085°C.

Some of the more convenient metals, such as tin (melting point 232°C), lead (mp 327°C), zinc (mp 420°C), aluminum (mp 660°C), and copper (mp 1084°C), can be used as practical, intermediate to higher temperature validation standards.

Research into energy storage has led to the assembly of compilations of the melting or freezing points of eutectic mixtures of salts and oxides (see www.nist.gov/system/files/documents/srd/NSRDS-61_Part-1.pdf). Table 3-2 has been compiled from the cited source and various additional sources to assemble many known eutectic melt mixtures to form a reference scale spanning the temperature range from room temperatures to 1250°C.

Extreme caution must be used in dealing with molten salts. Molten salts dissolve some metals, glass, and ceramics, causing unexpected failures with disastrous explosions, fires and often causing severe burns. If you are not familiar with working with molten salt, you should consult chemists or physicists who are familiar with it, or examine the original literature found in the reference listing of the NBS document from which numerous entries in Table 3-2 were extracted.

Platinum ware contains many but not all molten salts. Iron, nickel, and zirconium metalware can be used with some of the mixtures. Fused quartz, porcelain, and borosilicate glass vessels can contain various molten mixtures at temperatures below the containers melting points.

The mixtures selected for the tabulation have been chosen to contain readily available, inexpensive components that should fuse smoothly with little or no decomposition. If a temperature measuring system is to be validated, a mix with a melting point close to the desired temperature should be chosen, the ingredients collected, and the original literature or an expert in fusion work consulted to select an appropriate vessel to contain the melt. With a suitable heat source, the ingredients can then be fused, allowed to cool, and the resultant glass or melt broken up into pieces of a suitable size for testing the validity of the temperature measurement system.

Table 3-2. *Melting Point Mixtures*

Temperature	Compound Blend	Mol. %	T in deg C
rt to 100	$Ca(NO_3)_2 . 4H_2O - Zn(NO_3)_2 . 6H_2O$	51	25
	urea – KI – NaI	79-3-18	50
	$Cd(NO_3)_2 - NH_4NO_3$	23.5	74
	urea – NH_4NO_3	82.9	101.5
> 100	$Ca(NO_3)_2$ – urea – KNO_3	23.9 – 57.7 – 18.3	125
	CuCl – KCl	66	150
	$Cd(NO_3)_2 - KNO_3$	25	175
	$NH_4Cl - SnCl_2$	56	200
> 200	$NaCl - NaNO_3 - NaOH$	1.6 – 70.8 – 27.6	225
	KI – KOH	27	250
	LiCl – LiOH	34.5	274
	CuCN – KCL	41	275
> 300	$ZnCl_2 - ZnSO_4$	37	300
	CuCN – KCl	30	325
	$KCl - MnCl_2 - NaCl$	28.7 – 45 – 26.3	350
	$FeCl_2 - KCl$	40.7	350 +/– 2
	$FeCl_2 - NaCl$	44	374
> 400	$KCl - MnCl_2 - NaCl$	37.7 – 37.3 – 25	400
	$MnCl_2 - NaCl$	50	425
	$KCl - MnCl_2$	35	450
	$KSO_4 - ZnSO_4$	23	475
> 500	$CaCl_2 - NaCl$	52.8	500
	$Na_2S - PbS$	58.5 (app)	525
	$KCl - Na_2SO_4$	58.6	528
	$BaCl_2 - KCl - MgCl_2 - NaCl$	15.5 – 43.3 – 9.7 – 31.5	550
	$NaCl - NaF - Na_2CO_3$	42.5 – 20.5 – 37	575
> 600	$CaCl_2 - KCl$	26.6	600
	$BaCl_2 - CaCl_2$	54	624
	CaO – NaF	48	650
	$BaCl_2 - NaCl$	39.6	650
	NaCl – NaF	66	675
> 700	$K_2SO_4 - Li_2SO_4$	60	700
	$NaCl - CaSO_4$	79.8	725
	$K_2SO_4 - MgSO_4$	64.5	750
	$NaF - Na_2SO_4$	64	772
> 800	$CaO - CaCl_2$	70 – 77.5	800
	$Na_2CO_3 - Na_2SO_4$	62	826
	$Na_2O - TiO_2$	76	850
	$CaSO_4 - K_2SO_4$	39.7	875
	$BaCl_2 - BaO$	87.5	899
> 900	$NaF - TiO_2$	80	920
	$CaF_2 - CaSO_4$	50	951
	$Na_3AlF_6 - ZnO$	92.8	974
> 1000	$MgF_2 - NaF$	36	1000
	$Na_2O - SiO_2$	56.1	1022
	$CuO - Cu_2O - SiO_2$	40.8 – 48.4 – 10.8	1050
	$Al_2O_3 - CuO - Cu_2O$	2.8 – 55.9 – 41.2	1075
> 1100	$BaO - SiO_2 - ZnO$	23 – 59 – 10 (app)	1100

The higher heat and temperatures required to fuse most of the mixtures in Table 3-2 can be achieved with nichrome wire heating elements in the air. Nichrome melts at 1400°C (2550°F) but should be limited to operation below 1250°C (2282°F) with great care and below 1100°C (2212°F) for greater safety.

You must be careful because the components of the heating system are near their melting points at these elevated temperatures. The fusion of any of the materials of construction could cause spillage of the melt or electrical short circuits, either of which could cause fires or explosive dispersal of molten materials with disastrous results.

Safe, practical, high heat, high-temperature systems used for glass blowing, soldering, brazing, and welding are dealt with in reference texts and specialized publications (see *Building Scientific Apparatus*, 4th Ed. by John Moore et al (Cambridge University Press, 2009) and Jacobs-online.biz/nichrome_wire.htm). The final portions of the Measurement of Heat and Temperature dealing with thermocouples use small open flames to generate high temperatures for demonstration and testing purposes. Attempts to work safely at temperatures above 1100°C (2212°F) usually require special non-metallic heating elements, special power supplies, and inert atmospheres or vacuum chambers that involve expenses and techniques beyond the simplified nature of this book.

Subambient and Low Temperatures

Low-temperature calibrations should be limited to salt and water ice baths unless you are familiar with and equipped to handle volatile, toxic, explosive solvents and have access to cryogenic solids or liquids.

Physical chemistry that explains the changes in colligative properties of solutions, such as boiling point elevation and freezing point depression, can be used to establish reference temperatures for low-temperature thermal measurement system validation. As a solution dissolves in water, the freezing point of the solution goes down, while the boiling point goes up, in accordance with the concentrations of the dissolved solute.

By carefully controlling the nature of the solute, solute concentration, and heat flow into and out of the vessel holding the solution, stable sub-zero temperatures can be achieved. Stable, reproducible, sub-zero temperatures can be difficult to generate from ice and common, highly soluble chemical salts such as sodium and calcium chlorides because of varying concentrations as the ice melts. Researchers in plant physiology published a method for the preparation of salt-ice-based cryostats. The low-temperature baths were prepared from selected salts that are sparingly soluble in water.

Cryostats prepared from Dewar flasks (glass or metal vacuum jacket containers, thermos bottles), stirring equipment, and the appropriate quantities of the chosen salt, finely crushed ice, and water, are capable of prolonged operation at temperatures ranging from fractions of a degree below zero to several degrees are tabulated in Table 3-3 with data collected from several sources, including *Chemist's Companion: A Handbook of Practical Data, Techniques and References* by Arnold Gordon and Richard Ford (J. Wiley & Sons, 1972).

A two-phase three-component system is formed by using an excess of salt crystals from compounds with a limited water solubility. As the ice melts, more salt dissolves, thus maintaining a constant salt concentration and temperature. Table 3-3 is a tabulated collection of selected data assembled from referenced sources.

Table 3-3. *Cryostat Mixtures*

	Common Salt Cryostats			
Salt	Grams salt per 100 g ice	Bath temp deg C	Starting temperature	Chemical name and solubility
$Na_2B_4O_7 . 10H_2O$	20	-0.4		Borax 25.2 gm/l
$Na_2HPO_4 . 7H_2O$	100	-0.048		Sodium hydrogen phosphate 7.7 gm/100 ml
H_3BO_3	30	-0.7		Boric acid 57 gm/l at 25 deg. C
Na_2SO_4	50	-1.02		Sodium sulphate 4.76 gm/100 ml
Na_2CO_3	70	-2.08	-1 (ice)	Sodium carbonate 71 gm/l at 0 deg. C
$NaHCO_3$	70	-2.34		Sodium bicarbonate 69 gm/l at 0 deg. C
$NaHCO_3 + Na_2CO_3$	70 + 70	-3.26		
NH_4NO_3	106	-4	20	Ammonium nitrate 213 gm/100 at 25 deg, C
$NaC_2H_3O_2$	85	-4.7	10.7	Sodium acetate 54.4 gm/100 ml at 25 deg. C
NH_4Cl	30	-5.1	13.3	Ammonium chloride 39.5 at 25 deg. C
$NaNO_3$	75	-5.3	13.2	Sodium nitrate 91.2 gm/100 ml at 25 deg. C
$Na_2S_2O_3 . 5H_2O$	110	-8	10.7	Sodium thiosulphate penta hydrate 70.1 gm/100ml at 20 deg. C
$CaCl_2 . 6H_2O$	41	-9	-1 (ice)	Calcium chloride hexa hydrate 59.5 gm/100ml at 0 deg. C
KCl	30	-10.9	0 (ice)	Potassium chloride 281 gm/l at 0 deg. C
KI	140	-11.7	10.8	Potassium iodide 128 gm/l at 0 deg. C
NH_4NO_3	60	-13.6	13.6	Ammonium nitrate 213 gm/100 at 25 deg, C
NH_4Cl	25	-15.4	-1(ice)	Ammonium chloride 39.5 at 25 deg. C
NH_4NO_2	45	-16.8	-1(ice)	Ammonium nitrate 213 gm/100 at 25 deg, C
NH_4SCN	133	-18	13.2	Ammonium thiocyanate 128 gm/100 ml at 0 deg. C
NaCl	33	-21.3	-1(ice)	Sodium chloride 359 gm/l
$CaCl_2 . 6H_2O$	81	-21.5	0 (ice)	Calcium chloride hexa hydrate 59.5 gm/100ml at 0 deg. C
H_2SO_4 (66%)	23	-25	0 (ice)	Sulphuric acid is miscible with water
NaBr	66	-28	0 (ice)	Sodium bromide 90.5 gm/100ml at 20 deg. C
H_2SO_4 (66%)	40	-30	0 (ice)	Sulphuric acid is miscible with water
C_2H_5OH	105	-30	0 (ice)	ethyl alcohol (ethanol) is miscible with water
$MgCl_2$	85	-34	0 (ice)	Magnesium chloride 54.3 gm/100 ml at 20 deg. C
H_2SO_4 (66%)	91	-37	0 (ice)	Sulphuric acid is miscible with water
$CaCl_2 . 6H_2O$	123	-40.3	0 (ice)	Calcium chloride hexa hydrate 59.5 gm/100ml at 0 deg. C
$CaCl_2 . 6H_2O$	143	-55	0 (ice)	Calcium chloride hexa hydrate 59.5 gm/100ml at 0 deg. C

Subambient temperatures can also be created with electro-mechanical gas expansion/compression and solid-state semiconductor systems that can convert between heat and electrical energy and thus move or "pump" heat between thermally isolated environments.

Thermistor: Sensitive High-Resolution Temperature Measurements

Transition Metal Oxide Thermistors −40°C to 150°C

For biological, medical, and thermometric chemical analysis involving near ambient or room temperature solution chemistry, the thermistor is the most sensitive temperature sensor available at the time of writing. In addition to sensitivity, it is manufactured in micro-sized bead-shaped packages, is robust, inert, inexpensive, and exhibits a rapid response to temperature changes. A thermistor's non-linear nature is not of great concern when used with data processing software or to measure small or fractional degree temperature changes.

A 2004 STMicroelectronics application note AN1755, describes a method for using a 555 timer chip, a thermistor, and a microprocessor, to develop a high-resolution temperature measurement system (see `www.st.com/resource/en/application_note/cd00010962-a-high-resolutionprecision-thermometer-using-st7-and-ne555-stmicroelectronics.pdf`). The system converts temperature changes in the thermistor into variations in the output frequency of the timer chip.

Placing an NTC thermistor and a high-quality, low-leakage capacitor in the resistor/capacitor timing network of an astable configured 555 timer, the resulting duty cycle or pulse width ratios of the timer chip output vary as a function of the thermistor temperature. When measured in microseconds by a high-speed microprocessor with averaged multiple readings, the width of the output pulses provides a sensitive, high-resolution measure of the thermistor bead temperature. The microprocessor's digitized signal can then be streamed out to a computer serial port for a graphical display in a PC-based SCADA program.

In AN1755, the cycle timing of the 555 is discussed and displayed in two figures within the application note. However, the timer outputs a square-wave pulse train of high and low pulses as it cycles between one-third to two-thirds portions of the supply voltage. The resistance of the thermistor is a function of its temperature. Thermistor resistance partly determines the rate at which the capacitor is charged. It can be demonstrated from the mathematical expressions for the high and low time intervals t_1 and t_2, as follows.

$$t_1 = 0.693(R_{ntc} + R_2)C\text{--- }1$$

$$t_2 = 0.693(R_2)C\text{--- }2$$

thus

$$R_{ntc} = R_2(t_1 - t_2)/t_2\text{--- }3$$

Although the value of C does not directly enter the calculation of the value of R_{ntc} it does determine the value of the high and low t_1 and t_2 time values. If the difference between t_1 and t_2 is used as a measure of the temperature change and that change is measured in microseconds, the resolution of the temperature measurement can be markedly increased by using a large value of C.

In this application, C is a timing capacitor. It should be a plastic film, low-leakage type of device. Low-leakage, plastic film capacitors have very low polarity dielectric media that require large and expensive material packages to make devices of higher capacitance values. Smaller physical sizes are typically available in the pF and nF range capacitance values, but these too can be expensive and difficult to find. To maximize the Δt value, as large a value of a plastic film device as practical should be used where possible. Some of my development circuits were assembled with 1 µF polystyrene capacitors that were 5/32 × ½ × 1¾ in (4 × 10 × 45 mm) in size.

In theory, the frequency of the timer cycling is proportional to 1/ln(2)*(R1+R2)*C. If the cycle time is kept at 4 Hz or higher, the capacitor should not be over 18 µF. Low leakage plastic film capacitors generally begin to increase significantly in cost as the value rises past a couple of microfarads.

To assemble a high-resolution, high-sensitivity temperature monitor, you select an appropriate thermistor for the experiment. To provide a reasonable asymmetry in the 555 timer output signal, the fixed resistor of the RC network is then chosen to be approximately equal to that of the sensor at its intended operating temperature range. With the resistance values of the RC network fixed, only the capacitor value needs to be determined to provide a suitable output frequency compatible with the digital signal processing (DSP) capability of the microprocessor. The larger the capacitor in the RC timing network, the lower the oscillating frequency of the system. The 555 timer output signal must have a frequency low enough for the microcontroller code to measure the high and low pulse widths and then calculate the pulse width difference and average the numerical difference to provide a suitable level of noise reduction.

The Arduino is an 8-bit processor, so the pulse width difference is used rather than actual pulse widths. The number of elements in the moving average digital signal processing code must be small enough to avoid numerical overflow in the long integers used in the microprocessor code.

The thermistor measurement system can be calibrated by using a dry well temperature reference. Typical thermometric chemical analytical procedures only involve temperature changes in the order of a few to perhaps 8°C to 10°C. The linearity of the thermistor vs. temperature relationship can be examined and validated over a short high-resolution range.

Experiment Part A: Metal Oxide NTC Thermistors

To conduct sensitive high-resolution temperature measurements, an Arduino or similar microprocessor board should be independently powered with a battery or regulated supply to provide a virtually noise-free biasing +5 V and ground. With the appropriate NTC thermistor, capacitor, and reference resistor in the astable configuration timing network, the output of the 555 timer on pin 3 can be connected to digital pin 2 of Arduino boards. The Arduino board code in Listing 3-1 contains an n element moving average program that provides a smoothed stream of data for the DAQFactory graphical display. The code has been set to collect and average 16 data points.

Hardware

A 555 timer is configured as depicted in Figure 3-1.

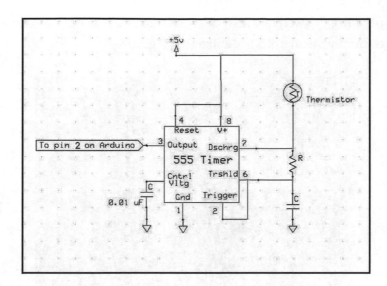

Figure 3-1. *555 timer output modulation by delta R of the thermistor*

C in Figure 3-1 circuit should be a high-quality Mylar or polystyrene, low leakage capacitor. The capacitor value is selected to ensure that the output signal frequency is low enough for the DSP code to measure and average the high and low portions of the rectangular, nominal 5 V output waveform. A discussion of the timing factors to consider when selecting the R, C, and thermistor resistance values for use in the temperature monitoring circuit is in the next section of this exercise.

Dry Well Temperature

A dry well consists of a cavity in a large thermal mass. The large thermal mass serves to maintain a known temperature in the well and moderate temperature fluctuations. Heated dry wells can be created from blocks or multiple plate laminations of metal, drilled, or notched to receive temperature measurement devices and sensors then insulated with any material possessing a substantial resistance to heat transfer such as foamed plastics, wood, plaster, or cement. If possible, programmable temperature dry wells should be fabricated from metals with their higher thermal conductivities.

Temperature programmable dry wells are more complex than static systems as a variable source of heat, and adequate insulation is required for the metal block containing the dry well. Dry wells operated at temperatures above ambient can optionally be controlled by proportional, integral, derivative process controllers (PID) to aid in the maintenance of their desired operating set point.

A low temperature dry well fabricated from 3 mm to 6 mm or ¼ in aluminum metal plates held together by metal bolts is depicted in Figure 3-2.

Figure 3-2. *A laminated aluminum plate dry well*

Using a laminated plate construction method greatly simplifies sourcing materials and shaping the finished dry well. The individual plates can be completely shaped with hand tools to accept the heating element, thermometer, and sensor or shaped to the desired outside profile, bolted firmly together, and drilled to a finished configuration.

In addition to the three-laminate dry well, depicted in Figure 3-2, my lab also has several wells constructed from six, ⅛ inch (3 mm) laminates fabricated from 2-inch-wide flat aluminum stock obtained from local hardware stores. The heating elements, whether square or cylindrical, should be fitted as tightly as possible to the block and coated with a silicone heat sink compound to provide maximum heat transfer. Ensure that the heating resistor leads are isolated from the metal block to avoid short circuits.

In Figure 3-2, the dry well's insulation has been cut from one-inch-thick Styrofoam sheet, using a plastic cutting tip on an electric soldering gun. The insulation jacket pieces for the block have been marked with "witness marks" and labeled with a felt tip pen to ease assembly. The individual plates of a laminated aluminum dry well should also be marked with "witness marks" to ensure the device's quick and easy assembly.

To use the block to create an elevated temperature, a power supply is required to heat the resistance embedded in the block. Low voltage DC supplies with low ohmic resistance values and multiple watt power ratings were chosen for use in my lab since these components were readily available. AC systems can be made to work and variable voltage AC transformers such as the Variac brand. Alternating current (AC) or line voltage wiring must follow local electrical wiring and building codes.

A typical dry well calibration, as used on the device depicted in Figure 3-2, consisted of setting a low voltage output on the supply connected to the well heating resistor or element and waiting until the temperature of the dry well stabilized. The voltage and temperature were recorded, and the voltage incremented slightly and the system allowed to equilibrate again.

A second set of voltage vs. equilibrium dry well temperature data was collected. The four points were then plotted to obtain some idea of the correlation between the applied voltage and resultant equilibrium dry well temperature. To validate the correlation between the magnitude of the applied voltage and the resulting equilibrium temperature, the slope of the plotted data can determine the applied voltage required to establish an approximate dry well temperature within the intended range of operation.

The predicted voltage to establish a third equilibrium temperature data point in the desired area of operation can often be used as validation of the voltage-temperature calibration data. A typical dry well temperature vs. DC voltage application is depicted in Figure 3-3.

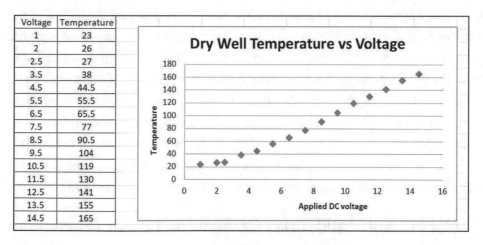

Voltage	Temperature
1	23
2	26
2.5	27
3.5	38
4.5	44.5
5.5	55.5
6.5	65.5
7.5	77
8.5	90.5
9.5	104
10.5	119
11.5	130
12.5	141
13.5	155
14.5	165

Figure 3-3. *Dry well temperature vs. applied DC voltage*

Although Styrofoam insulation is an excellent material to work with and is readily available, it is limited to operating temperatures under 150 to 160°C. The temperature restriction on the Styrofoam however, does not cause any concerns when used in a dry well calibrating system for thermistors that are best applied for measurements under 120°C.

Software

Microprocessor Code

The commented code in Listing 3-1 invokes the pulseIn() functions of the Arduino board to determine the time widths of the high and low pulses, then calculates the difference between the "mark" and "space" pulse widths. The individual time difference measurements are then averaged in a moving average function, implemented in the microprocessor code. The averaged time value is then streamed out on the serial port to the PC for graphical display. The microprocessor code is written entirely in integer format to minimize the time consumed in the digital signal processing (DSP) moving average.

A certain amount of experimentation with the microprocessor code and 555 timer frequency was required in developing the temperature measurement system. The hi/lo or mark/space-time must be within the range allowable for the pulseIn() function. The difference between the two values should simultaneously be as large as possible but small enough to permit long integers in the microprocessor code without incurring integer overflow in the moving average calculations.

Although the process measures the temperature of the thermistor bead, the bead sensor and microprocessor are running at a speed determined by the 555 RC timer circuit values and the rate at which the microprocessor code can calculate the desired average. The averaged data is sent to the PC in a serial format where the graphical display rate is determined by the rate of arrival at the serial port. If the serial port receives data faster than the display can handle, the screen and cursor response slow down.

To limit the rate at which data is sent out on the serial port, the main loop of the moving average program code contains a delay() statement to slow the data delivery rate down. Ideally, the 555 frequency, the number of iterations of the moving average, and the delay constant should be optimized by carefully recorded experiment.

DAQFactory Graphical Display Screen and Signal Processing

Sensitive or high-resolution temperature monitoring is best visualized in a graphical format to keep the trending of the monitored parameter continually on display. Although the absolute value of the temperature being monitored is generally of secondary importance at high sensitivity compared to the immediate or real-time heat and temperature changes of the system, the absolute temperature reading can be calibrated with reasonable accuracy.

All seemingly complex systems are composed of simpler subsystems. Temperature measurement is begun with the assembly of the NTC thermistor, 555 timer, and Arduino hardware. To ensure a relatively constant signal, the NTC thermistor is placed in an insulated dry well of the type depicted in Figure 3-2. The code in Listing 3-1 can be loaded into the microprocessor, run and the serial output monitor of the Arduino IDE used to confirm the validity of the data being sent out on the appropriate communications or com port.

Next, the DAQFactory program is configured to receive serial data on an appropriate channel and the inflow confirmed by observing the data being received with the correct serial port monitor. Figure 3-4 shows the data transmission time and the integer data value followed by the carriage return and line feed ASCII characters.

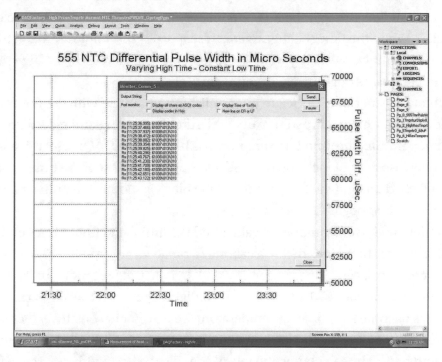

Figure 3-4. *DAQFactory serial port pulse width differential data from arduino moving average code*

Once the DAQ Factory screen can record the averaged pulse width time differential, the thermistor can be calibrated between two useful temperature points.

Observations and Calibration

To develop a thermistor calibration, it is necessary to create a reproducible temperature program. A dry well can create a temperature program by powering the heating element from a regulated supply for a timed period. By adjusting the voltage and time of power application, a temperature increases from ambient to a desired elevated level can be achieved. Once a reproducible program between ambient and the desired higher level has been established and validated, the DAQ Factory display can be calibrated.

In my lab, a mercury-in-glass thermometer in an additional dry well cavity was used as a primary standard for the calibration. A negative temperature coefficient thermistor is going to exhibit a lower resistance at a higher temperature. In our system being developed, the pulse width difference being measured has a "high time" dependent upon the current flow through the NTC thermistor and the reference resistor to charge the capacitor. When the timer changes state, the capacitor discharges through the reference resistor only. As the dry well block's temperature increases, the high time value inversely decreases, as does the NTC thermistor resistance.

A calibration experiment is begun by establishing a baseline with the thermistor immersed in the ambient temperature dry well. After measuring and recording the ambient temperature, the timed power interval is begun. The DAQFactory display trace begins to decrease as the block and dry well heats up. At the end of the timed period, the power is switched off, and the temperature of the block is monitored until it reaches its maximum value and begins to decrease.

The upper and lower temperature values and the initial and final values of the pulse width differential values define a calibrated range for the system. The procedure should be repeated several times to confirm and demonstrate reproducibility. Figure 3-5 displays the tracings from a set of three 3.0°C centigrade temperature changes. Drifting temperatures become a problem as temperature measurement sensitivity increases.

A correlation can be established between the measured pulse width difference and the temperature by calculating the rate of change of pulse width difference for the observed temperature differential. For the curves in Figure 3-5 and an additional six repetitions, the average ratio was 3140 PWD units/°C.

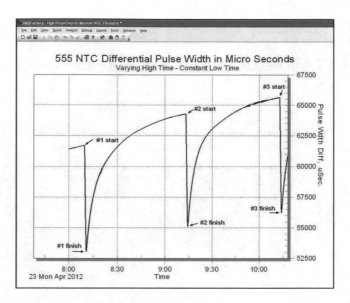

Figure 3-5. *Three-degree temperature changes*

Using the calculated slope and an accurate starting point of 17.0°C that was observed on several of the verification repetitions, the table, and graph depicted in Figure 3-6 were constructed. The constructed plot was then fitted to a standard y = mx + b format and the equation printed out on the chart. In Figure 3-7, the channel value for the streamed data from the Arduino 555 NTC timer was substituted in a re-arranged form of the y = –3140x + 117780 equation to produce the thermistor temperature measurement channel data trace. The trace is visible beneath the 2D Graph Component window at the left and right lower edges with the numerical value of 18.55°C in Figure 3-7.

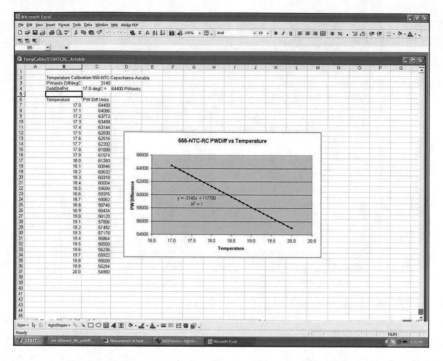

Figure 3-6. *Pulse width difference vs. temperature*

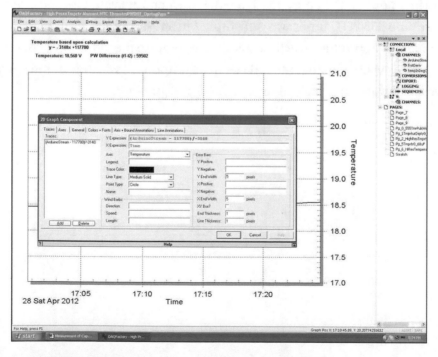

Figure 3-7. *DAQFactory graph component Y expression*

A useful feature in following titrations and other graphically displayed thermal phenomena is that of the first derivative of the primary trace, known as the *slope* of the data. The data slope at the point currently being displayed can be calculated from the differences in the values of the data points that have already been plotted and the times at which the data values were recorded.

$$slope = (X_{t1} - X_{t2}) / (t1 - t2)$$

Data in DAQFactory is maintained in the channels as a two-dimensional array of timestamped numerical values. Each channel created in the Channels table view has a properties window with five tabs containing the channel's basic properties, the options available for the channel, a graph of the channel data, a table of the channel data, and an event tab.

During development of this book, I used three channels to mathematically map or transfer from pulse width difference to highly sensitive temperature recording with an "on screen" first derivative of the temperature record.

The three channels were named Arduino Stream, which received the incoming data from the Arduino board, tempInDegC, which converted the pulse width data variations into graphical display values for the visual temperature monitor and frstDeriv calculates the numerical values for the first derivative of the data in the display.

Figure 3-8 shows the conversion code entered the Arduino Stream Event function tab that calculates the thermistor temperature from the measured pulse width difference data and inserts the calculated temperature and time value into the tempInDegC channel for graphical display.

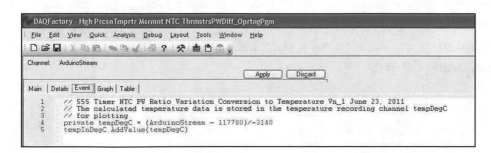

Figure 3-8. *Channel event conversion code*

Line 5 of the Arduino Stream channel event function transfers the calculated temperature into the tempInDegC channel for display. The second channel event function is programmed with the two long lines of code as shown. The lengthy lines calculate the first derivative of the temperature trace in the second channel. The second line transfers the data into the third channel for display.

```
1) private frstDiff = (Smooth(tempInDegC[0], 5) - (Smooth(tempInDegC[25],
   5))) / ((Smooth(ArduinoStream.Time[0], 5)) - (Smooth(ArduinoStream.
   Time[25], 5)))
2) frstDeriv.AddValue(frstDiff)
```

For ease of coding, control screen display and configuration development, I used three channels and assorted graphical displays of the intermediate values being calculated, to follow and validate the data transformation. For experimental applications, the three channels can be used with a single dual trace display.

Discussion

The 555 timer has been in use for over 40 years and is currently available in chips using either bipolar transistors or CMOS integrated circuitry. Chip power consumption, power delivery to external components, and operating frequencies are the main reasons to produce the two types of integrated circuitry, both of which operate equally well in this information processing, temperature measurement application.

Although the PC and the USB bus are capable of supplying the power required to drive experimental setups, the power is limited and can emit extraneous noise. Where possible, the Arduino and 555 chip of the setup should be powered by an independent dedicated supply. For highly sensitive low noise measurements, batteries provide the cleanest power. Figure 3-9 is a short-term or transitory "ringing or aliasing" in the temperature recording signal while drawing power from the computer's USB connection. These distortions are still seen but at significantly lower intensity when the Arduino is independently powered.

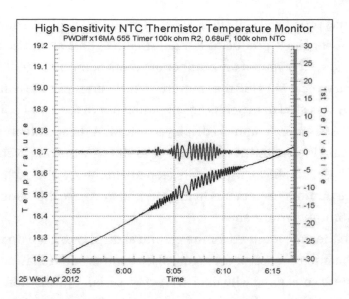

Figure 3-9. *Signal ringing or aliasing*

Thermistors or temperature-sensitive resistors are manufactured in several physical sizes and values of resistance, with that at 25°C being considered the unit's defining value. Temperature ranges greater than 10°C to 15°C the non-linear relationship between temperature and resistance may need to be corrected for some applications. The nonlinearity becomes less important for high-resolution temperature measurements limited to high and low spans of only several degrees.

Thermistors are temperature sensitive resistors that self-heat when a current flows according to the I^2R formula. By placing the thermistor in the R1 position (see the circuit in Figure 3-1) in an astable 555 circuit, the current flows through the thermistor–resistor series pair only when the capacitor is charging, thus lessening the self-heating current effect.

By installing a thermistor in the RC timing network, the duty cycle becomes a function of the thermistor's temperature. The analog temperature signal digitized by the 555 timer can be processed by a microprocessor to greatly improve the signal to noise ratio in the output signal by applying a moving average process to the measured pulse width data.

A moving average (MA) program executes a series of incorrect calculations until its averaging code reaches its nominal operating value. A nine-element moving average produces incorrect answers until it has processed nine data points. Once filled and operating, the array from which the averaged value is calculated produces a serial stream of data whose noise value has been reduced by a theoretical factor of 3. Once the moving average has processed sufficient values, it cycles through its code at the speed of the microprocessor clock, producing a serial stream of data at a noise reduction value proportional to the square root of the number of points being averaged.

Even though a typical MA DSP may require 15 to 20 lines of code to implement, the rate at which the processed data points are streamed out to the serial port is usually far too high for the DAQFactory graphical display to follow. A delay statement is usually required in the main loop of the microprocessor to slow the moving average code to the point at which the graphical display can keep up. In theory, the experimenter may want to adjust the number of elements in the MA and decrease the value of the delay statement for optimum performance.

In addition to the time required for the graphical display to keep up with the data reception rate, the microprocessor averaging also requires additional computing time. As additional time is consumed with data averaging, serial transmission, and graphical display, the time lag between changes in the system under study and the movement of the graphical display increases. The sum of all these delays is the "response time" of the measurement or system.

Care must be taken when increasing the number of elements in the moving average as the time lag of the display response increases but the improvement in signal to noise reduction only improves as the square root of the number of elements averaged. The experimenter must consider when assembling a temperature measurement system, the nature of the data to be collected and how much time can be used to smooth the data while maintaining a reasonable response time for the data display.

According to the IC timer datasheets, the output frequency of the astable configuration of the 555 timer is proportional to the values of the RC network. Large value capacitors together with large value resistors create large value time constants. The pulse width difference technique to measure temperature differences depends on the microprocessor measuring the difference between successive high times in the timer output signal.

The microprocessor code measuring the timer output uses 8-bit logic, so it has a limitation on the magnitude or size of the numerical values that can accurately be represented by the binary arithmetic. If the pulse widths become too high, the difference between successive difference measurements may cause numerical overflow in the microprocessor arithmetic coding. Long integers in the Arduino code can deal with numerical values up to 2,147,483,647. High-quality, low-leakage capacitors of several microfarads should provide ample temperature resolution for experimental work.

Experiment Part B: Silicon Carbide Thermistors −20°C to 450°C

Temperature-sensitive resistance has been recognized since 1833, when Michael Faraday noted the phenomenon in silver sulfide. Commercial production of thermistors began in 1930 and evolved into the inexpensive micro-glass or epoxy coated beads of mixed transition metal oxide devices used in Part A of this topic.

Silicon carbide (SiC), first manufactured as an abrasive and later used as a resistance heating element in high-temperature furnaces, is also a semiconductor. SiC has been fabricated into temperature-sensitive devices of decreasing resistance that greatly extend the upward temperature measurement range possible with regular transition metal oxide-based thermistor sensors and approximately doubles the rate of change of resistance per unit of temperature change (metal oxide 3% – 4% $\Delta R/°C$ vs. 7% – 8% $\Delta R/°C$ for SiC thermistors).

The monitored temperature range produces some materials selection problems for experimental work with the upper ranges of 500°C measurable with SiC devices. Mixed metal oxide thermistors are limited to temperatures below approximately 150°C. Tin lead solders and Styrofoam insulations are also limited to the lower portions of the 200°C range.

Figure 3-10 is a plot of a typical SiC thermistor correlation between the device resistance and temperature.

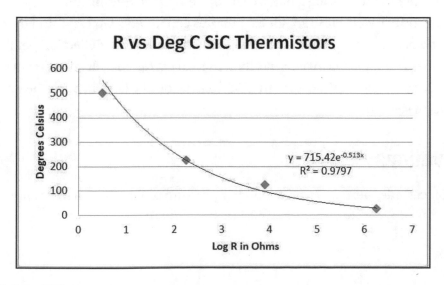

Figure 3-10. *SiC temperature range*

Semiconductor NTC thermistor temperature measurements can be made with the 555 timer circuit developed or with a traditional high resistance Wheatstone bridge circuit.

Experiment: 555 Timer Frequency Shift Temperature Measurements

Hardware

A National Semiconductor CMOS LMC 555CN was configured into an astable configuration with an Adsem silicon carbide TO-46 metal can "top hat" thermistor with a 25°C room temperature resistance of 1.750 MΩ and a 2.2 MΩ resistor. Recalling that in the astable configuration with R1varying with the SiC thermistor's temperature and R2 being the 2.2 MΩ fixed value reference resistor, the 555 timer has hi/lo or mark-space time duty cycle ratio of approximately 2:1 or 66%. A 10 nF (0.01 μF) capacitor was used with the SiC 2.2 MΩ combination to develop a theoretical output frequency of 25 Hz. (For the astable 555, f = 1.44/(R1 + 2R2)*C.)

The SiC thermistor was fitted into a 3/16 in (5 mm) diameter aluminum dry well in a Styrofoam insulated, laminated aluminum block; ½ in × 3 in × 2 in (12 mm × 76 mm × 50 mm), dry well heated with a 22.6 ohm, 5 W resistor. Block heater power was supplied by a 12 V, 1 A DC supply, and primary temperature determination was from a mercury-in-glass thermometer monitoring a block well adjacent to the thermistor.

Heating the dry well with 12 V for 2.0 minutes generated a 4.0°C ΔT and three, 4.0°C deflections were used to calculate an average value of observed deflection per degree Celsius value. The sensitivity value was then used to correlate deflection per degree and observed thermometer response for the SiC thermistor as was done with the epoxy metal oxide units in section A.

Observations

The silicon carbide thermistor deflection temperature plot is illustrated in Figure 3-11.

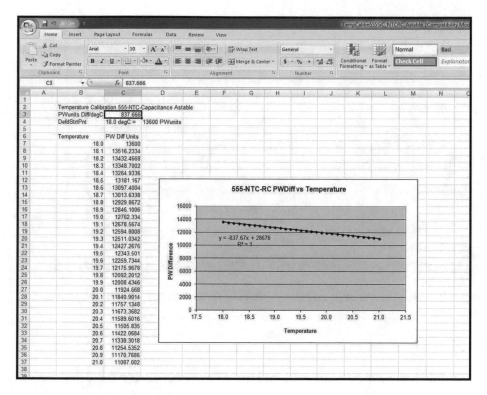

Figure 3-11. *SiC thermistor response data*

The typical abilities of the temperature measuring system were demonstrated and evaluated by generating and recording the measurement of a small temperature differential. The SiC thermistor was calibrated by measuring the PWD created by a 4.0°C temperature jump generated by 12 V DC applied for 2.0 min. To test the system, a 3-second power application should create a one-tenth degree differential as depicted in Figure 3-12. The power pulse was created by manually activating the power supply for a timed 3-second interval; the error in the timing of such a short pulse was relatively high.

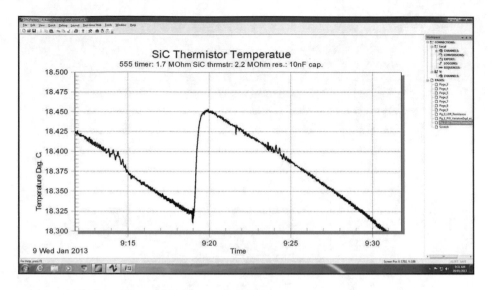

Figure 3-12. *SiC thermistor high-sensitivity temperature measurement*

Discussion

SiC thermistors have a significantly higher resistance and usable temperature range than do the metal oxide devices. Metal oxide devices have resistance values from hundreds of ohms to megohms and 4% – 5 % decreases in resistance per degree Celsius and rapidly lose sensitivity past the boiling point of water. SiC devices are usable from –20°C to 450°C and have resistance values in the megohm range with 8% decreases in resistance per degree Celsius temperature change.

The recorded trace in Figure 3-12 shows a repetitive ringing or aliasing just before 9:15 and 9:25 in the unsmoothed tracing. DAQFactory has several digital signal processing functions available for reducing the noise level in the data with each DSP function having its own merits and added time delay in signal response.

Figure 3-12 shows that the DAQFactory plot has major divisions equivalent to 0.025 degrees. With the baseline noise of approximately a fifth of the major divisions, a temperature resolution of 0.005 degrees should be feasible.

The high-resolution temperature graph illustrates one of the inherent problems in sensitive temperature measurements, heat leakage through insulation and the resulting temperature drifting. During the charging cycle, the USB-Arduino power supply is a nominal 5 V. At ambient temperatures, the thermistor and reference resistors sum to approximately 4 MΩ, resulting in a thermistor current of approximately 1.25 µA that only flows through the thermistor for 66% of the time (duty cycle = Hi time/total cycle time). The drifting is an electronic artifact, or the heat moves into or out of the dry well.

Experiment: SiC NTC Temperature Measurement with a Wheatstone Bridge

Wheatstone bridge circuitry, developed by Christie in 1833, was originally used to measure unknown resistance values in static systems. Static temperature measurements with thermistors and RTD are still in but dynamic temperature measurements have a wide variety of applications in experimental science and are the subject of this subsection.

Consider a Wheatstone bridge consisting of two voltage dividers assembled in a parallel configuration. If all four resistance values are the same in the two dividers there is no voltage difference at the division point between the two arms of the circuit. If a resistance value in one of the divider circuits does change, a voltage difference develops between the two division points in the circuit. For a certain range of resistance change, the voltage imbalance is directly proportional to the resistance variation. Resistance changes in the system at hand are temperature changes in the environment of the silicon carbide thermistor.

In Figure 3-13, the numerical relationship between the various components of the bridge configuration is displayed. If the formula for the bridge output is simplified by setting R1 = R2 = R, the output voltage follows the formula.

$$V_O = \frac{V_B}{4} \left[\frac{\Delta R}{R + \frac{\Delta R}{2}} \right]$$

Figure 3-13. *Wheatstone bridge output formula*

- V_o is the output of the bridge. V_B is the bridge or bias voltage.

- R is the value of the bridge resistors at balance.

- ΔR is the change in the active resistor or the change in the SiC thermistor value resistance.

The full formula and configuration are shown in Figure 3-14.

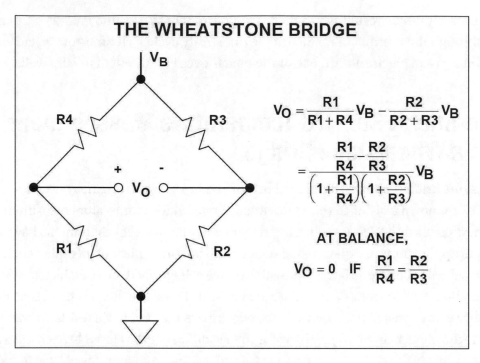

Figure 3-14. *A Wheatstone bridge circuit and formula*

Experiment

As seen in the circuit schematic in Figure 3-15, a bridge configuration was created with a variable and three fixed-value resistors. By selecting the resistance value of the three fixed-value units to be slightly above the room temperature resistance value of the SiC thermistor and adding an appropriately sized potentiometer, you can assemble a bridge circuit around the high resistance SiC thermistor that can be applied to heating or cooling operations.

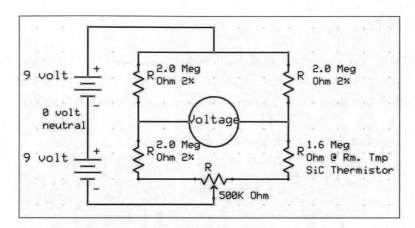

Figure 3-15. *SiC Wheatstone bridge*

For initial development work or experimental setups, the bridge imbalance can be monitored by any high impedance voltage measuring device. A dual battery power supply was chosen to provide a bipolar power source for an instrumentation amplifier.

While developing the temperature measurement process with the SiC thermistors, an archival record of the temperature calibration measurements was kept for use in the subsequent work of this section, involving heat movements and thermodynamics. Data was collected and displayed by monitoring and recording the deviation created in an initially balanced, equal arm Wheatstone bridge. A well-known temperature program was applied to the bridge SiC sensing element. As can be seen in the Figure 3-16 schematic, an AD 620 instrumentation amplifier in a unity gain configuration was used to buffer the bridge deviation signal to a differential input on a LabJack U12, which provides input for a DAQFactory graphical recording display.

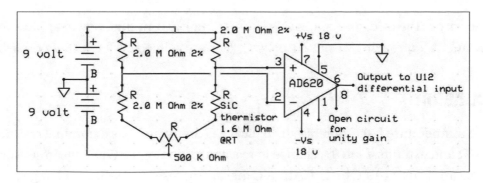

Figure 3-16. *AD620 instrumentation amplifier with SiC bridge*

Observations

A series of timed, 12 V DC power applications to the 22.6 Ω, 5 W resistance of an insulated, aluminum block, dry well, equipped with a mercury-in-glass thermometer, a type K thermocouple, and the SiC thermistor generated the data in Table 3-4.

Table 3-4. *SiC Bridge Calibration Data*

Min pwr	Initial T Hg	Final T Hg	Init K thrmcpl	Fnl K thrmcpl	Brdg Vltg DVM	Brdg Vltg DAQFct	Comments
1	17	20	18	20	0.24	0.24	Time scale 2400 sec
2	19.25	24.5	18	24	0.453	0.45	T.S 2400 +/- 1 volt DAQFt
3	19.5	28	18	27	0.723	0.7	T.S 2400 +/- 1 volt DAQFt
4	19.5	31	18	30	0.927	0.95	T.S 2400 +/- 1 volt DAQFt
5	18	32	17	31	1.213	1.2	T.S 4800 @+/- 1.5 volt
6	19.1	35.75	18	34	1.296	1.3	T.S 4800 @+/- 2 volt
7	18	37	17	36	1.617	1.6	T.S 4800 @+/- 2 volt
8	16.5	38	15	36	1.905	1.9	T.S 6000 @+/- 2 volt
9	18-18.5	41.5-43	16.5-17	41-43	1.8-2.1	1.75	T. S. 4800 @ +/- 2 volt
10	18	44.5	16.5	43	2.09	2	

Linearity in the bridge circuit begins to deteriorate at 8-minute power applications as the deviations approach 2 V from ΔT of 24°C. (Battery voltage 2×9 V = 18 V bridge bias.)

Discussion

At room temperature (20°C or 68°F) the typical SiC thermistor has a nominal resistance of 1.6 MΩ and exhibits a 7 to 8% change in resistance per degree C change in sensor temperature. Thus, at 19°C or 21°C, the SiC thermistor resistance should change by; 1.6 MΩ $\times$ 0.075 = 120 KΩ. Substituting the 120 KΩ value into the sensitivity formula finds that for the 2 MΩ bridge circuit that the sensitivity is 0.261 V/°C.

In theory, with the ability to easily measure voltages to the nearest millivolt each degree of temperature should be resolvable to the nearest millivolt or approximately 1/261 of a degree C. However, resistors are prone to noise, and with a 2 MΩ bridge, significant noise is anticipated and has been found as depicted in Figure 3-17.

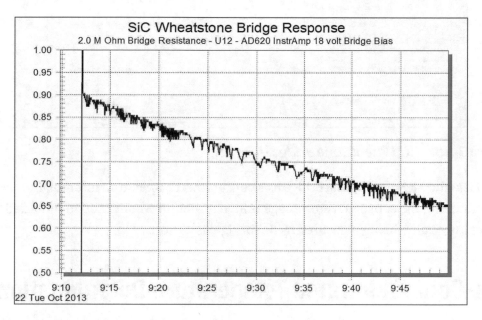

Figure 3-17. *High-sensitivity temperature measurement noise*

The averaging capabilities of the DAQFactory program could reduce the noise of the trace and simultaneously decrease the signal's response time.

By configuring the bridge as shown, you can balance the bridge to zero volts output by adjusting the potentiometer. The sensor measures heating or cooling operations.

Higher resistance values in bridge circuits are preferred with battery-powered systems as the current drawn is minimized, thus extracting maximum service life from the supply and limiting the current flow through the thermistor that limits self-heating. However, resistors generate noise in proportion to the magnitude of their resistance.

Although the bridge circuitry has a limited range in which the measured bridge output voltage has a linear relationship with the temperature-induced resistance change, Figure 3-18 shows the range is large enough to be useful so long as the bridge deviation voltage is kept within the linear range.

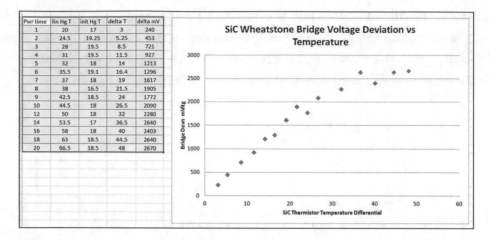

Pwr time	fin Hg T	init Hg T	delta T	delta mV
1	20	17	3	240
2	24.5	19.25	5.25	453
3	28	19.5	8.5	721
4	31	19.5	11.5	927
5	32	18	14	1213
6	35.5	19.1	16.4	1296
7	37	18	19	1617
8	38	16.5	21.5	1905
9	42.5	18.5	24	1772
10	44.5	18	26.5	2090
12	50	18	32	2280
14	53.5	17	36.5	2640
16	58	18	40	2403
18	63	18.5	44.5	2640
20	66.5	18.5	48	2670

Figure 3-18. *SiC Wheatstone bridge linearity*

To use the SiC Wheatstone bridge as a continuous temperature monitor, the temperature of the sensor at zero voltage bridge deviation would need to be added to the temperature value being measured by the bridge deviation.

Non-Contact Infrared Temperature Determination

The key advantage to infrared temperature measurement lies in making remote or "at a distance" temperature measurements optically, without physical contact. When interpreting IR temperature data, recall that the measurements are made optically. The transducer or detector converts only the invisible IR energy within a defined field of view (FOV) from distant objects or electromagnetic radiation sources into digital numeric values. The entire heat radiation collection system must follow the rules of propagation of electromagnetic radiation. The detector, available in numerous physical and optical configurations, must have an unobstructed, optically transparent path to collect and average all the heat radiation that falls within the field of view of the specific device.

Experiment

Hardware

A relatively low-cost ($20 CDN) IR detector such as the Melexis MLX90614, available from several online suppliers, can be used with the Arduino, two 4.7 KΩ "pull up" resistors, power, ground, and two data transmission lines to make non-contact temperature measurements. For temporary development work, I mounted the device in a mini-prototyping board and made the following connections (see Figure 3-19).

- – Pin 1 SCL to Analog pin 5 on the Arduino board

- – Pin 2 SDA to Analog pin 4 on the Arduino board

- – Pin 3 VDD to 3.3 V on the Arduino board

- – Pin 4 VSS to the ground on the Arduino board

- – A 4.7 KΩ resistor from pin 3 (VDD) to SCL

- – A second 4.7 KΩ resistor from pin 3 to SDA

Prototyping boards are useful for development work, but at the 3.3 V or 5 V level, the resistance of the "spring" contacts in the prototyping board may be sufficient to drop a contact voltage to the point at which the circuits do not work as intended. Several times during the development of the IR temperature measurement portion of this book, a correctly wired and powered circuit did not start until touched with the multimeter probe while troubleshooting. Printed circuit boards or hardwired circuits are to be preferred for actual data collection.

Figure 3-19 shows a circuit schematic.

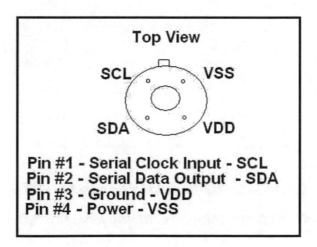

Figure 3-19. *Melexis 90614 IR detector pin-out*

Software

The IR chip can provide the temperature of objects in its field of view in either a pulse width format or serially in an integrated circuit to integrated circuit communication format (sometimes written as I²C but more often as I2C). The library required for the Arduino IR sensor communication to read the Melexis is part of the standard Arduino library and is loaded from the IDE menus and is listed as MLX90614.

Required Page Components

A visual temperature display can be configured in DAQFactory to accommodate the range available with the IR detector, as displayed in Figure 3-20.

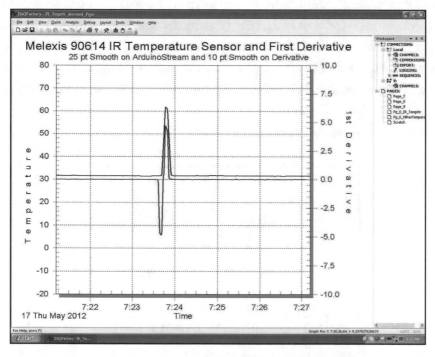

Figure 3-20. *IR detector temperature record and first derivative*

Required Scripting

The data streamed from the Arduino to the PC is the factory-calibrated temperature observed by the detector chip in degrees Celsius format. Figure 3-20 is displaying the temperature and the first derivative of the recorded temperature tracing. The algorithms and code structure remain the same as was used in the previous thermistor temperature measurement work. The IR detector produces the actual temperature, so no conversion is required. The first derivative is calculated as before. The sensitivity of the derivative function is determined empirically and depends on the temperature range being monitored.

Observations

The IR detector response is rapid and has a much larger linear range when compared to the thermistor. Figure 3-20 is a display screen that I set to measure from –20°C to 80°C for development validation purposes. The rapid large temperature changes are easily demonstrated by moving ice packs and hot drinks into and out of the detector's field of view.

Several easily conducted desktop experiments with a vertically faced sensor were used to graphically exhibit the care that must be used when collecting temperature data with infrared sensors. Because of the sensor's conical field of view (FOV), if a heat source such as a cup or mug filled with a hot drink or a frozen "cold pack" is held a few feet (a half meter) above the detector, the displayed temperature measurement is that of the ambient temperature of the environment in which the measurement is being made not that of the object of interest.

If the heat source is lowered to within a few inches (5 to 6 cm) of the detector, the displayed temperature trace rises or falls to display the surface temperature of the heat source. However, the heat source is a radiating body. If the power radiating is of sufficient intensity, it may affect the detector case temperature, along with the thermally sensitive detectors and the displayed reading drifts. The recorded temperature signal becomes noisy and biased when daylight, hand heat, and hot drinks are near the sensor case, even if not in the field of view of the detector.

As with all sensors, as the sensitivity is increased, the signal to noise ratio decreases and as the amount of signal averaging to reduce noise is increased, the response time of the display also increases.

The visual display created with the DAQFactory program required a delay of 200 ms to avoid an excessive streaming data rate that degrades the graphical display by causing the cursor to become sluggish and even non-responsive. I was able to add a 25-point average to the DAQFactory channel and decrease the delay in the Arduino code to 150 ms without noticeable degradation in the performance of the display screen cursor.

Optical temperature measurements are dependent on "line of sight" viewing. The heat source must be visible to the detector to be measured. Hot or cold liquids inside containers may need to be viewed from overhead to measure the temperature of the contents.

Discussion

A Melexis detector chip was identified with an MLX 90614 AAA part number. According to the manufacturer's datasheets, the first A indicates the unit was powered by 5 V (a 3.5 V unit is available) the second A indicating that the field of view is treated as a single object (a dual viewing zone detector is available). The final A indicates that the package is an industry-standard TO-39 case with a 45-degree field of view (FOV). Detectors are available with several FOV options from 5 to 35 degrees.

The datasheet contains the timing information for using the various data outputs and in-depth explanations of the detector's physical, electronic, and optical parameters. The window on the metal case holding the device can pass IR radiation between 5.5 and 14 micron).

The I2C library and the Arduino Melexis code are standard Arduino libraries accessible from the IDE. In some older versions of the libraries, the final few lines of the Arduino code, in a three-step, serial printing operation, send a mix of string characters and numerical digits to the serial port for assembly into a two-place decimal value, representing the average temperature of the objects within the detector field of view. If the mixed numerical and string character formats of the output value in the Arduino code are encountered, averaging and any desired data smoothing are probably best done with the signal processing capabilities of the DAQFactory channels and graphical displays.

The factory calibration and device firmware are based on the SMBus digital interface and allow access to the –70°C to 380°C temperature range. SMBus is an older, single-ended, two-wire communications protocol used for simple one-way data serial transfer. The System Management Bus protocol is usually compatible with the newer current I2C protocols.

Heat energy is transferred from one object to another by conduction, convection, or radiation. Radiative heat transfer involves electromagnetic radiation in the IR range with wavelengths from 0.7 to 1000 microns. (micron or sometimes μ are 10^{-6} meter) For practical reasons, the wavelengths between 0.7 and 14 microns are used for infrared temperature measurement. If an object in a field of view is illuminated by incident radiation, some of the radiation is absorbed, and some is reflected. The object's coefficient of reflectivity can vary from 0 to 100%. Rough, matte surfaces can have low reflectivity, whereas polished, glossy metal surfaces can be very reflective.

The positions of the source concerning the detector and the object's ability to transmit the IR wavelength being measured can also influence the temperature measured for an object in the field of view (see literature on spectroscopy or physics for more information on black-body radiation). The energy falling on the detector from an object in the field of view is affected by the coefficients of reflection, transmission, and absorption for the object, together with the wavelength of the IR radiation.

For accurate temperature determinations, the background around an object needs to be evaluated. The physical state of the surface needs to be determined, and the emissivity of that surface must be considered. Smooth or polished metal surfaces can act like mirrors for infrared radiation. A metal surface may indicate the temperature of its surroundings rather than the temperature of the metal itself. Bright aluminum surfaces may need to be coated with black high-temperature-tolerant paint or perhaps be anodized to allow an IR detector to measure the actual temperature.

For work involving an IR temperature measurement methodology, the system must be validated by observing and obtaining known object temperatures.

Thermocouple Temperature Determination

The Seebeck and Peltier effects describe the reversible electron flows that occur when the points of contact in a loop consisting of two dissimilar metals are at different temperatures. Figure 3-21 illustrates a typical dissimilar metal thermocouple measurement setup.

Typical voltage levels are in the microvolts per degree range, are reasonably linear and reproducible. Unknown temperature measurements are made by measuring the voltage in the dissimilar wire circuit when one of the two junctions is held at a known defined temperature, typically that of the ice-water point. Thermocouple voltages at ice water temperatures are of sufficient stability and reproducibility. Modern integrated circuits such as the MAX31855, AD594, and 595, can produce a reference voltage as a substitute for a second thermocouple junction at a given, fixed, 0°C temperature. With a fixed value, reference junction signal available from integrated circuitry, a single, bimetallic junction can determine unknown temperatures by measuring the voltage being generated at the point of contact. Thermocouples are self-powered sensors and require no excitation or external power source.

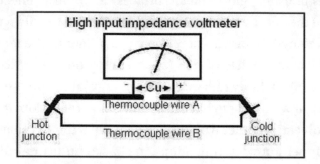

Figure 3-21. *A typical dissimilar metal thermocouple circuit*

The difficulty created by the small voltage values generated in thermocouples is, to a certain extent, offset by the wide range of temperatures over which the metals can operate. Relatively inexpensive alloys of nickel, chrome, iron, and copper are used to make the J and K-types of thermocouples that are the most popular sensors in use today. Thermocouples can be divided into the base and precious metal groups by virtue of the metals used to generate the heat-temperature-derived currents. Higher temperature measurement ranges between 1350°C to 1700°C or even higher must use the platinum group of metals with others such as tungsten, gold, and molybdenum to form the thermocouple junction, or the investigator can use optical methods. For high-temperature work and the correct applications of expensive alloys, you can find further information in literature.

A measurement range from cryogenic temperatures to approximately 1250°C can be realized with thermocouples manufactured from common metals such as those in Table 3-5. The base metal thermocouples are the emphasis of the work presented in the following texts.

K-type sensors consisting of chromel-alumel junctions generate 41 μV per degree C. The K-type sensor consists of a two-wire loop formed by welding together one wire of chromel alloy consisting of 90% nickel (Ni) and 10% chrome (Cr) with a second alloy wire called *alumel* made from 95% Ni, 2% manganese (Mn), 2% aluminum (Al), and 1% silicon (Si). The junction exhibits a 41 μV/°C voltage output and can measure temperatures within the range of –200°C to 1350°C.

J-type sensors called *iron-constantan* are made from constantan, an alloy of 55% copper (Cu) with 45% nickel and a higher purity iron (Fe) wire. The use of magnetic and relatively chemically reactive iron limits the range of utility to –40°C to 750°C. The advantage of the iron-constantan system lies in its relatively inexpensive materials of construction and a 55 µV/°C rate of signal generation. Table 3-5 was compiled from data listed in several sources, including the following.

- *The Art of Electronics* by Paul Horowitz and Winfield Hill (Cambridge University Press, 2015).

- `www.analog.com/media/en/technical-documentation/` `application-notes/AN-369.pdf`

Table 3-5. *Thermocouple Types*

ANSI Code (Type)	Alloy Combination	Maximum Temperature Range	mV Output
B	Platinum/Rhodium	0°C to 1700°C	0 to + 12.426
E	Chromel/Constantan	- 200°C to 900°C	- 8.824 to + 68.783
J	Iron/Constantan	0°C to 750°C	0 to + 42.283
K	Chromel/Alumel	- 200°C to 1250°C	- 5.973 to + 50.633
N	Nicosil/Nisil	- 270 °C to 1300°C	- 4.345 to + 47.502
T	Copper/Constantan	- 200°C to 350°C	- 5.602 to + 17.816

Metal wire diameters determine the strength of the thermocouple and hence its "in service" robustness. Wire diameters also influence the resistance of conductors and junction response times. Typical data for a chrome-alumel sensor with different wire diameters is tabulated in Table 3-6.

Table 3-6. *TC Wire Sizes and Effects on Sensor Response Times*

Wire inch	Diameter millimeter	gauge	Response Time(sec)
0.005	0.127	36	1
0.010	0.255	30	5
0.020	0.511	24	20
0.032	0.812	20	40

More discussions of the theory and practice of thermocouple heat measurements are discussed in *The Art of Electronics* and at www.analog.com. Virtually all the major integrated circuit manufacturers have specific application notes describing their circuitry available for thermocouple temperature measurements.

Experiment

When temperature measurement is implemented with thermocouples, the small-signal amplification and ice water reference signal requirements are best met with application-specific integrated circuits (ASIC) and commercially spot-welded sensors that are readily available, inexpensive, reproducible, and reliable.

Thermocouple junctions are spot welded to ensure complete physical and electrical contact. Commercially assembled sensors are usually supplied with specially manufactured, color-coded, male connectors for plugging into either female connector for single sensor systems or into manifolds for multiple sensor type networks as in many industrial applications. (Color coding varies outside North America.) For this exercise, the male thermocouple plug supplied with commercially manufactured J and K thermocouples from Omega Engineering connect to a red or yellow female receptacle connected with a twisted wire pair to the prototyping breadboard.

The plug-in breadboard allows for an easily assembled mounting and powering of the AD 595, ceramic, DIP, integrated circuit that provides an internal, electronic, ice-water reference voltage for K-type chromel- alumel sensors, signal amplification, and a high-impedance voltage reading. (The AD 594 DIP ceramic chip can be used with the J-type thermocouple.) The manufacturer's datasheets provide information on the following list of topics (see Figures 3-23 to 3-26).

– the basics of thermocouples

– temperature scale calibrations of the AD594 and 5 for J and K sensors

– power supply required for temperature range to be displayed and accuracy

– device output modes and implementing a thermocouple failure alarm

Initially, this book uses an AD595 installed on a prototyping breadboard and powered from a LabJack U3-HV interface. Electrical connections are made in the demonstration system with screw connectors and a twisted wire pair connecting the instrumentation amplifier to the industry-standard yellow K thermocouple's plug. A red LED continuity failure alarm is installed to ensure reliability.

One of the more difficult aspects of validating or demonstrating thermocouple temperature measurements and dealing with the material problems created by high-temperature experiments lie in making small, controllable, high-temperature sources.

The near 200°C temperature achieved in Figure 3-28 was created by encasing a 15 W "load lamp" bulb in a tin foil wrapped, corrugated cardboard radiant heat oven, as seen in Figure 3-22. The oven sits on a bottom plate, cut out to allow the load lamp bulb to be screwed into its socket. Care must be taken to ensure that the base plate sits snugly below the removable threaded porcelain ring encasing the light bulb socket in the CSA or UL approved lighting fixture. (Canadian Standards Association or Underwriters Laboratories—electrical fitting approval authorities). The walls and top of the oven are created by foil wrapping a heavy cardboard sleeve and square foil-covered cardboard plate. The lamp power can be controlled by either an approved light dimmer or the circuit in Figure 3-23.

If the TRIAC-powered A/C PWM circuit is chosen to control the power applied to the bulb, the timing capacitor should be a plastic film or a low leakage unit close to 1 µF to keep the timer IC output synchronized with the 60 Hz AC line voltage waveform. Recall that all AC wiring and electrical fittings must conform to local electrical or building codes.

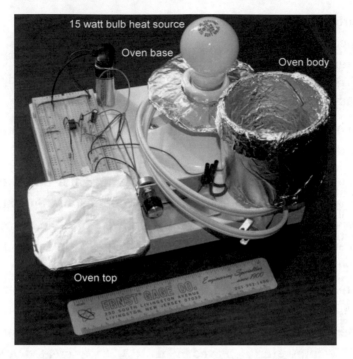

Figure 3-22. *Light bulb oven*

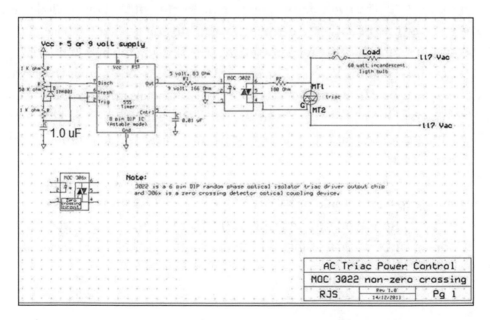

Figure 3-23. *A TRIAC-based AC power supply for the light bulb oven*

A series of circuit diagrams describing the variations in using the AD594/5 ICs to measure thermocouple temperatures are depicted in Figures 3-24 to 3-27.

To measure temperatures above the 300°C limit imposed using a +5 V supply (see Figures 3-24 and 3-26) from the U3-HV. To measure temperatures below ambient, a dual polarity, asymmetrical, power supply must be used, as depicted in Figure 3-25. Three 9 V batteries can be used by connecting the negative lead of a series-connected pair to the positive lead of the third 9 V battery. The common positive-negative connection has established a +18 V potential above "ground" or common and a –9 V below ground. The asymmetrical supply thus allows the AD595 and K thermocouple to measure from –200°C to 1350°C. The combined three batteries generate a total 27 V potential, three volts beneath the chip maximum of 30 volts.

The circuit in Figure 3-26 shows the connections for wiring an LED continuity indicator that should be installed on all thermocouple implementations.

Figure 3-27 illustrates a configuration in which the 595/4 chip can be used as a temperature sensor itself.

Hardware

A typical K-type thermocouple device may generate a 41 µV/°C signal while a J-type produces 55 µV/°C. Measurement of such small signals requires an "instrument amplifier" device that does not draw any appreciable current from the sensor. Dedicated high impedance instrument amplifiers are available in application-specific integrated circuits such as the Analog Devices 594 and 595 chips for J- and K-type thermocouples.

Soldering problems caused by temperature considerations and the chemical nature of the different alloys used to make thermocouples are circumvented by using mechanical connections to join the sensor to the electronics. A commercially available male socketed chromel-alumel, K-type thermocouple from Omega Engineering was plugged into a female K-type socket fitted with a twisted wire pair for plugging into a proto-typing breadboard. The prototyping board held the dual inline package (DIP) AD595, a 5 V supply from the LabJack, and the LED continuity indicator while providing easy connections to the U3-HIV interface.

Figures 3-24, 3-25, 3-26 are circuit schematics.

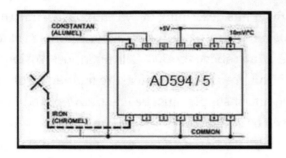

Figure 3-24. *Basic connection, single supply operation*

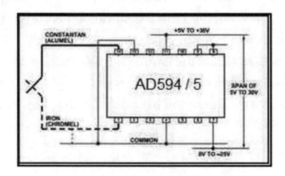

Figure 3-25. *Dual supply operation*

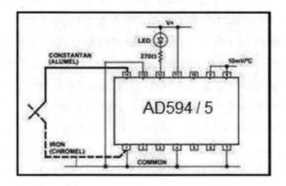

Figure 3-26. *Alarm configuration with LED*

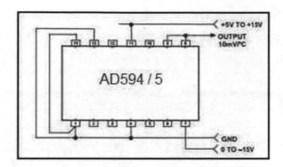

Figure 3-27. *ADC594/5 configured as a standalone Celsius thermometer*

Software

According to the manufacturer's datasheets, the ICs are factory trimmed for fixed gain operation at a nominal 25°C to generate the voltages that correspond to the ANSI values. To record the thermocouple temperature and output voltage of the AD595, breadboard mounting, and USB power supply combination, the graphical output of the channel used to follow the AD595 output can be adjusted to correspond to the ANSI standard by adding compensating values to the plotting function of the graphical display. For the J and K plots of temperature vs. voltage, the linearity of each is sufficient for most experiments. If more exacting temperature data is required, calibration over the area of interest is recommended.

A channel called thrmoCplU3 was created in DAQFactory to read the first analog input channel on a LabJack U3-HV interface. The results were plotted in black on a 2-D graphical display. A second plot in red on the right-hand axis was used to follow the actual voltage during the development stages.

Scripting is not required, but in the Y Expression box, the voltage of the AD595 output in volts is simply multiplied by 100 to plot the thermocouple temperature. The channel measures the 595 output voltage. When converted to millivolts and divided by 10mV/°C, it produces a multiplication factor of 100 to convert the observed amplified thermocouple voltage into degrees Celsius for plotting.

Observations

The temperature range measurable with the AD595 thermocouple amplifier is defined by the voltage of the power supply used to power the IC. Figure 3-28 displays a recording of both thermocouple amplifier outputs for 0 to 3.5 V and 0 to 300°C as was observed for the temperature in a simple load-lamp oven. The load lamp oven was devised to create adjustable, variable temperatures below the approximately 300°C degree limit imposed by the USB +5 V supply.

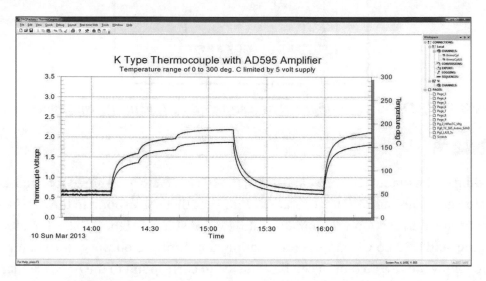

Figure. 3-28. *Surface temperature of incandescent light bulb*

The temperature tracing in Figure 3-28 represents the variation observed in the improvised load lamp oven as the on/off time of the load lamp is varied with the PWM power controller.

With the bipolar asymmetric power supply, the thermocouple can measure both below ambient and well above, with the upper temperature limit being defined by the melting points of the metals involved. In Figure 3-29, the different temperatures measured for the soldering iron demonstrate one of the problems encountered in measuring higher temperatures: corrosion products interfering with heat transfer.

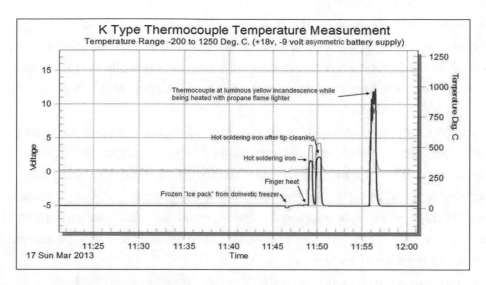

Figure 3-29. *Thermocouple voltage and higher temperature measurements*

Discussion

Thermocouples provide a means of temperature measurement above that obtainable with thermistors. Most thermocouples can provide data at temperatures approaching their melting points.

Science history notes that the thermoelectric effects were first discovered when the presence of magnetic fields around conductors immersed in a thermal gradient was discovered. It is often thought that the thermoelectric effect results from the contact of the dissimilar metals but fusion welding, flux-based brazing, or mechanical fasteners such as screws or bolts all produce the same results when the thermocouple is tested or validated. A thermoelectric effect is created along the length of the thermal gradient in the wire and not at the point of contact of the dissimilar metals that require only a sound electrical contact to complete the electrical circuit.

Attaining temperatures in excess of 650°C (1300°F) brings the equipment well into the range at which typical materials of construction such as tin-lead solder, zinc-galvanized coatings, tin, lead, and aluminum metals, plastics, soda-lime, and borosilicate glass, and many other materials, soften or melt. High-power electrical conductors insulated at lower temperatures may suddenly short out, possibly causing explosive vaporizations of molten and fused materials. The development of apparatus or supporting equipment to attain higher temperatures must be planned, fabricated, and brought to operating temperatures with carefully monitored and slowly incremented steps to ensure safety for all concerned.

Thermocouples, RTDs, or optical methods are the only means of measuring temperatures in excess of 650°C. Thermocouples are probably the simplest means of monitoring higher temperatures. K- and J-type sensors are popular for experimental work because they are inexpensive, rugged, and display high thermocouple junction voltages (41 µV/°C and 55 µV/°C).

The K-type thermocouple consisting of a chromel-alumel junction has lesser sensitivity but offers a higher temperature range and chemical inertness due to the aluminum and chromium oxide layers of the nickel, chrome, and aluminum components of the alloys. The J-type sensor, although generating the highest voltage of the thermocouple sensors, is composed of iron-constantan. The reactive nature of iron, together with a 770°C Curie point discontinuity in the temperature voltage correlation, limits the usable range of the sensor.

Care must be exercised when selecting thermocouples to measure high temperatures in enclosed environments because of possible corrosive off-gassing from the materials being heated. K-type thermocouples are protected by the refractory oxides of chromium and aluminum and provide full coverage of the sensor range in the air. J and T thermocouple types contain iron and copper, both reactive, native metals.

Atmospheres containing reactive and reducing gases such as ammonia, hydrogen, hydrogen halides, hydrogen sulfide, nitrogen oxides, oxygen, or sulfur oxides in major or minor relative abundances require you to review the pertinent literature for both chemical compatibility and temperature limitations.

Cryogenic measurement applications are generally in environments in which chemical reactivity is greatly suppressed by the cold temperatures and present fewer problems with sensor selection.

Increased temperatures proportionally increase the rates of chemical reactions, which include the reactions known as *corrosions*. While contacts between dissimilar metals are notorious for corrosive actions in mechanical structures, thermocouple metals are much less so, but high temperatures and high heats produce stressful conditions on virtually all materials. The installation of the LED continuity monitor illustrated in Figure 3-26 is a recommended practice in any TC temperature monitoring system.

Heat Transfer and Basic Thermodynamics

Thermal energy can be visualized as the molecular kinetic energy in the form of motion or vibration in a specific mass or system at a specific temperature. Theoretical physics calls the point at which all but zero-point molecular motion ceases as absolute zero on the temperature scale. From the concept of absolute zero, we can further differentiate between heat and temperature by considering two masses, one twice the size of the other, both with the same level of molecular kinetic energy. The two unequal masses are at the same temperature, but the heavier mass contains twice the heat of the lighter. Temperature describes the level of energy. Heat describes the quantity of energy.

Heat is a form of energy that can be transferred from one system to another by virtue of a difference in temperature between the two sites. Energy travels from hot to cold locations to achieve thermodynamic equilibrium. Convection, conduction, and radiation are the three main methods that transfer heat energy. Sir Isaac Newton's original publication on heat dealt with temperature measurement. The works of Fourier described the movement of heat energy.

A thermodynamic study of heat movement has been used as a traditional exercise in science or math education by modeling the cooling of heated objects. Newton's law of cooling is an application from which the exponential decay mathematical model can be developed.

Thus far, insulated metal block assemblies with internal electrical heaters and specially placed cavities to accept temperature sensors called *dry wells* were used in previous experiments involving temperature-monitoring studies. By recording the changes in temperature of the dry wells as they cool from a higher to a lower temperature, we can derive the cooling law and generate specific information about materials and predictive mathematical formulas.

Metals, glass, and plastics extensively used in our society are materials from which items are frequently manufactured from their higher temperature, liquid states. While the heated material remains in the furnace or oven, it is liquid or in a plastic state and can be shaped or squeezed into useful forms, then fixed into the desired final shape by cooling. Cooling is initiated by moving the hot formed product to a cooler environment to lose heat freely or in a controlled program.

In terms of a useful mathematical model, you can write

$$\frac{dT}{dt} = -k(T_i - T_e) -- 1$$

- – –k is a proportionality constant, dT/dt is the first derivative, or rate of change of temperature with respect to time

- – T_i is the initial temperature of the object

- – T_e is the temperature of the environment to which the object is losing heat.

To solve the differential equation and find the temperature T at any time desired, the time and temperature variables are separated. Each side of the equation is integrated to generate the expression.

$$-kt = \log(T_i - T_e) + \ln C \text{ or}$$

$$T_i - T_e = Ce^{-kt} \text{ from the initial conditions at time zero when}$$

$$C = T_i - T_e \text{ then we can substitute for C and write}$$

$$T = T_e + (T_i - T_e) e^{-kt} \text{ to relate object temperature and time passage.}$$

If the decrease in temperature is continuously recorded over a fixed time, you can use the decay curve as a source of data to evaluate parameters such as the effectiveness of insulations and the heat capacity of experimental setups.

A technique known as *Euler's method* converts the individual points of a recorded time and temperature curve into a format from which the numerical value of the proportionality constant in Newton's law formula can be derived.

Newton's law of cooling is used as an educational example of a differential equation because, unlike most differential equations, it can be resolved to an exact solution. Euler's method is a technique that generates both an approximate solution over a small range for differential equations that may not have an exact solution and to evaluate the constants in differential equations that do have an exact solution, as found in Newton's law of cooling.

Experiment

For chemists, biologists, and engineers, many experimental investigations require the monitoring of the development or loss of heat in closed systems. A simple approximation to a "closed system" has been used in previous sections of this book in the form of the aluminum block *dry well* used for creating both reproducible fixed temperatures and variable temperature profiles. Encased in a Styrofoam box as insulation but with openings for the heater power leads and for access to the dry well cavities in the metal block, the dry well approximates a *closed system*. By recording the decreasing temperature of the block as a function of time when it cools to ambient conditions after a temperature elevation perturbation, the data required to evaluate the proportionality constant k in equation 1 can be collected. If a timed power application to the block is made with and without the insulation layer in place, a numerical value can be derived for the insulative value of the layer. Using the SiC thermistor in a Wheatstone bridge as depicted in Figure 3-15, the cooling curves for the insulated and uninsulated dry well were recorded.

Observations

Figure 3-30 illustrates the tabulated time and temperature measurements read from the observed cooling curves for the 22.6 Ω dry well with and without its Styrofoam insulation layer. Blue is insulated cooling, and red is uninsulated cooling.

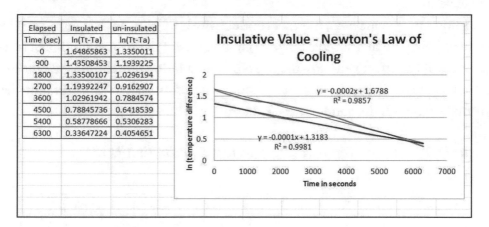

Elapsed Time (sec)	Insulated ln(Tt-Ta)	un-insulated ln(Tt-Ta)
0	1.64865863	1.3350011
900	1.43508453	1.1939225
1800	1.33500107	1.0296194
2700	1.19392247	0.9162907
3600	1.02961942	0.7884574
4500	0.78845736	0.6418539
5400	0.58778666	0.5306283
6300	0.33647224	0.4054651

Insulative Value - Newton's Law of Cooling

$y = -0.0002x + 1.6788$
$R^2 = 0.9857$

$y = -0.0001x + 1.3183$
$R^2 = 0.9981$

ln (temperature difference)

Time in seconds

Figure 3-30. *Effect of styrofoam insulation on the cooling rate of aluminum dry well block*

Discussion

Heat can be classified, rather simplistically, into two forms: *sensible* and *latent*. Sensible heat is the energy that, when added or removed from a mass, causes the temperature of the mass to change. Latent heat is the energy that must be added to or subtracted from the mass to effect a change of physical state and is non-sensible. Water has a specific heat of 4.186 J/g °C (80 cal/g °C), but at 0°C, the latent heat of fusion is 334 kJ/Kg (80 cal/g (calories per gram)). At 100°C, the latent heat of vaporization is 2260 KJ/Kg (540 cal/g).

We have used the latent heat phenomenon in calibrating the thermistors by measuring their resistance when immersed in a water/ice bath. If there is ice in the liquid bath, the temperature stays at 0°C until all the ice melts, at which point any heat that flows into the bath then causes the temperature of the system to rise (see Figure 3-49). At the other extreme, when using water as a calibrating fluid, a container of boiling or steaming water, when corrected for elevation or atmospheric pressure, remains at 100°C if liquid remains in the container.

At temperatures between the boiling and freezing points of water, the addition of one calorie of heat energy to one gram of water causes the temperature of the water to increase by one degree Celsius. Specific heat is the heat energy required to raise a unit of mass of material through one Celsius degree.

Water is the specific heat standard at one calorie per degree. The literature contains many tables of specific heat for elements, chemical compounds, and materials of construction in the form of liquids and solids. Gases require more care in the definition of specific heat.

In addition to specific heat, thermal conductivity is of value in designing systems to control heat flow. The measured change in cooling rate of the heated block can be taken as a measure of the effectiveness of the Styrofoam insulation and the closed nature of the system. Table 3-7 is a tabulation of the room temperature thermal conductivities of various materials with the conductivity, k, in watts per meter-degree Celsius.

Table 3-7. *Room Temperature Thermal Conductivities of Various Materials*

Material	k in W/m-°C	Material	k in W/m-°C	Material	k in W/m-°C
Diamond	2300	Lead	35	Wood (Oak)	0.17
Silver	429	Titanium	15.6	Helium (gas)	0.152
Copper	317	Mercury(liq)	85	Soft rubber	0.13
Aluminum	237	Glass	0.78	Glass fiber	0.043
Tungsten	180	Brick	0.72	Air (gas)	0.026
Zinc	112	Water(liq)	0.607	Urethane rigid foam	0.026
Iron	80.2	Human skin	0.37	styrofoam	0.033
Tin	64	Hydrogen (gas)	0.182	aerogel	0.025

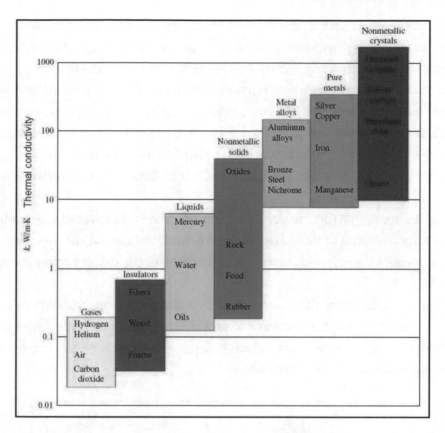

Figure 3-31. Graphical representation of selected material thermal conductivities (see http://what-when-how.com/energy-engineering/heat-transfer-energy-engineering/)

Thermoelectricity

It has long been known that mechanical energy can be converted into electrical energy by moving coiled wire conductors in magnetic fields. It is less well known that a thermal gradient along a conductor also produces a weak electric field in that conductor. The voltage that moves charge carriers across a thermal gradient can be measured by using a different metallic conductor to complete the measuring circuit, thus forming a thermocouple often used to measure the temperature at one end of the gradient.

Thermocouples are a well-known and familiar temperature measurement system. Thermocouple junctions are formed by electrically connecting two dissimilar metal wires, that when assembled into an appropriate, dual junction circuit, convert a temperature differential into a small measurable voltage. Thermocouples use the Seebeck effect that was discovered in the eighteenth century along with the Peltier effect relating current flow to heating and cooling in dissimilar metal junctions.

As the knowledge of the relationship between electrical energy, metallic conductors, and heat differences advanced, it became evident that the thermoelectric phenomena were weak in nature when compared to the forces of electromagnetic induction.

Heat, electric current, and power are related by Ohm's law and the power expression $P = I^2R$. Electric current moving through a metallic conductor, against resistance, creates heat.

Although the original thermoelectric phenomena were discovered with metal conductor interfaces, the same heat-electrical conversions can be affected with semiconductors. The semiconductor in most thermoelectric devices today is bismuth telluride (Bi_2Te_3).

In Figure 3-32, the reversible nature of the modern thermoelectric devices is illustrated by the direction of the heat or electrical energy flow. A single device can generate electricity if a temperature or heat gradient exists. Heat energy can be moved or "pumped" if electrical energy is available.

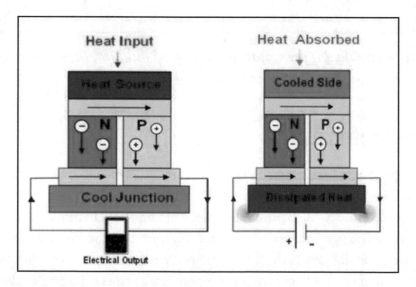

Figure 3-32. *A reversible thermoelectric device*

Figure 3-33 depicts the construction of a typical 40 mm^2 × 4 mm^2 ceramic encased thermoelectric plate.

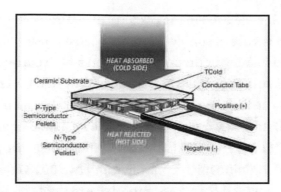

Figure 3-33. *A typical ceramic encased thermoelectric plate*

Thermoelectric Heating and Cooling

Thermoelectric devices are commercially manufactured to interconvert electrical and thermal energies. Solid-state thermoelectric devices can be considered reversible in that with no moving parts, they can use electricity to pump heat or use heat to produce electricity.

Optimization of the weak thermoelectric effect using semiconductors creates a heat movement technology with a similarly weak and limited, but still usable, capability. In addition to the weak nature of the effect, temperature differentials are also limited by the thermal conductivities of the materials of construction used to assemble the heat transfer devices and the radiative transfer of heat across the gradient established. As with electric resistance heating assemblies, care must be exercised so that the fusion temperature of the solder making electrical connections in the heat manipulating systems are not approached too closely or inadvertently exceeded. Virtually all semiconductor type devices are thermally sensitive and tend to operate better at ambient and lower temperatures. Datasheets from Tellurex, a manufacturer of 40 mm^2, bismuth telluride, alumina ceramic plate thermoelectric devices suggest upper temperature limits of 100°C.

Experiment

Flat plate, thermoelectric heat transfer elements require low-voltage, high-current DC excitation to move heat across their surfaces. Control of high DC currents at low voltages is conveniently implemented with microcontrollers and MOSFET devices.

The microcontroller code used in the circuitry in Figure 3-34 is a simple, manually activated increase or decrease of supply power through a pulse width modulation (PWM) application modulating or driving the gate on a high current MOSFET. Gate modulation thus regulates the 12 V, 8.5 A, DC power provided by a line-powered supply.

A thermoelectric heat pump demonstration cell was fabricated from a wooden base and a series of shaped, stacked wooden plates that form a dual-chambered test cell separated by a 40 mm² (1½ in) × 4 mm (⅛ in) thick, thermoelectric plate. A high current supply, terminal board, Arduino microcontroller, and two 30 KΩ thermistor temperature probes were all firmly mounted on the assembly base to safely power and monitor the temperature differential generated as the power to the thermos-electric cooling (TEC) plate is varied.

Figure 3-34 is a composite schematic showing the connections to the Arduino for the temperature monitoring and pulse width modulation (PWM) control of the high current MOSFET gate. Two 30 KΩ thermistors are mounted in the hot and cold chambers created on either side of a test cell in which the TEC plate separates the two chambers.

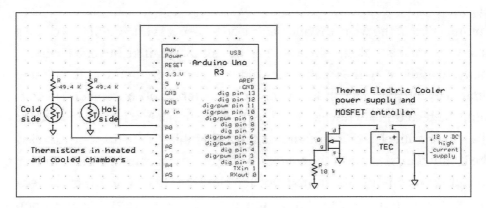

Figure 3-34. *Arduino TEC power control and temperature monitoring schematic*

As indicated in the schematic in Figure 3-34, the power control to the TEC and the temperature differential created by the TEC plate is controlled and displayed by an Arduino programmed with the code in Listing 3-4. The code controls a PWM pin whose output width is increased or decreased by the sending of "i" or "d" from the serial port that varies the time on and off the gate on a high current MOSFET switch. An FQP33N10 100 V, 33 A, 52 mΩ on resistance, N channel, enhancement mode power MOSFET, mounted on a 2 in × 2 in (50 mm × 50 mm) finned heat sink was used to control the current flow to the TEC. The temperature differential created by the TEC is monitored by two 30 KΩ epoxy bead thermistors mounted in the two chambers on either side of the TEC plate in the test cell.

Additional stability and increased accuracy are achieved in the temperature monitoring by using the 3.3 V supply on the Arduino, a 5x data average, and a Steinhart-Hart approximation relating resistance and thermistor temperature.

Each of the two thermistors used to monitor the relative temperature in each of the compartments formed by the division of the main chamber in two by the TEC plate was mounted on small hand-drawn circuit boards (see Figure RE-2) that were then fixed adjacent to access holes drilled into the centers of the top and bottom plates of the test assembly.

Listing 3-4 prints several intermediate values used in the control and monitoring algorithms to the serial port to aid in the configuration of the system. Once the test cell is functioning satisfactorily, you can comment out the lines of code printing the intermediate diagnostic values to clean up the serial port display as required.

In Figures 3-35 and 3-36, the TEC testing apparatus is shown in the assembled form and in a partially disassembled state to display its simple construction. The various components are identified by the numerical captions that are identified in the text following the figures.

Figure 3-35. *Arduino TEC testing chambers partially disassembled*

Figure 3-35 depicts the components used to make a 4 in² (10 cm²) dual-chambered test cell using four 3/8 in (9.5 mm) plywood plates in a partially disassembled state. Plates I and II have 1/8 in (3 mm) recessed ledges 1/16 in (1.5 mm) deep around an 1-5/16 in (3.3 cm) square opening to accommodate the 1-9/16 in (40 mm) TEC plate item 3.

Electrical connections to the plate are routed through the two recessed channels to the right of the cooling plate. The bottom plate of the cell is identical to caption 4 the top, with a 3/32 in (2.4 mm) hole bored through the geometrical center of the plate to accept the PCB mounted thermistor assembly as seen in Figure 3-36.

Four wooden dowels align the test cell assembly and position 4 in² (10.1 cm²) spacers that lift the entire stack ⅜ in (9.5 mm) off the top surface of the ½ in (12.2 mm) plywood base plate. The two terminal boards visible on either side of caption 5 are mounted on the base plate to provide secure fixtures for the wiring of the USB connected microcontroller (caption 6), the heat sink mounted MOSFET (caption 7) and the edge mounted high current 12 V supply (caption 8).

Figure 3-36 shows the top plate–mounted, hand-drawn, voltage divider circuit, PCB with the mounted thermistor and fixed value resistor. The top mounted PCB is identical to a second PCB assembly mounted on the bottom plate of the high current testing apparatus.

Figure 3-36. *Arduino TEC testing system fully assembled*

A TEC test is conducted by connecting the microcontroller to the computer hosting the Arduino IDE and applying power to the 12 V supply. Listing 3-4 is loaded into the microcontroller. The desired power to be applied to the TEC plate is incremented in 5 unit increments by sending an "i" from the serial monitor. The five-unit increment invoked by the "i" is mapped into a pulse width modulation range of 0 to 255 that adjusts the gate turn-on time to apply 12.5% of the available power to the TEC per 5-unit increment invoked or used.

Observations

Preliminary testing of the TEC in the wooden dual-chambered cell produced an overall cooling of the chambers. A single 5-unit increment of the Arduino code corresponding to a 12% PWM power delivery to the load cooled the thermistor on the cool side of the plate from an initial reading of 26°C to 1°C in an hour.

In the circuit diagram in Figure 3-34, the positive side of the power supply is connected to the red or positive terminal of the plate. The application of lower power levels causes the plate to cool, with one side cooling up to 5 or 6 degrees faster than the other. If the applied current is reversed, the opposite side cools more quickly, but only limited experimentation was conducted with the reversed current configuration.

In Figure 3-37, the amount of power applied to the TEC determines the degree of cooling realized from the cooling plate.

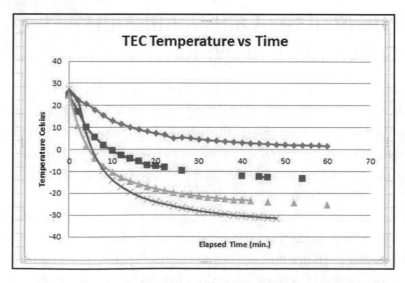

Figure 3-37. *Arduino TEC temperature vs. time for four applied power levels*

Discussion

Thermoelectric heat transfer requires the control of large currents at relatively low voltage levels. Power for the test cell TEC plate is derived from a line-powered, 12 V supply capable of an 8.5 A output. To use a PWM technique to control this current, an FQP 33N10 MOSFET was mounted on a 2 in × 2 in (5 cm × 5 cm) finned heat sink to handle the current demand of the TEC plate.

Dry wood was used as the basic material of construction because it is readily available, easy to work with, and both electrically and thermally non-conducting.

Listing 3-4 is an Arduino sketch that allows for TEC power control and prints the chamber temperatures to the serial port. The code uses the Steinhart-Hart equation to generate the degree Celsius temperature for each chamber. Only the cooling chamber data has been plotted as an example of the heat transfer capability provided by the TEC plate.

To fully utilize the heat transfer properties of the TEC plate, great care must be taken with insulations for both heat retention or heat exclusion. For instance, if substantial deviations from ambient temperatures are required for an experiment, the two-chambered test apparatus is a poor design because the pumped heat is not dissipated and builds up in the adjacent receiving enclosure to provide a close source of heat to flow back into the deficient chamber. As a minimum design parameter for a cooling function, the hot TEC surface should be open to the ambient atmosphere to allow the heat pumped to dissipate.

Measurement of Heat and Temperature with Raspberry Pi and Python

High sensitivity or high precision temperature measurements can be made and recorded with an Arduino microcontroller implementing a pulse width differential measurement technique on the output of a 555 timer chip, with a thermistor in its RC timing network. The pulse width differential variation created by temperature changes in the heat-sensitive thermistor can then be recorded and displayed with the Python Matplotlib strip chart recorder (SCR) display running on the RPi.

As presented in the DAQFactory implementation of the precision high-resolution temperature measurement method, the sensitivity of the thermistor measurement is expanded by using the pulse counting capability of the Arduino microcontroller to measure the time required to charge a high-quality, low-leakage capacitor through a fixed resistor and the series resistance of a negative temperature coefficient thermistor.

The method differs from the originally published technique. The pulse width differential time is used as the temperature change indicator rather than calculating the thermistor resistance and converting it into an absolute temperature (see www.st.com/resource/en/application_note/cd00010962-a-high-resolutionprecision-thermometer-using-st7-and-ne555-stmicroelectronics.pdf).

A continuous recording and plotting of the temperature data in the form of a pulse width differential numerical value require the plotting program to accept a varying number of digits, as explained in the Experiment section of this exercise.

Python code has been developed in Listing 3-2 to accept and evaluate a variable value of differing numerical digit width arriving at the serial port after broadcast by the Arduino microcontroller. However, in addition to the parsing out of the digital value transmitted, a clearing of the Python serial input buffer as seen in Listing 3-2 is sometimes necessary to stop the accumulation of garbage in the serial port buffer that causes the Python code to throw an error in subsequent plotting routines. You must also ensure that the Python input buffer clearing command and slice notations used are compatible with the version of Python in use for the plotting program.

The plotting code posted to the programming listings for this exercise as Listing 3-2 has been modified from the original Matplotlib strip chart recorder or oscillographic program in large part through a trial-and-error process. Attention is drawn to using the function len() to determine the length of a string and the slice() function for isolating a desired portion of the subject string. The Arduino output string may include several ASCII escapes characters such as \r, "carriage return" and \n, "new line" that len() and slice() treat as single characters. The serial read line function reads all characters up to the \r\n sequence that signals the end of the current line. The len() and slice() functions read these four characters as two singular units of \r and \n.

The Matplotlib plotting program has provisions for the labeling of the axes displayed. It allows the experimenter to choose either a rising or descending trace for changing data values by reversing the order in which the maximum and minimum limitations for the y axis are specified (see Figures 3-38 and 3-39). Positive and negative numbers are plotted above and below the zero axis by specifying the positive and negative maxima for the desired scale.

Ensuring that operating systems are updated, careful attention to backward compatibility, and a willingness to experiment with code to get a functioning program, are necessary prerequisites for using freely available open source systems.

Experiment

Figure 3-1 is a schematic diagram of the circuit used to implement the high resolution or precision thermistor temperature measurement setup.

To conduct high resolution or precision temperature measurement experiments, a choice should be made with respect to the assembly of the apparatus to be used. A solderless breadboard can quickly prepare a demonstration for one or two measurements or applications. Suppose a larger number of experiments with different values of thermistors, resistors, or capacitors are conducted. In that case, a printed circuit board or a hard-wired configuration on perf board, equipped with screw terminal connectors for component interchanges should be considered (see Figure 3-42).

In Figure 3-42, the device fabricated to demonstrate the effects of using different component values in the thermistor-capacitor timing network of the 555 timer RC consists of a perf board with soldered wire connections and three sets of dual terminal screw connectors.

After electrically configuring the RPi, the 555 timer-thermistor-Arduino combination, the power supply to the insulated dry well, then loading the Arduino moving average digital signal processing software and the RPi strip chart recorder (SCR) plotter program, the setup validation process can be started.

With the thermistor bead immersed into the dry well block that has stabilized at ambient room temperature, the serial monitor on the Arduino should generate a series of numbers that gradually rise to a steady numerical value. The rising numbers are the result of the moving average digital signal processing algorithm filling the averaging matrix and confirming the operation of the Arduino software.

Once the serial port output has been validated, the Python SCR plotter can be loaded and launched to display the pulse width differential count of the thermistor induced variation of the 555 timer high and low pulse widths.

To calibrate the plotter display a stopwatch should be used to measure the time width of the graphics display; or alternatively, the console display of the temperature could be timestamped with the Python asctime() function (https://docs.python. org/3/library/time.html). The timestamped temperature record can then be stored on an SD card, as explained in Chapter 10.

To thermally calibrate the system, a timed power pulse is applied to the heater element in the dry well block. The duration of the pulse and the voltage of the applied power should be determined by experiment as the size of the block, the wattage of the heater, and availability of power are all variable quantities in experimental work.

I used the dry well seen in Figure 3-2 with a 12 V, 3A power supply that was able to produce 2-to-5-degree temperature increases for 2-to-3-minute power pulses. The exact temperature differentials were read from a mercury-in-glass thermometer occupying one of the three wells in the block.

During the validation of the setup, the RPi display was invoked with both the console output and the plotter tracing being simultaneously displayed to provide an easily seen conformation of the values being received, manipulated, and displayed. Removal of the print statements in the Matplotlib code by converting them to comments displays only the SCR trace for repetitive experiments where archival data storage is not required.

Observations

A total of four calibration experiments were run with two different values of high-quality, low-leakage Mylar capacitors in the RC network of 555 timers. The y-value scales in the console record or the plotter trace in Figures 3-38 and 3-39 show that the PWD counts are in the 5000 to 6000 range. The PWD count for Figure 3-40 is an order of magnitude less with PWD counts in the hundreds. A 1 μF capacitor was used to collect the data in Figures 3-38 and 3-39. A 150 nF capacitor was used to generate the recorded data in Figure 3-40.

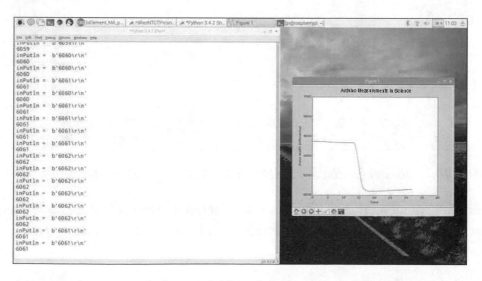

Figure 3-38. *Python console log and SCR plot of pulse width differential count during a known temperature change*

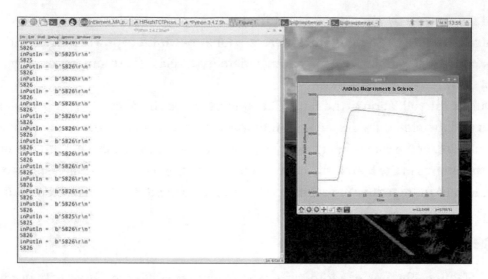

Figure 3-39. *Console log and SCR plot with inverted PWD count scale*

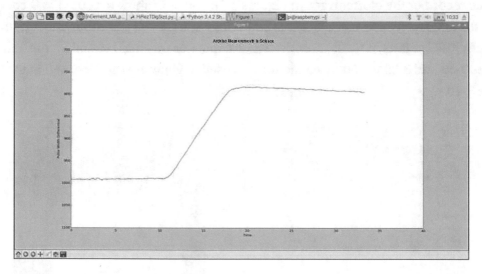

Figure 3-40. *Full-screen display option of Matplotlib SCR plotter programcs*

Table 3-8 is a tabulation of a duplicate set of temperature calibration experiments conducted with a 10 kΩ epoxy bead thermistor with a 10 kΩ 1% resistor in the R2 position of the 555 IC's timer network.

Table 3-8. *High-Resolution Temperature Calibration of a 10K Ω*
Epoxy Bead Thermistor

Expt.#	Capacitor	start PWD	Initial T	final PWD	final T	ΔT	ΔPWD	PWD/T	Heat Time
1	1 μF	6534	22-1/2	6041	24	1-1/2	493	328.7	1 min
2	1 μF	6470	22-1/2	5750	25	2-1/2	720	288	1-1/2 min
3	150 nF	696	22-1/2	800	27	4-1/2	169	37.6	2-1/2 min
4	150 nF	951	23	757	27-1/2	4-1/2	194	43.1	3 min
5	2 μF	13108	22	12144	24-1/4	2-1/2	968	430	1 min
6	2 μF	13406	21-1/2	12393	24	2-1/2	1013	405.2	1 min

Discussion

The timing in Linux-based operating systems is inconsistent. For accuracy, the time scale on the Matplotlib SCR plotting display should be calibrated with a stopwatch, or timestamped data can be saved on an SD card and displayed on the console.

By using a thermistor and a capacitor to form the RC timing network of a 555 timer, the small changes in thermistor resistance can be converted into changes in the ratio between the high and low times of the 555 timer square wave output. By monitoring the change in the ratio with microsecond resolution, small changes in thermistor resistance can be expressed in large numerical values that greatly increase the resolution or fineness with which the temperature can be monitored. As with all sensitive or high-resolution measurement systems, the calibration of the detector response over the intended range of use should be validated for both accuracy and reproducibility.

Table 3-8 indicates that approximately 300 counts are registered for each degree of temperature change experienced when a 10 kΩ thermistor, 10 kΩ resistor, and a 1 μF capacitor make up the RC network. If the plotter can read 30 counts above the baseline, then the temperature is monitored to 1/10 of a degree. If three counts are visible, the experiment is measuring 1/100 of a degree. In an electronic timing application, the size of the RC time constant is a linear function of the size of the individual components. When various sizes of low leakage capacitors are used in the high-resolution thermistor temperature measurement circuit, the PWD count becomes a linear function of the capacitor value for a constant thermistor-R2 combination, as seen in Figure 3-41. The equation of the line in Figure 3-41 is y = 6689.7x + 13.157.

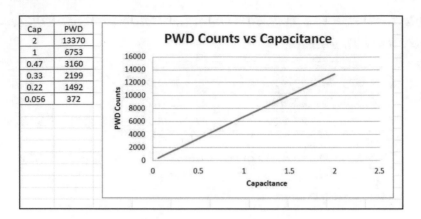

Cap	PWD
2	13370
1	6753
0.47	3160
0.33	2199
0.22	1492
0.056	372

Figure 3-41. *Effect of capacitor size in the high resolution temperature measurement circuit*

For high sensitivity measurements, attention to detail is required. Power supply noise must be minimized, or batteries used, electromagnetic shielding for all metal parts must be installed, and adequate insulation to stop thermal drifting must be considered. To maximize the sensitivity of the technique for a particular application, the RC combination needs to be optimized. That is probably best done experimentally after the noise reduction and thermal stability techniques have been implemented in the setup. As part of any optimization program, the thermistor's resistance value can be varied beyond the 10 kΩ and 30 kΩ units used in this book.

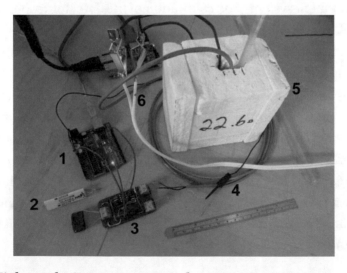

Figure 3-42. *High resolution or precision thermistor temperature measurement setup*

1) Arduino microcontroller board

2) 1 µF polystyrene capacitor

3) High-resolution thermistor 555 timer perf board, with three dual-
   wire, screw terminal connectors for component interchange

4) Thermistor twisted leads cable with grounded shielding lead
   (gray) and ground connection black clip

5) Dry well with mercury-in-glass thermometer for differential
   temperature testing

6) Heater power leads and clips with RPi in background

Non-Contact Temperature Measurement

Infrared sensors are available to measure the more intense 0.7-to-14-micron (10^{-6} meter)
radiation band of infrared emissions. As the IR is an optical measurement, the
precautions used in all optical determinations must be followed. Reflectivity,
transmissivity, field of view, and angle of view must be optimized for the measurement
to be reproducible and accurate.

A Melexis 90614 thermopile detector is used to measure temperatures between –70°C
and 380°C, with a single detector measuring the 5.5 to 10 microns infrared band from
objects within its 45-degree field of view.

Experiment

IR temperature measurements are made with the Arduino controlled detector then
recorded with the Matplotlib strip chart recorder program and the Python console.
Data is recorded graphically with the plotter and numerically with the console output.
The numerical data can be printed or stored on an SD card as required for subsequent
analysis.

The sensor is wired as depicted in Figure 3-19 to an Arduino microcontroller. The
microcontroller is programmed with a library available from the standard MLX90614
library collection accessed through the Arduino IDE.

As with all multiple hardware platforms, you should get the microcontroller wired to
the sensor, the appropriate software loaded into the microcontroller, and validate that

the Arduino is reading the IR sensor and sending the required data to the serial port. The standard library may contain lines or portions of text code containing the labels and values for the serial port display. The library may contain print statements and outputs for the ambient case temperature and the sensor object temperature in degrees Celsius for the first line and Fahrenheit for the second line. A third blank line was printed to the port to space out the output into a more readable format.

I commented out the Fahrenheit and blank line output print statements in the Arduino code to obtain a single line output for easier parsing of the data in the Python plotting program.

Once the Arduino sensor data stream has been configured and validated, the Python plotting code can be loaded into the RPi and the IR temperature monitored (see Listing 3-5).

If the data is to be recorded for later interpretation and analysis, a collection system could be configured to store the timestamped console output on an SD card, as explained in Chapter 10.

Observations

Figure 3-43 is a tracing of the IR detector response to a series of heated objects held two to three inches above the sensor mounted in a prototyping board on the desktop. At the extreme left is the "baseline" detector response to the open field of view (FOV) above the sensor. The first downward deflection is from a fresh polyethylene ice pack filled with frozen glycol-water, which registered –7.5°C.

The next upward deflection is from my hand heat, which registered 29°C. While the next large deflection is from the bottom of a hot-drink mug and registered 47°C. The next upward deflection to 32°C was the result of my hand heat after warming them on the sides of the hot drink mug. The last downward and upward deflections on the trace at –1°C to –0.75°C and at 40°C are the temperatures registered by the ice pack and hot drink mug bottom after having sat on the desktop for several minutes.

Previous experiments with hot water in a microwave container indicated a bottom surface temperature of 44°C. A mercury-in-glass thermometer indicated a liquid temperature of 58°C for the interior fluid.

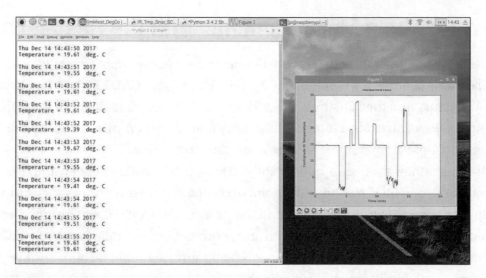

Figure 3-43. *Melexis 90614 infrared temperature measurements*

The sensor response is quickly appearing to be immediate.

Discussion

As seen in the demonstration readings and the inner and outer container measurements, the surface temperature is measured.

Radiated heat can cause the readings to drift if the heated object is substantially above the ambient temperature. The sensor object distance is small enough that the radiant heat can raise the temperature of the sensor case and its surroundings (within inches or less than 15 cm).

The total field of view is a 90° or 45° cone about the vertical axis. The sensor reads all the surface heat being radiated from the object within the field of view. If the object is small and the sensor distance is great, the sensor may be proportionally reading the object's background.

More information about the sensor construction, different models or options available, electronic configurations available, and optical properties are in manufacturer datasheets.

Thermocouple Measurements with the Raspberry Pi

With its robust nature and wide range of temperature measurement capability, the metallic thermocouple is a common industrial technology. SCADA systems such as the DAQFactory and the LabJack HMI are designed to accommodate thermocouple measurement systems. Most integrated circuitry manufacturers offer a selection of ASIC for thermocouple temperature measurement instrumentation.

Thermocouples produce approximately 40 to 50 µV/°C and require an amplifier to bring the microvolt signal up to the point of compatibility with devices such as the Arduino and its 5 V ADC. The temperature range from 0°C to 500°C can be measured, graphically displayed, and recorded with an Arduino microcontroller, an AD 595 IC, and an RPi. Special microcircuit breakout boards using surface mount technology integrated circuits are available from manufacturers that allow the RPi to access the –200°C to 1250°C temperature range available from K-type thermocouples (see Adafruit Industries Max31855 p/n 269; approx. $25 CDN at `www.adafruit.com`).

An AD595 DIP IC can be powered by the 5 V available from the Arduino to provide a direct, simple, Arduino ADC–compatible signal from a K-type thermocouple that can then be converted to a temperature value, streamed out to an RPi for plotting, and timestamped data storage.

Recall that wire size determines resistance, so the largest wire available provides the least resistance to the small voltages generated (see Table 3-6 for response times). I recommend that you use a twisted pair of wires for long thermocouple extensions, do an LED continuity check, and keep a log of thermocouple resistance. In electrically "noisy" environments, it may be necessary to place a capacitor of 0.01 to 0.1 µF across the thermocouple wires to minimize noise. Appropriate sheathing may be required for the thermocouple wires in hostile environments.

Experiment

The AD595 DIP IC can be mounted on a prototyping board and connected to a K-type thermocouple. Connecting the IC to the 5 V supply on the Arduino, connecting the grounds to power the IC, and wiring the output from the AD595 to the A0 input of the Arduino ADC completes the circuitry for measurement operations (see Figures 3-24 and 3-25).

After wiring the system, a normal assembly procedure should be followed by starting with the loading of the Arduino code (Listing 3-6) and validating by observing the collection and transmission of the data stream onto the serial bus of the Arduino serial monitor.

Once data transmission has been confirmed, the Python plotting code (Listing 3-7) can be launched and the console output and plotting graphics verified on the RPi monitor.

To circumvent the measurement limitations imposed using the Arduino's 5 V power supply with the AD595 an integrated circuit, the Maxim MAX31855 chip can be used instead to monitor a K-type thermocouple. The chip is a surface mount technology device. It is available from manufacturers in a miniature breakout board compatible with an Arduino microcontroller (available at `www.sparkfun.com` and `www.adafruit.com`). The breakout board has connections for power and the serial peripheral interface (SPI) used to convey thermocouple voltages to the microcontroller for display in the controller's serial monitor. An Arduino-compatible library is available from both manufacturers. It provides all the code necessary for continuous thermocouple temperature measurement. (Ensure that the RPi has been updated with the latest version of the Arduino IDE, as older versions of the SPI protocol are not compatible with the MAX31855 library.)

Observations

AD595/Arduino/RPi Temperature Monitoring

Figure 3-44 depicts the system response to the baseline established by the ambient room temperature (extreme left trace), my finger heat (the first small upward peak), placing the thermocouple between two freshly frozen ice packs (the first depression to 0°C and the temperature variations registered by moving the thermocouple around in the proximity of a candle flame.

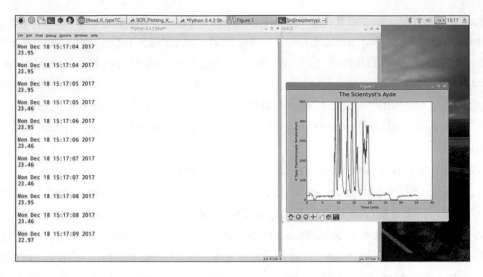

Figure 3-44. *K-type thermocouple response to various heat sources*

After cooling from the higher heats measured in the vicinity of the candle flame, the baseline, although appearing to be marginally higher than before exposure to the high heat, providing a normal response to finger heat and the ice packs.

MAX31855/Arduino /RPi Temperature Monitoring

To use the SPI protocol on the MAX31855 chip Arduino IDE revision, versions more recent than 1.6.6 are required. Newer versions of the IDE have a limited graphical data display capability coupled to the Arduino serial port.

Figure 3-45 depicts the serial port output from the thermocouple as it sits at ambient temperature on the desktop. The serial port displays two lines of data consisting of the temperature of the die on which the chip has been fabricated and the temperature of the thermocouple.

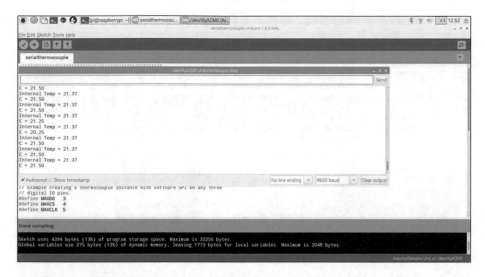

Figure 3-45. *MAX31855 serial port data output for ambient temperature response to K-type thermocouple*

The MAX31855 can measure the full range of temperatures accessible with the chromel-alumel K-type thermocouple that is –200°C to 1200°C with the 5 V supplied by the Arduino.

Fresh glycol ice packs from the freezer registered –10.5°C when the thermocouple was placed between two units. A small candle flame placed within one-eighth of an inch (3 mm) of the thermocouple indicated a temperature of 930°C and produced the Arduino serial port graphic recording in Figure 3-46.

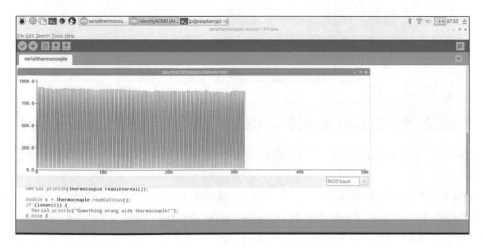

Figure. 3-46. *Arduino serial port graphic recording K-type thermocouple response to candle flame heat source*

A partial recording of the response as the thermocouple cools back to ambient temperatures and is reheated with my 32°C finger heat is depicted in Figure 3-47.

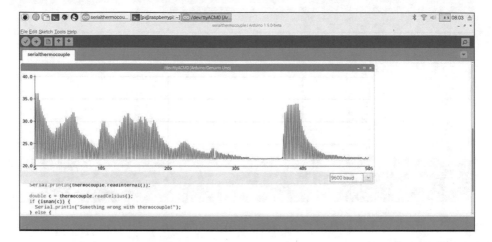

Figure 3-47. *K-type thermocouple cooling to ambient and effect of finger heat*

Figure 3-48 demonstrates the self-adjusting of the y-axis scale to lower temperatures.

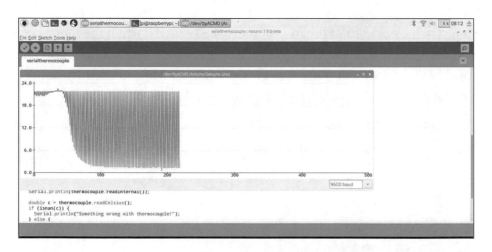

Figure 3-48. *Self-adjusting of serial plotter response to lower temperatures*

The Arduino's serial plotter is useful for graphical recording and displaying trends in data. To gain access to the more flexible Matplotlib strip chart recorder program and its scale expansion capabilities, the thermocouple reading program supplied by the board manufacturers must be modified. As in the previous serial port string to numerical

Matplotlib-compatible adaptations, the Arduino sketch needs to have the formatting and labeling code commented out. Only the temperature character string in the desired C or F temperature scale is printed to the serial port.

Listing 3-8 is only the generator function from the Matplotlib SCR program used to plot the Arduino data from the MAX31855. The remainder of the SCR code has been reproduced in the previous methods using thermistors, IR sensors, and the AD595 analog thermocouple temperature sensor. Experimental conditions require scale changes and axis labels as applicable for measurements.

The generator code in Listing 3-8 has a try/catch block around the serial port character input to numerical plotting value parsing and conversion code because of the frequent misreading of the character strings in the serial port. Thermocouples can be noisy, and for approximately 25% of the time, attempts to start the plotter failed with a ValueError exception terminating the program either before or shortly after starting. The errors were caused by the code attempting to convert a corrupted or non-convertible character string into a numerical value. The try/except block was set to catch the ValueError exception, then force another iteration of the readline() loop.

Figure 3-49 depicts the Matplotlib SCR plot of the thermocouple response to a sub-zero temperature measurement.

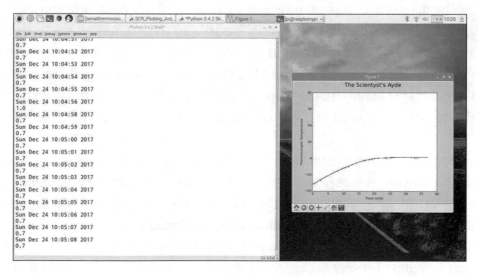

Figure. 3-49. *Sub-zero TC response and latent heat effects*

The low-temperature data in Figure 3-49 was obtained by placing the K-type thermocouple between two polyethylene glycol-water-filled freezer packs that were freshly removed from a freezer chest. As in previous versions of the SCR numerical value generator plotting code, a timestamped data printout has been included to print to the console a timestamped data stream for archiving.

Examining the plotter trace and timestamped data reveals a visual demonstration of the physics concept of latent heat in aqueous systems.

Discussion

Thermocouples are self-powered thermometric sensors with large dynamic ranges that to a first approximation are linear. Some thermocouples have discontinuities in their temperature-voltage relationship that is somewhat ignored by the software and instrumentation displaying the measured values. If accurate thermal measurement work is required, then the temperature range over which the thermocouple is to be used must be calibrated with standards in the tables.

The AD595 amplifier has an internally fixed gain resulting in an analog output of 10 mV/°C when connected to a K-type thermocouple. If the chip is powered from a 5 V supply, the maximum temperature measurable is 500°C. Higher temperatures can be measured by increasing the power supply to 10 V for the AD595 and applying a 2:1 voltage divider between the chip output and the Arduino ADC input to ensure the signal seen by the converter is 5 V or less (The ADC's maximum allowable signal strength.) When using a higher supply for the amplifier chip and a 2:1 voltage divider on the ADC input, the Arduino code must be adjusted to double the temperature value sent for plotting.

Thermocouple measurements into the cryogenic and flame temperature ranges can be made with only 5 V of power from the Arduino by using a type K thermocouple and the MAX31855 integrated circuit. The Maxim IC is a surface mount device that is available in a small printed circuit board format. The breakout board can be mounted on a prototyping board for temporary experiments or development work.

Thermocouples are noisy as they generally have long metal leads, are used in high power environments, and require large-signal amplifications to produce usable signals for driving displays. In some environments, a capacitor may be required across the two wires to moderate some of the spurious signals arising in the measurement system.

The noisy signal problem with the Matplotlib plotter serial port conversion code was minimized with an error catching Python function to ignore misread data with a try/except block.

Although the Arduino serial plotter with its fixed scales is useful, the Matplotlib SCR is more flexible since it can be adapted to display scale expansion, compression, or data varying into the positive and negative numerical domains.

Figure 3-49 provides a graphic visual display of the physics phenomenon of latent heat. The freezer packs cooled the thermocouple to an initial temperature of approximately –17°C and, in a linear manner, began to warm up. The time scale for this plotting was measured at forty minutes for the window as indicated on the time unit's scale. The temperature climbed steadily in a linear manner until about 12.5 minutes, when the effects of latent heat began to have a moderating effect on the temperature increase. After 20 minutes, the rate of temperature change stopped. The temperature remained in the 0.7°C area for hours as the melting ice within the packs absorbed the heat required for the solid to liquid phase change.

Passive Infrared (PIR) Heat Sensors

Devices are available that can be described as digital heat sensors. The heat sensing HC-501 PIR module is used extensively in security and personnel detection systems ($5 CDN). The device has a plastic domed Fresnel lens that can focus infrared light on thermally sensitive materials such as gallium nitride (GaN), cesium nitrate ($CsNO_3$), polyvinyl fluoride ($-CH_2-CF_2-)_n,$ organo-pyridines, and cobalt phthalocyanine complexes. Disturbances in the infrared radiation falling on the detector cause voltage fluctuations in the monitoring circuitry that change the high/low output state of the module.

Experiment

The PIR module is depicted in Figures 3-50 and 3-51.The three connection pins visible in Figure 3-51 from left to right are power, digital module output in the middle, and ground on the right. I connected module output to digital pin 2 on the Arduino for testing, demonstration, validation, and application development. I placed a red LED and 330 Ω current limiting resistor on digital pin 7. I placed a green LED and CLR on pin 8.

Listing 3-9 follows the activity on the PIR module output and activates the red-green diode array in accordance with the FOV activity level, and prints a written message to the serial monitor.

The PIR module has two potentiometers visible as the brick-red disks in Figure 3-50 and a position selectable jumper, the yellow rectangle (top-right of the circuit board) in Figure 3-51 that controls the operation of the device. The effects of these controls are presented and discussed in the Observations and Discussion portions of this section.

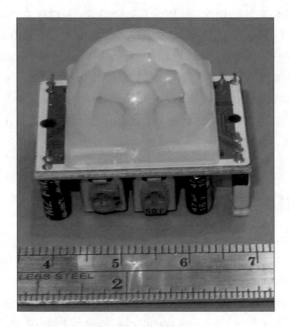

Figure 3-50. *The Fresnel lens top of HC-SR501 PIR*

Figure 3-51. *The circuit board of HC-SR501 PIR sensor*

Observations

It is noted in the manufacturer's datasheets that the device requires a full minute to stabilize after power is applied to the module.

The FOV of the lens is a 110–120-degree cone whose depth of field is variable from 3 to 7 meters (9 ft to 21 ft) and is adjusted with the right-hand potentiometer. In Figures 3-50 and 3-51, clockwise rotation increases the distance of surveillance.

The left-hand potentiometer controls the time delay from 5 seconds to 300 seconds with clockwise rotation (5 seconds to 5 minutes.)

A triggering option is selected by the position of the yellow jumper. In the top position or single trigger mode, the delay timer starts with the first motion-sensing signal. In the lower position or multiple trigger mode, the time delay is started each time a motion detection signal is detected

Discussion

To effectively use the PIR detector, the sensor must be placed in the correct orientation to detect differences in IR emissions within the FOV. The detector consists of two parallel rectangular surfaces coated with pyro sensitive material that, in quiescent conditions, both see the same IR emissions from the area monitored by the lens. A heated source entering the FOV at any angle not parallel to the centerline between the detector elements activates one element before the other. A differential signal is recorded as a disturbance in the background IR emissions. The sensor is a rectangular shape. The sensitive axis is parallel to the longer dimension.

The test circuit and colored diodes used in the Arduino program are solely to demonstrate the sensor's properties and allow the experimenter to develop a familiarity with the controls, response modes, sensor physical orientation, and evaluate sensor performance in daylight and extreme weather conditions.

Once the optimum operating conditions for a problem are achieved, the LEDs can be replaced with solid-state relays to activate night time cameras, lighting sources, or mechanical relays on detection of the motion of heated objects.

Code Listings

Listing 3-1. Arduino Pulse Width Difference Thermistor Monitor

```
// n Element Moving Average Dual Pulse Width Difference Measurement, Apr19/12
// Hi and Lo pulse widths read with pulseIn(pn#,HI/LOW). Difference value
// calculated and represents delta T of thermistor as Lo time is constant.
// Diff value accumulated in n element moving average for serial output
// of data
//
unsigned long duration;               // 1st pulse width
unsigned long duration_L;             // 2nd pulse width
unsigned long pwDiff;                 // pulse width difference
int const numReadings = 16;           // # readings averaged must be dclrd
                                      "const"

unsigned long readings[numReadings];  // individual readings
int index = 0;                        // readings array index
unsigned long total = 0;              // the running total
unsigned long average = 0;            // the averaged value
//
```

```
int inputPin = 2;                        // digital PWM pin #2 to be used for
                                         pulse counting
//
void setup()
{
  Serial.begin(9600);                    // set up serial comm
  for (int thisReading = 0; thisReading < numReadings; thisReading++)
  readings[thisReading] = 0;             // initialize readings array to zero
  pinMode(2, INPUT);                     // define input signal on PWM/dig
                                         I/O pins

}
//
void loop()  {
  duration = pulseIn(2, HIGH);           // fn waits for pin hi to start time
  duration_L = pulseIn(2, LOW);          // fn waits for pin lo to start time
  pwDiff = (duration - duration_L);
 // Serial.print("pwDiff =   ");
 // Serial.println(pwDiff, DEC);
  total = total - readings[index];       // subtract last entry
  readings[index] = pwDiff;              // collect current value
  total = total + readings[index];       // add current value to total
  //Serial.print("pre divide total =  ");
  //Serial.println(total, DEC);
  index = index + 1;                     // next array position
  if (index >= numReadings)              // if at end of array, wrap around
  {
  index = 0;
  }
  average = total/numReadings;           // calculate the average
  //Serial.print("average   ");
  Serial.println(average, DEC);
  //Serial.print("duration_L   ");
  //Serial.println(duration_L, DEC); // Comment out for DAQFactory usage
```

```
  //Serial.print("duration    ");
  //Serial.println(duration, DEC);
  delay(50);                              // slow rate down?
}
```

Listing 3-2. Matplotlib SCR Code for HiRezTempMonitor

```python
# RPi Python Strip Chart Recorder of Arduino Output
# SCR Plotting of serial data from Arduino output over serial port
# Arduino serial output must be numerical values only.
#
import matplotlib
import numpy as np
from matplotlib.lines import Line2D
import matplotlib.pyplot as plt
import matplotlib.animation as animation
import time
import serial
#
#
#
class Scope:
    def __init__(self, ax, maxt=40, dt=0.02):
        """"maxt time width of display"""
        self.ax = ax
        self.dt = dt
        self.maxt = maxt
        self.tdata = [0]
        self.ydata = [0]
        self.line = Line2D(self.tdata, self.ydata)
        self.ax.add_line(self.line)
        self.ax.set_ylim(1100, 700)  # y axis scale adjust size and order
                                        to suit application
        self.ax.set_xlim(0, self.maxt)

    def update(self, y):
        lastt = self.tdata[-1]
```

```
        if lastt > self.tdata[0] + self.maxt: # reset the arrays
            self.tdata = [self.tdata[-1]]
            self.ydata = [self.ydata[-1]]
            self.ax.set_xlim(self.tdata[0], self.tdata[0] + self.maxt)
            self.ax.figure.canvas.draw()

        t = self.tdata[-1] + self.dt
        self.tdata.append(t)
        self.ydata.append(y)
        self.line.set_data(self.tdata, self.ydata)
        return self.line,
#
ser = serial.Serial("/dev/ttyACM0", 9600, timeout=None)
#
def rd_data():
    ser.flushInput()  # flush the input buffer
    while True:
        inPutln = ser.readline()
        print("inPutln = ", inPutln)
        nbr_digs = len(inPutln) # detrmn len of string
        print("nbr_digs = ", nbr_digs)
        if (nbr_digs) == 5:     # there are 3 digits
            line = int(str(inPutln)[slice(2,5)]) # slice out 3 digits
        if (nbr_digs) == 6:     # there are 4 digits
            line = int(str(inPutln)[slice(2,6)]) # slice out 4 digits
        if (nbr_digs) == 7:     # there are 5 digits
            line = int(str(inPutln)[slice(2,7)]) # slice out 5 digits
        print(line)
        yield (line)

fig = plt.figure()
fig.suptitle("The Scientyst's Ayde", fontsize = 12)
ax = fig.add_subplot(111)
ax.set_xlabel("Time")
ax.set_ylabel("Pulse Width Differential")
scope = Scope(ax)
```

```python
# uses rd_data() as a generator to produce data for the update func, the
# Arduino LDC value is read by the plotting code in half second windows
# for the animated screen display. Software overhead limits response speed
# of display.
ani = animation.FuncAnimation(fig, scope.update, rd_data, interval=50,
blit=False)
plt.show()
```

Listing 3-3. Arduino TEC Power Control

```c
// A Thermo-Electric Power Controller with Temperature Differential Monitor
//
// This program uses the #3 PWM pin on an Arduino to regulate the power
// delivered to a Peltier plate. The Arduino controls a high power MOSFET
// gate to regulate the current flow to the heat transfer plate. Sending i
// or d from the serial port increases or decreases the power to the TEC plate.
// Two thermistor temperature sensors monitor the effect of the heat pumped
// by the TEC in two insulated chambers on either side of the TEC.
//
int peltier = 3; // the gate of the N channel MOSFET connects to Arduino pin 3
int power = 0;   // the power level varies from 0 to 99%
int peltier_level = map(power, 0, 99, 0, 255);  // power level mapping of %
                                            and 255
//
////thermistor analog pin connections defined
#define THERMISTORPIN A0
#define THERMISTORPIN1 A1
// resistance at 25 degrees C
#define THERMISTORNOMINAL 30000
// temp. for nominal resistance (almost always 25 C)
#define TEMPERATURENOMINAL 25
// averaging readings improves S/N by by the square root of
// the number of readings taken
#define NUMSAMPLES 5
// The beta coefficient of the thermistor (usually 3000-4000)
```

```
#define BCOEFFICIENT 3899
// the value of the fixed resistor in the voltage divider
#define SERIESRESISTOR 33000

int samples[NUMSAMPLES];

void setup(void) {
  Serial.begin(9600);
  analogReference(EXTERNAL);
  pinMode(peltier, OUTPUT); // set the peltier or MOSFET gate control pin
                            to output
}

void loop(void) {
  uint8_t i;
  float average;
  float average1;
  char option;  // action to be initiated; "i" increase, "d" to decrease
                powere input
//
  if(Serial.available() > 0)
  {
    option = Serial.read();
    if (option == 'i') // i sent from the serial port increases the power
                       to the load
    power += 5;
    else if(option == 'd') // d sent from the serial port decreases the
                           power to the load
    power -= 5;
//
  if(power > 99) power = 99;
  if(power < 0) power = 0;
//
  peltier_level = map(power, 0, 99, 0, 255);
  }
//
```

```
Serial.print("Power = ");
Serial.print(power);
Serial.print(" PLevel = ");
Serial.println(peltier_level);
//
analogWrite(peltier, peltier_level); // write the new levels % AND 0-255 to
                                     the port
//
//
// collect the data from thermistor #1
//
  // take N samples in a row, with a slight delay
  for (i=0; i< NUMSAMPLES; i++) {
   samples[i] = analogRead(THERMISTORPIN);
   delay(10);
  }

  // average all the samples out
  average = 0;
  for (i=0; i< NUMSAMPLES; i++) {
     average += samples[i];
  }
  average /= NUMSAMPLES;

  Serial.print("Average analog reading ");
  Serial.println(average);

  // convert the value to resistance
  average = (1023/average) - 1;
  average = SERIESRESISTOR / average;
  Serial.print("Thermistor resistance ");
  Serial.println(average);

  float steinhart;
  steinhart = average / THERMISTORNOMINAL;      // (R/Ro)
  steinhart = log(steinhart);                   // ln(R/Ro)
  steinhart /= BCOEFFICIENT;                     // 1/B * ln(R/Ro)
```

```
   steinhart += 1.0 / (TEMPERATURENOMINAL + 273.15); // + (1/To)
   steinhart = 1.0 / steinhart;                      // Invert
   steinhart -= 273.15;                              // convert to C

   Serial.print("Temperature ");
   Serial.print(steinhart);
   Serial.println(" *C");
// collect the data from thermistor #2

 // take N samples in a row, with a slight delay
  for (i=0; i< NUMSAMPLES; i++) {
   samples[i] = analogRead(THERMISTORPIN1);
   delay(10);
  }

   // average all the second data samples
   average1 = 0;
   for (i=0; i< NUMSAMPLES; i++) {
      average1 += samples[i];
   }
   average1 /= NUMSAMPLES;

   Serial.print("Average analog reading #2 ");
   Serial.println(average1);

   // convert the value to resistance
   average1 = (1023 / average1) - 1;
   average1 = SERIESRESISTOR / average1;
   Serial.print("Thermistor resistance #2 ");
   Serial.println(average1);

 // float steinhart declared in single device code
   steinhart = average1 / THERMISTORNOMINAL;      // (R/Ro)
   steinhart = log(steinhart);                    // ln(R/Ro)
   steinhart /= BCOEFFICIENT;                      // 1/B * ln(R/Ro)
   steinhart += 1.0 / (TEMPERATURENOMINAL + 273.15); // + (1/To)
   steinhart = 1.0 / steinhart;                   // Invert
   steinhart -= 273.15;                           // convert to C
```

```
  Serial.print("Temperature #2 ");
  Serial.print(steinhart);
  Serial.println(" *C");

  delay(1000);
}
```

Listing 3-4. RPi-IR Temperature Measurement and Plotting

```python
# RPi Python Strip Chart Recorder of Arduino Output
# SCR Plotting of serial data from Arduino output over serial port
# Arduino serial output must be numerical values only.
#
import matplotlib
import numpy as np
from matplotlib.lines import Line2D
import matplotlib.pyplot as plt
import matplotlib.animation as animation
import time
import serial
#
#
#
class Scope:
    def __init__(self, ax, maxt=20, dt=0.02):
        """maxt time width of display"""
        self.ax = ax
        self.dt = dt
        self.maxt = maxt
        self.tdata = [0]
        self.ydata = [0]
        self.line = Line2D(self.tdata, self.ydata)
        self.ax.add_line(self.line)
        self.ax.set_ylim(-10, 50)  # y axis scale
        self.ax.set_xlim(0, self.maxt)
```

```python
    def update(self, y):
        lastt = self.tdata[-1]
        if lastt > self.tdata[0] + self.maxt: # reset the arrays
            self.tdata = [self.tdata[-1]]
            self.ydata = [self.ydata[-1]]
            self.ax.set_xlim(self.tdata[0], self.tdata[0] + self.maxt)
            self.ax.figure.canvas.draw()

        t = self.tdata[-1] + self.dt
        self.tdata.append(t)
        self.ydata.append(y)
        self.line.set_data(self.tdata, self.ydata)
        return self.line,
#
ser = serial.Serial("/dev/ttyACM0", 9600)
#
def rd_data():
    while True:
        line = ser.readline()
        #print("line = ", line)
        ln_Ln = len(line)  #determines # digits in temp
        #print("Len line = ", ln_Ln)
        if (ln_Ln < 35):
            continue
        time.sleep(0.1)
        if (ln_Ln == 35): # the IR temp is < 10
            line = float((line)[slice(27, 31)]) # parse out & convrt to digits
        if (ln_Ln == 36): # the IR temp is < 100
            line = float((line)[slice(27, 32)]) # parse out & convrt to digits
        if (ln_Ln == 37): # the IR temp is = or > 100
            line = float((line)[slice(27, 33)])
```

```
          # decimal and single digit temperature values are processed by the code
          # double digit minus value may require additional processing code.
          print(time.asctime())                      # console print out of
          print("Temperature =",line," deg. C")   # timestamped data with a
          print()                                     # formatting blank line
          yield (line)

fig = plt.figure()
fig.suptitle("The Scientyst's Ayde", fontsize = 18)
ax = fig.add_subplot(111)
ax.set_xlabel("Time Units")
ax.set_ylabel("Centigrade IR Temperature ")
scope = Scope(ax)

# uses rd_data() as a generator to produce data for the update func, the
# Arduino IR value is read by the plotting code in 40 time unit windows
# for the animated screen display. Software overhead limits response speed
# of display.
ani = animation.FuncAnimation(fig, scope.update, rd_data, interval=50,
blit=False)

plt.show()
```

Listing 3-5. Arduino Code for K-Type Thermocouple Monitoring

```
/*
  Read a  K type thermocouple from an AD 594 IC
  Pgm reads an analog input on pin 0, converts it to voltage and for
  voltages < 5.00 directly
  converts the observed voltage into a Celsius temperature by x100 factor.
  Thermocouple voltages from temperatures over 500 C must be scaled down.
 */

// the setup routine runs once when you press reset:
void setup() {
  // initialize serial communication at 9600 bits per second:
  Serial.begin(9600);
}
```

```
// the loop routine runs over and over again forever:
void loop() {
  // read the input on analog pin 0:
  int sensorValue = analogRead(A0);
  // Convert the analog reading (which goes from 0 - 1023) to a voltage
     (0 - 5V):
  float voltage = sensorValue * (5.0 / 1023.0);
  float TempInDegC = voltage * 100;
  // print out the temperature
  delay(500);
  Serial.println(TempInDegC);
}
```

Listing 3-6. Python SCR Plotting Program for K-type Thermocouples (< 500°C)

```
# RPi Python Strip Chart Recorder of Arduino Output
# SCR Plotting of serial data from Arduino output over serial port
# Arduino serial output must be numerical values only.
#
import matplotlib
import numpy as np
from matplotlib.lines import Line2D
import matplotlib.pyplot as plt
import matplotlib.animation as animation
import time
import serial
#
#
#
class Scope:
    def __init__(self, ax, maxt=40, dt=0.02):
        """maxt time width of display"""
        self.ax = ax
        self.dt = dt
        self.maxt = maxt
        self.tdata = [0]
```

```
        self.ydata = [0]
        self.line = Line2D(self.tdata, self.ydata)
        self.ax.add_line(self.line)
        self.ax.set_ylim(0, 500)  # y axis scale
        self.ax.set_xlim(0, self.maxt)

    def update(self, y):
        lastt = self.tdata[-1]
        if lastt > self.tdata[0] + self.maxt: # reset the arrays
            self.tdata = [self.tdata[-1]]
            self.ydata = [self.ydata[-1]]
            self.ax.set_xlim(self.tdata[0], self.tdata[0] + self.maxt)
            self.ax.figure.canvas.draw()

        t = self.tdata[-1] + self.dt
        self.tdata.append(t)
        self.ydata.append(y)
        self.line.set_data(self.tdata, self.ydata)
        return self.line,
#
ser = serial.Serial("/dev/ttyACM0", 9600, timeout=1)
#
def rd_data():
    while True:
        inPutln = ser.readline()
        #print("inPutln = ", inPutln)
        if (len(inPutln) < 6):
            continue
        if (len(inPutln) == 6):                     # convert Arduino single
                                                       digit output stream
            line = float(str(inPutln)[slice(2, 6)])
        if (len(inPutln) == 7):                  # convert double digit
            line = float(str(inPutln)[slice(2, 7)])
        if (len(inPutln) == 8):                  # convert triple digit output
            line = float(str(inPutln)[slice(2, 8)])
```

```
        if (len(inPutln) == 9):
            line = float(str(inPutln)[slice(2, 9)]) # convert 4 digit output
        print(time.asctime())               # time stamp data
        print(line)                         # print data
        print(" ")                          # format print out with
                                              blank line

        yield (line)

fig = plt.figure()
fig.suptitle("The Scientyst's Ayde", fontsize = 20)
ax = fig.add_subplot(111)
ax.set_xlabel("Time Units")
ax.set_ylabel("K Type Thermocouple Temperature")
scope = Scope(ax)

# uses rd_data() as a generator to produce data for the update func, the
# Arduino LDC value is read by the plotting code in 10 minute windows for
# the animated screen display. Software overhead limits response speed
# of display.
ani = animation.FuncAnimation(fig, scope.update, rd_data, interval=50,
blit=False)

plt.show()
```

Listing 3-7. The Generator Code for Plotting of the MAX31855 Thermocouple Data

```
#
ser = serial.Serial("/dev/ttyACM0", 9600)
#
def rd_data():
    while True:
        inPutln = ser.readline()
        if (len(inPutln ) < 6):   # short character string fragment
            continue
        if (len(inPutln) > 9):     # long character string fragment
            continue
```

```
#
        try:
            if (len(inPutln) == 6):     # len for a single unsigned digit
                line = float(str(inPutln)[slice(2,5)])
                print(time.asctime()) # archival time stamp for
                                        console/data storage
                print (line)             # console display/archival data storage
                yield (line)
                #
            if (len(inPutln) == 7):     # len for a single unsigned digit
                line = float(str(inPutln)[slice(2,6)])
                print(time.asctime()) # archival time stamp for
                                        console/data storage
                print (line)             # console display/archival data storage
                yield (line)
                #
            if (len(inPutln) == 8):     # len for a single unsigned digit
                line = float(str(inPutln)[slice(2,7)])
                print(time.asctime()) # archival time stamp for
                                        console/data storage
                print (line)             # console display/archival data storage
                yield (line)
                #
            if (len(inPutln) == 9):     # len for a single unsigned digit
                line = float(str(inPutln)[slice(2,8)])
                print(time.asctime()) # archival time stamp for
                                        console/data storage
                print (line)             # console display/archival data storage
                yield (line)
        except ValueError:
            continue
```

Listing 3-8. PIR Sketch for Arduino

```
/*
 * PIR sensor demonstration and validation
 * when the IR in the field of view is low or inactive
 * light the green LED. When the IR  radiation increases
 * turn off the green and light the red LED.
 */

int pirPin = 2;              // choose the pin for the PIR sensor
int ledPinAct = 7;           // red led indicates ativity in FOV
int ledPinInact = 8;         // green pin for FOV inactive
//
int val = 0;                       // variable for reading the pin status

void setup() {
  pinMode(ledPinAct, OUTPUT);        // declare active LED as output
  pinMode(ledPinInact, OUTPUT);      // declare inactive LED as output
  pinMode(pirPin, INPUT);            // declare sensor as input
 //
  Serial.begin(9600);    // start serial port
}

void loop(){
  val = digitalRead(pirPin);  // read input value
  if (val == HIGH) {               // check if the input is HIGH
    digitalWrite(ledPinAct, HIGH);  // turn red LED ON
    digitalWrite(ledPinInact, LOW); // turn the green LED OFF
    Serial.println("Activity in FOV.");
  }
    if (val == LOW) {
      //
      Serial.println("No activity detected!");
      // green led on and red led off
      digitalWrite(ledPinInact, HIGH);
      digitalWrite(ledPinAct, LOW);
    }
    delay(10);
}
```

Summary

Heat and temperature are differentiated, and the extremes normally encountered in routine scientific work are discussed, along with some of the methods by which temperature scales can be calibrated and subsequently validated.

Numerous temperature sensors, their sensitivity ranges, output signal, and costs are explained.

Methods in which thermistors, thermocouples, and non-contact infrared sensors can produce high and normal resolution monitoring of temperatures are presented.

Thermoelectric heat transfers, insulation, mathematical cooling models, and IR security applications are investigated in modest detail.

Heat and temperature monitoring and control are both available with commercial, and the less expensive component assembled SCADA systems.

Heat in the form of infrared radiation forms part of Chapter 4 that explores the science of light, optical and photoelectric effects.

CHAPTER 4

Light, Optics, and Photoelectric Effects

Human vision evolved in daylight before civilization, creating the need for artificial lighting to see at night and illuminate enclosed protective dwellings. Artificial lighting, first based upon the incomplete combustion of carbon, created a red-yellow lighting characteristic of wood-fueled cooking fires, fat oils, and candles. Premixed oxygen fuel gas flames that could be adjusted to make brighter, cleaner lights were later developed. Eventually, electrical energy produced white light based upon the heat developed in an electric arc, an incandescent filament, and eventually electronic transitions.

Physics established the relationship between the color of light emitted when a black-body was heated to incandescence and provided the ability to define color in terms of the temperature, in degrees Kelvin, of the hot emitting body. The colors of visible light lie between 1000°K and 10,000°K.

Although artificial lighting has been developed using incandescent hot filaments, carbon arcs, the quartz iodine chemical cycle, electrically excited gases, and solid-state emissions, none of these illumination techniques can duplicate the colors as seen by the human eye in daylight.

In addition to illumination, light can be used as a scientific measuring tool, a visual recording, and data transmission medium or energy source. Light from the sun creates seasonal climate variations and daily weather as the orbital distance from the sun changes and the planet rotates. Sunlight and artificial light are used in farming and greenhouse operations. Photosynthesis produces biomass and oxygen from carbon dioxide and water.

This chapter discusses light, optics, and photoelectric effects. It examines the use of light in simple spectroscopic measuring applications and introduces basic quantum physics, simple computer imaging, computer vision, and energy collections and conversions.

© Richard J. Smythe 2022
R. J. Smythe, *Arduino Measurements in Science*, https://doi.org/10.1007/978-1-4842-6781-3_4

Discussions concerning the range of the electromagnetic spectrum visible to the human eye as colors are often measured with respect to their wavelengths that typically lie between the 390 nm to 700 nm (nanometer or 10^{-9} meter) portions of the electromagnetic spectrum. At longer wavelengths, the region of electromagnetic radiation is known as *infrared*. At shorter wavelengths, the radiation is known as *ultraviolet*. Birds, fish, and nocturnal animals can see partially into the infrared and ultraviolet regions visible to humans only through electro-optical photometric instrumentation.

Research into the electromagnetic spectrum and new technology developments are constantly advancing electromagnetic spectrum applications. As a result, many different terms for the energy contained in different portions of the electromagnetic spectrum have arisen.

Table 4-1 is a tabulation of the various named portions of the electromagnetic spectrum and the units of measurement to quantitatively describe the energy of the photons.

Table 4-1. *Energy Expressions for Sections of the Electromagnetic Spectrum*

Range	Subrange	Common notation	Electron-volts eV	Nano-meters nm	Wavenumbers cm^{-1}	Tera Hertz THz
Ultra-violet (UV)	Extreme UV	EUV vacuum for transmission	1240 - 12.4	1-100	$10^7 - 10^5$	$3^5 - 3^3$
	Vacuum UV	VUV, UV-C germicidal	12.4 - 6.53	100 - 190	100,000 - 52,600	3,000 - 1,580
	Deep UV	DUV, UV-C germicidal	6.53 - 4.43	189 - 280	52,600 - 35,700	1,580 - 1,070
	Mid UV	UV-B causes sunburn	4.43 - 3.94	279 - 315	35,700 - 31,700	1,070 - 952
	Near UV	UV-A non-ionizing ,fluorescence	3.94 - 3.26	314 - 380	31,700 - 26,300	952 - 789
Visible (Vis)	Violet	visible colour violet	3.26 - 2.85	380 - 435	26,300 - 23,000	789 - 689
	Blue	visible colour blue	2.85 - 2.48	435 - 500	23,000 - 20,000	689 - 600
	Cyan	visible colour cyan	2.48 - 2.38	500 - 520	20,000 - 19,200	600 - 577
	Green	visible colour green	2.38 - 2.19	520 - 565	19,200 - 17,700	577 - 531
	Yellow	visible colour yellow	2.19 - 2.10	565 - 590	17,700 - 16,900	531 - 508
	Orange	visible colour orange	2.10 - 1.98	590 - 625	16,900 - 16,000	508 - 480
	Red	visible colour red	1.98 - 1.59	625 - 780	16,000 - 12,800	480 - 384
Infrared (IR)	Near IR	NIR, IR-A NIR spectroscopy and	1.58 - 0.886	780 - 1,400	12,800 - 7,140	384 - 214
		NIR, IR-B communications, water blocks	0.886 - 0.413	1,400 - 3,000	7,140 - 3,330	214 - 100
	Mid IR	MIR, IR-C thermal IR imaging	0.413 - 24.8 meV	3 - 50 μm	3,330 - 200	100 - 6.0
	Far IR	FIR, IR-C thermal IR imaging	24.8 - 1.24 meV	50 μm - 1 mm	200 - 10	6.0 - 0.3
Terahertz (THz)		Spectroscopy for materials identification	124 - 1.24 meV	10 μm - 1 mm	1000 - 10	30 - 0.3

Table 4-1 covers only a small portion of the electromagnetic spectrum. Science and engineering have developed numerous technologies for instrumentation to monitor and use the listed wavelengths of electromagnetic radiation. When expressed in nanometers, these wavelengths differ by six orders of magnitude.

Quantitative and qualitative spectroscopic methods developed from visible and ultraviolet light utilization have traditionally designated the radiation used in these applications in terms of its measured wavelength in nanometers (10^{-9} meters) written as nm. Infrared spectroscopy and its "fingerprint" region (1500 cm^{-1} to 500 cm^{-1}) use units of waves per centimeter of length, known as *wavenumbers* (cm^{-1}). In the fingerprint region, infrared radiation is absorbed by the molecular structures that make up organic molecules.

Many structural features of carbon-based organic compounds produce unique, identifying patterns of infrared radiation absorption in the fingerprint region. Wave numbers are used to appreciate the physio-chemical interaction of structural features of organic molecules with the energy of the incident photon of IR radiation. Higher wave numbers are higher energy species.

The stretching, bending, and rocking vibrational modes of organic molecules can be assigned to a particular vibrational mode by measuring the energy of the IR photon absorption. The conversion factor between nm and cm^{-1} is 10^7, making the wavenumber single- and double-digit infrared spectroscopy values easier to use.

Mass spectrometry, semiconductor, and solid-state physics are primarily concerned with the energy of electrons that are physically manipulated or accelerated with magnetic fields or voltage potential; they are evaluated in electron-volts. High-energy photons of UV light measured or evaluated in terms of electron-volts remove electrons from gas molecules to create ions that can then be detected with electrometers for quantitative measurement of mass in the form of ion current collected. Collected currents above certain limits can activate alarms. Hazardous or poisonous gases are detected and quantified at very low levels of relative abundance with battery-powered, handheld meters using photoionization detectors (PID).

Instrumentation using radiation in the terahertz region is being developed as a soft, non-ionizing substitute for X-ray scanning and materials identification.

The study of the behavior of light and its interaction with matter forms a large portion of experimental science. A wide variety of solid-state devices are available to interconvert between light and electrical energy, enabling measurements of various physical and chemical parameters. LEDs, phototransistors, photodiodes, photoresistors, and photoelectric cells that interact electronically with various spectral wavelengths of light at varying sensitivities may be used for qualitative and quantitative light-dependent measurements.

With large area solid-state PN junctions, sunlight can be converted into electrical energy to add power to the electrical grid or power off-grid isolated electrical loads.

In keeping with the simplified nature of this book, only the portion of the electromagnetic spectrum accessible at ambient conditions with readily available electronic components is examined. At ambient conditions, active devices operate in the spectral range from the longer-wavelength infrared (IR) through the colors of the visible range and the shorter wavelength ultraviolet (UV).

Photovoltaic or solar cells are briefly examined in this section in respect to their sensitivity to artificial light sources. Their application as sources of power from sunlight is presented in Chapter 11.

Electro-Optical Components

Light Dependent Resistors (LDR)

LDRs are semiconductors that in darkness have few free electrons to move and exhibit a high resistance—usually many hundreds, kilo, or megaohm values. In the presence of light, the crystal structure absorbs light. Some of the lattice electrons are raised to an energy level at which they can break free and move (i.e., the conduction band of the crystal lattice), lowering the resistance of the device, often by values of thousands of ohms.

Common LDR devices are cadmium sulfide (CdS) that is sensitive to 545 nm green light. Cadmium selenide (CdSe) devices are sensitive to red 725 nm. Mixed CdS-CdSe devices are available with sensitivity to red-orange light of approximately 640 nm.

Time delays of 10 ms are noted between the onset of absorption of light and the drop in resistance. However, when a high flux of incident light ceases, periods of up to a second may be encountered as the conducting current falls off and resistance rises. Light-dependent resistance is temperature-sensitive, and the relationship between light flux and resistance is non-linear. Device resistance and luminous flux are described by an exponential relationship as follows.

$$R = A \times e^{a} \text{-- (1)}$$

R is the device resistance. A is a constant proportional to photon capture area for the material and e is the natural log base of 2.718. A is also a material-dependent constant that is 0.7 to 0.8 for CdS. (For design or calculation purposes, a straight-line approximation of a plot of log resistance vs. log lux for the device should be measured and constructed.)

LDRs are not suitable for high-speed monitoring of lighting changes and are limited to the visible and near-infrared radiation ranges. Lead sulfide and selenide are resistance-sensitive devices suitable for use in the mid- to far-infrared regions of the electromagnetic spectrum.

Photodiodes

Photodiodes have a reversed biased PN junction across which only a leakage or "dark current" flows until the device is illuminated by the correct energy of photons. Dark or leakage currents are typically in the nano-amp range. Some photodiodes are fabricated with a PIN junction that features an intentionally thick or wide intrinsic region situated between the P and N junctions. Increasing the intrinsic area degrades rectifier performance but enhances photosensitivity.

Light photons impinging on the intrinsic region create electron-hole pairs in proportion to the number of incident photons. The current produced is nearly a linearly proportional response to the flux of photons. Their response time is very fast, with frequency response typically into the low double-digit giga-Hertz range (1,000,000,000 or 10^9 Hz).

Depending upon the presence or absence of a biasing voltage, the PN junction can be a photoconductive or photovoltaic device. Solar cells are photodiodes with large surface areas (see Chapter 11).

Phototransistors

A phototransistor resembles a normal bipolar transistor in which the base electrical contact has been replaced with a light-sensitive surface. Illumination of the device causes the base current to flow and control a much larger collector emitter current. Many phototransistors are made with only two leads as the base is the photosensitive surface. (A phototransistor usually has a flat side on the emitter lead or a shorter lead length.) The PN junction response to the visible radiation extends from the 400 nm wavelength to well into the near IR with maximum sensitivity in the vicinity of 840 nm. A phototransistor uses a light-sensitive base structure to provide a base current proportional to the incident light intensity to activate a normal current amplifying transistor action in the device. A phototransistor is orders of magnitude more sensitive to light than a photodiode.

Figure 4-1 shows the spectral sensitivities of cadmium based LDRs and phototransistors. Cadmium sulfide devices exhibit a maximum sensitivity in the 550 nm range or green area of the visible spectrum. The phototransistor's maximum sensitivity is in the 850 nm or red/near-infrared portion of the visible spectrum. Photodiodes similar to phototransistors exhibit a broad spectral sensitivity with a maximum ranging from 800 nm to 1000 nm.

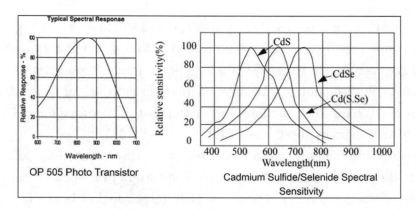

Figure 4-1. *Spectral sensitivities for cadmium-based LDRs and phototransistors*

Electro-optical Applications

LEDs are commonly used as visual indicators or power consumers in light sources or counting and timing events. IR photodiodes have been used as an indicator/detector of high-speed events with optical break beam systems. LDRs and photodiodes are integral parts of security systems.

Of particular value to experimental sciences is the development of the light-emitting diode in its various colors and wavelength capabilities. With a series of small, inexpensive, easy to use, readily available devices, the experimenter can generate and measure discrete segments of the electromagnetic spectrum that cover the range from the near-infrared to the ultra-violet. Many traditional colorimetric instruments required prisms or bulky filters and heavy, powerful light sources to isolate bands of the requisite color or energy of radiation to perform the desired experiment. LEDs, photoresistors or diodes, low-voltage power supplies, and simple light excluding cabinetry can be easily assembled into low-cost, working spectroscopic and photometric instruments from readily available materials and components.

Many substances have a molecular or atomic structure that interacts with portions of the visible light spectrum and thus appear to have color. Many light-interactive substances can be dissolved in a solvent to create colored, liquid solutions whose physical and chemical properties were found, in the late 1800s, to follow definitive mathematical relationships. Several scientific publications led to what is today called the Beer-Lambert law for dilute solutions. It is written as

$$A = \varepsilon c l -- (2)$$

A is the absorbance, a measure of the incident radiation that is absorbed. ε is the molar extinction coefficient of the absorbing species. l is the path length of the colored solution. c is the concentration in moles/liter of the colored agent.

Sunlight, when passed through a glass prism or refracted by raindrops, disperses into a rainbow of the individual colors that make up visible light. If the light from a monochromatic source such as a red LED is passed through a dilute solution of red beet juice, several physio-chemical events take place in accordance with the Beer-Lambert law.

The red color of beets and their juices are due to complex molecules called *betalains*, which are a mixture of betacyanins, a red pigment, and betaxanthins, a yellow pigment. The red betacyanins absorb red light with a wavelength of 535 nm and have a molar extinction coefficient of 60,000 L/(mole-cm). (Absorbance is a dimensionless concept, and the dimensions of ε must be 1/c-l.)

Some of the betacyanin molecules in the solution are in the path of incident red light photons, and the light is absorbed. Some of the incident photons pass entirely through the solution. As the number of betacyanin molecules per unit of volume of solution increases, the probability of absorption proportionally increases. As the thickness of the solution layer through which the photons must pass increases, the probability of absorption also increases.

The Beer-Lambert law describes how the absorbance of light in solutions is governed by the concentration of the colored agent in the solution, the path length through which the light must pass and a constant factor determined by the nature of the colored agent causing the absorption. The red betacyanins have a molar extinction coefficient of 60,000 L/(mol-cm) that is large. The large constant value indicates that the molecule has a large propensity to absorb red light. To keep the mathematical relationship described by the law valid, it can be applied only to very dilute solutions.

Colorimetric methods of analysis are found in a significant number of scientific disciplines where qualitative and quantitative identification and measurement of matter is required. Colorimetric methods of analysis are most often applied in a liquid format requiring equipment to accurately weigh samples, dilute volumes of solvent and measure solution absorbance. To demonstrate solution absorbance analysis, both a dry film, solid-state system, and a simple water volume-based exercise have been devised for use in this book.

Figure 4-2 is a basic block diagram of a light absorption experiment.

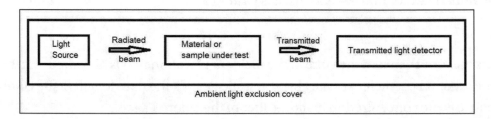

Figure 4-2. *A light absorption experiment*

For experiments using visible light absorption, an ambient light exclusion case is usually required to avoid external radiation interference. Infrared and ultraviolet experiments are often conducted under artificial lighting conditions but may need to be protected from sunlight or fluorescent lighting exposure containing long and short radiation wavelengths.

In terms of electro, optical, and mechanical configurations required to conduct qualitative or quantitative light absorption experiments, an apparatus known as an *optical bench* is used. The optical bench provides a means for mounting and adjusting the three basic components in Figure 4-2 that may be assembled in ambient conditions on a desk or lab benchtop or in a lightproof, temperature-controlled enclosure.

Experiment
A Simple Miniature Optical Bench

Light absorption experiments based upon the general process configuration depicted in Figure 4-2 using the miniature simple optical bench illustrated in Figure 4-3 requires the development of both an active light source and a method for determining the amount of transmitted light.

A basic introductory source and detector combination consisting of a LED illuminated with a constant current can provide a very narrow bandwidth, virtually monochromatic light source. A microcontroller or HMI can power or bias a light-dependent resistor and simultaneously monitor its output to quantify the transmitted light. The basic apparatus presented in the following text is an example of a simple piece of equipment able to measure the actual optical-electronic properties of several electro-optical devices.

A "mini-optical bench" can be fabricated from a small strip of rigid material, two screw connection terminal blocks, and some electrical wire, as illustrated in Figure 4-3. My system was fabricated from extruded aluminum angle that is readily available, inexpensive, lightweight, corrosion-resistant, and relatively easy to work. The two dual connector terminal blocks were mounted on the bench facing each other to provide an adjustable co-linear configuration between source and detector.

To use the bench, the detector and source are mounted in the appropriate terminal blocks. The devices are adjusted for collinearity using the screw terminals to hold the pieces in alignment.

Although simple, the device can produce reliable and useful data if you are careful in alignment and reproduce the distance between source and detector. Either altering the distance between the source and detector or controlling the power applied to the emitting source can regulate the radiant light energy falling on the detector.

My fabricated assembly resulted in a device whose spacing between the tip of an LED source and the top surface of a light-dependent resistor photodetector, as shown, could be extended out to approximately six inches (153 mm).

Since each LED produces a single wavelength of visible light and the detector response essentially is quantified by a microprocessor or LabJack 10 bit analog to digital converter (ADC), the detector counts can be used as a simple measure of quantitation of the system under study.

The simple device in this exercise generates empirical numerical measurements from both visible and invisible LED sources that demonstrate the spectral wavelength sensitivity of typical LDR devices, as seen in Figure 4-1.

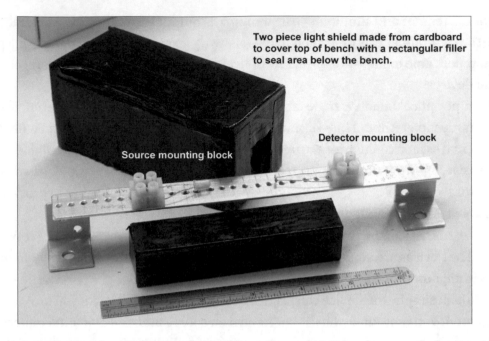

Figure 4-3. *A simple miniature optical bench*

A coarse evaluation of the typical sensitivity of a CdS LDR to the wavelength or color of the light falling on them can be demonstrated with the basic system depicted in Figures 4-2 and 4-3.

A DAQFactory SCADA software GUI program can implement the actual data generation, collection, and graphical display procedure for measuring LDR color sensitivity. An example of a working GUI control page is depicted in Figure 4-4. The control panel depicted in Figure 4-4 can be activated with the DAQFactory code from Listing 4-2 and a U12 LabJack. (Note that all code listings are provided at the end of the chapter.) The DAQFactory plotter can be configured to accept either LabJack or Arduino streamed data for plotting.

In the simple setup, the source power is controlled by the AO 0 (analog output terminal 0) on the LabJack. The detector output is monitored by an Arduino microcontroller applying a digital signal processing (DSP) program to the detector signal Listing 4-1 contains the code for a simple ten-element averaging that can, theoretically, produce an approximate three times enhancement of the signal to noise ratio in the detector signal streamed out to the device connected to the serial port. DAQFactory graphical display programs and Raspberry Pi plotters can be adapted to provide a graphical time-based display of the enhanced data arriving at the serial port.

Initially, the bench's detector was a cadmium sulfide LDR in series with a 10 kΩ, 1% metal film resistor. The voltage divider was biased with 5.0 V derived from an Arduino microcontroller running a ten-element, average DSP program before serially streaming the data to the PC hosting a much lower speed, DAQFactory graphical display. In Figure 4-3, a yellow LED is mounted in the source terminal block, and a ⅛ inch (3 mm) square cadmium sulfide (CdS) light-dependent resistor (LDR) is mounted in the detector block.

Hardware

The optical bench can be fabricated from any material stiff enough to firmly secure the terminal strips to hold the source and detector devices in a collinear configuration. Metal, wood, plastics, or even rigidly configured, heavy fiberboard can be used.

To achieve the maximum sensitivity and selectivity from the source and detector being used in a visible light measurement, it is best to exclude interfering ambient light with a bench cover or light shield. A cover can be fabricated from any opaque material sufficiently stiff or rigid enough to withstand the mechanical handling experienced in experimental setup or disassembly. A matt black coating aids in reducing the effect of stray light leakage and reflection.

Circuit Schematic

If indicator diodes such as the 5 mm T-1¾ (see the yellow LED in Figure 4-3) or 3 mm T1 LED devices are to be used as optical sources, then the maximum current through the diodes is usually limited to the 20 mA to 50 mA range. A LabJack or microcontroller analog output can be programmed to vary from 0 to 5 V, so you should install an appropriate current-limiting resistor value to ensure the diode current remains within the manufacturer's specifications during any voltage programming done in the experiment. A current limiting resistor also ensures that excessive or start-up surge current is not drawn from the LabJack or microcontroller (usually < 30 to 40 mA). A typical voltage divider circuit using a cadmium sulfide light-dependent resistor (LDR) as the upper resistance and 10 kΩ resistor to ground provides a measurable signal for the Arduino analog to digital converter (ADC) to process.

Software

To make optical-electronic measurements, the emitting source, radiant energy detector, and the controlling PC must be appropriately programmed.

To demonstrate an implementation of the optical bench presented here, I used both the LabJack and an Arduino microcontroller to provide two-way interactive control systems. The source is controlled by a DAQFactory script in Listing 4-2, which varies the output voltage on the AO 0 output on the LabJack to power the source. The detector is biased and monitored by the Arduino that provides the analog to digital conversion (ADC), and runs a digital signal processing (DSP) 10 element moving average program, as in Listing 4-1.

The Arduino streams the data out, on the serial port, for collection and display on a DAQFactory 2D graphical screen component on the host PC. The DAQFactory plotter displays both the LabJack voltage applied to the source and the ADC value received from the Arduino converter. (There is a significant difference between the analog output signal from the LabJack and that from an Arduino. The analog output from the LabJack U12 has 10 bits of resolution and passes through a first-order low pass filter with a 3db frequency around 22 Hz.

An analogWrite(m,n) instruction on an Arduino is not filtered and the microprocessor applies a 488 Hz PWM square wave signal to pin m with a duty cycle of n, where n has an 8-bit resolution of 0 to 255. The effect of the difference between a stepped analog signal as produced by the LabJack and the pulsed square wave from the Arduino can cause erratic values to be measured by a high-speed photodetector in a colorimetric measurement. A signal averaging DSP may be required to obtain a steady reading in some spectrophotometric measurements.)

A main display screen for operating the optical bench in an experimental mode is depicted in Figure 4-4.

My main GUI control panel screen for the optical bench consisted of the following.

- – a single 2-D time based graphical display with the voltage being applied to the source plotted on the left axis with a 0 to 5 V range for full-scale deflection (FSD), and the detector output plotted on the right with a range of 0 to 1025 FSD as created by the 10-bit ADC on the Arduino microcontroller

-   three edit boxes for entering the values of the starting value for the
    voltage to be applied to the source, the amount to increment the
    voltage ramp for each iteration, and the number of times to repeat
    the program cycle

-   a starting button to start the source power program

-   a text stating the time between power application increments

-   a spin control and text for manually controlling the voltage applied to
    the source.

-   a progress bar for following the source voltage value

-   two variable value displays for numerical readings of the source
    voltage and detector response

The spin control, progress bar, and two variable value components were not part of
the original control panel but were added later for other work and useful for evaluating
component electrical properties.

Required Scripting and Microcontroller Programming

Listing 4-2 is the autotest DAQFactory scripting activated when the Run Voltage Program
button is depressed. Listing 4-1 is an Arduino moving average that can be adapted as
needed to process the detector signal.

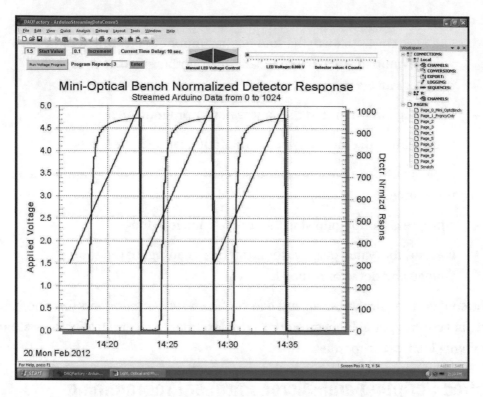

Figure 4-4. *Typical DAQFactory optical bench GUI control panel and data recordings*

Observations

At a source detector distance of 1.25 inches (32 mm), the autotest program incremented the diode voltage to 5.0 V through a 180 Ω metal film 1% resistor. The cadmium sulfide LDR signal is developed from a 10 kΩ 1% metal film resistor in series with the LDR, biased with 5 V from the microcontroller and monitored by the Arduino ADC. The signal was processed by a ten-element moving averaging program and streamed out to the PC hosting a normalized 1024 ADC unit graphical display. The various source diodes produced the following tabulated data in Table 4-2.

Table 4-2. *CdS LDR Response to LED Colours*

LED Colour	CdS Response	Wavelength	Emission Starting Voltage
Bright Green	960	565 - 555	2.1
Bright Blue	970	480-450	2.35
Bright Orange	940	605 - 620	2.4
Bright Red	890	700-640	1.6
IR Emitter	710	850 - 940	1.5
Standard Orange	600	620-605	1.75
Standard Green	400	555-520	1.8
Standard Red	180	633 - 660	1.5
Standard Yellow	620	390	1.8
UV Emitter	920	600-585	2.6
Bright White	960	3 bands 474, 535 & 638	1.6

The current limit on the diode power restricts the light output of the device, limiting the practical distance over which an optical beam can be monitored. Experiments with a bright, clear green 8000 mcd LED as the optical bench source and a CdS LDR with a ⅛ in × ⅛ in (3 mm × 3 mm) front surface area provided the data for Figure 4-5.

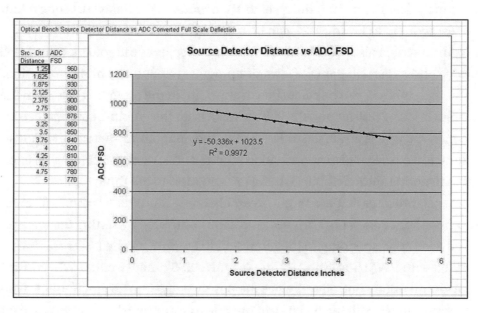

Figure 4-5. *Loss of intensity vs. LED detector distance*

Discussion

To demonstrate the basic management of variables possible with a SCADA software GUI using readily available and easily constructed mechanical equipment, the visible light spectral sensitivity of a typical CdS LDR has been measured. The observed data has been tabulated in Table 4-2. Based on the data in the table, the detector can be seen to exhibit a relatively good sensitivity to the components of the visible light spectrum and the fringes of its upper and lower wavelengths.

The DAQFactory GUI screen in Figure 4-4 has been configured with the manually adjustable spin control and coupled progress bar to allow you to adjust the applied voltage when testing diodes and circuits in configurations such as break beam interruption circuits. For simple quantitative measurements such as using the bright green LED to measure signal attenuation with respect to source-detector distance, a light shield can exclude stray visible light while conducting actual experiments.

The edit box entries allow convenient onscreen variation of test program parameters. If required, the sequence code can be altered to change the default time delay between voltage ramp cycles. The default time, set to 10 seconds in the delay(10) code of line 23 of the AutoTest sequence (Listing 4-2), can be manually altered as required.

The control screen also provides a simultaneous display of the voltage being applied to the device under test (DUT) in the form of a progress bar and as a numerical value. The current through the DUT can be calculated at any point in the program cycle from the value of the current limiting resistor and the voltage trace from the graphical output recording.

As seen in the traces displayed in Figure 4-4, the light output-detector response is a linear function of the voltage applied to the diode and its current limiting resistor. In addition to good reproducibility, careful examination of the three replicate measurements indicates that the bright green LED only illuminates when the voltage ramp reaches about 2.25 V. LED brightness can be controlled by setting the voltage to the desired level corresponding to the required LED output, or the LED brightness can be controlled with PWM from the Arduino or with a 555 timer circuit. PWM control with the Arduino microcontroller divides the power range into 255 increments while using a potentiometer with the 555 IC can provide a continuously variable pulse width over the entire duty cycle range (see `www.electronics-tutorials.ws/waveforms/555-circuits-part-1.html`).

The ADCs on both the Arduino and LabJack are 10-bit devices (2^{10} = 1024), creating a theoretical measurement capability of one part in 1024. One part in a thousand generally provides sufficient resolution for a graphical display following most physical phenomena, for the observer to follow any significant changes in the recorded signal. By careful selection of graphical recording and DSP conditions, a scale expansion can be achieved to provide substantial increases in sensitivity that could be used, for example, to monitor noise in the signal output.

The graphical display in Figure 4-5 demonstrates the concentrated power of the bright, high-power LEDs. Over the short distance measured, the detector response follows a gently sloping linear decrease in intensity as a function of separation distance. The highly concentrated light beam from the LED is to be expected as the clear lens and physical arrangement of the diode's anode and cathode are designed to keep the emitted light in as tightly focused a beam as possible. Typically, a point source of radiation has an inverse square exponential decrease in intensity as the distance between the source and detector increases.

It has been noted that LEDs are diodes that do not conform to Ohm's law. They require the application of approximately 1½ V to 3 V or 4 V to conduct current and illuminate with a characteristic color. It has also been established that the technique of PWM power application to LEDs can overcome the minimum activation voltage by using a variable duty cycle application of the full voltage available from the power supply. However, the response of some photodetectors can be compromised by the varying pulse wave signal.

For differential colorimetric analysis, a time averaging of the detector signal can mitigate the influence of the PWM signal on the collected spectroscopic data. A different easily implemented solution to the PWM compromised detector output is to use a DC signal to power the LED source.

Figure 4-18 shows a technique using a variable resistor to vary the voltage applied to the diode between the required turn-on voltage for the colored diode in use and the maximum available from the power supply. If at its minimum illuminated brightness, the light produced by the diode is too bright for the source in use, the diode to detector distance can be increased on the optical bench as demonstrated in Figure 4-5 to a point at which the detector output returns to a usable value. Although using a variable DC power source can significantly improve detector output signal stability, some signal averaging may be required to reduce electrical noise and drift.

The concepts of luminescence, radiance, and color temperature are discussed in the literature and care must be taken when dealing with visible and invisible radiation units. Table 4-2 has rendered all the different LED wavelengths of radiation into arbitrary units of 1024 ADC counts. LED intensity is specified in millicandela (mcd or cd/1000) in which the candela is the base unit of luminosity or brightness in the International System of Units. The relationship between lumens and candela is not a trivial matter. The conversion between the two requires definitions of angles of view, wavelength, and other factors that are best reviewed by the investigator in the pertinent literature if their use is required for the experimental work at hand.

LEDs are typical diodes in that they are devices that do not follow Ohm's law. Generally, as the diode color moves from red to blue, the starting voltage for light emission increases from approximately 1½ V to 4 V. The current should be limited to 20 mA to 30 mA unless specified otherwise by the manufacturer.

The simple optical bench with a microcontroller-computer readout and plotter display is the basis for making both electrical and spectral wavelength relative sensitivity measurements on individual pieces of electro-optical devices. By placing semitransparent materials into the optical beam between the source and detector, the optical bench becomes the frame of an experimental light absorption measurement instrument. Absorption instruments play a large role in both qualitative and quantitative physio-chemical experimental measurements.

A CdS or Phototransistor Detector Solid-State Colorimeter

As the name implies, a colorimeter is a spectroscopic device able to measure variations in color. A large literature exists detailing the development of colorimetric measurement techniques for analytes of interest in astronomy, biology, chemistry, engineering, geology, and medicine. To develop a more flexible colorimeter, the discrete wavelength diodes can be replaced by a single LED red, green, blue device that makes a continuously variable color source. A GUI control screen for the optical bench can be developed to configure the source's three primary colors into virtually any visible light color. The process developed here can be applied to developing colorimetric analysis methods for any experimental science investigation or research.

Composite light-emitting diodes capable of emitting red, green, and blue can be used with a microprocessor's PWM capability, such as that available with the Arduino, to act as a variable wavelength colorimetric spectroscopic source. A published visual experiment in which three equally intense colored spotlights obliquely illuminate a common area on a white screen, as seen in Figure 4-6, illustrates the effect of the overlap of the three primary colors. A wide distribution of synthetic colored light is available from the RGB LED by generating the three primary colors. Those colors available through the overlap or mixing of the primaries. Figure 4-11 illustrates the approximate colors expected from applying the nominal 0–255 PWM power settings to the RGB individual diode elements.

Figure 4-6. *The effect of primary light color combinations (see https://en.wikipedia.org/wiki/Image:RGB_illumination.jpg)*

Each of the three primary colors for the diode consists of electromagnetic waves of different wavelengths. A tri-color LED has typical RGB wavelengths of 624 nm, 525 nm, and 470 nm, with forward voltages of 2.25, 3.5, and 3.5 in a clear epoxy case with a 20-degree viewing angle. If two or three waves of different wavelengths, of constant amplitude, are simultaneously created within the same source, the waves combine to form a unique sum constituting a new wavelength. The various combinations of resultant colors for the equal mixing of the individual primary radiations are seen in the overlapped areas in Figure 4-6. To see the various colors by eye, a diffuser is often used to "mix" the colors for display. Viewing a multicolor LED from a short distance often results in the eye seeing only the individual diode colors illuminated.

To obtain the full range of visible light colors possible, each of the three primary color intensities must be variable from zero to full brightness (see Figure 4-11).

Although the concept depicted in Figure 4-2 is simple in theory, creating an instrument capable of measuring the intensity of light using PWM control of source illumination and light detection with LDR or phototransistors requires the consideration and accommodation of several additional factors.

PWM is a well-established technique for controlling power, as discussed in most electronics references, including *The Art of Electronics* by Horowitz and Hill (Cambridge University Press, 2015) and *Practical Electronics for Inventors* (McGraw Hill, 2013).

The PWM frequency for the Arduino pins is 488 Hz. A 5 V PWM pulse applied to RGB diode pins is well above the minimum typical "turn on" voltage of each of the individually colored LEDs in the device. At a frequency of 488 Hz, the diodes are turned on for the selected pulse width time then turned off. The 488 Hz cycling of the illumination from the individual colors of the RGB LED is too fast for the human eye to follow but not for the LDR or phototransistor light detectors.

Cadmium sulfide/selenide light-sensitive resistor specification sheets often report "latency" times. An LDR may respond within 10 ms to incident light with a sharp resistance decrease but can take much longer to re-establish the high resistance state after exposure to high-intensity illumination. Phototransistors have frequency response figures that are in the multiple digit kilo-hertz range that is dependent upon the size of the load being driven by the device. Both the CdS/Se and phototransistor devices are of sufficient response speed to be affected by the Arduino's PWM frequency.

Simple solutions to the photodetector following the profile of the pulsing width variation are to average the detector response over time or use an adjustable value DC voltage to power the source. A large window moving average such as the generic Arduino in Listing 4-1 generates a smooth average numerical detector output.

To measure a difference in light intensity transmitted, two stable numerical values are required to obtain the numerical difference. Listings 4-1 and 4-5 are DSP sketches for the Arduino microcontroller in general purpose (Listing 4-1) and specific application formats.

Experiment: CdS or Phototransistor Colorimeters

Visible light experiments can be conducted with the Windows-based DAQFactory GUI and the small optical bench or a slightly more improved enclosed instrument, all fabricated from readily available materials. In the following exercises, software management systems for the simple and enclosed color measurement equipment are developed in the Windows and Linux computing platforms.

Hardware: Small Optical Bench

To use the optical bench in Figure 4-3 and gain access to all the colors available in Figure 4-11, a red, green, blue (RGB) LED can be used as the instrument light source. To accommodate an RGB diode, the source block on the optical bench must be expanded to accept the typical four-lead common cathode device. If a single LED provides the requisite color needed to conduct an absorption experiment, no changes need to be made to the optical bench. The light shield may need to be adjusted to ensure the exclusion of stray light from ambient illumination.

Each color lead of the LED could be wired in series with an appropriate current limiting resistor and a pin of the Arduino PWM output. (Alternatively, for less precise color-intensity control, an appropriate resistor can be placed in series with the common lead and the power supply ground.) The required minimum value of the current limiting resistor can be calculated from the recommended maximum operating current for the safe operation of the device, as listed in the datasheet for the RGB or single LED being used as the source.

The CdS detector does not need any modification from its original voltage divider configuration. If a phototransistor such as the OP-505 is to be used as a detector, then the 5 V biasing voltage must be dropped to ground through a 10 kΩ "pull up" resistor and the phototransistor. The phototransistor's emitter is grounded, and the signal for the ADC on the Arduino A0 pin is taken from the collector-10 kΩ junction (see Figure 4-18).

Software: DAQFactory – Arduino

To select a single or combined color, each element of the RGB diode requires independent control. The serial communications link moves control information and observed data back and forth between the apparatus and the host PC display screen.

The Arduino microcontroller performs a multiple duty role in the colorimeter configuration, acting as an intelligent programmed source controller, a DSP calculator, and a serial communications terminal. The Arduino sketch code is shown in Listing 4-5.

While exerting full control over each primary color's intensity, the Arduino's PWM capability avoids the individual diode "turn-on voltage" requirement by applying 5 V timed width pulses to the light source.

The main portion of the GUI control panel screen seen in Figure 4-8 displays the CdS or OP505 detector response as a strip chart recorder with the display moving from the right to the left. Recall that the Detector Response scale on the left can be moved to the right by selecting the desired position from the Axis drop-down list on the Traces Tab of the 2-D Graph Component configuration window in the DAQFactory software, as seen in Figure 4-7.

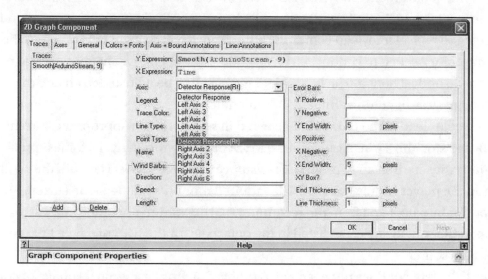

Figure 4-7. *DAQFactory axes selection*

Figure 4-8 depicts the DAQ Factory GUI OP505 colorimeter control panel screen. Beginning in the upper left-hand corner of the GUI control panel, there are three labeled edit boxes with push buttons to enter the values desired for the power to be applied to the RGB diodes of the composite LED source into the DAQFactory software. Recall that the three variables used to transmit the RGB values to the Arduino must be declared before they are usable in any scripting. The control screen in Figure 4-8 uses edit boxes, variable value displays, pushbuttons, a graphical display, and static text displays to provide and accept information.

Once the desired information has been entered into the control screen, the depression of the "RGB Transit" button activates the sequence codes to transmit the required red, green, and blue data values to the serial port for reading by the microcontroller and implementation of the requested power levels. Listing 4-2a contains the DAQFactory code for the button-activated transmission.

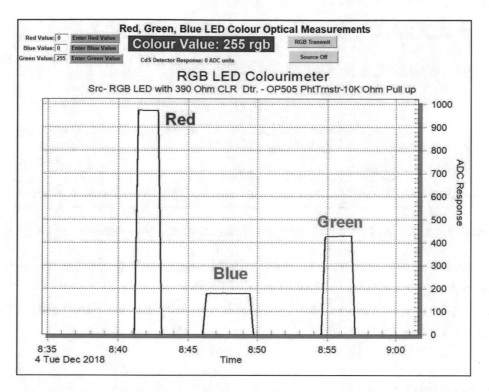

Figure 4-8. *Colorimeter GUI and OP505 detector response to RBG LED colors at full PWM power*

There is no scripting per se in the usage of the control panel. The scripting that has been written and is driving the actions is expecting three numerical values when the RGB Transmit button is keyed. All the boxes must contain a numerical value from 0 to 255. The Auto-Start feature of the scripting page and code (similar to Figure 4-9) must be used to ensure that the variables are declared.

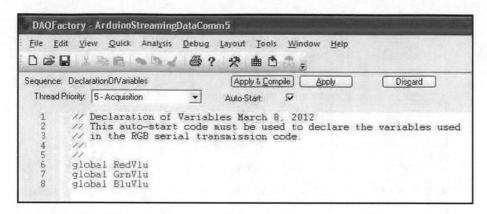

Figure 4-9. *Autorun DAQFactory code to declare required variables*

Figure 4-8 shows the buttons labeled "RGB Transmit" and "Source Off" configured to activate the sequence codes in Listings 4-2a and 4-2b.

Listing 4-5 is the Arduino sketch code that receives and implements the DAQFactory control panel serial transmissions.

Observations

If the Auto-Start option and declaration code is accidentally overlooked, some odd errors may occur when using the colorimeter.

Figure 4-8 depicts the OP505 detector response to the nominal colors and full PWM power levels that are entered into the RGB edit boxes of the GUI. The different colors can create different responses for the OP505 when compared to the CdS detector response to the bright LED colors, as observed in Table 4-2.

In Figure 4-10, the ADC count data obtained with an OP-505 phototransistor detector has been plotted against the Arduino PWM nominal values.

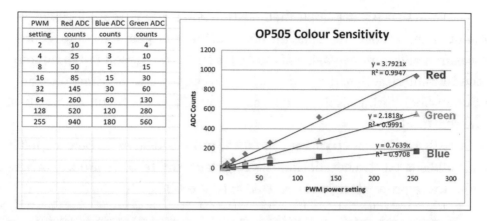

PWM setting	Red ADC counts	Blue ADC counts	Green ADC counts
2	10	2	4
4	25	3	10
8	50	5	15
16	85	15	30
32	145	30	60
64	260	60	130
128	520	120	280
255	940	180	560

Figure 4-10. *OP505 Phototransistor responses for RGB-PWM power levels*

Discussion

The Auto-Start checkbox causes the short sequence code to automatically load and run when the DAQFactory program creates the GUI page. Virtually all programming languages with variables must set aside memory space somewhere for numerical variables to reside. Usually, when a program, script, or sketch is written, there are provisions in the language for declaration and perhaps initialization of the symbolic variables used in the code following the declaration statements. In programs such as DAQFactory and other SCADA software, the main container for data is the channel that stores timestamped, numerical values. Channels are created and activated through the channel table. The Scripting page's Auto-Start feature allows coded sequences to be written and run that declare and initialize variables before being used by control screen component software code.

The cadmium sulfide detector is available in a wide range of resistance values that can vary from thousands of ohms in the light to tens of megohms in the dark. Recall that when using sensors in a voltage divider configuration for optimal performance, the experimenter should select a fixed resistance value that approximates the resistance of the sensor in the mid-point of its operating range.

LED power control with PWM can produce a certain amount of "flicker" in the light produced by the source device. Local temperature fluctuations from power application heating and electronic noise in the USB bus all contribute to noise in signal transmission.

In all quantitative spectroscopic methods and applications, reproducibility is of paramount importance. To obtain the reproducibility required in comparison light measurements, time averaging of the ADC signal is often required to smooth out electronic and stray light interference. Time averaging increases response times in continuous monitoring displays. Static colorimetric measurements do not affect experimental results.

A coarse RGB LED color creation chart using proportional PWM power applications has been published with a hexadecimal representation of the color proportions required to produce the appropriate light as depicted in Figure 4-11.

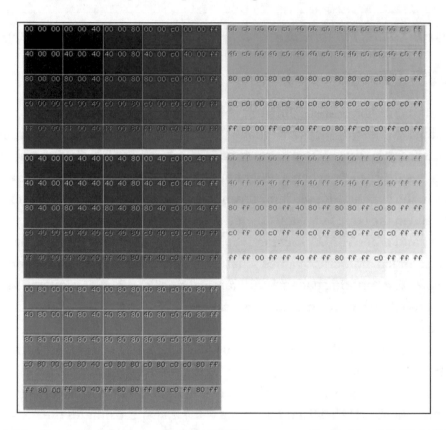

Figure 4-11. *Typical colors created by PWM power to individual RGB LED diodes (see* https://en.wikipedia.org/wiki/RGB_color_model*)*

Color and color perception are usually expressed rigorously in terms of black-body radiation in which the color temperature is expressed, for visible light, in the thousands of degrees Kelvin. The color chart and PWM settings are not rigorous definitions of the color that result when the appropriate numerical values from the chart are entered into the DAQFactory control panel. RGB diodes can vary in both the wavelength and intensity of the light emitted by each of the three luminous sources in each device.

In many experimental uses of a colorimetric comparison, an exact match between the source's spectra and the sample being analyzed is not required. A yellow material or solution can be examined for its color depth using the Beer-Lambert law at a slightly different yellow hue. By making several measurements at different sample thicknesses or concentrations at the slightly different shade or hue of yellow, accurate data can be obtained if the slightly different shade or hue of the yellow light from a source is not altered. Any discrepancies between the exact color of the source and the sample are canceled by the differential comparison technique.

Implementing Optical Bench Techniques with Raspberry Pi and Arduino

An Arduino-RPi combination can be used to assemble a setup to power an LED light source and photodetector combination mounted on a simple optical bench either open to the ambient lighting conditions as in Figure 4-3 or encased in an opaque enclosure as depicted in Figures 4-12 to 4-17.

An RPi-hosted Arduino IDE can provide graphical or numerical display options for the experimental work at hand. Reaction kinetics are often studied by following the rate of decay of a photoactive compound. An enormous amount of literature describing quantitative colorimetric methods of analysis has been published over the past 100 years in biology, chemistry, geology, and medicine.

LEDs are available that emit narrow bands of visible light varying from the deep red end of the visible spectrum to the blue. The individual colored LEDs should function as a light source for quantitative absorption measurements that can be made to determine the relative abundance of colored materials in both solutions and some semi-transparent solid phases.

Combining the RPi computational power and graphical data display capability combined with the source power control, data collection, conversion, and DSP abilities of the Arduino microcontroller should form an inexpensive, simple and easy-to-assemble colorimetric analysis system.

Recall that if a beam of colored visible light passes through a solution or solid of the same color, some of the photons are absorbed, and some pass through. The ratio of the incident light intensity to the intensity of the light transmitted through an absorbing medium is called *transmittance*. The transmittance is related to the amount of light absorbed in the medium under study by the following relation.

$$\text{Transmittance} = I_i / I_t \text{ and Absorbance} = -\log(T) = -\log(I_i / I_t)$$
$$\text{or Absorbance} = \log 1/T \text{ -- (3)}$$

I_i is the intensity of the light incident upon the medium. I_t is the intensity of the light transiting through the medium under study (or transmitted).

Absorbance is often called the optical density and it can be seen that as the absorbance increases the amount of light passing through the colored medium must decrease, giving rise to the inverse logarithmic ratio between absorbance and transmission.

Transmission can be measured, and absorbance must be calculated. The Beer-Lambert law relates absorbance to concentration in dilute solutions for constant path lengths. If absorbance and concentration are directly proportional, then a plot of measured absorbance for a series of known concentrations should result in a straight line. For rigorous quantitative analytical spectrophotometric analysis, linear calibrations relating to absorbance and concentration must be established. However, semi-quantitative, colorimetric analysis can be implemented with simple basic equipment capable of measuring light transmissions by establishing linear relationships between solution concentration and transmitted light intensity.

A simple, basic, colorimetric spectrophotometer as that being developed can measure the amount of light falling on a photoelectric detector after passing through a sample being tested. The ADC of the microprocessor monitoring the photodetector produces a digital value that is proportional to the light transmitted by the sample, which can be related to the concentration if a linear relationship has been established.

For more advanced investigators, the microprocessor in the instrument being developed can be programmed to calculate and display absorbance units for more rigorous and quantitative investigations.

Experiment

To obtain a true zero reading in an optical measurement system using a phototransistor as a light-sensitive detector, ambient or stray light must be excluded during the measurement experiment. An opaque enclosure should completely encase the optical bench holding the source and detector portions of the setup. The enclosure must also accommodate the placement of absorbing samples in the light path between the source and detector and allow the passage of electrical signals into the encased active components of the system.

To provide a dark environment for light intensity measurements, a hinged top, metal confectionery tin, 3½ × 11¼ × 2½ in (86 × 276 × 61 mm) was used (see Figures 4-12 to 4-17). A ⅜ in (9 mm) thick piece of plywood was cut to fit tightly into the bottom of the tin. The centerline of the base was marked along with two parallel lines ½ in (12 mm) on either side of the center. The outer rows were drilled from the bottom of the base. The holes are countersunk and tapped to receive 1 in #6 flat head machine screws (25 × 3 mm) on alternate half inch centers on the right and left ½ inch (12 mm) off-center lines (see Figure 4-13). When inserted back into the light exclusion box, two rows of holes were available on the base, each on ½ in (12 mm) centers. The technique of alternating the holes' positioning results in the post holes being on ¼ in (6 mm) centers with respect to positioning components on the centerline.

Note the following in Figure 4-12.

- Caption 1 is the LED light source (see also Figure 4-17), consisting of a double terminal, screw connector strip, bolted to a right-angle bracket and able to accept the anode and cathode of a colored diode.

- Caption 2 is the mounting post in one of the holes in the line opposite the hinge side of the center line with a right-angle bracket secured in place by a pair of hex-nuts to fix the source assembly at the correct height and collinearity with the detector phototransistor.

- Caption 3 is the detector phototransistor mounted in a double screw terminal connector strip is also bolted to a right-angle bracket to maintain collinearity with the source.

- Caption 4 is the threaded mounting post in one of the lines of holes on the hinge side of the centerline with a right-angle bracket that can be adjusted to the required height to maintain source detector co-linearity.

- Caption 5 is the electrical "feed-through" connecting the wiring for the source and detector to their respective microcontroller inputs and outputs (see also Figures 4-14 and 4-15).

- Caption 6 is the left-hand member of the post pair to mount a sample holder (see also Figure 4-16).

- Caption 7 is the matte black paper or cardboard liner to blacken the enclosure walls.

- Caption 8 is the inside black paper or cardboard liner for the top.

- Caption 9 is the left-hand line of mounting holes on ½ in (12 mm) centers on the opposite side of center line from the hinge (see also Figure 4-13).

- Caption 10 is the right-hand line of mounting holes on alternate ½ in (12 mm) centers on the hinge side of the centerline (see also Figure 4-13).

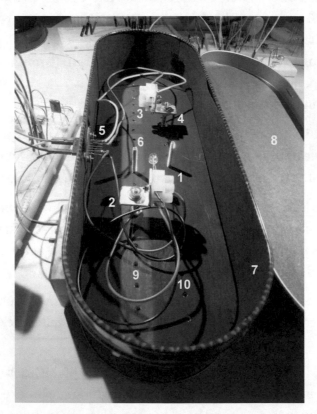

Figure 4-12. *Interior components of colorimeter*

The detectors and various sources were mounted in screw terminal connectors mounted on aluminum brackets drilled to fit over the #6 machine screws. A single locking nut fixed a mounting post at the desired height on the base. A second nut was threaded down the post so the source or detector could be adjusted for collinearity with its alternate component. A third nut locked the bracket component in place.

Figure 4-13 illustrates the technique I used to assemble an optical bench inside a lightproof container. Holes (#35 drill or 7/64 in) suitable for #6 flathead (3 mm) machine screws were drilled, countersunk, and threaded to accept the nominal screws on two lines parallel to the centerline spaced at ½ in (12 mm). The individual holes were bored on alternately spaced ½ in (12 mm) centers, so components could be adjusted to distances resolvable to ¼ in (6 mm) on the optical bench. The Phillips head, single screw, mounting posts for the source, detector, and the pair used for the sample holder are visible in the seventh position from the left on the bottom line, the fifth hole from the right on the top, and the tenth positions from the left in both the top and bottom lines.

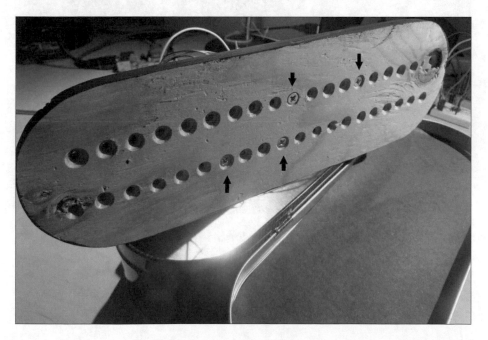

Figure 4-13. *Bottom view of the base plate with source, detector, and sample holder mounting posts in place*

Figures 4-14 and 4-15 depict the interior and exterior views of the electrical feedthroughs to provide isolated electronic access to the box interior. A slot was cut in the side of the light exclusion box to accept a four or six place stacking header connector. The connector block was epoxied to a small piece of perf board that had been drilled to accept two small bolts to mount the assembly on the box side to form an electrical feed-through for the source and detector connections.

Initially, the stacking header pins were soldered to the source and detector connections. Later versions of the instrument used standard 0.1 in (2.5 mm) spacing stacking headers that accept the normal jumper wires used on Arduino and prototyping boards (see Figures 4-19, 4-20, and 4-21).

Figure 4-14. *Interior view of the light excluding electronic connector*

Figure 4-15. *Exterior view of the opaque electronic connector and auxiliary breadboard*

The interior of the box and the top surface of the base were all blackened with black paper liners or paint to stop any internal reflections.

A pair of mounting posts positioned the sample holder. The sample holder consists of a ½ in (12 mm) aluminum angle drilled with a pair of offset holes to fit over the posts and hold solid sheets of cellophane in the light path. The sample sheets were held in place with ⅝ in (15 mm) pinch clamp paper clips (bulldog" clips), as depicted in Figure 4-16.

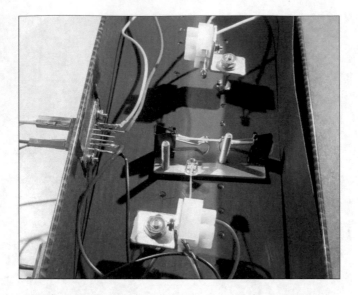

Figure 4-16.   *Sample holder with clips*

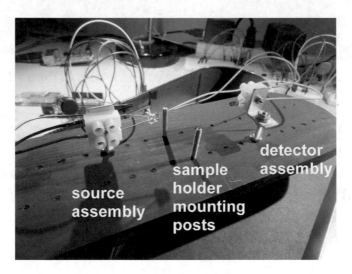

Figure 4-17.   *Essential components of optical bench*

An Arduino-RPi combination can control and power the LED source. The ADC on the Arduino can determine the amount of light falling on the detector. The 5 V supply on the Arduino powered the LED and the detector on the setup. The 5 V supply, collector on the OP-505, emitter, and 10 kΩ resistor were all connected in series as depicted in Figure 4-18. The voltage drop across the 10 kΩ resistor was recorded through the A0 connection to the ADC on the Arduino and read from the serial monitor.

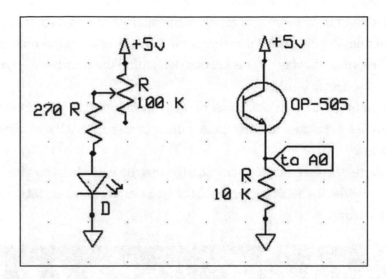

Figure 4-18. *Source and detector circuits for a colorimeter*

The source was powered from the 5 V supply of the Arduino. The current was routed through a 270 Ω current limiting resistor and one half of a 100 kΩ potentiometer. The voltage applied to the diode could be varied by adjusting the wiper position on the potentiometer. The inclusion of the 270 Ω current limiting resistor ensures the protection of the diode.

To begin absorbance experiments, you have several options. The phototransistor readout from Listing 4-3 that was originally written for static display with this chapter's DAQFactory control panels or Listing 4-3a can be used with the RPi's PIXEL home screen to display static absorbance readouts. From the Arduino icon on the PIXEL screen, the Arduino IDE can be launched. From the Tools menu, the serial monitor can directly display the Arduino ADC absorbance or transmission values. More advanced investigators can also use any of the Python serial port plotter programs in Chapter 1's Listing 1-3, in Chapter 2's Listing 2-1, and Chapter 3's Listings 3-2, 3-5, 3-7, or 3-8 to record kinetic data amenable to visual light optical monitoring.

With an empty sample holder in the light path and the light exclusion box closed, the potentiometer is adjusted to create an approximate ADC count of 900 units in red cellophane experiments. An approximate ADC count near 900 represents 100% transmission. A sheet of appropriately sized opaque material inserted into the sample holder should completely block the light path and establish the 0% transmission point.

Transmitted light measurements can then be taken of samples such as a red-colored cellophane. Reading the values for various thicknesses of the material from the Arduino serial monitor display on the RPi can determine the number of layers or mimic concentration changes in liquids.

Upon completing the desired number of measurements, the 100% transmission ADC value should be checked to determine if the system settings have drifted from their original set points.

To accommodate colored liquid samples, the instrument's interior can be modified to accept ¾ in outside diameter by 2 in tall (2 cm × 5 cm) clear glass vials, as depicted in Figures 4-19, 4-20, and 4-21.

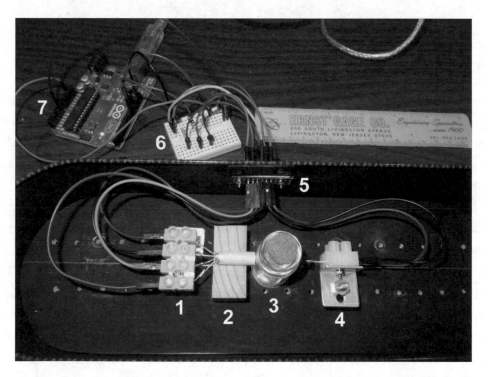

Figure 4-19. *Source, collimator, vial, and detector modifications for liquid samples*

The following describes the components in Figure 4-19.

- Component 1 is a four terminal screw connector block cut from a standard 12-unit terminal strip accepting the male end of a male-female prototyping jumper wire. The terminal block is mounted on a threaded post, as seen in Figures 4-12, 4-16, and 4-17. The block is bolted to an aluminum bracket that accepts the electrical connections and holds the RGB LED firmly in place when collinearity adjustments are being made.

- Component 2 is a wooden block that supports an aluminum foil, 5 mm diameter (¼ in) collimator that gathers the LED emissions into a rough beam collinear with the detector (4) on the opposite side of the sample vial. (3) (The collimator support block was painted black before entering service.)

- Component 3 is a soda-lime glass vial ¾ in (20 mm) diameter by 2 in (50 mm) in height. The vial is held in place by a ¾ in (20 mm) diameter hole cut into the base of the optical bench at its center.

- Component 4 is the detector assembly consisting of the aluminum bracket mounted 2 terminal polyethylene screw connector block. Again, the terminal strip provides two electrical connections and firmly fixes the OP-505 phototransistor detector in a collinear position with the source and sample vial.

- Component 5 is a 6-pin header strip that has been epoxy/cyanoacrylate glued to a perf board for mounting on the side wall of the lightproof box. A header strip is often used to mount breakout boards to prototyping breadboards and has male pins on either side (see Figure 10-2 in Chapter 10). A strip of dual male pins can provide a lightproof electrical connection for female prototyping jumper wires carrying current and detector signals.

- Component 6 is a small prototyping breadboard holding the optimized current limiting resistors to power the source in the large cell liquid instrument (see Figure 4-22).

- Component 7 is the Arduino that provides the PWM signals to supply the desired RGB diode currents from values entered into the serial monitor and read into the Arduino code with the Send button on the Arduino serial port screen. The microprocessor monitors the OP-505 phototransistor output with the 10-bit ADC and sends the values from 0 to 1023 to the serial port for Python processing.

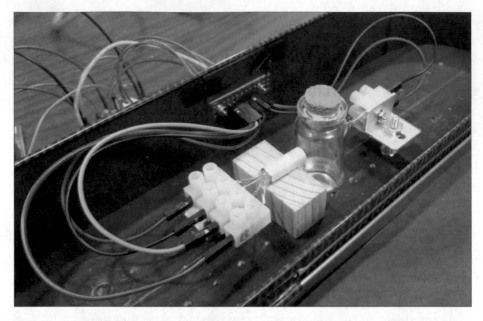

Figure 4-20. *Liquid sample modifications*

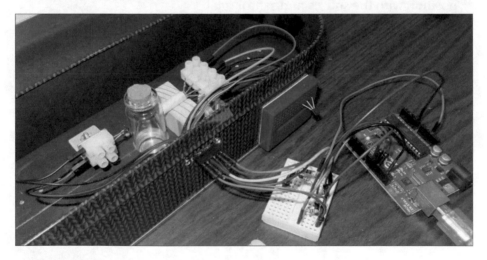

Figure 4-21. *Liquid sample modifications view 2*

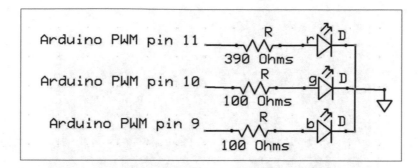

Figure 4-22. *Optimized current supply for RGB led source for large liquid cell colorimeter*

Colorimetric Light Intensity Determinations

A series of basic colorimetric measurements using the LDR, a phototransistor, or an OPT101 monolithic photodiode transimpedance amplifier IC detector can be made with the instrument depicted in Figures 4-20 and 4-21. For validation of the technique, a series of red, green, and blue solutions can be prepared from concentrated food coloring dyes or water-based food preparation solutions created by the processing of highly colored foods such as beets or blueberries.

Devices capable of dispensing a single liquid drop, such as one-piece plastic or two-piece glass tube rubber bulb droppers or eye medication drop dispensers, can be used to prepare a series of volume-on-volume known concentrations of the colored solution. A simple technique involves counting the number of liquid drops required to fill a known volume and then dividing to find the average volume of the individual drops. Inexpensive glass or plastic graduated cylinders, and 3 mL transfer pipettes (Pasteur pipettes) are available from online retailers in various sizes and material formats. A typical 10 mL graduated cylinder, and a plastic Pasteur pipette are depicted in Figure 4-23 and readily available small volume dispensing tools used for measuring medications.

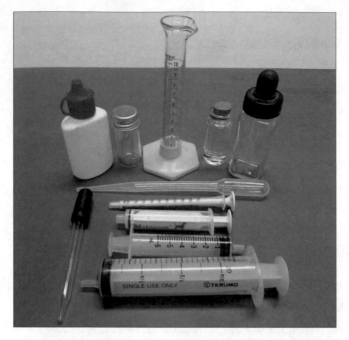

Figure 4-23. *Readily available implements for volumetric based calibrations*

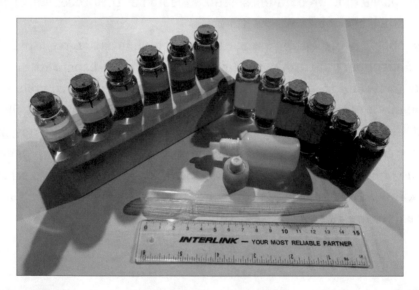

Figure 4-24. *Drop dispensing implements, diluted beet extract, and food dye calibration solutions*

Having used simple colored solids to introduce the concepts of light absorption by colored materials, the measurement of color in solutions with a sensitive detector can be examined. Although the instrumentation assembled thus far has not been involved with active optics in which the direction of light has been refracted, the use of cylindrical glass water-filled vials as sample holders causes a lensing effect that must be recognized and accommodated. A curved vial must be placed exactly on the optical bench's centerline to ensure that the maximum amount of refracted light falls evenly on the detector.

In Figure 4-24, the vials in the stand holding the red solution have been marked with a black line to ensure that the vials are placed in the sample holding block in the same position each time an absorption/transmission reading is taken. Each vial has been filled with water and placed in the instrument. The ADC value noted as the vial is rotated through each 45-degree position. The vials were then marked to ensure that when used and positioned with the indicator to the side opposite the electrical feed through the vials would have as close as possible to the same ADC value.

A specific integrated circuit is manufactured for visible and near IR light intensity measurements by Texas Instruments with the chip designation of OPT101 ($13 USD). Figure 4-25 contains a block diagram from the manufacturer's datasheet that illustrates the components that make up the inner circuitry of the device. A photodiode in the photoconductive mode (output current is proportional to incident light intensity) is used with a transimpedance amplifier to produce an output voltage proportional to the light intensity falling on the diode window. The spectral response for the incident light can extend from approximately 400 nm to 10000 nm and has a maximum sensitivity peaking at 850 nm in the near infrared.

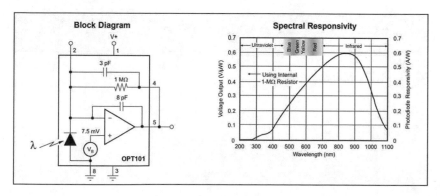

Figure 4-25. *Internal configuration and spectral response of Texas Instruments OPT101 IC*

Figure 4-26 illustrates the IC's mechanical layout and identifies the electrical pin connections for circuit implementation. A circuit for using the detector with an Arduino is depicted in Figure 4-27. Pins 2, 6, and 7 are not used in the circuit implementation. The Arduino provides power and an analog to digital converter to provide a numerical readout for the OPT101 transimpedance amplifier. The 100 Ω resistor in the power connection protects the integrated circuit. The two capacitors minimize noise on the power line. The Arduino also provides a moving average digital signal numerical smoothing since a manual readout and recording of the individual ADC representations of absorbance/transmission values is required.

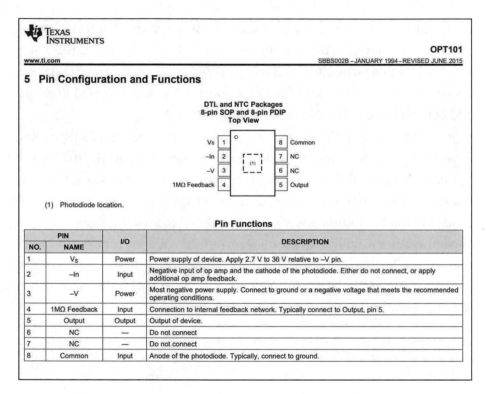

Figure 4-26. *OPT01 pin sssignment*

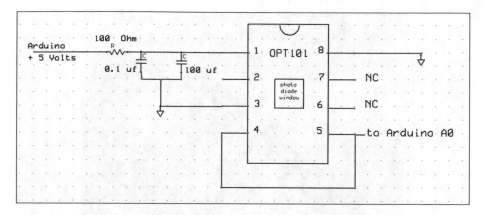

Figure 4-27. *A circuit diagram for reading the OPT101 with an Arduino*

In Figures 4-28 and 4-29, the numerical captions identify the various changes made to the instrument to accommodate the use of the OPT101 detector.

- Caption 1 identifies the RGB LED source mount and in Figure 4-28 an opaque plate with a ¼ in (6 mm) diameter aperture immediately in front of the LED lens cap.

- Caption 2 is a painted wood block drilled to hold the sample vial firmly in place. The block has two pins on the bottom that fit snugly into the alignment holes on the base of the instrument (see Figure 4-13).

- Caption 3 is a small perf board on which an 8-pin DIP socket has been mounted to accept the OPT101 chip. Figure 4-29 shows the back of the detector board with the threaded adjustable mount to the left and the detector board green screw terminal connectors to the bottom right.

- Caption 4 is a small prototyping board for power connections and component mounting.

- Caption 5 is a binary concentration gradient of blue food coloring dye.

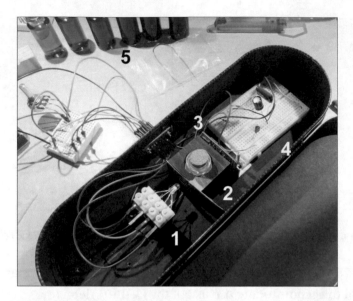

Figure 4-28. *OPT101 installation source view*

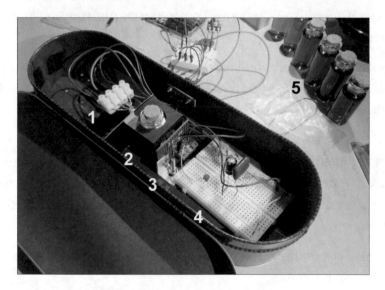

Figure 4-29. *OPT101 installation detector view*

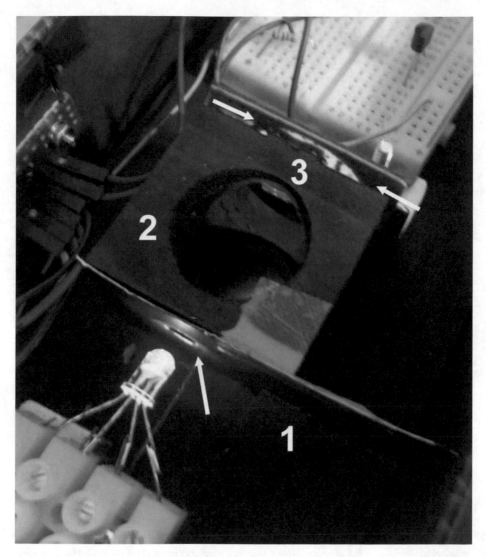

Figure 4-30. *Source light dispersion without glass sample vial in light path*

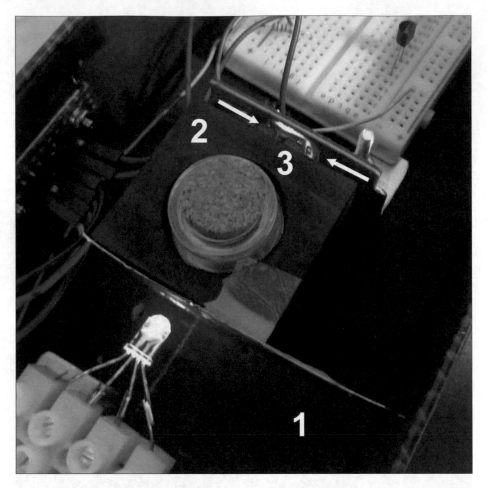

Figure 4-31. *Source light concentration with sample filled vial in light path*

Figures 4-30 and 4-31 depict the lensing effect of the sample vials when filled with a water-based solution. The source aperture is seen at the tip of the white arrow in Figure 4-30 on the opaque plate identified by the number 1. The interior of the sample holding block, identified by caption 2, appears to be completely illuminated by the light spreading out from the source aperture in Figure 4-30 without the glass cell in the holder. With the sample cell in place, the light beam appears to be condensed into the smaller oval visible in Figure 4-31, as indicated by the twin arrows identified by caption 3.

Measurements are made by assembling the LED source and detector to be used, aligning both with the appropriate sample holder. Once the mechanical components are mounted, electrical connections can be made. The Arduino IDE can be used with the appropriate software and power connections to illuminate and test the source. With the source generating the correct color for the measurement, the case can be closed, and the value from the Arduino ADC examined. A stable reading is necessary, and the number of readings averaged by the Arduino software may need to be adjusted to provide the required stability. The increase in the detector response time created by using a larger moving averages window is not of concern in these types of light intensity comparison measurements.

A certain amount of development may be necessary to obtain a stable detector response. With the water solvent in a sample vial in the sample holder, the detector response should be less than but as close to 1024 as possible. If required, either a diode power adjustment, a source detector distance adjustment, or both may be required to achieve a stable, measurable 0% absorbance/100% transmission baseline condition. Following the instrumental configuration for the lower end of the absorption measurement, an opaque object can be placed in the sample holder to establish the 100% absorption/0% transmission reading.

The difference between the ADC values needs to be high enough so that the individual absorbance/transmittance values from the gradient of colored standards form a linear calibration curve over the concentration range of interest.

Observations

In Figures 4-32 and 4-33, the simple colored dry cellophane system established a linear relationship between measured ADC count values and four layers of the red polymer. Additional experiments conducted with increasing numbers of layers of the cellophane polymer began to deviate from linearity due to the departure from the dilute solutions requirement for normal application of the Beer-Lambert law.

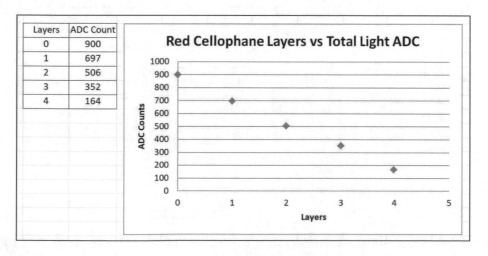

Layers	ADC Count
0	900
1	697
2	506
3	352
4	164

Figure 4-32. *ADC count vs. layers of red cellophane*

Figure 4-33 has been plotted with the full suite of data measured with eight sheets of translucent red cellulose wrapping. As seen in the trace of the plot, after four thicknesses of the sheeting, the linearity begins to deteriorate from excessive absorption.

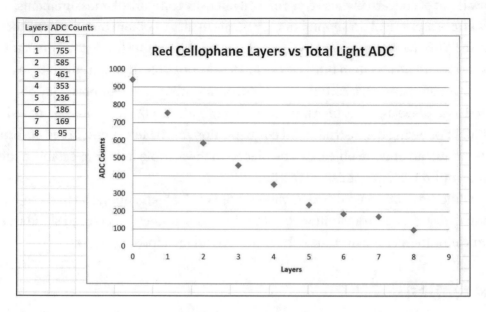

Figure 4-33. *Loss of linearity with excessive color density*

Red, green, and blue LED light sources were mounted in the instrument single diode configuration and all produced sufficient response with the CdS LDR to set the 100% transmittance ADC count to a stable value close to 900 to generate Figures 4-34 to 4-37.

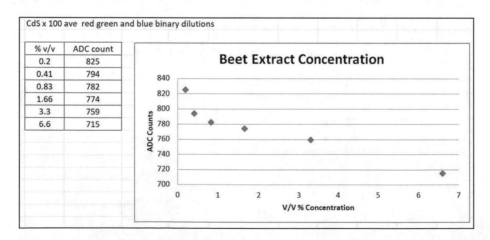

Figure 4-34. *RGB binary dilution calibrations with CdS LDR detector and signal averaging*

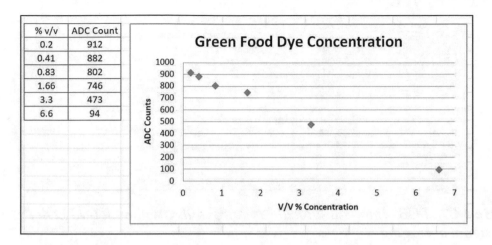

Figure 4-35. *RGB binary dilution calibrations with CdS LDR detector and signal averaging*

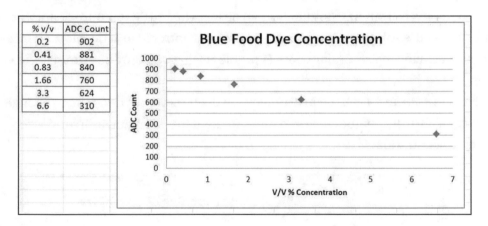

Figure 4-36. *RGB binary dilution calibrations with CdS LDR detector and signal averaging*

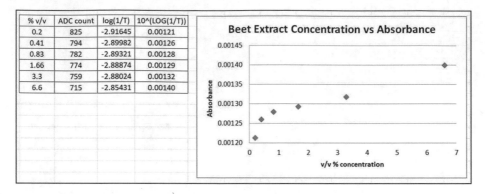

% v/v	ADC count	log(1/T)	10^(LOG(1/T))
0.2	825	-2.91645	0.00121
0.41	794	-2.89982	0.00126
0.83	782	-2.89321	0.00128
1.66	774	-2.88874	0.00129
3.3	759	-2.88024	0.00132
6.6	715	-2.85431	0.00140

Figure 4-37. *RGB binary dilution absorbance calibration with CdS LDR detector and signal averaging*

In Figure 4-34, the optical density of the red beet extract is too concentrated to form a linear plotting of detector ADC counts or transmittance with concentration. In Figure 4-37, attempts to convert from transmittance to an absorbance scale to improve linearity are not effective as the solution concentration is too concentrated and physio-chemical parameters are causing secondary optical problems that can only be eliminated by dilution.

In Figures 4-38 and 4-39, the instrument has been re-configured to use the high-sensitivity OPT101 IC photodetector to measure light transmission as a function of blue food dye concentration.

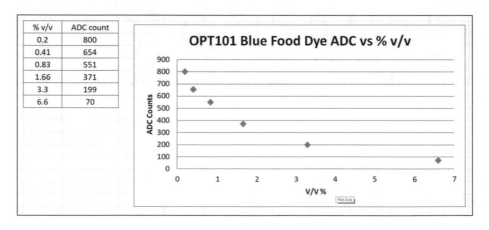

% v/v	ADC count
0.2	800
0.41	654
0.83	551
1.66	371
3.3	199
6.6	70

Figure 4-38. *Binary concentration vs. ADC calibration of blue food dye with OPT101 detector*

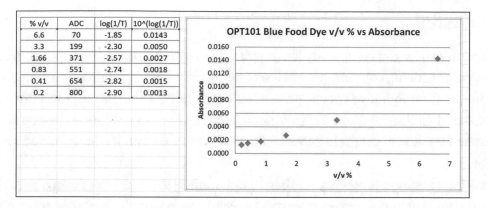

% v/v	ADC	log(1/T)	10^(log(1/T))
6.6	70	-1.85	0.0143
3.3	199	-2.30	0.0050
1.66	371	-2.57	0.0027
0.83	551	-2.74	0.0018
0.41	654	-2.82	0.0015
0.2	800	-2.90	0.0013

Figure 4-39. *Binary concentration vs. absorbance calibration of blue food dye with OPT101 detector*

Figures 4-38 and 4-39 demonstrate the improvement in linearity that can be achieved when the method or technique to measure the optical density changes.

Figure 4-40 is the OPT101 detector response in ADC units measured when the known nominal volumetric concentrations of a diluted beet extract were measured in the colorimeter using a DC powered monochromatic blue LED source. Figure 4-42 is the result of the binary dilution of a volume calibrated three-drop aliquot of a stock vegetable cooking extract. Three low incremental concentration dilutions were measured, with the third displaying the system response depicted in Figure 4-40. Concentrations down to the 50 parts per million (ppm) range are measurable.

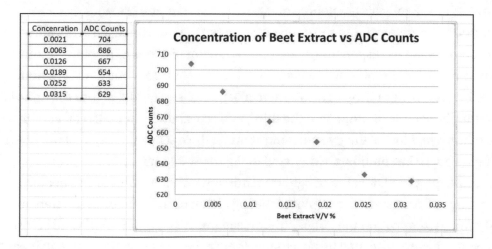

Concenration	ADC Counts
0.0021	704
0.0063	686
0.0126	667
0.0189	654
0.0252	633
0.0315	629

Figure 4-40. *Calibration of times three serial concentration of beet extract with OPT101 detector*

Discussion

To minimize costs and complexity for this introductory work, the traditional laboratory method of practicing colorimetric analysis has been somewhat modified to create a less rigorous semi-quantitative spectrophotometric technique. Concentrated solutions are dispensed by calibrated dropwise volumes for serial volumetric dilutions or dilution to a known volume to generate known volume on volume diluted concentration color gradients.

Standard solution preparation is begun by counting the number of drops required by the dispensing implement chosen to fill a well-known volume. A plastic polyethylene one-piece pipette, such as that in Figures 4-23 and 4-24, requires 350 drops to fill a 10 ml graduated cylinder to the 9 ml mark. Each drop from the pipette was 0.025 ml. Once the dispensing device is calibrated, it was marked to avoid errors. A second plastic pipette from the same bulk batch purchased for laboratory work produced drops of such a size that 280 drops occupied a volume of 9.6 ml, or each drop was 0.034 ml.

Two series of colored solutions were prepared for experimental work with the electronic absorbance measurement systems. Metal screw cap and narrow neck cork sealed vials (seen in Figures 4-23 and 4-24) were obtained from a craft store. They had 12 ml interior volumes. The narrow neck vials are easier to work with because the shoulder of the neck's restriction serves as a constant fill mark, much like a laboratory volumetric flask. (A series of laboratory-grade volumetric flasks of the same nominal volume has fill marks at different levels on the narrow neck. The assumption of equal volumes in the 12 ml vials is a source of random or systematic error.)

Solutions for determining the concentration range over which a linear calibration exists can be made by dispensing a binary progression of drops of a colored concentrate into six vials. The blue solutions in Figure 4-24 represent a concentration gradient created by dispensing 1 drop of a commercially purchased food dye into the first vial, 2 drops into the second, 4 drops into the third, and so on, until the sixth vial contains 32 drops of the dye. Plots of the dye concentration vs. the decreasing value of the blue light passing through the solution are depicted in Figures 4-34 and 4-35.

A simple plot of ADC value of light transmission vs. the V/V % is not linear over such a large range of concentration. A plot of the logarithm of the inverse of the transmission called the *absorbance* and the concentration can improve linearity. In some cases, a gentle smooth curvature may be acceptable for use. For investigations where linearity is required, a smaller color gradient can be used to make concentration measurements.

For dilute solutions, the Beer-Lambert law is postulated to be a linear relationship model of the absorbance, analyte concentration, and solution path length. In many experimental measurement systems, however, the calibration curves are not linear but are slightly curved. If the calibrations are reproducible, then the shape or curvature of the correlation between measurement parameters is not important if there is no radical change in concentration with measured absorption.

LEDs are not lasers. The light, although directed, is radiated out in a cone. Testing the simple system demonstrated that at an approximate 2 in (50mm) distance between the source and detector (OP-505 phototransistor) green, blue, and ultraviolet produced sufficient power to set the Arduino ADC to a steady count around the 900 value, sufficient for a series of absorbance measurements.

Although the OP-505 photo transistor peak spectral sensitivity lies, as do most PN junctions, in the IR region as depicted in Figure 4-1, the high-intensity output visible 5 mm diameter LEDs produce sufficient radiation to utilize most of the Arduino 10-bit ADC range for absorbance measurements (see Figure 4-10)

Examination of the spectral sensitivity curves for the three types of detectors indicates that the LDR is most sensitive in the green region of the visible spectrum. The PN junction-based devices have maximum sensitivities in the near IR. The OPT101 can function in the blue range of the spectrum (see Figure 4-38) and is reasonably sensitive in the red range (see Figure 4-40).

The photosensitive area of the LDR is ¼ in × 5/16 in (6 mm × 9 mm), OP-505 is ⅛ in (3 mm) diameter, and the OPT101 photoconductive diode is 0.090 in (2.29 mm) square. The use of LEDs as a source, with brightness and concentrated directional output allows the experimenter to assemble an instrument in which the components should be collinear for best performance.

Figures 4-32 and 4-33 demonstrate the non-linearity that exists as the optical density at the nominal wavelength increases, creating solid cellophane sheets—the same deviating effect that occurs in liquid solutions as they increase in analyte concentration.

The calibrations depicted in Figures 4-34 to 4-37 illustrate the effect of excessive concentration of the colored species of interest. In all four figures the sensitivity for red, green, and blue is sufficient to generate calibrations but only two the green and blue are linear. The red series of dilutions is too concentrated to exhibit a linear relationship in either the transmittance or absorbance mode of data plotting.

Figures 4-38 and 4-39 illustrate the improvement in linearity that may be obtained by altering the mode of data presentation from transmittance to absorbance.

Solutions can be prepared in which the concentration gradient standards are created by placing a linearly increasing number of drops in successive vials. Attempts to prepare calibrations with successive single and dual drop additions to sequential vials did not produce a reliable, reproducible decrease in the beet extract's observed ADC values. When three drop increments were used the calibration displayed in Figure 4-40 resulted. The calibration appears to be linear down to concentrations near 0.025 % V/V. The usable span of the red vegetable extract calibration covers the 20 to 250 parts per million v/v concentrations range.

Although the system assembled has not used any active optical elements, a substantial increase in sensitivity should be available if a simple hand-held magnifying glass collects the light passing through the sample (see Figure 4-31) and brings it to focus on the detector.

A Six Wavelength Spectrograph Using Reverse Biased LEDs

LEDs are a further development of the first solid-state signal or rectifier diodes fabricated from crystalline silicon or germanium. Metals and insulators are made from elements that form solids in which the multi-atom crystal structure forms energy bands that are partially full and allow electrons to move or are full and forbid conduction. Some elements can be blended to form materials that can act like metal conductors under controlled conditions.

Elements such as boron (B), aluminum (Al), and gallium (Ga) only have three electrons in their outer shell. Elements such as carbon (C), silicon (Si), and germanium (Ge) have four. Phosphorus (P), arsenic (As), and antimony (Sb) have five. If a material such as silicon or germanium is mixed with a small amount of boron, aluminum, or gallium and the mix is crystallized, a P-type semiconductor is formed. P-type materials consist of a bulk matrix in which the continuous structure of atoms with four outer electrons is sporadically interrupted with sites where the crystal atoms only have three electrons. An electron-deficient site in a bulk crystalline matrix can be considered as a positively charged hole.

If a four-electron material is mixed with a small amount of an element having five electrons in its outer shell and the mixture is crystallized, then an N-type semiconductor is formed. An N-type material consists of a bulk matrix in which the continuous structure of atoms with four outer electrons in their atomic structure is sporadically interrupted with sites where the crystal atoms have five electrons. A site with excess electrons can be considered as a negatively charged entity.

A PN junction is formed by fusing crystals of P-type semiconductor material with N-type.

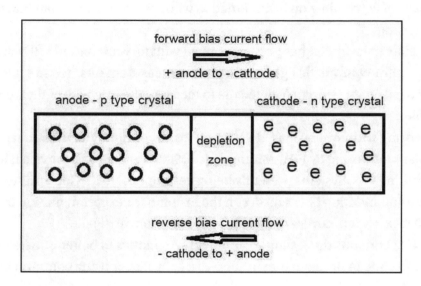

Figure 4-41. *A PN junction*

The fusion of the two crystal types causes the combination of holes and electron excess along the contacting interface resulting in the formation of an area with no mobile carriers, called the *depletion zone*. Current can only be forced to flow through the junction if a positive voltage is applied to the P side of the junction of sufficient strength to overcome the depletion zone energy gap of 0.3 V to 0.7 V, depending on the materials of construction.

As the basic building blocks of solid-state circuitry, single PN junctions form diodes that pass current in one direction, only functioning as a rectifier. Two PN junctions can form transistors such as the PNP or NPN types to control current flow. Four PN junctions in series form a thyristor or silicon-controlled rectifier. Reverse bias PN junctions form photocells and photodiodes.

Normal current flow through a PN junction releases energy as the holes and electron carriers cross the depletion zone in the form of infrared radiation. Diodes with PN junctions made from bulk semiconducting materials and minor quantities of elements such as gallium (Ga), arsenic (As), phosphorus (P), nitrogen (N), indium (In), and aluminum (Al) can be manufactured to produce radiation in the visible, near infrared and ultraviolet light ranges.

LEDs are photo emissive when forward biased and are photoconductive when reverse biased. In the photoconductive mode, the device passes a current in proportion to the amount of light falling on its PN junction whose energy is less than that of the PN junction band gap.

A solid-state colorimeter has been developed with forward biased LEDs functioning as a source of monochromatic light for absorption measurements. These same diodes can also be used as spectroscopic detectors to measure the intensity of their own nominal color.

Light sensing with reverse biased PN junctions in common LEDs has been used for solar monitoring by F. W. Mimms since 1988. It is the basis for visual light communication (VLS) systems presently being developed. Dr. M. Cook presented a method for implementing LED sensing on the Arduino for experimentation in 2008 (see www.thebox.myzen.co.uk/Workshop/Introduction.html).

Figure 4-42 contains three simple captioned schematics to better understand the algorithm and code to program the Arduino as a light sensor using common LEDs.

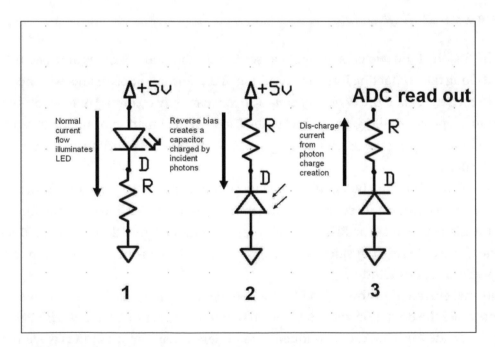

Figure 4-42. *Biasing of LEDs as color sensors*

By reversing the bias on an LED, the PN junction can be made to take on the properties and capabilities of a capacitor on which the junction charge is sustained by the presence of an insulator between the two semi-conducting material faces. The capacitance of the junction is typically in the picofarads range (10^{-12} F). If a reverse biased light-emitting diode is exposed to incident light with energy greater than the PN junction band gap, then electrons are pulled up into the conduction band, leaving holes behind in their place. Relaxing the reverse biasing voltage across the junction causes the holes and electrons to migrate, and a current proportional to the collected incident light intensity is created.

By allowing the accumulated charge to flow through a known resistor and measuring the time of the current flow, the quantity of the accumulated charge can be measured. The timing count can be determined with a microcontroller as a nominal 5 V biasing voltage across the capacitor formed by the PN junction decays back to a nominal 0 V or logic 0 through the known resistor. Recall that the integral of voltage change over time is a measure of the current or charge (see Chapter 1 equation 3).

There are several published reports in which the timed voltage decay/current flow from the discharging diode has been normalized into ADC counts as a measure of ambient illumination when the voltage on the diode is measured before and after discharge. Arduino sketch Listing 4-5 measures the accumulated charge on a single reverse biased LED. Also, the measured discharge time has been inverted to be expressed as a measure of darkness, to express diode emission in proportion to the ambient lighting conditions.

Since the color of a diode is determined by the energy difference of the PN junction band gap, it is to be expected that the junction is sensitive to its own wavelength of incident light.

Photon energy increases as the wavelength of the electromagnetic radiation gets shorter. A reversed biased PN junction originally fabricated for a longer wavelength should be sensitive to its own and shorter wavelengths.

Two techniques use reverse biased LEDs as light sensors with microprocessors. Both techniques expose the reversed biased PN junction to incident light, allow it to collect charge, and then discharge the diode through a resistor to ground, measuring either the voltage difference or timing the discharge. Experimentation has shown that using the voltage difference as a measure of incident light is suitable for a single LED but not for monitoring multiple diodes.

Most microprocessors have a single ADC and six or more multiplexed measuring channels. Observations made when using multiple diodes on a single ADC reveal that changes in one channel are often mirrored in the other channels. It has been suggested that residual charge in the multiplexer channels is probably responsible for the effect, often called *cross talk*.

By connecting a pair of digital pins on an Arduino microprocessor in series with an LED and a current limiting resistor, the use of the ADC multiplexer can be avoided, and the LEDs monitored independently with the code in Listing 4-4. A relatively simple sketch can be written to gauge the quantity of incident light falling on the diode junction with a wavelength shorter than that of the light emitted by the junction. As an Arduino has 12 easily accessible digital I/O pins, up to six different wavelength LEDs can be monitored by measuring the discharge time using the code in Listing of 4-4.

In Figure 4-10, the response of the OP-505 phototransistor to the three primary colors are different for each color. It is reasonable to expect that variations occur in the manufacturing process such that each diode in a given batch has a slightly different size of depletion zone and has a slightly different voltage difference across its PN junction. In addition to the small manufacturing voltage differences, there are larger values due to using different materials for manufacturing PN junctions of different colors. To use light-sensing LEDs in any form of quantitative or qualitative application, it is probably best to start any experimental measurements with the devices in the dark where their incident light collection is minimal.

Table 4-3 tabulates the measured response variation that exists in LEDs in reversed bias light sensing mode using the discharge time count as the incident illumination metric (colored devices are (clrd), and clear diodes are (clr)).

Table 4-3. *Timed Response Variation in Reverse Biased LED*

LED Reversed Bias Response to Ambient Lighting						
Specimen	red (clrd)	amber (clr)	orange (clrd)	yellow (clrd)	green (clrd)	blue (clrd)
1	30000	6000	10000	12000	2200	15300
2	15000	7300	10600	13000	2400	15600
3	17500	9100	105000	21000	2100	17000
4	30000	5100	9200	11500	2300	16000
5	27000	5000	11000	10500	2300	16000
6	12500	10800	no response	8700	2300	17100

Wavelength selective light sensing with reverse biased LEDs can be used in assembling an inexpensive demonstration of two important scientific concepts, one in theoretical physics and the second in astronomy. Light-sensing LEDs can selectively monitor the quantized black-body radiation from a hot object. Demonstrations of quantized radiation from heated objects are used as supporting evidence for one of the fundamental concepts of quantum mechanics in theoretical physics. Astronomical observations of the visible light color emissions from stellar objects are often used to determine object temperature.

Colors are often described as corresponding to the radiation given off by an incandescent or hot black-body at a specific temperature expressed in degrees Kelvin. A readily available black-body heated to a specific temperature is the tungsten filament of an incandescent light bulb.

A manageable, small, safe, easy to use, filamented light bulb can be obtained from any automotive supplier in the form of a 12 V vehicle tail light such as the Sylvania/Osram 1156 ($3 CDN; max. voltage 12.8, power rating 26.9 watts) along with the corresponding bulb mounting socket with wiring leads called a *pig tail* ($2.50 CDN). The small bulb usually draws a current slightly less than 2 A at full power, which is usually well within the ability of most kit built 30 V DC regulated supplies and the small bulb size requires minimal shielding to prevent burns from the hot glass envelope.

Examination of the correlation between temperature and radiated electromagnetic energy in the visible, IR, and UV ranges have been extensively studied with incandescent tungsten light bulb filaments. Incandescence in the tungsten filament is created through resistance heating of the metal element with DC or AC electrical energy. Tungsten filament temperature is measured by correlating the change in resistance of the elemental metal with known changes in temperature.

To conduct experiments with light sensing LEDs, the construction and assembly of a simple instrumental system for qualitative and quantitative measurements has been divided into two phases consisting of light emission source creation and selected light color detection.

Experiment: Light Source Assembly and Calibration

To use the tungsten filament/resistance temperature relationship, expressed as

$$T = T_0 + (R/R_0 - 1)/\alpha \text{ -- } (4)$$

the room temperature resistance R_0 measured at ambient or defined conditions of T_0 must be used with the filament resistance R-value calculated from the current and voltage data collected for the tungsten filament. α is the temperature coefficient of resistance for tungsten, reported as 0.004403.

Examining the temperature resistance relationship used to calculate the tungsten filament temperature requires measuring the wire resistance value at ambient conditions R_0. Typically, the low wattage 12 V lights have filament resistance values near half an ohm that requires careful measurement.

A low current adaptation of the technique can be used to accurately measure the low mass and fractional ohm resistance of the filament (see www.semanticscholar.org/paper/The-Ohmic-Region-of-a-Lightbulb-Grasel-Mudd/38ae1fbdf536b916adbc2965e3ad93eb6c79dbf7?p2df).

To minimize heating and a resistance perturbation of the low mass of material in the spiral filament and utilize reasonable cost meters to their best advantage, only the voltage drop across circuit components is measured.

In Figure 4-43, a low voltage power supply (3 V) has been connected in series with a 10 KΩ variable resistor, a high precision 1% 1 Ω power resistor, and the bulb filament. Two reasonably priced meters then measure the voltage drops across the filament and precision resistor as the variable resistor is adjusted to gradually increase the current through the circuit. In a typical experiment, the variable resistor was adjusted in 0.1 mV increments across the filament from 0 to 5.0 mV, and the millivolt drop across the precision resistor recorded for each increment.

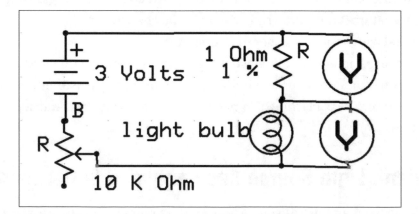

Figure 4-43. *Circuit for resistance measurement of low mass tungsten light bulb filament*

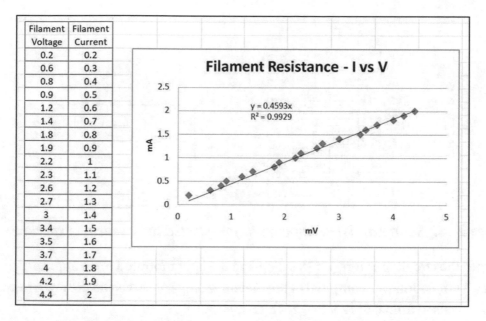

Filament Voltage	Filament Current
0.2	0.2
0.6	0.3
0.8	0.4
0.9	0.5
1.2	0.6
1.4	0.7
1.8	0.8
1.9	0.9
2.2	1
2.3	1.1
2.6	1.2
2.7	1.3
3	1.4
3.4	1.5
3.5	1.6
3.7	1.7
4	1.8
4.2	1.9
4.4	2

Figure 4-44. *Filament resistance from current vs. voltage graphic*

Figures 4-43 and 4-44 depict the circuit that powers the filament and the graphical determination of the filament resistance for the Sylvania 1156 bulb in these experiments. A high sensitivity Siglent SDM3055 digital benchtop meter using a low ohmic scale measured a filament resistance of 0.46 Ω. The low-power graphical procedure generated a value of 0.4593 Ω.

Experiment: Selective Color Light Sensing with Reverse Biased LED

Determining Temperature: Resistance Correlation for the Tungsten Filament

A small 12 V tungsten filament light bulb such as the 26.9 W Sylvania/Osram 1156 automotive tail light, illuminated by power from an adjustable voltage 2 A supply, makes an excellent incandescent source. Circuit A in Figure 4-45 depicts the circuit configuration used to measure the current and voltage delivered to the filament, allowing the determination of the filament resistance at each filament power setting.

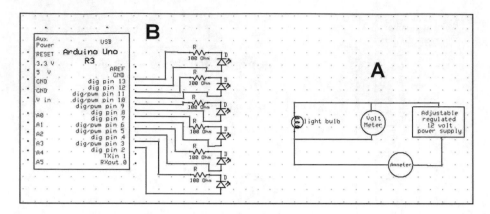

Figure 4-45. *Source and detector circuits for selected light-sensing experiments*

With the circuit in Figure 4-45A set up and the light mounted in an appropriate holder, a tabulation was compiled of the meter readings observed as the power supply voltage is raised from 0 to 12 V in 0.2 V increments.

A special notation of the filament power settings was made at the point where the central portion of the light bulb filament began to glow.

Table 4-4 tabulates the measured filament voltage and current in 0.2 V increments of the power supply settings from 0.2 to 12.0 V. The tabulation also contains the calculated resistance from a simple Ohm's law application and a temperature estimate approximated from the tungsten filament resistance value (see equation 4 and Chapter 7 for more on thermal coefficient of resistance or TCR).

Note   Calibration constants: tungsten (W) α coefficient = 0.0045, room temperature filament resistance = 0.46 Ω, and room temperature = 20.2°C.

Table 4-4. *Tungsten Filament Resistance vs. Temperature Calibration*

Filament Voltage	Filament Current	Fiament Resistance	Filament Temperature	Filament Voltage	Filament Current	Fiament Resistance	Filament Temperature	Filament Voltage	Filament Current	Fiament Resistance	Filament Temperature
0.087	0.076	1.145	351.0	2.56	0.956	2.678	1091.6	5.66	1.422	3.980	1720.8
0.162	0.141	1.149	353.0	2.67	0.975	2.738	1120.9	5.8	1.441	4.025	1742.4
0.235	0.2	1.175	365.6	2.85	1.004	2.839	1169.3	6.01	1.461	4.114	1785.2
0.316	0.262	1.206	380.6	3.03	1.035	2.928	1212.2	6.14	1.484	4.137	1796.8
0.416	0.333	1.249	401.5	3.14	1.052	2.985	1239.9	6.29	1.502	4.188	1821.0
0.495	0.383	1.292	422.3	3.3	1.078	3.061	1276.8	6.49	1.528	4.247	1849.9
0.636	0.451	1.410	479.2	3.45	1.1	3.136	1313.1	6.64	1.546	4.295	1872.8
0.71	0.49	1.449	498.0	3.67	1.136	3.231	1358.7	6.78	1.564	4.335	1892.2
0.791	0.571	1.385	467.2	3.81	1.156	3.296	1390.2	6.98	1.581	4.415	1930.8
0.913	0.618	1.477	511.7	3.95	1.178	3.353	1417.9	6.98	1.584	4.407	1926.8
1.077	0.664	1.622	581.5	4.09	1.2	3.408	1444.5	7.1	1.602	4.432	1939.0
1.244	0.704	1.767	651.6	4.29	1.23	3.488	1482.9	7.28	1.624	4.483	1963.6
1.333	0.722	1.846	689.9	4.46	1.255	3.554	1514.8	7.45	1.644	4.532	1987.2
1.531	0.763	2.007	767.3	4.6	1.275	3.608	1540.9	7.6	1.661	4.576	2008.4
1.628	0.785	2.074	799.9	4.71	1.291	3.648	1560.5	7.78	1.682	4.625	2032.5
1.794	0.817	2.196	858.8	4.86	1.313	3.701	1586.1	7.94	1.7	4.671	2054.3
1.917	0.841	2.279	899.2	5.04	1.337	3.770	1619.1	8.1	1.718	4.715	2075.7
2.11	0.875	2.411	962.9	5.18	1.359	3.812	1639.3	8.27	1.736	4.764	2099.3
2.22	0.897	2.475	993.6	5.35	1.382	3.871	1668.1	8.44	1.755	4.809	2121.2
2.42	0.932	2.597	1052.4	5.49	1.4	3.921	1692.4	8.57	1.77	4.842	2137.0
								8.74	1.789	4.885	2158.1

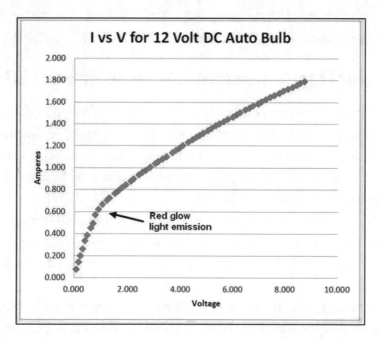

Figure 4-46. *Resistance change in Sylvania 1156 Tungsten filament with applied power*

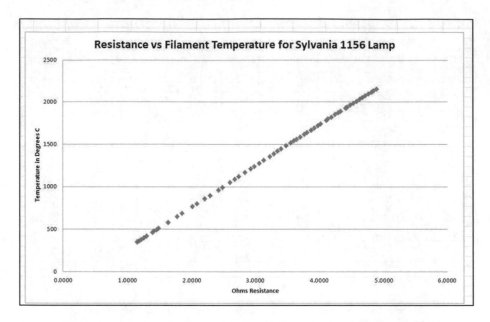

Figure 4-47. *Resistance vs. temperature for Sylvania 1156 light bulb*

Selective Color Light Sensing with Reverse Biased LED

To achieve independent measurement of the light sensed by different color reverse biased diodes arranged in an array (see Figure 4-49), a lightproof enclosure can be assembled to enclose both light source and sensors. The light source and detector circuitry in Figure 4-45 can be enclosed in a light excluding case fabricated from readily available components as seen in Figure 4-48.

The components depicted in Figure 4-48 have been fabricated from readily available, easy to work materials such as ¼ in (6 mm) plywood and fiber drum food containers, all of which have been painted with a matt black acrylic paint to reduce internal light reflection.

Item 1 is the base plate of the assembly that provides support for the Arduino microprocessor should the assembled unit be moved during experimentation. Items 2 and 3 are spacers providing adequate room for the microprocessor and, together with the small rectangular blocks, largely occlude stray light from infiltrating the microprocessor chamber. Item 4 is the top plate of the microprocessor compartment and the bottom plate of the cylindrical exposure chamber.

Both item 4 and the left half of item 5 have ⅛ in (3 mm) by 1½ in (40 mm) slots to accommodate the electrical connections between the microprocessor headers and the diode array. Items 1, 4, 2, 5, and 7 are cut from ¼ in (6 mm) plywood. The pair of components captioned as item 3 are cut from ⅜ in (9 mm) plywood to provide adequate clearance for the Arduino header arrays. All the wooden components constituting the base of the exposure chamber are 4½ in (11.5 cm) square.

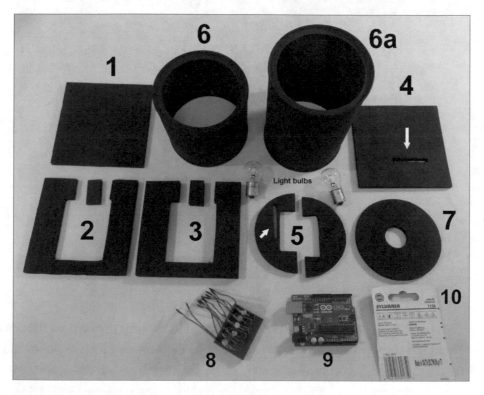

Figure 4-48. *Exposure chamber components*

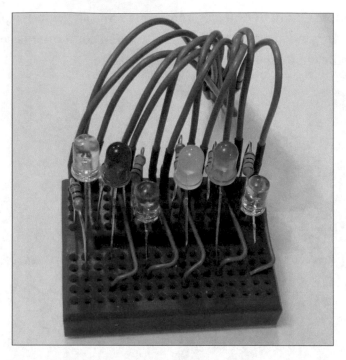

Figure 4-49. *Coloured LED diode array*

Item 5 consists of two plates that have been cut to fit around the base of the 1¾ in (45 mm) by 1¼ in (34 mm) prototyping board, as seen in Figure 4-9. The two plates fit inside the fiberboard cylinders so that the prototyping board and the aperture opening in item 7 are all concentric inside the different length cylinders 6 and 6a. Items 6 and 6a are 4 in diameter (10.2 cm) by 3¾ in (95 mm) and 5½ in (14 cm) long fiberboard cylinders cut from metal-rimmed, food packaging drums. The white arrows on items 4 and 5 indicate the slotted openings for the passage of the electrical connections between the diode leads and the Arduino digital pin access headers. The figure also depicts the diode array, Arduino microprocessor, and the packaging rear face displaying specification data for the two spare light sources.

Once the light exclusion case has been assembled and the Arduino is loaded with the five- or six-element light-sensing sketch in Listing 4-4, the Arduino serial monitor should display a streamed listing of the designated diodes (see Figure 4-50).

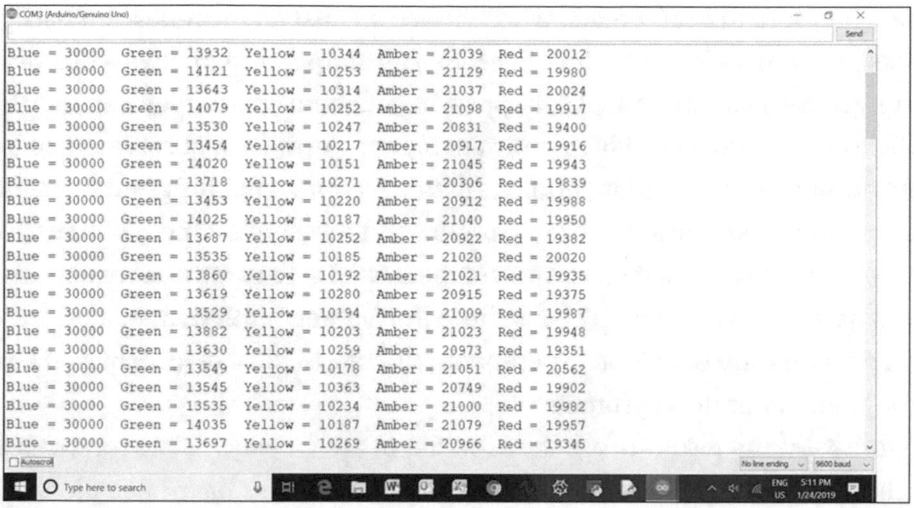

Figure 4-50. *Five-element reverse bias diode array serial monitor output*

Recall that the default option for the serial monitor output is to stream the data as it arrives and to manually record or inspect individual numerical values. The autoscroll checkbox in the lower-left corner of the screen window can be activated to "freeze" the display and stop the scrolling. (Use Ctrl+C to copy highlighted data to the clipboard.)

A 4 in (10.2 cm) tall cylinder is an appropriate exposure length for the approximately 30 W bulb and the ¼ in (5 mm) reverse biased LED light sensors, as depicted in Figure 4-49. Recall that the intensity of radiation for a point source follows an inverse square law with respect to distance.

Initially, with no power being applied to the light bulb filament, all the diode elements should be at their maximum time count values of 30,000 or less for some devices. Power is applied to the bulb filament in increments of voltage as was done in the filament resistance-temperature data collection experiment. As the voltage and current rise on the source, the serial monitor can be used to find the power setting in which each of the reverse biased diodes begins to respond to the photons generated by the heated filament. Table 4-5 tabulates the observed power settings at which the nominal diode color-sensitive PN junctions begin to respond to the filament emissions.

Reverse Biased LEDs as Optical Pyrometers

Non-contacting optical pyrometers are presently the only way to measure the temperatures of hot objects. Quantitative measurements of the power to heat a tungsten filament have been used to measure hot surfaces at temperatures up to the melting point of tungsten for more than 100 years. When viewed against an incandescent background, a hot tungsten filament becomes invisible when its temperature matches that of the heated surface being monitored. A "disappearing filament" pyrometer can only be used on a surface hot enough to produce sufficient light to permit the observation to be made.

In the primary and secondary portions of this section, a hot tungsten filament has been calibrated with respect to temperature and resistance. Once calibrated, the incandescent filament is used to find the temperatures at which the reversed biased LEDs see a particular wavelength of light from the filament emission. In a reversal of the selective light emission detection experiments, the response of reverse biased LEDs can form a rudimentary optical pyrometer.

In Figure 4-51, the results of a small experiment are displayed. The reverse bias LED discharge time responses for the nominal colored diodes have been plotted for the corresponding filament temperatures.

In addition to the multiple LED plots, trend lines are created for an exponential fit (see Figure 4-52) and a natural log fit of the red LED discharge time response vs. temperature graphics (see Figure 4-53). As seen in the reverse biased discharge times for the red diode, the natural log of the discharge time or current flow can form a reasonable linear based correlation between the diode stored charge and the calculated incandescent filament temperature.

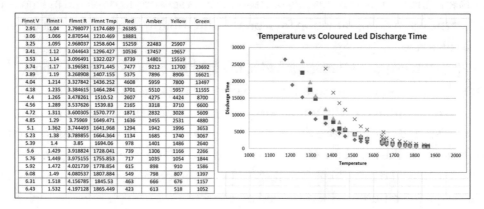

Flmnt V	Flmnt i	Flmnt R	Flmnt Tmp	Red	Amber	Yellow	Green
2.91	1.04	2.798077	1174.689	26385			
3.06	1.066	2.870544	1210.469	18881			
3.25	1.095	2.968037	1258.604	15259	22483	25907	
3.41	1.12	3.044643	1296.427	10536	17457	19657	
3.53	1.14	3.096491	1322.027	8739	14801	15519	
3.74	1.17	3.196581	1371.445	7477	9212	11700	23692
3.89	1.19	3.268908	1407.155	5375	7896	8906	16621
4.04	1.214	3.327842	1436.252	4608	5959	7800	13497
4.18	1.235	3.384615	1464.284	3701	5510	5957	11555
4.4	1.265	3.478261	1510.52	2607	4275	4424	8700
4.56	1.289	3.537626	1539.83	2165	3318	3710	6600
4.72	1.311	3.600305	1570.777	1871	2832	3028	5609
4.85	1.29	3.75969	1649.471	1636	2455	2531	4880
5.1	1.362	3.744493	1641.968	1294	1942	1996	3653
5.23	1.38	3.789855	1664.364	1134	1685	1740	3067
5.39	1.4	3.85	1694.06	978	1401	1486	2640
5.6	1.429	3.918824	1728.041	739	1306	1166	2266
5.76	1.449	3.975155	1755.853	717	1035	1054	1844
5.92	1.472	4.021739	1778.854	615	898	910	1586
6.08	1.49	4.080537	1807.884	549	798	807	1397
6.31	1.518	4.156785	1845.53	463	666	676	1157
6.43	1.532	4.197128	1865.449	423	613	518	1052

Figure 4-51. *Tungsten filament temperature vs. diode discharge time*

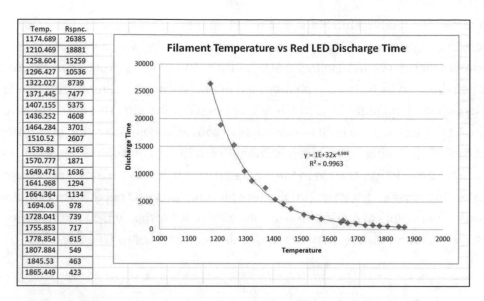

Figure 4-52. *Tungsten filament temperature vs. red diode discharge time*

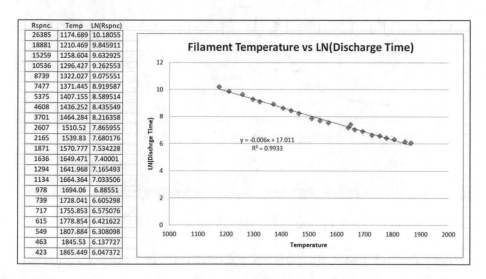

Figure 4-53. *Tungsten filament temperature vs. LN (diode discharge time)*

If the reverse biased LED light collection measurement is based on a voltage difference technique, the LED can operate in a color-selective, photodiode mode. A photodiode response should be a more linear relationship with the quantity of incident light. A single channel reading of the voltage difference on a reverse biased LED eliminates the ADC multiplexer "cross talk" problem. It should provide a more usable correlation between the hot surface temperature and the quantitative collection of light sensed by a reverse biased PN junction.

To record the relationship between a hot filament emission and the selected wavelength of light collected by a reverse biased LED, Listing 4-5 (for an Arduino microprocessor) can be used with a DAQFactory or RPi plotting program to record the data. Each diode to be tested can be mounted in the center of the small prototyping board as depicted in Figure 4-48 and 4-49 and placed in the 4 in (10.2 cm) exposure case with the 12 V Sylvania 1156 bulb as the emissive source. A data recording experiment is started by setting the filament voltage-current to a value slightly below the point at which the diode became active, as seen in the tabulated data in Table 4-5. A typical time-based data recording session using the DAQFactory plotting facility is depicted in Figure 4-54.

I tested four colors of diodes from the stock on hand with a typical result, as depicted in Figure 4-54, for a 5 mm (¼ in) diameter, clear green high-output device.

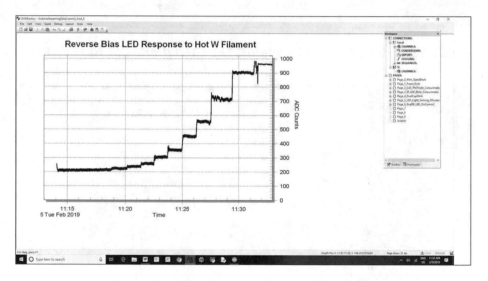

Figure 4-54. *Reverse biased green LED response to hot W filament*

To compile a correlation between the filament temperature and the reverse biased green LED response, the power supply incremental voltage settings and the measured filament current can establish the filament resistance and corresponding temperature at known times during the data recording session. For visualization, the filament temperature is then plotted against the corresponding recorded detector response. Figure 4-55 depicts the graphical correlation between the observed ADC counts of a reverse biased green, high output, clear, 5mm diameter LED and the calculated temperature of the incandescent Sylvania 1156, 12 V light bulb filament at a 4 in (10.2 cm) distance. Similar correlation curves were generated for an older green colored LED, an IR diode and a clear, high-output, blue device to cover various temperature ranges.

Observations

Table 4-5 is a tabulation of the source power values with calculated filament resistance and temperature. Beneath each nominal color heading is the initial time count for the point at which the reverse biased LED transits from being non-responsive (n/r) to actively measuring the light whose wavelength is shorter than that emitted by the forward biased diode.

Table 4-5. *Reverse Biased LED Response to Hot Tungsten Filament Radiation Emissions*

Supply Voltage	Filament Voltage	Filament Current	Filament Resistance	Filament Temperature	Reverse Biased LED Response						
					I R	Red	Amber	Yellow	Green	Blue	U V
2.8	1.7	0.793	2.14376	852	18943	n/r	n/r	n/r	n/r	n/r	n/r
4.4	2.91	1.04	2.79808	1175		26386	n/r	n/r	n/r	n/r	n/r
4.8	3.25	1.095	2.96804	1259			22483	25907	n/r	n/r	n/r
5.4	3.74	1.17	3.19658	1372					23692	n/r	n/r
10.2	7.82	1.697	4.60813	2070						27844	n/r
10.46	8.28	1.736	4.76959	2149							18092

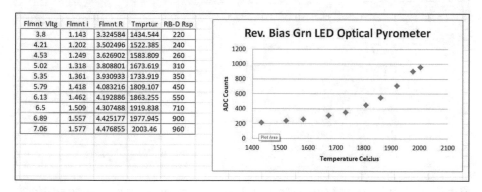

Flmnt Vltg	Flmnt i	Flmnt R	Tmprtur	RB-D Rsp
3.8	1.143	3.324584	1434.544	220
4.21	1.202	3.502496	1522.385	240
4.53	1.249	3.626902	1583.809	260
5.02	1.318	3.808801	1673.619	310
5.35	1.361	3.930933	1733.919	350
5.79	1.418	4.083216	1809.107	450
6.13	1.462	4.192886	1863.255	550
6.5	1.509	4.307488	1919.838	710
6.89	1.557	4.425177	1977.945	900
7.06	1.577	4.476855	2003.46	960

Figure 4-55. *A green reverse biased LED ADC count vs. temperature optical pyrometer correlation*

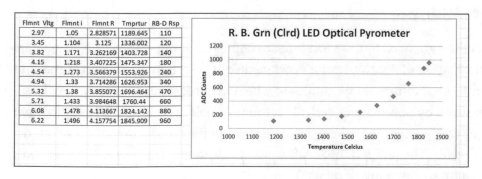

Flmnt Vltg	Flmnt i	Flmnt R	Tmprtur	RB-D Rsp
2.97	1.05	2.828571	1189.645	110
3.45	1.104	3.125	1336.002	120
3.82	1.171	3.262169	1403.728	140
4.15	1.218	3.407225	1475.347	180
4.54	1.273	3.566379	1553.926	240
4.94	1.33	3.714286	1626.953	340
5.32	1.38	3.855072	1696.464	470
5.71	1.433	3.984648	1760.44	660
6.08	1.478	4.113667	1824.142	880
6.22	1.496	4.157754	1845.909	960

Figure 4-56. *A green reverse biased LED ADC count vs. temperature optical pyrometer correlation*

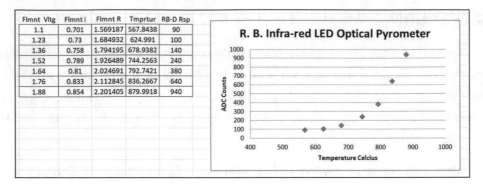

Flmnt Vltg	Flmnt i	Flmnt R	Tmprtur	RB-D Rsp
1.1	0.701	1.569187	567.8438	90
1.23	0.73	1.684932	624.991	100
1.36	0.758	1.794195	678.9382	140
1.52	0.789	1.926489	744.2563	240
1.64	0.81	2.024691	792.7421	380
1.76	0.833	2.112845	836.2667	640
1.88	0.854	2.201405	879.9918	940

Figure 4-57. *A reverse biased IR LED emitter ADC count vs. temperature optical pyrometer correlation*

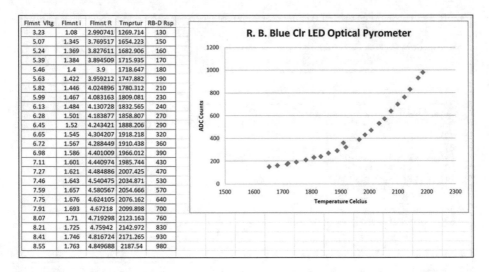

Flmnt Vltg	Flmnt i	Flmnt R	Tmprtur	RB-D Rsp
3.23	1.08	2.990741	1269.714	130
5.07	1.345	3.769517	1654.223	150
5.24	1.369	3.827611	1682.906	160
5.39	1.384	3.894509	1715.935	170
5.46	1.4	3.9	1718.647	180
5.63	1.422	3.959212	1747.882	190
5.82	1.446	4.024896	1780.312	210
5.99	1.467	4.083163	1809.081	230
6.13	1.484	4.130728	1832.565	240
6.28	1.501	4.183877	1858.807	270
6.45	1.52	4.243421	1888.206	290
6.65	1.545	4.304207	1918.218	320
6.72	1.567	4.288449	1910.438	360
6.98	1.586	4.401009	1966.012	390
7.11	1.601	4.440974	1985.744	430
7.27	1.621	4.484886	2007.425	470
7.46	1.643	4.540475	2034.871	530
7.59	1.657	4.580567	2054.666	570
7.75	1.676	4.624105	2076.162	640
7.91	1.693	4.67218	2099.898	700
8.07	1.71	4.719298	2123.163	760
8.21	1.725	4.75942	2142.972	830
8.41	1.746	4.816724	2171.265	930
8.55	1.763	4.849688	2187.54	980

Figure 4-58. *A blue reverse biased LED ADC count vs. temperature optical pyrometer correlation*

Discussion

Most of the light used by our visual senses comes from heated incandescent elements. An examination of light and color must involve at least a small portion of the study of heat and temperature. Temperatures at which incandescent objects emit light can only be measured by non-contact optical methods or power consumption approximations based upon the measured change in resistance of the conductor with respect to temperature. (The temperature coefficient of resistance, TCR is available for most metals, alloys, and many elements.)

Type K and J thermocouples can measure temperatures into the 1200°C to 1300°C range but are approaching the melting point of the sensor at higher temperatures. In the development portion of the reversed biased LED optical pyrometer project, the transformation of the curved data depicted in Figures 4-51 and 4-52 into that in 4-53 presents a method to gauge temperatures in the 1150°C to 1900°C range. Although the smooth curve depicted in Figure 4-52 is readable between 1400°C and 1900°C, the rate of change of discharge time and temperature between 1400°C and 1150°C is large and poorly defined. The natural log plotting of the discharge time vs. temperature in Figure 4-53 is far more definitive and precise.

Listings 4-5 and 4-4 measure the discharge time of one or more LEDs that have been reversed biased to collect a specific color of light. The decay time of the discharge is inversely proportional to the amount of light collected. A larger collection of light creates a bigger charge and a shorter discharge time in which plots of discharge time and temperature, as seen in Figures 4-51 and 4-52, are concave downward.

Listing 4-5 measures the microprocessor ADC voltage difference as a charged reverse biased LED discharges. Recalling that Q, the charge on a capacitor, is equal to the product of capacitance and voltage, a larger charge stored in the PN junction creates a larger ADC value on discharge. Plots of temperature vs. ADC counts are concave upward, as seen in Figures 4-55 to Figures 4-58.

Figures 4-55 and 4-56 demonstrate the slightly different sensitivities of clear and colored LEDs. The curve depicted in Figure 4-55 created by exposing a clear green epoxy reverse biased diode to the heated filament at 1430°C produces an ADC count of 200. A colored green reverse biased diode produces an ADC count of 200 at 1530°C.

The temperature scales in Figures 4-51, 4-55, 4-57, and 4-58 indicate that with the reverse biased LEDs, you should use the non-contact measurement method for temperatures approximately 550°C to 2200°C.

Non-ohmic resistance is presented in the discussion for this topic because of its importance to the generation of artificial lighting by way of electrically powered incandescent filaments. Incandescent tungsten filaments are used as a primary light source in light bulbs at an approximate temperature of 2700°C. Quartz iodine lamps also use a tungsten filament combined with iodine to redeposit evaporated tungsten as the tungsten filament temperature is raised an additional 250°C to approximately 2950°C for a brighter light with illumination characteristics closer to that of daylight.

Tungsten has the highest melting point of all the metal elements at 3695°K, 3422°C, or 6182°F. Tungsten metal has a temperature coefficient of resistance of 0.004403. Its high melting point allows approximate temperature calculations from metal resistance values over the temperature range of interest. Numerous numerical analysis techniques improve the accuracy of the simpler temperature-resistance approximation presented in this work.[1]

Ohm's law defines a fixed relationship between the current flow in a conductor, the conductor resistance, and the voltage impressed upon the system for a constant temperature. Resistance changes with the temperature. In fine tungsten filament conductors, a large change in resistance can be realized by heating the wire.

In Figure 4-4, the distinct change of slope as the filament begins to emit light as a visible red glow marks the point at which it could be said that the filament resistance is transitioning from an ohmic to a non-ohmic type of behavior.

In Figures 4-43 and 4-44, the apparent ohmic type behavior of the relatively cool filament has been taken to advantage by using only low current and voltage power applications to accurately determine the fractional ohm ambient temperature resistance of the tiny filament needed for temperature resistance approximations.

With a reasonable value for the small tungsten filament resistance, a correlation can be established between the filament resistance when heated with a controlled power input and the filament temperature as tabulated in Table 4-4 and displayed in Figures 4-46 and 4-47. An ability to control the heat applied to the filament and knowledge of the resulting temperature of the emitted radiation from that heated filament allows the demonstration of the basic radiated energy quantization explanation of black-body radiation through selected color light sensing with reverse biased LEDs.

An array of reverse biased, different colored LEDs, wired as depicted in Figure 4-45, assembled into an array as seen in Figure 4-49, then encased in the exposure chamber as depicted in Figure 4-48 demonstrates black-body radiation quantization. Experiments are begun at ambient conditions with no power being applied to the Sylvania/Osram 1156 lamp filament. At this point, the diode array output should all be indicating the empirically determined, maximum, 30,000-unit time count. An incremental increase in the power supply voltage powering the filament is implemented. After a short time, when the filament voltage and current have stabilized, the filament voltage and current power readings are recorded along with the reverse biased PN junction discharge time counts on each of the diode array elements. The data collection process is continued

---

[1]"Calibration and temperature profile of a tungsten filament lamp" Charles de Izarre and Jean-Michel Gitton, *Eur. J. Physics.* 31(2010).

until the filament is at full power. The data reduction process consists of entering the recorded power settings and individual averaged diode time counts into a spreadsheet as configured in Figure 4-59.

Flmnt V	Flmnt i	Flmnt R	Flmnt Tmp	Red	Amber	Yellow	Green
2.91	1.04	=B4/C4	=20.3+((((D4/0.46)-1))/0.004403)	26385			
3.06	1.066	=B5/C5	=20.3+((((D5/0.46)-1))/0.004403)	18881			
3.25	1.095	=B6/C6	=20.3+((((D6/0.46)-1))/0.004403)	15259	22483	25907	
3.41	1.12	=B7/C7	=20.3+((((D7/0.46)-1))/0.004403)	10536	17457	19657	
3.53	1.14	=B8/C8	=20.3+((((D8/0.46)-1))/0.004403)	8739	14801	15519	
3.74	1.17	=B9/C9	=20.3+((((D9/0.46)-1))/0.004403)	7477	9212	11700	23692
3.89	1.19	=B10/C10	=20.3+((((D10/0.46)-1))/0.004403)	5375	7896	8906	16621
4.04	1.214	=B11/C11	=20.3+((((D11/0.46)-1))/0.004403)	4608	5959	7800	13497
4.18	1.235	=B12/C12	=20.3+((((D12/0.46)-1))/0.004403)	3701	5510	5957	11555
4.4	1.265	=B13/C13	=20.3+((((D13/0.46)-1))/0.004403)	2607	4275	4424	8700
4.56	1.289	=B14/C14	=20.3+((((D14/0.46)-1))/0.004403)	2165	3318	3710	6600
4.72	1.311	=B15/C15	=20.3+((((D15/0.46)-1))/0.004403)	1871	2832	3028	5609
4.85	1.29	=B16/C16	=20.3+((((D16/0.46)-1))/0.004403)	1636	2455	2531	4880
5.1	1.362	=B17/C17	=20.3+((((D17/0.46)-1))/0.004403)	1294	1942	1996	3653
5.23	1.38	=B18/C18	=20.3+((((D18/0.46)-1))/0.004403)	1134	1685	1740	3067
5.39	1.4	=B19/C19	=20.3+((((D19/0.46)-1))/0.004403)	978	1401	1486	2640
5.6	1.429	=B20/C20	=20.3+((((D20/0.46)-1))/0.004403)	739	1306	1166	2266
5.76	1.449	=B21/C21	=20.3+((((D21/0.46)-1))/0.004403)	717	1035	1054	1844
5.92	1.472	=B22/C22	=20.3+((((D22/0.46)-1))/0.004403)	615	898	910	1586
6.08	1.49	=B23/C23	=20.3+((((D23/0.46)-1))/0.004403)	549	798	807	1397
6.31	1.518	=B24/C24	=20.3+((((D24/0.46)-1))/0.004403)	463	666	676	1157
6.43	1.532	=B25/C25	=20.3+((((D25/0.46)-1))/0.004403)	423	613	518	1052

Figure 4-59. *Data reduction spreadsheet for reverse biased led exposure to black-body radiation*

Table 4-5 contains the temperatures at which the emitted black-body radiation can create a photocurrent in the nominal reverse biased diodes. If the emitted wavelength of the radiation is such that its energy is too low to excite electrons in the colored PN junction, then the diode does not respond to the filament emissions. As the filament power is increased and the temperature on the filament is raised, the diodes are activated in the red, orange/amber, yellow, green, and blue sequence in accordance with their PN junction conduction initiation voltage. A simple explanation for the observed diode behavior is that the emitted radiation is quantized for the temperature at which it is emitted.

Reverse biased infrared and ultraviolet diodes respond to radiation emitted at filament temperatures below and above the reds and blues of the visible spectrum.

The gentle continuous curvature of the ADC counts and the calculated filament temperature provide a means of non-contact measuring of the hot surface temperature under constant defined conditions either through a table look-up or trend-line calculation method. Each diode used as an optical temperature sensor must be calibrated, as seen in Table 4-3.

A certain amount of experimentation is needed to select the best diode for use over a temperature range. The correct size of the increments of voltage or current applied to the filament that produces a final correlation plot with the gentle curvature or linearity permitting reasonably accurate estimations of the hot surface temperature from ADC response must be determined experimentally for the system at hand. Diode-emitter surface distances must be fixed during both calibration and experimental measurement. You must remember that most diodes are epoxy-encapsulated and heat-sensitive.

Lighting by Fluorescence

Much of the artificial lighting used for illumination in modern usage depends upon the process of fluorescence. Fluorescence is the emission of light by a material or substance that has absorbed light or other electromagnetic radiation. The energy-absorbing material is often called *phosphor*. Fluorescence has been used for many years as a more energy-efficient form of creating artificial illumination. An electric current passed through a glass tube containing argon gas, and a trace of mercury causes the emission of the strong mercury 254 nm radiation. The mercury radiation is absorbed by a phosphor coating on the inside of the tube and re-emitted as a mix of colors that the eye perceives as white light. White light LEDs also use various phosphor materials to transform an initial strong diode emission such as blue into a mix of colors perceived by the eye as white light. Filamented, fluorescent, and solid-state white lights are all seen as having a different effect on colors than daylight, with the LEDs being deemed the closest to daylight rendition.

Computer Imaging

Humans are visually oriented. A recurring theme in this book is the value of a real-time graphical display of numerical data to aid in the comprehension of phenomenon by visually observing for data trending. Images collected sequentially in various time frames then replayed in rates compatible with human comprehension reveal events missed in "real time". Mathematical examinations of the differences in the numerical values that make up the images can lead to computer emulation of human-like visual comprehension.

Remote imaging allows the observation of events and phenomena that would not be possible with a human presence or in environments that would not sustain a human presence.

In this basic experiment, the equipment is limited to the readily available and inexpensive RPi computer, simple web cameras, and open source software such as the Python programming language and the CV computer vision projects

Experiment

The RPi is based upon smartphone integrated circuitry. It can accommodate a digital camera peripheral. A Python library has been written for interfacing directly with the Raspberry Pi Foundation's picamera and software adaptations to interface with many other USB web cameras.

An open source project on computer vision began in the late 1990s. It is available at the OpenCV web site (http://opencv.org). A useful Python derivative is called SimpleCV. It can be used as an image capture, processing, and interpretation facility.

There are three image capture and display libraries readily available for download onto the RPi. The libraries are known as fswebcam (Figure 4-60), the picamera software from the Raspberry Pi Foundation, and SimpleCV from the OpenCV project.

All three software packages can be downloaded to the RPi. There are tutorials and supporting documentation online. The three packages are ordered in the degree of difficulty in use and the availability of power and flexibility.

Simple CV requires the downloading of several dependencies. At the time of writing, there were several versions of the procedure to be used. The following commands were successful for my RPi after the regular update and upgrade operations.

```
$ sudo apt-get install ipython python-opencv python-scipy
$ sudo apt-get install python-numpy python-setuptools python pip
$ sudo pip install svgwrite
Then SimpleCV is installed with;
$ sudo pip install https://github.com/sightmachine/SimpleCV/zipball/master
```

The package is approximately 54 MB and may take several minutes to complete the download. A USB camera can be connected to the system and the software activated with the SimpleCV command entry to bring up the console depicted in Figure 4-61.

SimpleCV tutorials are at SimpleCV.org. They should be reviewed by anyone not familiar with computer vision and the software. Figure 4-61 illustrates the four command-line instructions to collect and display a USB camera image.

Figure 4-60. *A fswebcam image*

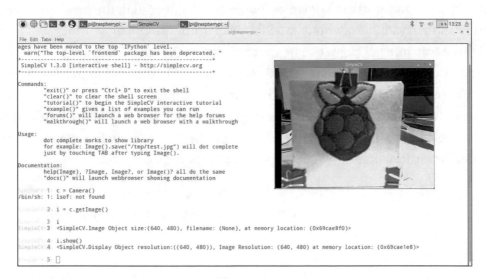

Figure 4-61. *A SimpleCV console session and captured image*

Discussion

The fswebcam package is a relatively simple software package that handles webcams compatible with the Linux operating system. Figures 4-60 and 4-61 were taken with a Logitech VUBM46 2Mp Auto Focus webcam.

The software downloads quickly and is simple to use with a limited image editing capability. A USB webcam can capture a single image, as depicted in Figure 4-60. The banner can be eliminated or edited, the image resolution adjusted, and time-lapsed sequences taken using the Linux cron time management facility.

The picamera is an image collecting device and software package from the Raspberry Pi Foundation. The camera is connected to the graphics processing unit (GPU) of the RPi with a short ribbon cable. The GPU takes some of the computation load required for image processing out of the CPU. USB webcam data is processed only by the CPU. Although the image processing should be faster with the dedicated picamera the ribbon cable is physically restricting while USB webcam locations are virtually unrestricted.

After the mechanical installation of the picamera the RPi must be re-configured to recognize the camera in the RPi configuration window. The window in Figure 1-16 and the camera selection box in Figure 1-17 in Chapter 1 are accessed from the PIXEL desktop main menu Preferences entry. The camera selection is enabled in the Interfaces tab, as seen in Figure 1-17. The Pi must be rebooted after the camera is enabled.

The Python camera control software allows for camera image capture, recording simple soundless video, 30 ms time-lapse photography, and various image-editing effects in both still and video images.

OpenCV is a computer vision project in which the computer can "see" through examining the differences between the numerical data files that make up images. Image files can be large, and examining the differences in the numerical values can become computationally intensive. Significant computing power must be available.

OpenCV is written in C and C++. SimpleCV is a *Python wrapper*. It is written around the OpenCV computer vision code.

Figure 4-61 is a screenshot of a minimal console session able to capture and display a Logitech web camera image. A tutorial at SimpleCV.org covers the following topics; basics of installation, interacting with the display, loading a directory of images, macros, binary vision, timing, monitoring changes in space or the field of view, manipulating or editing images, image arithmetic, and overlaying or layering images.

A series of computer vision exercises involving counting coins, motion detection, and facial recognition using SimpleCV are discussed in Chapter 8 of the *Raspberry Pi Cookboo*k by Simon Monk (O'Reilly Media, 2019).

Code Listings

Listing 4-1. Arduino Moving Average Digital Signal Processing Code

```
// Moving Averages Apr.3/11
// The size of the averaged array is numReadings
//
const int numReadings = 10;
//
int readings[numReadings];    // the number of readings collected from the
                                 analog input
int index = 0;                // the indexing value
int long total = 0;           // the running total
int average = 0;              // the average

int inputPin = A0;            //sensor input at Analogue Input 0

void setup()
{
  // initialize serial communications with computer:
  Serial.begin(9600);
  // initialize all the readings to 0:
  for (int thisReading = 0; thisReading < numReadings; thisReading++)
  readings[thisReading] = 0;
}

void loop() {
  // subtract the last reading:
  total = total - readings[index];
  // read from the sensor:
  readings[index] = analogRead(inputPin);
  // add the reading to the total:
  total = total + readings[index];
  // advance to the next position in the array:
  index = index + 1;
  // if at the end of the array..
```

```
if (index >= numReadings)
// .. wrap around to the beginning:
index = 0;

// calculate the average:
average = total / numReadings;
// send it to the computer (as ASCII digits)
Serial.println(average);
// SLOW THE ARDUINO TRANSMISSION DOWN
delay(100);
}
```

Listing 4-2. DAQFactory sequence code Electro-optics autotest

```
// "Electro-Optics Auto Test", Feb. 15, 2012.Rvn 2 Feb. 18/12 This sequence
// programs the power applied to the light source and detection system under
// test. The program is driven by a variable valued counter in a for loop.
// A page has been created on which the output from the photo detector is
// displayed in both graphical and numerical format. A manual slider
// control and spin button allow manual setting of the voltage delivered to
// the source device under test. Edit boxes, with a start button and
// variable value read outs on the page provide single or multiple
// cycling of the test protocol between selected voltage variables as
// determined by entries into the various button activated edit boxes.
// The time delay between increments is set at 10 seconds by default.
// Alterations to the time delay can be made by changing the value in the
// source code Delay () statement.
//
global VltgVlu = 0      // the value of the voltage being applied to the
                        //     device under test
global Start            // the initial voltage applied to the DUT
global Increment        // the voltage increment for each iteration
global cycles           // the number of program repeats
//
```

```
for (private.counter = 0, counter < cycles, counter ++)
//
VltgVlu = Start
//
while (VltgVlu)
//
   AppldVltg = VltgVlu     //AppldVltg is the digital to analog output
                           channel 0 ie. AO 0 on the LabJack
//
   delay (10)                // the timed interval
//
   VltgVlu = VltgVlu + Increment    // the applied voltage value is
                                    incremented
//
   if (VltgVlu > 5)    // the value of the incrementing voltage variable is
                       tested and if at the upper limit
      VltgVlu = 0       // of the range available the variable is reset to
                        zero terminating the while loop
   endif
   endwhile
//
AppldVltg = 0
VltgVlu = 0
Endfor
```

Listing 4-2a. DAQFactory sequence code to transmit RGB data on the serial port in use

```
// RGB Serial Transmission    Mar. 4, 2012
//The code serially transmits the desired RGB values.
//
//
global RedVlu
global BluVlu
global GrnVlu
//
```

```
//
device.Comm3.write("r")
device.Comm3.Write(RedVlu)
device.Comm3.Write(",")
device.Comm3.Write("b")
device.Comm3.Write(BluVlu)
device.Comm3.Write(",")
device.Comm3.Write("g")
device.Comm3.Write(GrnVlu)
```

Listing 4-2b. DAQFactory sequence code to shut off power to RGB diode

```
// Source Off Mar. 4, 2012
// The code transmits 0 for all three colour values to
// turn the tricolour LED Off.
//
device.Comm3.Write("r")
device.Comm3.Write(0)
device.Comm3.Write(",")
device.Comm3.Write("b")
device.Comm3.Write(0)
device.Comm3.Write(",")
device.Comm3.Write("g")
device.Comm3.Write(0)
```

Listing 4-3. Arduino Code for RGB LED Control

```
// CdS_RGB_DAQF_Serial_Photometer  Mar. 5, 2012
// A two-way serial link connects a DAQF control screen to an optical bench
// or photometer. The source wavelength is selected by choosing the RGB
// components from the control screen and transmitting the selection
// serially to the Arduino powering the LED. Once the source is lit the CdS
// response is read and serially transmitted back to the control screen for
// display. The CdS is in a 10K ohm voltage divider configuration biased
// with 5 volts. A moving average smoothing program is used to improve the
```

```
// data streamed out to the DAQFactory control screen display. To set/select
// source colour & intensity enter values between 0 - 255 in Edit Boxes
// of the DAQF Photometer control screen. For code usage without the
// DAQFactory GUI enter the desired data into the serial monitor send box as
// "r nnn,g nnn,b nn".
//
//
// LED on pins 9, 10, and 11 with 470 ohm CLR. Det on 5v gnd and analog
   input A0
//
char buffer[18]; // max length of buffer
int red, green, blue;
int RedPin = 11;
int GreenPin = 10;
int BluePin = 9;
// global variable declarations
long totalCnt = 0;
long avrg = 0;
int ttcntr = 0;

void setup()
{
    Serial.begin(9600);
    Serial.flush(); // clear the line of any characters
    pinMode(RedPin, OUTPUT);
    pinMode(GreenPin, OUTPUT);
    pinMode(BluePin, OUTPUT);
}
void loop()
{
   if (Serial.available() > 0) {  //as soon as characters arrive
    // start the following code
        int index = 0; // array index
        delay(100); // let the buffer fill up
```

```
    int numChar = Serial.available(); // character count input
  // plus the NULL on the end.
   if (numChar > 15) {
     numChar = 15;
   }
   while (numChar--) {  // post decrement operator
     buffer[index++] = Serial.read();
   }
   splitString(buffer); // turns source LED ON
 }
//
//
//
//times ten averaging code
ttcntr = ttcntr + 1;
if (ttcntr <= 10) {
  totalCnt = totalCnt + analogRead(0);
 }
 else {
   avrg = totalCnt/10;
     Serial.println(avrg);
     delay(250); // slow down loop
   // zero or re-zero counters and accumulating sum
   ttcntr = 0;
   totalCnt = 0;
 }
}
void splitString(char* data)  {
//Serial.print("Data entered: ");
//Serial.println(data);
  char* parameter;
  parameter = strtok (data, ",");
  while (parameter != NULL)  {
    setLED(parameter);
    parameter = strtok (NULL, ",");
  }
```

```
      // clear the text and serial buffers
      for (int x=0; x<16; x++) {
        buffer[x] = '\0';
      }
      Serial.flush();
}

void setLED(char* data) {
  if ((data[0] == 'r') || (data[0] == 'R')) {
    int Ans = strtol(data+1, NULL, 10);
    Ans = constrain(Ans, 0, 255);
    analogWrite(RedPin, Ans);  // red LED ON
//  Serial.print("Red is set to: ");
//  Serial.println(Ans);
  }
  if ((data[0] == 'g') || (data[0] == 'G')) {
    int Ans = strtol(data+1, NULL, 10);
    Ans = constrain(Ans, 0, 255);
    analogWrite(GreenPin, Ans);  // Grn LED ON
//  Serial.print("Green is set to: ");
//  Serial.println(Ans);
  }
  if ((data[0] == 'b') || (data[0] == 'B')) {
    int Ans = strtol(data+1, NULL, 10);
    Ans = constrain(Ans, 0, 255);
    analogWrite(BluePin, Ans);  // Bl LED ON
//  Serial.print("Blue is set to: ");
//  Serial.println(Ans);
  }
}
```

Listing 4-3a. A Simple Arduino RGB LED Diode Controller

```
//Serial Control of RGB LEDs
//Input 3 integers between the value of 0 and 255 the PWM limits from the
//serial port. The comma separated values are for the red, green and blue
//colour contributions. The colour values and detector response to the
//emitted light are printed back to the serial port.
//
char buffer[18]; // max length of buffer
#define red 11
#define green 10
#define blue 9
//
int tred = 0;
int tgreen = 0;
int tblue = 0;
int analogPin = 0;
int reading = 0;
//
//
void setup() {
  pinMode(red, OUTPUT);
  pinMode(green, OUTPUT);
  pinMode(blue, OUTPUT);
  Serial.begin(9600);
  color(0,0,0); // call the colour creation function
}
//
void loop()
{
    if (Serial.available() > 0) {  //as soon as characters arrive
    //
    tred = Serial.parseInt();
    tgreen = Serial.parseInt();
    tblue = Serial.parseInt();
    color(tred,tgreen,tblue);
```

```
    Serial.println("red " + (String)tred + " green " + (String)tgreen +
    " blue " + (String)tblue);
    // read the detector value
    int reading = analogRead(analogPin);
    Serial.print(reading);
    }
  }
//
void color(int cred, int cgreen, int cblue){
  analogWrite(red, cred);
  analogWrite(green, cgreen);
  analogWrite(blue, cblue);
}
```

Listing 4-4. Arduino Code for Reverse Bias LED Light Collection

```
// A six wavelength, reverse biased LED, electromagnetic spectrograph.
// 6 different colour LEDs are reverse biased on the digital pins of
// Arduino to form a diode array. 5 vlts to shrt cthd, anode to gnd through
// a current limit resistor 100 Ohm. Dig pins revrs bias diode, collect
// photon charge for timed period on pn junction capacitor then time
// discharge time. In photodiode mode, more light makes diode conductive
// and shortens time to discharge thru 100 ohm.
//
// Identify diodes in pin assignment definitions and in serial monitor
// output code
//
// define Arduino pin assignments
#define LED1_n_side 2    // first diode anode (long lead)      Blue
#define LED1_p_side 3    // first diode cathode (short lead/flat case +
                            resistor)
#define LED2_n_side 4    // second diode anode (long lead)     Green
#define LED2_p_side 5    // second diode cathode (short lead/flat case +
                            resistor)
```

```
#define LED3_n_side 6     // third diode anode (long lead)      Yellow
#define LED3_p_side 7     // third diode cathode (short lead/flat case +
                             resistor)
#define LED4_n_side 8     // fourth diode anode (long lead)     Amber/Orange
#define LED4_p_side 9     // fourth diode cathode (short lead/flat case +
                             resistor)
#define LED5_n_side 10    // fifth diode anode (long lead)        Red
#define LED5_p_side 11    // fifth diode cathode (short lead/flat case +
                             resistor)
#define LED6_n_side 12    // sixth diode anode (long lead)
                          UV or Infrared Emitter
#define LED6_p_side 13    // sixth diode cathode (short lead/flat case +
                             resistor)
//
void setup() {
  Serial.begin(9600);  // start serial port for display
}
void loop() {
  unsigned int j; // declare time counter index for first diode
  unsigned int k; // declare 2nd counter index for second diode
  unsigned int l; // declare 3rd counter index for third diode
  unsigned int m; // declare 4th counter index for fourth diode
  unsigned int n; // declare 5th counter index for fifth diode
  unsigned int o; // declare 6th counter index for sixth diode
  //
  // first diode readout
  //
  //
  // Apply reverse voltage and allow LED-Capacitor to charge
  pinMode(LED1_n_side, OUTPUT);
  pinMode(LED1_p_side, OUTPUT);
  digitalWrite(LED1_n_side, HIGH);
  digitalWrite(LED1_p_side, LOW);
```

```
//isolate the cathode-shrt end of the diode by changing it from
// OUTPUT HIGH to INPUT LOW (high impedance input with internal
// pull-up resistor off)
pinMode(LED1_n_side, INPUT);
digitalWrite(LED1_n_side, LOW);  //turn off internal pull-up resistor
//count time to discharge cathode-shrt charge to logic 0
for (j = 0; j < 30000; j++){
//Serial.println(j);  // diagnostic for debug
if(digitalRead(LED1_n_side) == 0)break;
}
// int avg_timeCnt[jc] += timeCnt[jc]/avrg;
int timeCnt1 = j;
//
//  Second diode readout
//
// Apply reverse voltage and allow LED-Capacitor to charge
pinMode(LED2_n_side, OUTPUT);
pinMode(LED2_p_side, OUTPUT);
digitalWrite(LED2_n_side, HIGH);
digitalWrite(LED2_p_side, LOW);
//isolate the cathode-shrt end of the diode by changing it from
// OUTPUT HIGH to INPUT LOW (high impedance input with internal
// pull-up resistor off)
pinMode(LED2_n_side, INPUT);
digitalWrite(LED2_n_side, LOW);  //turn off internal pull-up resistor
//count time to discharge cathode-shrt charge to logic 0
for (k = 0; k < 30000; k++){
//Serial.print(k,DEC);  // diagnostic for debug
if(digitalRead(LED2_n_side) == 0)break;
}
int timeCnt2 = k;
//Serial.print("Green = ");
//Serial.println(timeCnt2,DEC);
//
```

```
//    third diode readout
//
// Apply reverse voltage and allow LED-Capacitor to charge
  pinMode(LED3_n_side, OUTPUT);
  pinMode(LED3_p_side, OUTPUT);
  digitalWrite(LED3_n_side, HIGH);
  digitalWrite(LED3_p_side, LOW);
  //isolate the cathode-shrt end of the diode by changing it from
  // OUTPUT HIGH to INPUT LOW (high impedance input with internal
  // pull-up resistor off)
  pinMode(LED3_n_side, INPUT);
  digitalWrite(LED3_n_side, LOW);  //turn off internal pull-up resistor
  //count time to discharge cathode-shrt charge to logic 0
for (l = 0; l < 30000; l++){
  //Serial.print(l,DEC);  // diagnostic for debug
  if(digitalRead(LED3_n_side) == 0)break;
}
int timeCnt3 = l;
//Serial.print("Yellow = ");
//Serial.println(timeCnt3,DEC);
//
//    fourth diode readout
//
// Apply reverse voltage and allow LED-Capacitor to charge
  pinMode(LED4_n_side, OUTPUT);
  pinMode(LED4_p_side, OUTPUT);
  digitalWrite(LED4_n_side, HIGH);
  digitalWrite(LED4_p_side, LOW);
  //isolate the cathode-shrt end of the diode by changing it from
  // OUTPUT HIGH to INPUT LOW (high impedance input with internal
  // pull-up resistor off)
  pinMode(LED4_n_side, INPUT);
  digitalWrite(LED4_n_side, LOW);  //turn off internal pull-up resistor
  //count time to discharge cathode-shrt charge to logic 0
```

```
for (m = 0; m < 30000; m++){
  //Serial.print(m,DEC);  // diagnostic for debug
  if(digitalRead(LED4_n_side) == 0)break;
}
int timeCnt4 = m;
//Serial.print("Amber = ");
//Serial.println(timeCnt4,DEC); // diagnostic for debug
//
//     fifth diode readout
//
// Apply reverse voltage and allow LED-Capacitor to charge
  pinMode(LED5_n_side, OUTPUT);
  pinMode(LED5_p_side, OUTPUT);
  digitalWrite(LED5_n_side, HIGH);
  digitalWrite(LED5_p_side, LOW);
  //isolate the cathode-shrt end of the diode by changing it from
  // OUTPUT HIGH to INPUT LOW (high impedance input with internal
  // pull-up resistor off)
  pinMode(LED5_n_side, INPUT);
  digitalWrite(LED5_n_side, LOW);  //turn off internal pull-up resistor
  //count time to discharge cathode-shrt charge to logic 0
for (n = 0; n < 30000; n++){
  //Serial.print(n,DEC);  // diagnostic for debug
  if(digitalRead(LED5_n_side) == 0)break;
}
int timeCnt5 = n;
//
//     sixth diode readout
//
// Apply reverse voltage and allow LED-Capacitor to charge
  pinMode(LED6_n_side, OUTPUT);
  pinMode(LED6_p_side, OUTPUT);
  digitalWrite(LED6_n_side, HIGH);
  digitalWrite(LED6_p_side, LOW);
```

```
  //isolate the cathode-shrt end of the diode by changing it from
  // OUTPUT HIGH to INPUT LOW (high impedance input with internal
  // pull-up resistor off)
  pinMode(LED6_n_side, INPUT);
  digitalWrite(LED6_n_side, LOW);  //turn off internal pull-up resistor
  //count time to discharge cathode-shrt charge to logic 0
for (o = 0; o < 30000; o++){
  //Serial.print(o,DEC);  // diagnostic for debug
  if(digitalRead(LED6_n_side) == 0)break;
}
int timeCnt6 = o;
//
//
// data output
//
//Horizontal data display
Serial.print("Blue = ");
Serial.print(timeCnt1, DEC);
Serial.print("  ");
Serial.print("Green = ");
Serial.print(timeCnt2, DEC);
Serial.print("  ");
Serial.print("Yellow = ");
Serial.print(timeCnt3,DEC);
Serial.print("  ");
Serial.print("Amber = ");
Serial.print(timeCnt4,DEC);
Serial.print("  ");
Serial.print("Red = ");
Serial.print(timeCnt5,DEC);
Serial.print("  ");
Serial.print("I-Rd = ");
Serial.println(timeCnt6,DEC);
}
```

Listing 4-5. An Arduino single reverse bias diode light sensor using discharge
voltage difference to measure incident light

```
// Single LED Light Sensor
// Light sensed with A0 voltage measurement of discharge of reverse
// biased LED thru 220 ohm resistor. Anode to pin 2 (long lead)
// cathode (short lead) to A0.
//
// define variables
byte anodePin = 2;                    // led anode pin connection
byte cathodePin = 14;                 // A5 digital pin number
int vltg_s = 0;                       // starting voltage
int vltg_f = 0;                       // final voltage
//
void setup() {
  // global disable pull up resistors
  _SFR_IO8(0x35) |= 0x10;
digitalWrite(anodePin, LOW);          // initialize pin as low on output
                                         declaration

pinMode(anodePin, OUTPUT);            // declare anode pin as output
pinMode(cathodePin, INPUT);           // declare cathode as input
//
Serial.begin(9600);                   // start serial port
//
}
void loop() {
  digitalWrite(anodePin, HIGH);       // configure pins
  pinMode(cathodePin, OUTPUT);        // to turn led on
  digitalWrite(cathodePin, LOW);      // discharging capacitor residual
  //
  // allow led to accumulate charge
  digitalWrite(cathodePin, HIGH);
  digitalWrite(anodePin, LOW);
  // put cathode into measuring state
```

```
pinMode(cathodePin, INPUT);
// read initial voltage level
vltg_s = analogRead(14);
// set led discharge time
delay(30);
//
vltg_f = analogRead(14);   // read the voltage after discharge
//
pinMode(cathodePin, OUTPUT);
digitalWrite(cathodePin, LOW);
Serial.println(vltg_s - vltg_f);
}
```

Summary

Modern light-sensitive solid-state electronics and integrated circuitry can interact with the visible light portion of the electromagnetic spectrum and a small portion of the longer and shorter wavelength radiation found in the near infrared and near ultraviolet.

Solid-state electronics, simple optical benches, and SCADA software systems are configured into spectroscopic measurement systems for colorimetric analysis.

PN junctions and their general methods of construction and opto-electronic interactions and applications were presented.

Reverse biased LED devices are used as qualitative and quantitative color selective light sensors to demonstrate a basic concept of quantum physics and a practical application in astronomy.

Artificial illumination techniques, the concepts of color temperature, and introductory computer vision were discussed briefly.

Less complex methods for measuring magnetic fields are presented in Chapter 5.

Magnetics, Magnetoresistance, and Hall Effects

For millennia, pieces of naturally occurring magnetic minerals have been used to determine direction during journeys over land and sea. In the 1800s, the relationships between electric current flow and electromagnetism were distinguished from natural magnetism in minerals. The creation of electromagnetism then led to the explanation of the observed forces of attraction or repulsion created by magnetic poles.

Applications such as spinning magnetic fields are the source of most of our electrical energy. Magnetically driven motors convert that energy into mechanical actions that form a large part of present-day technology. The focus of this section is on the measurement of magnetic field strengths.

The Hall effect and magnetoresistance are two important physical phenomena that measure magnetic field strengths.

In 1892, the Hall effect was discovered involving magnetic fields' effect on currents moving through conductors. The Hall effect remained a laboratory novelty until the development of semiconductor materials enabled the effect to measure magnetic field strengths.

The second important phenomenon discovered is *magnetoresistance*, which is the variation in the resistance of conductors under the influence of magnetic fields.

There are numerous techniques for measuring both high- and low-level magnetic fields, as depicted in Figure 4-1. The main portion of the following text centers on readily available, less expensive, magnetic field measurement integrated circuitry involving the Hall effect or magnetoresistance.

© Richard J. Smythe 2022
R. J. Smythe, *Arduino Measurements in Science*, https://doi.org/10.1007/978-1-4842-6781-3_5

Measurements of very low-level magnetic field strength usually involve complex and expensive apparatus that are beyond the introductory nature of this book. Extensive information on low-level magnetic field detection is available in the literature.

Integrated circuitry to measure magnetic fields is predominately available in surface mount technology. SMT devices are used on breakout boards and are manufactured and sold by several suppliers.

Although magnetic fields arise from the actions of electrons it has been traditional to use two notations to completely describe magnetic field strengths. Induced magnetic fields the subject of Ampere's and Biot-Savart discoveries are represented by the vector quantity symbol **B**. When an induced magnetic field envelops a mass of material a new magnetic field results that is represented by the vector quantity symbol **H**. Both **H** and **B** have the units of ampere/meter. **B** and **H** can only be equal in a vacuum since they differ when a material able to augment or decrement the strength of the induced magnetic field is present. Substances that can increase or concentrate the lines of magnetic flux are called *paramagnetic*. Those that dilute or spread apart the lines are called *diamagnetic*. (For rigorous mathematical considerations, the quantities are vectors).

A measure of magnetic field strength in the centimeter-gram-second (CGS) system is called an *oersted* (Oe). An oersted exists when two like poles of two identical magnets placed one centimeter apart cause a repelling force of one dyne. In the International Standard system of units, an oersted is equal to $(1000/4\pi) \times (A/m)$, where A is amperes and m is meters.

A similar measure of *electromagnetic* field strength is an infinitely long wire wound into a coil of a fixed number of turns per meter carries one ampere of current. The magnetic field at the center of the coil is then described in amps per meter. The force and current based measures are related by the ratio 1 A/m = 79.58 Oe.

Magnetic field strength can be visualized in terms of magnetic field lines. The more lines there are in a given area, the stronger the field. The number of field lines in a fixed area is called the *magnetic flux*, and the unit of magnetic flux in terms of square meters is called a *tesla*. Tesla = $kg/A \times s^2$ or $V \times s/m^2$ (in SI units of kilogram, amperes, and seconds).

The properties of static and induced magnetic fields are defined and expressed in various units, as detailed in Table 5-1.

Table 5-1. *Magnetic Field Strengths*

Unit System	Magnetic Induction B	Magnetic Field H
SI units	tesla: 1 T = 1 V×s/m²	A/m
Traditional	gauss: 1 G = 10⁻⁴ T	oersted: 1 Oe = (10³ / 4π) × A/m

	mT (tesla)	G (gauss)	kA/m	Oe (oersted)
1 mT	= 1.000	= 10.000	= 0.7960	= 10.000
1 G	= 0.1000	= 1.000	= 0.0796	= 1.000
1 kA/m	= 1.2560	= 12.560	= 1.000	= 12.560
1 Oe	= 0.1000	= 1.000	= 0.0796	= 1.000

You may say that a current flowing in a wire creates a magnetic field in the air, which is represented by the symbol **B**. If the electromagnetic field envelops a material and a change in field strength results, the new entity is represented by the symbol **H** and it can be written that $B = \mu_0 \times H$. μ_0 is a proportionality constant called *magnetic permeability*. μ_0 can vary from unity in air or vacuum to more than 1000 for soft iron materials. Recall that **H** and **B** are vector units consisting of the magnitude of the force and its direction.

Ampere's law relates the magnitude of **B** to the current flow in the conductor that determines the value of **H** when the electromagnetic field is manipulated by coiling a conductor around an iron core.

Solenoid is the term introduced in 1832 by Andre-Marie Ampere to describe a tightly wound helical coil of conductor used to form a homogeneous electromagnetic field within the coiled wire cylinder when current is passed through the helix.

Field strengths within the solenoid are estimated with the following expression,

$$B = \mu_0(n)I$$

where μ_0 is the magnetic permeability of air, n is the number of wire turns per unit of length and I is the current through the coil.

By forming an iron core solenoid and powering the coil with a varying current, it is possible to create a variable magnetic field and, with a magnetic material, convert between electrical current, magnetic field strengths, and mechanical motion.

Field strengths can be determined by numerous methods depending on the fields' strengths to be measured, as depicted in Figure 5-1.

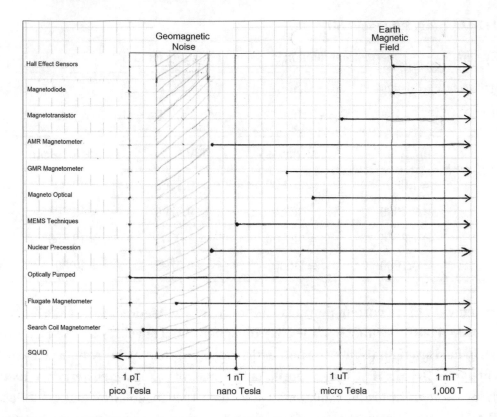

Figure 5-1. *Range of detection for magnetic field measurements*

Many of the measurement methods or techniques depicted in Figure 5-1 are complex implementations involving cryogenic coolants, sophisticated electronics, and research-grade medical or physical laboratory facilities.

A summary of various instrumentations and units of measurement are available at en.wikipedia.org/wiki/Orders_of_magnitude_(magnetic_field). You can also refer to "Magnetic Sensors and Their Applications" by J. Lenz and S. Edelstein in *IEEE Sensors Journal* (Vol. 6, No. 3) if greater detail is needed.

Three of the more common and easily implemented magnetic field measurement techniques involve differences in physical phenomena created by the flow of current in the presence or absence of a magnetic field is the focus of this chapter.

Hall effect detectors, anisotropic magnetoresistances, and giant magnetoresistance arrays create measurable voltage differentials in the presence of magnetic fields. The Hall effect, anisotropic magnetoresistance, and giant magnetoresistance cover a large portion of the detectable range over which modern technology can measure magnetic field strengths.

Hall Effect Measurements

In 1892, Edwin Hall discovered that a magnetic field caused a deviation in the current flowing through thin gold foil, which resulted in a measurable voltage difference between the sheet metal faces. A block diagram of Hall's experiment is depicted in Figure 5-2.

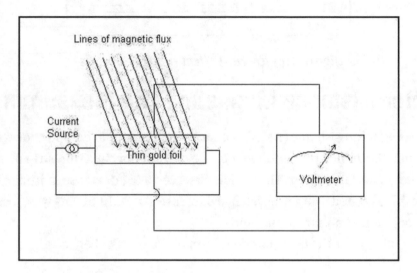

Figure 5-2. *The Hall effect measurement*

The small size of the voltage difference was not usable until the development of semiconductors made practical measurements possible. InAs (indium arsenide) and GaAs (gallium arsenide) are used in thin films fabricated into application-specific integrated circuits (ASIC) using chopper-stabilized operational amplifiers to measure the small voltages developed in the Hall effect. The thin film detector is figuratively depicted in Figure 5-3.

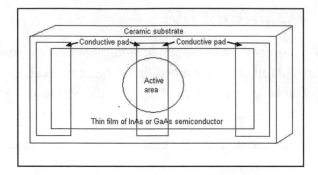

Figure 5-3. *ASIC configuration for Hall effect measurements*

Magnetoresistance Magnetic Field Measurements

Anisotropic magnetoresistance (AMR) occurs in ferromagnetic compounds when a magnetic field is applied perpendicular to the current flow in a thin strip of ferromagnetic material. William Thompson observed a 5% decrease in iron resistance in 1856. Nickel exhibited a larger resistance decrease. An AMR of 50% was observed in some ferromagnetic uranium compounds.

Figure 5-4 illustrates the basic configuration of the physical effect.

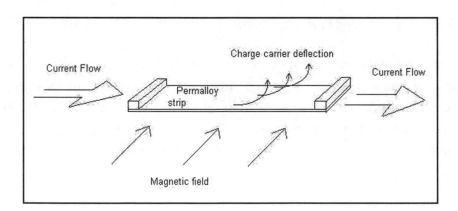

Figure 5-4. *AMR mechanism*

In the absence of a magnetic field, the current in Figure 5-4 moves from the left hand rectangular electrical contact through the metal strip to the right. When a magnetic field is placed parallel to the plane of the permalloy strip (80% Ni and 20% Fe) but perpendicular to the current flow, the magnetization vector attempts to rotate. The strip's resistance increases as the rotation angle of the vector increases.

Anisotropic magnetoresistance sensors have been engineered and fabricated with geometrical and material improvements that greatly increased the sensitivity of magnetic field measurements. Multiple "Barber Pole" geometry, with transducers configured into a Wheatstone bridge and amplified signals from chopper-stabilized op-amps make such increased sensitivity possible.

Giant magnetoresistance is found in multilayer constructs of ferromagnetic alloys and ultrathin conducting layers of materials. Iron chromium (Fe/Cr) and cobalt copper (Co/Cu) multilayer stacks can exhibit over 100% drops in resistance in the presence or absence of magnetic fields. Sensors are also typically configured into Wheatstone bridge configurations to provide field strength proportional analog outputs.

Not all sensors for measuring magnetic fields are manufactured in analog formats. Some sensors are considered "digital output" devices. The digital output sensors exhibit a "snap-action" behavior, and in the absence of a magnetic field, produce virtually no output. In the presence of a field strong enough to activate them, switch to "full on." Digital sensors are specified in accordance with the field strengths required for them to turn on and release.

Surface mount technology has added a level of complexity to experimental development. In the following exercise on measuring magnetic field strengths, one sensor is available in a format compatible with the commonly available prototyping breadboards as a single inline package (SIP), while two are not. Surface mount technology (SMT) chips are designed for mounting directly onto circuit boards. To use SMT with solderless prototyping boards, the devices must be mounted on microcircuit board adapters that can be connected electrically to pins compatible with prototyping breadboards.

Magnetoresistive sensors are dependent on changes in the resistive properties of the materials chosen for use in detecting or measuring the presence of magnetic fields. Many of the resistance type sensors form the sensing elements into a Wheatstone bridge configuration to provide an easily measurable bridge imbalance voltage, proportional to the strength of the enveloping magnetic field.

Sensitive magnetoresistive sensors that can detect low-strength magnetic fields are susceptible to the effects of local stray magnetic fields and may themselves become magnetized or distorted in the presence of strong fields.

To allow the use of high-sensitivity field detectors, some manufacturers build magnetic offset coils into their devices and provide conductors able to accept currents large enough to restore magnetoresistive properties after high field exposure has disrupted the normal sensor functions (see `https://aerospace.honeywell.com/content/aero/en/us/home/learn/products/sensors/low-field-high-precision-linear-1-and-2-axis-analog-magnetic-sen.html`).

Magnetic Field Lines and Field Strengths

Magnetic field strengths are characterized by the number of field lines that pass through an area of space. The lines are loops, do not cross one another, and point to or flow from the north to the south pole outside the magnet. Because the field lines are loops, great care must be taken when attempting to relate field strengths to the positions and distances from magnets. Typical images of iron powder particles tracing out the magnetic lines of force produced by a bar magnet show high densities of highly curved, individual field lines at either pole and gently curved lines connecting the curved polar ends. Figure 5-5 depicts the typical cross-section area of the magnetic field generated with a rectangular magnet.

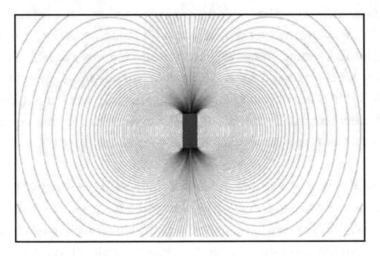

Figure 5-5. *A typical magnetic field from a rectangular magnet*

The magnetic field is a three-dimensional entity. To fully visualize the magnetic field, the lines depicted in the drawing must be rotated 360 degrees about the vertical axis at the center of the rectangular core. Qualitatively, the magnetic field lines decrease in density as the distance between the surface of the magnet and any point on the drawing increases. Quantitatively, the field lines that originate collinear with the vertical axis of the magnet diverge in a conical expansion, and then turn perpendicular to the original axis. While still expanding, they eventually turn roughly parallel to the main axis to complete the field line loop outside the magnet on the opposite pole. The lines continue inside the magnet, returning to the north pole to form closed loops.

There are no simple mathematical expressions to calculate the magnetic field strengths for permanent magnets other than those developed for the highly symmetrical simple cube, cylinder, and ring. The following is an equation for the cylindrical magnet used in the experiment portion of this exercise.

$$B = B_R / 2 \left(\frac{D+z}{\sqrt{R^2 + (D+2)^2}} - \frac{z}{\sqrt{R^2 + z^2}} \right)$$

B is the magnetic field strength. B_R is the magnet's remanence (the strength of the magnet's residual field after magnetization during manufacture). D is the length of the magnet cylinder. R is the radius of the cylinder. z is the distance along the primary axis at which the magnetic field strength is calculated.

Near the magnet pole face, the field strength is approximately proportional to the inverse square of the distance and at greater distances is proportional to the inverse cube. For work done with $\frac{1}{8} \times 1$ in (3 × 24.5 mm) rare-earth (RE) magnets, the inverse square relationship extends out to about an inch (2.45 cm) and the inverse cube relationship beyond that. A rule of thumb states that additive magnetic field strengths can be created by stacking together discs until the stack's thickness equals the diameter of the discs.

Rare-earth magnets made from samarium-cobalt compositions are the strongest, most compact, and expensive of the magnetic materials. Neodymium, iron, and boron compositions are comparable in strength to RE materials but less expensive. NdFeB (neodymium, iron, and boron) compositions are temperature sensitive but, if not overheated, lose only 5% of their initial strength in 100 years. NdFeB magnets can also be coated for corrosion protection or decorative appearance. Alnico is a type of alloy containing aluminum, nickel, cobalt, iron, and other additives that can be varied in composition to provide a material with a wide range of physio-chemical properties. Certain compositions can be made into very strong magnets with a low-temperature sensitivity. High-strength alnico magnets are less expensive than RE but more so than most other magnetic materials. Ceramic magnets made from barium or strontium ferrite are poor conductors of heat and electricity, are chemically inert, and less expensive than alnico devices. Iron chromium magnets can have magnetic properties similar to lower grades of alnico materials but are soft enough to be worked with normal machining techniques before a final hardening for use. There are ductile copper/iron/nickel alloys known as *cunife magnets* that can be shaped and formed as required and flexible plastic and rubber composites of barium or strontium ferrites that can be shaped as required.

Typical magnetic field strengths such as the earth's magnetic field at 0.25 to 0.65 G and refrigerator magnets at 100 G are two commonly encountered low strength magnetic fields. RE, NdFeB, and alnico magnets can have field strengths in the range of 11,000 to 13,000 G at their pole faces. (10,000 G = 1 tesla)

Iron is one of the few materials that can effectively shield against or contain magnetic fields. The iron must be of sufficient thickness that the magnetic field does not saturate the shielding and thus transmit the magnetic lines of force.

Experimental: Hall Effect Sensors
Allegro Microsystems LLC

The A1326 sensor has three pins. When viewed from the domed side of the device (the front), the left-hand pin is connected to a 5 V supply, the middle pin serves as the ground, and the right-hand pin is the sensor output. Normally, when connected to a 5 V supply in the absence of any magnetic field, the nominal output is one-half of the nominal 5 V supply. If a magnetic field is brought to the front of the device, a north pole causes the output voltage to rise toward the V_{cc} or 5 V rail. Conversely, the presence of a south pole causes the voltage to drop toward the ground value of zero. The factory calibration of 2.5 mV/G for the A1326 p/n is then used to determine the field strength.

Next, let's discuss the circuit connections and field strength testing protocol. Connecting the Allegro 1326's three leads to 5 V, ground, the LabJack U3-HV's AI0 terminals, and a DAQFactory plotting program are required to measure magnetic fields with the device. The device consists of a micro-sized die, 1.5 × 4 × 1.5 mm in the form of a single inline through hole pack with three 15 mm leads. The device and connecting wires to the LabJack HMI can all be mounted in a 1¾ × 1¼ in (44 × 34 mm) 170 pin mini-prototyping board for easy assembly.

Each of the three sensors selected for evaluation was tested with a strong, rare-earth disk magnet (REM) to provide a simple measure of relative sensitivity to magnetic fields. The 1 in diameter × ⅛ in (3 mm × 24.5 mm) magnets are used as cabinet door closing fixtures in woodworking. The actual field strength of the REM is unknown but is constant throughout the testing of the individual sensors.

Sensor relative evaluations were gauged by affixing the sensor to the 0 end of a 6-inch scale (152 mm) and placing the magnetic disk at various measured distances from the field detector.

Software

Figure 5-6 illustrates the page components to monitor the Allegro sensor's output as a 1-inch diameter rare-earth permanent magnet (PM) was placed at measured distances from the sensor. Since the Allegro sensor generates an output voltage proportional to the magnetic flux density and the supply is a nominal 5 V, a single DAQFactory channel can receive the sensor output. The left trace in black records the sensor output voltage that should be half of the nominal 5 V supplied by the LabJack power terminal in the absence of a magnetic field. The right-hand trace depicts, in red, the magnetic field strength in gauss as calculated from the sensor input voltage. (V_S on the LabJack U3-HV was measured at 4.24 V.)

North and south pole sensitivities result in a deflection toward or away from the midpoint of the supply voltage of a nominal 5 V. If the no field baseline is set to 0 G, the upward or downward deflection can quantify and qualify the nature and strength of the field being sampled.

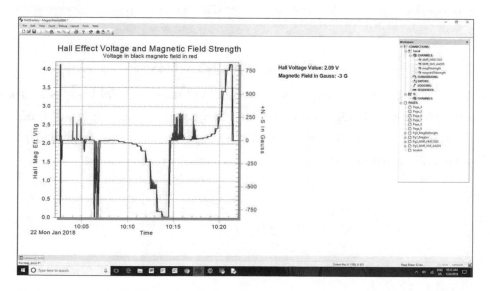

Figure 5-6. *Magnetic field and sensor voltage response to a rare-earth PM at fixed distances*

Two variable value displays provide digital numerical values of the voltage and magnetic fields measured at individual distances between the Hall effect sensor and the RE PM.

Table 2 tabulates the data collected during the simple relative sensitivity measurements.

NVE Corporation AA005 Analog Magnetic Sensor

The NVE sensor is a giant magnetoresistance based device configured into a Wheatstone bridge. In the absence of a magnetic field, the bridge is balanced, and both outputs are at half the supply voltage. A magnetic field increases the resistance of bridge components, and the outputs generate different voltages. A noise-free, highly stable power supply must be used to bias the bridge. A high-impedance differential amplifier must read the bridge imbalance without loading and disturbing the bridge deviation.

The sensor's linear range is from 10 G to 70 G. It saturates at 100 G. Device power can be up to 24 V and has an output at a maximum field of 60 mV/V per G. Device sensitivity is in the plane of the package, so the field lines being sensed must be parallel to the package surface. Sensor configuration is such that the device is *omnipolar*, responding to either field polarity with a positive voltage output.

Wheatstone bridge sensitivity for magnetoresistance systems can be expressed as follows.

$$\text{Sens} = mV_{Dvn} / V_{BrdgBs} / \text{gauss (or Oe)}$$

Figure 5-7 depicts the circuitry I used to record the magnetic field response from sensors using resistance bridge configurations. In the coarse measurements made for sensor comparison, a 1 kΩ 5% metal film gain resistor was used with the AD 620 to provide an amplifier gain of 50.

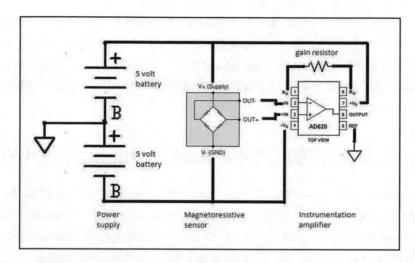

Figure 5-7. *A readout circuit for magnetoresistance sensors configured as Wheatstone bridges*

Figure 5-8 depicts the recorded traces from three experiments measuring the magnetic field from a disk REM at several fixed distances from the sensor.

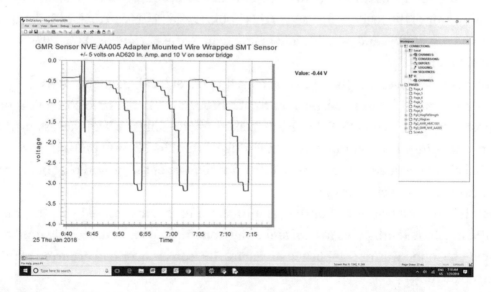

Figure 5-8. *AA005 measured REM magnetic field strength with GMR sensor at fixed distances*

The AA005 is a 1/8 × 3/16 × 1/16 in (3 × 5 × 1 mm) SOIC-8 SMT device mounted on a 11/16 mm × 3/8 in (17 × 11 mm) board fitted with two rows of four pins each to fit into a prototyping board. (Breakout boards prepared by Proto-Advantage.com) The board's sensor was aligned with the distance measurement scale's zero position using double-sided adhesive tape for the measurement experiments recorded graphically in Figure 5-8 and numerically in Table 5-2. The output pins of the boards using Wheatstone bridge detectors were wire-wrapped to provide adequate flexibility during the distance vs. field strength measurements.

Honeywell HMC 1001 Single-Axis Magnetic Field Sensor

Honeywell sensors are anisotropic, magnetoresistive, four-active-element, Wheatstone bridge-based devices with very high sensitivity. The sensors can measure field strengths from microgauss to six gauss values. The SMT sensor used in the measurement exercise is a single axis sensitive device with 8 pins mounted on a 1⅛ × ½ in (30 × 12 mm) breakout board with 8 inline pins to fit a prototyping board. The board-mounted sensor was fixed to the zero position on the distance scale and powered with the dual battery circuit depicted in Figure 5-7.

According to the manufacturer, the HMC 1001's magnetic field measurements should be limited to less than 5 G. Although the device is equipped with an 8-pin I/O array, only four of the leads were used in this book. Large fields can distort the output, disturb the sensitivity, and possibly add magnetism to the permalloy (80%/20% Ni/Fe) sensor elements.

The Honeywell sensors have internal coils that offset local magnetic fields. Connections called *set* and *reset* pulse currents through the detector to correct the effects of exposure to large magnetic fields. For this experiment, only the leads accessing the Wheatstone bridge's power inputs and the bridge output leads were utilized. The set/reset and offset coil leads were plugged into unused rows of the prototyping board to ensure no accidental circuitry shorting.

Baseline output was re-established empirically after overexposure by rapidly moving the REM north or south poles toward and away from the sensor in the test jig until a quiescent baseline was re-established. In Figure 5-9, sensor overload occurred at 9:56 and again at 10:04.

Data was collected by quickly moving the REM from its undetectable remote position to a predetermined measurement mark on the distance scale with the pole of interest facing the detector. The distance was recorded along with the numerical value in the variable value readout for each point.

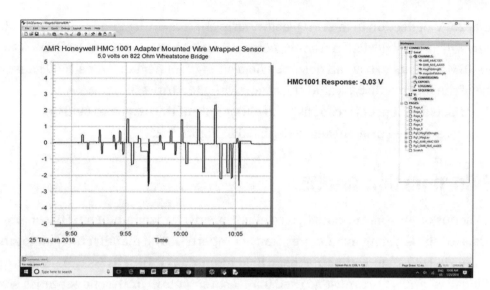

Figure 5-9. *HMC 1001 magnetic field response*

Observations

A high magnetic field strength REM provided a constant, high-value, standard field for use in comparing the relative sensitivity of the three readily available, inexpensive, easy-to-use, small, solid-state magnetic field sensors.

Table 5-2 contains a graphical tabulation of the individual detector response to the REM field present when the field source is placed at a fixed, known distance from the respective magnetic field sensor. Distances are presented in ¼ in (6 mm) intervals. The field values measured at each distance are reasonably reproducible for simple comparisons.

Allegro Microsystems

The Allegro Microsystems Inc. Hall Effect sensor used in the exercise (p/n A1326) was factory calibrated to have a 2.5 mV/G sensitivity. The red trace in Figure 5-6 reaches full-scale deflection at values near 725 to 750 gauss. Extra measurements made with the REM and the bead sensor at 1/8 in (3 mm) and 1/16 in (1½ mm) indicated field strengths of 755 and 818 gauss that indicate that the measurement system is saturated and probably past the point of reliable use.

Permanent magnets made from rare earths are reported to have magnetic field strengths at their faces that can be as high as a thousand or more gauss. The REM used in testing was obtained from a woodworking hardware supplier. It easily produced a nominal 2.5 V deflection in the DAQFactory strip chart recorder graphical display shown in Figure 5-6. A 2.5 V deviation from $V_{cc}/2$ is equivalent to 2.5 V / (2.5 × 10^{-3}) mV/G = 1000 G. The REM appears to have an observed field strength of near or over a 1000 gauss at the surface of the magnet disc, a value consistent with literature estimates.

The Hall effect sensor is responsive to either pole of the magnetic field being sampled, as expected from the effect depicted in Figure 5-2.

NVE Corporation AA005

The AA series of sensors are classified as high-sensitivity magnetometers, based on materials exhibiting giant magnetoresistance properties. The manufacturer states that unlike the Hall effect and other magnetic field monitors, GMR sensors can measure in the milligauss range. Care must be used in measurements in the fractional gauss levels, as the earth's magnetic field is typically in the 0.5 G to 0.65 G range.

The sensor is responsive to only one pole of the rare-earth magnet and has a linear range of sensitivity below 5 gauss. The values represented by the field strengths at distances under 3 inches (75 mm) are increasingly at odds with the values recorded for the Hall effect data.

Honeywell HMC 1001

Initial attempts to measure the field strengths with the REM held at the top end of the distance scale at 6 in (15.2 cm) with the HMC 1001 and a gain of 50 for the instrumentation amplifier drove the readout to the rail voltage. With a gain resistor of 47 kΩ and an amplifier gain of 2, the data in Table 5-2 were collected. However, without using the manufacturer's recommendations to properly re-zero the detector with the proper currents through the set/reset current straps, the numerical values contain a substantial systematic offset error. Using the manufacturer's calibration data, the numerical values collected in Table 5-2 result in numerical magnetic field strengths of 8 and more for the closer distances that are clearly beyond the linear range of +/– 2 gauss for the sensor. Although the qualitative recording indicates a relatively long-range proportional sensitivity to the RE magnet, the numerical data has errors.

Table 5-2. *Magnetic Field Strength Measurements At Known Distances*

Distance	A1326 Gauss test 1	test 2	Average Field Strength	AA005 Voltage test 1	test 2	test 3	Average Field Strength	HMC 1001 Voltage test 1	test 2	Average Field Strength
6								0.48	0.47	>2
5 3/4										
5 1/2										
5 1/4										
5								0.75	0.69	>2
4 3/4										
4 1/2										
4 1/4										
4				0.53	0.48	0.47	1.6	1.48	1.44	>2
3 3/4										
3 1/2									1.96	>2
3 1/4									2.34	>2
3				0.59	0.53	0.52	1.8			
2 3/4										
2 1/2		5	5	0.68	0.62	0.63	2.1			
2 1/4		8	8	0.8	0.72	0.73	2.5			
2	20	11	15	0.94	0.85	0.88	3.0			
1 3/4		17	17	1.22	1.17	1.19	4.0			
1 1/2	32	27	30	1.75	1.69	1.84	5.9			
1 1/4	46	42	44	3.02	3.05	2.96	10.0			
1	67	70	69	3.17	3.17	3.17	10.6			
3/4	120	127	124	3.17	3.17	3.17	10.6			
1/2	238	254	246							
1/4	522	526	524							
0	770									
1/8	770	755								
1/16	831	818								

Table 5-2 demonstrates the relative sensitivities of the Hall effect, GMR, and AMR magnetic field sensors. The Hall effect sensor has the largest dynamic range in field strength measurement, and the GMR and AMR are more sensitive with the expected narrower dynamic ranges.

Discussion

Exercise care when working with rare-earth magnets to avoid material fracture. Several of my discs shattered into small sharp fragments when subjected to a violent impact resulting from the unrestrained attraction between two discs or an iron surface.

Detailed overviews of magnetic field detection and sensing with ICs are available from several manufacturers (see sensing.honeywell.com/hallbook.pdf, www.allegromicro.com/hall-effect-sensor-ic-publications, or www.nve/ SensorAppsList).

Magnetic field strength is the determining factor for the detector selected for the measurement at hand. Strong fields are measured with Hall effect sensors. Moderate fields can be evaluated with GMR, and low-level fields are sampled or measured with suitably shielded and calibrated AMR devices. As with all measurement techniques, the more sensitive the determination, the more complex the measurement system required.

A Hall effect sensor can be fabricated so that only a biasing voltage and a reasonably high impedance voltmeter readout system are required to implement a measurement system. While the GMR and AMR sensors are fabricated with a Wheatstone bridge, the output signals usually require a high-impedance differential amplifier to produce a reasonable signal. Sensitivities such as that exhibited by the AMR devices also require additional circuitry to address external and internal effects that interfere with the measurement.

As with most physio-chemical sensing operations, as the system's sensitivity increases, so does the implementation cost. Allegro HE sensors are $3, NVE GMR sensors are $11, and Honeywell HMC 1001 are $29.

High sensitivity measurements in any experiment require intensive attention to detail. The Honeywell HMC 1001 shows a qualitative response to the standardized magnetic source at distances well beyond the GMR and Hall effect sensors. The voltage measured by the sensor is incorrect, however, and appears to have a substantial and systematically high numerical error. Honeywell has published several application notes on bridge balancing, removing residual magnetic effects on the sensors, and magnetic field current sensing. (Honeywell AN 209, AN 212, and Honeywell 1 and 2 axis Magnetic Sensors HMC-1001/1002/1021/1022). The manufacturer's literature indicates that overexposure to high magnetic fields can cause the AMR sensors to "stick" at incorrect output levels.

Allegro Microsystems LLC: Linear Hall Effect Sensors A1324, A1325, and A1326

Allegro's sensors are available with 5.0, 3.125, and 2.5 mV/G sensitivities. The three-lead single inline package (SIP) integrated circuits can be easily assembled into a wide dynamic range magnetic field measurement probe requiring only three wires carrying power, ground, and the readout signal voltage.

The block diagram depicted in Figure 5-10 represents the configuration that measures magnetic field strengths with the A1326 through hole 3 lead package configured as a moveable magnetic field probe. The die contains the sensor, amplifiers, offsets, tuned filters, and additional electronics to generate the analog voltage proportional to the sampled magnetic field . The manufacturer's literature indicates that the ASIC combines a chopper-stabilized operational amplifier, filters, and temperature compensation along with the Hall effect sensor.

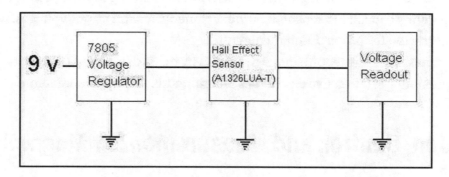

Figure 5-10. *Block diagram for a portable HE magnetic field probe*

9 V batteries can power a 7805 regulator in a portable device, or a regulated 5.0 V supply from either a "stand-alone" unit or a "fixed in place" setup with a LabJack-type HMI can power the device. The proportionally scaled voltage readout from the A1326ALU-T can be displayed in a DAQFactory graphic.

Pololu Robotics supplies a 0.8 × 0.7 in (18 × 20 mm) breakout board that is reportedly a simple carrier of Allegro's ±15.5 A ACS711 Hall effect-based linear current sensor with overcurrent fault output. It offers a low-resistance (~0.6 MΩ) current path and electrical isolation up to 100 V. This version accepts a bidirectional current input with a magnitude up to 15.5 A and outputs a proportional analog voltage centered at $V_{cc}/2$ with a typical error of ±5%. It operates from 3 V to 5.5 V, so it can interface directly to both 3.3 V and 5 V systems (www.pololu.com/product/2197).

NVE Corporation Magnetometers

Magnetometer part numbers from AA002-02 to AAK001-14 are available, covering the magnetic field range from 1.5 to 2500 Oe (1 Oe = 1 G). The devices are SMT packages with the sensing elements configured in a Wheatstone bridge that exhibit sensitivities from approximately 10 to 0.0025 mV/V/G depending on the field strength being monitored. The devices are mono-polar, producing a differential output compatible with the instrumentation amplifier.

Honeywell HMC 1001

Although Table 5-2 and Figure 5-9 record a semi-proportional increase in response for the HMC1001 at higher distances from the common magnetic field source, the measurement is disturbed or distorted by excessive field strengths. The proximity of high fields apparently caused the sensor to output erroneously high bridge voltages, which must be corrected for proper implementation.

If the measurements require the high sensitivity offered by the AMR sensors, you must implement the corrective electronics recommended by the manufacturer.

Creation, Control, and Measurement of Magnetic Fields

Electrical engineering has taught the principles of feedback control using graphically spectacular demonstrations of electromagnetic suspension. A steel ball bearing is suspended in mid-air beneath an electromagnet. In some of the first teaching units, interrupting the light in a beam illuminating a photocell determined the steel ball's position. The light beam intensity transmitted to a photodetector varies in accordance with the sphere's position, which controls the power delivered to the electromagnet.

There are currently numerous examples of magnetic levitation apparatus available. They vary from commercially available assembled desktop units, complete kits with circuit boards, and published methods for educational or science fair projects that use permanent magnets, steel, or soft iron objects as cores for controlled magnetic suspension from electromagnets. The initial system assembled for the development of this exercise was an analog computing system able to support magnetic materials or permanent magnets by changing the voltage of the power supply driving the electromagnetic coil.

Two forms of feedback controllers are examined in this exercise: an analog computer and a microprocessor. The multi-component analog computer is built from four of the dependable and readily available 741 op-amps, while the single unit feedback controller is configured with the Arduino microprocessor. All feedback mechanisms require monitoring a process to create a signal to be "fed back" to the process input stage.

A light beam and photocell are the traditional means for creating an error signal in a negative feedback magnetic levitation system. The Hall effect sensors that measure the change in magnetic field intensity can also be used.

Magnetic suspension or levitation uses a current-controlled electromagnetic field to counter the force of gravity pulling down on a suspended object. The electromagnetic field must be strong enough to couple with a permanent magnet in the suspended mass or induce in a magnetizable material, a magnetic field strong enough to permit levitation.

To calculate the strength of the electromagnetic field required to suspend either type of mass is not a trivial matter and is best evaluated by direct measurement.

Experiment

A. Magnetic Suspension/Levitation with an Analog Computing System

To achieve levitation, a non-magnetic supporting framework is required to fix the electromagnet in place. The electromagnet would typically be mounted in an adjustable, vertical position. The mass to be weighed can hang, unobstructed from the magnetic field created just off the core's tip. Depending on the method chosen to monitor the position of the suspended mass, the supporting frame may be fabricated in the form of a single pedestal for use with Hall effect sensors or as an inverted "U" with two sides on which to mount the light beam emitter and sensor.

The hardware configuration must allow mechanical adjustment of the vertical distance between the tip of the electromagnet and the IR beam if the light-beam method of measuring the suspended object is chosen.

Circuit Schematic: Analog Computer Control

Figure 5-11 illustrates the circuit schematic used for an analog computer, feedback power controller that creates a magnetic suspension or levitation field. Obstructing the beam lowers the power delivered to the electromagnet coil. Increasing illumination of the photocell detector increases the power delivered to the coil.

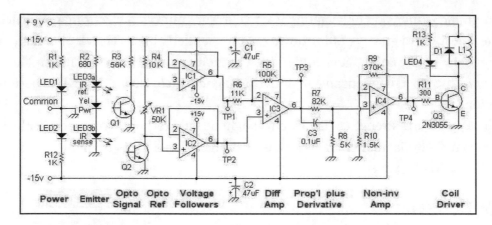

Figure 5-11. *An analog computing controller for magnetic levitation*

The circuit in Figure 5-11 is a modified version from one at `www.coilgun.info`. In the circuit that I assembled, a small Potter & Brumfield electromagnet (1 in × 1¼ in frame with an 11/16 thick × 1 in diameter, nominal 6 V DC coil) was used with a coil resistance of 18 ohms. In addition to the manufactured coil, a yellow LED power pilot light for the IR emitting diodes were added to the original circuitry together with an independent reference beam set of IR transmitter and receiver. The smaller P&B coil has a higher resistance than the custom-built coil but was available in my lab and required only minor changes to the proportional-plus-derivative resistor values to achieve magnetic field stability.

A feedback monitor and power controller assembled from op-amps is an analog computer of considerable complexity. The simplicity, stability, and robustness of the 741 op-amp renders the complexity of the analog computer into a state of manageability. After assembling the electronic components on the breadboard and validating all the connections, each op-amp's inverting and non-inverting inputs are grounded. With the inputs, grounded power can be applied to the op-amps, and the trim potentiometer for the amplifier is adjusted to balance the output to zero volts.

Once the four amplifiers are balanced, the analog computer's inputs can be adjusted to control the magnetic field strength. Each op-amp has a bipolar power supply. For the best performance, it should be biased with LED movement on the monitor beam and VR1 on the reference beam to operate near the 0-output level. This means having +/- 15 V available to swing in either the positive or negative range in response to deviations created by the magnetically suspended object's movement. As illustrated in Figure 5-11, there are two IR beams: one that monitors the position of the suspended object and one for the ambient light level.

B. Microcontroller Magnetic Suspension/Levitation

1) A microcontroller can greatly reduce the development time required to create a magnetic suspension/levitation demonstration. A microcontroller replaces most of the analog circuitry with programming. The optical mechanical construction and assembly remain essentially the same for both systems. The microcontroller's operation is easier to understand because of the explicit nature of the programming and its algorithm.

There are many magnetic suspension demonstration resources available for experimentation. The system to generate magnetic fields for measurement in this book is a well-established and relatively robust system described in Chapter 13 of *15 Dangerously Mad Projects for the Evil Genius* by Dr. Simon Monk (McGraw-Hill, 2011). The device uses an Arduino microcontroller board, and the text and drawings provide a complete description of construction, assembly, testing, operation, troubleshooting, control algorithm code, and operating theory.

When the system is properly adjusted and working, you can feel the correct position for object suspension through the vibration of the object in response to the control system attempting to stabilize the object's position.

Rather than tune the PID algorithm, I used a trial-and-error method to trim the weight on a suspended magnetic "bob" until the weighted magnetic bob hung quiescently beneath the electromagnet. After assembling the magnetic levitation apparatus, downloading the microcontroller code from the book's website, and powering up the entire system, the trial-and-error process began.

A ½-inch (12 mm) cylindrical iron magnet was held beneath the electromagnet and moved up and down to activate the coil current. As the electromagnet began to exert force on the magnet, it was pulled down to find the release point.

I balanced the magnet on my finger beneath the release point and slowly raised it into the IR beam to add power to the coil. If the magnet flew up immediately to the coil, a paper clip was added to the magnet and the experiment repeated. To keep the mass added to the magnet under control, I used a piece of cellophane tape to hold a paper tube to the edges of the cylindrical magnet. The bottom of the tube was flattened and folded over to form a container for the additional paper clip weights added to the bob.

After several trials, the bob floated quiescently beneath the electromagnet, as depicted in Figure 5-12. The paper tube on the bob was banded with a marking pen to aid visibility.

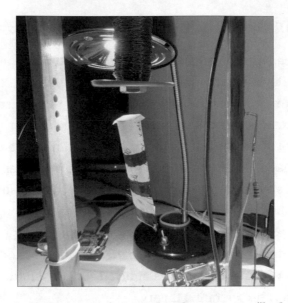

Figure 5-12. *Magnetic levitation of a weighted magnetic "bob"*

As the bob hung suspended in the electromagnet's field, an attempt was made to measure the field strength with a Hall effect probe assembled as depicted in Figure 5-10. The probe was powered from the nominal 5 V supply of a LabJack U3-HV, and the readout was recorded with a copy of DAQFactory Express on a laptop (see Figure 5-14). Care must be taken in using the probe, as seen in Figure 5-13, not to block the IR control beam. Although the probe works as expected, the rapid change in the field must be recorded or averaged electronically to obtain any quantitative numerical values.

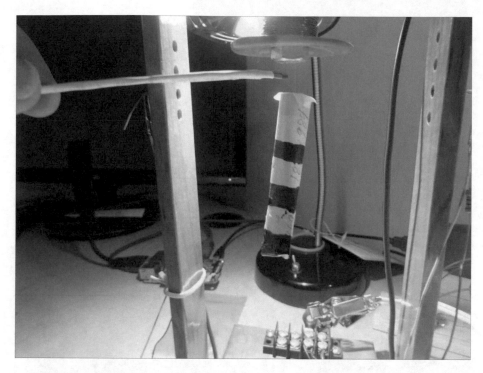

Figure 5-13. *A Hall effect magnetic probe*

Figure 5-14 shows the desktop magnetic levitation device and recording laptop. Figure 5-15 records the magnetic and voltage values during a levitation experiment. (Note the spiking traces in the upper-left corner of recorded data.)

Figure 5-14. *A magnetic levitation experimental setup*

In Figure 5-14, the area labeled 1 shows the LabJack U3-HV in red, and the Arduino and the prototyping board behind it and to the left. The area labeled 2 shows the suspended bob, the Hall probe in a white tube, and an electromagnetic copper wire coil overhead. The area labeled 3 shows the wood support frame with an IR beam position detector. Also on the desktop are my laptop, two desk lamps, a 12 V mains-powered DC coil power supply, and an ammeter behind the host computer display.

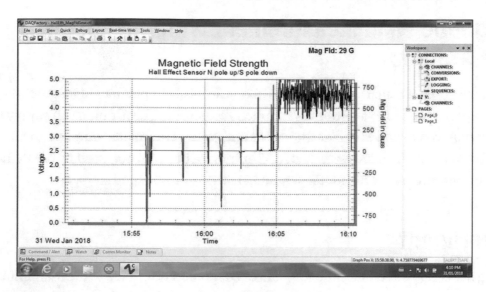

Figure 5-15. *Magnetic levitation field strength recording*

Discussion

Do not attempt to balance the bob with the Hall probe in place as the magnet bob may have sufficient mass to damage the probe die when drawn violently up to the electromagnet face pole.

By assembling the levitation apparatus detailed by Dr. Monk a large amount of successful experimental development work can be used and the experimentalist can focus on the development of magnetic measurement techniques.

Two suspension bobs were assembled: a heavier piece that weighed 23.26 g and a lighter version (seen in Figures 5-12, 5-13, and 5-14) that weighed 9.85 g. The lighter bob suspended at about ½ inch (12.5 mm) beneath the coil with a coil current that varied from 0.52 to 0.62 A. Experiments with the heavier bob suspended the weight at a lower point below the coil. The weight jumped erratically for short periods of time before falling out of the suspending field. A lighter bob and moving the IR beam diodes closer to the coil suspended the bob smoothly with only small minor movements and held the weight in suspension for as long as power was applied to the system.

Figure 5-15 indicates that the controller algorithm adjusts the coil current and electromagnetic field intensity at a rapid rate. The Hall effect sensor appears to be working near the upper limit of linearity in the 600 to 1000 G range.

A magnetic levitation demonstration is always a graphic display of process control and makes an interesting problem illustrating probe-type magnetic field measurements.

Magnetic Field Measurement with the Raspberry Pi and Arduino

A Hall effect sensor such as the Allegro A1326 is an easily implemented magnetic field sensor when coupled to an Arduino/Raspberry Pi pairing. The Arduino can supply both the 5 V required to power or bias the sensor and convert the analog output into a 10-bit digital signal. The Arduino writes the ADC output to the serial port read by the Python plotting software on the RPi for display and archival timestamped storage.

Experiment

Listing 5-1 is very short and simple. A simple adaptation was made to the Matplotlib strip chart recorder code's input generator function in Listing 5-2 (all code listings are provided at the end of the chapter). Since the Allegro sensor outputs a linear voltage proportional to the magnetic field strength, a simple linear transform can convert the ADC output to gauss.

Allegro's device uses a 5 V potential to establish a no field or zero field level at one-half the biasing span. Magnetic fields of increasing strength with a north polarity cause the voltage and ADC to rise toward the 5 V or 1023 maximum value of the readout system. Increasing magnetic fields with a south polarity cause the voltage output and ADC value to decrease toward the minimum output of zero at ground potential. By subtracting the no field or mid-span potential from the ADC reading to transform the voltage output and using the factory calibration of 5 mV/G the ADC output can be converted to a positive-negative magnetic field value to be archived and plotted.

A demonstration of the sensor capability was conducted by placing magnets of varying strengths at a fixed distance from the sensor head. After recording the field strength for an individual magnetic disc face, the disc or stack was turned over, and the opposite pole strength was measured and recorded. The numerical captions identify the number of discs in the stack whose north and south magnetic field strengths are being recorded. The discs were from a set of six $\frac{1}{8}$ in × 1 in diameter (3 × 24.5 mm) ceramic magnets obtained from a woodworking supply.

Observations

Figure 5-16 is a screen capture of the RPi display on which the console output of the timestamp and the magnetic field values are displayed as archived. The plot to the right is the graphic display of the measurements made to gauge the increase in total field strength as discs were stacked together.

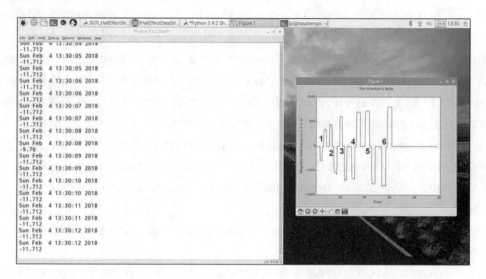

Figure 5-16. *Magnetic field strength increase from stacking disc magnets*

Discussion

Figure 5-16 depicts the effects of stacking together disc magnets to create a stronger magnetic field. The rule of thumb states that the fields will add until the stack's depth equals the diameter of the individual discs.

Although the Arduino code is very short, simple, and straightforward, the Python serial port code for reading the incoming data must again be written to accommodate the variable width of the numbers streamed out from the sensor. The code is heavily commented on copying and pasting, but I left the comments in place so that you can follow the logic without having to look back to see the purpose of a statement or operation.

Natural Magnetic Fields and the Magnetometer Compass

Life on earth is protected from solar radiation by the planet's magnetic field. The earth's iron core generates a magnetic field whose presence is often visible in northern and southern latitudes as the aurora borealis and aurora australis. The lights are created when high energy particles from the sun, collected by the earth's magnetic field lines, collide with the gas molecules and atoms in the earth's upper atmospheric layers.

Although on geologic time scales, the poles of the core's magnetic field move and occasionally reverse, the northern and southern poles are sufficiently stable over several years to be used as a direction indicator for navigation. At the earth's surface, the magnetic field is typically between 0.25 to 0.65 G (or microtesla).

Solid-state magnetometers can be fabricated to read the direction of the local magnetic fields and determine the direction of the northern magnetic pole. The position of the magnetic pole can then be used to determine the direction to the geographic North Pole.

There are many solid-state compass devices available in surface-mount technologies that incorporate motion-sensing units.

Next, two compass units demonstrate direction-finding capability as part of larger navigation facilities.

Experimental

A breakout board from Adafruit Industries that combines a three-axis accelerometer with a compass and the output of the Sense HAT board are two devices that read the earth's magnetic field to determine the direction of magnetic north. The Sense HAT is a fully assembled board that mounts directly onto the RPi. The Adafruit board requires soldering a row of header pins if the board is used in a prototyping setup.

Adafruit Industries, Inc.: LSM303DLHC ($15 CDN)

Compass information from an SMT module mounted on the Adafruit board can be collected and interpreted with the Arduino microcontroller. A pair of software libraries enables the magnetometer reading and conversion of the data into a numerical compass heading or direction that is subsequently broadcast onto the serial port.

Both DAQFactory and Python can read data from a microcontroller serial port and display the compass heading. The libraries to program the microcontroller can be downloaded from the online repository at `https://github.com/adafruit/Adafruit_LSM303DLHC`. In addition to the microcontroller software, there are examples of programs to read the compass heading and the three-axis accelerometer on the breakout board (see Chapter 6).

A USB connection between the host and microcontroller supplies power and communication to the microcontroller. The +5 V and ground connections from the breakout board can be connected to the microcontroller for power. The SDA and SCL serial bus communication connections on the sensor board can be connected to the Arduino A4 and A5 inputs to complete the system wiring.

Once the libraries are installed on the host computer in use, the magnetometer compass program can be run, and the serial port output from the microcontroller validated. (At the time of writing, the RPi hosted Arduino IDE requires removing any non-alphabetic or numeric values in the titles of the Adafruit libraries stored in the libraries folder of the sketchbook. The IDE program can read the alphabetic-numeric titles at initialization.) The most recent version of the Windows-based Arduino IDE contains the required libraries.

Once the microprocessor compass heading readings have been validated on the Arduino IDE's serial port monitor, the "Compass Heading" portion of the output can be removed to ease the parsing required by DAQFactory or Python serial port monitors. In the magnetometer compass, program the lines to be by-passed by commenting out are as follows.

```
Serial.println("Magnetometer Test"); Serial.println(""); in the setup
function and the line;
 Serial.print("Compass Heading: ");
```

By commenting out the above code lines only the numerical value is printed to the serial port.

DAQFactory can be configured to receive the compass data on a com port. As explained in the *DAQFactory Serial Communications Manual* (`www.azeotech.com/dl/serialguide.pdf`), the data can be appended to a channel for use in the DAQFactory displays. Figure 5-17 depicts the compass display properties panel, and Figure 5-18 the compass display.

Compass Headings RPi and Python

Python and the RPi can be used to display the numerical values of compass headings derived from either the Arduino or the Sense HAT board.

The serial port's digital values can be read by simple Python code for a streamed display on the console or a static real-time Tkinter-based GUI display, as depicted in Figure 5-19. The code for Figure 5-19 is provided in Listing 5-3.

Direction information can also be read by the RPi from the Sense HAT board magnetometer compass. The code in Listing 5-4 reads a single compass heading. If the code were enclosed in a while loop, the compass data could be streamed out on the Python console for archiving.

Observations

The properties selection panel allows you to change the color and sizes of the disks and text on the DAQFactory compass icon. (The icon is not available in the Express version.)

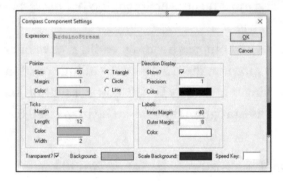

Figure 5-17. *Properties selection panel for DAQFactory compass display*

After several minutes of observation, the digital numeric display fluctuates from electronic noise but remains pointed in a specific direction.

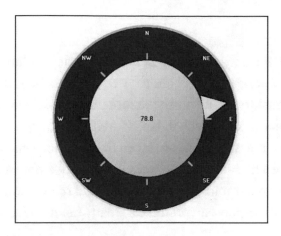

Figure 5-18. *DAQFactory compass display*

Figure 5-19. *RPi Tkinter GUI real-time display of compass heading from Arduino and the Adafruit LSM303 board*

Discussion

The earth's magnetic field is weak. The presence of magnets or large portions of magnetic metals can affect compass readings. The compass heading is a magnetic bearing, and its relationship to true north is a function of several variations determined by the geographical locale from which the measurement is taken.

Most solid-state compass readings are taken from magnetometers incorporated into systems to provide a high-speed determination of position. Graphical displays are relatively slow to respond to rapidly changing data, and hence averaging the compass heading readings before display can produce a steady heading indication.

Code Listings

Listing 5-1. Arduino Streaming Data from Hall Effect Sensor

```
// Hall Effect Sensor Data Stream
// the HES is connected to +5 volts, AO and gnd
//
int analogPin = 0;
//
void setup()
{
  Serial.begin(9600);
}
//
void loop()
{
  int reading = analogRead(analogPin);
  Serial.println(reading);
  delay(500);
}
```

Listing 5-2. Python Plotting Code for Hall Effect Sensor Magnetic Field Strength Data

```python
# A Strip Chart Recorder for Raspberry Pi with Serial Input
# SCR Plotting of changing Hall Effect sensor data from Arduino A0 input.
# ADC count is approx 2 Gauss + data is a north pole - is a south pole.
#
import matplotlib
import numpy as np
from matplotlib.lines import Line2D
import matplotlib.pyplot as plt
import matplotlib.animation as animation
import time
import serial
#
#
#
class Scope:
    def __init__(self, ax, maxt=10, dt=0.02):
        """maxt time width of display"""
        self.ax = ax
        self.dt = dt
        self.maxt = maxt
        self.tdata = [0]
        self.ydata = [0]
        self.line = Line2D(self.tdata, self.ydata)
        self.ax.add_line(self.line)
        self.ax.set_ylim(-1000, 1000)  # y axis scale
        self.ax.set_xlim(0, self.maxt)

    def update(self, y):
        lastt = self.tdata[-1]
        if lastt > self.tdata[0] + self.maxt: # reset the arrays
            self.tdata = [self.tdata[-1]]
            self.ydata = [self.ydata[-1]]
```

```python
            self.ax.set_xlim(self.tdata[0], self.tdata[0] + self.maxt)
            self.ax.figure.canvas.draw()

        t = self.tdata[-1] + self.dt
        self.tdata.append(t)
        self.ydata.append(y)
        self.line.set_data(self.tdata, self.ydata)
        return self.line,
#
ser = serial.Serial("/dev/ttyACM0", 9600)  # serial port instance
#
def rd_data():
    while True:
        inPutln = ser.readline()
        # print("inPutln = ", inPutln) # for error diagnostics only
        if (len(inPutln ) < 3):    # short character string fragment
            continue
        if (len(inPutln) > 6):     # long character string fragment
            continue
        #
        if (len(inPutln) == 3):    # len for a single unsigned digit
            line = int(str(inPutln)[slice(2,3)])
            print(time.asctime()) # archival time stamp for console/data
                                storage
            print ((line - 516) * 1.952) # console display/archival data
                                    storage
            yield (line - 516) * 1.952
        #
        if (len(inPutln) == 4):    # len for double unsigned digit
            line = int(str(inPutln)[slice(2,4)])
            print(time.asctime()) # archival time stamp for console/data
                                storage
            print ((line - 516) * 1.952)  # console display/archival data
                                    storage
            yield (line - 516) * 1.952
```

```python
        #
        if (len(inPutln) == 5):    # len for a triple unsigned digit
            line = int(str(inPutln)[slice(2,5)])
            print(time.asctime()) # archival time stamp for console/data
                                storage
            print ((line - 516) * 1.952)  # console display/archival data
                                    storage
            yield (line - 516) * 1.952
        #
        if (len(inPutln) == 6):    # len for a quad unsigned digit
            line = int(str(inPutln)[slice(2,6)])
            print(time.asctime()) # archival time stamp for console/data
                                storage
            print ((line - 516) * 1.952)  # console display/archival data
                                    storage
            yield (line - 516) * 1.952

fig = plt.figure()
fig.suptitle("The Scientyst's Ayde", fontsize = 12)
ax = fig.add_subplot(111)
ax.set_xlabel("Time")
ax.set_ylabel("Magnetic Field Gauss (n > 0 < s)")
scope = Scope(ax)

# uses rd_data() as a generator to produce data for the update func, the
# Arduino LDC value is read by the plotting code in 10 minute windows for the
# animated screen display. Software overhead limits response speed of display.
ani = animation.FuncAnimation(fig, scope.update, rd_data, interval=50,
blit=False)

plt.show()
```

Listing 5-3. A Python Tkinter GUI to Read the Serial Port

```
# -*- coding: utf-8 -*-
"""
A Utility Program to Read the Serial Port for Magnetic Heading Display.

Sensor data collected by Arduino is first read from its serial port and
validated as being a numerical data string. The serial port is closed and
this program launched. The string data is read parsed and displayed
in the Python - Tkinter GUI.

The parsing code has been written for multiple digit floating point
character strings not numerical values. This default pgm reads Arduino ADC
integer value and potentiometer floating point voltage value as a
transmitted single character string. Tkinter textvariables are by default
set to display adc_numeric and wpr_flt with an appropriate banner in the
default Tkinter GUI. If not being used comment out the banners and set the
textvariables to None.
"""
import serial
from tkinter import *

ser = serial.Serial("/dev/ttyACM0", 9600)
ser.baudrate = 9600

def update(): # called after millisec by main loop
    while 1:
        reading.set(ser.readline())  #tkntr StringVar() set to seql input
                                     char strng
        string_val = reading.get()  #string_val variable for slice operations
        #print(string_val, "len string_val, ", len(string_val))
        # diagnostic print diagnostic
#
        if len(string_val) == 13: # ADC is 1 digit
            adc_numeric.set(int(string_val[2:-10])) # slice out and set
                                                    IntVr() numerical
                                                    integer string
```

```
            wpr_flt.set(float(string_val[3:-5])) # slice and set DoubleVar()
                                              numerical floating point
#

    if len(string_val) == 14: # ADC is 2 digits
        adc_numeric.set(int(string_val[2:-10])) # slice out and set
                                              IntVr() numerical
                                              integer string
        wpr_flt.set(float(string_val[4:-5])) # slice and set DoubleVar()
                                              numerical floating point
#

    if len(string_val) == 15: # ADC is 3 digits
        adc_numeric.set(int(string_val[2:-10])) # slice out and set
                                              IntVr() numerical
                                              integer string
        wpr_flt.set(float(string_val[5:-5])) # slice and set DoubleVar()
                                              numerical floating point
#

    if len(string_val) == 16: # ADC is 4 digits
        adc_numeric.set(int(string_val[2:-10])) # slice out and set
                                              IntVr() numerical
                                              integer string
        wpr_flt.set(float(string_val[6:-5])) # slice and set DoubleVar()
                                              numerical floating point
#

    root.update()
#
root = Tk()
#
w = Label(root, text="Magnetic Compass Heading ",background="white",
        foreground="red", font="Arial 20")
w.pack()  #1st display label
#
# 2nd label is string value of serial input displayed in real time
reading = StringVar()  # tkinter StringVar variable, reading created
w = Label(root, textvariable= reading, font="Arial 15") #label up-dated
w.pack()
```

```
#
"""
#3rd label is title for sensor's fp vltg and int ADC value
w = Label(root, text="Potentiometer Wiper Voltage and ADC Outputs", background=
          "white", foreground= "red", font="Arial 16")
w.pack()
#
"""
# 4th label is 3 sgnfcnt fig fp wiper vltg
wpr_flt = DoubleVar() #tkinter double fp var created for display
w = Label(root, textvariable= None, font="Arial 15")
w.pack()
#
#5th label is the 3 dig int ADC val from A0 input
adc_numeric = IntVar() #tkinter int val var created for display
w = Label(root, textvariable= None, font="Arial 15")
w.pack()
#
root.after(1, update)  # a new value is read
root.title("The Scientyst's Ayde")
root.mainloop()
```

Listing 5-4. A Single Reading of the Sense HAT Magnetometer Compass Heading

```
# Sense-Hat Programming
#
from sense_hat import SenseHat
#
sense = SenseHat()
# A message for matrix display
sense.set_rotation(180)
north = sense.get_compass()
print("North: %s" % north)
```

Summary

Magnetic fields are classified as arising from static magnetic materials, such as permanent magnets, or being generated by electric currents and classified as *electromagnetic*.

Materials are classified as paramagnetic or diamagnetic depending on whether they concentrate or disperse magnetic fields.

Permanent magnets with a substantial range of field strengths are available made from a host of metal alloys and ceramics.

Magnetic field strengths can be measured with Hall effects or one of the forms of magneto resistance.

A large dynamic range of magnetic field strengths can be measured with commercial and less expensive component-based SCADA systems.

Numerous solid-state sensors available in miniature formats can read the earth's magnetic field for navigation.

In Chapter 6, navigation aids are used when traveling over great distances as part of the study of motion and vibration.

CHAPTER 6

Motion and Vibration

Experiments often require monitoring movement that may be too small for the eye to see, easily seen by the eye, or over distances too great for either the eye to see or the mind to comprehend.

Recordings of movement can be made electronically by using various transducers to determine both time and position. The range of movement recorded varies from minute, elastic material expansions requiring Wheatstone bridge strain gauges to following transcontinental migrations of species or determining astronomical distances. Continuous recordings of time and position can calculate speed, acceleration, and directions, as required for navigation.

A coarse determination of motion in the vertical plane on the earth's surface can be followed by measuring the atmospheric pressure. Barometric pressure sensors such as the BMP180 or the Sense HAT board's pressure sensor monitor the ambient pressure that decreases at a predictable rate as the elevation above sea level increases (see Chapter 9).

Vibration is a repetitive movement associated with oscillations around a point of normal rest. The oscillations may be periodically repetitive or random. Vibrations are often described in terms of frequency as cycles per second (cps) or Hertz (Hz) because of their repetitive nature. They can be used in a constructive mode or be inadvertently the source of uncontrolled, resonant, destructive actions.

Mechanical vibrations in water, the earth, or the ambient atmosphere between certain frequency ranges are the source of sounds for various species. Piezoelectric and electromechanical transducers can interconvert motion and electrical energies, thus monitoring sound frequency ranges above and below what is accessible to the human ear.

Distance and time are two fundamental parameters required in the study or discussion of movement or motion. The quotient of distance and time is speed, and the rate of change of speed is acceleration, the result of an unbalanced force acting on a mass.

© Richard J. Smythe 2022
R. J. Smythe, *Arduino Measurements in Science*, https://doi.org/10.1007/978-1-4842-6781-3_6

Distance on a Grand Scale

Dead Reckoning

Navigation based on starting from a known position and using the speed and direction traveled to estimate the current position has been in use for hundreds of years and is known as *dead reckoning*. Errors in measuring the direction, time, and distance traveled since the last known position are cumulative and usually increase in proportion to the distance traveled.

Inertial Navigation

Inertial navigation is a self-contained technique (see `http://www.eng.hmc.edu/NewE80/` `PDFs/IntroToInertialNavigation.pdf`). As with dead reckoning, the technique starts from a known position and orientation then through recording the passage of time, the effects from measured accelerations and gyroscopes, the inertial navigation unit determines the current position and orientation of the object at hand.

Devices fabricated with three orthogonal rate-gyroscopes and three orthogonal accelerometers measuring angular velocity and linear acceleration are called *inertial measurement units* (IMUs). The processing of signals from these devices establishes position and orientation.

Micromachined electromechanical systems (MEMS) fabricate micro inertial navigation systems (INS).

Inexpensive self-contained INS units and IMU devices are available to record both motion and position. As with traditional dead reckoning, the systems have inherent errors that can accumulate as direction, distance, and time change.

Determining and describing the position of objects moving through space has led to the development of the terminology of *degrees of freedom*. Objects confined to a single line of motion, such as a ball rolling down an inclined track, have a single degree of freedom. A ball free to roll about on a level flat plane has two degrees of freedom. A ball with a hook suspended from a lifting crane boom has three degrees of freedom.

If an aircraft or an unmanned aerial vehicle (UAV) moves through space, its position to the earth can be expressed in terms of three degrees of freedom. Its orientation to pitch, yaw, and roll may require the addition of three more degrees of freedom to accurately describe its complete position and orientation in space.

Global Positioning System (GPS)

Satellites that broadcast well-regulated time signals orbit around the Earth. The broadcast signals are derived from oscillators using large atom, atomic, electron energy level transitions for radio frequency (RF) modulators. Oscillators using heavy atom vapors such as cesium for resonant frequency bases are often referred to as *atomic clocks*. Since many radio transmissions are limited to "line of sight," the number and positioning of the satellites are arranged so that the earth's entire surface is continually covered by their transmissions.

Microcomputing systems equipped with receivers on the earth's surface within the field of view of multiple satellites can compute their position from the satellite transmissions. If time signals from ground-based stations are simultaneously available with multiple GPS satellite signals, positions on the earth's surface can be determined within centimeters or inches.

GPS receiver antennas must have a clear, unobstructed view of the sky with multiple satellites within the field of view to function. Position determinations may take 1 to 5 seconds to compute, depending on the desired positioning resolution. Supplementary fixed in position ground stations often provide local high-resolution positioning information.

Reflective Distance Determinations

Radar (radio detection and ranging) is the acronym describing systems using radio wave reflections to detect and determine the range to solid objects within the broadcast antenna's field of view. Radar systems measure distances in feet or meters as ground penetrating radar (GPR) to interplanetary distances.

Lidar systems are laser powered distance measurement techniques in which pulses of reflected light measure distances from the transmitter. Aerial vehicles carrying IR Lidars map surface topology beneath forest canopies and ground-based systems accurately measure earth-to-moon distances.

Large arrays of optical and radio frequency telescopes measure interplanetary and stellar distances difficult for the mind to comprehend.

Distance on a Visible Scale

Range Finders

At normal temperatures and pressures of 20°C in dry air, sounds (or *atmospheric pressure waves*) have been measured to travel at a speed of 343.2 m/s or 1126 ft/sec.

With the aid of a microprocessor and appropriate transducers, a short pulse of ultrasonic waves can be broadcast into a volume of space that is subsequently monitored for reflected waves from any solid objects that may be present. An object's range can be calculated by measuring the time between the broadcast of the ultrasonic pulse and its return to the receiving transducer. Dimensional analysis (meters/second × seconds = meters) allows the calculation of distance and direction. Using repetitive timed measurements, the velocity or acceleration of objects can also be calculated.

Square wave pulse trains of infrared light measure distance and direction using the time elapsing between broadcast and return of the reflected pulse train.

Lidar and radar are distance and direction measuring range-finding devices that use light and radio waves, respectively, to determine distances. Instruments using pulsed laser light and long radio waves measure distances in feet and inches in ground-penetrating radar, lidar mapping of building interiors, and aerial topology surveying.

Distance in the Invisible Scales

The constructive and destructive combination of waves of light, called *interference*, has been used for over a hundred years to measure distances on the scale of the wavelengths of light with a technique known as *interferometry*. In an experiment using interference, light from a common source is divided into two beams passed through different path lengths or paths in different materials before being recombined. Light has the properties of a wave phenomenon. It is subject to the superposition principle, which stipulates that two waves in phase constructively interfere with augmenting or increasing their combined amplitude. Waves out of phase destructively interfere and cancel or reduce their total amplitude or intensity.

An observer watching the intensity or brightness of a recombined beam sees it vary from black to full brightness as the path lengths of either beam changes. Interferometers are perhaps the instruments with the largest dynamic range available. Spread across continents, they measure astronomical distances and gravity waves. In infrared spectrometers, they measure the size and shape of organic molecules. Experiments that require interferometric methods require you to study the relatively abundant and extensive chemistry, physics, and mathematics on the subject that can be found in the current literature.

The inverse square law limits the range of distance measurement systems using broadcast sound or light energy as a reflected medium for distance measurement. A narrowly focused beam of energy should extend the range of measurement in proportion to the width of the beam. Lasers measure the earth-moon distance by reflecting pulsed beams from shaped reflectors left on the moon's surface by explorers.

Any distance measuring technique that depends on reflectance is influenced by the size, shape, surface texture, and material composition of the object being detected. A soft cotton surface may not reflect an ultrasonic pulse, and a radar pulse may pass completely through a flock of birds.

Strain Gauge

A plastic insulating film with a thin metallic foil deposited on its surface can measure very small mechanical displacements. A typical gauge element consists of many thin parallel lines of a resistive metal alloy deposited on a plastic film. The alloy changes resistance if deformed by a stress applied to the plastic medium to which the multiple parallel arrays of conductors are bonded. Strain gauge elements are also manufactured in spiral configurations. A strain gauge manufacturer has published detailed gauge information at `www.vishaypg.com/docs/11055/tn505.pdf`. In the reference, it is noted that the most common thin-film alloy is constantan (45% Cu and 55% Ni used in J type thermocouples). The alloy has a high sensitivity to strain or gauge factor, high resistivity, and relatively low-temperature sensitivity. The high resistivity is desirable as a small grid of the alloy has a suitable resistance value to aid in measurements of small changes. Constantan also has a relatively high elongation capability and a good fatigue life.

Backing material for the alloy grid must be a plastic, deformable, insulating medium sturdy enough to permit handling and mounting on the substrate to be monitored. Polyimide polymers and glass fiber-reinforced phenolic epoxy are two of the more commonly used backing materials.

As discussed in Chapters 3 and 5, a Wheatstone bridge detects small changes in the resistance elements that make up the bridge. Multiple strain gauges are often used as arms in the bridge. You can augment the signal generated by a mechanical deformation if two gauges simultaneously measure tension-based expansion, and the concomitant compression in the arms of the Wheatstone bridge monitoring a bending or flexing action.

Capacitor Distance Measurement

Capacitance and capacitors (see Chapter 1) are important electrical circuitry components but can measure weight, force, pressure, and small distances. The energy stored in a capacitor depends on several physical and chemical parameters, including the distance between the conducting plates.

Chapter 9 describes a multiple plate capacitor's compression to measure weight or force and angle of inclination. By calibrating the capacitance as a function of known distance in a multiple, parallel plate capacitor, it should be possible to use the device as a small or short distance measurement transducer.

Velocity and Speed

Velocity is a vector quantity obtained by dividing the displacement distance by the transit time. Velocities possessing both magnitude and direction can determine positions in the past or future (velocity = displacement/time). Speed is a scalar quantity determined by dividing the distance between two locations by the time required to transverse the distance.

Acceleration

According to Newton's second law of motion, to set a mass at rest in motion, energy must be applied to the body by an unbalanced force acting over a displacement to increase its velocity from zero to some finite value. If the time required to change the velocity from zero to its final value is recorded, you can determine the vector acceleration using acceleration = velocity change/time of velocity change.

Velocity and acceleration were examined and modeled with mathematical relationships by Galileo Galilei near the end of the sixteenth century. Galileo devised several innovative technologies and experimental techniques to examine the relationship between the gravitational force and its actions on free-falling bodies. He slowed the rate at which gravity causes bodies to accumulate higher velocities by using an inclined plane down which gravity caused a bronze ball to accelerate. He measured the timing of the increasing ball velocity with an ingenious method using the weight of water flowing through an orifice as a timing clock. From many trials conducted with careful observations and recording data, he could derive the relationships between distance, speed, and acceleration caused by gravity.

Galileo also studied pendulums and the simple harmonic motion resulting from the variations in the physical lengths and masses of the oscillating systems.

Vibration

A vibration can be envisioned as a repetitive or random oscillation of a system's mass about its normal "at rest" position or point of equilibrium.

Vibrations are often associated with a rotary motion that may occur as a continuous action or a series of regularly spaced discrete steps of movement occurring in fixed units of time or as steps occurring at randomly spaced intervals.

Continuous

DC motors convert electric energy into continuous rotational energy. The speed, direction of rotation, and torque (twisting strength) delivered by the motor can be varied by controlling the motor's voltage. A continuous vibration is often generated by a rotating object not having a symmetrical distribution of its mass about the axis of rotation.

Often rotational speeds of objects such as fans and motors can be monitored by counting the interruptions caused in a beam of infrared radiation by the passing blades or measuring the number of magnetic pulses created by magnets mounted on a rotating shaft in fixed units of time.

Discrete Steps

Relays, mechanical solenoids, stepper, and servo motors produce vibrations when activated. The vibration frequency, determined by the individual mechanical actions, may be repetitive or random.

Vibration Detectors and Generators

Recent advances in materials science have allowed the first practical applications of graphene. Graphene is a single-atom thick sheet of carbon atoms bound together in a planar hexagonal configuration. Graphene sheets are strong, flexible, and lightweight. They are used in manufacturing speakers and microphones capable of operational frequencies from less than 20 Hz to more than 500 KHz.

Piezoelectric materials display a voltage in response to applied physical stress. Certain organic polymers and inorganic crystals generate electrical signals in response to rapid compressive or bending stresses and convert compressions and bending vibrations into measurable electrical signals.

Crystals and Plastic Polymers

In 1880 and 1881, the Curie brothers first reported the generation of voltages when certain types of inorganic crystals such as quartz, topaz, and Rochelle's salt were subjected to mechanical stress. In the following year, physicist G. Lippmann reported the reverse effect of expansion and contraction when a voltage was applied to these same crystals.

Interconversion of electrical voltage and mechanical volume change led to the development of high-frequency sound generation and its application to sonic range-finding. Research and development efforts to improve the sound electricity transducer produced three piezoelectric materials: barium titanate ($BaTiO_3$), lead zirconium titanate ($Pb[Zr_xTi_{1-x}]O_3$) (PZT), and lithium niobate ($LiNbO_3$).

The piezoelectric phenomenon is found in ionic crystals with unit cell configurations that lack a central or center of symmetry with respect to charges. An application of stress produces a net distortion of the positive and negative charges with respect to each other, resulting in an electric dipole formation or polarization. For some materials, the effect can be augmented by heating the crystalline structure under the influence of a strong DC electric field to allow the structure's polarized domains to align and then cooling the crystal to fix the aligned domains in place.

An organic polymer, polyvinylidene difluoride (PVDF) $[-CH_2-CF_2-]_n$ exhibits a strong enough piezoelectric voltage generation to be used as a flexible film vibration detector.

Experiment: Distance, Time, Velocity, and Acceleration

A modernized study of motion and vibration fundamentals can be implemented with the physical computing systems developed thus far and a repetition of two basic experiments done by Galileo more than 500 years ago. The value of g, the gravitational constant, can be measured by observing the speed of a ball rolling down an inclined plane or by determining the length and period of a simple pendulum. (Recall air drag influences both experiments, and mechanical friction causes the ball to spin as it rolls down the inclined plane, transforming some of the gravitational potential energy into rotational kinetic energy.)

The two experiments are relatively easy to implement, are a classical study in experimental design, and both can use the well-known, well documented IR break beam technology (see https://learn.adafruit.com/ir-breakbeam-sensors).

To implement a break beam timing gate, a pair of small printed circuit boards can be etched and drilled to mount the IR emitter and either a photodiode or phototransistor to implement the circuitry in Figure 6-1.

In Figure 6-1, two caption arrows indicate the two halves of the circuit that must be mounted on two boards to form a break beam gate through which an object being timed must pass. Gate pairs of hand-drawn circuit boards are visible in Figures 6-3, 6-4, 6-5, 6-6, and 6-29, each of which is mounted on adjustable wood U-shaped mounts. For pendulum timing, only one pair of boards is required, while a dual rail track representation of an inclined plane may require five pairs to divide the track into four equidistant quarters. (Recall that the RPi GPIO logic levels of 1 and 0 are represented by 3.3 V and near 0 while the Arduino is 5 V. Signals with a voltage level over half the logic 1 value are interpreted as high. Signal voltages below the 50% level are low or 0. An accidental application of a 5 V signal to a pin of the RPi GPIO array may damage the computer.)

You can eliminate timekeeping problems in the host computer by using the Arduino's crystal-controlled oscillator clock and connecting one or more photogates to the microcontroller using the circuit shown in Figure 6-1.

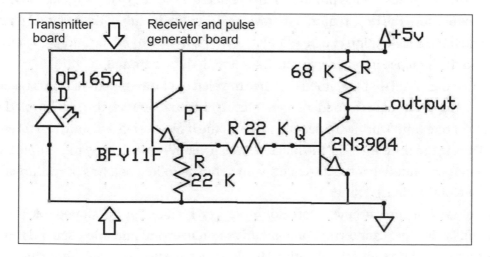

Figure 6-1. *A 5 V IR break beam timing gate circuit*

Figure 6-2 depicts a circuit configuration for a series of 5 timing gates that can be placed at known intervals along an inclined track to measure the time at which a rolling ball passes the individual locations.

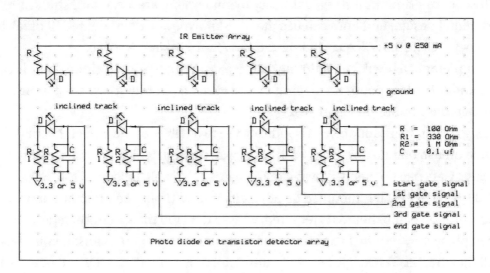

Figure 6-2. *A five gate IR break beam timing circuit for Raspberry Pi data collection*

Galileo reasoned that an inclined plane slows down the rate at which an object is accelerated by gravitational force. A vertical track is equivalent to a free-falling body. As the angle decreases from 90 degrees toward the horizontal, you should see a decrease in the acceleration measured in proportion to the decrease in the plane's slope. Two timing gates can measure the time required to traverse the entire length of the inclined plane from which the acceleration can be calculated, or the track can be monitored by multiple gates and the increase in speed over the track length demonstrated.

Galileo observed that the timed distance traveled over the sloped track increased in a ratio proportional to the odd integers. During the first interval, the ball traveled a distance of one unit. During the second interval, the ball traveled a distance of three units. During the third interval, the ball spanned five units. After many measurements, Galileo demonstrated that the distance spanned by the rolling ball was proportional to the square of the elapsed time.

Accurate time measurement depends on several factors. For the sloped track and pendulum swing, either interrupt or logic-driven millisecond and microsecond time resolution should be sufficient. Arduino Uno boards have two external, hardware interrupt terminals on pins two and three.

The external interrupts can monitor the pendulum swing and the total span of a sloped track. If multiple photogates are used, the pin change interrupts system available on the Atmega 328 chips can also be used. However, a simpler logic-driven system developed and reported in an article in a teaching journal[1] a can be modified to accommodate multiple timing gates (see Listing 6-1 at the end of the chapter).

A three-foot section of aluminum U-channel ⅝ inches wide by ½ inches deep (900 mm × 15 mm × 12 mm) was mounted on a supporting wooden frame prepared to accept five IR emitter/phototransistor photogates that divided a track into four quarters. A ¾-inch hole (18 mm) bored into one end of the supporting frame accepts a dowel that fits into an adjustable clamp on a vertical member of a lab stand to allow for variation of track slope, as depicted in Figure 6-3.

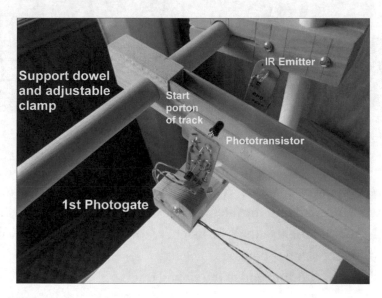

Figure 6-3. *Top end of the sloped track*

Five photogates were mounted to divide the track into four equal quarters. Figure 6-4 shows a typical timing gate.

---

[1]"An Arduino-Controlled Photogate" by C. Galeriu in *The Physics Teacher*, Vol. 51, March, 2013.

Figure 6-4. *Typical photogate mounting detail*

Each U-shaped gate was fixed to the mainframe with a #10 bolt (⅛ in or 3 mm), as shown in Figure 6-4. The bolt head is in the center of the U-shaped gate frame's bottom plate. Spacers were inserted or removed from between the top of the gate frame and the bottom of the mainframe to adjust the height of the IR beam above the track rails to accommodate different-sized spheres.

Figure 6-5 shows the bottom end of the sloped track.

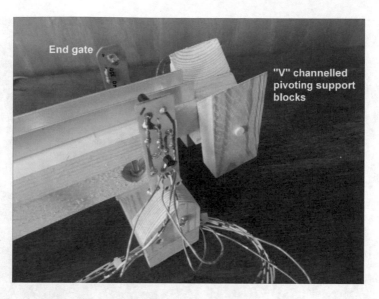

Figure 6-5. *The bottom end of the sloped track*

To catch the test sphere at the end of an experiment, a *catch block* was fabricated from a 3½ in × 4 in × 1¾ in (90 mm × 112 mm × 45 mm) block of wood with a 2 inch (51 mm) diameter × 1 inch (24.5 mm) deep boring on one face to hold the captured sphere. The catch block is seen in place for service in Figure 6-6 and holding the test spheres in Figure 6-7.

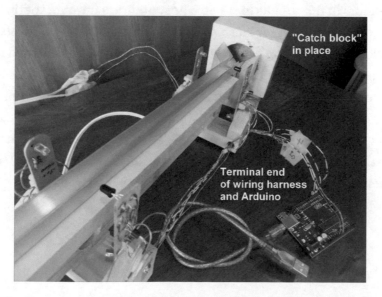

Figure 6-6. *The bottom end of the sloped track with the catch block in place*

Figure 6-7. *The test spheres, catch block, and elevation adjustment blocks*

A USB-powered Arduino has limited current to drive external circuitry, so a 5-IR emitter system should be powered by an external supply. To ensure an intense IR beam, my setup used a 9 V, 1.5 A DC regulated laboratory supply to power the five parallel wired IR emitters creating a 27 mA current in each LED. The bright IR beam current caused the ¼ W 330 Ω resistors in the circuits to run in a hot condition during experimentation.

To ensure sufficient power for biasing the five phototransistor detectors, an auxiliary 1.5 A, DC regulated 5 V supply was connected to the Arduino. A measured current draw for the five-element detector array was 2.5 mA.

Once the sloped track and timing gates are functional, the distance time measurements can be made. With Listing 6-1 loaded into the Arduino, selecting the serial monitor in the Tools menu brings up the blank screen and starts the internal timer. Placing the test ball on the track above the first gate and releasing it to roll "downhill" prints the system time to the serial monitor as each gate is passed.

In Figure 6-8, an experiment with the sloped track generates five "tick count" times consisting of the system microsecond count at the time the individual photogates are tripped. The data consists of the start gate time, the first quarter finish time, followed by the second, third and fourth quarter finish times. The elapsed times for each quarter are obtained by taking the difference between the finish and start time tick counts for the quarter.

The data is transferred by highlighting the data, pressing Ctrl+C to copy it to the operating system clipboard, and then pasting it to the desired spreadsheet or software for data processing.

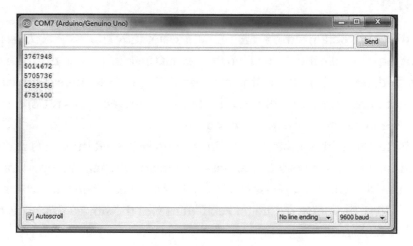

Figure 6-8. *A typical sloped track data collection display*

To duplicate the experiments done by Galileo, a series of glass spheres of assorted sizes were obtained from a large toy distributor in the form of a small bag of children's marbles. Table 6-1 tabulates the diameters, weights, and corresponding colors of the test spheres.

Table 6-1. *Physical Parameters of Glass Test Spheres*

Diameter (mm)	Weight (g)	Color
16	6.69	white
22	14.24	green
24	21.72	blue
40	91.12	red

Observations

By keeping the construction simple, an inherent systematic source of error is introduced into the apparatus to collect data. Galileo noted that the ball's speed during its descent along the track depended on its starting position. In Figure 6-3, there is no fixed starting position. For accurate measurements with spheres of different sizes the spheres must all start from the same point of contact with the track.

The initial testing of the photogate inclined ramp collected three sets of data from six repetitions of the passage of a white, glass sphere down a gently sloped track (slope = 1.9 cm rise in an 88.0 cm run, or ¾-inch rise × 34½-inch run). The data was pasted into a spreadsheet, where the elapsed time for each quarter of the sloped track was calculated, as tabulated in Table 6-2.

Table 6-2. *Initial Sloped Track Testing Data*

Gate pass time usec	Elapsed time		Gate pass time usec	Elapsed time		Gate pass time usec	Elapsed time
2829364	1278216		7172064	1283240		2749988	1323056
4107580	797508		8455304	810668		4073044	793640
4905088	659572		9265972	672160		4866684	655200
5564660	594456		9938132	608136		5521884	586964
6159116			10546268			6108848	
1358656	1286876		3023392	1283968		4957680	1349388
2645532	799468		4307360	800192		6307068	793496
3445000	662772		5107552	660956		7100564	652140
4107772	597076		5768508	594896		7752704	579400
4704848			6363404			8332104	
3157188	1294584		2379456	1322008		10069892	1431628
4451772	795688		3701464	813656		11501520	817556
5247460	659136		4515120	669028		12319076	680132
5906596	592416		5184148	601588		12999208	603824
6499012			5785736			13603032	
2867044	1303320		3208624	1368196		6506156	1394408
4170364	822756		4576820	810232		7900564	796548
4993120	688740		5387052	665976		8697112	654476
5681860	614536		6053028	595916		9351588	583328
6296396			6648944			9934916	
1911508	1350380		2123220	1315968		11237728	1371844
3261888	807036		3439188	809288		12609572	800236
4068924	665392		4248476	666628		13409808	652856
4734316	598384		4915104	597232		14062664	580904
5332700			5512336			14643568	
3467480	1296620		2670760	1325564		13824176	1436200
4764100	792116		3996324	813588		15260376	800604
5556216	651576		4809912	669900		16060980	651840
6207792	588488		5479812	598384		16712820	584388
6796280			6078196			17297208	

A second sloped track experiment was conducted with the gentle slope (1.9 in 88.0 cm) configuration using different-sized spheres as test objects. Table 6-3 tabulates the "tick count" data recorded and the calculated quarter track velocities for the different test spheres.

Table 6-3. *Sloped Track Velocity for Different Sizes and Mass of Spheres*

White	Elapsed Time u sec	Velocity	Green	Elapsed Time u sec	Velocity	Blue	Elapsed Time u sec	Velocity	Red	Elapsed time u sec	Velocity
2749988	1323056	16.63	5919112	1276392	17.24	2399680	1275136	17.25	6457120	1191452	18.46
4073044	793640	27.72	7195504	697608	31.54	3674816	671412	32.77	7648572	622884	35.32
4866684	655200	33.58	7893112	555820	39.58	4346228	528536	41.62	8271456	489612	44.93
5521884	586964	37.48	8448932	493184	44.61	4874764	465688	47.24	8761068	429744	51.19
6108848			8942116			5340452			9190812		
4957680	1349388	16.30	3306184	1282208	17.16	2646676	1230196	17.88	9696160	1212556	18.14
6307068	793496	27.73	4588392	697968	31.52	3876872	664932	33.09	10908716	621840	35.38
7100564	652140	33.74	5286360	556328	39.55	4541804	525336	41.88	11530556	488212	45.06
7752704	579400	37.97	5842688	494568	44.48	5067140	463652	47.45	12018768	428848	51.30
8332104			6337256			5530792			12447616		
10069892	1431628	15.37	3549472	1295084	16.99	2409428	1252156	17.57	2577196	1135760	19.37
11501520	817556	26.91	4844556	697672	31.53	3661584	665660	33.05	3712956	619460	35.51
12319076	680132	32.35	5542228	555676	39.59	4327244	523084	42.06	4332416	485104	45.35
12999208	603824	36.43	6097904	492024	44.71	4850328	460740	47.75	4817520	428728	51.31
13603032			6589928			5311068			5246248		
6506156	1394408	15.78	3330772	1224820	17.96	1161352	1232884	17.84	5331340	1227244	17.93
7900564	796548	27.62	4555592	690912	31.84	2394236	667848	32.94	6558584	622812	35.32
8697112	654476	33.61	5246504	552036	39.85	3062084	526720	41.77	7181396	488228	45.06
9351588	583328	37.71	5798540	489260	44.97	3588804	465248	47.29	7669624	429528	51.22
9934916			6287800			4054052			8099152		
11237728	1371844	16.04	3309824	1254052	17.54	2302340	1210192	18.18	5543848	1117296	19.69
12609572	800236	27.49	4563876	692292	31.78	3512532	661880	33.24	6661144	613272	35.87
13409808	652856	33.70	5256168	551816	39.87	4174412	521776	42.16	7274416	483796	45.47
14062664	580904	37.87	5807984	487008	45.17	4696188	459864	47.84	7758212	426252	51.61
14643568			6294992			5156052			8184464		
13824176	1436200	15.32	7758528	1260172	17.46	2266180	1266044	17.38	6260764	1097648	20.04
15260376	800604	27.48	9018700	697676	31.53	3532224	667556	32.96	7358412	609788	36.08
16060980	651840	33.75	9716376	553716	39.73	4199780	524248	41.96	7968200	482628	45.58
16712820	584388	37.65	10270092	491124	44.80	4724028	462336	47.58	8450828	425380	51.72
17297208			10761216			5186364			8876208		

A third experiment with the sloped track and green sphere was conducted with track slope increasing toward the vertical. The data collected was processed into quarter track increments, and the acceleration calculated only for the transit time of the first quarter of the track length where the starting speed was essentially zero and the short formula of $s = \frac{1}{2} a t^2$ could be used. The data is tabulated and graphically displayed in Figure 6-9.

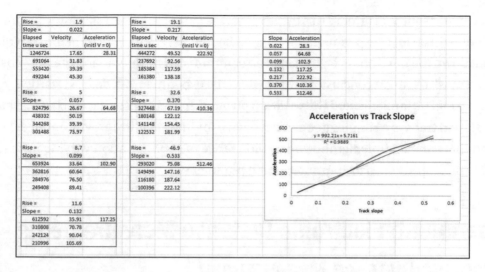

Figure 6-9. *Measured acceleration vs. track slope*

Discussion

Photogates built with phototransistors are of such sensitivity to a broad range of visible light that great care must be taken when commissioning new measuring systems. Daylight from a window caused reflective objects to physically pass through the photogates' IR beam, but reflect enough daylight into the phototransistor to not trip the digital read logic. The apparently errant gate worked normally when the curtains were drawn over the window. In addition to stray light elimination, the blocking object or obscuring media should be of sufficient size to eliminate transmission of the emitted radiation from reaching the photodetector.

An Arduino has a 16 MHz crystal-controlled oscillator that provides the time basis for the microcontroller. The megahertz clock speed executes lines of code at such a high rate that a compact and efficient logic-driven sketch can read milli and micro accurately. (Recall +/- 4 μs rounding in Arduino timing) In Figure 6-9, at a slope of 0.5, the test sphere is taking 100,396 μs to transit the fourth quarter of the track. Any discrepancy between using a logic-driven vs. an interrupt-driven time measurement technique is of minimal consequence.

The collected data shows that within experimental error, the spheres' size and mass do not alter the rate at which they transit the sloped track. Examining the transit times for the four quarters shows the increasing speed as the spheres descend the track. The graphical display in Figure 6-9 indicates that the increasing acceleration as the ramp's slope increases are approximately 992 cm/s/s (cm/s^2) when the track is in a vertical orientation.

The major source of error in this technique is the lack of a defined starting point for the spheres. In an ideal experiment, the spheres should have zero velocity at the start of a descent down the track however, the small error introduced by the variable starting positions does not mask the main conclusions drawn from the experiments. A defined starting position could be implemented with a tilt-up pivoting, hinged, or sliding mechanical barrier.

A sloped track is a simple mechanical device for investigating gravity-induced motion that can be implemented with a wide range of sophistication varying from sloped boards and stopwatches to computer timed photogates.

Experiment: Electronic Distance Measurements

Ultrasonic Distance Measurement

Sound vibrations travel through the air at approximately 344 m/s, and the speed varies slightly with the relative humidity. For accurate velocities under varying ambient conditions, corrections can be made using online calculators (see resource.npl.co.uk/acoustics/techguides/speedair/).

Ultrasonic range-finders consisting of a side-by-side high-frequency sound transmitter and receiver are used with computers and microcontrollers to monitor distances up to 200 centimeters. A relatively inexpensive, easily obtained, and simple to use ultrasonic range-finder is the HC-SR04. The device has four connections: power, ground, trigger, and echo. When connected to the +5 V, ground and #9 and #10 digital pins of the Arduino, programmed with the code in Listing 6-2 in the following listings, a stream of distance measurements to the nearest object in the device field of view (FOV) is streamed out to the serial monitor.

A number of variables are involved with the application of the ultra-sonic reflection, range finding technique that is presented in the Discussion section of the following text.

Experiment

A ⅛-inch (3 mm) plywood mounting yoke was cut out to accept the transmission and reception tubes of an HC-SR04 ultrasonic range-finder. The yoke's dual openings were offset from a hole bored in the plate to accept a #10 (⅛ in or 3 mm) bolt and wing nut used as a compression fitting in an adjustable clamping arrangement (see Figure 6-10). The SR04 was connected to an Arduino microcontroller board programmed with the code in Listing 6-2.

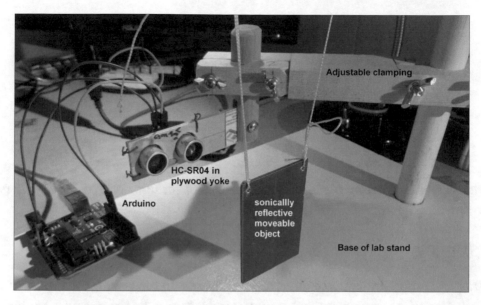

Figure 6-10. *An ultrasonic range-finder distance to pendulum experimental setup*

Observations

When tested with a centimeter scale and a block of wood, the SR04 exhibited a fluctuating distance measurement error of less than ½ cm (¼ in) over the 2 to 50 cm (¾ in to 2 in) range. When the block was removed from the field of view (FOV), the device measured the distance to the wall at 174.3 cm (71 in).

Attempts to follow the motion of a moving object led to the development of the flat steel plate suspended from a pair of threads, as depicted in Figure 6-10. (A dual-string pendulum is sometimes referred to as a *bifilar* or *two-wire pendulum*. A bifilar pendulum is often used to determine the center of mass in a suspended object.) The dual filament arrangement is used in this experiment solely to keep the moving mass centered in the SR04 FOV. With the plate's horizontal motion restricted, the semi-quantitative plotting function of the Arduino serial monitor could record the back-and-forth motion of the plate, as graphically displayed in Figure 6-11, when acting as a pendulum "bob" with the mechanical configuration seen in Figure 6-10. A detailed explanation of the Arduino serial monitor plotter operation, adjustments, and limitations are at the following online sources.

- www.arduino.cc/reference/en/libraries/plotter/

- https://github.com/devinaconley/arduino-plotter

- https://learn.adafruit.com/experimenters-guide-for-metro/
  circ08-using%20the%20arduino%20serial%20plotter

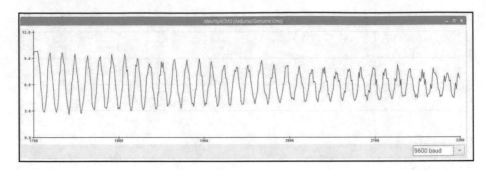

Figure 6-11. *A recording of simple harmonic motion with an HC-SR04 ultrasonic range-finder*

Discussion

An ultrasonic range-finder determines distance based on measuring the time required for a high-frequency, multiple wave, sound pulse or "chirp" to bounce off an object of interest. Because the system is a point source of radiation reflected off a reflective surface, the inverse square law and initial power determines system performance. In addition to the inherent dispersive nature of the broadcast signal, textured, small, or curved reflective surfaces, oblique-angled reflections, subject motion, and minimum and maximum detection distances are some reasons why objects are not seen by the device. The large flat steel surface (at right angles to the source and receiver modules, as seen in Figure 6-10) resulted from a small experimental testing project conducted to get reproducible results in attempts to use the SR04 in the pendulum and sloped track motion studies.

The range-finder's optimal performance is realized in conditions mimicking those described earlier and seen in Figure 6-10. However, the recording system suffers from numerous deficiencies with respect to quantitative data collection.

The oscillations' amplitude is recorded by a distance-measuring sensor calibrated before or after the experiment. The period between oscillations becomes a little more difficult to calibrate. Try some experimentation with a stopwatch and manual oscillation counting or a first derivatives software monitor similar to the one used in Chapter 3 for following the slope of temperature recordings.

Although producing a steady, strong recording of the pendulum oscillation, the pendulum is a massive source of air resistance. It should be possible to reduce the large air resistance by using a plate drilled with holes or a metal grating if a longer time of oscillation decay is required. A perforated or metal grille pendulum would need to be tested to see at what point the ratio between open and closed surfaces affects the reflection of the ultrasonic pulse.

Infrared Electromagnetic Proximity Sensors and Distance

Rangefinders

Proximity sensors are qualitative positional indicators consisting of a pulsed infrared emitter and a reflected IR pulse detector. An IR diode and an IR photodiode are mounted in a parallel orientation pointing in the same direction. The IR photodiode sees only the background emission. An object opaque to IR that enters the emitter FOV can reflect some of the IR to the photodiode FOV and cause an increased current flow in the diode circuit. The more IR reflected, the more current flows in the photodiode circuit, which can gauge proximity between the emitter-detector couple and the reflector. An OSEPP IRDET-01 is an inexpensive adjustable distance proximity sensor.

STMicroelectronics manufactures a surface mount technology (SMT) integrated circuit laser ranging sensor with a part number VL53L0X that determines distance measurements up to 2 meters (7 ft).

Experiment: Proximity Sensing

An OSEPP IRDET-01 was connected to the 5 V power and ground connections of an Arduino while the signal pin was connected to the A0 analog input. With an arrangement similar to that depicted in Figure 6-12, the sensor can be calibrated. The blue box with the slot screw adjustment in the board's upper-right corner is the ten-turn distance setting adjustment.

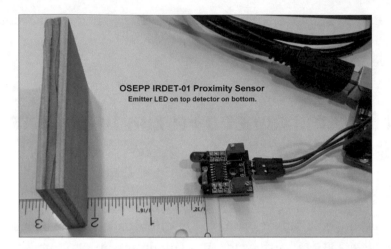

Figure 6-12. *Establishing the IRDET-01 active proximity range*

To calibrate, connect the device to the Arduino, load the sketch from Listing 6-3, and set up the measurement scale and detectable object. Move the object back and forth until the SMT LED on the detector board between the emitter diode and the receiver flashes steadily at a rate of 30 flashes in 20 seconds. Carefully move the object toward the board, and stop when the SMT-LED turns on and stays on.

A steady illumination marks the closest point of the proportional sensing range for the given potentiometer setting. Carefully move the object away from the sensor. When the steady flashing stops, the object is at the furthest distance of the operational range for the given distance potentiometer setting. Having noted the closest and furthest active points, the distance control can be rotated one full circle in either the clockwise or counterclockwise direction.

After making the known variation on the distance control, the closest and furthest active points can be measured again. The increase or decrease in the range can be determined by examining the previous distance setting data. Using the technique described, the position of the distance potentiometer created the proximity sensing zones tabulated in Table 6-4. The data describing the active range is tabulated with the imperial measurements on the left and the corresponding metric values on the right.

Table 6-4. *IRDET-01 Active Ranges for Potentiometer Settings*

Position of Potentiometer	Active range	Min to Max
Fully CCW	2⅛ to 2-½	54 to 64 mm
1 turn CW	2⅛ to 2-⅝	54 to 64 mm
2 turns CW	2⅛ to 2¾	54 to 70 mm
3 turns CW	2¼ to 2¾	58 to 70 mm
4 turns CW	2½ to 3	58 to 64 mm
5 turns CW	2⅝ to 3¼	67 to 82 mm
6 turns CW	2⅞ to 3½	72 to 89 mm
7 turns CW	3⅛ to 4	80 to 102 mm
8 turns CW	3⅜ to 4½	85 to 114 mm
9 turns CW	5¼ to 8¾	133 to 214 mm
10 turns CW	7⅛ to ∞	175 to ∞

Observations

When the Arduino sketch in Listing 6-3 runs, only two ADC values are observed. At the approximate minimum values tabulated in Table 6-4, the digital values streamed to the serial monitor switch between 1023 and 12 or 13. The IRDET-01 is acting like a digital sensor at the minimum proximity distance set by the distance potentiometer.

Discussion

Unlike larger multi-turn potentiometers, the miniatures may not exhibit a mechanical stop at the end of wiper travel. Hence, you must "orient" the potentiometer wiper's current set position with the approximate values in Table 6-4.

The manufacturer suggests that the frequency at which the pulsed IR operates can be adjusted if interfering radiation is present. My experiments have shown that adjusting the frequency potentiometer also alters the range settings set by the distance potentiometer. Experiments that require frequency adjustments should re-adjust any previously set distance calibrations or define the ranges after altering frequency settings.

To use the proximity sensor with analog input, an IF logic statement must determine any actions to be taken when the detector causes the analog input to switch from 1023 to 12 or 13.

Experiment: IR Time-of-Flight Distance Measurement

Several manufacturers, such as Adafruit Inc. and Pololu Corp., use the VL53L0X Time-of-Flight (ToF) distance sensor from STMicrocircuits Inc. as a range-finder. The nominal device used in the following experiments is a 200 mm range SMT chip that is reported to measure distances from approximately 3 cm (1.19 in) to 2 m (81.5 in) with a 3% to 10% accuracy, depending on the ambient lighting and temperature conditions under which the device is used.

A quantitative distance measure is derived from travel time taken by a reflected pulsed IR beam. The miniature circuit boards populated with SMT IC components accept 5 V power and communicate with the I2C protocol that the Arduino type microcontrollers receive on the A4 and A5 analog input pins. (Pololu Corporation offers three ToF carrier boards with ranges of 60 mm, 200 mm, and 400 mm (24 in, 81 in, and 162 in)).

There are two libraries with examples of code to read the sensor in a continuous mode or a single measurement mode. Both libraries are available on the GitHub repositories at `https://github.com/pololu/vl510x-arduino` and `https://github.com/adafruit/Adafruit_VL53L0X`. Each provides an Arduino-compatible library with the chip manufacturer's suggested application program interface (API).

To test and validate the range-finding carrier boards, the flat plate pendulum and a suitable clamping system eliminate many problems with broadcast radiation in range-finding systems. Virtually every device that relies on broadcast radiation and the capture of the reflected signal must meet the criteria of having the emitter, target, and detector all in the system field of view (FOV), the target having a reflective surface and the reflected radiation being in the detector's FOV. The bifilar, flat plate pendulum meets all the criteria outlined in the presentation on using ultrasonic detection with the SR04 device. The testing and validation set up for the ToF IR range-finding experiments are depicted in Figure 6-13.

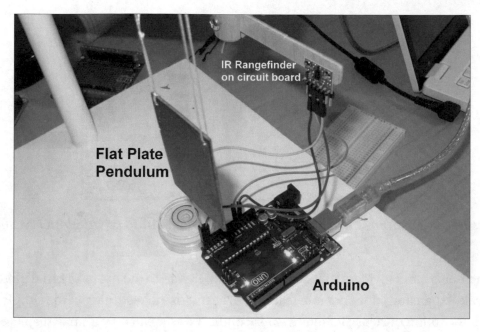

Figure 6-13. *Testing and validation setup for ToF IR pulse range-finder*

Observations

Figure 6-14 shows the ToF detector's signal on the Arduino serial plotter. The Arduino microcontroller runs a continuous data collection program from the Pololu Corporation library. Although the plotter records static distance measurements from 85 mm to 96 mm, the actual distance between the sensor and flat plate measured 75 mm (3 in). A repeat static distance measurement a day later (see Figure 6-15) indicates that the distance measured appears to be between 66 mm and 68 mm (2⅝ in and 2¾ in).

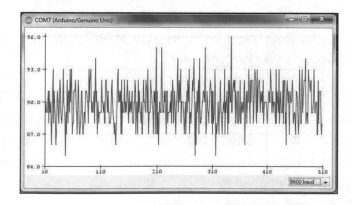

Figure 6-14. *Distance measurements collected by Arduino serial plotter*

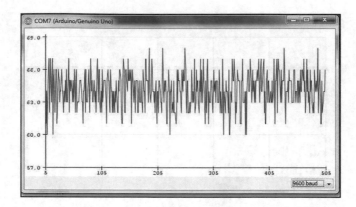

Figure 6-15. *Distance measurements collected by Arduino serial plotter the next day*

The noise band (evident in Figures 6-14 and 6-15 due to the Arduino serial plotter's autoscale expansion) does not noticeably interfere with the recording of the simple harmonic motion of 20 oscillations in 27 seconds. It was created by a small displacement of the bifilar pendulum from its rest position at 75 mm (3 in), as depicted in Figure 6-16.

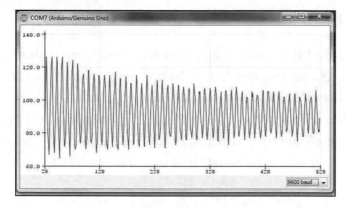

Figure 6-16. *Recorded simple harmonic motion of bifilar flat plate pendulum with a Time-of-Flight IR pulse range-finder*

One of the intended applications of the ToF IR pulse distance range-finder is as a hand-motion detector. Three experiments were conducted with the Arduino serial plotter as the microcontroller ran the Pololu continuous monitoring program. I inserted my hand into the device FOV and moved it toward and away from the stationary carrier board. The detector was positioned 82 cm (33½ in) from the wall and at the end of the desktop on which the experiments were conducted.

Figure 6-17 depicts the Arduino serial plotter in its initial default mode. It records the default full-scale display of the Pololu software in the absence of any obstruction or moving object in its emitter and detector FOVs of 35° and 25°, respectively.

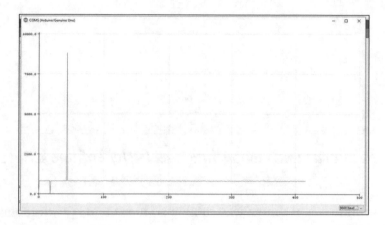

Figure 6-17. *Arduino serial monitor output for a clear ToF FOV*

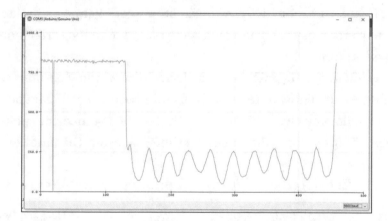

Figure 6-18. *Recorded hand motion autoscaled by Arduino serial plotter software*

In Figure 6-19, the plotter software's autoscaling has reverted to its initial default settings.

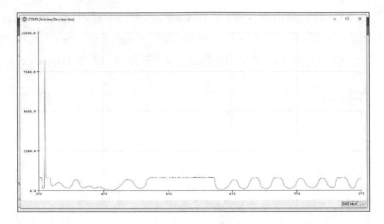

Figure 6-19. *Recorded hand motion auto-rescaled by Arduino serial plotter software*

A semi-quantitative experiment was conducted to evaluate the influence of ambient lighting conditions on the range-finding values. A thin, flat plastic ruler, orthogonal or at right angles to the vertical and horizontal axes of the sensor, was placed 129 mm from the ToF carrier board. In a room lit by overhead fluorescent light on a desktop 3 feet from a window on an overcast day, 22 data points were recorded in the serial monitor screen on my Windows/Arduino setup.

Immediately after the data points were collected, the window curtains were drawn, the overhead fluorescent lights were turned off, and a second set of data points were collected. On the following clear, bright day, a third set of distance data points were collected. Table 6-5 summarizes the three experiments' results (distance in mm).

Table 6-5. *The Effect of Ambient Lighting Conditions on Response of VL53LOX*

Light Conditions	Data Points Collected	Average	Standard Deviation
Darkened room	28	124.9	2.086
Over cast window	21	123.1	1.571
Bright day window	27	119.4	1.638

Discussion

According to the theory of special relativity, the motion of massless photons is the upper limit of the magnitude of relative velocity in the universe (186,000 miles/second, or 299,792,458 m/s). Over short distances, special techniques and electronics are required for reflected light measurements. Illuminating the subject with a pulsed, modulated sine or square waveform IR beam from a laser operating in the 850 nm–940 nm range, and then collecting the reflected energy pulses with a single-photon avalanche diode (SPAD) with fast electronics able to time a pulse of 6.6 picoseconds in duration can achieve 1 mm distance resolution. The phase difference between the emitted and captured reflected pulse is proportional to the time of flight or distance.

Measuring only the reflected pulses out of the ambient background improves the signal to noise ratio (see Table 6-5). Close examination of the actual measured distance and the ToF reported distance on the serial monitor reveal some discrepancies and errors that are obvious and somewhat predictable. For the set distance of 129 mm, measured values of 125, 123, and 119 are generated for the three lighting condition variation experiments.

The manufacturer specification sheet indicates a 3% to 10 % error, and the three measurements have 3%, 4.7%, and 7.75% errors, respectively. The solid-state device is temperature-sensitive but specified for operation between –20°C and 70°C and is factory calibrated, presumably for 20°C/25°C or room-temperature operation. The datasheet indicates that calibration is not valid if the temperature during measurement is greater than 8°C off from the factory calibrated conditions.

For experimental work requiring modest accuracy, the ToF sensors should be tested and validated under the lighting variations and temperature changes encountered in the actual measurement environment.

Measuring the differences in pulse time shift results in aliasing, limiting the range over which the pulse frequency can determine distances. Other ToF chip models are available to measure shorter distances.

As of version 1.6.13 of the Arduino IDE, the axes on the serial plotter were not adjustable. The serial plotter software utility graphically displays incoming USB serial data values on a dynamic x/y axes screen. The vertical y axis (ordinate) automatically adjusts as the numerical value of the output increases or decreases. Each tick on the x axis (abscissa) is equal to an executed serial println statement in the Arduino sketch. Hence, the rate at which tics are displayed depends on the rate of execution of the sketch. The x-axis display in the serial port window is limited to 500 tick counts.

For more controllable plotting of distance measurements and following target motion or position, data from the Arduino can be streamed out to the serial port and either the Windows DAQFactory or the RPi Python Matplotlib strip chart recorder displays can be used to view the data in a quantifiable graphical format. The slower response plotting programs may need to have the streamed data rate slowed or data stored in memory for plotting offline later.

Three-Dimensional Positioning and Motion
Accelerometers, e-Compass, and Tilt Correcting

Microcontrollers like the Arduino read the output from solid-state accelerometers, compasses based on magnetometers, and global positioning system receivers. Surface mount technology reduces the size and response time of the position and motion sensing devices to the point at which small remotely controlled and autonomous flying machines that are the size of large insects and birds have become commonplace surveillance devices for wildlife biology and aerial geological/geographical field investigations.

There are many sensors available for measuring both time and motion in three dimensions that can be used with an Arduino microcontroller. The magnetic compass capability of the STMicroelectronics LSM303DLHC output was demonstrated, and the accelerometer and magnetic capabilities are further developed here.

Both Adafruit and Pololu develop electronic compass boards and software. Pololu uses a newer revision of the accelerometer-magnetometer electronics (LSM303D) to produce a tilt-corrected compass. Both manufacturers provide extensive software libraries to demonstrate the accelerometer and compassing functions.

The newer LSM303D chip is a system-in-package featuring a 3D digital linear acceleration sensor and a 3D digital magnetic sensor.

Observations

Figure 6-20 shows the serial monitor output obtained from the Adafruit software and LSM303DLHC carrier or breakout board, operating in the digital compass mode. The board was mounted in a small desktop adjustable stand that was rotated by hand to record the changing compass headings.

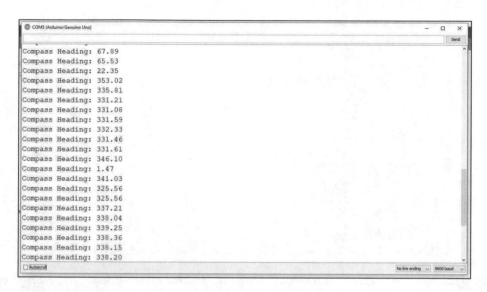

Figure 6-20. *Arduino serial monitor compass headings*

Figure 6-21 shows the serial monitor's output when the Arduino was programmed with the Adafruit magnetometer software and the author brought a rare earth magnet near the detector board.

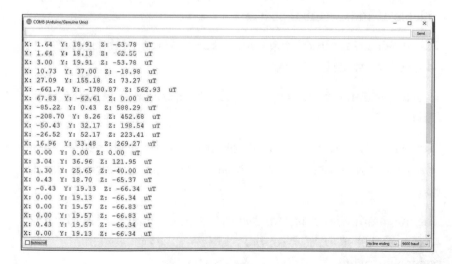

Figure 6-21. *Three axis magnetometer response to the proximity of a rare earth magnet to the LSH303DLHC*

Figure 6-22 shows the serial monitor response obtained when the author picked up and shook the desktop stand in which the accelerometer/magnetometer board was mounted.

341

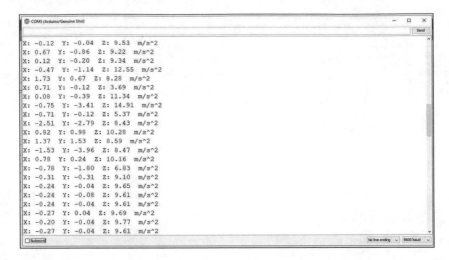

Figure 6-22. *Recorded accelerometer readings from handshaking the mounted LSH303DLHC board*

Discussion

Figures 6-20, 6-21, and 6-22 display the serial monitor outputs from the sensor as received by the Arduino using the three sketches provided by the Adafruit programs and libraries available on the GitHub repository.

- The multisensor interfacing library is at `https://github.com/adafruit/Adafruit_Sensor`.

- The device library is at `https://github.com/adafruit/Adafruit_LSM303DLHC`.

- The LSM303DLHC tutorial and compass code is at `https://learn.adafruit.com/lsm303-accelerometer-slash-compass-breakout/coding`.

- The magnetometer program is at `https://github.com/adafruit/Adafruit_LSM303DLHC/blob/master/examplesmagsensor/magsensor.pde`.

- The accelerometer program is at `https://github.com/adafruit/Adafruit_LSM303DLHC/blob/master/examples/accelsensor/accelsensor.pde`.

For more information on the LSM303DLHC's properties and capabilities, consult the manufacturer's datasheet at www.st.com/en/mems-and-sensors/lsm303dlhc.html. The datasheet describes the range of sensitivities available on the 3D accelerometer and the 3D magnetometer and many other device features.

The breakout board communicates with the Arduino through the I²C (or I2C) serial bus interface that supports standard and fast mode 100 kHz and 400 kHz operation. The system can be configured to generate interrupt signals by inertial wake-up/free-fall events and the device's position. Thresholds and timing of interrupt generators are programmable by the end user. Magnetic and accelerometer blocks can be enabled or put into power-down mode separately.

Raspberry Pi Motion Detection, Recording, and Visualization

Traditionally, the terms to describe the motion of ships and boats at sea also apply to aircraft moving through the air. When traveling in an x direction, in three-dimensional space, rotational motion about the three axes is referred to as *roll*, *pitch*, and *yaw*, as illustrated in Figure 6-23.

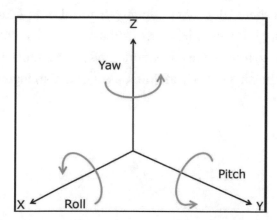

Figure 6-23. *Roll, pitch and yaw axes*

The RPi Foundation has developed and provides a multipurpose motion and environmental monitoring board called the Sense HAT (hardware at top). Sense HAT was developed for the annual Astro-Pi competition. The best student-derived code for measurements using the board's sensors and displays were loaded on the two RPis equipped with the Sense HAT boards taken aboard the International Space Station in 2015.

A Sense HAT sensor board mounts directly onto the RPi GPIO pin array or can be connected to the Pi by a 40-pin ribbon cable. Although much larger than the smaller Arduino, accessible carrier, or breakout boards, the multipurpose Sense HAT is capable of physical computing. It is an educational demonstration platform and a fully functional sensor array. A Sense HAT is easy to handle. A complete tutorial on programming Python to extract data from onboard sensors is available on GitHub (see `https://github.com/raspberrypilearning/sense-hat-data-logger/blob/master/worksheet.md` or `https://projects.raspberrypi.org/sense-hat-data-logger/4`).

Experiment

By following the worksheet or projects tutorial, you can develop a data logging program that records all the sensor outputs from the board in a timestamped, comma-separated value format that most spreadsheet programs can read.

Figures 6-24 and 6-25 show some of the columns in the data file after having been imported into the LibreOffice spreadsheet calc program on the RPi.

Selective data logging for positional or navigation determinations can use the techniques explained in the worksheet2 tutorial on the GitHub repository to isolate the accelerometer, gyroscope, magnetometer/compass readings, and the timestamp.

The tutorial in worksheet2 describes applying true/false Boolean logic to the general-purpose data logging program, created in the primary tutorial to collect the desired parameters. In addition to a selective collection, the second tutorial guides you through the process of varying the data collection times, as depicted in Figures 6-26 and 6-27.

Observations

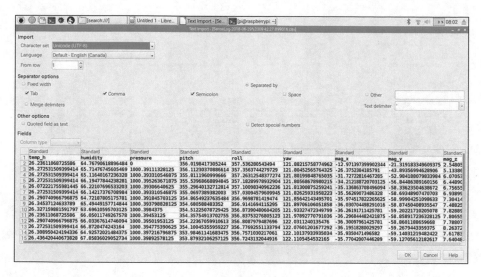

Figure 6-24. *Left rows and columns of Sense HAT data recordings in LibreOffice calc spreadsheet*

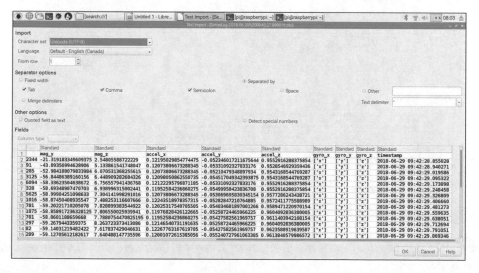

Figure 6-25. *Right rows and columns of Sense HAT data recordings in LibreOffice calc spreadsheet*

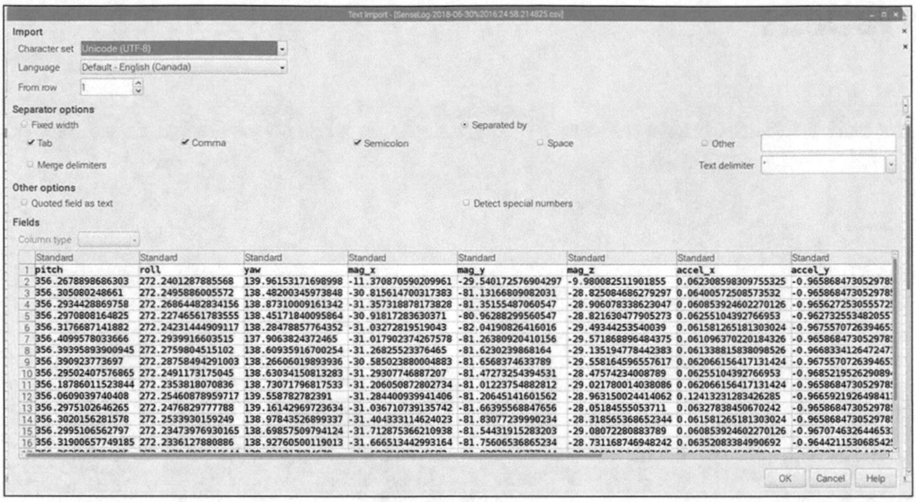

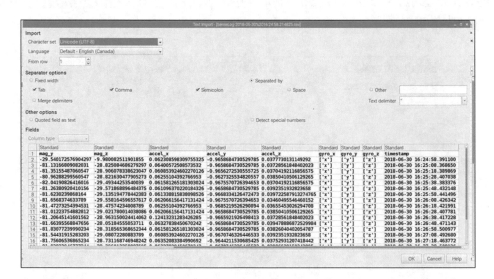

Figure 6-26. *Data logging of navigational sensors with selected time interval left columns*

Figure 6-27. *Data logging of navigational sensors with selected time intervals right columns*

Discussion

The timestamps in Figure 6-27 reflect the 10-second interval I chose to demonstrate the Sense_Logger_v4 code capabilities.

In addition to numerically recording position, movement, and orientation, the RPi and Sense HAT board can generate an interactive, graphical, three-dimensional image display. The board's sensors can create a software or virtual IMU from the outputs of the accelerometer and gyroscope to control a three-dimensional, graphical image display.

Figure 6-28 shows the 3D Apollo-Soyuz image on the RPi monitor that follows the orientation of the sensors making up the roll, pitch, and yaw inputs to the virtual IMU of the sensor board.

Any motion or movement imparted to the board mounted on the RPi is mirrored by the 3D image of the docked spacecraft (see https://github.com/astro-pi). As described in the GitHub ReadMe file, by keying certain entries, the effect of removing various inputs to the IMU can be evaluated.

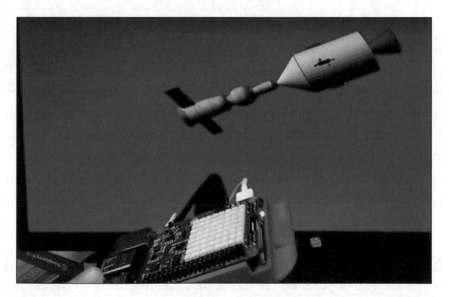

Figure 6-28. *Control of a 3D image with an IMU*

Image motion is limited to the primary three degrees of freedom—roll, pitch, and yaw. Actual forward translational movement along the x axis is not transferred from RPi to image. Separating the Sense HAT board from the computer with a ribbon cable lessens the strain on the RPi and its power and input-output cables.

Repetitive Motions and Vibration

A truly ancient building tool, the *plumb bob*, consists of a mass suspended by a string from an overhead structure. At rest, the supporting string of the plumb bob, under the influence of gravity, forms a plumb, true, or vertical reference line.

A plumb bob is also a simple pendulum. Displacing and releasing the suspended mass results in the bob swinging back and forth about its equilibrium point in an oscillation called *simple harmonic motion* (SHM). The pendulum swings in a back-and-forth motion across its point of equilibrium until the drag from air friction dissipates the energy of the force that was required to initially move its mass. In the seventeenth century, Galileo observed that the time required for the pendulum to swing back and forth for small distances depends only on the length of the pendulum.

The following mathematical expression governs an oscillation time for a simple pendulum subjected to a small angular displacement.

$$T = 2\pi(L/g)^{1/2}$$

T is the time in seconds, L is the length of the pendulum in meters and g is the acceleration due to gravity.

In a typical experiment, the pendulum bob is displaced a horizontal distance from its rest position and released. Gravity pulling down on the bob causes it to accelerate toward the low energy rest position, and the bob experiences an increasing velocity as it accelerates downward and travels inward. The velocity increases until the mass passes through the rest position. At this point, the pull of gravity begins to decrease the elevated velocity as it moves outward and upward against the gravitational force. Eventually, the outward and upward velocity decreases to zero at the point of maximum angular displacement from the rest position, and the simple harmonic oscillation cycle begins again.

Aerodynamic drag caused by the air's friction being displaced by the moving pendulum eventually dampens out the oscillations and returns the pendulum/plumb bob to its rest position.

A re-arrangement of the pendulum time period expression can generate a means for measuring "g"—the local gravitational acceleration.

$$g = L/(T/6.2832)^2$$

The rearranged expression for measuring g involves determining the pendulum length, L, and the period of oscillation, T.

Galileo observed that the length of the pendulum determined the period or time of oscillation and that the pendulum's mass does not affect the time of oscillation.

Experiment

Figure 6-29 depicts the setup to collect the data in Table 6-6.

Figure 6-29. *Photogate pendulum timing data collection setup using an Arduino microcontroller*

To repeat the observations made by Galileo, a series of graded weights as used with fishing tackle were obtained from a sporting goods store to serve as different pendulum weights or masses.

Each of the weights was painted with a matte black acrylic paint and weighed, as tabulated in Table 6-7. Individual polyester threads were cut and provided with a loop on both ends to prepare pendulums of the nominal lengths listed. To aid in fabricating the desired length of pendulum, a thin scrap of wood had small (¾ in or 20 mm) finishing nails partially driven in at the 0 cm, 12 cm, 24 cm, 48 cm, and 96 cm marks (4.9 in, 9.8 in, 19.6 in, and 39.2 in). Each weight is equipped with a wire loop to accept a quick release clip. The quick-connect fittings are the same length, so as one polyester thread-fitted for a pendulum of 48 cm total length can be quickly fitted with all five weights without effectively changing the length of the pendulum. The length of each looped thread was adjusted so the pendulum's length from the top supporting hook to the midpoint (center of mass) of the weight was within a millimeter or two of the intended nominal length.

The Arduino was programmed with the code in Listing 6-4.

Each period measurement experiment requires the loading of the sketch into the Arduino and drawing back the pendulum "bob" out of the photogate's IR beam. The serial monitor is then activated, and the weight is released to oscillate. Each time the "bob" passes through the IR beam, the system time in ms or millis() is printed to the serial monitor. After collecting approximately 25 to 30 oscillations, the autoscroll option in the bottom left of the serial monitor window is turned off, and the screen scrolled back to the first data point collected. The column of data is then highlighted with the cursor, and the Ctrl+C key sequence is entered to copy the column of data to the operating system clipboard.

An Excel or other spreadsheet is opened, and the column of data pasted into the worksheet. A half swing timing of the pendulum is found by determining the time difference between individual entries. Twenty or so half swing times can be averaged, and then the average doubled to get the full period of oscillation in milliseconds.

Data was collected by fitting the top loop of a polyester thread to the overhead hook on the lab stand and fitting the thread's bottom loop to the quick connect fitting on the weight to be tested. Using a sequential progression of thread, length and weight increase or decrease any large-scale variations in experimental conditions immediately stand out as anomalies in the data collected and transferred.

Observations

In Table 6-6, the pendulum period decreases as the length decreases, and for any given length, the period remains relatively constant as the weight of the "bob" changes.

Table 6-6. *Pendulum Period Data for Weight and Length Differences*

Length	Wt. 1	Wt. 2	Wt. 3	Wt. 4	Wt. 5
96 cm	1.96	1.96	1.95	1.94	1.93
48 cm	1.38	1.38	1.37	1.37	1.36
24 cm	0.98	0.97	0.97	0.96	0.95
12 cm	0.71	0.70	0.70	0.69	0.69

In Figure 6-30, the pendulum period is virtually a linear function of its length.

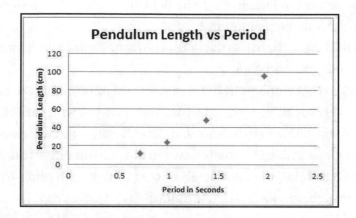

Figure 6-30. *Pendulum length vs. period*

Table 6-7. *Value of "g" from Pendulum Data with Measured Weight and Length Differences*

Length	15.3 gm	11.8 gm	8.2 gm	6.2 gm	4.5 gm
96 cm	9.87	9.87	9.97	10.07	10.17
48 cm	9.87	9.95	10.10	10.10	10.25
24 cm	9.87	10.07	10.07	10.28	10.50
12 cm	9.40	9.67	9.67	9.95	9.95

Discussion

An Arduino microcontroller using the IR break beam techniques and millisecond time measurements must be converted into seconds to validate Galileo's original observations and calculation of the local gravitational acceleration.

In Table 6-7, the effects of air resistance and pendulum length become graphic as the mass of the pendulum bob decreases and the length of the supporting thread increases.

Further insights into the decay in amplitude as seen in the recordings of simple harmonic motion as seen in Figures 6-11 and 6-16 are dealt with in a rigorous mathematical analysis of the pendulum.[2]

DAQFactory and the RPi can use the data generated by the microcontroller to process the pendulum motion data.

Experimentation that employs IR LED emitters and phototransistors in a break beam configuration is a very sensitive technique that must be used with care. A phototransistor is most sensitive in the 850 mm to 950 nm wavelength range, but it is sensitive to other wavelengths with diminishing sensitivity down to the 400 nm range (blue light). Strong direct daylight can cause false or completely missed signals with phototransistor circuits. In several cases, experiments worked in the morning but not in the afternoon unless an opaque light shield was placed between the phototransistor and the daylit window.

The photogates used thus far in this book are based on 940 nm IR beams generated by LEDs and monitored by phototransistor detectors. Photodiode current output is linear over seven to nine orders of magnitude, while the phototransistor range of linearity is only three to four decades. Phototransistors are up to a thousand times more light-sensitive than photodiodes and act as a mechanical switch in the presence or absence of light. When light is present, the phototransistor can sink or pass a substantial current. While in the dark, it passes typical dark currents in the range of 10 nA to 100 nA. Phototransistors are much slower in frequency capability than photodiodes but of sufficient speed for the motion detection studies encountered in mechanical systems.

Measurement of Vibration Motions at Higher Frequencies

Pendulum simple harmonic motion is visible, but as the frequency of the motion increases past one-thirtieth of a second, the eye is no longer able to see the continuously changing position of the mechanical oscillator.

In addition to navigation, accelerometers are used extensively in monitoring vibration. Vibration at higher frequencies between 20 cycles per second and 20 to 40 thousand cycles per second is the audio frequency range of human hearing. Higher frequency mechanical vibrations are deemed to be in the ultrasonic realm.

---

[2]The Pendulum: Rich Physics from a Simple System, R. A. Nelson and M. G. Olsson, Am. J. Physics 54(2), Feb 1986.

Because vibrations are typically a cyclic motion, there are large changes in acceleration at the extremes of the oscillation or erratic motion from random impacts that can be monitored with the change in force that must accompany the change in direction and acceleration of a mass.

Piezoelectric, optical, and microelectromechanical systems (MEMS) are some of the techniques used to measure changes in acceleration. There are numerous methods and techniques for monitoring vibrations. Two industrial organization publications describe vibration monitoring. National Instruments reviews vibration monitoring with integrated electronic piezoelectric (IEPE) industrial sensors in a white paper entitled "Measuring Vibration with Accelerometers" at www.ni.com/en-us/innovations/white-papers/06/measuring-vibration-with-accelerometers.html. Texas Instruments has a white paper titled "IEPE Vibration Sensor Interface Reference Design for PLC Analog Input" at www.ti.com/lit/ug/tidud62/tidud62.pdf.

Most of the robust sensors described in the two industrial papers are represented in the non-industrial prototyping area by relatively common and inexpensive piezoelectric stud and screw- or bolt-mount knock sensors (see Figure 6-31).

SparkFun Electronics manufactures a three-axis accelerometer in a ½ in × ¾ in (12 × 18 mm) SMT board containing an Analog Devices ADXL345 and supplies the software required to display the sensitive outputs of the breakout board also seen in Figure 6-31.

A third, different technique using a sensor manufactured by Measurement Specialties consists of a thin film of piezoelectric PVDF polymer film, laminated to a polyester backing, to form a small, flexible, rectangular tab with two electrical connectors. Bending or flexing the plastic tab causes the polymer laminate to generate a substantial voltage spike.

Experiment

The sensors in Figure 6-31 are readily available vibration detectors for physical computing or experimental work with excitation and output display provided by the Arduino microcontroller. Listing 6-5 is the Arduino code for monitoring the knock and leaf sensors.

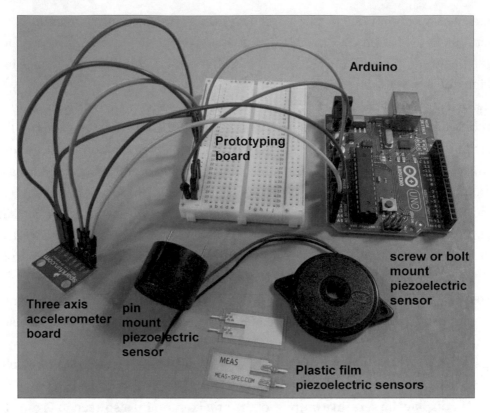

Figure 6-31. *Piezoelectric sensors*

Communication between the high-resolution triple-axis accelerometer (4 mg/LSB, milligravitational acceleration/least significant bit) and the microcontroller is via the two-conductor I2C protocol.

The library is provided by the manufacturer at `https://github.com/sparkfun/ SparkFun__ADSL345_Arduino_Library`. The manufacturer-specified connections between the board and Arduino are detailed in Table 6-8.

Table 6-8. *Arduino/ADXL345 BoB Connections*

Arduino Pin	ADXL345 Board Pin
GND	GND
3V3	V_{CC}
3V3	CS
GND	SDO
A4	SDA
A5	SCL

The displays seen in Figures 6-32 and 6-33 were obtained by running the Arduino Sketch: ADXL345 Example program in the SparkFun library. The code indicates that the x, y, and z positional values are plotted by the Arduino with traces of x in blue, y in orange, and the z coordinate in red.

In Figure 6-31, the two black piezoelectric sensors—one a cylindrical "stud" or pin mount and the other a flat disk screw or bolt mount—have positive terminals connected to the Arduino ADC's A0 (analog input pin 0) input. The second terminal on the devices is connected to ground. A 1 MΩ resistor is connected across the A0 and ground connections. The resistor protects the input circuitry on the ADC converter as the piezo element can produce 90 V spikes under certain high stimulus conditions. (Connections can be made on the prototyping board for testing.)

The MEAS leaf sensor from MEASUREMENT SPECIALTIES company (now part of TE Connectivity, see DigiKey distributor p/n 223-1321-ND, $10 CDN) plastic film sensors are active cantilever accelerometers that produce a pulse DC voltage of 1.1 V per g of acceleration. The device resonates at 75 Hz and generates 6 V at this frequency. The 5 V input limitation on the Arduino ADC may require a voltage divider to protect the converter. The device can be mounted directly on a breadboard or there are Amphenol FCI Clincher connectors available for installations requiring cabled connections to experiment setups.

I suggest that a 1 MΩ resistor be placed across the leaf sensor's electrodes to protect the Arduino ADC. With the protective resistor in place, the two electrode lead connections on the leaf can be connected to A0 and ground for data display.

Observations

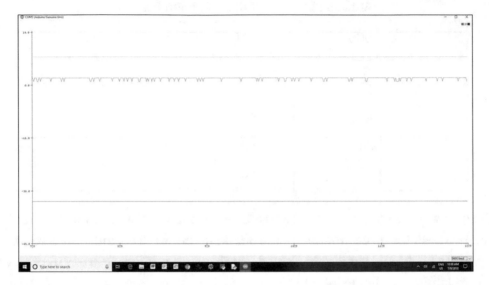

Figure 6-32. *Arduino serial plotter recording of quiescent accelerometer board conditions*

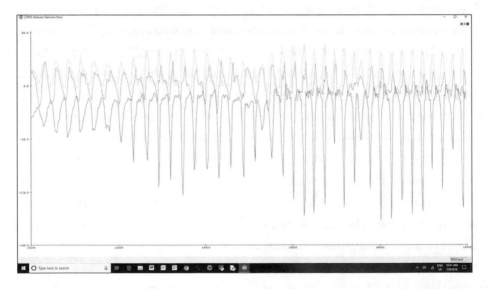

Figure 6-33. *Arduino serial plotter recording of accelerometer board being shaken*

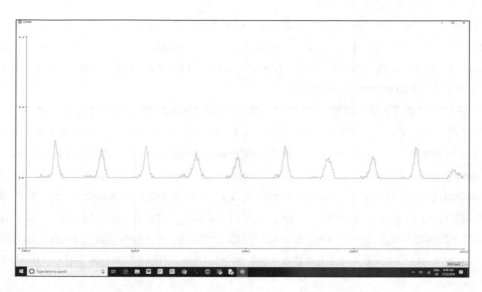

Figure 6-34. *Arduino serial plotter recording of plastic film sensor response to slow bending*

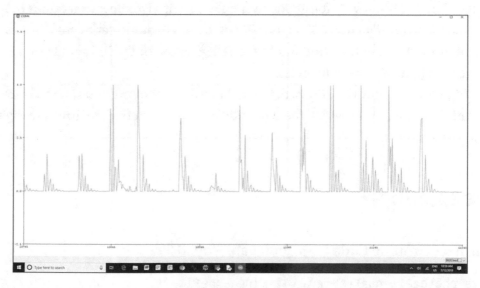

Figure 6-35. *Arduino serial plotter recording of plastic film sensor response to passing impact deflection and resulting flexings*

Discussion

There is extensive literature on applying small computing systems such as the RPi and Arduino microcontrollers to the measurement and display of vibration motions, especially in production equipment.

For vibration to be examined, it must first be detected by a sensor or transducer, which converts mechanical motion into an electrical signal. Several sensors in Figure 6-31 are designed to be securely fixed to solid surfaces with fasteners, and some can respond to vibrations transmitted through the air.

Vibrations can be classified into two broad categories that may require two different techniques to record for analysis. Rotating machinery or servo activations can produce repeated disturbances amenable to frequency counting determinations for recording and subsequent analysis.

Random vibrations such as those created by vehicle suspension moving over uneven terrain are not readily amenable to frequency counting techniques. Random vibrations may be recorded with high-speed data acquisition systems recording mechanical displacement amplitude and time that may be plotted offline for detailed visualization and analysis.

An Arduino's serial plotter is an excellent transient real-time visualization utility. The image of the signal being plotted can be saved with the print screen function on the host computer. The quantitative information available is limited to the x-axis values that are tick counts of println functions. To archive the data, the Arduino serial port signals must be routed through either the Windows-based DAQFactory or the RPi serial ports for graphing or logging at low frequencies.

For higher frequency vibrations, the digital inputs on the Arduino can measure the vibration frequency, provided there is sufficient signal strength to drive the digital detection electronics.

Code Listings

Listing 6-1. Arduino Code for 5 Photogate Sloped Track

```
// Five photogate quarter track timing experiment
// Photogates connected to D2 to D6 and when gate goes high during beam
// blockage the time is recorded and displayed on the serial monitor.
// Trigger code ensures that the time is recorded only once as the object
// causing beam blockage passes through the gate.
//
```

```
int photogate, photogate1, photogate2, photogate3, photogate4;
// 1 = object in photogate path
int trigger, trigger1, trigger2, trigger3, trigger4;
// 1 = photogate ready to trigger
unsigned long time0, time1, time2, time3, time4; // time in microseconds
//
void setup() {
Serial.begin(9600);
pinMode(2, INPUT); // set up digital pin 2 as input
pinMode(3, INPUT); // set up digital pin 2 as input
pinMode(4, INPUT);
pinMode(5, INPUT);
pinMode(6, INPUT);
//
trigger = 1;  // initialize trigger variables
trigger1 = 1;
trigger2 = 1;
trigger3 = 1;
trigger4 = 1;
}
//
void loop() {  // digital pins checked at the rate at which loop cycles.
  photogate = digitalRead(2);
  time0 = micros();
  //
  photogate1 = digitalRead(3);
  time1 = micros();
  //
  photogate2 = digitalRead(4);
  time2 = micros();
  //
  photogate3 = digitalRead(5);
  time3 = micros();
  //
```

```
photogate4 = digitalRead(6);
time4 = micros();
//
if((photogate==1) && (trigger==1)) // if 1st time pin 2 is high record time
{
  Serial.println(time0);
  trigger = 0;
}
if ((photogate==0) && (trigger==0))  // if beam still blocked leave
                                     trigger as 0
trigger = 1;
digitalWrite(2, LOW); // turn on pull down resistor
//
//
if((photogate1==1) && (trigger1==1))
{
  Serial.println(time1);
  trigger1 = 0;
}
if ((photogate1==0) && (trigger1==0))
trigger1 = 1;
digitalWrite(3, LOW); // turn on pull down resistor
//
//
if((photogate2==1) && (trigger2==1))
{
  Serial.println(time2);
  trigger2 = 0;
}
if ((photogate2==0) && (trigger2==0))
trigger2 = 1;
digitalWrite(4, LOW);
//
//
```

```
  if((photogate3==1) && (trigger3==1))
  {
    Serial.println(time3);
    trigger3 = 0;
  }
  if ((photogate3==0) && (trigger3==0))
  trigger3 = 1;
  digitalWrite(5, LOW);
//
//
  if((photogate4==1) && (trigger4==1))
  {
    Serial.println(time4);
    trigger4 = 0;
  }
  if ((photogate4==0) && (trigger4==0))
  trigger4 = 1;
  digitalWrite(6, LOW);
//
}
```

Listing 6-2. An Arduino Sketch for the HC-SR04 Ultrasonic Rangefinder

```
const int trigPin = 9;
const int echoPin = 10;
//
float duration, distance;
//
void setup() {
  pinMode(trigPin, OUTPUT);
  pinMode(echoPin, INPUT);
  Serial.begin(9600);
}
//
```

```
void loop() {
  digitalWrite(trigPin, LOW); //strobe the pulse output
  delayMicroseconds(2);
  digitalWrite(trigPin, HIGH);
  delayMicroseconds(10);
  digitalWrite(trigPin, LOW);
  //
  duration = pulseIn(echoPin, HIGH);
  distance = duration*0.0343/2;
  Serial.print("Distance ");
  Serial.println(distance);
  delay(100);
}
```

Listing 6-3. Arduino Sketch for the OSEPP IRDET-01

```
/*
Infrared proximity sensor on the Arduino A0 input.
An OSEPP IRDET-01 on board LED flashes when an object is between the distances
measured by the user for a given setting of the distance potentiometer.
The LED is continually on when the object is inboard of the pre-set range
and off when outside the range.
Range width or depth of field is adjusted and set with a 10 turn potentiometer.
*/
int IR_Pin = A0;     // define sensor input
int ledPin = 13;     // Arduino board LED
int IR_Value = 0;    // sensor variable 0 -1023

void setup() {
  // set the ledPin as an OUTPUT:
  pinMode(ledPin, OUTPUT);
  Serial.begin(9600);
}
//
```

```
void loop() {
  // read the value from the sensor:
  IR_Value = analogRead(IR_Pin);
  Serial.println(IR_Value);
 }
}
```

Listing 6-4. Arduino Sketch for Plum Bob Timing

```
// Break Beam Pendulum Timing for the Measurement of "g" with period averaging
// Oscillation times are measured about the point of equillibrium to avoid
// alignment problems Pgm starts from hi or low state of IR beam
//
const int switchPin = 2;              // pin input
const float pndlm_lngth = 71.9;       // pendulum length
float g;                              // the gravitational constant variable
int oscl_time;                        // oscillation time
int counter = 0;                      // counter for while averaging loop
int n = 5;                            // number of successive periods to time.
//
long startTime;                       // value returned from millis to start
                                      //     high timing

//
//
void setup()
{
  pinMode(switchPin, INPUT);
  //
  Serial.begin(9600);
}
//
```

```
void loop()
  {

    if(switchPin == HIGH)                          // start with beam broken
      {
        while(digitalRead(switchPin) == HIGH)
        {
          if(digitalRead(switchPin) == LOW)
           {
             break;                                // exit loop when pin
                                                   //    goes low

           }
        }
    startTime = millis();                          // start the cycle timer
    //
     while (counter < n)                           // start the while loop
                                                   //    to determine the time
                                                   //    for n periods

      {
          while(digitalRead(switchPin) == LOW)  // follow low till goes hi
          {
            if(digitalRead(switchPin) == HIGH)
           {
            break;   // exit loop
           }
          }
           while(digitalRead(switchPin) == HIGH)
             {
                if(digitalRead(switchPin) == LOW)
                  {
                    break;   // exit loop
                  }
             }
          while(digitalRead(switchPin) == LOW)
            {
```

```
            if(digitalRead(switchPin) == HIGH)
              {
                break; // break out of the loop and stop the timer
              }
            }
        counter ++;  // increment counter for timing the next period.
      }
    oscl_time = (millis() - startTime)/n;
    g = (39.44 * pndlm_lngth) / ((oscl_time) * (oscl_time));

    Serial.print("g = ");
    Serial.println(g);
  }
//
if(digitalRead(switchPin) == LOW)    // the beam is clear
  {
    while(digitalRead(switchPin) == LOW)
      {
        if(digitalRead(switchPin) == HIGH)
          {
            break;  // on low to hi start timer on exit from loop
          }
        }
    startTime = millis();  // start time
    //
    while (counter < n)  // start the while loop to determine the time for
                         n periods
    {
      while(digitalRead(switchPin) == HIGH)
        {
          if(digitalRead(switchPin) == LOW)
            {
              break;  // exit loop
            }
          }
```

```
     while(digitalRead(switchPin) == LOW)
      {
         if(digitalRead(switchPin) == HIGH)
           {
             break;  // loop exit
           }
      }
    while(digitalRead(switchPin) == HIGH)
     {
         if(digitalRead(switchPin) == LOW)
          {
            break;  // exit loop
          }
     }
    while(digitalRead(switchPin) == LOW)
     {
         if(digitalRead(switchPin) == HIGH)
          {
            break;  // exit loop to stop time
          }
     }
   }
   //
  oscl_time = (millis() - startTime)/n;
  g = (39.44 * pndlm_lngth) / ((oscl_time) * (oscl_time));
  Serial.print("g = ");
  Serial.println(g);
   }
 }
```

Listing 6-5. Arduino Code to Measure Knock/Leaf Vibration Sensor

```
 // Piezoelectric Knock/Leaf Vibration Sensor Monitor
// Knock/Leaf vibration sensors are pulse DC sources and can use A0
// ADC input directly. If the voltage may rise continuously past 5 volts a
// divider may be required to protect the ADC. Use 1 M Ohm across
```

```
// Knock/Leaf electrodes for spike protection then ground one lead or
// negative if marked and monitor voltage with A0
//
int sensorPin = A0;          // select the input pin for the voltage reading
int sensorValue = 0;         // variable to store the value coming from the
                             //     analog input
//
void setup() {
  // start the serial port for data display
  Serial.begin(9600);
}
//
void loop() {
  // read the values from the sensor pin
  sensorValue = analogRead(sensorPin);
  //
  // slow the program to regulate data delivery rate to the serial port
  delay(50);
  //
  //Serial.print("ADC value = "); // comment out for serial plotter display
  Serial.println(sensorValue); }
```

Summary

Long linear and shorter relative distance displacement measurements can be made by numerous techniques involving radars, GPS, laser, ultrasonic range-finders and strain gauges.

Timed motion over a distance can navigate or detect the presence of destructive vibration.

Galileo used classical experiments timing motions to determine the acceleration due to gravity four hundred years ago.

Miniature sensors using piezoelectric crystals and MEMS in surface mount technologies can provide sensors for SCADA systems to control equipment operating in multiple degrees of freedom.

In Chapter 7, the measurement of electrical resistance and conductivity are investigated.

CHAPTER 7

Resistance and Conductivity

Resistance is a measure of a material's opposition to electric current flow when exposed to a voltage difference. Impedance is also a measure of the resistance to the flow of electrical energy. Impedance occurs in alternating current circuits, for example, those including capacitors and inductors, and depends on the AC's frequency. Resistance is a linear quantity; impedance is not.

In a complete electrical circuit, Ohm's law relates the electric field's voltage, causing a flow of current and the total resistance in the circuit impeding the current. Resistance to current passage depends upon many factors, such as the chemical composition, cross-sectional area, length, and temperature of the materials carrying the current through the circuit.

The Ohmite company, a manufacturer of electrical and electronic resistive components, published a paper titled "Resistor Terminology" and "Resistance Values" (`www.ohmite.com/assets/docs/res_select.pdf`). It describes the availability of standardized resistance values and the terms commonly used with discussions involving electrical or electronic resistance. It includes several useful tables and nomenclature that describes fractional resistance values (i.e., 1/1000 or milliohms ($M\Omega$) to 10^{12} or teraohms ($T\Omega$)).

Traditional chemistry divided the elements into metals and non-metals. The metallic elements are usually electrical conductors, while the non-metals are usually insulators. Metallic elements are characterized by having low tendencies to restrict electrical current flow. Resistivity symbolized by ρ (rho) measured in ohms/meter is the numerical value of the material's normalized resistance.

Total resistance for a conductor depends on physical parameters such as the length, cross-sectional area, and temperature of the conductor. For a given fixed temperature,

$$R = \rho \times L / A$$

© Richard J. Smythe 2022
R. J. Smythe, *Arduino Measurements in Science*, https://doi.org/10.1007/978-1-4842-6781-3_7

L is the conductor length, A is the cross-sectional area, and ρ is the resistivity of the metal or alloy.

In addition to the conductor's physical dimensions, the observed resistance is also dependent upon the temperature at which the observation is made. A portion of the numerical resistivity value is due to the rate of collisions between charge carriers, and that collision rate increases with increasing temperature. A quantity symbolized by α (alpha) is known as the *temperature coefficient of resistivity*. The empirically measured value of the change in resistivity with temperature over a limited range is shown in the following expression.

$$\rho(T) = \rho_o[1+\alpha(T{-}To)]$$

$\rho(T)$ is the resistivity at temperature T. ρ_o is the resistivity at reference temperature T_o.

The temperature coefficient of resistance is usually specified for the resistors used in assembling electronic circuitry. For electronic resistances of equal values, the units with the lower temperature coefficient of resistance (TCR) tend to be more expensive.

Resistance and resistivity are usually a concept associated with electrically conducting materials such as metals and semiconductors.

Conductivity, the reciprocal of resistance, is used in association with insulators and poorly conducting media such as solid insulators or metal oxides, carbon-based organic compounds, liquid solutions, and gases. Electrical conductivity, the reciprocal of resistance, is symbolized by the Greek letter σ (sigma) and is expressed in units of siemens/meter $(S = 1/\Omega)$.

Conductivity is often measured by assembling a capacitor type device in which the physical parameters of the conductor plates are well defined, and the material under test forms the dielectric of the capacitor like measurement system. When a DC voltage is applied to the assembled device, current flows through the capacitor and the material under test. It can be measured with a current measuring device or electrometer. From the measurement of the current flow and the capacitor's known parameters, the resistivity of the material under test can be calculated (see Chapter 2).

Several forms of resistance require special techniques to monitor and evaluate. Internal and equivalent series resistances are two such parameters.

Internal resistance is the term applied to batteries and other sources of power. The techniques for measuring internal resistance are discussed in Chapter 11.

Equivalent series resistance is a term used with capacitors and inductors. It describes the deviation of a given type of component from the ideal in ohmic resistance.

Once measured with analog volt-ohm meters (VOM), resistance is measured with digital voltmeters (DVM) capable of three-to-four-digit accuracy over resistance values typically from 200 MΩ to 200 Ω for reasonably priced meters. ($25–$100 CDN) For measurements of resistance below an ohm, more expensive meters (> $500 CDN) are available that can use two or four-wire connections and selectable input impedances to measure mΩ resistance values (mΩ = 1/1000 Ω).

Experimental science often involves the continuous recording of resistance or measurement of values either above or below the range displayed by conventional DVMs. The following three sections are divided into low, normal, and high ohmic value measurements.

The Experimental Measurement of Resistance

Electrical resistance may also be viewed as analogous to mechanical friction. If a current flow is forced through a conducting medium or material that exhibits only a moderate ability to conduct electricity, the conductor begins to heat. In the extreme, the conducting medium can be brought to its melting point. Heat energy, electrical resistance, and current flow are related by the following expression.

$$P = I^2R$$

- P is the power defined in watts.

- I is the current flowing through the resistance in amperes.

- R is the resistance value in ohms.

Heating a conductor such as a copper wire or a precision resistor usually causes a decrease in a material's conductivity that becomes detrimental to certain types of measurements, such as the determinations of low ohmic values of resistance. To measure small resistances, you can determine the voltage across the device under test (DUT) with increased current while recognizing the power-current relationship's limitations.

Low ohmic measurements use a *Kelvin connection*, named after Lord Kelvin, in which four wires assess a small voltage drop across a low resistance object, carrying a large current.

In a Kelvin connection, one pair of wires passes an excitation current through a resistance. The second pair of wires is connected to the voltage sensing device and across the resistance. The separated voltage sensing circuit is minimally affected by the circuit's resistance carrying the excitation current.

In Figures 7-1 and 7-2, the circuits represent the electrical current flow through the wiring of the actual devices to determine low resistance values. Figure 7-1 shows the voltage measurement across the leads of the known resistance and then repeats the second measurement across the leads of the unknown. The potential difference is always measured between or "inside" the current connections.

Within limitations, the lower the value of R, the higher the current can be passed through the DUT to produce a higher voltage drop across the device.

Experimental Measurement of Fractional and Low Ohmic Values

Method 1

Often it is necessary to measure the resistance of low voltage, high current circuit components as may be found in heater, motor, or electrochemical systems involving battery charging or electrolytic refining. Using a constant current flow through two resistors, one known and the other under test, then measuring the voltage drop across each resistor, the unknown value can be determined by simple calculation.

In a voltage divider arrangement of two resistors as depicted in Figure 7-1, the same current flows through each resistor. Ohm's law applies to both the known resistor and the unknown, as follows.

$$V_1 = R_1 * I \text{ and } V_2 = R_2 * I$$
$$\text{from which } V_1/R_1 = I = V_2/R_2 \text{ and } V_1/R_1 = V_2/R_2$$
$$\text{so } R_1 * V_2/V_1 = R_2$$

The simple circuit in Figure 7-1 is discussed on the Robot Room (www.robotroom.com) hobbyist website. It can be assembled on a breadboard and powered by any convenient regulated 5 V supply. Two optional capacitors dampen any noise on the power supply and consist of a ceramic capacitor of 0.1 μF and a higher value electrolytic in the 10 μF range.

To minimize drift from temperature effects, R_{known} in a 5 V test system should be approximately 220 Ω and have as high a power or wattage rating as possible.

A low-value resistance determination is made by assembling the following circuit with the DUT in the bottom portion of the voltage divider circuit. After power is applied to the circuit and a stable current flow established, the voltage drops across the known resistor and DUT can be measured. For low values of resistance in the DUT, the meter's millivolt scale needs to obtain sufficient resolution to generate an accurate calculation. The DUT resistance is as derived earlier and determined from the following formula.

$$R_{Dut} = \text{Volt drop } R_{Dut}/(\text{Volt drop } R_{known}/R_{known})$$

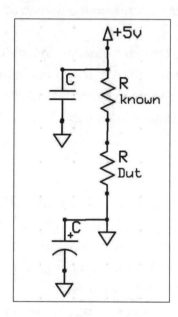

Figure 7-1. *Circuit for measurement of low resistance values*

When VR_{Dut} is measured in millivolts, the appropriate factors must be used in the calculation. (For lower values of millivolt readings, the voltage follower electrometer depicted in Figure 2-3 in Chapter 2 can be used.)

Observations

A simple validation test conducted with a breadboard and the 5.10 V supply taken from a LabJack U3-HV with no smoothing capacitors and a nominal 220 Ω ¼ watt resistor (measured resistance 217 Ω) generated the following values on a 1 Ω 1% power resistor.

$$R_{known} = 217\ \Omega;\ VR_{known} = 5.04\ V$$

$$VR_{Dut} = 23.3\ mV\ that\ yielded\ R_{Dut} = 1.0032\ \Omega$$

This data was measured with a moderate cost meter, and a repeat measurement with an inexpensive troubleshooting meter yielded the following data and resistance value.

$R_{known} = 217\ \Omega;\ VR_{known} = 5.00\ V$ and $VR_{Dut} = 23.1\ mV$ that yielded $R_{Dut} = 1.0025\ \Omega$.

Fourteen-gauge copper wire is reported to have a resistance of 0.40160 Ω per 100 feet of length. A single foot of wire should thus be .0040 Ω. With the 5.10 V excitation supply, the 217 Ω resistor displayed a 5.06 V voltage drop, and the one foot 14-gauge copper wire DUT displayed a 2mV voltage drop. The one-foot length of copper wire has a measured resistance of 0.0047 Ω.

The technique's limitations are determined by the millivolt resolution of the meter measuring the voltage drop across the DUT. In the validation measurements made, if 0.1 mV is taken as the minimum value that can be read, then the minimum theoretical resistance value that can be measured is 0.1 × 217/5000 or 4 mΩ.

Method 2

For practical benchtop determinations of low resistance, the current through a low resistance DUT can be set and regulated to100 mA by an appropriately programmed voltage regulator, such as the LM317. The construction of an op-amp IC-based DVM, low-ohm adapter is discussed at All About Circuits (see www.allaboutcircuits.com/projects/build-your-own-low-resistance-meter).

A power source of 5 V capable of delivering 100 mA is required to drive a voltage regulator such as the LM 317. The LM317 is programmed for current delivery by applying this formula: $i_{out} = 1.25/R_{adjust}$. A 100 mA constant current source can be realized by inserting a suitably sized resistance, recall I^2R, of the value of R (12 Ω) between the "adjust" and "output" terminals of the regulator chip. (Since the LM 317 can regulate currents up to 1 A, a 100 mA current regulation requires a 12 Ω resistor, 1.25/12 = 0.1A).

Figure 7-2 depicts the general wiring and configuration that pass a 100 mA current through the load resistor or device being tested. The higher constant current enables you to measure lower resistance values in the device being tested.

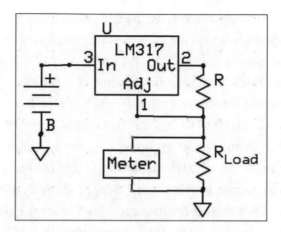

Figure 7-2. *Circuit for constant current determination of low-value resistance*

The components selected should ensure that the current through the DUT is maintained at a relatively constant value in the 100 mA range. With an increased nominal 100 mA current passing through the unknown resistance, the voltage drop across the load can be measured to determine the DUT's resistance. The exciting current and voltage measuring meter are connected in a Kelvin configuration. The load voltage measurement meter is connected close to the DUT to measure only the load resistance voltage. Any effects of the leads carrying the exciting current are bypassed. The power connection is made "outside" of the voltage measurement contacts so that the current flow does not affect the voltage measurement.

Observations

A 100 mA current is created using the nominal 5 V supply from a device such as LabJack U12, U3 or a plugin "wall wart" supply and a 12 Ω programming resistor on an LM 317 voltage regulator configured for constant current service. A 105.1 mA excitation current was created with the 5 V from a LabJack U3, and a 104.8 mV drop was measured across a 1 Ω, 1%, 12.5-watt resistor. The device had an apparent measured resistance of 0.9971 Ω. A similar measurement with a 1-foot length of 14 ga copper wire indicated a voltage drop of 0.3 mV that, with the previously measured current flow of 105.1 mA, indicated a resistance of 0.0029 Ω.

I conducted several additional validation experiments to demonstrate a basic tenant of low level or high sensitivity measurements.

During the resistance measurements of the 1 ft (30.5 cm) of 0.040 in (1.02 mm) 18 ga copper wire, the voltage drop across the wire was measured with two moderately priced handheld digital multimeters (< $150 CDN). A voltage drop of 0.3 mV was observed on the 200 mV scale of the DMM. The input impedance of the meters is 10 MΩ, and the readings were at the limit of the meter's capabilities. With the 0.3 V reading, the wire's resistance was calculated to be 0.0113 Ω. A 200 mV digital panel meter with an input impedance of 100 MΩ repeated the 18 ga copper wire measurement. A 0.2 mV drop was observed across the wire length. The wire resistance was then calculated to be 0.0076 Ω.

The third set of measurements of 0.215 mV were made with the 10 TΩ input impedance electrometer, which was in close agreement with the 100 MΩ value of 0.2 mV.

Engineering tables indicate that the 18 ga copper wire should have a resistivity of 0.00636 Ω/ft. (Recall resistance is temperature-dependent, see Discussion) The 10 MΩ DMM reading is high by 0.0114 − 0.00636 = 0.005 Ω while the higher input impedance DPM is also high but by 0.0076 − 0.00636 = 0.00123 Ω.

The measured values of the wire resistance, an improvement of almost five times, are obtained with the higher impedance voltage measurement instruments' improved millivolt capability.

Intermediate or Moderate Resistance Value Measurements

Most reasonably priced digital voltmeters can measure resistance values from 1 to 10 Ω up to 1 to 10 MΩ with accuracies of 3 or 4 significant figures. However, for monitoring a continuously changing resistance a quickly changing digital numerical display is of limited value.

A time-based graphical display of the recorded resistance value often provides more information about the experimental system by providing trending information.

A dynamic monitoring technique has evolved from the static resistance bridge method developed by S. H. Christie in 1833 to measure the resistance of unknown entities. It was modified by Sir Charles Wheatstone in 1843 and is still very much in use today.

A Wheatstone bridge circuit can be visualized as two voltage divider circuits in parallel, as depicted in Figure 7-3. The main use of the bridge today is for the continuous dynamic measurement of small resistance variations or changes generated by various physical sensors represented by R_x. Continuous monitoring of thermistor temperature sensing, magnetically sensitive magnetoresistance elements, and strain gauge detection of mechanical structure flexing are three of the more common uses for resistance bridge circuits.

A bridge can be used in either a static mode to measure an unknown value of resistance or in a dynamic mode to continuously monitor small variations in a resistor. When a meter determines the null point at which the voltage at the nodes are equal and have no current flows, it can be shown using voltage divider equations that $R_x = R_2 (R_3/R_1)$. The accuracy of the measurement is determined by the accuracy of the known resistor values.

The second form of bridge usage monitors the voltage difference between the nodes. When both sides of the bridge are of equal resistance, no voltage difference exists at the division nodes, and hence no current flows between them. As the unknown resistance value fluctuates, the voltage at the divider points also fluctuates, and the bridge goes out of balance. The signs of voltage fluctuations or the direction of current flow can impart important information about the nature of the physical phenomenon being monitored by the bridge's resistance elements.

Application-specific integrated circuits (ASIC) in instrumentation amplifiers can measure the voltage variation between the two bridge nodes as R_x changes. High input impedance instrumentation amplifier ICs, such as the AD620, are specifically designed for these applications (see Figure 3-16 in Chapter 3).

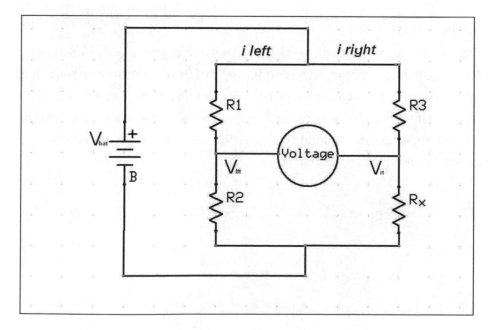

Figure 7-3. *A Wheatstone bridge circuit*

Bridge circuits are often fabricated into application-specific integrated circuits such as the anisotropic and giant magnetoresistance magnetic field detectors described in Chapter 5.

Analog Devices AD620 is a popular instrumentation amplifier often applied to monitoring the voltage differences that are generated at the bridge nodes of the circuit depicted in Figure 7-3 (also see the circuits depicted in Figures 3-14, 3-15, and 3-16 in Chapter 3).

Measurements of High Resistance Values

Resistance values measured in double-digit megohms are often beyond the measuring ability of most benchtop and handheld volt-ohm-meters. Commercial instruments using thousands of volts to drive currents through high-value resistances are available when required. High resistance value measurements based on Ohm's law invoke the measurement of low currents when common battery voltages are used as the driving potential for the measurements. Low current measurements can be made with the current electrometer described in Figure 2-3 in Chapter 2.

The TIA-based circuit in Chapter 2 (see Figures 2-1 and 2-4) with its high input impedance can measure currents into the 10^{-12} A range; if used with a 12 V excitation battery, it should provide resistance measurement capabilities into the 1.2×10^{12} or gigaohm values (GΩ).

Current electrometers measure leakage currents in capacitors. Liquid-type electrolytics are also a measure of the conductivity of the dielectric. The same technique that measures capacitor leakage can measure any material's high resistance and conductivity that can be placed between two conducting plates to form a capacitor.

Figure 7-4 illustrates the general configuration to measure the material's conductivity or resistance between the DUT's plates.

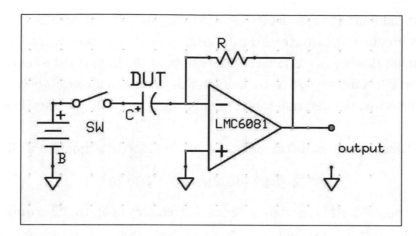

Figure 7-4. *TIA electrometer configuration for low-level current determinations*

Discussion

Odd or unusual resistance values or shapes of resistance elements can be fabricated from resistance wires obtainable from several supply sources (for example, see `https://jacobs-online.biz/nichrome_wire.htm` and `www.omega.com/en-us/`).

In the normal work encountered in digital and low voltage signal processing from analog systems, the resistance values encountered are in the ranges accessible with handheld meters. The manual handling of circuit boards and resistance values have no detrimental consequences. When high-value or low-value resistance objects or devices are encountered, surface contamination (from skin oils, moisture from humidity, or atmospheric contamination) can have detrimental effects on circuit performance. Resistors of extremely high or low resistance must be kept clean and protected from all forms of contamination.

Although the crystalline metals have free electrons in their bulk formats that are free to move within the metal under the influence of an electric potential difference, the degree of freedom varies in accordance with the atomic structure of the element and the physical conditions under which the potential difference field is applied. The measurable term given to the opposition of electron flow in a bulk metal is resistance. All materials possess temperature-dependent resistance. However, some elements can lose their resistance at low cryogenic temperatures to become "superconductors," Their resistance drops to virtually zero. SQUIDS used to detect low-level magnetic fields and whole-body magnetic resonance imaging (MRI) medical diagnostic systems operate at liquid helium temperatures of –269°C or 4°K.

Resistors manufactured for use in electronic circuitry are available in several formats that use different materials to create the desired nominal resistance value. Carbon, thin films, and metal alloy wires are some of the materials used to manufacture resistors. You can often select the desired resistance value from several materials of construction. Cost and the desired temperature coefficient of resistance (TCR) are often the deciding factors.

The TCR defines the change in resistance as a function of temperature difference.

$$TCR = ((R2 - R1)/R1(T2 - T1)) * 10^{-6}$$

TCR is in ppm/°C, R1 is resistant at room temperature in ohms. R2 is resistance at operating temperature in ohms T1 is the room temperature. T2 is the operating temperature, both in °C.

Table 7-1 tabulates the TCR for an assortment of common materials and elements. The published data should be considered reasonable approximations for ambient temperatures at which electronic circuit boards are expected to see service. The coefficients are dependent upon the purity of the nominal materials, and many TCR values are not linear over extended temperature ranges. Literature should be consulted for use in resistance-heating applications (see Chapter 3).

Table 7-1. *TCR Values for Metals and Alloys*

Material	Composition	TCR/°C
Aluminum	Al	0.0039
Carbon	amorphous	-0.0005
Calcium	Ca	0.0041
Constantan	Cu 55% / Ni 45%	0.000008
Copper	Cu	0.0039
Iron	Fe	0.005
Germanium	Ge	-0.048
Gold	Au	0.0039
Lead	Pb	0.0039
Lithium	Li	0.006
Manganin	Cu 86% / Mn 12% / Ni 2%	0.000005
Mercury	Hg	0.009
Nickel	Ni	0.006
Nichrome	Ni 80% / Cr 20%	0.0004
Platinum	Pt	0.00392
Silicon	Si	-0.075
Tin	Sn	0.0045
Tungsten	W	0.0045
Zinc	Zn	0.0039

Conductivity

The traditional concept of resistance and Ohm's law (when used with the crystalline forms of the common metallic elements such as copper, aluminum, iron, nickel, chrome, tin, lead, and zinc together with specific alloys made from these elements) must be revised when the crystalline form of the metals is not the conducting medium carrying the current flow. *Conductivity* is the term often applied to the transfer of current through non-crystalline metallic media.

Under certain conditions, metal elements can be distinguished by losing electrons to form stable positive ions known as *cations*. Non-metals can gain an electron to form stable negatively charged species called *anions*.

Complete chemical compounds could gain or lose electrons to form positive and negative ions, which, under the influence of an electric field, can conduct electrical current by transferring electrical charge.

At ambient conditions, matter or materials are present in gases, liquids, or solids. Each physical form of the conducting medium has its own method of passing current. Metals pass current with electrons moving in the crystal structure's conduction band. Solutions pass current with the physical motion of cations and anions through the liquid phase. Gases pass current through the process of migration and diffusion of ionized species.

Plasmas, discovered in the 1920s, are ionized gas containing energy sufficient to separate electrons from the core nuclei of atoms. The separated electrons remain close to the nuclei and usually travel with it when the plasma moves. Because the plasma is composed of charged entities, it is subject to the influence of electric and magnetic fields. The sun's core, lightning, and the northern and southern lights are examples of plasmas.

Conductivity in Solids

Conductors

Chemistry divides the elements into two classifications of metals and non-metals depending upon the elemental atomic propensity to gain or lose electrons. Many of the elements such as silver, copper, gold, aluminum, zinc, tin, lead, iron, nickel, chrome, and platinum and alkali earths and metals are excellent conductors of electricity. Metallic elements in their crystalline form have energy level bands in which electrons can move easily under the influence of an applied electrical potential difference. Although there are great differences in the ability to pass current among the metals, the conductivity is so high that it is usual to compare metals by their resistance or resistivity.

Insulators

Elements such as silicon and sulfur that lack low energy conduction bands when in their solid mineral format are insulators, along with virtually all metallic oxides as the conducting energy level bands are filled. True insulators should exhibit no electrical conductivity, but material and surface impurities often contribute to a small but finite current passage capability.

Semiconductors

A PN junction can be formed by adding trace quantities of elements able to accept or donate electrons from their outer layers to crystals of atoms with the opposite tendencies. Solid-state devices such as transistor switches, light-emitting, and photosensitive diodes can be fabricated from these semiconductor materials (see Figure 4-41 in Chapter 4 and Figure 11-3 in Chapter 11).

Conductivity in Liquids

Liquids are non-compressible, fluidic materials that conform to the shape of the container in which they reside. Conductivity in liquids depends upon the chemical properties of the materials that make up the liquid.

Ionic Electrolytes

Liquids composed of materials whose atomic or molecular structure allows them to dissociate into positively and negatively charged species at or near ambient temperatures are called *ionic liquids*. Traditionally ionic compounds such as sodium chloride (also known as common table salt) and other salts are solid crystalline materials that only dissociate into positive and negative ionic species in a suitable polar liquid solvent such as water. However, many salts with melting points in the range of ambient temperatures are commercially available today, and these materials are referred to as ionic liquids. Ionic liquids are room-temperature fluids composed of positively charged cations and negatively charged anions.

In an aqueous solution containing dissolved positively and negatively charged ions, any application of a DC electric field between two conductive electrodes inserted into the solution creates polarization layers around the two electrodes. Upon initial application of the voltage, the ions diffuse to the opposite charge's electrode and eventually cover the entire surface of the electrode. Current flows only as the ions migrate. When the surface of the electrodes is covered, the main current flow ceases. The layer of ions covering the electrode of opposite charge attracts the ions of the same polarity as the electrode. An electrical double layer results on both electrodes, as depicted in Figure 7-5.

Measuring a dissolved salt solution's electrical conductivity is not a trivial exercise, as demonstrated and developed in the following experiments.

Non-Ionic Liquids

Water consists of an oxygen atom bonded to a pair of hydrogen atoms. It is a covalent molecule since the atoms only share portions of the electrons. In salt, the electrons are donated by half of the molecule and accepted by the other to form an entity held together by the electrical attraction of the newly created positive and negative charges.

If two plates are immersed in a liquid, and a voltage is applied across the two in an ionic liquid, it is expected that the positively charged portion of the liquid should migrate to the negative plate. The negatively charged species migrate to the positively charged plate. The applied voltage has caused charges to move in the ionic liquid that conforms to a current flow. On the other hand, if the liquid is a covalent type of molecule, there are no ionic species attracted to the charged plates created by the impressed voltage. With no charges to migrate, the liquid performs like an insulator.

An insulating liquid such as water can be turned into a conducting medium by adding an ionizable, water-soluble, crystalline salt to form a liquid solution of mobile cations and anions.

Capacitively Coupled Contactless Conductivity Detection (C4D)

C4D uses a high-frequency transmitter electrode to irradiate a region of a conductive liquid sample with a large amplitude electromagnetic signal. A corresponding attenuated AC signal is received by a receiver electrode either immersed in or surrounding the liquid, and a DC signal is extracted for recording. An advantage of the C4D technique is that it is a non-contact technique in which transmitting and receiving electrodes are not wetted by the fluid under test. As a result of not having to contact the fluid, the technique can be applied to small samples and is used in capillary chromatographic separation techniques. The technique uses complex high-frequency electronics and is used in more advanced research work.

Conductivity in Gases

Gases are compressible materials that expand to fill and conform to the shape of the container that holds them.

Most gases are covalent or monatomic entities that do not conduct electricity under normal conditions. High voltages or special conditions such as exposure to high energy-ionizing radiation must convert gases into electrically conductive media.

Gas is a collection of unconnected, thermally excited, vibrating, individual molecules. Any ionized or charged species created in a gas at atmospheric pressures must overcome the continual collisions with other molecules to migrate under the influence of an electric field or voltage differential present. A gas's conductivity depends on many factors, such as its chemical structure or composition, temperature, pressure, and the magnitude of the applied voltage.

Arc and Spark Discharges

Although most gases are insulators under increasing voltage levels, several forms of conductivity can occur. Dry atmospheric conditions as occur in cold winter climates can lead to static accumulations that eventually breakdown the air resistance, and an arc spark allows the electrons to move to neutralize the static voltage imbalance (see Chapter 8). Lightning appears to be a large-scale arc discharge.

Flame Ionization

Combustion can be defined as a chemical reaction that produces noticeable heat and light. Combustion can only occur in the gas phase and is a free radical chemical reaction mechanism. Free radicals are molecules or atoms with unpaired electrons that may exhibit a positive or negative charge and thus be able to carry a current when subjected to an electric field. Hydrogen-based flame ionization detectors (FID) are used extensively in gas chromatographic analysis of hydrocarbon molecules.

Nitrogen, phosphorus, sulfur, and halide atoms in organic compounds can be detected by adding ionization catalysts to the flame ionization detector method.

Typical flame ionization detectors use an electrometer to measure picoampere currents that flow when electrodes biased at 400 V cause ion migration in an FID device's combustion zone.

Glow Discharges

Under high voltage, electric fields electrons can be extracted from gas molecules, typically at 2 kV to 3 kV. Free electrons accelerate toward the positive anode, and the positively charged ions migrate toward the cathode.

Depending on the gas pressure, which determines a parameter called the *mean free path*, the ions may or may not be able to gain enough kinetic energy to create additional ionizations on impact and thus produce a self-sustaining "avalanche" chain able to conduct electrical energy. The collisions and electron impacts excite the electrons on the gas atoms to higher energy levels that radiate photons when they return to their normal energy level. The emitted photons are a characteristic color emissions seen in neon tube lighting. The inert gases of helium, neon, and argon make glow discharge light generators of various colors.

Neon gas discharges are sometimes used as voltage regulators in high power electrical circuitry.

Applications of Gas Conductivity in Chemical Analysis

Inductively Coupled Argon Plasma Optical Emission Spectroscopy and Mass Spectrometry

For optical emission spectral analysis, an inductively coupled plasma (ICP) is created at the outlet tip of a small quartz tube called a *torch*. A vertical plasma is created in a steady flow of inert gas (usually, argon) that flows from the entrance at the bottom end of the tube to the top exit end, where the plasma is formed just above the end of the tube, hence the name *torch*.

A water-cooled copper tube is coiled three or four times around the outside of the quartz tube near the exit end of the torch. A high-frequency AC signal is driven through the copper tube coils, which creates a substantial magnetic field within the coil, quartz tube, and argon gas.

The generated magnetic field creates forces on electrons that create collisions, ionizations, and containment with theoretical temperatures equivalent to the 6000°K to 10,000°K range. By injecting a nebulized solution of fine droplets into the base of the torch with a pump, any atoms within the solution have their electrons excited and can be ionized as they pass through the plasma. As the excited electrons drop back to their normal energy levels, they emit photons characteristic of the energy level difference for the atom on which they reside.

Separating the individual wavelengths of light produced by the atoms passing through the plasma with a spectrometer provides qualitative identification from the wavelength and quantitative information from the intensity of the emitted wavelength. Sensitivities from parts per thousand to parts per billion and sometimes beyond are possible.

Since the species created in the plasma torch are charged and influenced by electric and magnetic fields, mass spectrometry techniques can be applied to separate the entities according to their atomic mass. Traditional mass separation techniques of ion extraction, magnetic deflection, and electrostatic focus achieve up to one part per quadrillion sensitivities (one part in 10^{15}).

Ion Mobility Spectrometry (IMS): Plasma Chromatography

Gases can be ionized under ambient conditions by several techniques, one of which involves using emissions from radioactive elements. Nickel Ni^{63} and americium Am^{241} are used as sources of beta particles or high energy electrons that can ionize a gaseous molecule or atom. In IMS, certain chemical structures preferentially ionize and under a strong uniform electric field migrate or drift toward the electric field plate of opposite charge. The drift time is characteristic of the molecule under study. During the original development of separations, the technique was called *plasma chromatography,* but the modern term *ion mobility spectrometry* is now in use. Many explosive compounds are nitrogen-containing species for which the IMS has picogram (10^{-12} gram) sensitivity.

Photoionization

Gas ionization can be accomplished by irradiating atoms and molecules with high energy ultraviolet photons. Many volatile organic compounds have a structure that presents a large area for photon absorption, resulting in the ejection of an energetic electron and molecular ion formation. Many explosive and poisonous gases can be quickly detected and quantified by collecting the ionized current generated by short-wavelength photoionization lamps. Table 4-1 in Chapter 4 lists the energy levels used in photoionization detector lamps (PID).

Experiment

Many of the electrical conductivity applications used extensively in instrumentation to measure a large number of physio-chemical parameters are too complex to be used as exercises in this simple work. Two of the more common, less complex applications that make use of conductivity measurements are readily demonstrated when measuring the electrolytic conductivity of water or salt solutions and determining the relative humidity in an atmosphere.

Measurements of moisture in a gas volume are made by determining water adsorbed conductivity onto a catalytic surface. Measuring the equilibrium relative humidity in a closed volume containing a material under test can determine the test sample's water activity. Water activity is an important parameter in predicting food safety.

The basic concepts governing aqueous electrolytic conductivity measurements in liquids are best demonstrated with modest concentrations of one ionizable electrolyte in solution. Common food grade table salt and distilled water are two readily available materials from which definitive aqueous conductivity measurements can be made.

Electrolytic Conductivity Measurements in Aqueous Solutions

Salts are the products of reactions in which acids react with bases forming water as a byproduct. Many salts are water-soluble and dissociate into ions when dissolved. As a polar molecule, water can stabilize in a solution the electrically charged components of salts that have positive or negative charges, or cations or anions, respectively. When an electrical voltage is applied to two conducting plates immersed in a water solution containing a dissolved salt, the positively charged salt components are attracted to the negatively charged cathode from which the word *cations* is derived. The negatively charged components are attracted to positively charged anions.

When two electrodes are placed in a water-based solution that contains a dissolved ionic salt such as common table salt (sodium chloride), and a small DC voltage is placed across the electrodes, the current flow between the two conductive plates have the same type of curvature observed when a capacitor is charged (see Figure 1-1 in Chapter 1).

The initial application of the voltage to the plates draw the cations or sodium ions to the negative cathode and the anions or chloride ions to the positive anode. An initial high current flow tapers off as the ions collect around their respective electrodes.

Eventually, the current flow stop as the electrodes are surrounded by oppositely charged ions. Figure 7-5 depicts the double-layer formation.

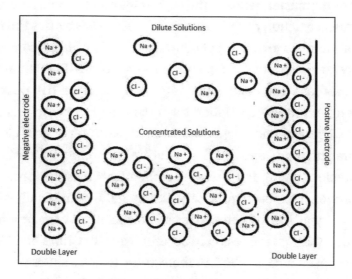

Figure 7-5. *The electrical double layer in dilute and concentrated aqueous solutions*

The current flow stops because the small DC voltage applied to the solution does not have the electrical energy required to discharge the ions collected at the electrodes.

At low voltages, water is a stable polar solvent. The minimum theoretical voltage necessary to start water decomposition or electrolysis is 1.229 V.

$$2H_2O + \text{electrical energy} \otimes O_2 + 2H_2$$

To measure the electrical conductivity of water-based or aqueous solutions, the impressed voltage should be kept below the point at which the water decomposes. To avoid the formation of the insulating double layer around the electrodes, an AC excitation signal has traditionally been used.

An electrode surrounded by attracted ions is *polarized*. A polarized electrode again attracts ions of the opposite charge. An electrical "double layer" may form with a DC voltage impressed upon the two electrodes. Polarization and double-layer formation during conductivity measurements has traditionally been avoided by using an alternating voltage excitation signal, usually in the low kilohertz range that stops ionic migration toward either electrode. (Recall from the examination of capacitance that a capacitor stops a DC current but inverts and passes an AC signal.)

When using alternating polarity voltages in water-based salt solutions for conductivity determinations, the applied voltage should not be high enough to cause excessive electrons to transfer between the electrodes and the ions surrounding them in an electrochemical reaction called *electrolysis*. Electrolysis causes the neutralization of the charged ions and the formation of neutral atoms. The atoms combine to form hydrogen and oxygen gas bubbles on the separate electrodes. Elemental hydrogen, oxygen, chlorine, sodium, and many metals are all manufactured in bulk by large-scale industrial processes or produced in laboratory quantities by electrolysis reactions.

Traditionally electrochemical experiments used platinum or gold electrodes for their inertness. Graphite, titanium, and stainless steel are economical materials that can be substituted for precious metals in many electrochemical investigations.

If an ionic solution is exposed to a low peak voltage, symmetrically oscillating polarity, electrical signal, it is expected to act somewhat like a capacitor and pass the electrical oscillation through the circuit in accordance with Ohm's law. The combination of resistance and capacitance is called an *impedance*, which at intermediate frequencies is treated like a resistance in the basic current- voltage relationship.

In theory, high purity water should not contain any impurities, and thus only the hydroxide anion and proton from self-ionization should be present. The chemical literature indicates that the product of the proton and hydroxide ion concentrations is a low value of 10^{-14} for such a theoretical situation. In aqueous solutions, the presence of such a small number of ionized species is not going to carry an easily measured current.

As depicted in Figure 7-5, the dissolution of a salt in an aqueous medium produces an electrically neutral solution of individually charged cations and anions. Opposite charges attract, and similar charges repel, so at low concentrations, when the ions are well spaced from one another, there is little interaction between like and unlike electrically charged species. At high concentrations, when the electrically charged entities are closely packed, ionic interactions are expected. The expected linear relations between ionic concentration and measured conductivity may not be observed.

Conductivity is represented by G and set to the reciprocal of resistivity, which suggests that the higher the resistance, the smaller the conductance's value.

Compensation for a non-linear concentration-conductivity response can be achieved using a varying "cell constant" derived from measuring the cell or probe response to known conductivity standards. Specific conductivity (SC) is defined as the product of the measured conductivity G and the empirical cell constant K. The cell constant compensates for variations in cell geometry and experimental conditions by acting as a normalizing factor for expressions of conductivity in units of siemens/cm.

$$SC = G * k - siemens/cm$$

Traditionally, the units of conductance (1/r in ohms) were called *mho*. They were renamed *siemens* to form the current specific conductance units of S/cm. A siemen is a large unit. mS or 1/1000 S and μS or 1/1,000,000 S are more commonly used.

Temperature differences can affect measured conductivity by 4% to 5% in aqueous solutions. To avoid thermally related errors, conductivity measurements, solution preparations, and standardizations should be performed at the same temperature.

Generating accurate aqueous conductivity measurements depends on the use of salt solutions with accurately known compositions over the expected concentration range of the solutions under test (see Table 7-3).

Aqueous conductivities can vary over a wide range of values. Distilled water may have a typical resistance of 18 MΩ or exhibit a conductivity of 1 μS/cm. Tap water is typically 5 kΩ or 50 μS/cm. Seawater is typically 20 Ω or 50 mS/cm.

In industrial applications, compensation for dilute or concentrated solutions are optimized by adjusting the measurement excitation technique, size, shape, construction materials, and separation of the cell electrodes. For more than 100 years, the robustness and utility of the simple two-electrode, parallel plate arrangement, and low voltage AC excitation for conductivity measurement cells have been demonstrated and validated. For most general-purpose investigations and routine laboratory work, the low-voltage AC system developed in this section is less expensive but has more robust configuration and reproducibility and wider applicability than most other published measurement systems.

Experiment

Traditional electrolytic conductivity measurements have been made with low voltage sine wave excitation of the solution under test. The varying voltage was applied to a pair of electrodes in the solution. The signal passed through the impedance presented by the electrodes and the conductive ionic solution between them, in proportion to the ionic concentration of the liquid in accordance with Ohm's law. The alternating polarity signal passing through the sample was then rectified and read as a strip chart recorded DC voltage signal, proportional to the conductivity of the solution.

Figure 7-6 depicts a circuit derived from one published in the *Journal of Chemical Education* in May 1997 (as discussed in more detail later in this chapter).

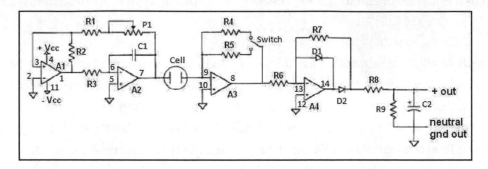

Figure 7-6. *A circuit for electrolytic conductivity measurement*

In Figure 7-6, amplifiers A1 and A2 are configured as an oscillator. A3 amplifies the signal passing through the cell, A4 rectifies the signal, and the output resistance capacitor network is a low pass filter. The following section discusses the IC in use.

The circuitry in Figure 7-6 was assembled and tested on a prototyping breadboard before hardwired onto a printed circuit board for assembly onto a metal base to form a conductivity measurement instrument (see Foreword and Figure RE-1, the plastic-wrapped circuit test prototype board PC-102). The assembled instrument is depicted in Figure 7-7.

The circuit depicted in Figure 7-6 is set to provide an output in volts for visualization with a digital multimeter. The calibration factor corresponds to 10 mS/cm per volt on the normal scale and 100 µS/cm on the ×100 expanded scale. You may create calibrations using the standard sodium chloride solutions prepared to measure cell constants or validate instrumental response as required.

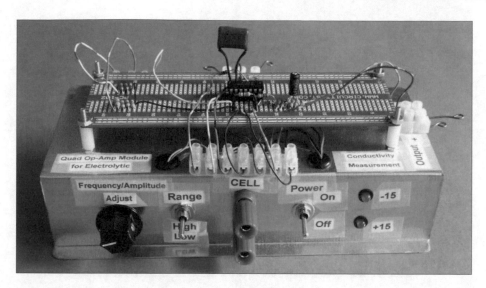

Figure 7-7. *An electrolytic conductivity measurement instrument*

The instrument controls' nominal functions are marked, and the instrument is powered by a bipolar 15 V supply connected to the labeled three terminals visible at the rear of the chassis.

A bipolar power supply can be configured from two battery packs consisting of either a 9 V battery connected in series with four AA cells or a 12 V battery connected in series with two AA cells. The bipolar supply is assembled by connecting the negative supply from the first 15 V battery pack to the positive lead from the second battery pack. The negative-positive connection is the common ground. The positive lead from the first supply is the +15 V supply. The negative lead from the second battery pack is the –15 V supply. See the battery pack configurations in Figure 2-3 in Chapter 2.

Figure 7-8 depicts an oscilloscope display of the excitation signal applied to one of the conductivity probe plates.

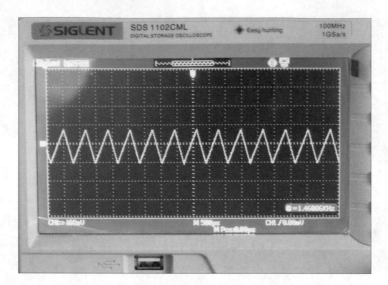

Figure 7-8. *The electrolytic conductivity (EC) excitation signal*

A low-cost conductivity probe was fabricated from stainless steel. The probe plates, 10 × 20 mm (⅜ in × ¾ in) were cut from the ½ in (12 mm) wide band-straps of an old stainless steel hose clamp. Electrical connections were made to the electrodes by silver soldering copper wires to the back faces of the plates. The plates' front surfaces were polished to a mirror finish with wet silicon carbide abrasive papers starting at 400 grit and using finer grits until the desired luster was obtained. The probe elements were mounted with the front surfaces of the plates parallel at 1 cm spacing, and all other exposed surfaces and wiring of the probe were epoxy resin-coated (see top probe in Figure 7-14).

Although numerous designs for electrolytic conductivity probes have been published for diverse uses (such as monitoring natural waters in the environment to recording the ionic strength of nutrient solutions in hydroponic indoor gardening systems), only easily assembled two-electrode probes are tested in this book.

Preparation of Ionic Solution Standards

To make useful ionic conductivity measurements without resorting to expensive and fragile laboratory volumetric glassware, a procedure for the preparation of known quantities of dissolved ionic standards is presented. Common food grade table salt is a readily available, inexpensive, powdered crystalline format standard, available from most grocery or food suppliers. If the dry, free-flowing powder is continually added to distilled water until no more dissolves, and a distinct portion of salt crystals remain undissolved on the bottom of the container, a solution of well-known composition can be prepared. The exact composition of a saturated salt or sodium chloride solution prepared as described earlier has the nominal composition at the given temperatures, as defined in Table 7-2.

Table 7-2. *Temperature Dependence of Saturated NaCl Solution Composition*

Temperature F°	Temperature C°	Density gm/ml	Weight %
50	10	1.204	26.35
59	15	1.204	26.40
68	20	1.200	26.43
77	25	1.198	26.48
86	30	1.196	26.56

Once a solution of known, fixed sodium chloride concentration is prepared, various concentrations of lower levels of sodium chloride solution can be prepared usuing proportional dilutions. By mixing one volume of saturated solution with nine volumes of distilled water, a solution of one-tenth the concentration of the original concentrated, saturated stock solution is created. A binary-based series of known concentrations can be generated by initially diluting the saturated stock in a one-to-one proportion, then re-diluting the 1:1 dilution again in a 1:1 proportion. A binary dilution scheme can be implemented and repeated as many times as is required to produce the desired lower-level concentration.

Better accuracy and reproducibility can be realized in a repetitive dilution scheme using the following suggestions.

- – Pick a volume-measuring container of sufficient size to produce enough of the final dilution solution to cover the electrodes in the conductivity cell being used for the determinations and permit any further dilutions required to be made. Plastic pill vials or condiment containers of approximately 1 oz or 30 ml volumes (as seen in Figures 7-12 and 7-13) can be used.

- Use the same volume container for measuring both the initial concentrate and the single-volume distilled water diluent in a binary dilution scheme or multiple volumes of distilled water in a proportional dilution scheme. By measuring the dilution water in the same container that measured the concentrate being diluted, any residual traces of the concentrated solution that did not get transferred to the final volume container are washed out by the distilled water additions into the final volume of solution.

- To minimize "carry-over contamination," always wash the volumetric container after dispensing the final portion of dilution water with distilled water and dry the volume measuring container before measuring out the next required volume of concentrate.

Table 7-3 tabulates the specific conductance for various concentrations of sodium chloride solutions.

Table 7-3. *Conductivity of Sodium Chloride Solutions*

Parts per million	µS/cm or µmho/cm	Parts per million/%	mS/cm or mmho/cm
1	2.2	5000	8.2
3	6.5	1%	16.0
10	21.4	2%	30.2
30	64	5%	70.1
100	210	10%	126
300	617	20%	204
1000	1990	24%	222
3000	5690		

To minimize errors during conductivity, measurements using any cell probes other than platinum, wash and dry the electrodes between measurements of individual standards and samples.

A second useful technique during the measurement of a series of varying standard concentrations begins with the most dilute and work toward the most concentrated. The effect of any inadvertent carry-over is minimized.

Electrolytic Conductivity Measurements: 555 Timer

Several applications allow the RC time constant of the 555 timer IC to monitor a physical parameter, causing either a varying resistance or capacitance value in the circuits making up the timing regulator. The circuit in Figure 7-9 can produce the classical bipolar excitation signal in Figure 7-10 to measure electrolytic conductivity.

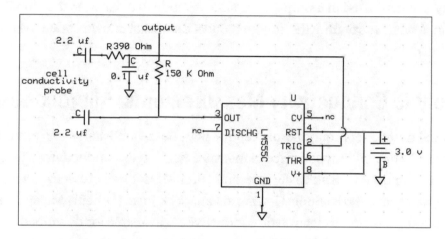

Figure 7-9. *A 555 timer circuit for electrolytic conductivity measurement*

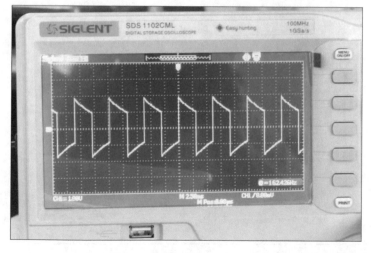

Figure 7-10. *Excitation signal from 555 timer for conductivity measurement*

The simple circuit has a low component count and is easily assembled on a prototyping breadboard. The circuit is an AC, bipolar excitation type measurement, and the output conductivity data is contained in the frequency of the oscillation of the timer. The frequency can be measured or read with either an Arduino configured with the frequency reading library or an oscilloscope.

The timer-based circuit works well with the stainless-steel probe described previously. It can be used in a simple comparative study to determine the circuit performance while measuring the conductivity of a series of known concentration table salt solutions.

Electrolytic Conductivity Measurements: Microcontroller

A substantial number of proposals and reports have been published using an Arduino microcontroller or similar type device to measure electrolytic conductivity. Figure 7-11 shows the circuit used with an easily fabricated probe described in *Environmental Monitoring with Arduino* by Emily Gertz and Patrick Di Justo (O'Reilly Maker Press, 2012). The code to read the electrolytic conductivity is available for download at GitHub (`https://github.com/ejgertz/EMWA/tree/master/chapter-5`).

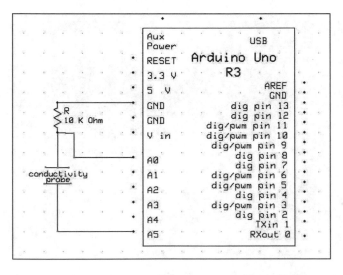

Figure 7-11. *Measuring electrolytic conductivity with Arduino*

Many Arduino-based systems use the microcontroller ADC to read the voltage on an electrolytic cell plate after the electrode is polarized. The book's code and the circuit in Figure 7-11 can be used with the stainless-steel probe described previously. The circuit performance can be evaluated in a comparative study by measuring the conductivity of a series of table salt solutions.

Observations

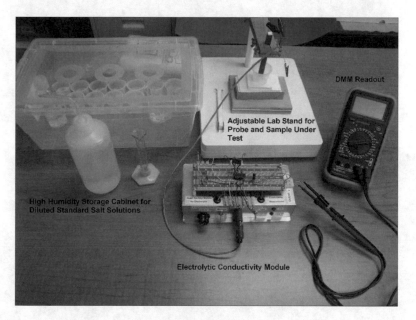

Figure 7-12. *The EC testing of serial dilution standard salt solutions*

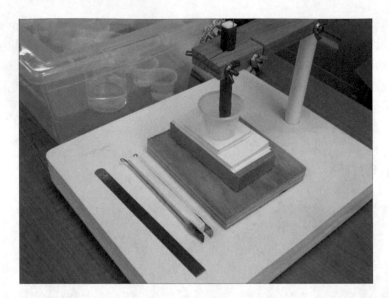

Figure 7-13. *Sample containment for serial dilution testing of salt solutions*

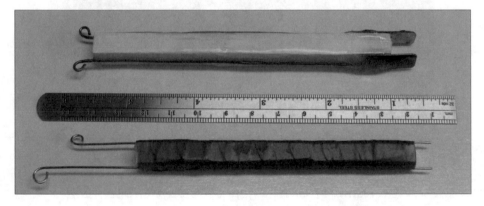

Figure 7-14. *The probes used for testing serially diluted salt standard*

Dilution of Sat. Soln.	Fractional Value	gm/ml of NaCl	Voltage Response	Concntn mg/ml	Conductivity mS/cm
1	1	0.357	4.27	357	42.7
1/2	0.5	0.1785	4.26	178.5	42.6
1/4	0.25	0.08925	4.23	89.25	42.3
1/8	0.125	0.044625	4.14	44.625	41.4
1/16	0.0625	0.0223125	3.8	22.3125	38
1/32	0.03125	0.01115625	3.14	11.15625	31.4
1/64	0.015625	0.005578125	1.958	5.578125	19.58
1/128	0.0078125	0.002789063	1.013	2.789063	10.13
1/256	0.0039063	0.001394531	0.552	1.394531	5.52
1/512	0.0019531	0.000697266	0.285	0.697266	2.85
1/1024	0.0009766	0.000348633	0.1707	0.348633	1.707

Conductivity of NaCl Serial Dilutions

Figure 7-15. *Concentration vs. mS/cm conductivity for 10 binary dilution span*

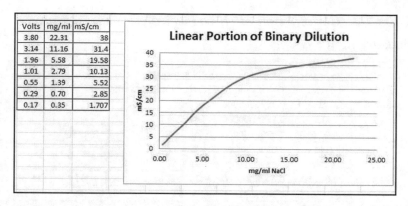

Figure 7-16. *Concentration vs. measured conductivity for lower/linear range*

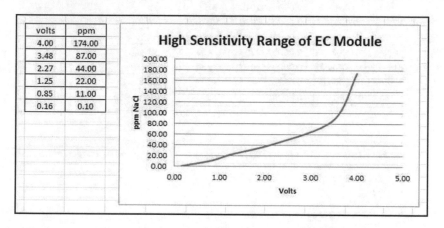

Figure 7-17. *Scale expansion of the electrolytic conductivity module*

A series of table salt solutions were prepared and analyzed to compare the various techniques available for monitoring the conductivity of aqueous solutions. The data obtained from the individual analytical techniques are tabulated in Table 7-4.

Table 7-4. *Comparison of Three Electrolytic Conductivity Measurement Systems*

Solution Preparation	Reduction Factor	gm/ml NaCl Concentration	LC-HP IC (nr) E. C. Module	LC-HP IC (hr) E. C. Module	Arduio EMWA	555 Timer (KHz)
saturated	1	0.3170000000	42.8			
1/2	0.5	0.1585000000	42.8			
1/4	0.25	0.0792500000	42.6		806	
1/8	0.125	0.0396250000	41.4		676	
1/16	0.0625	0.0198125000	38.1		621	
1/32	0.03125	0.0099062500	31.6		517	11.70
1/64	0.015625	0.0049531250	20.2		442	11.23
1/128	0.007813	0.0024767210	11.05		353	10.41
1/256	0.003906	0.0012382020	5.96	453	320	9.08
1/512	0.001953	0.0006191010	3.12	452	279	7.12
1/1024	0.000977	0.0003097090	1.626	443	230	5.02
1/2048	0.0004883	0.0001547911	0.868	422	184	3.27
1/4096	0.0002441	0.0000773797	0.457	372	133	2.00
1/8192	0.0001221	0.0000387057	0.254	252	93	1.142
1/16384	0.00006104	0.0000193497	0.162	1616	63	0.795
1/32768	0.00003052	0.0000096748	0.139	1351		0.662

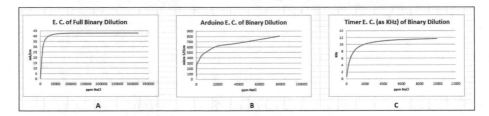

A   B   C

Figure 7-18. *Electrolytic conductivity plots of binary dilution from three measuring systems*

Discussion

More than 125 years ago, German scientists published studies that examined the passage of electrical energy through aqueous solutions of various salts and water-soluble compounds. A theory was developed correlating the unusual electrical conductivity of solutions with the concentration and degree of ionization that occurred when the substance of interest was dissolved in water.

Many measurements of the electrical conductivity at various solution concentrations led to the development of the strong, intermediate, and weak electrolyte descriptions of water-soluble compounds and a reasonable theory to explain the observed unusual behavior of concentrated, strong electrolytes. In highly concentrated solutions of strong electrolytes, the electrical attraction of the oppositely charged species causes a partial cancellation of their individual ionic charge. It hence reduces their ability to respond to externally applied potentials. In the graphs shown in Figure 7-18, the concentration of NaCl rises above certain levels the measured solution conductivity changes little.

Detailed qualitative and quantitative explanations of the theory of ionic solutions can be found in any textbook of physical chemistry.

For this simple exercise, only the linear portions or the more dilute concentration of the conductivity vs. concentration curves are used for solution monitoring.

This exercise first develops a rigorous, well-defined methodology for solution conductivity determinations that can validate simpler Arduino, RPi, and 555 timer IC–based measurement approximations.

A modern solid-state, electrolytic conductivity measurement system adhering to the traditionally developed unit operations consisting of a low voltage, AC test cell excitation, signal rectification, and DC voltage readout, was presented in 1977 by M. Ahmon.[1] The circuit presented used a quad, op-amp chip, LM348, in which the four amplifiers (741s) were configured into a sine wave generator, an amplifier, rectifier, and low pass filter.

In the ensuing decades, many variants of the original circuit have been used in a host of practical applications and as a chemical laboratory instrument for educational purposes.

Figure 7-6 is derived from a May 1997 article titled "A Low-Cost and High-Performance Conductivity Meter" by Rogerio T. da Roche et al. in the *Journal of Chemical Education* (Vol. 74, No. 5, pg. 572–574).

The 741 op-amp is still available, but the 411 has replaced it in many applications, and the quad op-amp chips TL074 and TL084 are 411-based replacements for the LM348, with the TL074 having a lower noise generation value. The module assembled from the cited reference has a triangular, low voltage, alternating polarity excitation signal applied to the conductivity probe. The signal passing through the ionic solution is amplified, rectified, and filtered to provide a DC output proportional to the solution conductivity. A range switch is provided in the circuitry to allow a 100-fold amplification gain in the output signal (see Figure 7-17); this accommodates the large conductivity differences between natural sources such as seawater and rainfall.

---

[1] "Electronics" September 15, 1977, pages 132 and 3, M. Ahmon, "Engineer's notebook"

In addition to the electronic circuit module, the authors present a method for producing a robust, easy to assemble conductivity probe from readily available materials. The probe is of a large surface area and can accommodate a strong, stable signal for experiments. In Figure 7-14, the upper conductivity probe is fabricated from 2 cm × 1 cm (¾ in × ⅜ in) stainless-steel plates and coated with epoxy, as described by Brazilian educators in the May 1997 *Journal of Chemical Education* article. The lower plastic electrical tape wrapped probe was constructed from 20 ga (0.812 mm, 0.0320 in) stainless steel wire. Each probe has a 1 cm wide plastic core setting the electrode spacing at 1 cm. The wire probe is simple and easy to assemble, eliminating silver soldering and epoxy coating.

Despite the large number of simple microcontroller-based conductivity measurement systems described in current literature, the more complex, traditional AC excitation method is used in this book because of its robustness and wide applicability.

A low-voltage AC excitation avoids water electrolysis and can be used on either a static, quiescent sample or on a stirred or flowing system without concerns about double-layer formation. The instrumentation is assembled around a single, readily available, low cost, integrated circuit, easily assembled on either a temporary prototyping breadboard or instrumentation mountable, universal printed circuit board, as seen in Figures 7-7 and 7-12.

The system can be calibrated and validated with an innocuous, easily obtained, standard salt that can be quantified and diluted without any expensive lab scales or dangerously fragile laboratory glassware.

Traditional graphical recording methods used for determining the electrical conductivity of aqueous solutions have been implemented with low voltage, applied AC signals that must be rectified, filtered, and amplified to produce a DC signal suitable for recording. The educational circuitry developed with the TL074 IC ($0.65 USD) produces an analog signal on the 0 V to 5 V scale that can be directly converted into a digital signal by either the Arduino microcontroller or the RPi connected to a 10- or 12-bit ADC for continuous strip chart display.

A continuous electrolytic conductivity monitor applies the technique to process control systems or chemical analysis procedures, such as conductometric titrations.

Continuous electrolytic conductivity monitors based on the 555 timer are remarkably simple in implementation as depicted in Figure 7-9 and provide the desirable low voltage, AC excitation signal, as seen in Figure 7-10. The plot of frequency vs. ppm of sodium chloride NaCl, as seen in Figure 7-18 graph C, is the shape expected or normal for the dilute to a concentrated range of the binary dilution series of salt solutions.

Many Arduino-based conductivity measurement systems are single readout methods that determine the voltage on an immersed probe after a fixed time or when the voltage on the electrode stabilizes. The data collected and plotted with the code in *Environmental Monitoring with Arduino* is reported in microsiemens and is derived from the final stable voltage exhibited by a probe plate in the solution under test.

Intuitively, the final measured voltage should be proportional to the charge that accumulates around the plate while under the influence of the nominal 5 V electric field imposed by the Arduino's output pin voltage. Intuitively, the higher the ionic concentration, the stronger the charge stored in the double layer around the immersed electrode plates.

Several cautions and limitations must be recognized when making or using electrolytic conductivity measurements experimentally.

- To obtain proportional, reproducible data measurements or monitor concentration trends, solute levels at which inter-ion interactions are detectable should be avoided. Measurements should be made in the steeply rising or falling portions of the curves seen in many EC vs. concentration plots.

- Electrolytic conductivity values can only be established and validated by comparison with known standards and appropriate cell constant calculation.

- Conductivity measurement systems using voltages above 1½ V to 2 V can cause electrochemical reactions at the electrode surfaces, resulting in the formation of gases or the accelerated corrosion of the conductivity probe electrodes.

- Platinum electrodes may be required for conductivity measurements made in strong acids or bases.

Conductivity: Relative Humidity

At 100% relative humidity, mist, fog, or rain is seen in the atmosphere, and the air is saturated with water vapor. How far below the water vapor saturation points a parcel of air may be indicated by relative humidity (RH) values less than 100%.

Ambient temperatures determine the amount of water vapor that air can theoretically hold. In cold climates, the low temperatures create dry conditions that give rise to static accumulations. Hot summer conditions near large bodies of water raise the relative humidity (RH) to the point at which static electric demonstrations are virtually impossible.

RH values can be measured with sensors manufactured with moisture sensitive, metal oxide ceramic foams. Typical detectors consist of a moisture-sensitive plate sandwiched between two conductive metal electrodes. The sensor absorbs moisture from the air, and on the surface of the oxide, in a thin molecular layer, the water ionizes. As the mass of ionized water on the oxide surface changes, the conductivity of the detector changes and a measure of the RH is generated.

Table 7-5 tabulates the properties of two RH detectors, the DHT11 and DHT22 ($12 and $22 CDN), which are readily available from many online sources or local electronics suppliers.

Table 7-5. *Properties of DHT11 and DHT22 RH Sensors*

Parameter	DHT11	DHT22
Temperature	$0 - 50^{\circ}C$ / +/- $2^{\circ}C$	$-40 - 125^{\circ}C$ / +/- $0.5^{\circ}C$
Relative Humidity	20 – 80% / +/- 5%	0 – 100% / +/- 2-5%
Sampling Rate	1 Hz. (1 reading/sec)	0.5 Hz. (1 reading/2 sec)
Detector Size	15.5 x 12 x 5.5 mm	15.1 x 25 x 7.7 mm

The metal oxide surface has a limited ability to disperse a water film, and the excess vapor or liquid water can saturate the surface, virtually short-circuiting the detector. Saturated detectors can be restored by eliminating the excess water in a procedure by the manufacturer.

Experiment

A DHT11 or 22 sensor can be connected to an Arduino microcontroller to measure and display the temperature and relative humidity (RH) of the gas environment in which the sensor resides.

Measurements of the ambient RH can be made with the lower resolution DHT11. The higher-resolution DHT22 can be used in experiments or measurements that require a higher resolution or larger dynamic range of RH determination as in water activity evaluations.

The library required to read the sensor can be downloaded from the device manufacturer, supplier, or the Arduino website, along with several Arduino readout programs that appear in the "examples" entry of the nominal library's available code menu. DAQFactory and RPi computing systems can follow and plot any data streamed to the Arduino serial port. The Arduino libraries provide code to read the sensor for RH and temperature. By modifying the exemplar, read program outputs to stream only a comma-delimited numerical pair to the serial port, the control computers can read and plot the data.

All descriptive printings to the serial port should be commented out in the Arduino code. The first numerical data value is output with the line Serial.print(nn.nn); followed by the line Serial.print(","); and finally, Serial.println(nn.nn);. The serial port should then display the desired data format consisting of a column of dual, floating-point digits, separated by a comma.

An RH measurement begins by validating the Arduino serial port output that should result in a stream of comma-separated floating-point values down the left-hand side of the serial monitor output window. The Arduino had to be started on my Windows system, the output validated, and the serial monitor shut down before the DAQFactory program was started. Failure to follow the initializing sequence resulted in either program throwing a "port in use error."

For the DAQFactory serial port to read and parse comma-separated value (CSV) data, the I/O data parsing code at the end of the chapter was installed in the "on receive" event of the DAQFactory serial port.

A water activity measurement in a tested material involves using a small volume, low surface porosity, insulated, humidity monitoring chamber. Figures 7-19, 7-20, and 7-21 illustrate my device. An experiment is begun by starting the software and establishing a stable baseline for the empty but closed chamber. Once a stable baseline is established, the chamber's bottom drawer is filled with freshly prepared silica gel drying agent and then inserted into the bottom compartment, the top and bottom front shutters are fixed in place, and the interior RH value allowed to drop to a steady value.

When the chamber's inside moisture content has reached its minimum value, the isolation partition can be inserted between the chambers. The sample is inserted through the opening in the top shutter, and then the sampling door is sealed.

You can then let the chamber RH and the graphical display rise to a steady value representing the equilibrium relative humidity (ERH) value.

Assembly of an Equilibrium Vapor Pressure Chamber

The assembly and construction of an ERH chamber are depicted in Figures 7-19 through 7-24. When using the ERH described next, a simple but significant modification of routing the wiring out the rear of the chamber to not interfere with the sample insertion and recovery became evident.

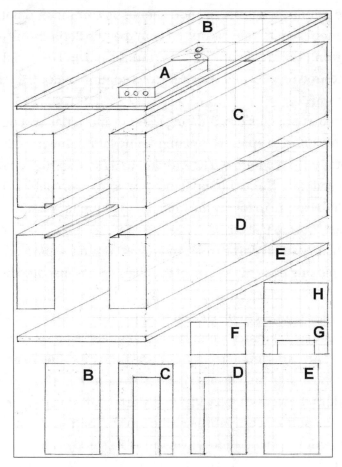

Figure 7-19. *ERH chamber component outline drawings*

Table 7-6 describes the components in Figure 7-19.

Table 7-6. *ERH Chamber Component Data*

Part	Component or function	Material of construction	Dimensions	Comments
A	DHT Sensor			
B	Top plate of chamber	thin lexan or plastic sheet	2-1/2 x 4 in (65 x 102 mm)	thick PET (polyethylene terephthalate)
C	Walls of ERH chamber top compartment	"U" shaped wood	(3/4 x 1-1/2 stock) 2-1/2 x 4 in. (18 x 37 mm stock)	bottom inner edges cut for isolation plate + bottom drawer
D	Walls of ERH chamber bottom compartment	"U" shaped wood	(3/4 x 1-1/2 stock) 2-1/2 x 4 in. (18 x 37 mm stock)	top inner edges cut for isolation plate + bottom drawer
E	Bottom plate of chamber	1/8 in (3 mm) plywood	2-1/2 x 4 in (65 x 102 mm)	can be fixed in place if desired
F	Sample port cover/door	thin lexan or plastic sheet	2 - 1/2 x 1 - 1/4 (65 x 32 mm)	movable for port access ie hinged, pivot point, slotted end
G	Top chamber front plate with sample port	1/8 in (3 mm) plywood	2 - 1/2 x 1 - 1/4 (65 x 32 mm) and 1-1/4 x 1/2 (32 x 12 mm)	can be fixed in place if desired
H	Bottom chamber front plate	1/8 in (3 mm) plywood	2 - 1/2 x 1 - 1/2 in (65 x 37 mm)	must be removable to change silica gel desiccant

Figure 7-20. *Top view of ERH chamber with saturated salt humidity standard*

Figure 7-20 is labeled as follows.

- A is a Lexan top with brass fastening screws.

- B is a DHT sensor with power, signal, and ground connections.

- C is silica gel desiccant.

- D is a sample dish with saturated sodium chloride humidity standard.

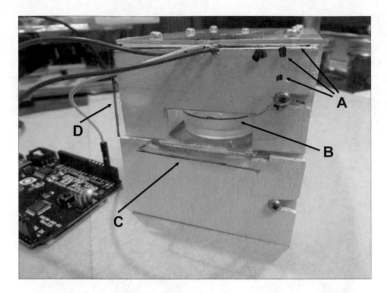

Figure 7-21. *Front view of ERH chamber with humidity standard solution*

Figure 7-21 is labeled as follows.

– A shows felt-tip pen marks on a Lexan sample port cover.

– B is a standard salt humidity solution in sample holder dish.

– C is a Lexan chamber isolation plate.

– D is the left end of the sample port cover.

All wood surfaces exposed to the interior of the ERH must be painted or varnished with several coats of the finish and sanded smooth between coats to seal off porous surfaces to minimize surface water adsorption/desorption.

Silica Gel Desiccant Preparation

Heating silica gel in a conventional oven at temperatures between 125 and 150°C (257°F–302°F) then allowing the adsorbent to cool to room temperature in a sealed 125 ml (¼ pt) preserving jar produces a desiccant that provided an ERH chamber RH value of approximately 66%. Increasing the oven temperature to 175°C (347°F) and cooling the gel to room temperature in the drying column equipped storage vessel (see Figure 7-22) produced an ERH chamber RH value of 35%. Additional experimentation with higher temperature silica gel conditioning at 225°C (437°F) and cooling in the drying column equipped vessel was able to lower the ERH chamber to 26.3% RH in 10 to 15 min.

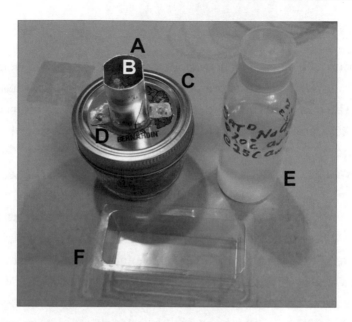

Figure 7-22. *Silica gel dry cooling/storage vessel, salt humidity standard, and bottom desiccant drawer*

Figure 7-22 is labeled as follows.

– A is a thin wall tube that can withstand 225°C hot silica gel beads.

– B shows a charge of ¾ inch to 1 inch (20 mm – 25 mm) depth portion of freshly heat-treated silica gel.

– C is a sealing ring of preserving jar to seal the lid to the jar and force cooling air to be drawn through the desiccant filled tube.

– D is a jar top with pinholes in the center of the drying tube and silicone sealant.

– E shows a saturated sodium chloride humidity standard.

– F is a desiccant drawer cut from appropriately sized, rectangular, PET, hardware, bubble packaging.

Observations

Omega Engineering published data based on a large set of peer-reviewed ERH values for saturated salt solutions at various temperatures (see www.omega.com/temperature/z/pdj/z103.pdf). The data for a saturated sodium chloride solution indicates an ERH value of 75.47 at 20°C and 75.29 at 25°C. A saturated salt solution was observed to create chamber RH values of 78.8%, 79.0%, and 78.6% for an average value of 78.8%. The high ERH for the saturated salt solution suggests a systematic error in the measurement system of +3.4%.

Figure 7-23 shows a duplicate measurement of the water activity in a bran flakes breakfast cereal. Between each of the measurements collected, the isolation plate to separate the silica gel adsorbent from the measurement chamber was removed to lower the chamber RH value as low as possible to minimize any residual moisture in the measurement chamber on the ERH of the sample under test. (The next section discusses the low magnitude of any possible moisture residual in this type of testing.)

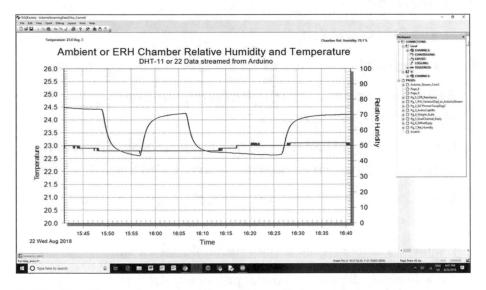

Figure 7-23. *Duplicate determination of bran flakes water activity*

The initial water activity determination began at 15:57 and terminated at 16:07. The second measurement began at 16:27 and terminated at 14:41. An initial ERH value of 70.8% and a second value of 70.0% were recorded.

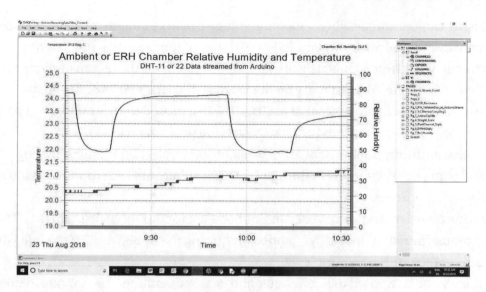

Figure 7-24. *ERH of maple syrup and peanut butter*

Table 7-7. *ERH of Foods and a Pharmaceutical*

Sample No.	Material	ERH %
1	Bran flakes	70.8 70.0
2	Glycerine USP	66.2
3	Maple syrup	85.6
4	Marmalade (Orange)	86.9
5	Peanut butter	72.4

Discussion

For the RH sensors to work, the ambient atmospheric moisture must diffuse onto the surface of the ceramic transducer. The measurement is known as *diffusion controlled*. Gaseous diffusion at ambient temperatures and pressures is a relatively slow process. It is the major contributor to the large one or two seconds per reading response time of the sensors. The one- and two-second sampling rates are thus needed to ensure that any local atmospheric moisture content changes have time to equilibrate with the molecular layer of water on the metal oxide foam surface. For analysis and trending purposes, RH data is best followed by graphical displays provided by computer plotting of the generated data as a function of time.

The RH can determine whether a static charge can accumulate on insulated objects within the monitored environment. Prof. T. B. Jones of the Electrical Engineering Department at Rochester University lists a series of electrostatic demonstrations on the following website. The last entry on the list describes the effects of RH on the demonstrations. Prof. Joes notes that at 60%–70% RH, most demonstrations will probably not work (see www2.ece.rochester.edu/~jones/demos/index.html).

Relative humidity is important for weather observations and predictions. Fog, mist, and water condensations in the ambient atmosphere are hazardous to vision and transportation systems.

The inexpensive RH sensors used in this book are for indoor measurements. They are not robust, and they are easily "flooded," requiring the application of the following restoration procedure.

If the sensor is exposed to liquid water and ceases operation, the ceramic foam surface must be re-equilibrated to restore its conductive catalytic activity. The plastic structure will not tolerate any sustained excessive heat, UV light, or prolonged exposure to direct sunlight. A manufacturer or supplier, dual step recovery program is suggested in which the detector is first heated to 50°C–60 °C at <10% RH for 2 hours (122°F–140°F) and is then followed by heat treatment of 20°C–30°C at <70% RH for 5 hours (68°F–86°F).

RH sensors based on PTFE polymer bases are available for remote, field-based weather observation stations exposed to high humidity, sunlight, and actual liquid water.

Water Activity

Although the conductivity RH sensors are useful in measuring ambient relative humidity, a lesser-known but important use of these devices is in the study of microbial growth, food preservation, and food safety. Food preservation depends on stopping or severely restricting microbial activity. Microbes usually need water to grow. Restricting the amount of water available for microbial growth can extend the storage life of many foods and pharmaceuticals. The US Food and Drug Administration published an online Water Activity in Foods memo at www.fda.gov/ICEC/Inspections/InspectionGuides/ InspectionTechnicalGuides/ucm072916.htm. Prof. M. Chaplin discusses the theory and effects of water activity at www1.Isbu.ac.uk/water/water_activity.html.

The US FDA document defines water activity and its relationship to the equilibrium relative humidity. It draws attention to the fact that water activities at or above 0.95 can support microbial growth. The document also points out that foods in which the moisture content is reduced to create water activities less than 0.85 cannot support microbial growth and are exempt from certain government regulations.

A paper on the application of the ERH chamber technique to solid pharmaceuticals[2] discusses the low values of error that carefully designed ERH chambers create.

A traditional method for preserving food is to pack the material to be stored in salt or another moisture absorbent such as sugar. The large presence of salt absorbs a significant portion of the free water needed for microbial growth. The activity of the water is reduced to the point that microbial spoilage is severely retarded or virtually halted.

Water activity is written as a_w and is scaled from 1 to 0 in which free pure water has an activity of 1, and a dry water-free environment is 0. Water activity scales well with the water's partial pressure in an aqueous or biological system.

From thermodynamic considerations, it can be shown that

$$a_w = P/P_o = ERH(\%)/100$$

P is the partial pressure of water above the material of interest. P_o is the partial pressure of pure water at the same temperature. ERH is the equilibrium relative humidity expressed as a fraction.

To measure the ERH, an example data display program from the Arduino library chosen for the DHT sensor must be modified by the experimenter so that only the comma-separated relative humidity value and temperature are streamed out to the serial port. Validation of the Arduino serial port output should result in a stream of two comma-separated, digital floating-point values down the left-hand side of the serial monitor output window. On my Windows system, the Arduino had to be started, the output validated, and the serial monitor shut down before the DAQFactory program started. If the initializing sequence was not followed, "port in use" errors were thrown.

The DAQFactory serial port monitor validated reception of the relative humidity and temperature data parsed by the simple script in Listing 7-1 into two channels named tempDegC and relHmdty for graphical display.

The DHT11 and 22 are well suited to determining the ambient or open-air RH, but the DHT22 is better suited for monitoring the ERH chamber and the ERH of materials under test. In Figures 7-23 and 7-24, the time scales on the bottom were expanded to record an hour or more of data. The small chamber method and isolation technique are

---

[2]Data & Review , Feb. 2007 Pharmaceutical Technology, pg 56-71, "Implementation of Water Activity Testing to Replace Karl Fischer Water Testing", Snider, Liang and Pearson

based on an equilibrium between the reduced water content of the material under test and the thin molecular layer of water on the detector sensor, metal oxide foam. Many foodstuffs with a high-water activity can take a substantial amount of time to effuse sufficient water to bring the chamber water vapor content and the mass of water in the material under test into a state of equilibrium. The human eye easily sees a flat line at the end of a recorded analog transition. The measurement is complete.

DAQFactory Serial Port I/O Data Parsing Code

I used the following code in the "on receive" event of the serial port named Comm6. It is defined as com 6 in the DAQFactory identification window entry. I set up two channels in the channel entry table: relHmdty as channel 0 and tempDegC as channel 1. The following code parsed out the RH value and loaded the entries into relHmdty[0] and the corresponding temperature values into tempDegC[0].

```
if (strIn == Chr(13))
    private string datain = ReadUntil(44)
    Channel.AddValue(strDevice, 0, "Input", 0, StrToDouble(DataIn))
    Private string datain = ReadUntil(13)
    Channel.AddValue(strDevice, 0, "Input", 1, StrToDouble(DataIn))
Endif
```

Summary

Techniques for the measurement of low values of resistance in mΩ range were discussed: the continuous measurement of normally encountered resistance values in the Ω range and the measurement of high values of resistance in the gigaohm (GΩ or 10^9) and teraohm (TΩ or 10^{12}) ranges.

Wheatstone bridge and Kelvin connection concepts and techniques that are nearly two hundred years old and still heavily in use today are demonstrated and evaluated for making resistance measurements.

Electrical resistance is a function of temperature. The temperature coefficient of resistance is measured and published for numerous elements, metals, materials, and alloys.

Conductivity is defined and evaluated in solids, liquids, and gases.

Two specific techniques and applications for measuring conductivity in liquids and gases are presented and evaluated.

An IC-based, high-frequency AC, low-voltage instrument is presented for making conductivity measurements in ionic solutions able to be read by a SCADA system or a simple handheld VOM for field use.

Low values of the water content of foodstuffs can be measured with ICs able to measure the conductivity of atmospheric water vapors in relative humidity (RH) determinations in ERH chambers.

Chapter 8 examines the measurement of voltage, the last of the three values in Ohm's law.

CHAPTER 8

Voltage

This chapter discusses the origins of voltage differences and presents several less expensive and practical techniques for determining the magnitudes of potential differences. High-voltage, low-current-based power supplies are described in Chapter 11.

Voltage is commonly accepted as a measure of the potential energy that makes electrons or a charged entity move during an electrical flow. It is defined as the energy per unit charge or energy = E/Q. A volt is a joule/coulomb. An electric field is created when electrons are removed from the atoms or molecules in one area of a material and concentrated in another. The work needed to separate the electrons and create the areas of positive and negative charge creates an electric field in which potential energy is stored. Voltage is a measure of the restorative trying to neutralize unbalanced charges. As one of the variables in Ohm's law, voltage may be quantified by measuring the amount of current it can draw through a known resistance (V = IR).

Voltages can be created by different physio-chemical actions that separate or move electrons resulting in unbalanced charges that create an electric field between the separated charges. Some of the more familiar methods in which voltage differences are formed are outlined briefly in the following passages.

Voltages can be created through chemical actions in a conducting medium when elements able to release electrons are placed near those able to accept them. Spontaneous electron transfer reactions are used in the design and manufacturing of batteries produced in two formats. Single-use batteries are made from non-rechargeable or primary cells. Rechargeable batteries are made from rechargeable or secondary cells. In primary cells, electrical energy from chemical reactions can be stored and released only once, while in secondary cells, a recharging cycle can be repeated many times over. Electrochemical phenomena are based on the electromotive series listing certain elements ranked according to the voltages required or created when they gain or lose electrons. The electromotive series has applications in energy storage and generation,

© Richard J. Smythe 2022
R. J. Smythe, *Arduino Measurements in Science*, https://doi.org/10.1007/978-1-4842-6781-3_8

corrosion science, and analytical chemistry.[1] Many biological systems, such as central nervous systems, function through electrochemical processes and related phenomena (see Chapter 11).

Electron flow can be created by moving a magnetic field relative to a conductor. *Magnetic induction* is the basis by which electrical or mechanical energies can be interchanged. Motors and generators have been engineered to optimize the interchange between rotational motion and electrical energy, as seen in the various types of motors available and the different kinds of generators currently in existence.

Alternating current/direct current (AC/DC) motors generators and alternators are all in use as required by the service's needs. Using rotational motion to spin magnets or conducting coils creates or consumes alternating current electrical energy that changes direction on each rotation.

AC voltages have a distinct advantage over DC in that AC voltages can be "stepped up" or "stepped down" with simple transformers. Electrical transformers use an AC current in a coiled wire called the *primary* to create a varying intensity magnetic field that induces a current flow in another electrically isolated coil called the *secondary*, immersed in the fluctuating magnetic field. The voltage and currents induced in the circuits connected to the transformer's primary and secondary windings are directly proportional to the number of turns in the two coils (see Chapter 11).

Voltage differences can be created by illuminating PN junctions in photovoltaic cells constructed from silicon-based semiconductor materials. Although the voltage generated is on the order of a half volt per cell, the cells can be fabricated from large areas and connected in series and parallel configurations to supply virtually any current and voltage desired from sunlight (see Chapter 11).

Piezoelectricity is the voltage produced when certain, highly polar crystals or molecular structures are deformed by pressure. Piezoelectric crystals such as tourmaline, quartz, topaz, and Rochelle salt (sodium-potassium bitartrate, $NaKC_4H_4O_6.4H_2O$) are all electro-active materials able to produce electrical impulses when deformed by mechanical forces or mechanically deforming when stimulated by electrical energies.

Polyvinylidene fluoride or polyvinylidene difluoride (PVDF) plastic is an organic polymeric material with a polar molecular framework: $(CH_2-CF_2)_n$ – CAS Number 24937-79-9). Bending or deforming the bulk polymer material's physical shape forces areas

---

[1]*CRC Handbook of Chemistry and Physics*, 84th ed., by David Lide (CRC Press, 2003).

of different charge to move and can create measurable voltage differences during the deformation. Plastic material has many advantages over a rigid crystalline substance (see Chapter 6).

Voltages are also developed when junctions of dissimilar metals or certain semiconductors are heated or cooled. Thermoelectric voltages and currents are small but can be amplified and measure temperatures and even pump heat (see Chapter 3).

Thermionic emission in vacuum tubes occurs when the electrons' energy in a heated filament becomes sufficient to overcome the potential barrier known as the *work function* for the metal or material and are ejected from the filament. The electrons only contain a few electron volts of energy and form a space charge.

The utility of the vacuum tube, the predecessor of transistors and integrated circuits, is only realized with the application of external voltages that greatly overpower the tiny voltages created by the space charge cloud formation. Impressing an external voltage on a wire close to the incandescent filament in the vacuum tube controls the emitted current flow through the tube. Electronics based on vacuum tube technology was virtually confined to analog circuitry. The first computers and operational amplifiers were vacuum tube devices, but energy consumption, size, heat generation, and short service lives limited their development.

Many of the preceding voltage sources generate potential differences that are quite small and can only be measured with instrumentation systems of high input impedance. The smaller the value of the potential difference to be measured, the higher the input impedance of the measurement system to minimize the current drawn from the source under test (see Chapter 2).

Several measurement techniques for low-level electronic signals have been described, starting with Figure 2-3 in Chapter 2. In Figure 2-3, the voltage follower electrometer presents an input impedance to the potential difference generating source of 10 TΩ (10^{12}) that draws little current from the source under test.

Many moderately priced (< \$150 CDN) digital multimeters (DMM) or digital panel meters (DPM) have 200 mV scales that monitor millivolt sources. High input impedance measurement systems, usually over 10^8 Ω, are needed to measure voltages in the low or fractional millivolt range.

A short discussion and tabular summary of available op-amp integrated circuits and their input impedances are in Table 2-1 in Chapter 2.

High voltage, high current electrical energy is not considered in this book. High-energy electricity requires special knowledge, training, and equipment to be handled safely and is far too dangerous to be in this simple experimental work. High voltage low current electrical energy is required for many experimental investigations, and the safe generation and handling of these high voltage sources are dealt with in Chapter 11.

Most analog and digital scientific measurement systems work in the low voltage range under 50 V. Biochemical research, biochemical analysis, and chemical analysis techniques involving molecular or atomic ionization all make extensive use of low-current, high-voltage electrical potentials. Static electric voltages, with potential differences of hundreds or thousands of volts, are in this section because of their frequent occurrence in nature, their importance in causing measurement noise, ignition in flammable gas or dust accumulations their destructive capability with respect to integrated circuitry.

Static Electrical Charge and Measurement

Static electric charges, known from the ancient Greek philosophers, were first studied qualitatively with pivoting needles called *versorium* devised by William Gilbert around 1600. A semi-quantitative knowledge of static phenomena evolved with the development of the gold leaf or pith ball electroscopes.

Static electric voltage measurements differ from all previous measurement techniques in two aspects, the first being a requirement for non-contact sensing and the second being in the substantially larger magnitudes of the voltages to be determined.

Static electrical phenomena are often created by frictional forces or physical contact between different materials and have been traditionally demonstrated by rubbing insulating materials such as glass rods or resinous materials with silk cloths or animal furs.

Tribologic science deals with the interactions of surfaces in contact or moving with respect to one another. An ordering of materials that spontaneously develop a static electrical charge on contact with one another, much like the electromotive series, but known today as the triboelectric series, has been in existence since the mid-1700s.

The triboelectric series features materials with a tendency to gain or lose electric charge when in contact with one another. The understanding and control of static electrical charges is required for safety in fire and explosion prevention, is a serious concern for micro-miniaturized integrated circuitry, must be considered in the measurement of electrical signals, and is essential for many practical problems such as photo-copier design and the precipitation of nuisance dusts in environmental pollution controls.

Several large organizations must deal with static electrical phenomena, including NASA (Handbook 8739.12), the Electrostatic Discharge Association, and the Electrostatics Society of America. All three organizations are authoritative sources on static electricity.

Recent investigations into the nature of negative and positive static charges in insulators and conductors show the presence of several physio-chemical mechanisms at work. Static voltages are created when electrons and actual mass is transferred between contacting bodies. Research has also demonstrated that the distribution of electrical charge in insulators is localized, while in conductors, it is distributed. Studies have quantified the tribologic series; the results by AlphaLab Inc. are available at `https://www.alphalabinc.com/triboelectric-series/`.

Static charge accumulations are essentially surface phenomena that create localized electric fields. An electrostatic discharge (ESD) between charged entities in the form of an arc or sparking current flow can cause catastrophic damage to microcircuits or a source of ignition for an explosion or fire.

Determining the presence of a static field has traditionally been achieved by qualitatively observing the non-contacting repulsion and attraction of like and opposite static charges. Traditional methods consisted of gold leaf and pith ball electroscopes. An unknown static charge in a material either spread the gold leaves or repelled/attracted the suspended pith ball. The electric field in a charged material was brought near the electroscope.

Some traditional electroscopes were modified to measure the angle between the leaves of the gold leaf instrument or deflection from the vertical of a pith ball suspended by a thread to provide semi-quantitative field strength measurements.

The magnitudes of voltages involved in static electrical phenomena can be somewhat deceiving for experimental investigators or educational demonstrators that work with low-voltage digital and mains electrical systems. Potentials of thousands of volts cause static electric sparks that result in arcs as a result of walking on a carpet. Traditional gold-leaf electroscopes used to detect electrostatic charge on glass tubes or rods rubbed with hair or furs can create electric fields of sufficient size to activate the gate areas on field-effect transistors. A voltage impressed upon an active FET can thus regulate the current flowing in the device's main channel and provide a means of measuring the electric field voltage without disturbing the field.

The sizes of static voltages developed in dry conditions associated with people moving about an indoor environment can run into the thousands of volts that destroy most integrated circuits if discharged near the circuitry. Experimentally exposing solid-state devices intentionally to electrostatic fields must be done under controlled conditions to not destroy the inorganic thin films within the devices.

In addition to electric fields, it was found that non-contact electrical energy can be transferred between two sources or electrical circuits by induction and capacitive couplings. As indicated by the name, capacitive coupling involves transferring electrical energy through the insulated medium in capacitors.

In the measurement of capacitance and charge,

$$C = Q/V \text{ or } C = (I \times t)/V \text{ and } C = k \times (A/d)$$

C is the capacitance, Q is the charge, V is the voltage, I is the current flow into the capacitor, t is the time of current flow, A is the area of the capacitor plates, d is the distance between plates, and k is a proportionality constant.

$(kA/Q) \times V = d$ indicates that for a system of constant plate area and system charge, the system voltage varies in proportion to the distance between the plates of the charged capacitor.

Objects with a static charge separated from a detector, such as a metal foil electroscope, form a capacitor. The motion of a plate in a charged capacitor creates variation in the voltage of the capacitor system, thus making high sensitivity electroscopemeasurements motion-sensitive.

The earlier attempts to replace electroscopes with high-input impedance electrometers were made possible by technology improvements in first vacuum tubes and then in solid-state systems. Electrometers are characterized by high input impedances that make non-contact voltage measurements of electric fields associated with static charges.

Using solid-state devices called *junction field effect transistors* (JFET), investigators use simple circuits to detect the electric field created by static charges. By monitoring the current flow through circuits connected to the main body of JFET detectors, electric fields from static charges could be detected with impressive sensitivities.

However, although the drain-source voltages on these three terminal devices can be up to 100 or so volts, gate voltages on the semiconductor junction controlling the current flow in the main channel are usually limited to typically 20 V maximums.

Commercial non-contacting voltage measurement devices called *field meters* use rotating, grounded, metal shutters in the form of segmented, rotating disks or tubes to create AC signals from alternately exposing sensing electrodes to ground then the electric field under study. Although the AC voltage generated by the field meter simplifies the electronics required to amplify the measurement signal, the complexity of the rotating electrode exposure "chopper" greatly increases the complexity and cost of the devices. Instructions for the construction of a field mill device are at `www.precisionstrobe.com/jc/fieldmill/fieldmill.html`.

Several manufacturers of static electricity meters have generated substantial literature on the nature and characteristics of static electrical surface charges, the tribologic series, and energy-harvesting applications.

Inverse Square Laws

Theoretical considerations indicate that the magnitude or intensity of the attractive or repulsive forces generated by static electric charges follows the inverse square law, gravity, nuclear radiation, and light. A basic theory for an inverse square law can be derived by envisioning the radiated emanation as an expanding, spherical shell originating from a point source.

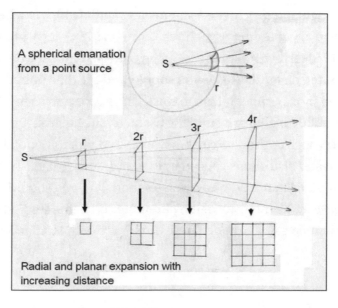

Figure 8-1. *Inverse-square law intensity*

425

The surface area of a sphere of radius r is given by $4\pi r^2$. If a static charge of Q coulombs is located at the source S, then the intensity of the radiated electric field at a distance r from the point source is the total emitted field divided by the area of the expanding sphere.

For a point source charge of Q coulombs, at the center of a spherical expansion of radial field lines, the field intensity at a distance r is

$$E_r = (Q/\varepsilon_0)/4\pi\, r^2 \text{ (where } \varepsilon_0 \text{ is the permittivity of free space)}$$

As is seen in Figure 8-1, the electric field is spreading out in proportion to the expanding area through which the field lines must pass. Since the spherical surface area is increasing as the square of the distance r from the point source charge, the intensity of the electric field is diluted by the increasing area which it is permeating.

A useful quantitative property inherent in the inverse square law relationships can be derived by considering the intensity of the emanation at two different distances from the point source, as follows.

$$E_n / E_f = (4/3\,\pi\,(r_n)^2)/\,(4/3\,\pi\,(r_f)^2)$$
$$\text{or } E_n / E_f = (r_n)^2/(r_f)^2$$

E_n is the nearest electric field intensity, E_f is the further value, and r is the corresponding distance from the source of the two measurement locations.

Graphical representations of inverse square law relationships can be presented in a hyperbolic form on x, y coordinates, or linear form on log x – log y plotting. When the data points from an ideal inverse square function collected from a true point source of radiation are plotted on log/log axes, you should find the data points, although randomly dispersed by experimental error, clustering about a straight line with a slope of –2. Deviations in both the linearity and the predicted negative slope can be caused by experimental effects such as the source of the emanated phenomenon being spread over a large surface area and distortions caused by experimental artifacts.

To study phenomena that follow an inverse square law, you should be prepared for a very rapid decrease in the intensity of the phenomenon being studied with relatively small increments in increasing distance from the source of the radiation being studied.

Solid-State Devices for Static Voltage Measurements

Static electric phenomena, known since ancient Greek civilization, can be qualitatively explained in terms of modern atomic theory by dividing materials into conductors and insulators. In keeping with the simple approach, conductors have conduction bands in their molecular structures in which electrons can flow, while insulators do not.

Static electrical charges can arise from the simple mechanical contact between certain materials. Mechanical contact permits the transfer of surface electrons from one material surface to another, which results in one surface having excess electrons while the other is electron deficient. Positively and negatively charged surfaces are the result of unbalanced electron distribution.

Static charges follow two rules.

- Accumulated unbalanced charges create electric fields whose strength follows an inverse square law with distance.

- Like charges repel while opposite charges attract.

Induction is a consequence of these two statements in that a charged body can induce opposite polarity charging in materials brought into proximity to the original electrified surface. Induction causes dust, plastic wrap, and foam packing beads to stick together and cause lint and other small particles to cling tenaciously to non-conducting material surfaces.

As investigated in capacitance measurements, a voltage or charge difference established between two surfaces separated by an insulator form a capacitor. A static charge on a surface forms a capacitor when the charge's electric field induces an opposite charge in any material that enters the electric field. The induction of an opposite charge in conductors near charged entities is called *capacitive coupling*. Capacitive coupling can be prevented by placing grounded metal shielding around one or both conductors.

Although the phenomenon called static electricity was discovered, developed, and explained in terms of conductors and insulators, modern transistors and integrated circuits use a third type of material called a *semiconductor* to manipulate and control electrical energy flow. Semiconductors are manufactured in formats where high purity crystals of silicon are treated with specific atomic impurities to regulate actual electron flow in N-type semiconductor materials. Silicon crystals are also manufactured with

427

measured, trace atomic impurities to regulate the flow of crystal artifacts lacking a balanced electrical condition called *holes* that can be considered "positive" electrical energy flow in *P-type semiconductor materials.*

Traditionally, electroscopes used the mechanical displacement of thin metal leaves and suspended pith balls to visualize the presence of repulsive and attractive electric fields created by like and opposite charges. Modern technology has developed electronic semiconductor devices called *field effect transistors* (FET) that function as traditional electroscopes. Numerous simple and complicated designs for "electronic electroscopes" have been published over the years since inexpensive FET and integrated circuit op-amps using FET inputs have become commercially available.

FETs are well suited for measuring static electric fields by virtue of their construction and method of operation. Field effect transistors are three-terminal voltage-controlled devices that possess high input impedances and can regulate the passage of current between their main input and output terminals, called the *drain and source*, in accordance with the electric field impressed upon their third terminal, called the *gate*. Gate input impedances for FET type devices can be in the hundreds of MΩ. Input impedances of such high magnitudes virtually draw no current load from the source being measured and meet the requirement for measuring static charge accumulations of not noticeably affecting or disturbing the source being measured.

FETs manufactured in both N- and P-type semiconductors with gate sensitivities to the impressed electric field's polarity should allow the detection and measurement of the electric fields generated by both forms of static electrical accumulations.

The extreme input impedance and the virtual absence of a gate current, characteristic of FET devices, led to their widespread use in a large-scale integrated circuit, digital logic chips, and the low-voltage microprocessor control of small and large currents, in power control applications. Improvements in basic FET devices resulted in the development of metal oxide semiconductor field effect transistors (MOSFET) with substantially increased gate input impedances, and channels can easily handle currents in the 25 A to 50 A range.

FET and MOSFET devices are manufactured in different formats for signal amplification and power control applications. The schematic symbols for the different field effect devices are depicted in Figure 8-2. (MOSFET symbols may have a fourth terminal, indicating a metal mounting tab that is connected to the drain or source, and MOSFETs are also manufactured with dual control gates on the source drain channel.)

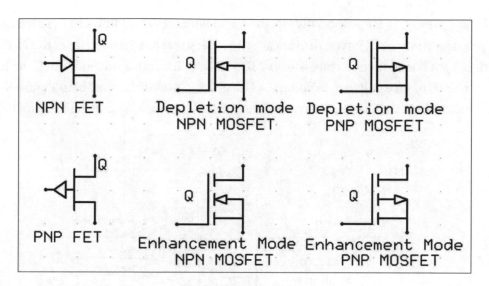

Figure 8-2. *Schematic symbols for field effect devices*

MOSFET devices are manufactured to control the current flow through the transistor's main channel by a depletion or enhancement mode action. Enhancement mode N-channel devices are the most used of the MOSFET family. P-channel enhancement and depletion mode devices are manufactured, but applications for these devices are much less common than those for N-channel enhancement mode transistors.

FETs are voltage-controlled devices with the typical features and parameters depicted in Figure 8-3.

Modern field effect transistors are three or four-terminal devices consisting of a bar of P- or N-type of semiconductor material called a *channel*, through which an electric current can pass from the bar ends known as the *source and drain*. At right angles to the main channel or conducting bar are two or more electrically connected pads of semiconductor material of the opposite polarity to that of the main channel, covered with an insulating layer of metal oxide. Electrical contacts on the two insulating pads are connected to the gate or third terminal of the device that allows impressed voltages to regulate the current flow through the main channel of the transistor.

Figure 8-3 is a composite displaying typical FET and generic MOSFET circuit symbols, structures, and voltage-current characteristics for simple field effect transistors (FET) and metal oxide semiconductor field effect transistors (MOSFET) devices.

The simpler FETs are a normally ON device in which current flows in the absence of an applied gate voltage. (P-type devices are the reverse electrical polarity of the N-type materials with base junction transistors). MOSFET devices are a normally OFF device in the absence of an applied gate voltage. (The generic MOSFET symbol in Figure 8-3 is found in actual circuit diagrams as one of the more descriptive symbols in Figure 8-2.)

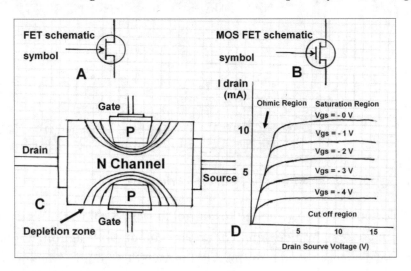

Figure 8-3. *Typical N-channel FET and MOSFET characteristics*

Both FET and MOSFET devices are designed and manufactured as amplifiers or power control elements. Of particular interest is the area labeled the Ohmic Region in the partial reproduction of a set of typical voltage-current curves for these devices. If the drain-source voltage is kept low so that the device does not enter its designed saturation operating range, the size of the current flow through the device is close to being linearly controlled by the voltage between the gate and the source.

Of particular interest is that voltage alone controls the current flow in the channel, the voltage range over which the current flow is regulated, and the input impedance to these devices is measured in the hundreds of MΩ for FET and significantly higher for MOSFET devices.

Reported Static and Electric Field Detectors

Field effect transistors are voltage-controlled devices with input impedances ranging into the hundreds and thousands of MΩ that should function as a non-contact, electric field, voltage sensor. At the FET's high input impedances, virtually no current flows from the static charge being monitored.

Two interesting qualitative electronic electroscope reports are discussed on the Internet. The first presented by W. J. Beaty was written in 1987. It consisted of an FET, LED, and a 9 V battery (see `http://amasci.com/emotor/chargdet.html#16`).

The second is by Dr. J. Ahrens, reported on in 1999 (see `www2.ece.rochester.edu/~jones/demos/index.html`). It was a device using a CMOS 4011 IC to identify the polarity of a charge (see Figure 8-7).

Over the past several decades, there have been a significant number of internet postings on methods for detecting static electrical charges or assembling "electronic electroscopes" with field effect transistors and metal oxide semiconductor field effect transistors (MOSFET). Most of the circuitry described uses an ammeter deflection for visualizing the presence of static electrical charge by monitoring the current flow through the main conducting channel of an FET often assembled into a battery-powered Wheatstone bridge configuration.

Investigators examining the various circuits described for "electronic electroscopes" find two basic types of devices: single and dual detector entities. Single detector devices are simple: a positive or negative charge moves electrons back and forth on the single FET controlling gate on the biased P- or N-channel semiconductor.

The channel current varies when the device's correct polarity voltage is applied to the gate electric field signal collector or antenna. If the circuit for the electroscope has two different polarity FET detectors, then some form of diode-based logic must be incorporated into the circuitry to accommodate the motion of electric charges. When an emanated electric field envelops both the gate antennas as the charge approaches and recedes the detection device, both detectors are activated at different times as the charge moves (see Figure 8-7).

Most electronic electroscopes indicate only qualitative information by illuminating red or green LEDs in accordance with the polarity of the electric field under test. The following technological review and preliminary experimental development work was undertaken to add at least a semi-quantitative ability to the simpler FET-MOSFET qualitative static charge detection schemes.

Wheatstone Bridge Circuits and Positive/Negative Field Detectors

The qualitative use of simple, highly sensitive, static charge detectors or *electronic electroscopes* has been the subject of numerous reports beginning with W. J. Beaty in 1987. It continued with incorporating the FET transistor device into a Wheatstone bridge type of detector in 2005 by A. Yates. Numerous bridge concept variations have been reported since, using both N- and P- channel devices. Figures 8-4 and 8-5 depict generic bridge-type static electric field detectors. The original circuits described with an ammeter have been modified to use a transimpedance amplifier (TIA) op-amp circuit to replace the electro-mechanical gauges.

Figure 8-4 depicts a sensitive circuit that used an MFP 102 FET, a 1 MΩ gate protection resistor, and an alligator clip as the field sensing antenna. The MFP 102, 2N5116 in Figure 8-5, and the 2N3518 in Figure 8-6 are generally available from distributors and mail-order houses, but some are considered obsolete and are not available from manufacturers.

I reproduced and verified the circuits' functioning in Figures 8-4, 8-5, and 8-6.

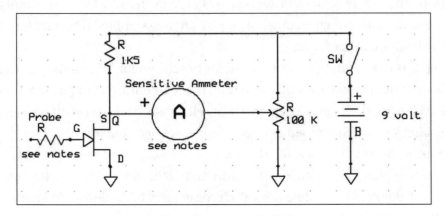

Figure 8-4. *Circuit schematic for N-FET bridge static detectors*

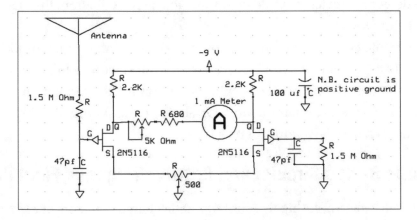

Figure 8-5. *Circuit schematic for P-FET bridge static detectors*

Care must be taken in assembling either of the circuits in Figures 8-4 or 8-5. I used separate +/– 9 V bipolar supplies to power the LF411 op-amp TIA monitoring the bridge currents. Figure 8-5 is a negative ground, and Figure 8-6 is a positive ground circuit.

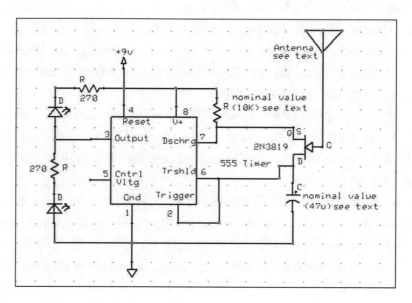

Figure 8-6. *A 555 timer static charge detector*

The circuit depicted in Figure 8-6 uses the 2N3819 as a variable resistor in the timer's RC network. The IC device charges the timing capacitor through the series resistor pair R1 + R2. When the capacitor's charge reaches two-thirds of V_{cc}, the timer cycles and discharges the capacitor through R2. The FET transistor datasheets indicate that the device has a channel resistance of 100 ohms at a gate voltage of –7 V and a resistance of 400 Ω at –1 V. The oscillating frequency of the system can be calculated from the following formulas.

$$t_1 = 0.693 \times (R1 + R2) \times C \text{ and } t_2 = 0.693 \times R2 \times C$$

$$T = t_1 + t_2 = 0.693 \times (R1+R2) \times C$$

$$f = 1/T = 1.44/((R1 + R2) \times C)$$

With the 10 kΩ timing resistor, 47 µf capacitor and the 2N3819 FET with a 100 to 400 Ω resistance variation, the calculated frequency of the astable 555 configured chip at the midpoint of the FET resistance variation is 3.2 Hz.

Human vision is reported to have an average flicker fusion threshold (FFT) at 15 Hz. An FFT of 15Hz suggests that most people see a pair of LED lights switching on and off at a rate faster than 15 Hz as being on continuously.

To quantify the rate at which the 555 timer is oscillating and attempt to correlate the FET resistance to the magnitude of the electric field being sampled by the device gate, the frequency measuring capability of the LabJack U3-HV and the DAQFactory SCADA software can be used. (An Arduino configured with the frequency library used as a frequency meter may also be implemented).

To study the detector responses generated by electrostatic charges reported for the various bridge-type static monitors, a survey was made of the ammeters used in various N and P static detector bridge circuits. Ammeters capable of displaying from 10 μA to 1 mA have been reported.

A transimpedance amplifier (TIA) capable of displaying current flows from $10 \times 10-6$ to $1 \times 10-3$ A in three ranges was chosen to record the various detector responses. The TIA was configured around a LM411 FET input op-amp using 10 kΩ, 100 kΩ, and 1 MΩ feedback resistors to provide 0 to +/- 10 V output, for current input ranges of 1 μA, 500 μA and 1 mA (see Figure 8-8 and Chapter 2). The TIA was used to drive a LabJack U3 HV capable of displaying +/- 10 V for recording on a DAQFactory strip chart recorder display.

Before experimenting with the recording of bridge circuitry output a static charge polarity detection circuit depicted in Figure 8-7 was assembled.

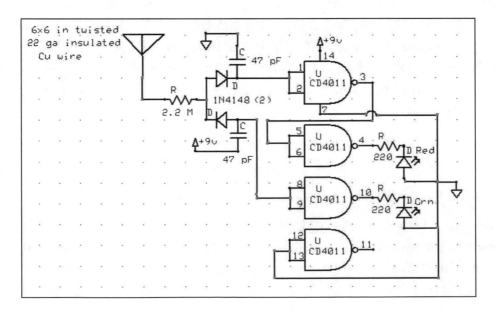

Figure 8-7. *Static charge polarity detection circuitry*

In Figure 8-7, a solid-state polarity detector is depicted based on the original design reported by Dr. J. Ahern as discussed in Prof. Jones web site (www2.ece.rochester.edu/~jones/demos/index.html). A table is available on the web site that explains the illumination of the individual LEDs in accordance with the motion of either positive or negative charges toward or away from the detector antenna (CD4011 $0.81 CDN).

The use of the ammeter readout circuits and handheld static sources such as glass and plastic objects can be quite confusing, with the needle swinging back and forth as the charged object is moved about. A recording system brings a more understandable display of the static phenomenon being demonstrated, measured, or followed. The construction of a small, inexpensive handheld positive and negative electrostatic field detector is described at www.techandgeek.com/electrostatic-polarity-detector/. The device uses a small plastic bottle. A 9 V battery powers an FQP27P06 ($2.02 CDN) and an HPF730 (IFR840 $1.69 CDN) TO-220 case format pair of MOSFET devices to illuminate a colored LED to determine the presence of a positive or negative electrostatic field.

Quantitative Measurement of Accumulated Static Charges

To explore the possibility of developing a method for quantitatively evaluating the magnitude of the static charge accumulated on tubes, small objects, and various materials, as traditionally used in demonstrating static electric phenomenon, a graphical recording system was assembled to record the observed phenomenon.

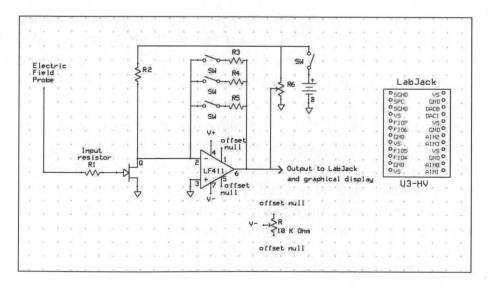

Figure 8-8. *Circuit schematic for N-FET TIA bridge static detectors*

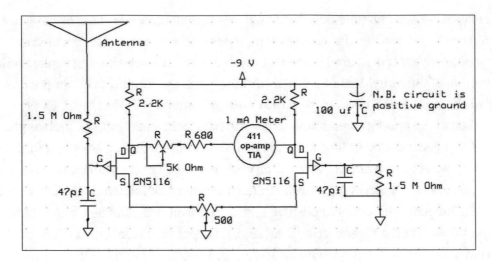

Figure 8-9. *Circuit schematic for P-FET bridge static detectors*

In several of the preceding figures, there are no descriptions of the electric field probe or the antenna because these components are best determined by experimental development. The size of the probe or antenna determines the sensitivity of the system. If the antenna is too large, it picks up the 60 Hz noise from the building wiring, and if too small, the system will not detect the fields of interest. Qualitative, static charge experiments with glass or plastic tubing and the appropriate fur/fabric cloths can test and adjust the size of the antenna for the FET detector in use and the size of the circulating bridge current.

Numerous resistance values in the Figure 8-8 schematic are not specified but determined by the experiment and the choice of FET. Most gate connections in a FET or a MOSFET are static discharge sensitive. Depending on the likelihood of an electrostatic discharge strong enough to destroy the FET sensor, you may choose to add a protective MΩ value series resistance to the input circuit of the gate.

When using either P- or N-FET bridge circuitry, the experimenter must be careful in interpreting the deflection tracings resulting from simple quantitative experiments. Moving static charges created by friction in a glass rod or tube with wool or fur into the detectable range of the probe attached to the device gate generates responses in accordance with the charge and direction of motion as described by Dr. J. Ahern.

Excessive and motion-induced sensitivity in the bridge circuitry led to the experimentation and implementation of the much simpler and robust MOSFET field detector depicted in Figure 8-10.

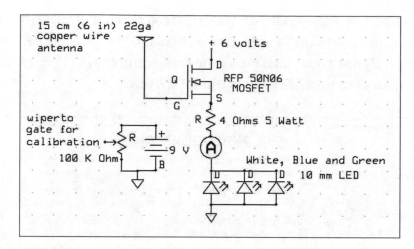

Figure 8-10. *N-channel MOSFET electric field monitor*

I empirically developed the electric field monitor circuit depicted in Figure 8-10 through a trial-and-error methodology. The data in Figure 8-11 was collected after establishing the correlation of the gate/source voltage level with a 9 V battery and a 100 kΩ potentiometer to vary the voltage applied to the gate, then measuring the channel current with an ammeter in series with a 6 V drain-source power supply for individual gate-source voltage levels.

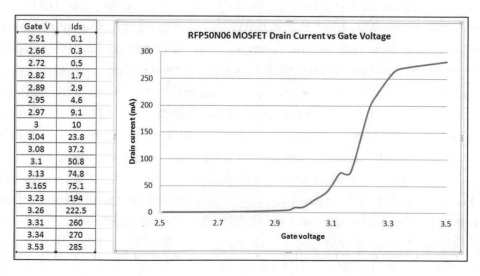

Gate V	Ids
2.51	0.1
2.66	0.3
2.72	0.5
2.82	1.7
2.89	2.9
2.95	4.6
2.97	9.1
3	10
3.04	23.8
3.08	37.2
3.1	50.8
3.13	74.8
3.165	75.1
3.23	194
3.26	222.5
3.31	260
3.34	270
3.53	285

Figure 8-11. *N-channel MOSFET gate vs. drain-source current*

An additional data set was collected with a 2N7000 N-channel MOSFET and a sigmoidal curve as depicted in Figure 8-12 was obtained. In Figures 8-11 and 8-12, the 2N7000 exhibits almost a one-volt difference in controlling 60 mA of current while the RFP50N06 requires less than half a volt to control 250 mA.

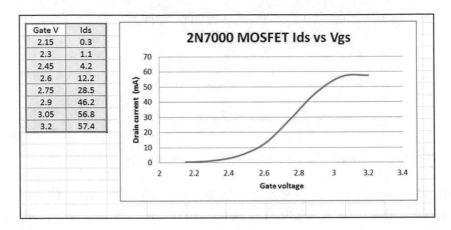

Gate V	Ids
2.15	0.3
2.3	1.1
2.45	4.2
2.6	12.2
2.75	28.5
2.9	46.2
3.05	56.8
3.2	57.4

Figure 8-12. *Gate voltage vs. drain current for 2N7000 (N-channel)*

Figures 8-11 and 8-12 show the calibration of the drain-source current flow with gate voltage establishes a quantitative relationship between the gate voltage and the resulting current passing through the main body of the device under test (DUT). If the gate is connected to an antenna and the FET device current is measured, then a means is available for measuring the electric field in which the antenna is immersed. If the distance between the antenna and the static charge creating the electric field is measured, then the inverse square law can determine the magnitude of the static charge.

Graphical displays of the state of charge on either a glass or a CPVC tube can be recorded by monitoring the voltage drop across the LED current limiting resistors in circuits using the configuration displayed in Figure 8-10. During the initial development of a reproducible positive and negative static charge creation method with nominal ¾ in or 2 cm ID tubing of soda-lime glass and CPVC plastic (chlorinated polyvinyl chloride), a typical static charge decay curve was recorded as depicted in Figure 8-13.

The DAQFactory display in Figure 8-13 was set to record the voltage drop across a 220 Ω resistor used as a current limit for a 5 mm red LED functioning as a visual monitor in an RFP50N06 MOSFET electric field monitoring circuit. The voltage drop across the resistor was monitored with a LabJack U3-HV interface capable of monitoring 0 to 10 V signals. (the DAQFactory channel named staticVoltage was set to record a 0 to 5 V drop across the LED current limiting resistor). A 6 V drain-source supply was used, and the gate was connected to a 3 foot 22 ga. (900 × 0.64 mm) insulated copper wire, folded into a flat parallel array of 6 inches (150 mm). The curve displayed depicts the time-based discharge of the static charge created on the glass tube by rubbing it with a wool cloth. The charged tube was positioned parallel to the antenna. The distance between the antenna and the tube was adjusted to obtain medium brightness on the LED before recording the discharge display.

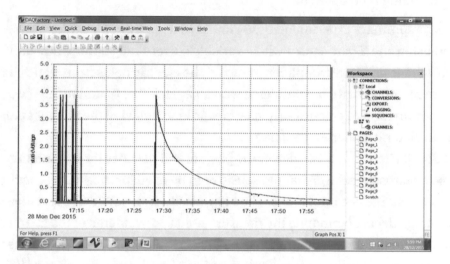

Figure 8-13. *Decay of static charge on a glass tube*

Development experiments were confined initially to the glass tube and the N-type MOSFET, as the sensitivity of the N semiconductor-based monitor or the intensity of the charge accumulated on the soda-lime glass was far more intense than that displayed by the P-type monitor and the CPVC plastic tubing.

A distance-measuring capability was added to the simple qualitative LED brightness assembly to begin the process of developing a quantitative measurement system.

During the initial experimentation with the glass tube and the qualitative visual brightness LED display, I found that if the glass tube was not rubbed evenly, localized surface charges resulted from the abrasion. Holding the tube in one hand and rubbing it on a wool sweater charged only the contacted area of the tube. If the charged tube was rotated about its longitudinal axis in the proximity of the antenna, the LED brightness was maximized when the charged surface was physically facing the antenna.

Measures should be instituted to bolster reproducibility and minimize the effects of surface charge localization.

- The outer surfaces of the antenna and tubular charge carriers must be parallel to one another, with the charged area of the carrier facing the antenna.

- The tube should be mounted on a fixed distance peg as soon as charging is completed.

During preliminary experimentation, I found that each circuit could be assembled and tested using a FET gate sensor with a variable current range, transimpedance current to voltage converter amplifier, to record the electric fields from static charges. Traces were recorded as a 0 to 10 V signal with a LabJack U3 HV and the DAQFactory software combination to create a strip chart recorder displaying the voltages created by the induced electric field from the charge.

Virtually all circuits published over the past several decades for assembling "electronic electroscopes" were far too sensitive to be used for measuring friction induced static charge accumulations. The high sensitivity resulted in capacitive and other coupling effects dominating the measurements. Movements of the charged bodies to and away from the sense antennas caused full scale and spurious deflections that were both non-reproducible and difficult to assign. (See the circuit in Figure 8-7 and interpretation of the diode illumination on the Electrostatic Demonstrations website).

After a good deal of experimentation, I was finally able to partially control and account for the FET gate's extreme sensitivity to accumulated static charge, charge motion, and antenna parameters by using simpler circuitry based on the configuration depicted in Figure 8-10.

Experiment
FET and MOSFET Static Electric Field Sensors

In theory, any wiring connected to the gate of a FET with a few volts induced in it by the presence of an electric field should create measurable variations in the current flowing through the channel. The current-voltage curves in Figure 8-3 are typically provided by manufacturers for designers to use for applications in which the FET and MOSFET devices are used as current controls.

The small section of the curves called the *ohmic region* is a useful area in which to operate a device for the voltage applied to the gate. It is quantified by measuring the current flowing through the device's channel.

The range of gate voltage over which a predictable channel current results is narrow. To use the linear or Ohmic region of an N- or P-channel FET or MOSFET device, you must control the distance variable. Controlling the distance variable is greatly aided by a recording of the circuit output to visually indicate when the field source is too close or too far from the detector to impress an "on scale" or usable signal on the detector's gate.

MOSFET Calibration

I chose MOSFETS because of their robustness, abundant availability as power control devices, low cost, high current carrying ability (60 A), and simplicity of calibration for use as a static field detector. Figures 8-14 and 8-15 show the circuit configurations to calibrate the current flow in the main channel of the individual device with the voltage impressed upon the gate lead.

Numerical data must be collected for incremental gate voltage values and graphed against the channel current as depicted in Figures 8-16 and 8-17. A numerical relationship is then computed from a straight-line approximation of the data to compute a reasonable value for the gate or antenna voltage from the measured channel current.

Although Figure 8-14 depicts only the circuitry to calibrate the N-type MOSFET, Figure 8-15 contains the circuitry to convert from the calibration to the measurement configurations. The measurement circuits replace the potentiometer, voltmeter, and ammeters in the calibration configuration with the gate connected antenna. The normally open (NO) push-button switch grounds the "floating" gate after each measurement operation, as the gate has virtually no means of dissipating any accumulated charge that may build up in the device during measurements.

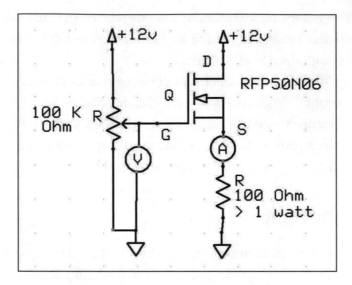

Figure 8-14. *Circuit for N-channel MOSFET calibration*

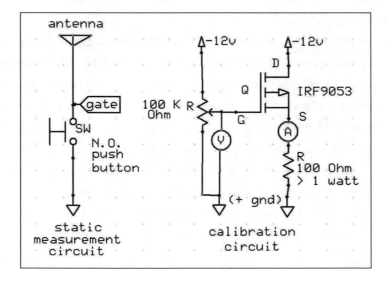

Figure 8-15. *Circuit for P-channel MOSFET calibration*

Having calibrated the MOSFETs and converted the calibration circuits to the much simpler measurement configurations, the DAQFactory graphical display can be configured by connecting the LabJack U3–HV device to measure the voltage drop across the 100 Ω load resistor. (Recall that the LabJack is a laboratory interface for measuring primarily voltage-based signals.)

Equations 1 and 2 were generated by the statistical packages in the Excel spreadsheet program to plot the data. Recalling that the N-channel measures positive gate voltage electric fields because the current flow through the channel is regulated by the value of the positive voltage impressed upon the gate, all the numerical data collected for the voltage-current correlation are positive numerical values. When the data is collected for the P-channel device, the current in the channel is regulated by the negative electric voltage impressed upon the gate. For the statistical data processing algorithms, the sign of the numbers is equivalent for positive and negative numbers since the sign represents a physical, not a mathematical difference.

The positive gate voltage N-mode device has the gate voltage, the x value, in terms of the source drain current relationship, the y value, as follows.

$$Y = 8.6212x - 20.174 \text{ --- } (1) \; R^2 = 0.9965$$

The negative gate voltage P-mode device has the gate voltage source drain current relationship of

$$Y = 7.6448x - 22.389 \text{ --- } (2) \; R^2 = 0.9871$$

As seen in the circuit diagrams in Figures 8-14 and 8-15, when the circuits are re-wired for electric field measurement, the impressed electric field on the antenna determines the current flow through the 100 Ω load resistor. The current through the load resistor creates a voltage drop of $100 \times I_{ds}$ in accordance with Ohm's law, but I_{ds} is related to the gate voltage by equations 1 and 2.

From the observed value of the voltage drop across the load resistor (V_{lr}), the N MOSFET positive gate voltage (V_g) is given by the following formula.

$$V_g = ((V_{lr} * 10) - 20.174)/8.6212 \text{ --- } (3)$$

A similar formula for the P MOSFET generates the negative gate voltage.

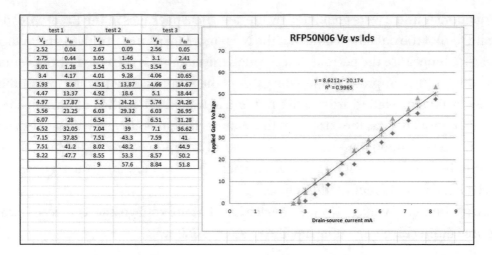

test 1		test 2		test 3	
V_g	i_{ds}	V_g	i_{ds}	V_g	i_{ds}
2.52	0.04	2.67	0.09	2.56	0.05
2.75	0.44	3.05	1.46	3.1	2.41
3.01	1.28	3.54	5.13	3.54	6
3.4	4.17	4.01	9.28	4.06	10.65
3.93	8.6	4.51	13.87	4.66	14.67
4.47	13.37	4.92	18.6	5.1	18.44
4.97	17.87	5.5	24.21	5.74	24.26
5.56	23.25	6.03	29.32	6.03	26.95
6.07	28	6.54	34	6.51	31.28
6.52	32.05	7.04	39	7.1	36.62
7.15	37.85	7.51	43.3	7.59	41
7.51	41.2	8.02	48.2	8	44.9
8.22	47.7	8.55	53.3	8.57	50.2
		9	57.6	8.84	51.8

Figure 8-16. *Gate voltage vs. source-drain current for RFP50N06 MOSFET*

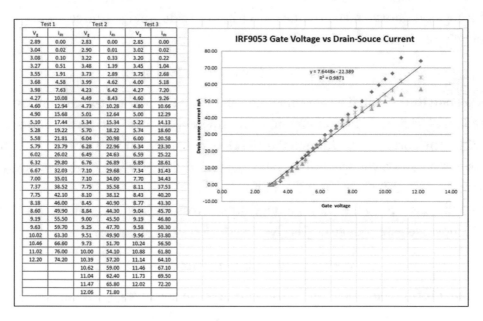

Test 1		Test 2		Test 3	
V_g	i_{ds}	V_g	i_{ds}	V_g	i_{ds}
2.89	0.00	2.83	0.00	2.85	0.00
3.04	0.02	2.90	0.01	3.02	0.02
3.08	0.10	3.22	0.33	3.20	0.22
3.27	0.51	3.48	1.39	3.45	1.04
3.55	1.91	3.73	2.89	3.75	2.68
3.68	4.58	3.99	4.62	4.00	5.18
3.98	7.63	4.23	6.42	4.27	7.20
4.27	10.08	4.49	8.43	4.60	9.26
4.60	12.94	4.73	10.28	4.80	10.66
4.90	15.68	5.01	12.64	5.00	12.29
5.10	17.44	5.34	15.34	5.22	14.13
5.28	19.22	5.70	18.22	5.74	18.60
5.58	21.81	6.04	20.98	6.00	20.58
5.79	23.79	6.28	22.96	6.34	23.30
6.02	26.02	6.49	24.63	6.59	25.22
6.32	29.80	6.76	26.89	6.89	28.61
6.67	32.03	7.10	29.68	7.34	31.43
7.00	35.01	7.10	34.00	7.70	34.43
7.37	38.52	7.75	35.58	8.11	37.53
7.75	42.10	8.10	38.12	8.43	40.20
8.18	46.00	8.45	40.90	8.77	43.30
8.60	49.90	8.84	44.30	9.04	45.70
9.19	55.50	9.00	45.50	9.19	46.80
9.63	59.70	9.25	47.70	9.58	50.30
10.02	63.30	9.51	49.90	9.96	53.80
10.46	66.60	9.73	51.70	10.24	56.50
11.02	76.00	10.00	54.10	10.88	61.80
12.20	74.20	10.39	57.20	11.14	64.10
		10.62	59.00	11.46	67.10
		11.04	62.40	11.73	69.50
		11.47	65.80	12.02	72.20
		12.06	71.80		

Figure 8-17. *Gate voltage vs. drain-source current for IRF9053 P-channel MOSFET*

The data table to the left of the curve is a composite made up of three repetitions of gate voltage variation experiments. Within experimental error, the curves are reproducible.

Both high-power MOSFET devices used to develop the measurement technique are large TO-220 packages with massive semiconductor dies capable of working with large currents. The devices are designed to be used with robust turn on signals such as those generated with microprocessor-controlled pulse width modulation techniques. The manufacturer's datasheets indicate that the gates can withstand up to 20 V of signal strength and typically require at least 2 to 4 V to turn on. The data in Figures 8-16 and 8-17 indicate a 2.52 and –2.89 V signal is required to initiate any channel current at a drain-source voltage of a nominal 12 V.

The detector circuits can be built on a prototyping board or on a screw terminal strip as depicted in Figure 8-18 for use in a portable device using battery power and a small laptop for a graphical display.

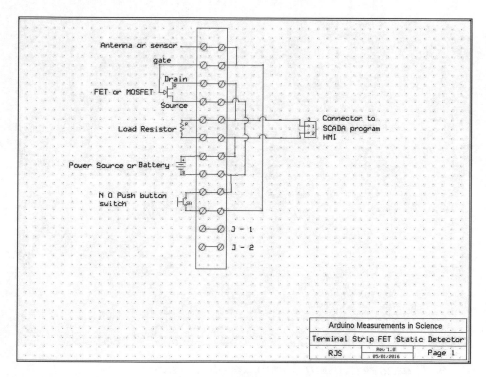

Figure 8-18. *A static detector for positive electric fields mounted on a terminal strip*

The circuits in Figures 8-14 and 8-15 are compact, neat and the screw terminals provide a positive contact for all the connections. A negative charge detector was assembled using the same mechanical construct but followed the circuitry in Figure 8-15.

To generate reproducible static electric fields with simple equipment is a difficult task. Examination of a current triboelectric series published by Alpha Labs indicates that polyurethane foam sustains a positive charge when rubbed with an animal fur–based material such as wool. Teflon and chlorinated polyvinyl chloride (CPVC) sustain a negative charge (see www.alphalabinc.com/triboelectric-series/). One of the best materials for manipulating a positive electrostatic field is polyurethane foam insulation.

A convenient positive charging surface can be created by spreading a thin layer of an adhesive or insulating urethane foam over a suitable wooden surface. Urethane adhesives and insulating foams suitable for positive static charge generation are based on toluene di-isocyanate formulations, and for safety, label instructions must be followed. Figures 8-19 and 8-20 show a collection of classical static electricity demonstration equipment built with readily available materials and common workshop tools.

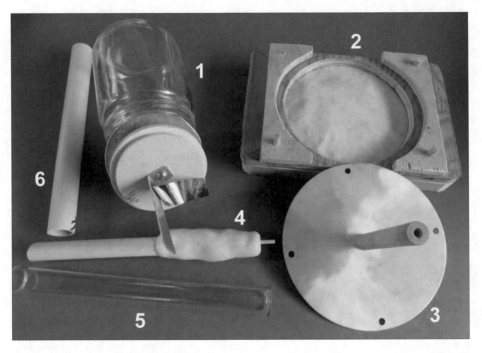

Figure 8-19. *Classic electrostatic demonstration equipment*

Item 1 in Figure 8-19 is the assembled metal foil electroscope that consists of a ½ in × 3 in (12 × 75 mm) strip of aluminized mylar foil (survival blanket) bolted to a bent aluminum strip of ⅝ in × 3½ in (15 × 80 mm) metal with the metalized side of the mylar facing the aluminum bracket. The electroscope has a 3 in (75 mm) aluminum disc on top. It is held in place by a ⅛ in (3 mm) diameter threaded brass rod that passes through two plywood discs, as seen in Figure 8-20. The upper disc is cut slightly larger than the inner diameter of the glass jar used to house the hanging foil. The lower disc is cut to fit inside the diameter of the glass container.

Items 5 and 6 are ¾ in (18 mm) soda-lime glass and CPVC tubes for positive and negative charge creation, while 4 is a ⅝ in (15 mm) wooden dowel coated with a layer of polyurethane foam for positive charge creation. In Figure 8-20, the dowel is drilled to receive an ⅛ in (3 mm) pin shown installed in Figure 8-19. The pin allows the foam holder to be fitted into the drilled holes on a distance positioning board.

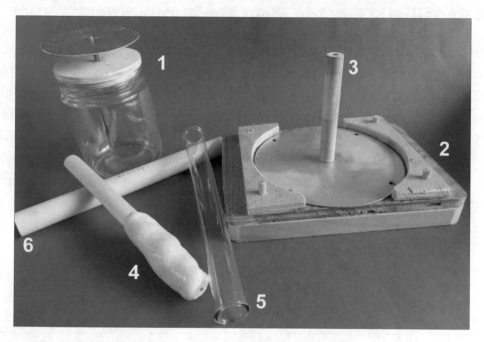

Figure 8-20. *Classic electrostatic demonstration equipment*

The shop-built apparatus in Figures 8-19 and 8-20 validates the operation of the solid-state electric field detectors. In Figure 8-20, the electroscope's top assembly is turned inside out to illustrate its configuration.

Items 2 and 3 make up an *electrophorus*, demonstrating the phenomenon of induction and produces electrostatic charges of defined polarity. In Figure 8-19, the interior of the base for the device consists of a tan-colored, smooth, thin layer of cured polyurethane foam. The foam layer is spread on the wood base plate, seen as the bottom layer in Figure 8-20. The center portion of the foam layer is encircled with the edge of ¼ in (6 mm) plywood to support the aluminum disc at a small but fixed distance above the foam.

When in place, as seen in Figure 8-20, the positive charge on the foam induces a polarization in the metal disc that, when grounded, creates the negative charge on the aluminum disc. Wood is used in the device construction as an insulator; the entire assembly is held together with four ¼ in (6 mm) diameter wooden pegs.

The plywood disc alignment and positioning guides are temporarily removed to charge the electrophorus. The foam can be rubbed with wool or another animal fur to create a positive charge on the urethane foam. On reassembly of the alignment guides, the aluminum disc can be repeatedly charged negatively by induction.

High Sensitivity Electric Field Measurements

The circuits in Figures 8-4, 8-5, and 8-6 were all built, tested, and modified with op-amp transimpedance or feedback ammeters to evaluate their applicability for making quantitative measurements of electric fields. The noise, unpredictable responses, and unwieldy sensitivities prompted using a much simpler circuitry, augmented with an analog/digital signal recording capability to try and elucidate the confusing, transitory meter-based response observed with the bridge amplifier and frequency change circuits.

An Arduino microcontroller monitored the output from a simple circuit, as depicted in Figure 8-21.

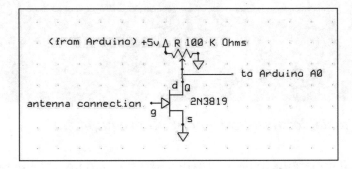

Figure 8-21. *Circuit for high-sensitivity electric field testing*

The circuit in Figure 8-21 was also used with a P-channel FET 2N5460 to test the suitability of the detector for examining negative electric charges and their associated electric fields. (For the P-type FET, the current flow is reversed).

The Arduino test circuitry produced a serial port data output of ADC values between 0 and 1023 that were streamed out from the microcontroller to the host Windows computer. The streamed serial port data were received by the comm 4 port of a DAQFactory plotting program for a graphical display of the positive and negative static detector responses on a 0 to 1025 full-screen deflection (FSD) display.

Observations

A normally open (NO) push-button grounding switch is suggested for positive and negative charge FET/MOSFET detection circuits since an accumulating or accidentally induced charge on the "floating" gate system must be neutralized before making any measurements. The insulated metal oxide gate and its electrical contact form a capacitor that should have a path to ground to return the device's input to neutrality before each electric field measurement is made.

Unlike the simple MOSFET devices used in the previous experimentation with their robust, large massive dies, the smaller and more sensitive FET devices can be used with the Arduino for measurement experimentation. The smaller FET devices' high gate sensitivity does not seem to be affected by their lower input impedances that are relatively high but not as large as the bigger MOSFET devices.

During the initial development of a reproducible positive and negative static charge creation method with nominal ¾ in or 2 cm ID tubing of soda-lime glass and chlorinated polyvinyl chloride plastic (CPVC), typical static charge decay curves were recorded as depicted in Figures 8-22 and 8-23. (Figure 8-22 is reproduction in Figure 8-13 for visual comparison.)

The curve displayed depicts the time-based discharge of the static charge created on the glass tube by rubbing it with a wool cloth. The charged tube was positioned parallel to the antenna. The distance between the antenna and the tube was adjusted to get nearly full-scale deflection of the recording trace.

During the experiment, if the glass tube was not rubbed evenly, localized surface charges resulted from contact. Holding the tube in one hand and rubbing it on a wool sweater charged only the contacted area of the tube. If the charged tube was rotated about its longitudinal axis in the proximity of the antenna, the recorder trace rose and fell according to the position of the charged face of the tube with respect to the antenna.

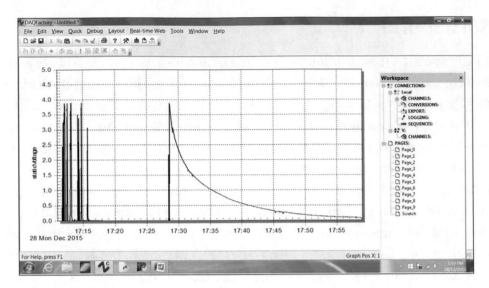

Figure 8-22. *(13) Decay of static charge on a glass tube*

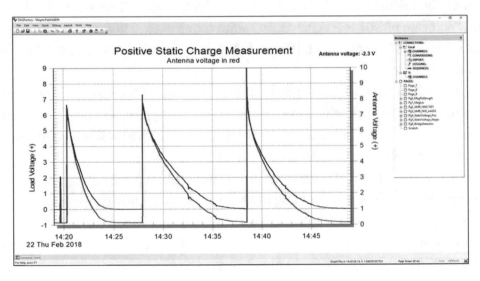

Figure 8-23. *Decay of static charge on a polyurethane foam deposit*

Using distance control to regulate the static electric field voltage sensed by the MOSFET device and measuring the current flow through the main channel at a fixed drain-source voltage difference, an observed current flow can be correlated to a given gate voltage exposure. With an electric field value measured at known distances from the static charge, the static charge value can be calculated by applying the inverse square law.

To increase the sensitivity of the electric field detection methodology, a simple circuit based on an Arduino microcontroller was assembled (see Figure 8-21) with an initial 18 in (456 mm) antenna of insulated 22 ga. (0.64 mm) copper wire with a half-inch (12 mm) bare antenna exposed at the end to facilitate finger-touch grounding. Recall that a MOSFET/FET gate is a capacitor.

After assembling the circuit on a prototyping board, the Arduino program electrometer was loaded and launched (see Listing 8-1). Figure 8-21 shows the data generated by the analog to digital converter (ADC) on the serial port was the voltage drop across the FET that acts as a voltage-controlled resistor. It was found that fluctuating ADC values near zero could be cleared with a finger touch to the antenna. The Arduino serial plotter displayed the trace provided by the ADC output. Potentiometer adjustment established a full-scale deflection (FSD) of approximately 1000 ADC counts. By reducing the antenna to 4½ inches (112 mm), the recorder tracing was brought to a state that the serial port data quickly varied between the baseline and values at FSD or lower. With additional experimentation, it was found that a noisy but relatively stable baseline could be recorded if statically charged entities were kept several feet away (0.5 m) from the antenna.

To display the charge state as a function of time, the digitized Arduino ADC output was collected by the serial port of DAQFactory for display, as depicted in Figure 8-24.

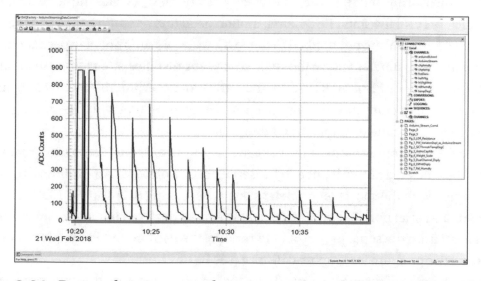

Figure 8-24. *Decay of static source charge on a polyurethane foam deposit with high sensitivity 2N3819 FET detector*

As indicated in the recorded display in Figure 8-24, the gradually decreasing ADC peak heights appear to be an exponential charge decay, as seen in Figures 8-22 and 8-23.

Each of the peaks recorded in the apparent charge decay was created by moving the dowel mounted polyurethane foam deposit seen as item 4 in Figures 8-19 and 8-20. The foam deposit had been charged with a wool cloth approximately 5 minutes before the FSD peaks at 10:20 were recorded. The peaks from 10:21 onward were created by quickly moving the horizontally oriented foam deposit vertically, five times at 12 inches (approx. 0.3 m) from the vertically oriented 4½ in (110 mm) antenna.

In addition to electronic noise, spurious signal interference from materials moving with my arm, varying distance moved, and varying speed at which the hand-powered charge motion was conducted, the voltage induced on the detector gate due to a remote charge motion is remarkably reproducible.

Recording Electrostatic Effects with Arduino and Raspberry Pi

Many electrostatic charge and electromagnetic wave detectors can be used with the Arduino and the RPi to produce recordings of the detector responses.

When measuring and recording the effects of static charges with the large MOSFET field indicators and the small FET charge motion detectors operating at 12 or 9 V, ensure that voltages over 5 V are not applied to the ADC. A certain amount of experimental development is required to place the static charge at a distance sufficient to maintain an FSD for the 10- or 12-bit ADC used at the start of an experiment. Antenna lengths coupled to the detector gates may also need adjusting to get reproducible starting conditions for static measurement recordings.

Once the positioning of the static voltage charge and antenna size is configured, data can be collected and streamed to the serial port for plotting. An Arduino can be programmed with the short electrometer sketch (see Listing 8-1) and the ADC values printed to the serial port. Recording the data streamed out from the microcontroller can be collected from the serial port by an RPi running the Python-coded Matplotlib strip chart recorder program for graphical display (see Listing 8-2).

As an example of recording capabilities, the circuit to generate the data recorded in Figure 8-25 was the TIA modified version of that depicted in Figure 8-4 (Yates 2005) with a 2N3819 FET as the detector. I produced the detector response by quickly moving a glass tube, held in the horizontal position, up and down, a vertical distance approximately equal to the length of the short wire antenna with an alligator clip on the end (4 in or 100 mm). The glass tube was 3 in (80 mm) from the antenna and had been initially charged with a wool cloth several hours before.

Figure 8-25 records the console output diagnostic data used to adjust the plotter code parameters to accept the varying data widths of the streamed data. For actual experiment data archiving the ADC counts and the corresponding output timestamp could be saved.

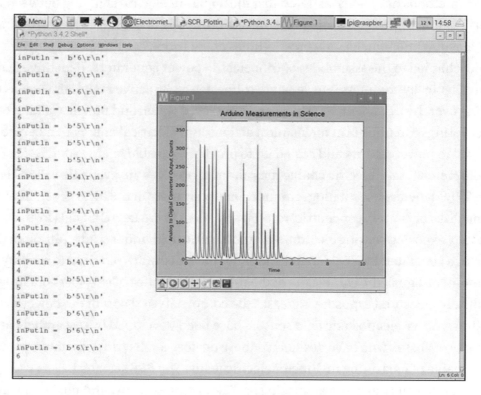

Figure 8-25. *RPi graphical recording of charged glass tube movements*

Discussion

Static electrical phenomena created by the physical contact of different materials have been studied since the times of Thales of Miletus (c. 624–546 BC) in ancient Greece. The first listing of common materials that could reproducibly create electric potential static phenomena was published in 1757 by J. C. Wilcke. Static electric phenomena created by contact with materials is known as *triboelectricity.* The listing of common materials employed to generate static electric charges is called the *triboelectric series.*

There are numerous triboelectric series listings. AlphaLab Inc., a supplier of commercial static charge measuring equipment, published a modern, tested listing (`www.alphalabinc.com/triboelectric-series/`). It is a semi-quantitative numerical data compilation of a charge affinity nC/J (nano coulombs of transferred charge/joule) that can be interpreted as a measure of the relative strength of the triboelectric effect for a material entry.

A theoretical basis for the triboelectric series has not been developed. Modern research methods have demonstrated that the apparent electric charging between the various conducting and insulating materials in the listing depends on several atomic and molecular phenomena. Advanced studies of the triboelectric effect in polymer materials has led to the assemblies of triboelectric power generators. Repetitive actions that mechanically compress and separate triboelectrically active materials such as cars traveling over the pavement, wave actions in bodies of water, and people walking over floor coverings can transform mechanical actions into electrical energy that can be harvested to power sensors and scaled up to provide a useable energy source.

Commercial static electric charge measurement devices are available called "Field Meters". Field meters use rotating, grounded metal shutters in the form of segmented rotating disks or slotted, concentric, rotating cylinders to create AC signals from alternately exposing sensing electrodes to the electric field under study. Although the AC voltage generated by a field meter simplifies the electronics required to amplify the measurement signal, the complexity of the rotating electrode or "chopper" creating the periodically measured exposure increases the complexity and cost of the devices.

Ultrasensitive electrostatic field sensors have been developed by researchers at the University of Sussex who have designated these devices as electric potential sensors (EPS) capable of measuring mV/meter electric fields. The EPS sensors have a wide range of applicability in medical imaging or diagnostics, security, and nuclear magnetic resonance spectroscopy (NMR spectroscopy).

Recent works by researchers from NASA have developed a method for using static electric fields and an electric field generator as an imaging system. A series of patent applications and conference presentations describe the system.[2]

---

[2]"Electric potential and electric field imaging" by E. R. Generazio. American Institute of Physics Conference Proceedings 1806, (2017).

Researchers have recently reported applying a FET as a cellular voltage sensor in which the regulated drain-source current measures the voltage generated by neurotransmitter molecules fixed to the gate.[3]

The static discharge is familiar to most residents of northern climates as a predominantly wintertime effect. In hot summer conditions, high humidity tends to nullify static discharge hazards before they form. In the winter, when the air is cold and moisture content is low, static electric activity is noticeable (see `www2.ece.rochester.edu/~jones/demos/`).

Rubber-soled shoes rubbing against nylon carpet is an example of two insulators exchanging charge. Electrons are transferred to the rubber soles from the carpet as the individual walks across the floor covering. An accumulating negative charge on the insulator soles induces a positive charge into the body of the individual wearing the shoes to produce an electrical discharge if the individual gets close to an earth ground.

Static accumulations from common actions at different humidity levels are listed in Table 8-1.

Table 8-1. *Common Static Accumulations at Various RH Values*

Human Motion or Actions	Relative Humidity Levels		
	10%	40%	55%
Crossing a carpet	35,000	15,000	7,500
Crossing a vinyl floor	12,000	5,000	3,000
Motions of individuals not grounded	6,000	800	400
Removing bubble packaging	26,000	20,000	7,000

At a measured relative humidity level of 74% on a day in late spring, I could not generate or measure any electrostatic activity. I had to postpone experimentation until dryer weather conditions of 65% RH arrived.

Electrostatic damage to integrated circuitry is classified into three categories: catastrophic, parametric, and latent. Catastrophic failures destroy a circuit immediately upon electrostatic discharge. Parametric damage occurs when a circuit still operates after a discharge but not up to its original design specifications, and latent failures occur after a circuit has gone into active service.

---

[3]"Learning the brain's chemical language." *Neuroscience*. Sept. 10, 2018,

Integrated circuitry can be damaged by electrostatic discharges (ESD) at the levels listed in Table 8-2.

Table 8-2. *ESD for IC Damage*

Circuit or Device Type	Electrostatic Discharge Voltage Level
MOSFET	10 – 100
EPROM	+ 100
CMOS	200 – 3000
JFET	400 – 7000
OP-Amps	190 – 2000

Human-awareness levels of static electric discharges are tabulated in Table 8-3.

Table 8-3. *ESD and Human Senses*

Feel static discharge if	> 3500 volts
Hear static discharge if	> 5000 volts
See static discharge if	> 8000 volts

Static accumulations can be prevented by grounding conductors, raising the humidity to dissipate the charge in insulators, and using air ionizers. Grounded metallic shielding can protect static sensitive equipment, areas, and sensors.

Detecting and Measuring Static Electric Accumulations

When experimenting with FET and MOSFET devices as static electric charge detectors, the researcher must be aware of the environment in which the investigations are carried out. Areas of North America around the oceans and great lakes that experience high relative humidity can make electrostatic demonstrations virtually impossible to conduct. High relative humidity causes frictionally generated test charges to be weakened and decay in minutes. In drier inland portions of the continent, static charges can inadvertently accumulate to destructive levels for electronic devices and integrated circuits on creation.

The significant difference in sensitivity seen between the tiny plastic case TO-92 FET transistors (typical weight 2N3819 – 0.198 g) and the relatively massive TO-220 MOSFET devices (typical weight RFP05N06 –2.00 g) led to the adoption of the power MOSFETs as more robust static charge detectors. In addition to significantly more controllable sensitivity, the power control devices can manage currents of 10 A or more over a gate input voltage range of 20 V. The FET is typically limited to fractions of an ampere over the same gate voltage limitation.

An additional feature in high-power MOSFET devices that may be an advantage in some high field detection applications is the "turn on voltage" of 2 V to 3 V that probably reduces sensitivity to electric fields and noise-induced electromagnetic interference.

The N- and P-channel devices that I chose for static electric field measurement were taken from my supply of power-control devices. Some smaller FET devices were difficult to work with and did not show linear gate voltage to source drain current relationships in the configurations used to collect the data in Figures 8-16 and 8-17.

There are several manufacturers of power MOSFET devices. The units from different manufacturers can be tested for suitability in this application. Other investigators have used FQP27P06 and HPF730 (or IRF840) as suitable detectors. A dual MOSFET array (the FDS8958 in a surface mount technology package) has also been reported as being suitable for detecting both positive and negative electric fields.

There are a large number of published schematics for electronic electroscopes that vary from the simple circuits as seen in Figures 8-4, 8-5, 8-6, and 8-10 to the complex logic gate adaptations in Figure 8-7. The inclusion of the logic gates and diodes in many electroscope circuits appear to be directed at eliminating much of the confusion caused by the detector responding to the approaching and receding motions of statically charged objects.

Code Listings

Listing 8-1. Arduino Electrometer Code

```
// Arduino Electrometer code.
// Program monitors the voltage on an FET configured as a
// variable resistor with an antenna controlling the gate voltage
// The FET source drain current is the current through the
// variable resistor monitored by the ADC
//
void setup() {
  // open serial port
  Serial.begin(9600);
```

```
  //
}
void loop() {
  // stream out the FET data
  Serial.println(analogRead(A0));
  delay(200); // adjust value for plotting code in use
  //
}
```

Listing 8-2. RPi Strip Chart Recorder Display

```python
# RPi Python Strip Chart Recorder of Arduino Output
# SCR Plotting of serial data from Arduino output over serial port
# Arduino serial output must be numerical values only.
#
import matplotlib
import numpy as np
from matplotlib.lines import Line2D
import matplotlib.pyplot as plt
import matplotlib.animation as animation
import time
import serial
#
#
#
class Scope:
    def __init__(self, ax, maxt=40, dt=0.02):
        """"maxt time width of display"""
        self.ax = ax
        self.dt = dt
        self.maxt = maxt
        self.tdata = [0]
        self.ydata = [0]
        self.line = Line2D(self.tdata, self.ydata)
        self.ax.add_line(self.line)
        self.ax.set_ylim(0, 1023)  # y axis scale
        self.ax.set_xlim(0, self.maxt)
```

```python
    def update(self, y):
        lastt = self.tdata[-1]
        if lastt > self.tdata[0] + self.maxt: # reset the arrays
            self.tdata = [self.tdata[-1]]
            self.ydata = [self.ydata[-1]]
            self.ax.set_xlim(self.tdata[0], self.tdata[0] + self.maxt)
            self.ax.figure.canvas.draw()
        t = self.tdata[-1] + self.dt
        self.tdata.append(t)
        self.ydata.append(y)
        self.line.set_data(self.tdata, self.ydata)
        return self.line,
#
ser = serial.Serial("/dev/ttyACM0", 9600)
#
def rd_data():
    while True:
        inPutln = ser.readline()
        print("inPutln = ", inPutln)
        nbr_dgts = len(inPutln)
        if (nbr_dgts > 6 or nbr_dgts < 3): # skip noise or corrupted data
            continue
        if (nbr_dgts == 3):      # there is only 1 digit
            line = int(str(inPutln)[slice(2,3)])
        if (nbr_dgts == 4):      # there are 2 digits
            line = int(str(inPutln)[slice(2,4)])
        if (nbr_dgts == 5):      # there are 3 digits
            line = int(str(inPutln)[slice(2,5)])
        if (nbr_dgts == 6):      # there are 4 digits
            line = int(str(inPutln)[slice(2,6)]) # convert arduino serial
                                                  output stream
        # to a Python string, parse out the numerical symbols and convert
          to a value
        print(line)
        yield (line)
```

```
fig = plt.figure()
fig.suptitle("The Scientyst's Ayde", fontsize = 12)
ax = fig.add_subplot(111)
ax.set_xlabel("Time")
ax.set_ylabel("Analog to Digital Converter Output Counts")
scope = Scope(ax)
# uses rd_data() as a generator to produce data for the update func, the
# Arduino ADC value is read by the plotting code in 20 or so minute windows
# for the animated screen display. Software overhead limits response speed
# of display.
ani = animation.FuncAnimation(fig, scope.update, rd_data, interval=50,
blit=False)
plt.show()
```

Summary

Voltage is a form of potential energy created by the separation of electric charge.

Numerous actions can create voltage differences, including chemical processes in the construction of batteries, moving magnets, contact with materials in the triboelectric series, sunlight impinging on PN junctions, and biological systems.

Static electric voltages are examined because of their high voltage nature that can destroy ICs, ignite fires, and the special non-contact techniques required to estimate their stored potential energy.

In Chapter 9, a novel technique is developed to measure weight and force.

CHAPTER 9

Weight, Mass, and Force

Experimental sciences frequently require the measurement of the amount of the materials being tested, analyzed, or aliquoted. Mass can be measured in a gravity field by determining the balancing point of leveled levers from which are suspended the item under test and a known standard mass. Only in a gravitational field, when a force is exerted on the mass in an object, can the experimenter determine its weight. The purpose of this multi-sectioned chapter is to measure mass in terms of weight with a simple electrical transducer.

Modern laboratory balances able to weigh in grams, milligrams, or micrograms use a combination of electrical and mechanical leverage for balancing reference weights against the load. Usually, optical-electromagnetic servo type mechanisms digitize and display the system point of balance. For some experimental work, these fragile, expensive, but very sensitive systems must be used with appropriate calibration.

Purely electronic methods can measure forces and masses by determining the resistance change that occurs when a mechanical strain is applied to a resistor. Resistance based "load cells" use Wheatstone bridge-instrumentation amplifier pairings to follow resistance changes in one or more bridge elements fixed to a deformable, mechanical component under stress. "Peel and stick" resistive load cell foils are commercially available that can be applied to mechanical systems under load to measure any deformation or movement. Strain gauges are typically long, thin, film, parallel, or spiral deposits of Constantan (45% Cu – 55% Ni as used in J-type thermocouples) that have a large resistance change when placed under a mechanical load. Resistance load cells usually measure kilograms of weight or newtons or more of force with instrumentation amplifiers reading the resistance bridge imbalance. Resistance bridges are often configured with multiple active sensor arms to augment the system imbalance signal as the substrate deforms under load.

© Richard J. Smythe 2022
R. J. Smythe, *Arduino Measurements in Science*, https://doi.org/10.1007/978-1-4842-6781-3_9

Determination of Weight and Mass

For many years, the physics of magnetic fields has been taught with devices known as *current balances*. There are several commercially available educational units and a significant number of Internet postings describing student lab demonstration equipment of varying degrees of sophistication that can be assembled by individuals or educators. In both the commercially available and experimenter assembled apparatus, the relationships between magnetic fields, created by measured currents flowing through wires and gravitational weight forces, can be explored. Current balances are usually delicate, limited weight range, sensitive devices that are not easily adapted to measuring unknown weights or masses.

Resistive load cells and current balances either lack sensitivity or are too delicate and complex to be easily adapted to the discrete or continuous measurement of weight, force, or masses in experimental setups. A simple, robust methodology is outlined in the following exercise. A capacitor, assembled from multiple flat plates of conductors and dielectrics, changes capacitance in response to being compressed by weight loads on the multilayer device. (The advantages and limitations of capacitor-based load cells are discussed later in this exercise.)

Only recently have the industrial applications and technology for the use of compression of specially fabricated capacitors as industrial load cells become available. The following text is a further development of my initial work done in the mid-1990s in which the measurement of fractional gram loads was desired for scientific experimentation. Initially, development work was limited to a digital readout of the capacitance value. A continuous real-time graphical display was beyond the capability of the computing facilities available for personal or home use. Further development of the capacitor as a load cell has been made possible by monitoring the device output as a function of time. A "strip chart recorder" display on a host computer establishes when the loaded device has reached equilibrium, displays the relative magnitude of the device response, the noise in the signal, and indicates drifting in the signal value.

The following text is compiled from my research notes during the development of a reasonably sensitive and reproducible compressive weight sensing device. A significant amount of detail and exploratory testing was included for the benefit of investigators wishing to duplicate the methodology or further develop this technique.

Capacitors consist of two conductor plates separated by an insulator. Normally capacitors are used in electrical circuits to store electrical energy, filter out DC signals, create timed delays, or set a resonance point in circuits with alternating currents. Device capacitance is proportional to the area of the plates, the chemical nature of the dielectric insulating medium between the plates, and the distance between the conductors.

Classical theory expresses the capacitance of a device as the ability to store charge in the following formula.

$$C = k\,A\,/\,d \text{ --- } 1$$

C is the device capacitance. k is a proportionality constant composed of the permittivity of free space plus the dielectric constant of the insulating medium between the conducting plates. A is the active area of the conductors and dielectric plates. d is the distance between the conductors.

Commercially available capacitors come in many physical forms (see Figure 1-2 in Chapter 1) and charge storage capabilities that exhibit capacitance values from picofarads, written as pF and representing $1/10^{12}$ farads, to many Farads as discussed in Chapter 1. Very high resistance, low current leakage devices are manufactured from rolled, metalized, plastic films of polyethylene, polystyrene, and Mylar which suggested the format for the first experiments I conducted, as described next.

Development History

Conceivably, a calibrated, coiled metal spring from which masses are suspended for weighing should be replaceable with a stack of capacitor plates fitted with deformable plastic dielectrics between the conductive plates. Compression of the stack by a gravitational force acting on a mass, placed on top of the interleaved assembly, should compress the distance between the plates and change the device's capacitance.

Two conducting plates on either side of an insulator form a single capacitor device. As depicted in Figure 9-1, five tabbed metal plates, denoted by the letters A to E separating four insulating dielectrics, denoted by the numerical values from 1 to 4 makes a four capacitor device. A multiple plate capacitor of n units contains n+1 conducting plates separating n dielectrics. Multiple plate capacitor load cells (MPCLC) are the devices formed from these multi-layered assemblies.

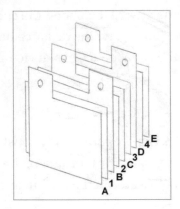

Figure 9-1. *A multiple plate capacitor load cell*

In the capacitor formula in equation 1, an inverse proportionality between device capacitance and plate distance is shown. A theoretical plot of arbitrary units of device capacitance vs. a monotonic decrease in arbitrary interplate distance generates the expected inverse ratio curvature, as seen in Figure 9-2.

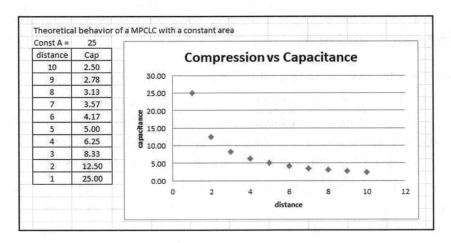

Figure 9-2. *Capacitance vs. interplate distance*

As is evident from the plot in Figure 9-2, the linear portion of the curve between 0 and 2 to 3 distance units is the area in which the relationship between the measured device capacitance and the degree of compression is reasonably predictable.

Figure 9-3 depicts the power expression mathematical model to which the capacitance compression curvature plotting belongs.

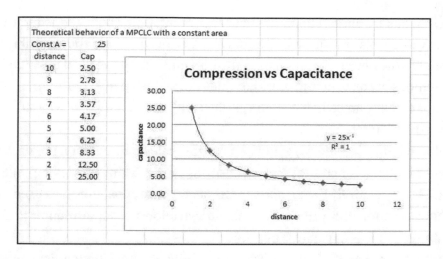

Figure 9-3. *Mathematical expression for capacitance vs. interplate distance plot*

Figures 9-1 to 9-3 depict a set of ideal conditions and theoretical considerations that practical devices built with multiple capacitor units, connected in parallel, will probably not exhibit. A host of variables involving materials of construction, variations in assembly, electronic, mechanical, and environmental noise, or perturbations contribute to deviations from ideal behavior. The effects of materials of construction, plate shape, the number of device leaves, and device orientation on the performance of the assembled device are explored later.

An unexpected proof of concept was observed as the first experimental units were assembled for testing. Stacking the plates and insulators on top of one another increased the overall capacitance of the device in an inordinate amount that was proportional to the number of insulators and conductors used. As the number of leaves of the devices increased, the weight of the materials in the upper layers compressed the lower leaves and inordinately increased the observed "at rest" capacitance of the sensor. The contribution of the self-compression effect could be measured by both monitoring the increase in total capacity as the device is assembled in the horizontal plane or by observing the change in capacitance that occurs as the device is rotated from the horizontal to the vertical plane around the axis at the tabbed or the free end of the individual leaves.

Simple, single tabbed, square plate devices, as depicted in Figure 9-1, are the easiest to build and measure larger weights. Single tabbed triangular plates are more difficult to prepare but are more weight sensitive (see Figures 9-26 and 9-27). Single tabbed square or tapered shapes are limited to horizontal experimentation. Higher-sensitivity devices used in the vertical plane require individual leaf mounts that hold the assembly securely in alignment as the device is rotated from the horizontal to the vertical position.

The methods of constructing more complex devices used in experimental measurements at any angle between the vertical and horizontal are discussed throughout this chapter.

To utilize a multiple plate capacitor as a weight scale, load cell, or a possible inclinometer, a means for continuously measuring or displaying the device capacitance is required. Many relatively inexpensive multimeters have capacitor measurement scales. There are numerous programs available that allow the experimenter to use microcontrollers or PCs as capacitance meters.

Experimental research often involves determining the physio-chemical properties of very small amounts of organic, biological, or medical materials that are difficult to obtain and small amounts of material that are all that is left of a substance of interest. In developing a weight-sensitive transducer that converts compressive force into a varying capacitance, it is desirable to measure the smallest possible weights. In addition to the transducer responding to small increments of weight change, the software and display should also follow these very small changes with a minimum time delay for thermometric studies.

In Chapter 1, an Arduino capacitance measurement sketch using the calibrated, internal stray resistance and capacitance (ISRC) of an individual Arduino board was presented. Capacitance meters using internal Arduino component calibration have no external circuitry other than the DUT.

In this weight measurement exercise, an additional sensitive capacitance measurement sketch requires some external circuitry. In 2013, several contributors to the Arduino forum presented a capacitance measurement technique that uses the input capture feature of the Arduino's ATmega328 microprocessor chip timer (ICFT) and external circuitry to achieve sensitive and accurate, continuous, capacitance measurements in July 2013 (see gammon.com.au/forum/?id=12075).

In the following text, weight measurement programs explore the use of different dielectric materials and a device's physical parameters to evaluate the relationships between device construction and applied weight induced capacitance changes with respect to linear dynamic range and transducer sensitivity. Both types of microprocessor capacitance measurement programs were used along with data smoothing code in both the Arduino microcontroller and the DAQFactory display to achieve a maximum amount of noise reduction and still maintain a reasonable transducer response time.

The capacitance measuring microprocessor coded sketch for a given experiment or calibration has been modified from the original ISRC or ICFT code. The sketches were modified to include a moving average digital signal processing (DSP) and take capacitance measurements on quarter-second time intervals (250 ms). The DAQFactory display uses a 16 point or higher smoothing of the Arduino data. (Recall that averaging decreases response time and that the increase in benefit or decrease in noise with an averaging is proportional to the square root of the number of points averaged.)

Some of the data presented in the following passages does not require extensive digital signal processing (DSP) for noise reduction, but as the sensitivity of the desired weight measurement increases, DSP smoothing of the data becomes important.

For noise reduction at increased sensitivity, the battery power option of the Arduino must be used. In Figure 9-4, the noise reduction seen in the black recorder trace at 9:03, resulting from transferring the Arduino's power source from the USB's nominal 5 V to a nominal 12 V, rechargeable, lead-acid battery, is substantial (see the discussion on batteries in Chapter 11).

A battery is a storage "reservoir" of electrical energy. To realize the benefits available from the constant DC power supply, the "reservoir" needs to be large enough to appear as a "constant voltage" source when power is drawn from the device. The batteries I used were 4.0 and 4.5 ampere hour units (3½ × 2½ × 4 in, or 9 × 6.5 × 10 cm, weighing 3 lbs or 1.4 kg). The batteries could run the Arduino for 12 to 16 or more hours before the output voltage dropped below 12 V. After recharging a lead-acid battery, the voltage can rise to over 13 V but stabilizes at a value in the upper 12 V range after several hours. As a precaution against damage to any circuitry, a freshly charged battery was not used to power a microcontroller until its output voltage dropped below 13 V. Battery power was discontinued when the voltage dropped below 12 V, at which point the power source was recharged.

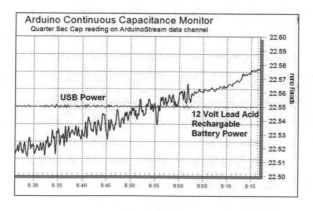

Figure 9-4. *Signal noise reduction from 12 V battery power*

In Figure 9-4, although the black baseline noise is reduced from 0.02 nF to 0.007 nF, the drift is unaffected.

There are additional sources of noise and drift in the signals created using multiple parallel capacitors at higher sensitivity consisting of air currents, temperature changes, and induced electromagnetic or static electric fields. In Figure 9-5, the black signal trace before 6:35 is unshielded while the signal after that is protected.

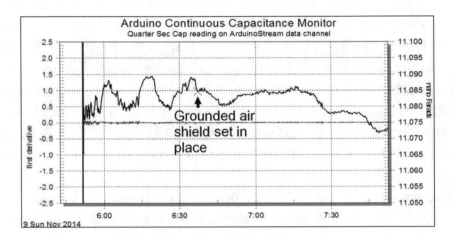

Figure 9-5. *Signal noise reduction from thermal, electrical, and mechanical shielding*

The signal noise reduction in Figure 9-5 was achieved with a thin cardboard structure painted black on its inner surface and covered in aluminum foil on the outside. The aluminum foil on the outer surface was cut to a shape larger than required to effectively cover the cardboard's total area. The excess of the foil wrapping was folded into a flat tab or rolled into a "pigtail" grounded to the shielding of the twisted pair cable connecting the DUT to the Arduino board. An alligator clip on a jumper wire established the required electrical grounding connection (see item 3 in Figure 9-6).

The design of the shielding assembly is determined by the configuration of the device assembled by the researcher. I assembled many different shielding configurations in the development of these devices, one of which is depicted in Figure 9-6. The shield depicted is a compromise solution that covers and protects most of the transducer's active area. The open-ended nature of the shielding allows the tip of the transducer to be loaded and cleared of test weight loads, either manually or with special jigs, to minimize upper plate disruptions during weighing operations.

The development of the MPCLC devices outlined in this book is the result of a typical sequence of experiments in which small attempts to improve a simple device leads to further insights as to the mechanism by which the DUT operates. Increased knowledge of the operational mechanism leads to further experimental refinements that increase the understanding of the device and subsequently increase or decrease its complexity to enhance performance.

In developing the capacitive load cell, the first simple device consisting of a square, easy to assemble apparatus led to the more complex, difficult to assemble, tapered, thin layer and composite film devices with vastly increased sensitivities.

Weight sensitivity becomes the determining factor for the type of apparatus to be built by the experimenter. A simple square device with readily available materials can be cut out by hand to demonstrate the effect and measure grams and ounces of weight. Measurements of fractions of grams may require the construction and assembly of the more sensitive, tapered devices that require more care, time, and effort to build and use. For very low masses, the stiffness of the plates in the sensor determines the lower limits of sensitivity.

Experiment

The captioned Figure 9-6 depicts several different multiple-plate capacitive load cells and the various accessories initially used to fabricate and operate these devices.

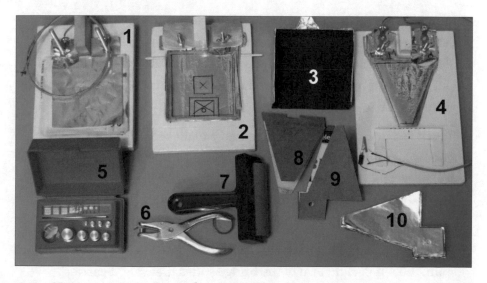

Figure 9-6. *Various MPCLCs and accessories*

- Item 1 is the original device. It consists of tabbed, square, (approx. 4 in or 10 cm) aluminum foil, conductor plates, with common connections on the left and right, separated by polyethylene sheet dielectrics cut from plastic bags.

- Item 2 is a square plate device made from Mylar film with a deposited aluminum layer. The leaves of the device were cut from an aluminized Mylar "survival blanket." (Rolls of "Silver" Al-Mylar giftwrap were found to be 0.0011 in (0.029 mm) virtually twice the thickness of the blanket material). The composite is coated on one and hence both left and right hand plates must be cut out from the stock sheet material. The edges of the plates may need to be cleared of metal to avoid shorting of the device.

  Being metalized on one side only, an electrical contact must be made between plates. The electrical contact consisted of a folded strip of aluminum foil with a hole punched in either end (see Figure 9-7). Attempts to use a fold-over tab to eliminate the tin foil bridge do not provide a robust, usable electrical contact that frequently fails during assembly or while in service. Although the polymer film stretches or compresses on the inside or outside curvature of a fold or bend, the aluminum film often breaks when on the outside of a fold or bend in the sensor leaf.

- Item 3 shows the inside view of an air current and electromagnetic field interference shielding cover made to fit item 4. The interior of the open box was painted matt black, the exterior covered with aluminum foil, and the foil folded to provide a ground connection tab visible at the top edge of the cover.

- Item 4 is a device displaying increased weight sensitivity, assembled from triangular, etched edge, tapered plates made from aluminized Mylar. Weights were added or removed from the tip of the device with the custom-built sliding cardboard "bridge" visible just below the apex of the capacitor plates, in the retracted position.

  To use the bridge, weights were placed onto the center of the span, the left or right arm of the bridge slides the weight carrier far enough over the capacitor tip so the weight could be pulled or pushed off the center of the span, to be deposited onto the mid tip of the load cell beneath.

After the measurement was taken, the arm of the bridge could move the bridge back to the retracted position, usually pushing the weight off the load cell in the process.

Also visible in the photo are both ends of the twisted pair, shielded cable, used to transfer electrical signals. The end tabs of the conducting plates were connected by a number 10 bolt with 32 threads per inch, using a wing-nut for compressing the left and right plate stacks together. (#10 is 3/16 in diameter, or 4.6 mm.)

Electrical contact was made with a large area, copper strapping adapter, soldered to the red and black wires of the signal transfer cable. The end of the cable that connects to the Arduino has two pins that fit snugly into the appropriate analog input header pins and an alligator clip on the metal shielding to grip a pin fitting snugly into one of the Arduino's ground pin headers.

- Item 5 is the calibration weight set.

- Item 6 is a ¼ inch paper punch (6 mm).

- Item 7 is a silkscreen printing roller to smooth and flatten the foil capacitor plates.

- Item 8 is a template for tapered dielectrics.

- Item 9 is a template for tapered foil conducting plates.

- Item 10 is a supply of tapered conducting plates.

Items 8 and 9 are cardboard templates to cut out tapered foil conducting plates and dielectric sheets. The templates attempt to make multiple, uniform, triangular reproductions of the desired shapes so that the tips of the assembled device, both metal foil and dielectric insulators, all align with one another. The templates are used with folded sheets of aluminum foil and dielectric to simultaneously create four or five identical pieces at once.

Variation of Dielectric Composition, Discrete Plates, and Metalized Plastic Films

Although the original concept for the multiple plate capacitor load cell was assembled from materials at hand, consisting of kitchen-grade, rolled aluminum foil and dielectrics cut from the polyethylene film of plastic bags, an increase in sensitivity should be possible by altering the chemical composition of the dielectric. Mylar, paper, and many water-soluble salts have higher dielectric constants than polyethylene. By changing the dielectric chemical composition, creating a more weight sensitive load cell should be possible. As with commercial capacitors, "load cells" can be assembled from composite materials, such as dry papers, or dried papers soaked in various salts or polarizable compounds such as glycerin and from metallic layers deposited on insulating plastic films, such as aluminum on Mylar. There are several considerations to take into account that are discussed later. The service required of the device should be examined before selecting the materials to be used in sensor fabrication.

Assembly of a multiple plate capacitor is best done in incremental stages. Each device I assembled was fabricated in steps of five or ten dielectric plates, between which the open circuit nature of the device was confirmed, and the total device capacitance was measured. Incremental confirmation of electrical properties guaranteed a fully functioning device before attempting the collection of experimental data. The experimenter should find that the total device capacitance initially increases in significantly larger portions than is expected in a simple linear relationship between the device's total capacitance and the number of plates being incrementally added. A source of nonlinearity is self-compression that is discussed later.

Larger square devices with dimensions of 2 to 4 inches (5 to 10 cm) on a side are the easiest to build, exhibit reasonable capacitance values, and are easily loaded with weights in the gram and higher ranges. To measure the capacitance change response to loadings in fractional gram ranges, smaller devices with mechanical jig assistance in device loading or unloading are necessary to achieve working, reproducible, sensitive devices.

Aluminum Foil and Sheet Polyethylene

The original square, proof-of-concept, experimental device assembled from household materials was fabricated in 1997. Capacitance change was initially monitored with a Commodore-64 using an add-on capacitance meter board employing a 555 timer. The timer circuit read the RC time constant created by the varying capacitance DUT and a known precision resistor value. Calibration and coarse test measurements were achieved by hand plotting of the data.

The metal plates for the capacitor depicted in item 1 in Figure 9-6 can be cut from a roll of household or kitchen-grade aluminum foil. The dielectrics can be cut from polyethylene plastic bags, clear mailing wrappers, or PE drop cloths. Very thin layers of plastic film "sealing or cling wraps" do not allow the conducting plates and dielectrics to slide over one another and do not make usable, multiple plate capacitor load cells (see Table 9-1).

Initially, the holes in the individual aluminum foil plates were made with a ¼ in (6 mm) diameter handheld paper punch. The plates and dielectrics were cut out using the templates shown, and the multiple plate capacitors were assembled on the painted wooden bases depicted in the various photos. Later experimental devices were built with smaller holes cut with a "leather punch" (see item 3 in Figure 9-26).

Papers, Treated Papers, and Cellulose Films

Papers that are made from wood fibers consisting of carbohydrates tend to have higher dielectric constants than polyethylene. Papers are manufactured in many different thicknesses and come in various formats such as bond papers, newsprints, tracing paper, glassine paper, parchment papers, and onion skin. Many papers are "wettable" and can be permeated with water-soluble chemical compounds, then dried to increase the overall capacitance of devices assembled from these materials. Clear cellulose films, as used by food manufacturers and florists, can also be used as dielectrics to increase device capacitance.

Aluminized Mylar Film

Aluminized Mylar, commonly sold in outdoor and camping supply outlets as "survival blankets" or in 30-inch-wide rolls as giftware wrapping, has an aluminum coating on one side of a remarkably durable, thin, stretched polyethylene terephthalate film known by the tradename Mylar. A capacitor can be formed by cutting out tabbed squares (see Figure 9-7), but with mirror-image left and right tabs to accommodate the single side nature of the aluminized coating. With the left- and right-hand configured sheets, an interleaved multiple plate capacitor can be formed with the Mylar side preferably "up" and the aluminum side "down."

To assemble a usable multiple plate capacitor from aluminum foil plates and individual discrete sheets of a dielectric, the insulators are cut to a size slightly larger than the active area of the aluminum plates. The left- and right-hand plates are mounted on their respective fixed terminals on either side of the positioning block with the insulating dielectrics interleaved between the fixed plates to avoid the conducting plates coming into contact with one another and shorting out the device.

To avoid interplate short circuits in a device assembled from a deposited aluminum layer, the conducting metal can be removed from a thin strip around the edges of the individual composite plates. Alternatively, an insulating strip of paint, ink, or wax coating can be deposited around the edges of the aluminum layer to minimize the possibility of the interleaved plates short-circuiting (see discussion on noise generation).

Thin strips of metal (approximately ⅛ in or 3 mm) can be removed from coated foils with an aluminum etch solution, consisting of 15.7 gm of blue copper sulfate, 10 gm NaCl common table salt, and 50 ml of water. To apply thin bands of etchant to the edges of the coated films, I used the edge of a ⅛ in thick rectangle of plywood of the appropriate length, wrapped in cotton cloth. The edge of the cloth wrapped plywood was first soaked in the etch solution and then pressed against the supported aluminum side of the leaf being treated to remove the outer edges of the plates active aluminum coating. The plate being etched was supported on a wet piece of flat glass to handle the thin film during etching and washing. Care must be taken to not allow the etchant to contact the central portion of the capacitor plate. The author created several plates with virtually perfect copies of his fingerprints etched into them.

Electrical connection between the two layer tabs requires bridging the dielectric layer between the aluminum leaves of each adjacent capacitor cell. Initially, a connector was made from a ¾ (2 cm) × 3 in (7.5 cm) strip of aluminum foil with two ¼ in (6 mm) holes punched in either end of the strip. When folded in half and placed over each tab so that all three punched holes lined up, all the individual capacitor cells formed became connected in a parallel configuration as desired.

Figure 9-7 shows the left- and right-handed plates and the connecting foil bridge. Each plate, both left- and right-hand, requires a connecting foil bridge. Attempts to simplify construction by simply folding over the tabs of the leaves cause the deposited aluminum foil to break when the foil layer is on the outside of the bend. Assembled and tested devices fabricated with folded tabs that suddenly failed during experimental testing returned to service when each leaf was bridged with a folded foil bridge, as depicted in Figure 9-7.

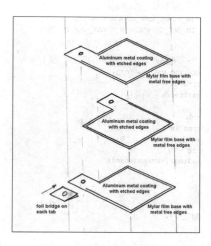

Figure 9-7. *Etched edge aluminized Mylar plates and foil bridges*

The aluminum foil coated side of the Mylar film can be identified with a resistance reading or continuity check function on a digital multimeter (DMM) or volt-ohm-meter (VOM). When cutting multiple layers of the Mylar film at once from folded stock, ensure that the correct number of left- or right-handed plates results before cutting the folded material.

Software

Two Arduino sketch programs are available for continuous monitoring of these sensors. Listing 9-1 uses accurately known resistors and capacitors to evaluate the Arduino board's internal stray resistance-capacitance (ISRC). The internal calibration is accomplished with the formulas presented in Chapter 1. The ISRC code can continuously monitor the device capacitance for graphical display.

Listing 9-2 is the second capacitance measurement program using the input capture feature of the timer (ATmega328) (ICFT) method and a moving average DSP code is presented in the exercise listings. Accurate and sensitive measurements are created using precisely-defined external circuitry and the ICFT code to make capacitance measurements (see Figure 9-8).

For convenience and noise reduction, the voltage divider circuit, capacitor charging, and discharging resistors, as depicted in Figure 9-8, were soldered onto an Arduino shield after primary development on a prototyping board. The D*x* designations are the nominal digital signal I/O pins on the Arduino.

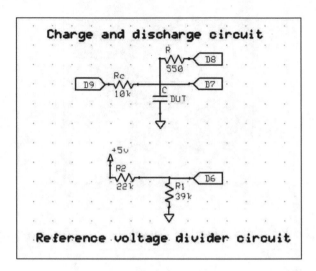

Figure 9-8. *External circuitry for using the input timer capture feature of the Arduino*

Slope or First Derivative Software

In addition to the two different techniques for measuring the capacitance of the DUT, the ability to measure the first derivative of the signal being recorded is a useful facility for these types of measurements (see Chapter 3, where the digital implementation of the first derivative in the event tab of a channel in DAQFactory is discussed.)

The basic derivative software can be coded into the event tab of a channel with the following long and short lines of code.

```
private frstDiff = (Smooth (ArduinoStream[0],4) - (Smooth
(ArduinoStream[25],4))) / (Smooth (ArduinoStream.Time[0],4) - (Smooth
(ArduinoStream.Time[25], 4)))

frstDeriv.AddValue(frstDiff)
```

In terms of the x vs. time plot displayed by the DAQFactory program, the derivative is the "rise" over the "run" or the rate of change of the x value with time. The two-line code was developed while experimenting with the silicon carbide high-temperature resistors. The height of the "rise" and the length of the "run" values are empirically derived. A slope value calculated over 25 data points from the streamed Arduino values is multiplied by another empirically derived scale factor to create a visually useful first derivative trace. Figure 9-11 displays an application for the derivative trace in locating a possible primary capacitance change due to an applied weight. (See discussion on polyethylene dielectrics.)

Smooth(Value, Amount) is the "moving average" command of DAQFactory. (Value is the entity or channel being plotted. Amount is the number of points to average or smooth.) In the DAQFactory code for frstDerv, the most recent four data points are averaged. The value from the average of four points that were recorded 25 data points earlier is subtracted to determine the difference in the x value (the "rise" over the length of the time of the "run"). Division of the delta x by the time index difference between the current and 25 data values creates the slope or first derivative value.

In Figure 9-11, the first derivative trace value was multiplied by 50, then displayed between +/- 3 on the screen set for a full-scale deflection of 2.0 nF between MPCLC values of 19.3 to 21.3 nF as weights between 100 mg and 1 g compressed the device (see discussion on scale expansion).

Observations

Simple Systems: Aluminum–Polyethylene Sheet

Although the original system developed in 1997 produced a rough linearity between measured capacitance and weight on the load cell, the relatively simple computational system, with a single value numerical readout, did not have the resolution or continuous recording capability to display an inherent phenomenon that limits the simple use of polyethylene sheet in this type of capacitor load cell application. As the weight used in the calibration experiments increases, the system response takes increasing lengths of time to stabilize. A typical response is displayed in Figure 9-9.

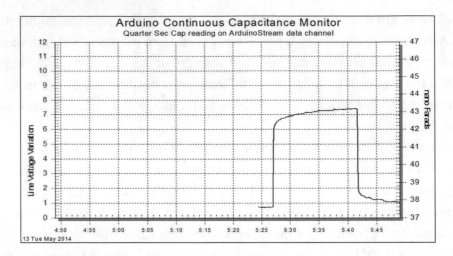

Figure 9-9. *Signal drifting with polyethylene dielectrics*

The data in Figure 9-10 was collected after discovering the long-term equilibration time and confirming its reproducible nature.

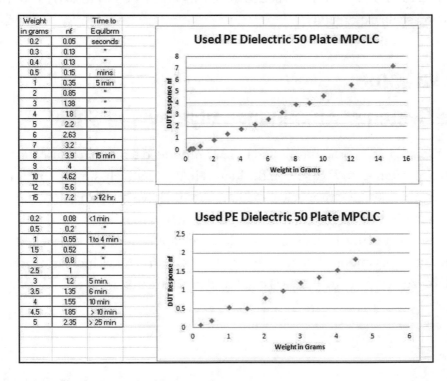

Figure 9-10. *Polyethylene drifting study*

The time required for the system to reach a constant measured capacitance seems to increase with the magnitude of the load and requires care in usage at higher weights when in a continuous display mode.

Another option for compensating for the long-term drifting, possibly a result of some form of secondary compression in the polyethylene dielectric layers of a device, is to monitor the first derivative of the transducer output. A first derivative can be calculated and transferred to a second channel for display with the last two lines of DAQFactory code.

To evaluate the utility of a first derivative mapping of the capacitance change observed during the initial displacement of a used polyethylene MPCLC, a 100 mg to 2 g calibration was recorded, as depicted in Figure 9-11.

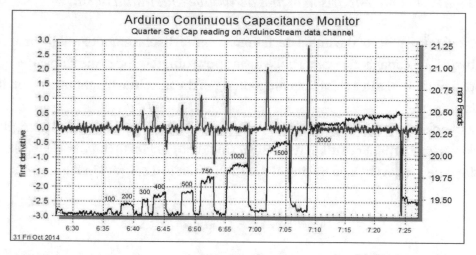

Figure 9-11. *First derivative recording of polyethylene MPCLC Weight response*

The calibration traces were recorded with a 50 dielectric, tapered plate device, made from used clear polyethylene magazine mailing wrappers and thin aluminum foil. The Arduino was running the ICFT calibrated resistance measurement program using a 32-point moving average smoothing before sending the data to the DAQFactory program for display. The DAQFactory used an 8-point average on the channel input, a 32-point smoothing of the capacitance value, and a 64-point smoothing of the first derivative for the graphical strip chart recorder displays. The first derivative's amplitude was adjusted to the display scale by multiplying the smoothed plot by an arbitrary value of 250 for the display being shown. The device used for the 100 mg to 2 g data collection was open to the ambient room conditions.

The data in Figure 9-12 was obtained when the initial deflection and the absolute height of the triangular first derivative traces were measured in millimeters (mm) and plotted against the nominal weights.

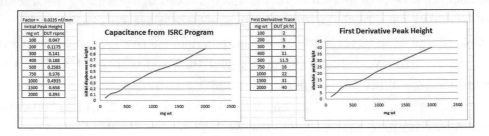

Figure 9-12. *Data comparison of first derivative and initial deviation*

Although the plots of the initial deviation baseline displacement and the first derivative of the capacitance value trace have approximately the same slope, the derivative plot's linearity is less than the plotting of the absolute height of the initial deviation.

A second set of calibration data was collected at higher sensitivity after a simple black construction paper cardboard air-heat shield protected all but the 1¼ in (32 mm) tip of the tapered device. The tracing of the calibration is displayed in Figure 9-13.

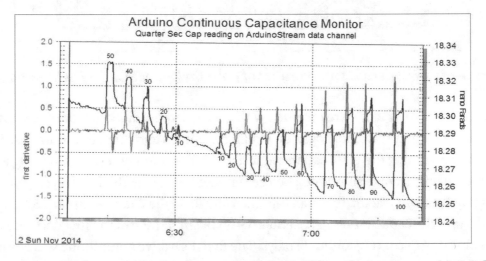

Figure 9-13. *Higher sensitivity data comparison of first derivative and initial deviation*

Figure 9-14. *Data plots of initial baseline displacement and first derivative peak height*

As seen in the two plots, the initial displacement values have better linearity than the peak height of the first derivative display. The first derivative's value lies in determining the points at which to measure the start and finish of the weight-induced capacitance change in devices with polyethylene dielectrics.

After collecting the data in Figure 9-14, a source of thin polyethylene was found in "produce bags" used in fruits and vegetable departments in most supermarkets. The sensitivity for weighing was extended down to 10 mg using the thin PE and a later four-post design of the plate and dielectric mounting technique. Figure 9-15 plots the curvature of a large weight range and the linear portion of that range. The values for the data plotted in Figure 9-15 were noisy, but with the first derivative tracing, the initial deflection heights of the capacitance tracing were measurable.

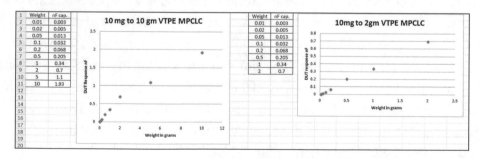

Figure 9-15. *Data plots of initial baseline displacement from first derivative slope changes*

Simple Systems: Aluminum–Cellophane Sheet

Sheets of cellophane (23½ in × 19½ in or 58 cm × 48 cm) (polymerized wood cellulose, extruded into thin sheets with glycerin added as a plasticizer) obtained from a local florist were cut to the nominal sizes to fit the aluminum foil plates and mounting bases in use. During the assembly of the units, the foil plates were rolled flat with a 1¼ in diameter by 4 in long (3 × 10 cm) hard rubber roller as used for silkscreen printing (see item 7 in Figure 9-6).

The cellophane device was calibrated with weights and generated the data tabulated and graphically displayed in Figure 9-16.

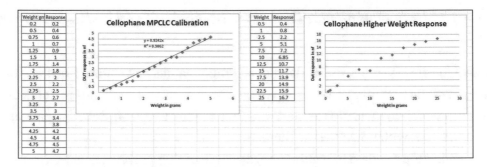

Figure 9-16. *Cellophane MPCLC weight vs. capacitance*

Simple Systems: Aluminum–New and Used Newsprint

A 50 dielectric and 51 conducting plate, multiple plate capacitor was assembled from 3¾ in (9.5 cm) square active area, aluminum foil plates with 4¼ in (10.5 cm) square dielectrics. The dielectrics were cut from ordinary printed newspaper pages and had a thickness of 0.060 in for a stack of 20 leaves for an average thickness of 0.030 in (0.76 mm). Before being calibrated, the 50-cell sensor was compressed with a 3 lb weight (1.4 kg) and allowed to relax three times before settling to a nominal 30.25 nF capacitance value which then exibited a 0.05 nF baseline noise on a scale of 29 to 31 nF. Under a 3 lb load, the cell had a measured capacitance of 92 nF. Capacitance values for known weights were measured in triplicate over several days. The data for the first calibration was plotted, as shown in Figure 9-17.

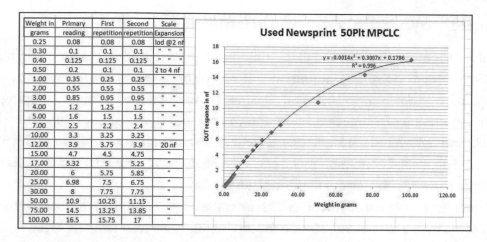

Weight in grams	Primary reading	First repetition	Second repetition	Scale Expansion
0.25	0.08	0.08	0.08	lod @2 nf
0.30	0.1	0.1	0.1	" " "
0.40	0.125	0.125	0.125	" " "
0.50	0.2	0.1	0.1	2 to 4 nf
1.00	0.35	0.25	0.25	" "
2.00	0.55	0.55	0.55	" "
3.00	0.85	0.95	0.95	" "
4.00	1.2	1.25	1.2	" "
5.00	1.6	1.5	1.5	" "
7.00	2.5	2.2	2.4	" "
10.00	3.3	3.25	3.25	" "
12.00	3.9	3.75	3.9	20 nf
15.00	4.7	4.5	4.75	"
17.00	5.32	5	5.25	"
20.00	6	5.75	5.85	"
25.00	6.98	7.5	6.75	"
30.00	8	7.75	7.75	"
50.00	10.9	10.25	11.15	"
75.00	14.5	13.25	13.85	"
100.00	16.5	15.75	17	"

Figure 9-17. *Used newsprint MPCLC weight vs. capacitance*

New sheets of newsprint are thicker than printed materials. Large compression forces from the rollers used in the printing process compress the paper stock during its processing. Used material has a thickness of 0.0025 in or 0.06 mm, and the new newsprint is 0.005 in or 0.12 mm. A similar weight vs. capacitance plot for new newsprint is depicted in Figure 9-18.

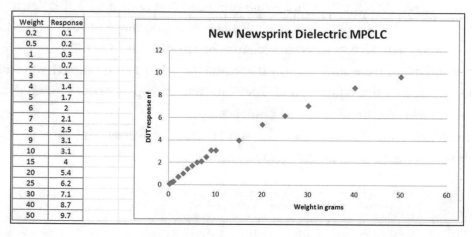

Weight	Response
0.2	0.1
0.5	0.2
1	0.3
2	0.7
3	1
4	1.4
5	1.7
6	2
7	2.1
8	2.5
9	3.1
10	3.1
15	4
20	5.4
25	6.2
30	7.1
40	8.7
50	9.7

Figure 9-18. *New newsprint MPCLC weight vs. capacitance*

Complex Systems: Aluminum-Mylar Composite

A 50 dielectric and 51 conducting plate, multiple plate capacitor was assembled from 3¾ in (9.5 cm) square active area, aluminum foil–Mylar composite plates that were cut from an aluminum-Mylar "survival blanket." The blanket was obtained from the camping supply department of a large retail store and was cut into square shapes with a 1 in² (2.45 cm) left- and right-hand tab for electrical contact. To assemble a reliable, reproducible device, the deposited aluminum metal had to be etched away from the outer edges of the Mylar film to avoid shorting out of the individual plates.

By etching a nominal eighth of an inch from the edges of each plate, a somewhat irregular 3¼ in (8.3 cm) square aluminum conducting plate resulted. The Mylar dielectrics remained as 3¾ in (9 cm) square sheets supporting the deposited aluminum conductors. Because the aluminum was deposited on one side of the Mylar film and the Mylar was now the main structural material of the device, the aluminum layers on each device plate had to be connected with aluminum foil "bridges," as shown in Figure 9-7.

A 30-unit stack of plates cut from the "survival blanket" material had a thickness of 0.06 inch for an individual leaf thickness of 0.002 inch or 2 mil (0.051 mm). As with the simple systems, before being calibrated, the 50-cell unit was compressed with a 3 lb weight and allowed to relax three times before settling to a nominal 96 nF capacitance value with a 0.05 nF baseline noise on a full-scale deflection range of 96 to 96.5 nF. Under a 3 lb load, the cell had a measured capacitance of 410, 425, and 420 nF.

Capacitor values were continuously determined by the Arduino capacitance meter program cycling four times per second. The DAQFactory display of the streamed Arduino data was smoothed with a 32-point average.

Capacitance values for known weights were measured over several days. The data for the calibrations was plotted, as shown in Figure 9-19.

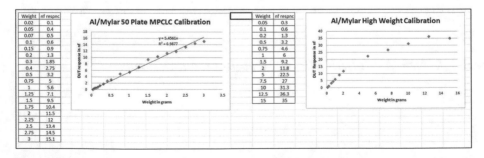

Figure 9-19. *Etched edge Mylar-Aluminum MPCLC weight vs. capacitance for high and low weights*

In addition to the more complex etched plate capacitor, numerous experiments were conducted with several different materials as dielectrics. A simple rectangular device constructed from aluminum foil and sheets of different dielectric materials was used to gather data. The results of the various experiments are compiled in Table 9-1.

Table 9-1. *Properties of 50 Plate Capacitor Load Cells with Various Dielectric Materials*

Physical and Electronic Properties of 50 Plate Capacitor Load Cells						
Dielectric Material of Construction	Dielectric Thickness	Stack Thickness	nf Nominal Capacitance	Sensitivity nf/gram	Linear Range	Comments
aluminum on mylar	0.0005"/0.013 mm	1/4"(4.2 mm)	95 - 100 nf	4.2	2-3 gm	y = 5.4561x, R^2 = 0.9877: complex construction
cellophane	0.0011"/0.027 mm	1/4"/6mm	68-73 nf	0.9	7 - 12 gm	y = 0.9242x, R^2 = 0.9862: simple construction
newsprint (new)	0.005"/0.12 mm	0.75"/19 mm	25 - 30 nf	0.25	10 -20 gm	y = 0.2895x, R^2 = 0.9735 : device constructed from readily
newsprint (used)	0.0025"/0.06 mm	0.75"/19 mm	25 - 30 nf	0.225	20 gm	y = 0.2472x, R^2 = 0.9905 : available materials
onionskin paper	0.0015"/0.04 mm	0.5"/12 mm	42 - 47 nf	0.50	30	y = 0.54656x, R^2 = 0.9935 : " " " "
paper - glycerine	see tracing paper	20 plate stack	150 nf	n. d.	n. d.	high capacitance, relaxation time in hours, integral use
polyethylene (printed/used)	0.007"/0.017mm	0.5"/12mm	48 nf	0.46	16 gm	y = 0.4656x, R^2 = 0.9973 : slow to stable readings
polyethylene (new rolled)	0.0008"/0.02mm	0.625/15 mm	120 nf	0.175	none	concave upward slope, no inter plate motion
tissue (gift wrap pink)	0.001"/0.025 mm	0.5"/12 mm	50 nf	0.43	15 - 16 gm	y = 0.4240x, R^2 = 0.9856 : simple construction
tracing paper	0.002"/0.047 mm	0.625"/15 mm	50 nf	0.67	12 - 15 gm	y = 0.7187x, R^2 = 0.9710 : slow to stable readings

Notes: 1) aluminum foil - mylar capacitor plates active area after etching approx 3-7/8" or 97 mm square.
 2) aluminum foil plates nominal 4" or 102 mm square and 0.001" or 0.0245 mm thick
 3) DAQFactory display x32 smooth and Arduino stream rate 250 ms (4 /sec.)

To determine the reproducibility of this weighing technique, the aluminum-Mylar, cellulose, and onion skin paper devices were each calibrated three times over longer ranges and then within their linear ranges. Data from the Al-Mylar system was typical of that observed for the other two devices and is displayed in Figure 9-20.

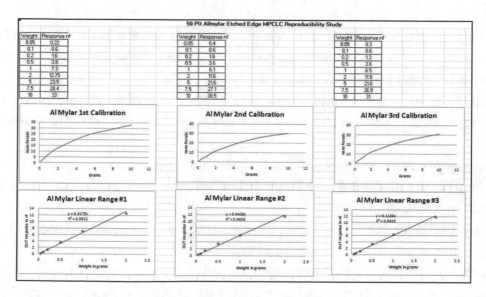

Figure 9-20. *Typical system reproducibility*

A series of calibrations were run on the onion skin, cellulose, and Al-Mylar devices for their individual responses within their linear ranges. The typical data observed for these devices is depicted in Figure 9-21.

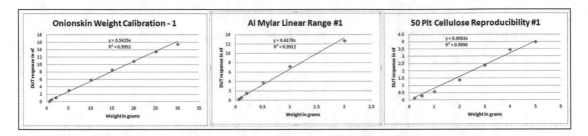

Figure 9-21. *Linear response of onionskin paper, cellulose film, and aluminum Mylar composite*

Complex Shaped Systems

Although the capacitance value of a device is dependent on the area of the plates and dielectrics in contact with one another, the larger area is also responsible for an increase in the frictional forces experienced when the plates slide over one another in this type of device application. If the plates and dielectric were triangular, as the plate's width decreased, the frictional and bending forces should also decrease, making a more weight sensitive device.

Triangular plates should be more sensitive to smaller weights but must be validated for linearity. Oddly shaped devices also present difficulties in assembly. Jigs for cutting and assembly may be required during construction.

Initially, to aid in the assembly of tapered devices, blocks of wood were mounted on the supporting bases to aid in the alignment of the pointed ends of the device being built.

Initial experiments used 4 in (10.2 cm) square aluminum plates trimmed to taper to ⅜ in (1 cm) as the conducting plates with dielectrics cut to overlap the conductors by ⅛ in (3 mm) per side.

The capacitance of a device is proportional to the area of the plates in use, and reducing that area to decrease friction and increase weight sensitivity requires increased sensitivity in the ability to measure small changes in the DUT response. To accommodate the smaller changes in system capacitance that would be expected to result when both the device itself and the weight applied both decrease in magnitude, the ICFT program and weight handling devices were used to collect data.

A typical experimental setup for data collection and small weight manipulation is depicted in Figure 9-22 and described as follows.

- Item 1 is the Arduino and an Arduino "shield" with the external charging-discharging and voltage divider reference resistor circuitry mounted on top.

- Item 2 is the 12 V, 2.4 Ah, rechargeable, sealed, lead-acid battery power source for the Arduino

- Item 3 is the air-electromagnetic shield, consisting of a thin, fitted cardboard base completely covered with aluminum foil. The aluminum foil has a tapered tab visible at the lower-left corner of the shroud that connects to the shielding on the twisted pair input signal cable connected to an Arduino ground pin.

  The shroud has two notched rectangular openings at the rear to accommodate the perforated copper strip electrical contacts of the multiple plate capacitor. To manipulate the weights and their sliding bridge, the shield does not cover the entire length of the shaped device.

- Item 4 is the base plate with two threaded metal posts and central white spacing block at the left end that both position and provide electrical contacts for the left- and right-hand conducting plates of the capacitor.

- Item 5 is the center of a cardboard bridge that slides over the tip of the capacitor. In the photo, the top view of the bridge resembles a squared "C". The top and bottom arms of the "C" are stacks of thin cardboard shims that have progressively been glued together to elevate the bridge to the point at which it just clears the top leaf of the capacitive load cell.

  The bridge is a thin piece of cardboard folded at right angles to the deck of the bridge. When viewed from the side end, the bridge deck has a cross-sectional "L" shape with the long arm forming the deck. Both the bridge deck and the center of the load cell tip were marked with a center line to ensure reproducible positioning from measurement to measurement.

With the bridge to the right of the capacitor tip, a weight is loaded onto the center line of the deck. The bridge is then moved to the left until the two tips of the center lines match, and the weight is carefully pulled or pushed off the bridge onto the upper plate of the load cell. When the measurement was made, the bridge was pulled back to the right, and the weight slid off the load cell.

- Item 6 indicates the set of wooden blocks to position the conducting plates and the dielectrics during assembly of the device.

Figure 9-22. *Tapered MPCLC*

A weight manipulating bridge is custom built to work with an individual capacitive load cell. Shims are added to each of the top and bottom arms until the bridge just clears the top plate of the cell without disturbing it mechanically. If the distance between the top plate and the capacitor is too great, the weight will not be pushed off the load cell when the bridge is moved to the right for reloading. You must manually try to move the weight without disturbing the cell's configuration.

The close proximity of the bridge to the load cell affects the baseline trace, as shown in Figure 9-23.

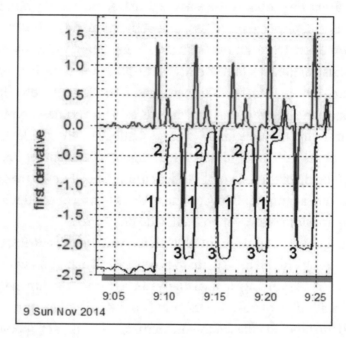

Figure 9-23. *Baseline response to weight manipulating bridge movement*

The baseline originally seen at the bottom left of the figure is elevated as indicated by the portion of the trace labeled with the caption 1, by moving the bridge to the left and covering the tip of the load cell. After a short period of time elapses, and the weight is pushed off the bridge onto the top plate of the load cell, and the weight induced capacitance change is recorded as portion 2. Sliding the bridge to the right pushes the weight off the top plate of the cell, and the baseline returns to the position marked with caption 3. The red first derivative peak of the capacitance tracing marks the inflection points in the recording.

Experimental Refinements of Tapered MPCLC Devices

Later experiments with tapered cells combined several techniques to develop a sensitive, inexpensive, easy-to-assemble device.

Polyethylene films are probably the least expensive, most easily obtained and with their chemical and physical inertness, one of the more desirable insulators for MPCLC experimentation. Experiments with thin "cling wrap" polyethylene films were unsuccessful because of the lack of flexibility of the assembled device.

A second source of very thin, semi-transparent, non-clinging polyethylene film in the bags used to package fresh produce in grocery stores. The film has a typical thickness of 0.0075 in (0.184 mm) for 16 sheets for an average 0.00047 in film thickness (0.011 mm).

Earlier experiments with tapered devices, as depicted in Figure 9-22, attempted to bring the width of the tip of the assembled capacitor load cell down to ⅜ in, (1 cm) but in the image, variation in alignment between the various leaves of the device resulted in an assembled device tip width well over an inch wide (2.45 cm).

To aid in the alignment of the conducting plates and the dielectrics, two steel pins were added to the design of the base plate to position the insulators with tension, rather than using wooden blocks relying on a virtually non-existent rigidity in the polyethylene films. By careful positioning of the two steel pins on the base plate and adding two perforated tabs to the tapered sides of the dielectrics, the insulators could be mounted in place more firmly.

In addition to a more firmly mounted dielectric, the variation caused by cutting and perforating the dielectrics could be minimized by turning the insulating film over to attain better alignment of the tip portions of the device being assembled.

By adding two steel pins to the base board to fix the dielectrics in place, several additional experiments and applications of the device were made possible.

Previous initial experiments using a sliding bridge for weight manipulation with high sensitivity devices caused the baseline deviations depicted in Figure 9-23. A second technique for avoiding the effects of freehand addition of weights disturbing the positioning of the tapered portion of the device plates was devised through the use of the electronics concept of biasing. A taper was introduced into the device design to decrease frictional forces, and a narrowing cross-sectional area of the plates resulted. A small tripod device with threaded legs and a large hole in the center was fitted over the tip of the load cell, and its height was adjusted until the tips of the device plates were placed into a lightly compressed state.

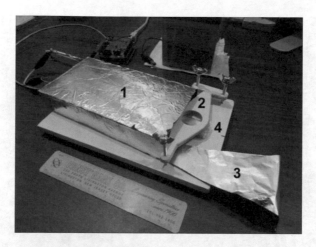

Figure 9-24. *Thin polyethylene tapered MPCLC opened*

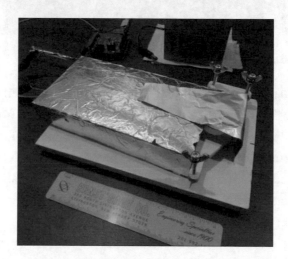

Figure 9-25. *Thin polyethylene tapered MPCLC cover closed*

Figures 9-24 and 9-25 show the initial setup to evaluate the thin polyethylene film dielectrics in an MPCLC application. The capacitor device is similar to the tapered device seen in Figure 9-22; however, it has an isosceles triangle configuration with a base that is half the length of the sides as opposed to the first tapered device experiments in which square plates were cut to a ⅜ in (9 mm) tip.

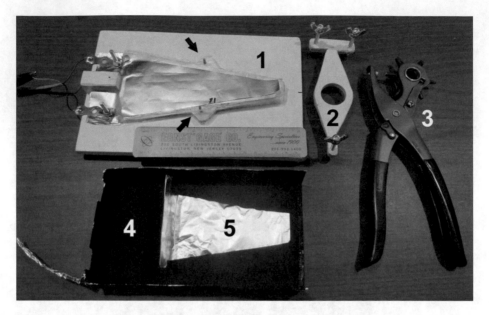

Figure 9-26. *Thin polyethylene tapered MPCLC*

In Figure 9-26, two black arrows indicate the steel pins between which the thin dielectrics were tightly fitted approximately one-third the way up from the base of the triangular device and ⅛ in (3 mm) wider than the normal width of the dielectrics for this shaped device. The extra width pins hold the insulators in place. A tripod bridge, item 2, has slightly compressed the capacitor's tips to establish an adjustable capacitance, baseline value, in much the same manner as transistors are voltage biased to establish their operating points.

The large opening in the center of the tripod allows the forceps assisted addition and removal of weights. The tripod was shaped to maximize the tapered tip area and fit as far under the thermal and electromagnetic shielding, items 4 and 5, as possible. Item 3 is an adjustable hole size, "leather" punch to cut the 3.5 mm (⅛ in) holes in the shaped dielectrics and conductor plates.

Using the device depicted in Figures 9-25 and 9-26, a capacitance vs. weight calibration from 50 mg to 600 mg (mg or mgm is milligram, 0.001 or 1/1000 gram) was conducted. The data measured in the calibration is presented in Figure 9-22 in tabular and graphical form.

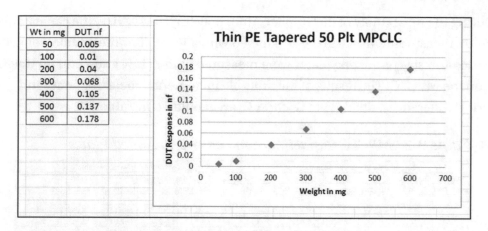

Wt in mg	DUT nf
50	0.005
100	0.01
200	0.04
300	0.068
400	0.105
500	0.137
600	0.178

Figure 9-27. *50 to 600 mg weight calibration*

Figure 9-28 illustrates the effects of ambient room temperature variations created by the cyclic effects of North American domestic, wintertime, central heating.

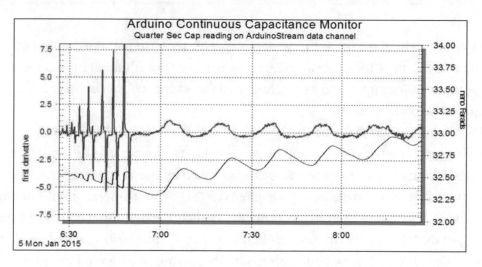

Figure 9-28. *Baseline drift from central heating*

As seen in Figure 9-28, significantly more thermal insulation is needed to maintain a reasonably stable baseline for conducting experiments at higher sensitivities.

To confirm the absence of short circuits during device assembly, it was noted that as the number of plates in an MPCLC increases, the device capacitance appears to get inordinately larger. To work at increased device sensitivity, a much thicker heat shield was constructed. The thin polyethylene device was disassembled while fitting the heat-EMF shielding and making modifications to the base plate to fix the position of the compression "biasing" bridge.

During the reassembly of the 50-plate, thin, polyethylene device, the capacitance validation measurements normally conducted with a VOM after the addition of five dielectrics and six conducting plates were measured with 2, 1, ½ gram and no weight loads on the MPCLC. The results of the multiple incremental measurements and numerical differences, titled "Dlta C" for Δ C, are tabulated in Table 9-2.

Table 9-2. *MPCLC Capacitance Increase with Added Plates*

Free and Weight Biased Capacitance Value Increases During Very thin polyethylene MPCLC Assembly							Dlta C for	Dlta C for	Dlta C for	Dlta C for	Average C
Number Dielectrics	Conductor Plates	2 gm bias	1 gm bias	0.5 gm bias	no bias wt		2 gm bias	1 gm bias	1/2 gm bias	no bias	per DE plate
5	6	1.58	1.54	1.50	1.36	nf					0.27
10	11	3.80	3.71	3.62	3.42	nf	2.22	2.17	2.12	2.06	0.34
15	16	6.60	6.52	6.43	6.23	nf	2.80	2.81	2.81	2.81	0.42
20	21	11.05	11.03	10.83	10.56	nf	4.45	4.51	4.40	4.33	0.53
25	26	14.07	13.93	13.70	13.36	nf	3.02	2.90	2.87	2.80	0.53
30	31	17.95	17.60	17.35	17.05	nf	3.88	3.67	3.65	3.69	0.57
35	36	20.38	20.05	19.76	19.48	nf	2.43	2.45	2.41	2.43	0.56
40	41	24.18	23.86	23.66	23.38	nf	3.80	3.81	3.90	3.90	0.58
45	46	28.36	27.96	27.69	27.36	nf	4.18	4.10	4.03	3.98	0.61
50	51	32.00	31.56	31.25	30.86	nf	3.64	3.60	3.56	3.50	0.62
Average delta C increase per 5 unit increment over 15-20 dielectric plates =							3.63	3.34	3.31	3.28	

On the far right of the table, the average capacitance based on the number of dielectrics in the stack increases steadily as more leaves are added to the device. The average capacitance appears to be increasing as the added weight of leaves compresses the capacitance cells beneath.

The average weight of the polyethylene and the aluminum foil plates were measured to get an idea of the weight being added as the device was assembled and to determine how much compression would be induced by the added leaves. Ten very thin polyethylene (VT-PE) film dielectrics weighed 0.6604 gm. Ten tapered aluminum foil conductor plates weighed 2.9186 gm. Individual average weights of 0.0660 and 0.2919 gm. suggest that the weights of the aluminum foil conducting plates are not negligible as the size of the MPCLC increases and are probably causing an observed increased total capacitance as the number of plates in the device increases.

Plotting the total observed capacitance against the number of dielectrics and foil conducting plates gives the curve depicted in Figure 9-29.

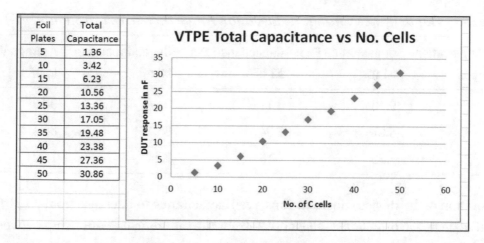

Foil Plates	Total Capacitance
5	1.36
10	3.42
15	6.23
20	10.56
25	13.36
30	17.05
35	19.48
40	23.38
45	27.36
50	30.86

Figure 9-29. *Observed total capacitance vs. number of foil conducting plates in MPCLC*

In Figure 9-29, the graphic is not linear. It exhibits a slightly upward concave curvature that is probably due to the self-compression resulting from the accumulating weight of the plates on top compressing those beneath.

One of the problems encountered in building longer and more tapered devices is keeping the tips of the aluminum foil conducting plates aligned. The dielectrics can be stretched over the alignment pins and need not be carefully aligned if they overlap the edges of the foil conducting plates far enough to avoid shorting out the devices.

If the foil plates are not aligned carefully, the capacitance change as each new cell is added causes excess variation in the measurements taken as the device is built up and may mask any trends seen in the tabulated data.

As the data for Table 9-2 was collected, the misalignment of the plates became quite noticeable and had spread out from an intended ⅜ in (1 cm) to well over ¾ in (2 cm) wide.

With the dielectrics fixed in place between two steel pins, a simple experiment was conducted, in triplicate, to evaluate the effects of self-compression on the observed capacitance of the 15 VT-PE dielectric device. By rotating the capacitor through 90 degrees, the downward force from gravity on the capacitor should decrease in proportion to the cosine of the angle of inclination (see "inclined plane" discussion), as tabulated in Table 9-3.

Table 9-3. *Capacitance Change as Elevation Angle Increases in 15 Plate VT-PE*

Angle of elevation in degrees	Capacitance Exp. #1 nF	Capacitance Exp. #2 nF	Capacitance Exp. #3 nF	Average Value in nF
0	9.18	9.11	9.02	9.10
45	8.97	8.94	8.91	8.94
90	7.35	7.16	7.14	7.22

Rotation of the device causes the observed capacitance to decrease from 9.10 to 7.22 nF, a decrease of 1.88 nF (see Figure 9-43 for the theoretical relationship between observed capacitance and angle of inclination for an MPCLC).

A four-pin mounting arrangement for both the conducting plates and the insulating dielectrics was developed from the two-pin concept to increase the reproducibility and sensitivity of the devices. Base plates were built with four linear, equally spaced mounting points, (¾ in (18 mm) center to center) consisting of two outer threaded metal #8 × 32 tpi (⅛ in or 3 mm diameter bolt with 32 threads per inch or 2.45 cm) screw mounting posts, with wing nuts, for electrical contact and two inner ⅛ in (3 mm) diameter wooden dowels. The dielectrics were symmetrical and fit over the two inner wooden posts. The conducting plates were left and right mirror images that fit over the conducting terminal and the far wooden post.

By supporting the dielectrics and conducting plates from two points, the device components remained in relative alignment as the angle of inclination increased.

After developing a basic understanding of the compressive behavior of the MPCLC devices, a series of additional experiments were conducted in which levers suspended weights at the end of a moment arm to augment the compressive effects imparted to the weight sensor.

Augmentation of Force Created by Weighing Operation

Sensitivity and reproducibility in the weighing operation were maximized using a second-class lever principle, traditionally studied in physics as a "nutcracker." The lever was then coupled with a simple mechanical mechanism for raising and lowering the weight-bearing beam, as depicted in the sketch in Figure 9-30. The etched edge, square, aluminum Mylar device shown in Figure 9-30 is depicted as item #2 in Figure 9-6.

The plate mounting and electrical bridging information are shown in Figure 9-7. An open-ended shielding consisting of a rectangular cardboard structure covered with grounded aluminum foil and painted black on the interior was constructed to fit over most of the device structure. The open end of the shielding cover was of sufficient size to allow the manual raising and lowering of the weighing beam.

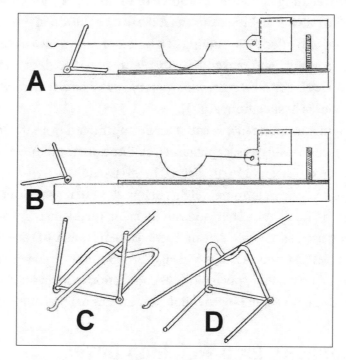

Figure 9-30. *A simple levered weight determination apparatus*

Lifting the lever off the sensor between weighing allowed the capacitor to expand back to its rest position and re-establish the baseline. Visual attainment of the baseline condition was monitored with the DAQFactory strip chart recorder display. When the display visually appeared to be constant with time, the capacitance's actual numerical value was read off the input channel value table to define the baseline. While in its elevated position, the beam was loaded with the weight to be measured. Loading the elevated beam ensured that the capacitor plates were not disturbed or compressed accidentally.

To begin the weight determination the beam and weight were lowered back onto the sensor, which begins to respond to the compression. The DAQFactory display also monitored the increase in capacitance of the sensor from the new loading. When the increased load tracing became constant with time, the actual numerical value of the DAQFactory channel table was again read and recorded.

To determine the device's actual response to the applied weight, the tare weight of the empty beam must be subtracted from the total weight measurement. In the current good laboratory practice (cGLP) protocol, a "standard" weight is weighed before and after the processing of a batch of samples to determine their weights. In keeping with the cGLP protocol, the empty beam weight correction can be measured several times before starting the weighing of a series of known or unknown weights and once or twice after completing the batch weighing exercise. A close correlation of the observed beam empty weight before and after the weighing of a batch of calibration or unknown weights assures you of the reliability and reproducibility of the observed data for the batch at hand (see *Standard Methods for the Examination of Water and Wastewater*, 23rd ed. (American Water Works Association, 2017)).

The beam weight correction factor can then be subtracted from the total values measured to generate the weigh vs. capacitance calibration or unknown weights of the batch processed (see the discussion on levered beam usage).

Attempts to use levers to determine weights below 20 to 10 mg are limited by the downward force of the small mass being measured, being unable to bend or move the leaves of the MPCLC being used as a weight sensor. To measure between 100 and 10 milligrams, the small triangular MPCLC seen as item A in Figure 9-33 can be used with a battery-powered Arduino and an auxiliary powered USB connection to generate the calibration data required for use in this low weight range without any additional mechanical aids.

Design Parameters for a Weighing Device

To design, build and validate a weighing device, the experimenter may find a modular system is the most flexible and useful. A certain amount of modularity has already been developed in the separation of the capacitor sensor, microprocessor data collection, and host computer windows or Python/Linux graphical trace-numerical display.

Capacitive sensor design depends upon the application. Weighing requirements involving grams can be realized with discrete plates made from aluminum foils and dielectrics in accordance with Table 9-1. For samples of very small mass and weighing tasks involving fractional gram measurements, smaller square plates or triangular forms of capacitor plate which are more difficult to fabricate and assemble can be used (see devices A and B in Figure 9-3).

Simple square and rectangular devices are by far the easiest to build. If the extra effort to add additional supporting tabs is put into the device construction, the sensor can be used in the vertical plane to measure force or angle of inclination. Rectangular or square devices are also the most robust when in service, especially with devices fabricated from aluminum Mylar composites with their lower component count and higher sensitivity in terms of capacitance change per unit of weight (see Table 9-1).

Intuition suggests that the thicker the sensor, the more compressive range is available for making measurements. Sensor sensitivity appears to increase if the square plate format is tapered to minimize the sliding friction between the plates. In Figure 9-31, the sensitivity is gained at a loss in the dynamic range of measurement.

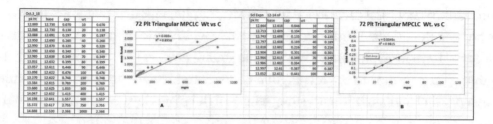

Figure 9-31. *Weight vs. capacitance for a small triangular Al-Mylar sensor*

Figure 9-31 shows that as the size of the mass being weighed increases, the quality of the least squares' linearity fit deteriorates. The R^2 variance is 0.8958 for the 1000 mg range in A. It rises to 0.9815 in the 100 mg range. (Recall that in statistical analysis theory, a perfect least squares fit has a variance of 1.)

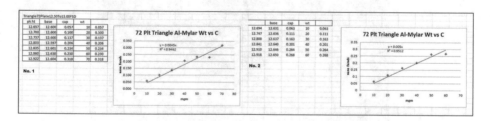

Figure 9-32. *A reproducibility study for a small triangular Al-Mylar sensor*

Figure 9-32 is a dual graphical display prepared from the data collected during a repetition of the determination of the capacitance values measured from a 10 mgm to 60 mgm loading of the tapered capacitor.

In Figure 9-33, the square capacitor device, depicted as item B in Figure 9-34, was used at different scale expansions to measure the detector response to capacitor loadings varying from 10 to 100 mgm.

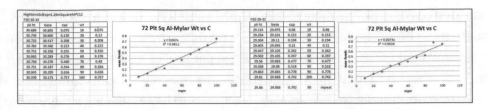

Figure 9-33. *A small square Al-Mylar sensor high sensitivity display*

After a great deal of experimentation with square and triangular devices, a compromise concept was envisioned for the MPCLC. Rectangular plates are more easily created than tabbed squares. If the length to width ratio of the rectangle is large, the "wedge" formation problem distorting the square devices could be eliminated. By assembling the sensor with the rectangular plates at right angles to one another rather than in a parallel configuration, the long length of the plates lays flat on one another and only form a compressible capacitor, where the square area of the ends overlap.

A high number of plates can easily be assembled into a relatively flat, uniform small area surface. Device C in Figure 9-34 is the first iteration of a long-leaved, overlapping ends sensor. Rectangular plywood stiffeners were needed to keep the long plates from buckling when heavier weights were applied to the sensing overlapping plate area.

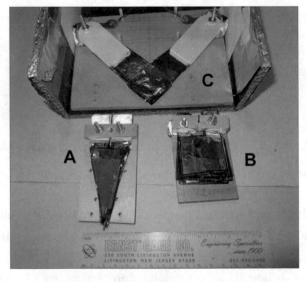

Figure 9-34. *Three Al-Mylar experimental sensors*

Figure 9-35 displays a plot of the device capacitance against the weight applied to the sensor. The overall response curve displays the inverse curvature expected for these devices, as originally predicted in Figure 9-2.

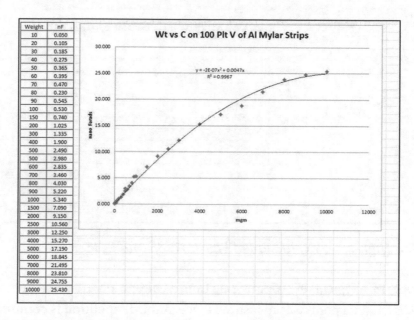

Figure 9-35. *Wt. vs. C for 100 plt. Al-Mylar V -shaped MPCL*

Figure 9-36 depicts the linear portion of the observed detector response in Figure 9-35.

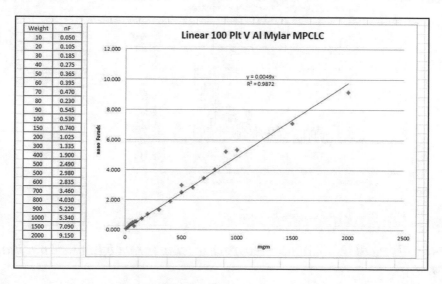

Figure 9-36. *Linear portion of Figure 9-34*

Figure 9-37 indicates that if the setup can resolve capacitance values less than 0.050 nF, the detector should detect single-digit milligram weights.

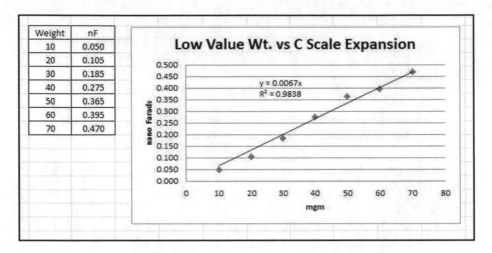

Figure 9-37. *High-scale expansion of Figures 9-35 and 9-36*

In Figure 9-38, a typical recorder tracing from a calibration measurement session is displayed. Each data point was measured twice. A third repetition is conducted in data pairs in which the difference between the two repetitions appears to be larger than expected.

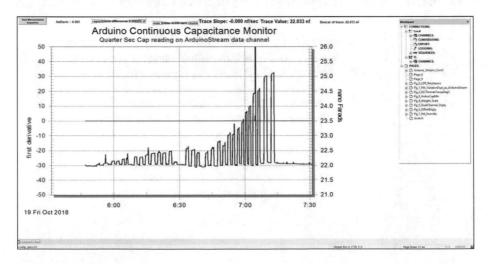

Figure 9-38. *Typical DAQFactory recorder tracing for weight vs. capacitance experiments*

While attempting to extend the weighing technique to lower limits, the 100-plate device began to show erratic and sometimes no response to weights in the 10 to 20 mg range. It was suspected that the small weights did not have sufficient mass to overcome the stiffness of the capacitor plates to generate a measurable compression. After being relieved of heavier weights, the plates returned by expanding their original configuration in a reasonably reproducible manner.

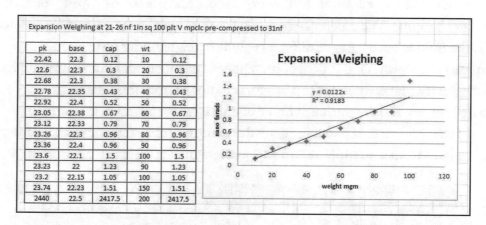

pk	base	cap	wt	
22.42	22.3	0.12	10	0.12
22.6	22.3	0.3	20	0.3
22.68	22.3	0.38	30	0.38
22.78	22.35	0.43	40	0.43
22.92	22.4	0.52	50	0.52
23.05	22.38	0.67	60	0.67
23.12	22.33	0.79	70	0.79
23.26	22.3	0.96	80	0.96
23.36	22.4	0.96	90	0.96
23.6	22.1	1.5	100	1.5
23.23	22	1.23	90	1.23
23.2	22.15	1.05	100	1.05
23.74	22.23	1.51	150	1.51
2440	22.5	2417.5	200	2417.5

Figure 9-39. *Sensor expansion weighing*

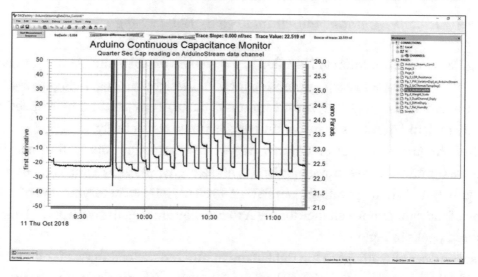

Figure 9-40. *Recorder tracing from compression-expansion weight calibration*

Expansion weighing was conducted by compressing the sensor with a bar on two adjustable supports to the point at which the device registered a 31 nF value. In the compressed state, with the trace off the top of the scale, a weight was placed on the sensor. The compressing bar was then removed and the sensor allowed to expand, carrying the weight to be measured. The trace dropping in value comes back on the scale and drops to a position above the original baseline where it can stabilize. Removing the weight from the sensor allows for further expansion, and the trace drops to the vicinity of the original baseline. The difference between the final baseline value and the "plateau" value is the induced capacitance difference for the weight under test.

Expansion determinations occasionally appear to suffer from the same inability to move the device plates when the test weight is removed from the sensor.

To definitively explore the lower limits of the 100 plate "V" sensor, a series of milligram weights were prepared from regular grade aluminum foil. Figure 9-41 depicts a set of weights from a nominal 12.9 to 1.07 milligrams.

Figure 9-41. *Representative milligram weights 12.9 to 1 mg*

Regular grade aluminum foil is rolled to a thickness of 0.016 mm. Aluminum has a density of 2.70 g/cm³ and a square centimeter of foil weighs 4.3 mg. In Figure 9-42, A, B, and C are folded and single thickness coupons of 3 cm², 2 cm², and 1 cm², respectively. D and E are half and quarter square centimeter fractions, respectively.

When the Arduino is powered by a battery or 12 V regulated supply, the noise from the USB is removed from the system display, and a high scale expansion can be used (see Figure 9-4.) When operating at an FSD of 0.150 nF, a DAQFactory tracing of a double reading of the capacitance change for the A to E milligram weights is displayed in the numbered peaks in Figure 9-42.

A second set of readings to the right of the numbered deflections was completed. Although plagued by baseline shifts, they were not markedly different in basic numerical capacitance difference values than the initial measurements.

The use of weights with a nominal mass value of 1 mg indicates that the aluminum-Mylar plates respond to such small entities and do so with reasonable reproducibility.

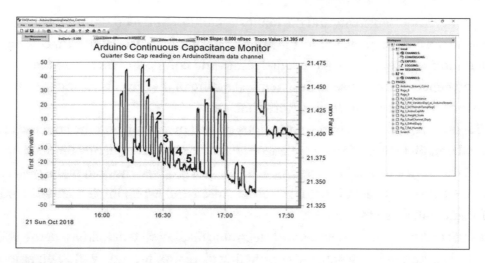

Figure 9-42. *Recorder tracing from nominal 12.9 to 1.07 mg weights*

Discussion

Static Friction and Self-Compression

Although the sensor has no moving parts, it has surfaces that move with respect to each other. Motion between surfaces in direct contact with one another is impeded by friction. Friction is further classified into static and sliding. Sliding friction is usually lower than static, which is consistent with our physical observations that once an object is moving, it is easier to keep it moving than it was to "break it free."

Insights into the physics of large, flat-plate capacitors are found in physics literature (see https://pdfs.semanticscholar.org/ff77/36f012a67a6d29fe3a6da29d46a7a51 af930.pdf).

Increasing the sensitivity of the multiple plate capacitor load cells is an example of the development methodology in which a simple concept of initially successful experimentation can logically develop a more refined and useful device.

The initial concept of using a multiple leaved capacitor as a replacement for a "spring" or "leveled levers" envisioned a simple square device mounted on a flat plate with two bolted electrical contacts through tabs on the right and left upper corners of the capacitor. Initial success led to further work, in which a more sophisticated electronics capacitance measurement technique and a visual display program were added to continually monitor and display the capacitance changes as weights or compression were applied to the DUT.

With increased sensitivity and the ability to monitor and record the capacitance changes in the capacitor over time, the limitations of the square, large surface area configuration were evident. Different dielectrics and composite "metal-on-plastic" films measured capacitor response as the chemical nature of the dielectrics and the physical dimensions or shape of the devices were changed.

With large square devices, the limitations caused by friction and the stiffness of the metal and dielectrics plates were encountered. It was subsequently reduced by tapering the device to a point. Tapering of the device reduced the area of the plates. More sensitive electronic detection systems were required and, when implemented, produced the predicted increased sensitivity.

As the sensitivity of the devices and electronic display system increased, the effects of physical alignment of the tapered conducting plate tips, together with their smooth, flat surface texture became important. Attempts to improve the alignment problem in the tapered devices led to extra pins in the base plate to hold both the conductors and dielectrics in place. Experiments with dual tabs on the device plates and the addition of alignment pins between the threaded electrical contact posts gave more consistent alignment.

The fragile nature of the materials of construction suggests that new devices should be assembled carefully and tested for freedom from short circuits as the number of conductor plates and dielectrics increases. As the number of leaves of each new device assembled increased, it is expected that the device capacitance should increase proportionally; however, observations showed that the incremental capacitance went up at a rate higher than expected for the number of new plates and dielectrics added. A simple explanation for the inordinate increase in observed capacitance lies in realizing that although the fragile, tapered aluminum foil plates and dielectrics are very thin and lightweight, their weight is not negligible. As the number of plates increases, their combined weight compresses the layers beneath, elevating the observed device total capacitance above that expected from the added incremental number of plates.

Determining Self-Compression and Angle of Inclination

While attempting to quantitatively evaluate the relationship between capacitance increases with the plate addition, I realized that self-compression added to the device total capacitance. Self-compression could be eliminated by rotating the DUT from the horizontal to the vertical about the axis running through the clamped ends of the device.

Rotation of a tapered device assembled from materials producing the best sensitivity to date, behaves as expected and separates the inherent device capacitance into two values with and without self-compression.

A simple set of experiments using drafting triangles to set the DUT to the common angles of 30, 45, and 60 degrees revealed that the device self-compression capacitance could measure a rough approximation of the angle of device inclination.

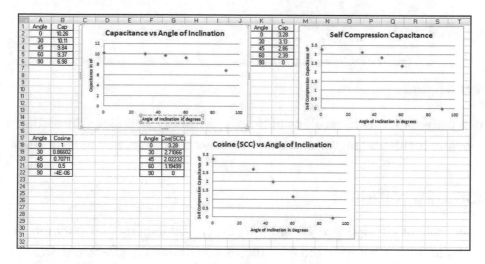

Figure 9-43. *Capacitance values and angle of inclination*

In Figure 9-43, the total observed capacitance drops as the DUT is rotated about an axis in the plane of the base and perpendicular to the triangular shape center line. Rotation separates the inherent capacitance of the device from that due to self-compression. The upper left plot varies from 10.26 nF at zero degrees of inclination to 6.98 nF in the vertical position. Plotting the capacitance due to self-compression (i.e., observed total capacitance–inherent device capacitance) against the angle of inclination produces the expected curve seen in the upper-right plot in Figure 9-43.

If a rigorous physical analysis is conducted on the system, then the downward weight vector at no angle of inclination is due to the gravitational pull on the mass of the plates in the capacitor. Rotation of the device out of the plane at right angles to the gravitational pull vector divides the force into two components, as depicted in Figure 9-44 of the inclined plane. The gravitational force is given by $F = m \times g \times \cos\theta$, where θ is the angle of incidence in radians, m is the mass of the object, and g is the local gravitational constant.

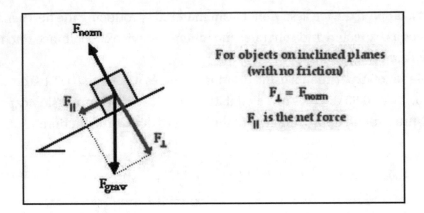

Figure 9-44. *Inclined plane*

A plot of the capacitance resulting from the downward gravitational force (determined by the angle of incidence) produces the linear relationship illustrated in Figure 9-44.

Device Capacitance

In the four drawings in Figures 9-45 and 9-46, the typical incremental assembly of a multiple plate capacitor assembled from discrete components is depicted. In each frame, the conductive plates are labeled alphabetically. The insulating dielectrics are numbered. Each increment in the illustrative device is a single capacitor unit consisting of a dielectric between two conducting plates.

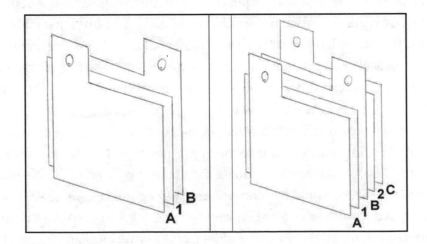

Figure 9-45. *Two and three plate devices forming single and double capacitor sensors*

In Figures 9-45 and 9-46, the total number of capacitor units is one less than the number of plates in the sensor unit. The presence of the conducting plates limits the charge collection or capacitor effect to a single insulator plate. Each insulator plate has an air gap on either side for devices built with discrete components.

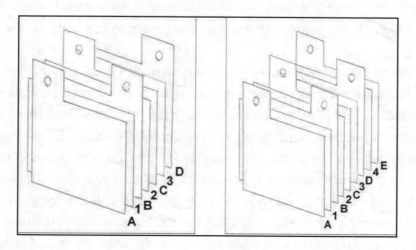

Figure 9-46. *Four and five plate devices forming three and four capacitor sensors*

Classical physics provides the mathematical relationship between the capacitance storage capability of a three-plate device and its physical and chemical properties of the dielectric and space between the conducting plates, in the form of the following mathematical model.

$$C = kA/d$$

C is the device capacitance. k is the proportionality constant determined by the nature of the dielectric between the plates and the permittivity of free space and air. A is the area of the conducting plates. d is the distance between the conductors.

In terms of the three-plate device, you could write the equation as

$$C_{Total} = k * A_{A-B} / d_{A-B}$$

Since the total capacitance of two devices connected in parallel is additive, we could write the following for the five-plate device.

$$C_{Total} = (k * A_{A-B} / d_{A-B}) + (k * A_{B-C} / d_{B-C})$$

For a horizontal device, the weight of plates B, C, and dielectric 2 compress the device and decrease the distance d_{A-B}, making the total device capacitance higher than the simple sum of the two parallel plate devices.

When the number of capacitors increased to three parallel units, the total number of plates increased to seven. The bottom-most device was compressed by the weight of the two units on top of it. The middle device was compressed by the weight of the topmost unit.

If the three-plate capacitor incremental units were all a relatively uniform weight, then the weight induced compression would increase as the horizontal stack gets thicker. The increase in total device capacitance for the horizontal unit being assembled should be a linear function of the number of capacitors in parallel and the increase in capacitance from the weight induced compression of the lower members of the device.

A semi-quantitative estimate of the contribution to the device's total capacitance resulting from self-compression can be made by rotating the device 90 degrees. The observed capacitance due to self-compression of the 15 dielectric VT-PE device was seen to be 1.88 nF. The total horizontal capacitance value of 9.10 nF decreased to 7.22 nF as the device was rotated from the horizontal to the vertical. The larger 50-plate tapered VT-PE went from a horizontal capacitance of 27.72 nF to 22.71 nF in a vertical position. The 15 dielectric device displayed a 20.6% reduction in observed capacitance during the rotation. the 50 dielectric device displayed an 18.1% decrease. A carefully built, Al-Mylar, 80 plate, triangular device with etched edges transited from 85 to 52 nF when rotated from horizontal to vertical, a decrease of 39%.

An assembled sensor has an inherent wedge-shaped air gap from the tightened threaded fasteners to ensure electrical contact. Each device's capacitance is unique when assembled. rotation appears to expand and reduce the angle of the "wedge," altering the inherent capacitor value by amounts varying from about 20% to 40%.

Initial experimentation with devices having short electrical connection tabs caused the MPCLC sensors to form wedge-shaped air gaps. Wedge-shaped air gaps are most disruptive in tapered plate sensors. Poor tip alignment, ample plate flexibility, and lack of mechanical support from the underlying capacitor plates made the initial tapered sensors susceptible plate distortion during load manipulation. Only later was the need for longer tabs realized to reduce or minimize the wedge shaping in the active area of the weight transducer. An MPCLC with a wedge-shaped profile, when viewed from the side, has the same profile as a lever. The further the weight being tested is from the fulcrum, the larger is the moment arm. The device becomes sensitive to the position of the weight.

Intuition suggests that increasing the number of plates should make a "bigger spring" with a wider dynamic range. If much longer tabs are created, and an alignment tab is added to the plates, the problems of a wedge-shaped air gap and plate tip misalignment can be minimized. Longer and multiple tabs on the plates increase the time and effort required to build, assemble, and validate the device.

Materials of Construction

To convert force to capacitance, the multiple plate transducer must be compressed to decrease the distance between the plates causing the device capacitance to rise. Metals are considered incompressible. The dielectric and air gap between the plates are the components doing most of the compacting. Premium grades of heavier aluminum foils are less desirable in this application than inexpensive, thinner grades of material that have more flexibility.

The same "thinner is better" criterion should apply to the selection of the dielectric. New thin "stretch and seal" polyethylene films virtually do not work in this application. The "stretch and seal" films are manufactured to adhere to the substrates over which they are stretched, which is exactly the opposite of the physical action required for this application. The very thin polyethylene films used in the "produce" bags or numerous other polyethylene film bagging or wrapper applications that utilize the "non-stick" property of this inert plastic can assemble reasonably inexpensive, fully functioning devices.

After assembly and before conducting any experimental measurements, the device should be tested with a VOM for short circuits caused by misalignment of the plates and dielectrics, or some other source of leakage, such as over-tightening of the threaded connectors, or tab clamps, causing a mechanical failure of a structurally fragile, dielectric or foil plates.

The original envisioned concept for the capacitance load cell consisted of a stack of independent, parallel, conducting plates and insulating dielectrics. Experimental improvements have shown that longer tabs, plates with additional alignment tabs and tapered composite materials can produce sensitive devices.

The simplest and most easily assembled form of weight sensor is produced from rectangular aluminum foil plates with many types of commonly available materials as insulators. Each device must be checked for linearity or utility over its desired range of use. The shape of each individual device plotting of capacitance vs. weight must be examined to determine its useable linear or curved range of utility.

The sensitivity of these devices is limited by small weights not exerting enough force to overcome the coefficient of static friction between the plates of the stack. A small weight must depress the stack. Since the device is a collection of interleaved equal length plates emanating from a common point, the stacked assembly forms a series of radials or a segment of a circle when viewed in cross-section. Depressing the top plates causes the contacting surfaces to slide over one another. If the coefficient of static friction is too high, the plates will not move, and no change in capacitance is measured.

Minimization of friction (as found in load cells made from the single sheet aluminum deposited onto Mylar) is probably one of the major contributors (in addition to having only one air gap per plate) to the high sensitivity of these cells. In contrast to the Al/Mylar devices, load cells made from aluminum foil plates and "stretch wrap" cannot flex or and hence exhibit concave upward curved, limited utility, weight vs. capacitance change, responses.

Changing the nature of the dielectric to a softer, more compressible medium such as a paper-type material greatly extends the dynamic range of the device, as seen in Table 9-1.

Weight Manipulation, Data Generation, and Interpretation

Because the capacitance of these devices varies with the pressure applied to the top plate, manually placing and removing the weights can cause spikes and baseline shifting when the plates are depressed or shifted sideways by an unsteady hand. For larger weights that are easier to grip and manipulate, disturbing the plates is a relatively minor problem. With small weights such as 10 mg, disturbing plate alignment or depressing the plates at high sensitivity settings can destroy reproducibility and the ability to collect usable data. Mechanical transporting devices in which the weight sits on a bridge that slides over the capacitor produces the experimental capacitance recordings seen in Figure 9-47.

Although the sliding bridge can minimize plate disruption, it causes the complex tracings seen in Figure 9-47. Even with the bridge supporting the tiny weight, the plates are often inadvertently depressed when sliding the weights off the bridge, as in repetitions 10 and 12.

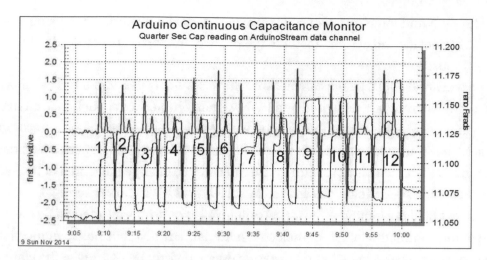

Figure 9-47. *10 mg weight measurement repetition*

A system of direct upward lifting with a weight tray that is only lifted upward can be devised to minimize plate disturbance when changing weights. A second-class lever or an arrangement of hooks and loops can produce direct vertical only motion. An alternate option uses a light plate compression to "bias" the baseline and minimize plate disturbance (see Figures 9-39 (expansion weighting), 9-72, 9-73, and 9-74).

You must be prepared to experiment and investigate the properties of the device fabricated for a specific purpose. Problems such as the time required for the device to stabilize under compression, re-establish a baseline when unloaded, whether a re-zeroing mechanism must be implemented, system linearity, system noise both random or systematic and the problem of sensitivity and "sticking plates" must all be evaluated when creating a weight sensor.

Measurement of Force

An Experimental Anemometer and Wind Pressure Gauge

When mounted in the vertical plane, the MPCLC sensor responds to any force that compresses the multiple plate capacitor leaf array. If the MPCLC were to be mounted vertically in a vented box and a moving air stream is directed to impinge at right angles to the plane on the vertical front surface of the hanging array, flow over the plate and exit the box at the rear of the sensor, a signal proportional to the wind speed can be created.

A simple "wind force" proof of concept experiment can be performed using a powered fan positioned at right angles to the plane of the top plate of a vertically mounted sensor.

A pocket wind speed gauge can measure the gas velocity generated by the fan as the power to the fan motor is regulated by a PWM signal. The sensor capacitance change can be calibrated in the horizontal position with a series of known weight values. Once calibrated and returned to the vertical position, the windspeed or airspeed velocities can be correlated with resultant pressure by the capacitance change measured at the various wind speed or airspeed velocities created by the various PWM power settings.

In the vertical position, the sensor capacitance is not primarily affected by the weight of the conducting plates or dielectric material. The distance between the plates is still expected to be wedge-shaped, tapering down to virtually nothing at the clamped electrical contacts at the top of the device. At the opposite end of the sensor or "bottom end," the free-hanging plates are only influenced by plate weight through the small-angle formed between the vertical and the angle of the "wedge" (see Figure 9-43). Intuition suggests, and observation confirms that as the device is rotated from the horizontal to the vertical, the interplate distance, especially at the bottom edges, increases.

Device sensitivity in the vertical orientation is expected to be similar to that seen in horizontal weighing applications and is limited by the flexibility of the capacitor plates. The deforming force must bend the plates whether plate stiffness is due to the coefficient of static friction or the rigidity of the material of construction.

Experiment

To function in the vertical plane, a dual tabbed triangular plate MPCLC was assembled from 80 plates of Al-Mylar composite. Plates were 3½ in (9 cm) wide at the base and 4 in (10.2 cm) at the apex. Electrical contact was established in the usual manner, with the outside tab of the left- and right-hand plates being mounted with the requisite electrical contact foil bridge on a threaded rod. The inner tab of each plate was fitted over a fixed wooden dowel positioned to hold the plate in a fixed alignment.

During the assembly and testing of the vertical mounting of the device, the final sensor capacitance at rest was measured with an Extech EX505 multimeter at 94 nF. When the device was placed into service with the DAQFactory SCR display, the baseline was stable at 90 nF. Further adjustments on the tilting mount electrical connections disturbed the sensor plates. A second meter reading of 84 nF was confirmed with the

DAQFactory displays during sensor calibration in the horizontal position. Figure 9-48 is a recorded trace of the dual measurement of a series of weights between 20 mg and 1½ g.

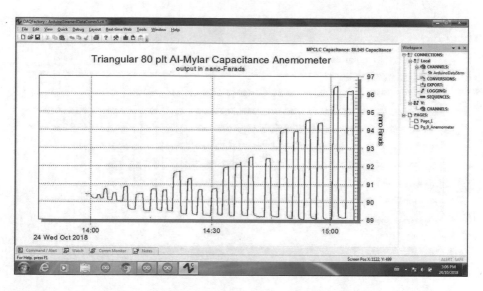

Figure 9-48. *Anemometer sensor horizontal 20 mgm to 1½ gm calibration (deflections not in order of ascending mass)*

The numerical data corresponding to the chart deflections in Figure 9-48 represent the weight vs. capacitance change data presented in Figure 9-49.

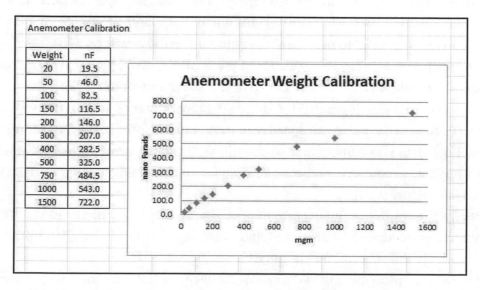

Figure 9-49. *Anemometer sensor horizontal weight calibration*

515

The data generated when the anemometer sensor is moved between the vertical and horizontal is depicted in Figure 9-50.

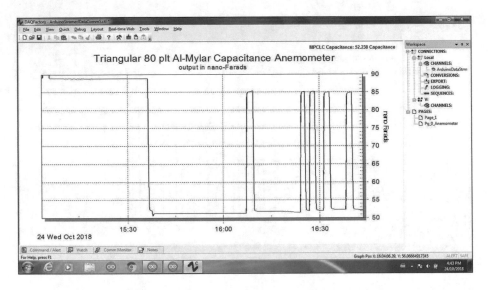

Figure 9-50. *Anemometer sensor horizontal to vertical transition capacitance change*

Variable Speed Wind Generator

To provide a controlled but variable wind speed, a fan powered by a 12V DC brushless motor (BLDC) can be used with a microcontroller or computer-generated pulse width modulation (PWM) signal to provide a programmable wind pressure.

A current control methodology using the pulse width modulation (PWM) technique was assembled with a TIP 122 Darlington pair transistor and an RPI GPIO pulse generator, as depicted in Figure 9-51. A simple Python Tkinter slider GUI from the library was used to control the fan motor speed with PWM pulse widths set by the Python-Tkinter Slider GUI. When implemented, the RPi-GPIO library array output was only able to exert coarse control over the motor speed and proved not suitable for the control required (see Figure 9-55).

Initially, the control circuit using the TIP122 Darlington pair with the RPi GPIO 3.3 V output had to be replaced with an Arduino PWM signal at a nominal 5 V output to provide a much better fan motor control with Listing 9-3.

Figure 9-51 depicts the schematic used initially to control the wind source power for the anemometer.

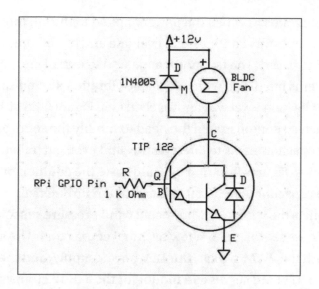

Figure 9-51. *Anemometer fan motor speed control circuit*

In Figure 9-52, a pocket wind speed gauge correlates the velocity of the air being moved by the fan. The gauge was mounted on a pair of threaded rods to estimate the air velocity at various distances from the fan.

Figure 9-52. *Wind velocity correlation with fan motor speed*

Experimental programs in which the power applied to the fan motor was incremented in 10% units was conducted to evaluate and record the capacitance change as the wind speed increased. The fan motor appeared to initially respond to the RPi-GPIO PWM increments but did so with noticeable vibration and noise and lost speed as the 100% power application level was approached (see Figure 9-55 at 17:05 and beyond).

The experiment also demonstrated the need to modify the setup as air currents caused the fragile capacitor plates to lift, separate, and even get pulled up-stream into the rotating fan blades. Figures 9-53 and 9-55 illustrate the addition of a cardboard cover plate to protect the capacitor leaves from the air stream turbulence.

Figure 9-53 depicts the vertical un-protected wind pressure sensor, fan, and the small circuit board with three sets of green screw terminal connectors. The screw terminals accept the wires with the PWM signals, the 12 V power supply, and the connections to the fan motor. The perf board serves as a mount for the TIP 122 transistor, diode, and resistor components of the circuitry depicted in Figure 9-50.

In Figure 9-53, the triangular cover plate was cut from thin cardboard like that used in office file folders. It only has two perforations to fit over the threaded rod binding posts. The cover plate hangs loosely from the binding posts at ¾ in (18 mm) from the base plate as determined by the lengths of the wooden dowel capacitor plate positioning posts.

Figure 9-54 illustrates the sensor cover plate mounted in position over the pressure sensor.

Figure 9-53. *Wind velocity sensor setup with air turbulence protector*

Figure 9-54. *Wind velocity setup with air turbulence protector in place*

A second wind speed experiment was conducted using the PWM drive from an Arduino Uno. Pulse width values for a program of increasing fan power were entered manually into the Arduino code in Listing 9-3 using the serial port to transmit the required numerical values. A series of 16 entries of digital values incremented from 0 to 255 in 16-unit intervals were used to collect the measured capacitance as a function of wind pressure.

The fan motor responded smoothly in a quiet and virtually vibration-free incremental power increase from nothing to full power when the PWM signals were generated by the microprocessor.

Observations

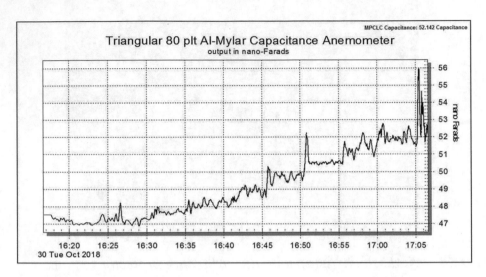

Figure 9-55. *Measured capacitance at ten percent increments of PWM fan motor power from RPi GPIO pin 18*

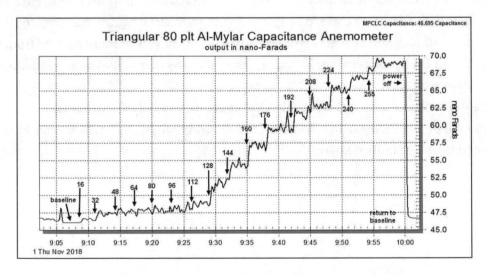

Figure 9-56. *Measured capacitance at indicated RPi-Arduino PWM power levels*

A continuous correlation between the airflow velocity measured with the hand-held meter and the PWM power applied to the fan motor was not observed or measured. In low-power-level applications, the wind speed produced does not move the gauge indicator into stable, clearly defined numerical ranges. The gauge fluctuations are unreliable at values under 3 meters/second. Power applications of 240 and 255 place the gauge indicator at 4 m/s (9 mi/h).

If the data in Figure 9-49 estimates the slope of the linear portion of the weight vs. compression capacitance calibration plot between the 50 and 100 mg standards, then

```
Slope = (543) / (1000)
      = 0.543   nF/mg
```

Division of the slope by the observed, estimated nF capacitance from the compression at full fan power from Figure 9-55 of 69 nF suggests a compression force of 127 mg.

Discussion

Figure 9-55 was reproduced on two different occasions. It appears that the PWM signals from the RPi are suffering from the timing errors known to be caused by the operating system. Figure 9-55 shows substantially more noise and erratic incremental power responses than Figure 9-56.

Substitution of the Arduino for the RPi GPIO PWM signal source is unnecessary if any one of the software upgrades for correcting or bypassing the timing conflicts of the GPIO array is installed.

Figures 9-48 to 9-56 individually depict and document the development of a proof-of-concept anemometer and wind pressure gauge utilizing a MPCLC as a sensor. The setup was assembled from repurposed components developed or assembled for other exercises in this work.

Figure 9-49 shows that the plot of weight vs. nF is reasonably linear with a slope of the plot calculated at 0.543 nF/mg. In Figure 9-49, the sensor's change in capacitance is reproducible and varies between 85 nF and 52 nF.

In a horizontal position, the sensor has a measured capacitance of 85 nF due to self-compression that changes to 53 nF when the device is rotated to the vertical configuration and the direction of the weight is no longer a compressing factor. The rate of change of measured capacitance with increasing weight applied to the top plate of the sensor remains constant for incremental weights up to about 1500 mg, according to Figure 9-49.

If a series of weight determinations are made between 100 mg and 300 mg, the graphical trace shows that the same rate of change of capacitance for the increment of weight exists for a series of weight determinations made between 400 mg and 500 mg. Figure 9-48 shows that a series of weighings made at two or more points within the linear portions of the calibration curve must have the same slope or sensor response factor.

If no alterations are made to an apparatus other than rotating a calibrated MPCLC sensor from the horizontal to the vertical configuration, the sensor response factor remains constant. Figure 9-50 records a loss difference of 32 nF between the horizontal and vertical orientations of the sensor. The position change shifts the apparent vertical sensor response to a value 32 nF lower than that observed in the horizontal position. In Figure 9-50, a 32 nF shift in the capacitance axis is well within the linear range of the sensor calibration.

Figure 9-56 indicates that driving the fan at full power creates sufficient pressure on the MPCLC to generate a 69 nF response and register a wind speed of 9 miles per hour (4 m/s).

As calculated, the vertical sensor response of 127 mg at full fan power is equivalent to a total weight applied over the entire surface area of the top plate of the sensor. Each triangular plate is 3.5 in (8.8 cm) at the base 4 in (10.1 cm) with a tip ⅜ in (1 cm) wide. The triangular plates are a trapezoid with an area of 7.75 in^2 or 48.8 cm^2 that can calculate the wind pressure on a per unit area base.

Figure 9-56 suggests possible linearity between the upper half of the fan motor power range that may be useful in measuring wind speed and wind pressure. The initial minimal response to increasing wind speed may be due to several factors. A shield had to be placed over the top plate of the sensor to keep the leaves in place at higher wind velocities. The relatively heavy cardboard may be absorbing a portion of the wind energy.

A second factor contributing to the low slope at low wind speed may be the high number of 80 plates in the sensor. Recall that in attempts to measure low values of weights, MPCLC with a smaller number of plates and a smaller surface area provided better sensitivity.

Figures 9-49, 9-50, and 9-51 indicate that the concept does work and that the system can be scaled with an experimental development program to suit your needs.

Pressure

Mathematically pressure can be modeled as the quotient of force, and area thus measurements of pressure are in dimensions of force per unit of area. Pressure can be created by a gas, liquid, or solid pressing against a surface.

Measurements of Pressure

Recalling the general physical properties of definitions of solids, liquids, and gases, pressure measurements are relatively simple for non-compressible liquids and finely divided solids in a gravitational field. The pressure at any depth in these materials is given by the total weight of the material above the point of interest divided by the area supporting the weight.

Measurements of gas pressures require more sophisticated transducers than those used to measure weights and areas. In 1634, E. Torricelli described a 34 ft high (10.4 meter) water column barometer for measuring the atmospheric pressure. Torricelli later developed a more compact device with mercury that was only approximately 80 centimeters in height that became known as a *mercury barometer*.

In 1646, Pascal suggested that the air had weight since as the observer went upward in altitude, the weight of the atmosphere above the observer's position became smaller, and the atmospheric pressure lessened. In 1654, Otto von Guericke publicly demonstrated the air pump he had invented and illustrated the immense force with which the air pressure would seal together a pair of copper hemispheres with smoothed contacting surfaces. The demonstration used what became known as the Magdeburg Hemispheres that are still used in physics education today.

Many units for measuring atmospheric or barometric pressure have been developed for earth sciences, weather forecasting, altitude determinations, and medical applications. At sea level and 20°C, the various atmospheric pressure units are tabulated in Table 9-4.

Table 9-4. *Atmospheric Pressures*

Imperial Measure	Metric Units
14.696 pounds/square inch	101325 Pascals (N/m^2)
29.9212 inches of mercury	760 mm of mercury

Atmospheres and bars are units that often refer to elevated pressures expressed in multiples of the unit sea level pressure at either the standard temperature of 0°C or the normal temperature of 20°C.

Since the atmospheric pressure is known to decrease at a known rate as altitude increases, it is possible to use a barometer as an altitude indicator. The following formula calculates a pressure altitude in meters above sea level.

$$\text{Pres. Alt.} = 44330 \times [1 - (P / P_o)^{1/5.255}]$$

P is the measured pressure at altitude. P_o is the atmospheric pressure at sea level. If the altitude is accurately known at the point at which a pressure measurement is made, then it is possible to rearrange the formula above to get the sea-level atmospheric pressure as follows.

$$P_o = P / [\, 1 - (\text{Altitude} / 44330)]^{5.255}$$

The known altitude is meters above sea level. Engineering and climatology references have the corresponding calculations in both imperial pressure units and inches or millimeters of mercury column heights.

The Bosch company used the piezoelectric crystals discussed in Chapter 6 to develop the BMP180 and BMP280 pressure sensors. The miniature sensors are 3 mm square by 1 mm thick, SMT, IC devices available from several manufacturers on 1.5 cm square prototyping or breakout board mounts. Adafruit Industries supplies the board mounted sensor and Arduino libraries to implement an atmospheric pressure monitoring system. (Adafruit BMP280 I2C or SPI Barometric Pressure & Altitude Sensor, P/N 2651, $10 USD.)

Atmospheric pressures usually vary over many hours or days unless weather extremes are involved. A more useful readout for these devices consists of the traditional strip chart record. By converting the Arduino code created by the sensor board supplier to print only the raw temperature and pressure data as a continuous sequential stream to the serial port, as depicted in Figure 9-56, the DAQFactory charting modules can be used for long recordings.

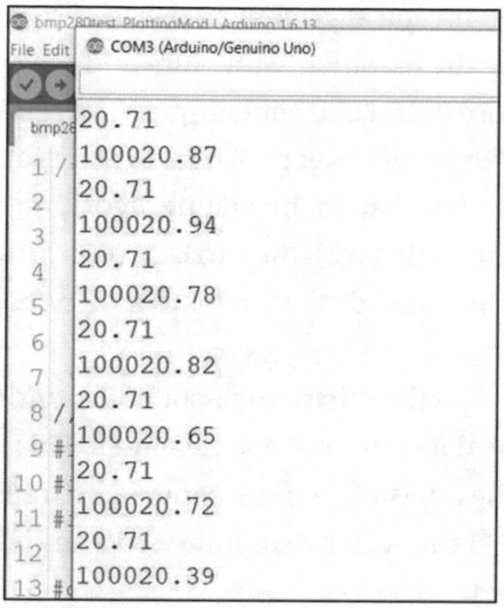

Figure 9-57. *Arduino serial monitor output of temperature and pressure for DAQFactory plotting*

Two DAQFactory sequence codes for processing multiple sequential data values appearing on the serial port are presented as Listings 9-5 and 9-6. Program 9-5 was initially developed to process the data stream seen in Figure 9-57. After several tests, the simple logic of the program would randomly interchange the barometric pressure and temperature data on the plotting display as it simply read the first number in the cleared buffer.

Examining the code shows that each data point sent from the Arduino was transmitted with a line feed and a carriage return to signal the end of the data transmission. The DAQFactory sequence is written, so the first parsing based on a ReadUntil(13) locates the first data point and transfers the data to a channel identified as data0 holding the data from the first variable being charted. A second parsing code locates the second value of the dual parameters being charted. It transfers it to a second channel named data1, holding the data points of the second variable to be plotted. The code in this sequence is for use only with dual data points that are significantly different in magnitude. The ambient temperature can only vary from subzero to 45°C, so the need to distinguish which channel to plot, as the temperature is axiomatic. The plotting channel assignment may need to be changed each time a new plotting session is started since this simple code can start reading data as either temperature or pressure in the first channel.

While attempting to modify the algorithm to always assign the larger number to the channel representing the barometric pressure and the smaller number to the temperature channel, a more useful and general-purpose serial port processing utility was developed. Listing 9-6 expects a stream of data to arrive at the serial port in a sequential comma-delimited format. In the polling algorithm, the code finds the end of the comma-delimited data string with the carriage return/new-line combination (CHR13), then parses out the single data values and assigns each to a data channel for plotting.

Both programs require that the microprocessor code sends the correctly formatted data to the serial port. If the data format seen in Figure 9-57 is used, the plotter assignments may need to be adjusted. A more general and reproducible DAQFactory code sequence in Listing 9-6 can read two or more comma-delimited data points streamed into the serial port.

Figure 9-58 depicts a DAQFactory page containing a graphical display of the temperature and atmospheric pressure surrounding the sensor board on my desktop. Three variable value displays were added to the graphical record to adjust the graphical scales for temperature and pressure should the traces drift off the scale and determine the sea level pressure for the local atmospheric pressure being recorded.

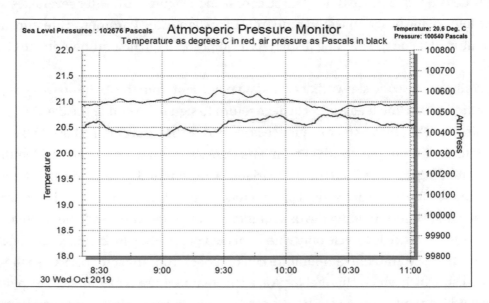

Figure 9-58. *A Typical DAQFactory atmospheric temperature and pressure display*

Instruments to measure atmospheric pressures with columns of liquid are not flexible, portable, nor robust. Unwieldy columns of liquid led to the development of aneroid systems that were without fluids. Aneroid barometers use the flexing motion of diaphragms or bellows to measure pressure. Gas and liquid pressures are commonly measured with a compact aneroid device known as a Bourdon tube. Eugéne Bourdon, a French watchmaker and engineer, invented the tube in 1849. Curved, flattened Bourdon tubes, the elastic element in most dial-type pressure gauges, as seen in Figure 9-59, are still in common use today.

Bourdon pressure gauges operate on the principle that when the interior of the flattened tube is pressurized, the tube attempts to re-inflate. Having been formed into a "C" shape, tube inflation causes the structure to expand. The mechanical force generated is used to move a lever, connected to an indicator sweeping over a calibrated, circular dial face. Bourdon tubes are manufactured in C, helical, and spiral shapes. The thickness and type of material from which the flattened tube is made determine the range of pressure measured with these devices.

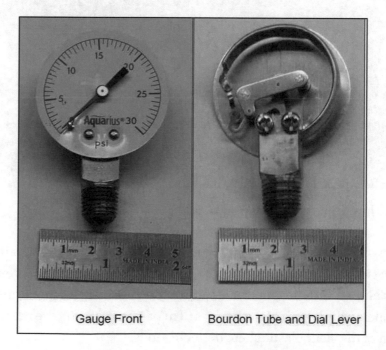

| Gauge Front | Bourdon Tube and Dial Lever |

Figure 9-59. A Bourdon gauge

Bourdon tubes are typically manufactured from stainless steel and phosphor bronze.

Part C: Sensor Construction, Calibration, and Optimization

Sensor Construction

For the construction of smaller, sensitive devices, jigs to promote uniformity in the size and shape of the components being fabricated are recommended. For experimenters assembling aluminum-Mylar devices that may require many aluminum foil, electrical contact bridges, several jigs to aid in cutting and perforation can be fabricated from readily available materials. Figure 9-60 displays several of the jigs used in the construction of weight sensing devices.

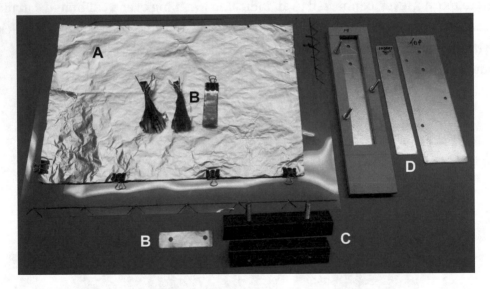

Figure 9-60. *Jigs for component preparation*

Item A is a triple layer of kitchen or regular grade aluminum foil a foot in width (30.5 cm) and often cut in about 14 in to 16 in (34 cm to 39 cm) lengths. The three sheets are aligned and clamped with the paper clamps, as shown. A marking pen is then used to lay out lines parallel to the length of the bridges (3 in or 76 mm) using the markings visible on the bottom of the clear plastic sheet under the foils.

Perpendicular to the broadly spaced lines, the closely spaced marking indentations lay out the parallel lines of the bridge widths of ¾ in (18 mm). The clamped foils are then cut along the ¾ in lines to form 1 foot long (30.4 cm) strips of ¾ in (18 mm) wide foil marked at 3 in (76 mm) intervals. The bridge "blanks" are then cut from the long strips to generate ¾ × 3 in foil strips (18 × 76 mm). The blanks are then stacked into groups of 100 as seen in the clamped bunches B. (Alternatively, 3 in or 76 mm wide columns can be cut and sectioned into ¾ in or 18 mm wide strips for perforation in jig C.)

When cut and stacked, the blanks are clamped between C, the angle iron jig faces, and the bolts are tightened until the foils form a hard aluminum bar. Then the hard compaction is drilled with a ¼ in bit (6 mm) to form the final bridge foil, as seen beside the white B (see also Figures 9-61 and 9-62).

Item D is the jig to perforate rectangular Al-Mylar plates. Rectangular blanks of the composite material are cut from the larger sheets and loaded into the plywood form with the drilled metal bottom. When all the blanks are loaded into the jig, the drilled metal insert is placed on the top of the blanks and the jig top plate added with any spacers required to compress the blanks with the bolts through the assembly. When tightly compressed, a hammer and a leather punch can be used in the top holes to perforate the blanks with the requisite number of holes. (Use a wooden base when driving the punch to avoid damaging the cutting edge of the hole cutter.)

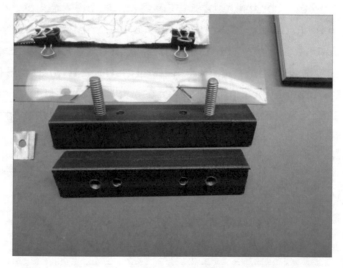

Figure 9-61. *Details of foil bridge preparation jig*

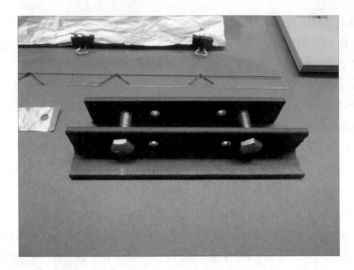

Figure 9-62. *Details of foil bridge preparation jig*

Sensor Calibration

Certified weight standards consisting of stainless steel or brass defined masses can be
expensive and difficult to obtain. In North America, electrical wiring for homes and
businesses is regulated for safety. The allowable size of the copper wiring used in various
electrical power supply systems is defined by the American Wire Gauge (AWG) system.
Table 9-5 tabulates some physical properties of a small selection of the commonly
encountered AWG copper wiring used in light-duty, domestic wiring applications.

Table 9-5. *Copper Wire Physical Properties*

AWG	O. D. in	O. D. mm	lb/1K ft	Ω/1K ft
12	0.0808	2.053	19.8	1.59
14	0.0641	1.628	12.4	2.52
16	0.0508	1.291	7.8	4.02
18	0.0403	1.024	4.92	6.39

Copper has a density of 8.96 g/cm³ at room temperature (20°C/68°F) and is relatively corrosion-free if kept at room temperatures and at moderate relative humidity. Number 14 gauge copper wire, as used in housing applications, is a readily available material from which a selection of relatively accurate, known masses of copper can be prepared.

Electrical wiring is prepared in large quantities with a relatively constant diameter, as suggested in Table 9-5. The constant diameter of a #14 ga Cu wire is specified as 1.628 mm. If the wire diameter is constant and known, the weight of a given length of the wire can be calculated from the following formula.

$$Mass = ((dia./2)^2 \times \pi \times length) \times density$$

In the formula, *dia.* is the measured diameter of the wire, π is approximately 3.1416, *length* is the accurately known length of a wire coupon, and *density* is the known density of copper metal.

A series of compromises must be accepted when generating an inexpensive substitute for an expensive set of calibrated weighing standards. The inexpensive, readily available, easy-to-work-with constant composition material is only available in one physical format consisting of a long thin wire. The range of mass standards that can be fabricated from manageable lengths of short wire is limited. Handling wire lengths less than a quarter of an inch or 6 mm is difficult. The lower weight limit is that represented by a 6 mm wire coupon. Wire coupons over two inches in length or 48 mm are in some cases too long for the weight, mass, and force testing sensors to accommodate and defines the upper limit of the mass range set of standards. Higher lengths than 2 inches or 50 mm can be prepared and carefully bent double or into whatever shape is desired if required.

To evaluate the errors to be expected in preparation of a set of known copper mass standards, four sets of eight calibration units each were prepared in my workshop and then weighed on a laboratory 1/10 milligram analytical balance or scale. The lengths of coupons cut were in the nominal form of the nearest whole millimeter metric equivalents of wires varying in lengths from a quarter of an inch or 6 mm to 2 in or 48 mm. The coupons were cut in ¼ in or 6 mm increments. Figure 9-63 depicts the four sets of test specimens that I prepared.

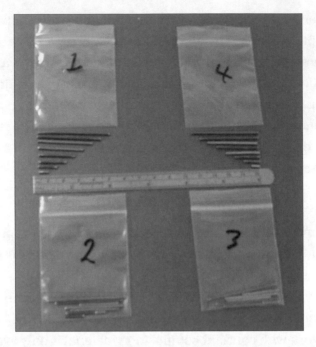

Figure 9-63. *Copper wire mass standards for statistical analysis of typical preparations*

The individual units were created from wire lengths cut several mm longer than the intended final length of the standard being prepared. The initial wire cuts were made with a pair of hand-operated side cutters that produced a pair of beveled ends on the coupon cut (see the large cutters in Figure 9-64). The wire standard being prepared was then gripped in a pair of square nosed pliers with the beveled end protruding in an orientation perpendicular to the plane formed by the edges of the plier jaws (see Figure 9-65). The protruding beveled copper end was then hand filed to a smooth circular cross-sectional area, at right angles to the wire length.

Figures 9-64 and 9-65 depict the hand tools and techniques to prepare and trim to size the required wire lengths for creating the standard copper masses.

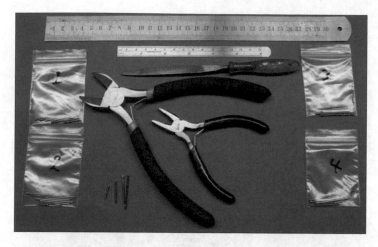

Figure 9-64. *The hand tools to prepare copper wire mass standards*

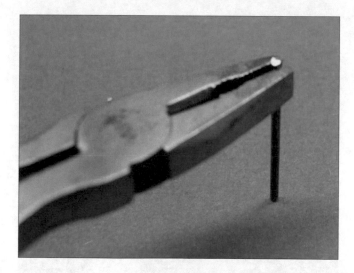

Figure 9-65. *A copper wire gripped and positioned for end face filing*

The second beveled end of the cut standard was then filed to a flat square end, and the length of the wire coupon measured on the millimeter scale. The length of the coupon under preparation was adjusted by filing the ends of the wire while being held in the vertical position with the pliers. Care must be taken in gripping the coupon being prepared to minimize the damage to the outer surface of the piece and ensure that the end face is as close to being a "square cut" as is possible.

Figures 9-66 and 9-67 are magnified images of the beveled ends as cut on the left and prepared for length determination on the right.

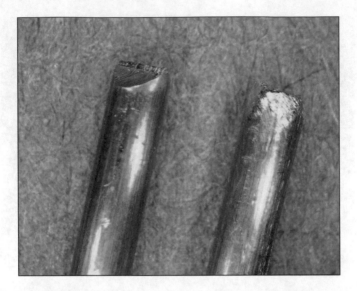

Figure 9-66. *Copper wire ends*

Figure 9-67. *Copper wire ends*

Table 9-6 tabulates the data collected and calculated for the four sets of prepared standard weights. The copper wire diameter was measured at 1.61 mm, consistent with the #14 ga marked on the cable insulation. The diameter was used with the individual coupon nominal lengths and the published density for copper at room temperature to calculate the mass of the standards.

Table 9-6. *Measured and Calculated Physical Properties of Prepared Copper Wire Mass Standards*

Preparation and Validation of Copper Wire Masses For Use As Standard Weights									
Cu wire diameter =	1.61	(#14 AWG)	Volume factor =	0.01824109					
Wire length mm	Measured Weight							Theoretical Weight	Percentage Error
	Set 1	Set 2	Set 3	Set 4	Average	Std. Dvn.	Diff in Avrg		
6	0.1107	0.1141	0.1165	0.1086	0.1125	0.00351	0.1063	0.1094	-2.77
12	0.2205	0.2186	0.2189	0.2170	0.2188	0.00143	0.1099	0.2189	0.07
18	0.3331	0.3251	0.3309	0.3254	0.3286	0.004	0.1099	0.3283	-0.09
24	0.4274	0.4396	0.4461	0.4410	0.4385	0.00793	0.1100	0.4378	-0.17
30	0.5468	0.5476	0.5546	0.5449	0.5485	0.00424	0.1141	0.5472	-0.23
36	0.6682	0.6613	0.6593	0.6614	0.6626	0.00389	0.1005	0.6567	-0.89
42	0.7664	0.7581	0.7607	0.7671	0.7631	0.00438	0.1108	0.7661	0.40
48	0.8706	0.8742	0.8780	0.8727	0.8739	0.00312		0.8756	0.19

Table 9-6 has a column labeled "Diff in Average" in which the incremental difference between the average value for the next longer coupon and the previous coupons is calculated. Each increment in the length of the series is 6 mm. The theoretical weight for a 6 mm increment is 0.1094. The reasonably close values in the column serve to validate the incremental mass value increases in the averaged data.

The percentage error of the averaged data with respect to the theoretical values also suggests that the technique is relatively reproducible. A measure of the typical error to be expected with the technique can be estimated by examining the spread in observed masses with respect to the expected theoretical value. Table 9-7 tabulates the typically expected error as seen from the spread of measured weights in the four prepared sets of standard copper wire masses.

Table 9-7. *Typical Error from Spread in Observed
Mass Values of Copper Standards*

Standard Length	Theoretical Weight	High Value	Low Value	Spread Value	Percentage Error
6	0.1094	0.1165	0.1086	0.0079	7.2
12	0.2189	0.217	0.2205	0.0035	1.6
18	0.3283	0.3331	0.3251	0.008	2.4
24	0.4378	0.4461	0.4274	0.0187	4.3
30	0.5472	0.5546	0.5449	0.0097	1.8
36	0.6567	0.6682	0.6593	0.0089	1.4
42	0.7661	0.7671	0.7581	0.009	1.2
48	0.8756	0.878	0.8706	0.0074	0.85

Examining the values in the "Percentage Error" column conforms to an often-observed effect in which the error analysis reveals the decreasing effect of errors made in determining the length of the coupon as the overall length of the DUT increases. The shortest and longest entities have the highest and lowest errors, respectively.

A lower number gauge of copper electrical wiring, being a thicker or heavier material per unit of length, can be used to fabricate heavier masses. A longer length of a higher gauge or narrow electrical wire can be weighed to determine the approximate weight per unit length and then cut to the lengths required to create lower mass standards.

After fabrication, the copper rods should be washed with soap and water or a solvent to remove any finger oils, grease, or dirt that may be on the surface of the standards. Once cleaned, good laboratory practice (GLP) recommends that only forceps or tweezers handle the standard masses.

For standard masses below the nominal 100 mg copper unit, 1.0 centimeter-wide strips of regular-grade aluminum foil can be used. For the regular grade of foil, the thickness is 0.016 mm. Each square centimeter of the foil is $1.0 \times 1.0 \times 0.0016$ or 0.0016 cm^3. Aluminum has a density of 2.70 g/cm³. Each centimeter of the strip is 4.32 mg (see Figure 9-41).

Weight or Force Sensor Optimization

In summary, an MPCLC is a flat, very thin, inexpensive sensor that is easy to build and use. Devices can be built in a small or shaped format for sensitive low mass applications or larger, more robust devices for use with heavier masses and forces.

MPCLCs are nonlinear over much of their sensitive range, require time and care to assemble, calibrate, and often require multiple readings to improve accuracy.

As a final portion of this weight, mass, and force exercise, instrumental systems were assembled using several techniques and methods developed during the years over which the properties of this type of sensor were examined.

To optimize the signal obtained from a MPCLC the following operations and techniques are suggested.

- To minimize the noise present in the recordings of the capacitance tracing the Arduino should be powered from a battery and connecting USB cables should have ferrite beads or collars to reduce high frequency noise.

- The conducting plates of a capacitor can act as an antenna for electromagnetic interference, be disturbed by air currents and expand and contract with temperature differences. These perturbations caused by exposure to the local environment can be lowered by encasing the sensor in a thermally insulated, grounded metal shielding.

- Situate the sensor on a level, vibration free surface.

- For both discrete aluminum foil plates and insulating dielectrics or Al-Mylar composites the capacitor insulators must be wide enough to prevent short circuiting between conducting plates (Al-Mylar etched or coated edges).

- Alignment posts in addition to electrical contact posts on all plates can aid in plate alignment and reduce signal variation during compression and expansion.

- High sensitivity systems using the thin aluminized Mylar foils need some form of mechanical mechanism whose action can reproducibly and uniformly apply the forces created by masses under test to the compressive capacitor plates without disturbing the alignment of the interleaved sensor during test mass changes.

- Simple rectangular plates are the easiest to fabricate and assemble.

- When an MPCLC is fabricated, the top plate that receives the compressive force should be a non-conducting dielectric, and any pressure distribution plates used can be perforated with ¼ in (6 mm) lightning holes.

Thus far, the capacitance of the MPCLCs was monitored by using the Arduino to measure the point at which the capacitor reaches the voltage equivalent to one time constant or 63.2% of the expected full charge. (Nominally the 5 V of the charging supply.)

A second technique for making high-resolution temperature measurements can also be used with a 555 timer IC to measure capacitance.

Figure 3-1 in Chapter 3 illustrates a 555 timer astable configuration in which the upper resistor in the R1-R2 RC network was replaced with the NTC thermistor to generate a pulse width differential in the timer IC output as the thermistor resistance varies with temperature.

A datasheet on any typical 555 timer shows that the frequency of the output in the astable state can be written as

$$\text{Frequency} = 1/\text{Time Period} = 1.44 / ((R1 + 2R2) * C)$$

If accurately known resistance values are placed in the Ra and Rb positions, respectively, the preceding frequency expression can be rearranged to the following.

$$\text{Capacitance} = (1.443 * T) / (R1 + 2*R2)$$

Since the time period of the 555 IC output and frequency bear an inverse relationship, any program able to measure the frequency of the timer IC output can be modified to measure the capacitance of the MPCLC. As seen in the preceding equation, the values of the charging resistors are in the denominator of the expression. If the values of these components are varied, the frequency and time period can be changed.

Listing 9-4 was written for 10 kΩ and 1 kΩ resistors that generate an approximate 6 KHz frequency with a 25 nF MPCLC.

The Arduino has a pulseIn() function to return the high and low microsecond times of the respective portions of a rectangular wave applied to the designated digital pin on the microprocessor. An output frequency of the timer chip can be obtained from the following three lines of code.

$$\text{hiTime} = \text{pulseIn}(2, \text{HIGH});$$
$$\text{lwTime} = \text{pulseIn}(2, \text{LOW});$$
$$\text{freq} = 1 / (\text{hiTime} + \text{lwTime});$$

Listing 9-4 implements the high, low pulse width summation method for using a 555 timer IC frequency to monitor the capacitance of an MPCLC. (A similar but higher resolution pulse width measuring function is the pulseInLong() that measures in microseconds. The long function has other program requirements. The Arduino documentation for the expression should be examined before the implementation of the function.)

Preliminary experiments invoking the concept of using an external source of a known defined electronic waveform, such as a 555 timer output that could then be passed simultaneously through two MPCLCs (one as a load sensor and the other as a reference to create a differential measurement to gain access to higher sensitivities for small mass determinations) were of limited success. The complex, high parts count, differential electronic systems, and multiple MPCLCs were difficult to assemble and coordinate. A better, much simpler method for determining the weights of small masses was developed.

Table 9-2 was assembled to document the small inordinate increase in capacitance due to self-compression as an MPCLC device is assembled. Intuitively the device response is expected to be proportional to the thickness of the "stack" of compressible capacitor plates. A thicker device with a larger number of plates should exhibit a high capacitance, a higher degree of compressibility, and a significant increase in capacitance under compression.

Table 9-2 reveals that the change in capacitance of the device when the plate number is increased from 5 to 10 with no compressive weight was 2.06 nF. The device has a capacitance of 0.206 nF (206 pF) per plate. The transition from 45 to 50 plates showed a no weight capacitance change of 3.50 nF or 0.07 nF per plate (70 pF). A smaller number of plates should provide a larger signal to noise ratio to weigh a smaller mass.

Experiment

To minimize the disturbance to the stacked plates' alignment and reduce EMI, a grounded, metal-encased overhead design was adopted to develop a prototype weighing apparatus, as depicted in Figures 9-68, 9-69, 9-70, and 9-71.

Figure 9-68. *A prototype overhead multiple plate capacitor load cell (OH-MPCLC) weighing system*

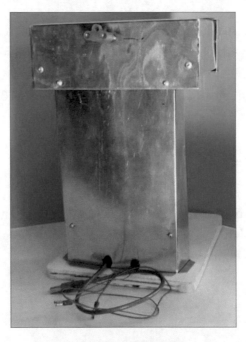

Figure 9-69. *Rear metal case panel of OH-MPCLC*

The red "banana plug" visible on the upper surface of the aluminum EMI and insulating rear panel is an electrical connection to the V-shaped MPCLC seen in Figure 9-71. Direct access to the load cell was created for validating capacitance measurements with external meters, which occur in low weight determinations or for invoking diagnostic processes to locate potential electro-mechanical failures in weighing operations.

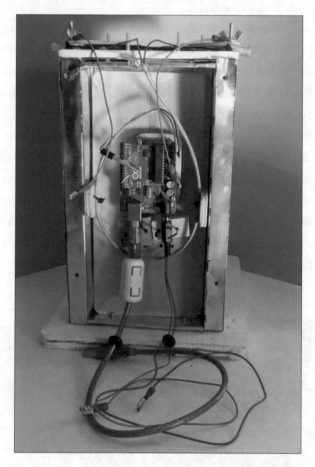

Figure 9-70. *Microprocessor mount, USB cable, and auxiliary power connections*

In Figure 9-70, the large white cylinder on the short insulated blue USB cable is an add-on ferrite bead, high-frequency noise attenuator that converts electromagnetic energy into heat. A metal box completely encases the microprocessor and MPCLC to minimize atmospheric and EMI interference. The metal case is connected to the ground pin on the Arduino headers. The red and green leads are the connections for the auxiliary battery supply that reduces the noise generated by the internal power supply of the Arduino (see Figures 9-4 and 9-5).

In Figure 9-71, you can see a clear plastic, diamond-shaped "pressure plate" with lightning holes. A thin, spring steel wire was glued to the plate with cyanoacrylate glue to form an attachment yoke with hooks at each end. The valleys in the hooks are centered in the holes immediately beneath the yoke ends so as the aluminum wires supporting the thin aluminum pan (see Figure 9-68) with an insect's exoskeleton, can be connected to the yoke and the compressive sensor.

The "weighing pan" is a thin aluminum disk bonded to the U-shaped aluminum wire suspension structure with cyanoacrylate glue. All the cyanoacrylate bondings had the surface area of contact maximized by forming a "Z" shape into the wire component of the joint being formed to fix the desired shape of the assembly while maximizing the strength of the bonded structure.

Thin plywood plates cover the long capacitor leaves to stop plates from buckling. At the rear of the sensor, the threaded rods compress the microprocessor copper connectors, aluminum foil bridges, capacitor plates, load spreading washers, and the red external banana plug connections. The load spreading washers are only visible as a gray arc beneath the plywood covers. The external connections to the banana plug terminate in the male portions of male-female disconnect electrical wiring fittings so the rear panel of the prototype instrument with the fixed banana plug feed-through can be separated from the unit for any required servicing or modifications.

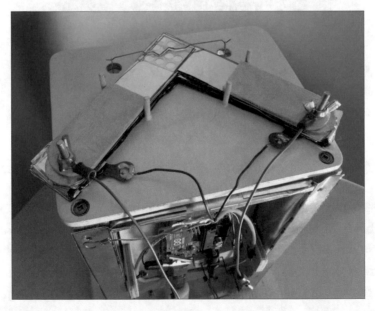

Figure 9-71. *The top plate of the OH-MPCLC*

A rectangular capacitor sensor leaf with a square right-angled overlapped compressive area was selected for ease of construction and assembly (see Figure 9-34 item C).

A spring steel wire yoke was initially epoxied to a thin aluminum pressure plate to minimize localized disturbance to the stacked leaves of the sensor. Each end of the yoke was bent into a hook shape to receive the ends of an aluminum wire "U" serving to support a weighing pan.

The arms of the "U" pass through two ⅜ in (1 cm) holes in the overhead platform to connect with the weight transfer yoke. A thin PET plastic pressure distribution plate perforated with ¼ in (6 mm) lightning holes was subsequently created for use on the OH sensor to lessen the weight of the sample, supporting assembly contribution to the total load on the capacitive sensor. The prototype unit contained a 160 plate MPCLC.

Simple over the center-offset round levers can vertically elevate the weight pan to minimize the transfer of mechanical disturbance to the leaves of the sensor. The actual lifting platform "floats" on a horizontal pin and can be lifted or shimmed as required to adjust the height at which the platform engages the bottom of the weighing pan. Figures 9-72, 9-73, and 9-74 depict a vertical lifting device in the elevated and lowered position and provide a close view of the lift components.

Figure 9-72. Weighing pan arrestor lowered position

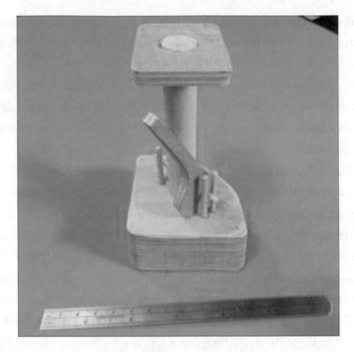

Figure 9-73. *Weighing pan arrestor elevated position*

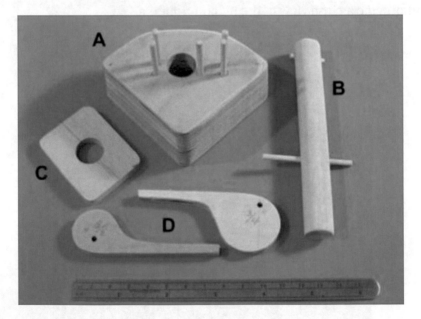

Figure 9-74. *Components of weighing pan arrestor*

A construction drawing is not presented as the arrester should be scaled to the device in use and fabricated from the materials at hand. My lift was built from plywood and wooden dowels and to avoid static accumulations was left in the unfinished state after sanding.

Item A in Figure 9-74 is the massive base block bored to accept a ⅝ dowel (15 mm) lifting post and 5, ⅛ in (3 mm) positioning dowels. Item B is the lifting post with the elevating axel at the bottom and the pin to support the movable top plate. Item C is the top plate. The items above and below D are a pair of offset center elevation levers providing a ⅜ in (1 cm) and ¾ in (19 mm) lift, respectively. The four outer paired pins serve to keep the lifting post axel in place as the post is raised and lowered. The inner pin adjacent to the lifted post serves as the inner retainer for the offset lever axle placed between the two outer post pairs on the extreme left and right in item A in Figure 9-74.

Figure 9-77 shows that weighing masses greater than 100 mg and up to 5 gm is possible without further calibration or device modification on the OH-MPCLC. The prototype device response for 20 to 10 mg is approaching the level of the baseline noise and is of limited utility for these lower weight values.

To determine weights at and below the 10 mg level, two devices were used: a 10-plate MPCLC assembled from tapered left- and right-hand leaves (see Figure 9-33 item A) and a baseline adjusting bridge (see Figure 9-26 item 2). The biasing bridge and weight sensor are depicted in the following two figures.

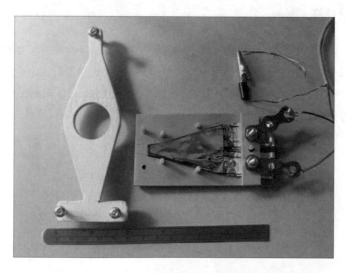

Figure 9-75. *A 10-plate isosceles triangle low weight MPCLC and biasing bridge*

Figure 9-76.   *Low mass weighing assembly with bias bridge in place*

In Figure 9-76, the ⅛ in (3 mm) diameter pins hold the bridge in place over the tapered leaf weight sensor. The baseline can be adjusted by raising or lowering the two screws on the long arm of the bridge. The left-hand edge of the hole in the bridge also places the calibration or test weights into the same position each time a mass-capacitance measurement is made.

Observations

A prototype OH-MPCLC (see Figure 9-68) generated the curve seen in Figure 9-77. With USB power, no air or EMF shielding, and a DAQFactory 64-point smoothing of the plotted tracing, the prototype could resolve 20 mg of weight. Powering the Arduino from a 9 V battery reduced the noise, so 10 mg was just resolved by the 1 in (24.5 mm) V-shaped sensor.

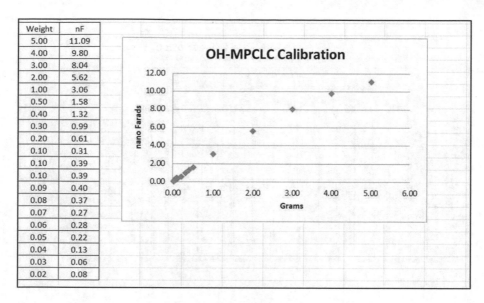

Weight	nF
5.00	11.09
4.00	9.80
3.00	8.04
2.00	5.62
1.00	3.06
0.50	1.58
0.40	1.32
0.30	0.99
0.20	0.61
0.10	0.31
0.10	0.39
0.10	0.39
0.09	0.40
0.08	0.37
0.07	0.27
0.06	0.28
0.05	0.22
0.04	0.13
0.03	0.06
0.02	0.08

Figure 9-77. *OH-MPCLC prototype 5 gm to 20 mg weight calibration*

In Figure 9-78, the noise reduction in the recorded tracing is again seen as the Arduino power supply is changed from the noise laden USB +5 V to a 9 V battery at 6:47. The baseline undergoes a substantial change from 34.9 nF up to 35.4 nF as the internal supply is supplanted by the battery power. (The Arduino can accept any battery or regulated power supply between 7 and 12 V.)

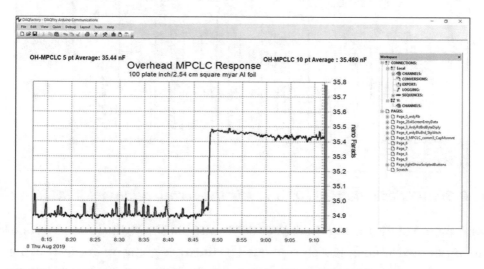

Figure 9-78. *Battery power noise reduction in OH-MPCLC baseline*

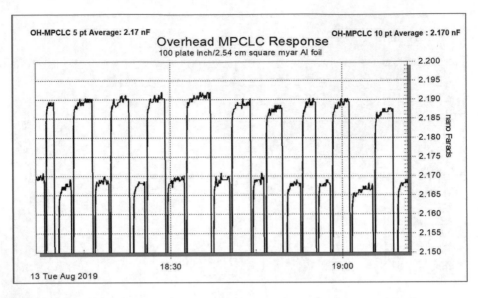

Figure 9-79. *Ten repetitions of 100 mgm weight with pulse width determination method*

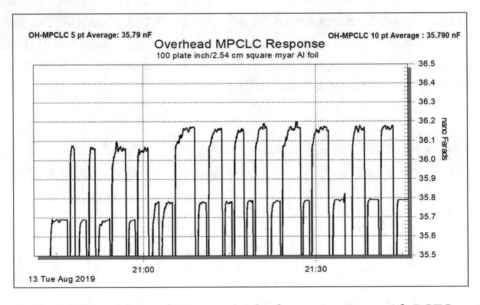

Figure 9-80. *12 Repetitions of 100 mg weight determinations with RCTC method*

Examination of the tracings in Figures 9-79 and 9-80 shows the lower baseline levels and the upper measurement levels separated by the trace going off the scale at the bottom, as the pan, pan support wire, and test weight, if present, are removed from the sensor by the pan arrestor (see Figures 9-68, 9-72, and 9-73).

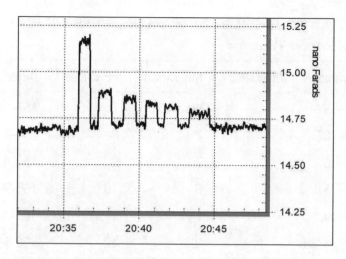

Figure 9-81. *100 mg to 10 mg calibration on 72 plate 1¼ x 2¼ in isosceles triangular MPCLC*

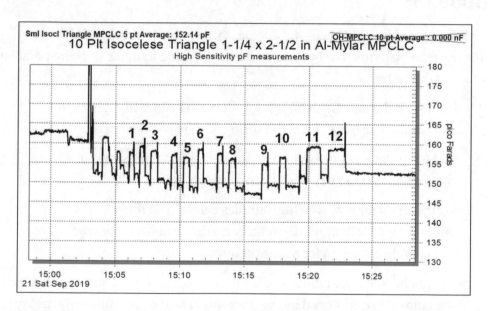

Figure 9-82. *Recording of 12 Repetitions of 10 mg weight determinations*

Table 9-8. *12 Numerical Height Measurement Repetitions of 10 mg Weight Determination Recorder Tracings*

Repetition	pF values	Difference	Repetition	pF values	Difference
1	157–152	5½	7	157–150	7
2	159–152	7	8	156–149	7
3	158–151	7	9	155–147	8
4	157–151	6	10	156.5–149.5	7
5	156–149	7	11	159–151.5	7½
6	158 – 148.5	9½	12	158.5–152	6½

Discussion

Using the optimized weighing scale prototype is much like handling any delicate scientific instrument in that the operator needs to become familiar with the peculiarities and foibles of the system.

1) Do not lift the pan any higher than what is required to separate the aluminum wire hooks from the spring steel yoke bent ends.

2) Move the elevation lever slowly and ensure that the spring steel yoke stays centered in the platform through holes.

3) Position and remove weights/samples carefully. If the pressure plate is disturbed, carefully realign everything before resuspending the pan for a mass determination.

Figures 9-79 and 9-80, both the single time constant measurement and the 555 timer duty cycle variation programs used by the microprocessor to continuously measure the capacitance, do not appear to differ measurably in their ability to reproduce weight-capacitance correlations. I preferred the simplicity of the RC-TC measurement technique implementation.

There seem to be several advantages and disadvantages to using the overhead sensor technique. Each sensor has a fixed capacitance when leveled and at rest with no added compressive load that is fixed by the self-compression caused by the plates' weight. As weights are added to the top of the stack, the distance between the plates decreases. The device sensitivity should theoretically move toward the left in the curve depicted in Figure 9-2 or toward increased sensitivity as interplate distance decreases. A decreasing plate distance caused by increasing sensor load simultaneously decreases the compressing sensor's dynamic range as the curvature rises toward the vertical with decreasing interplate distance.

Heavier weights compress a multiplate stack more than lighter masses and cause a larger measurable change in capacitance if the curvature of the capacitance—plate distance plot does not get too close to the vertical.

To monitor heavier weights or forces, identical rectangular plates are easy to fabricate, mount and, when used with a pressure plate, are less prone to mechanical disruption during service. An overhead configuration of the sensor and the mass allows the use of a vertical lift to minimize the disturbance to the leaves of the sensor stack. Variation in the vertical application of compressive forces during weight changes resets the baseline each time the device makes a measurement.

Lighter masses with lesser bending weight forces are best monitored with thinner, sensitive sensors consisting of tapered, left- and right-tabbed plates. The shaped leaves are more difficult to fabricate and mount, but fewer are required for a thin stack of increased weight sensitivity.

In Figure 9-82, the microprocessor continuous capacitance monitoring software automatically switches from measuring nanofarads to picofarads as the value of the input signal changes. The switch from nano to picofarads requires a reconfiguration of the DAQFactory display.

Experiments were conducted with levers in attempts to increase sensitivity, but only limited success was realized. In a normal lever configuration with the sensor beneath the fulcrum, the lever's weight compresses the MPCLC necessitating a thicker sensor. Preliminary experiments with inverting the lever and sensor so when at rest the sensor expands under gravity and is compressed when weight is added to the long arm of the sensor work, but the complexity of the setup was not further developed because I favored the more sensitive, thinner sensor seen in Figures 9-75 and 9-76.

Figures 9-34 A and 9-75 reveal that the 10-plate higher-sensitivity tapered sensor has had the plate tips cut off to form a uniform plate length of 2 in (49 mm). Removal of the bent and distorted pointed apex of the individual plates should allow them to lie flat against one another to produce a smoother, more reproducible bending action as the sensor flexes in service.

The tips of the 72-plate sensor in Figure 9-34 were bent in all directions and spread out over an eighth of an inch or several millimeters, both horizontally and vertically, so the sensitive tip areas of the device would not slide smoothly over one another as the tips flexed. The larger number of plates generated a capacitance in the 14 to 15 nF range that probably masked the rough behavior of the tip portion of the sensor in the compression of the thicker portions of the plates.

In Figure 9-81, the noise level of the 72-plate device is approximately 0.05 nF or 50 pF. In the trimmed 10-plate device in Figure 9-81, the noise level is approximately 1 pF.

Table 9-8 indicates that with the 10-plate triangular device, a 7 pF response was recorded for multiple replications of the 10 mg mass, weight determination. For weight determinations in this mass range, the area, shape, and thickness of the load sensor can be optimized through a development program and the DSP and display scale expansion of the SCADA software. The sensor and software optimization methods may need to be developed for handling and manipulating very small quantities of material.

Experimental development programs for optimizing the sensitivity of capacitor load cells are only limited by the time you have available since the cost of the materials used in the load cells is low.

Code Listings

Listing 9-1. Arduino Capacitance Measurement Using the ISRC Method

```
//CAPACITANCE Monitor with Moving Average
//Basic pgm clbrtd from knwn caps to vlu intrnl resistance
const int OUT_PIN = A2;
const int IN_PIN = A0;
const int numReadings = 32;   // MA array size
//Capacitance between IN_PIN and Ground
//Stray capacitance value will vary from board to board.
//Calibrate this value using known capacitor.
const float IN_STRAY_CAP_TO_GND = 24.48;
const float IN_CAP_TO_GND = IN_STRAY_CAP_TO_GND;
//Pull up resistance will vary depending on board
//Calibrate this with known capacitor.
const float R_PULLUP = 35.9;  // in K ohms
```

```
const int MAX_ADC_VALUE = 1023;
float capacitance = 0;
float uFcapacitance = 0;
//Moving Averages parameters
int index = 0;
float avrgdVlu = 0;            // MA value
float total = 0;              // sum of MA array
float MovAvrg = 0;
float readings[numReadings];    // # readings in MA
//

void setup()
{
  pinMode(OUT_PIN, OUTPUT);
  //digitalWrite(OUT_PIN, LOW; //This is the default state for outputs
  pinMode(IN_PIN, OUTPUT);
  //digitalWrite(IN_PIN, LOW);

  Serial.begin(9600);
  //
  // clear the MA array
  for (int thisReading = 0; thisReading < numReadings; thisReading ++)
  {
  readings[thisReading] = 0;   // zero the matrix elements
  }
}
//
//*************************************************************************
//
//*************************************************************************
//
void loop()
{
  //Capacitor under test between OUT_PIN and IN_PIN
  // Rising edge on OUT_PIN
  pinMode(IN_PIN, INPUT);
```

```
  digitalWrite(OUT_PIN, HIGH);
  int val = analogRead(IN_PIN);
  digitalWrite(OUT_PIN, LOW);
  if (val < 1000)
{
  //Low value capacitor
  //Clear everything for the next measurement
  pinMode(IN_PIN, OUTPUT);

  //Calculate and print result

  float capacitance = (float)val * IN_CAP_TO_GND / (float) (MAX_ADC_VALUE - val);

//***************************** MOVING AVERAGE *************************
  total = total - readings[index];  // subtract last reading
  readings[index] = capacitance;    // next cap reading
  total = total + readings[index]; // add cap to array
  index = index + 1;                  // increment index
  if (index >= numReadings)          // test position in array
  index = 0;                         // wrap around
  float average = total / numReadings;  // calculate average

  Serial.println(average, 6);
}
else
{
  //Big capacitor - so use RCX charging method
  //
  // discharge the capacitor (from low capacitance test)
  pinMode(IN_PIN, OUTPUT);
  delay(1);
  //
  // Start charging the capacitor with the internal pullup
  pinMode(OUT_PIN, INPUT_PULLUP);
  unsigned long u1 = micros();
  unsigned long t;
```

```
  int digVal;
  //
  //Charge to a fairly arbitrary level mid way between 0 and 5 v
  //Best not to use analogRead() here because it's not really quick enough
  // next is a do - while loop
  do
  {
    digVal = digitalRead(OUT_PIN);
    unsigned long u2 = micros();
    // next line selects either:or
    t = u2 > u1 ? u2 - u1 : u1 - u2;
  } while ((digVal < 1) && (t < 400000L));
  //
  pinMode(OUT_PIN, INPUT);   //Stop charging
  //Now we can read the level the capacitor has charged up to
  val = analogRead(OUT_PIN);
  //
  //Discharge capacitor for next measurement
  digitalWrite(IN_PIN, HIGH);
  int dischargeTime = (int) (t / 1000L) * 5;
  delay(dischargeTime);  //discharge slowly to begin with
  pinMode(OUT_PIN, OUTPUT);  //discharge remainder quickly
  digitalWrite(OUT_PIN, LOW);
  digitalWrite(IN_PIN, LOW);
 // calculate and print result
float capacitance = -(float)t / R_PULLUP / log(1.0 - (float)val / (float)
MAX_ADC_VALUE);
//
if (capacitance > 1000.0)
{
  // ***********************MOVING AVERAGE ***************************
  float uFcapacitance = capacitance/1000.0;
  total = total - readings[index];  // subtract last reading
  readings[index] = uFcapacitance;    // next cap reading
```

```
  total = total + readings[index]; // next position in array
  index = index + 1;
  if (index >= numReadings)         // test position in array
  index = 0;                        // wrap around
  float average = total / numReadings;  // calculate average
  Serial.println(average, 6);
}
else
{
//************************* MOVING AVERAGE ****************************
  total = total - readings[index];  // subtract last reading
  readings[index] = capacitance;    // next cap reading
  total = total + readings[index]; // next position in array
  index = index + 1;
  if (index >= numReadings)         // test position in array
  index = 0;                        // wrap around
  float average = total / numReadings;  // calculate average
  Serial.println(average, 6);
  }
}
while (millis() % 1000 != 0);
}
```

Listing 9-2. Arduino Code for ICFT Measurement of Timed RC

```
// Capacitance Meter Output in nano-farads
// A voltage divider forms a reference voltage of 2/3 or 66% of the final
// 5 volt charge Internal timers of the Arduino can be used to measure tau
// the RC time constant. With a defined precision 10K ohm resistor the
// capacitance can be calculated.
//
#define Rc 10000.0 // determine the actual resistance by measurement or
                        purchase
#define Rd 55.0
```

```
#define R1 40100.0
#define R2 21000.0
#define clockRate_us 16.0
//
const float k = 1/(clockRate_us*Rc*log((R1+R2)/R2));
volatile uint8_t TIFR1_Copy;
volatile uint16_t ICR_Copy;
volatile uint8_t ICR_Flag = 0;
volatile uint16_t TOV1_Ctr;
//***************************Moving Average Variables*********************
const int numReadings = 64; //a times 5 improvement in noise
float capacitance = 0;
int index = 0; //MA index variable
float total = 0; // MA total
float avrgdVlu = 0; //value of MA
float readings[numReadings]; //the MA array

void setup() {
  Serial.begin(9600);
  //Serial.println("OK");
  //clear the MA array
 for(int thisReading = 0; thisReading < numReadings; thisReading ++)
 {
 readings[thisReading] = 0; //zero the matrix elements
 }
  //
  MCUCR |= (1<<PUD); // Globally disable pullup resistors

  TCCR1B = 0; //Noise canceller off; Normal mode; falling edge; stopped
  TCCR1A = 0; //Normal code;
  TIMSK1 = (1 << ICIE1) | (1<< TOIE1); // Input Capture and Overflow
                                  interrupts

  DIDR1 |= (1 << AIN1D)|(1 << AIN0D); //Disable digital buffer on com
                                  inputs
  ACSR = (1 << ACIC); //Enable comparator capture
```

```
  pinMode(8, OUTPUT);
  pinMode(9, OUTPUT);
  digitalWrite(8, LOW);
  digitalWrite(9, LOW); //Both pins low - discharge

  delay(1000); // wait plenty of time for discharge
}

void loop(){
  float C;
  uint16_t dischargeTime;

  ICR_Flag = 0; //Initialize counters and flag
  TOV1_Ctr = 0;
  TCNT1 = 0;

  pinMode(8, INPUT); //Pin 8 set to input - high impedance
  cli(); // No interrupts between starting charge and starting timer
  PORTB |= (1 << 1); //Pin 9 set high - start charging
  TCCR1B = (1 << CS10); // Start Timer1
  sei(); // Let interrupts happen now
  while(!ICR_Flag) {} // Wait for charging to finish

  pinMode(8, OUTPUT); // Pin 8 set to output
  digitalWrite(8, LOW);
  digitalWrite(9,LOW); // Pins 8,9 low - start discharge
  // Calculate capacitance
  //Adjust overflow counter - if TOV1 is on and ICR is low -
  if ((!(ICR_Copy & (1 << 15))) && (TIFR1_Copy & (1 <<TOV1))) {
    TOV1_Ctr++;
  }
  C = k * (float)(((uint32_t)TOV1_Ctr << 16) | ICR_Copy);
  //****************************Moving Average****************************
 total = total - readings[index]; //subtract last reading
 readings[index] = C; // next cap reading
 total = total + readings[index]; // next position in array
 index = index + 1; // increment
 if (index >= numReadings) // test position in array
```

```
  {
  index = 0;
  }
  float avrgdVlu = total/numReadings; //calculate the average
  C = 1000 * (avrgdVlu); // convert micro to nano farads
  //
  Serial.println(C, 6);
  //Serial.print( "uF");Serial.println();
  dischargeTime = 1 + (uint16_t)(10.0*Rd*C/1000.0);
  delay(dischargeTime); // Wait at least 10 time constants
  if (dischargeTime < 250) {
    delay(250-dischargeTime); //Wait some more to limit printing
  }
}
ISR(TIMER1_CAPT_vect){
  TCCR1B = 0;   //Stop Timer1- CS12:CS10 = 0
  TIFR1_Copy = TIFR1; // Get overflow interrupt status
  TIFR1 = (1 << TOV1); // Clear overflow
  ICR_Copy = ICR1; // Get the ICR
  ICR_Flag = 1;   //Set the flag
}
ISR(TIMER1_OVF_vect) {
  TOV1_Ctr++; // Bump the overflow counter
 }
```

Listing 9-3. Arduino Anemometer Fan Motor Speed Control with Manual Serial Port Input

```
// Manual Set of PWM from Serial Port
// PWM pin 9 has a value set by the integer between 0 and 255
// entered from the serial port. (PWM pins 3,5,6,9,10 & 11)
//
int pwmPin = 9;
//
void setup() {
  // set pin mode and activate serial port
```

```
  pinMode(pwmPin, OUTPUT);
  Serial.begin(9600);
  }
 //
 void loop() {
  //check for serial input
  if (Serial.available())
  {
    int pulsWdth = Serial.parseInt();
    analogWrite(pwmPin, pulsWdth);
  }
}
```

Listing 9-4. Capacitance Measurement from 555 Timer Output Frequency
Variation

```
// n-Element Moving Average Frequency Determination Capacitance
// Measurement, Aug16/19 Hi and Lo pulse widths read with pulseIn(pn#,HI/
// LOW). Hi time and lo time values summed to get total cycle time that is
// inverted to get the 555 output frequency.
// Capacitance value calculated from Cv = 1.44/(21000 * freq). (times 10
// expn 9 nF) (Recall for floating point division f = (float)i / (float)j
// cast all ints to floats before division)
// diagnostic print lines and value identifications commented out for
// DAQFtry Python plotting from serial port data transmission
//
unsigned long duration;                 // 1st pulse width high signal
unsigned long duration_L;               // 2nd pulse width low signal
unsigned long tmSum;                    // pulse widths sum
float freq;                             // the frequency variable
int const numReadings = 16;             // #readings averaged must be
                                        //   dclrd "const"
unsigned long readings[numReadings];    // individual readings
int index = 0;                          // readings array index
unsigned long total = 0;                // the running total
unsigned long average = 0;              // the averaged value
```

```
//
int inputPin = 2;                              // digital PWM pin #2 to be used
                                               // for pulse counting
float capTnc = 0;                              // capacitance value of DUT
int Rc = 10000;                                // value of first charging
                                               // resistor in 555 RC cct
int Rd = 1000;                                 // value of second charging or
                                               // discharge resistor in RC cct
//
void setup()
{
  Serial.begin(9600);                          // set up serial comm
  for (int thisReading = 0; thisReading < numReadings; thisReading++)
{
  readings[thisReading] = 0;                   // initialize readings array
                                               // to zero
}
  //
  pinMode(2, INPUT);                           // define input signal on PWM/
                                               // dig I/O pins

}
//
void loop() {
  duration = pulseIn(2, HIGH);                 // fn waits for pin hi to
                                               // start time

  duration_L = pulseIn(2, LOW);                // fn waits for pin lo to
                                               // start time

  tmSum = (duration + duration_L);
  //Serial.print("tmSum =  ");                 // diagnostic
  //Serial.println(tmSumDiff);
  total = total - readings[index];             // subtract last entry
  readings[index] = tmSum;                     // collect current value
  total = total + readings[index];             // add current value to total
  //Serial.print("pre divide total =  ");      // diagnostic
  //Serial.println(total);
```

```
  index = index + 1;                          // next array position
  if (index >= numReadings)                   // if at end of array, wrap around
  {
  index = 0;
  }
  average = total / numReadings;              // calculate the average
  freq = 1 / (float)average;                  // calculate frequency from
                                              // square wave period

  // recall C/C++ requirement to cast ints to floats before division
  capTnc = (1.44/(21000 * freq)) * 1000;      // nF calculation
  //Serial.print("average  ");                // diagnostic
  //Serial.println(average);
  Serial.println(capTnc, 2);                  // output value to serial port
                                              // with 2 decimal places

  //Serial.print("duration_L  ");             // diagnostics
  //Serial.println(duration_L, DEC);          // comment out for DAQFactory
Python serial port usage
  //Serial.print("duration    ");
  //Serial.println(duration, DEC);
  delay(50);                                  // slow rate down?
}
```

Listing 9-5. DAQFactory Sequence Code to Parse Dual Sequential Serial Port Data Points

```
// This sequence auto polls Comm7 for streamed Arduino data
// ensure the null protocol has been selected in the protocol window
// and that the correct data is streaming into the DAQFactory serial
// port
// clear the buffer
device.comm7.Purge()
while(1)
   try
      private string datain = device.comm7.ReadUntil(13)
      private data = strToDouble(datain)
```

```
      ArduinoStream.addValue(data0)
    private string datain = device.comm7.ReadUntil(13)
      private data = strToDouble(datain)
      ArduinoStream.addValue(data1)
    catch()
      delay(0.1)
    endcatch
endwhile
```

Listing 9-6. DAQFactory Sequence Code to Parse Multiple Serial Port Data
Points for Plotting

```
// Parse Multiple Values from Serial Port in the order in which they are sent.
// Sequence auto polls COM3 for streamed comma delimited Arduino data.
// the order in which the data stream is to be parsed for the 1st, 2nd etc
   data points.
// Ordering the data plotting ensures the same variable is always assigned
   to the same trace.
// ensure the null protocol has been selected in the protocol window
// and that the correct data is streaming into the DAQFactory serial
// port. Data on the SP must be a carriage return/newline separated stream
   of n comma delimited values.
// Create n channels to hold the data for plotting ardyValu_1, ardyValu_2 etc.
// To parse out the data use a loop to find he cr/nl delimiters convert to
   numbers and Parse(datin,position #, ",").
// into data1, data2 etc values and then use channel.addValue(datan) to
   assign numerical values to the channels.
//
// clear the buffer
device.Com3.Purge()            // clear old data lines
device.Com3.ReadUntil(13)      // clear any partial line reads
//
while(1)
   try
```

```
    //parse first data point for plotting
      private string datain = device.Com3.ReadUntil(13)
      //?datain
          private data1 = StrToDouble(Parse(datain,0,","))
          ardyValu_1.AddValue(data1)
          private data2 = StrToDouble(Parse(datain,1,","))
          ardyValu_2.addValue(data2)
          private data3 = StrToDouble(Parse(datain,2,","))
          ardyValu_3.addValue(data3)
    catch()
      delay(0.5)
    endcatch
endwhile
```

Summary

A novel method for the determination of weight by following the change in capacitance in a compressible capacitor weight sensor with a microprocessors and host computer SCADA system was presented.

Compressive weight-sensing capacitors can be assembled from various inexpensive, readily available materials to determine sample weights over a substantial range of weight values.

Constructing a microprocessor-controlled weighing scale and instrument calibration weights assembled from inexpensive, readily available materials with simple hand tools was discussed.

Pressure and force measurement applications using commercial and experimenter assembled equipment were presented.

The techniques for collecting and storing experimental data are examined in Chapter 10.

CHAPTER 10

Data Collection, Storage, and Networking

This book was developed around the concept of using SCADA software systems to monitor and control scientific experiments. Many experimental systems are monitored in real-time, often through a visual graphic representation of the experiment called a *human-machine interface* (HMI).

An HMI allows for operator observation and possible intervention in the experiment. Unmonitored experiments conducted in very short or lengthy time scales, isolated or remote locations, or under unique conditions usually cannot be followed with the HMI. Data from experiments whose progress can't be followed requires data collection or acquisition systems that must read, timestamp, and store values to be retrieved, reviewed, and interpreted later.

Data logging is the term to collectively describe all the unit operations required to accumulate and store the history of the results from remote, isolated, or autonomous, unmonitored investigations.

Data logging operations are also required to conduct certain types of experiments and permanently record quality control and quality assurance measurements. Unit processing operations in which organic materials such as foodstuffs or pharmaceutical preparations are dried to specified water activity levels to avoid microbiological spoilage are monitored by measuring and recording the water activity of the product inside sealed and isolated testing chambers. Autonomous battery-powered data collection modules equipped with sensors can be placed inside sealed chambers to measure and record a time-based profile of the physio-chemical conditions within the chamber. This provides permanent documented evidence that the correct physio-chemical conditions were achieved and maintained in past production or testing operations.

R. J. Smythe, *Arduino Measurements in Science*, https://doi.org/10.1007/978-1-4842-6781-3_10

In keeping with the simple nature of this book, invoking only readily available, inexpensive components, the data acquisition rates in this exercise are limited to those available with the Arduino microcontroller.

For all the topics presented so far in this book, and in keeping with the introductory nature of this book, the data collection rate available with an Arduino microcontroller using a secure data (SD) storage medium for timestamped data is adequate. (There are several newer higher-capacity SD cards. You must ensure that the cards and their increased capacity are compatible with your storage system.)

For high-speed data acquisition rates, the reader is referred to the literature concerning the data streaming capabilities of the LabJack HMI devices or to the literature of chemical spectroscopic analysis.

Time Measurement

The autonomous collection of experimental data from sensors or apparatus that are not constantly monitored by humans requires an independent, accurate timekeeping data source. Independent timekeeping data is available from digital integrated circuits known as *real-time clocks* (RTC).

There are several sources of accurate timekeeping signals available for use in data collection.

- Global Positioning System (GPS) broadcasts time signals from orbiting satellites

- Universal Time Coordinates (UTC) require a GPS receiver module.

- Internet Network Time Protocols (require an Ethernet connector to access the Internet)

- Broadcast radio time signals use a radio receiver to monitor time signals from atomic clocks (DCF77 receiver hardware required)

- Serial time messages from a computer

555 timers are integrated circuit oscillators that produce a continuous square wave output of fixed or variable frequency for as long as power is applied to their circuitry. External components determine the frequency or high and low time periods of the rectangular wave output produced by the integrated circuit timer. Relative time information is determined by counting or comparing pulses. The temporal information

produced is limited to a single varying digital signal. Microcontrollers like the Arduino record relative time passage by counting microsecond and millisecond intervals in appropriately sized binary registers from the start time of the session in progress. The millisecond and microsecond counters overflow and reset every 70 minutes and approximately 50 days, respectively.

Autonomous data collection from remote or very long experiments must be "timestamped" as collected and stored so that an accurate history of the recorded experimental values can be reconstituted later for reviewing, interpretation, display, or numerical processing. Timestamping data usually consists of the standard epoch time defined as the number of seconds since January 1, 1970. The timestamp expression consists of the current year, month, day of the week, hour of the day, minute of the hour, and seconds of the minute.

Application-specific integrated circuits (ASIC) such as the surface mount, Maxim IC, DS1307 are low-power, serial, binary coded decimal, calendar-clock devices. The nominal real-time clock (RTC) chip that provides year, month, day, hours, minutes, and seconds is accurate within a minute per month. (A similar temperature compensated device called the ChronoDot is accurate to a minute per year.)

A real-time clock is an assembly of components that provide not only a continuous, on-demand time function to the client software but also maintain an accurate time reckoning when the client software or microcontroller is turned off. Data from the DS 1307 chip is serially transmitted via an I²C (inter-integrated circuit) binary coded decimal (BCD), bidirectional bus, and software protocol that uses only two wires to implement the bus and data transfer. (Analog In pins 5 and 4 on the Arduino.) Normally the RTC draws power from the USB or microcontroller; however, the clock-calendar chip is operated with circuitry that automatically powers the chip from a 3 V lithium primary cell if the client software or microprocessor is turned off. The 3 V lithium cell can provide three years of continuous power for the clock-calendar chip, so that accurate timekeeping is assured for many years.

Several commercial suppliers offer complete RTC assemblies ready for use in rapid prototyping applications or kits that require minimal assembly before use.

The most recent version of the Arduino IDE has a selection of simple programs in the Examples menu under the RTClib entry. The demonstration program entry of most interest is the simple program ds1307 (see Listing 10-1) that prints the current time and date to the serial monitor, and then does several illustrative date and time calculations after setting the RTC with a call to the host computer.

An additional time library Time.h is available for download as a zip file and provides additional functionality for the Arduino controller with or without external hardware. The Time library allows for setting and synchronizing the microcontroller with an RTC to Internet time services, GPS systems, and serial time messages from computing systems. Additional explanations and examples of time functions with sample programs are provided in the Time library.

Data Storage

Appropriately timestamped experimental data collected over days, weeks, or months can be stored on large capacity, non-volatile memory, SD cards. SD cards are interchangeable memory devices able to be written to and read from, as an auxiliary drive by computers and microcontrollers. Data logging SD cards can be formatted in a FAT 16 or 32 file system to store data in a comma-separated values format (CSV) readable by many spreadsheets and data manipulation or display software applications. The cards are robust, easy to handle, inexpensive, readily available, have large storage capacities, are physically small and compact, being available in regular and microphysical sizes. All sizes of SD cards combined with simple adapters/holders are compatible with all desktop, workstations, and laptop computing hardware operating with Windows, Apple, or Linux operating systems.

SD cards are 3.3 V technology, while the Arduino is a 5 V system. Adaptive circuitry is required in read and write electronics when interfacing SD cards with microcontrollers. Micro-miniaturization and surface mount technology are rapidly replacing the older socket mount and "through hole" format circuit boards.

To accommodate the breadboard assembly of prototype devices, micro miniature, surface mount systems are available in breakout boards (BoB) that allow the handling and mounting of this tiny circuitry on conventional prototyping equipment. Breakout boards are available for both the RTC and the SD cardholders that accept batteries to provide auxiliary power and adapters to permit the experimenter to use either SD card size in their data collection systems.

Special circuit boards called *shields* that fit over the Arduino and plug into the I/O, power pins, and headers of the microcontroller so that complete, compact, dedicated devices can be built are available for data logging applications. The Arduino data logging shields contain both the battery-powered real-time clock and the SD cardholder. An Arduino microcontroller and a data logging shield combination form a compact system packaged into a robust housing for autonomous service in severe field or isolated laboratory conditions.

Data transfers to and from the SD cards use the serial peripheral interface protocol (SPI). SPI implementation uses a four-line bus to connect devices in a master-slave-oriented topology. In this exercise, the SPI code was and a working data logging system was created to monitor the output from a solid-state, humidity, temperature sensor designed to be encased in a sealed chamber. I²C and SPI programming is covered in *Practical Electronics for Inventors* by Paul Scherz and Simon Monk (McGraw-Hill, 2016). This exercise focuses on modifying published data logging codes required to record data from different sensors or sensor arrays.

The SD Library used in programming the Arduino defines an SD class of functions to define and manipulate files and directories on SD cards and a File class for writing to and reading from the individual files on SD cards. A brief review of the following library features can be augmented with information from the Arduino language reference site and online forums.

SD Class

- begin() – SD.begin() or SD.begin(cspin) initializes the SD card, the SD Library and prepares the SPI bus on digital input/output (DI/O) pins 11, 12, and 13 for operation. The function also sets the SS (slave select) pin, usually DI/O pin 10 on the Arduino board, for output, as default. If the SS DI/O pin is changed to a unique value designated by "cspin" (chip select pin) it must be set as an output, or the SD Library will not work.

- exists() – SD.exists(filename) returns true if the filename exists. Directory presence can be confirmed by combining the forward-slash notation in the filename character string.

- mkdir() – SD.mkdir("a/b/c") creates three directories a, b, and c on the SD card.

- open() – SD.open(filepath, mode) opens the file for reading by default. Reading defaults to the beginning of the file and writing to the end of the file.

- remove() – SD.remove(filename) removes the named file from the card directory.

- rmdir() – SD.rmdir(directory) removes empty directories only from the SD card.

File Class

- available() – file.available() returns the number of bytes available for reading in the named file.

- close() – file.close() closes the file and ensures that all data is written to the SD card.

- flush() – file.flush() ensures that all bytes written are saved to the SD card.

- peek() – file.peek() reads a byte from the file without advancing to the next one.

- position() – file.position() returns an unsigned long integer indicating the position of the next byte to be read from or written to.

- print() – file.print(data) or (data, BASE) prints the nominal data to the already opened for writing file, with the optionally specified base for numerical values.

- println() – file.println() prints or adds a carriage return and newline after printing.

- seek() – file.seek(pos) seeks out a new position in the file at hand where position is an unsigned long integer with a value between 0 and the file size.

- size() – file.size() returns the size of the file as an unsigned long integer.

- read() – file.read() returns the next byte of the file or -1 if none are available.

- write() – file.write(data) or (buffer, len) writes the data to the file, where data can be the byte, char, or string (char *) to be written. Alternatively, a buffer or an array of characters of length len can be written to the file.

- isDirectory() – *file*.isDirectory() returns a boolean indicating whether an entry is a directory or not. Directories (or folders) are special kinds of files. This function reports if the current file is a directory (see SD Library entry in Arduino Language Libraries reference for code example).

- openNextFile() – *file*.openNextFile() Reports the next file or folder in a directory (See SD Library entry in Arduino Language Libraries reference for code example).

- rewindDirectory() – *file*.rewindDirectory() returns focus to the first file in the directory, used in conjunction with openNextFile().

SD cards should be formatted only when required to prolong their useful service life. Adhering to the good scientific practice of incrementally developing complex systems from simpler fundamentals, this chapter develops an RTC that is read by the Arduino serial port, then visually displays the time and date on a multiline LCD before moving to the assembly of the data logging function in which both timestamp and sensor data are read from sources and written to a SD card for storage. Listing 10-3 is an Arduino sketch for timestamped data logging provided at the end of the chapter.

Liquid Crystal Displays (LCD)

LCD is a multilayer, thin-film technology in which an illumination source is obscured when viewed through two 90 degree crossed polarizing filters placed on either side of another multilayer assembly containing a material known as a *liquid crystal*. The liquid crystal layer is placed between two optically transparent Indium Tin Oxide (ITO) electrodes. When a voltage is applied to the transparent ITO electrodes, the liquid crystal molecular structure changes, causing the plane of polarization of the light traveling through the crystal to rotate and the lighted area between the electrodes to become visible.

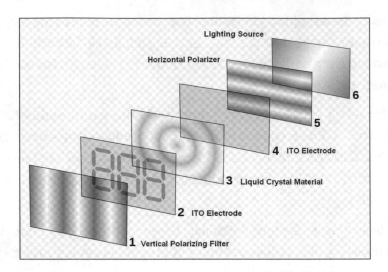

Figure 10-1. *A three-character LCD*

By depositing the ITO electrodes on glass substrates in pixilated rectangular arrays, custom created and standard alpha-numeric characters can be displayed. LCDs are manufactured in various formats, from single-line character displays to large format graphical displays and computer or television screens. (Figure 10-1 graphic from Wikipedia)

LCD displays can be driven from microcontrollers. The Arduino software has a full set of commands and libraries for all displays compatible with the Hitachi HD44780 chip. The Arduino serial monitor and the LCD share many common commands as essentially serial communication-based devices.

This exercise is based upon using an inexpensive LCD configured with a fixed four lines of 16 characters each. More expensive LCDs are available with graphics capabilities, but they are not required for this project.

Printing text to the LCD is similar to the instructions to print to the serial monitor. Any position in the matrix is determined by the row number from 0 to 3 and the column number from 0 to 15.

There are many LCD systems available based on the standard HD44780 chips. There are several different memory mapping software/hardware system implementations to control multiline displays. Because of the differences between manufactured LCD memory management systems, scrolling display screens often produce unexpected and confusing results. The visual effect of a scrolling display is not required for most scientific data recording operations and is not considered in this exercise. An Arduino sketch for RTC timestamped LCD data display is in Listing 10-2.

As more components are added to the data logging project, the pins available on the Arduino microcontroller are used, and the wiring in the prototype becomes complex. Care must be taken, as the complexity of the project grows to ensure that the RTC, SD card, and LCD display are all correctly wired and that the software has assigned the correct function to the appropriate chip pins. The increasing complexity of the project can be simplified by using the shields plugin boards that fit over the I/O pins of the Arduino. Complete data logging boards containing the RTC, voltage reduction electronics, and SD cards are available as kits or fully assembled from various suppliers.

A fully assembled data logging shield is used in the last portion of this exercise to build a battery-powered autonomous module that measures the conditions inside isolated chambers. An autonomous data logger can be used in refrigerators, cold storage units, sealed chambers with special atmospheres, or closed system biology experimentation to measure or validate the environmental conditions within the sealed chamber.

As a development exercise, a data logging application will be developed using an Arduino Uno as a controller. The controller drives a four-line by 16-character LCD monitor to provide a visual display of the experimental data being logged or stored, obtain the current time from an RTC to assemble a line of timestamped data, and then record and store the timestamped data on an SD card. Data is generated by and streamed from a DHT–22 temperature–humidity sensor to determine water activity in organic materials. (See the relative humidity sensor discussion in Chapter 7.)

An autonomous data logging recorder is assembled from an Arduino, a data logging shield, a light-dependent resistor, an Analog Devices TMP 36 solid-state temperature sensor, and a battery pack. Initially, the device is connected to the host computer, and the required programming in Listing 10-4 (presented at the end of the chapter) is uploaded to the Arduino controller. After confirming the system's operation with both the USB and battery pack power, through the display provided by the serial monitor, the data logging apparatus is disconnected from the USB cable and allowed to run on battery power alone.

By recording the time at which the autonomous data logging experiment begins, and by occluding the room light falling on the LDR, an artificial data variation can be created and confirmed by removing the SD card and examining the data on it with a spreadsheet. The simple light occlusion test and recorded data examination validate the system operation before implementing the device in a much longer monitoring program.

Experiment

Hardware

Integrated circuits are manufactured in surface mount technology to be used in automated circuit board assembly lines. To use single pieces of surface mount micro-miniature integrated circuitry, small circuit boards known as *breakout boards* (BoB) must be prepared to use the chips in prototype experimentation. The breakout boards generally hold ICs of interest and other assorted electronics components, power, data I/O facilities, and mounting hardware required for integrating a board into a project or prototyping setup.

The two breakout boards used in this exercise to hold the real-time clock and the microSD card are available from several suppliers as fully assembled miniature circuit boards or kits that require the assembly of mounting hardware. The kits are reasonably easy to assemble, but their small size requires some care in soldering.

Real-Time Clock and Breakout Board

Several suppliers of DS 1307 real-time clock chip (RTC) kits can be used for this exercise, and the Adafruit Industries kit, product number 264, was used for this project. RTCs must run off battery power when the host that they normally draw power from is turned off. The Adafruit kit contains a lithium button cell battery that automatically switches over to battery power when the Arduino microcontroller is powered down. The lithium cell can supply continuous power to the RTC that draws 500 nA for up to three years. The date and time count from seconds to years is valid until 2100. (Boards and kits vary from $10 to $30 CDN).

In Figures 10-2 and 10-3, the top and bottom of the assembled breakout board are shown with reference to a millimeter rule.

As an initial test of the RTC, the program included in the Arduino IDE examples listing, called DS1307 in the RTCLib menu, can be loaded and run after the RTC breakout board has been assembled and connected to the Arduino. The breakout header pins for ground and 5 V are connected to the Arduino board. The SCL is connected to Analog In pin 5 and SLA to Analog In pin 4.

Figure 10-2. *Top of RTC breakout board*

Figure 10-3. *Bottom of RTC breakout board*

A DateTime object is returned by the RTCLib function now(). The object describes the year, month, day, hour, minute, and second, when the function was called.

SD Card Holder and Breakout Board

An Adafruit Industries kit, product number 254, using a microSD card, was chosen for the data logging exercise. The kit is completely compatible with the Arduino microcontroller, having a built-in 5 to 3.3 V converter. The microSD card is 3/8 in (1 cm) wide, 5/8 in (1.5 cm) long, and 1/16 in (1 mm) thick. The breakout board is 1 in (2.45 cm) by 1¼ in (3 cm) and 1/16 in (1 mm) thick. The SD BoB is depicted in Figure 10-4 with an 8 GB microSD card.

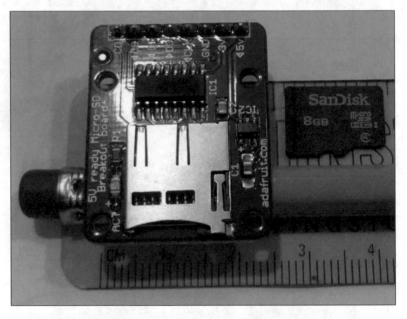

Figure 10-4. *Top view of breakout board and microSD card*

The next photo depicts the bottom of the SD breakout board with the 1/10 in (2.45 mm) spaced header pins. The header pins are spaced to be compatible with a standard 1/10 in spacing used on prototyping breadboards, as depicted in Figure 10-5 and seen in Figure 10-6.

Figure 10-5. *Bottom view of the breakout board and 8 GB microSD card*

New SD cards are often sold in FAT16 format if less than 2 GB in size and FAT32 if larger than 2GB. To reuse SD cards previously used in logging data or for other purposes, such as cameras or music recordings, the formatting utility on a computer can clear the card of the files and create the appropriately sized new file system for the card.

It is not recommended to reformat the SD cards too often. Files that have been written to the SD card and are no longer needed can be deleted by using Windows Explorer or its equivalent file manager utility and the Delete key in the manner usually applied to deleting files from the C drive.

Liquid Crystal Display

A Samsung DCM 16433, from Jameco Electronics, four-line by 16-character, non-backlit display, compatible with the HD44780 standard, was chosen for the data logging project. With a four-line display, it is possible to observe the time and date from the real-time clock together with the temperature and humidity data stream from a sensor mounted in a window equipped sealed chamber as the data is being recorded on the microSD card.

A sealed chamber is used to measure the water activity of materials under test. A four-line display allows for both data monitoring and a display of the equilibrium conditions within the chamber.

LCD ICs have a 14-pin connection strip or header for control and data transfer and may have two additional connections for a backlighting capability. Arduino's IDE has a built-in library called LiquidCrystal.h that has a series of nineteen programming functions that control the character display providing for display illumination, accepting serial input, blinking, and creation of non-standard characters. (See Arduino LCD library language reference). (LCD displays using I^2C are currently available that only use VCC, GND, SDA, and SCL, leaving four digital pins on the Arduino).

An LCD requires power and ground that are usually the first two connections on the LCD terminal board. The manufacturer's reference literature should be examined to confirm the remainder of the connections required to control and activate the display. In addition to the power connections, the four-line by 16-character display I used had the wiper of a 10 kΩ potentiometer bridging the ground and 5 V supply, connected to pin 3 of the display header to control image contrast. The image contrast control voltage is known as V_o for the display used in this exercise.

In addition to the electrical connections controlling power, ground, and image contrast, six more are required to operate the LCD.

Although the LCD can accept 8-bit data for display, only four bits are normally used. For most applications, the difference between 8- and 4-bit operations is not noticeable in the display, and the 4-bit methodology leaves four digital I/O lines available for other uses on the microprocessor. The 6-pin assignments between the digital I/O on the Arduino and the LCD header can vary as required by the application if the correct assignment is made in the appropriate line of code.

LiquidCrystal lcd(RS, enable, D4, D3, D2, D1); // lcd connection assignments

Arduino's IDE has several simple demonstration code examples of LCD use, while the following code demonstrates LCD programming useful in scientific applications.

Software

To ease cross-referencing of text and LCD Listings 10-1 and 10-2 have been integrated into the following passages discussing this subject rather than being listed separately.

Listing 10-1 addresses an Arduino real-time clock's serial monitor display. The data logging project's initial phase is to assemble or acquire a real-time clock based upon the Maxim 1307 device. This clock chip is a compromise between cost and capability. It provides sufficient accuracy for most data logging operations that might be used with experiments designed from the exercises presented in this book. Arduino code for an RTC with the Maxim 1307 can be found in the examples provided with the IDE as listed next.

The code following from the IDE Examples "ds1307" menu selection uses the rtc. adjust() function to set the time and date from the host computer the first time the code is run. Once the RTC has been initially set to the correct time and date, the RTC runs if there is power. Power can be drawn from the USB, an auxiliary Arduino power source (i.e., a battery or separate power supply energizing the Arduino), or if the Arduino is off, from the RTC's own coin cell. The current time/date can be obtained using the rtc.now() function.

Listing 10-1. Setting the Time and Day

```
// Date and Time Functions Using a DS1307 RTC Connected via I²C and Wire Lib
#include <Wire.h>
#include "RTClib.h"
RTC_DS1307 rtc; // declare the rtc object

void setup () {
  Serial.begin(9600);
#ifdef AVR
  Wire.begin();
#else
  Wire1.begin(); // Shield I2C pins connect to alt I2C bus on Arduino Due
#endif
  rtc.begin();

  if (! rtc.isrunning()) {
    Serial.println("RTC is NOT running!");
    // following line sets the RTC to the date & time this sketch was
      compiled
    rtc.adjust(DateTime(F(__DATE__), F(__TIME__)));
    // This line sets the RTC with an explicit date & time, for example to
      set
    // January 21, 2014 at 3 am call the following code:
```

```
    // rtc.adjust(DateTime(2014, 1, 21, 3, 0, 0));
  }
}

void loop () {
    DateTime now = rtc.now();

    Serial.print(now.year(), DEC);
    Serial.print('/');
    Serial.print(now.month(), DEC);
    Serial.print('/');
    Serial.print(now.day(), DEC);
    Serial.print(' ');
    Serial.print(now.hour(), DEC);
    Serial.print(':');
    Serial.print(now.minute(), DEC);
    Serial.print(':');
    Serial.print(now.second(), DEC);
    Serial.println();

    Serial.print(" since midnight 1/1/1970 = ");
    Serial.print(now.unixtime());
    Serial.print("s = ");
    Serial.print(now.unixtime() / 86400L);
    Serial.println("d");

    // calculate a date which is 7 days and 30 seconds into the future
    DateTime future (now.unixtime() + 7 * 86400L + 30);

    Serial.print(" now + 7d + 30s: ");
    Serial.print(future.year(), DEC);
    Serial.print('/');
    Serial.print(future.month(), DEC);
    Serial.print('/');
    Serial.print(future.day(), DEC);
    Serial.print(' ');
    Serial.print(future.hour(), DEC);
    Serial.print(':');
```

```
    Serial.print(future.minute(), DEC);
    Serial.print(':');
    Serial.print(future.second(), DEC);
    Serial.println();

    Serial.println();
    delay(3000);
}
```

In Listing 10-2, a visual display of the current time can be created by extracting the time data described in the previous program and displaying it in the first two rows of the LCD. The following code provides an RTC LCD time clock.

Listing 10-2. RTC LCD Time Clock

```
// Date and time functions using a DS1307 RTC connected via I2C and Wire lib to
// Arduino and an LCD. (The digital time is available on the serial monitor
// but scrolls rapidly.)

#include <Wire.h>
#include "RTClib.h"
#include <LiquidCrystal.h>
// initialize the LCD and pin assignments
LiquidCrystal lcd(9, 8, 7, 6, 5, 4);
RTC_DS1307 rtc;

void setup () {
  Serial.begin(9600);
#ifdef AVR
  Wire.begin();
#else
  Wire1.begin(); // Shield I2C pins connect to alt I2C bus on Arduino Due
#endif
  rtc.begin();
  lcd.begin(16, 4);
```

```
  if (! rtc.isrunning()) {
    Serial.println("RTC is NOT running!");
    // following line sets the RTC to the date & time this sketch was compiled
    rtc.adjust(DateTime(F(__DATE__), F(__TIME__)));
    // This line sets the RTC with an explicit date & time, for example to set
    // January 21, 2014 at 3am the investigator would call:
    // rtc.adjust(DateTime(2014, 1, 21, 3, 0, 0));
  }
}

void loop () {
    DateTime now = rtc.now();
    lcd.clear();
    Serial.print(now.year(), DEC);
    lcd.print(now.year(), DEC);
    Serial.print('/');
    lcd.print("/");
    Serial.print(now.month(), DEC);
    lcd.print(now.month(), DEC);
    Serial.print('/');
    lcd.print("/");
    Serial.print(now.day(), DEC);
    lcd.print(now.day(), DEC);
    Serial.print(' ');
    lcd.print(' ');
    lcd.setCursor(0,1);
    Serial.print(now.hour(), DEC);
    lcd.print(now.hour(), DEC);
    Serial.print(':');
    lcd.print(":");
    Serial.print(now.minute(), DEC);
    lcd.print(now.minute(), DEC);
    Serial.print(':');
    lcd.print(":");
```

```
   Serial.print(now.second(), DEC);
   lcd.print(now.second(), DEC);
   Serial.println(); //a scrolling display in serial monitor.
   delay(10);
}
```

Listing 10-3 reads the data from a solid-state humidity and temperature sensor and logs the data on a formatted 8 GB microSD card with a timestamp. The relative humidity temperature sensor has its own library, DHT.h, that enables the Arduino to read the sensor output. The DHT 22 is an equilibrium sensor and is only read every three seconds.

A continuous visual display of the localized atmospheric conditions around the DHT-22 sensor is displayed on a four by 16-character LCD as the experimental conditions are recorded.

Figure 10-6 depicts the crowded prototyping board with the LCD display, Arduino board, and the USB cable. The RTC (1), SD (2), DHT-22 (3), 10 KΩ LCD contrast adjusting potentiometer (4), and microSD card adapter (5) are as captioned.

Figure 10-6. *Timestamped relative humidity and temperature data collection and microSD card data storage*

The code for the data logging project follows.

An Arduino with shield-mounted, compact, battery-powered, and autonomous data collection system is depicted in Figure 10-7.

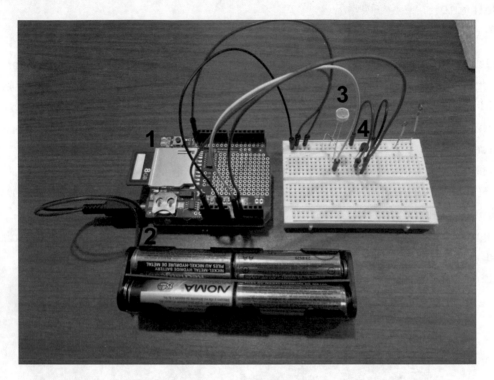

Figure 10-7. *Autonomous light and temperature data collection module*

In Figure 10-7, the caption (1) indicates the regular-sized SD card on which data is recorded or logged, (2) indicates the battery-powered RTC, (3) is the light-dependent resistor, and (4) is the solid-state temperature sensor.

Figure 10-8 depicts the underside of the plugin data logging shield and the Arduino controller board.

Figure 10-8. *The connecting pins of the data logging shield*

The Arduino data logging shield in Figure 10-8 was purchased fully assembled from Adafruit Industries. It was modified with the optional stacking headers to allow the logging assembly to be used with either additional shields or a prototyping breadboard.

Using my assembly with the optional stackable headers, the LDR and LM 35 temperature sensors were mounted on a small prototyping breadboard in accordance with the circuit depicted in Figure 10-9.

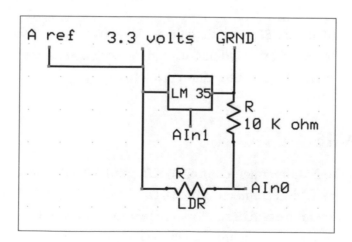

Figure 10-9. *Arduino LDR and temperature sensor circuitry*

The system was assembled in accordance with the suggested configuration for the example software provided by the supplier. The system was powered from the 3.3 V supply that has the advantage of being regulated down from the noisy USB supplied 5 V and should be a voltage supply with a much lower noise level.

The suggested circuitry for the light and temperature sensors involves configuring the LDR in a voltage divider circuit to convert the degree of illumination into a measurable voltage. The non-linearity and unusual behavior of this type of sensor configuration are presented and mathematically modeled in Chapter 6 of *Practical Electronics for Inventors*.

The purpose of assembling the autonomous system is to place the unit inside a refrigerated container to validate the return of internal temperature to its set point and confirm the absence of light. The LDR should vary from a low resistance value when illuminated during chamber opening to its maximum resistance in the dark when the chamber is closed. The recorded data on the SD card should thus be characterized by an analog drifting in the temperature data and a "digital" type switching from low to high in the illumination data.

The Arduino sketch in Listing 10-4 has been modified from the data logging shield manufacturers' examples. It records the time, temperature, and illumination as a 10-bit ADC scaled numerical value.

To use the recorder, the system is assembled, connected to the battery pack, and the data recording session started by accessing the serial monitor. When the serial monitor displays all the initialization and start-up messages and begins listing data, the USB cable can be disconnected and the module placed in the environment to be monitored.

While connected to the USB, each time the serial monitor is accessed, a new file is created. Clearing the SD card of old files with an operating system file management utility resets the numerical file identification program.

Observations

After assembling the Arduino microcontroller, RTC, and SD data cardholders on a prototyping breadboard and connecting the DHT-22 sensor to the Arduino's digital I/O pin 2, the room temperature and humidity were recorded for 41 minutes. The default collection time in the data logging program is 20 samples per minute. A record of 820 readings was collected in 41 minutes.

The data collection was terminated by removing the 8 GB microSD card from its holder. The microcard was mounted in a regular-sized SD cardholder/adapter for insertion into a desktop workstation to examine the collected data. SD cards are recognized by the host computer as an additional regular drive and assigned an appropriate drive number or letter. According to the header on the SD card, 41 minutes of data collection resulted in a file size of 34 KB.

Examining the true file size with the computer's file properties utilities indicated a total file size of 65,536 bytes that includes the file system overhead. With the 3-second data collection rate and the 41-minute collection interval resulting in 820 lines of data, the system is consuming a total of approximately 1.5 kB/min. The 8 GB card has space for 8 GB/(1.5 KB/min) or 5,293,211 minutes, or 3,675 days of continuous data collection.

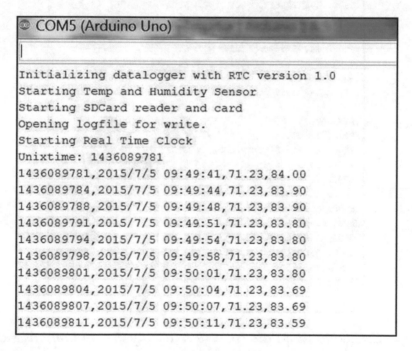

Figure 10-10. *Serial monitor record of temperature and humidity data*

```
COM7 (Arduino Uno)

Initializing SD card...card initialized.
Logging to: LOGGER01.CSV
millis,stamp,datetime,light,temperature
999, 1439195607, "2015/8/10 8:33:27", 707, 68.46
1998, 1439195608, "2015/8/10 8:33:28", 706, 68.46
2999, 1439195609, "2015/8/10 8:33:29", 702, 68.46
3999, 1439195610, "2015/8/10 8:33:30", 700, 68.46
5000, 1439195611, "2015/8/10 8:33:31", 701, 68.46
5998, 1439195612, "2015/8/10 8:33:32", 701, 68.46
6999, 1439195613, "2015/8/10 8:33:33", 703, 68.46
7999, 1439195614, "2015/8/10 8:33:34", 706, 68.46
8998, 1439195615, "2015/8/10 8:33:35", 706, 68.46
9999, 1439195616, "2015/8/10 8:33:36", 711, 68.46
10999, 1439195617, "2015/8/10 8:33:37", 710, 68.46
12000, 1439195618, "2015/8/10 8:33:38", 706, 68.46
12999, 1439195619, "2015/8/10 8:33:39", 18, 67.88
14000, 1439195620, "2015/8/10 8:33:40", 3, 67.88
14998, 1439195621, "2015/8/10 8:33:41", 4, 67.88
16000, 1439195622, "2015/8/10 8:33:42", 0, 68.46
17000, 1439195623, "2015/8/10 8:33:43", 0, 68.46
17998, 1439195624, "2015/8/10 8:33:44", 0, 68.46
18999, 1439195625, "2015/8/10 8:33:45", 0, 68.46
19998, 1439195626, "2015/8/10 8:33:46", 0, 68.46
21000, 1439195627, "2015/8/10 8:33:47", 0, 68.46
21999, 1439195628, "2015/8/10 8:33:48", 0, 68.46
22999, 1439195629, "2015/8/10 8:33:49", 0, 67.88
24000, 1439195630, "2015/8/10 8:33:50", 712, 68.46
24999, 1439195631, "2015/8/10 8:33:51", 712, 68.46
26000, 1439195632, "2015/8/10 8:33:52", 712, 68.46
26999, 1439195633, "2015/8/10 8:33:53", 707, 68.46
28000, 1439195634, "2015/8/10 8:33:54", 699, 68.46
28999, 1439195635, "2015/8/10 8:33:55", 701, 68.46
29999, 1439195636, "2015/8/10 8:33:56", 711, 68.46
```

Figure 10-11. *Serial monitor data collection display in autonomous mode*

The data collected from the battery-powered autonomous module displays the Arduino ADC values recorded for the LDR when exposed to room lighting. Normal overhead illumination from incandescent lighting creates illumination values in the 700 ADC counts range while covering the LDR with a pen top, drops the reading to zero.

Recovery of the data collected in the autonomous operation of the data collection module is achieved by removing the card from the module and inserting it into the SD card slot on a computing system or SD card reader. The files on the card are displayed as depicted in Figure 10-12.

Name	Date modified	Type	Size
LOGGER00	01/01/2000 12:00 AM	Microsoft Office E...	1 KB
LOGGER01	01/01/2000 12:00 AM	Microsoft Office E...	4 KB

Figure 10-12. *SD files generated by battery-powered autonomous data collection module*

Opening the Logger01 file in Microsoft Excel provides the tabular data array depicted in Figure 10-13. The spreadsheet headings are created with the following line.

```
logfile.println("millis,stamp,datetime,light,temperature");
of the Arduino "DataLoggingLightAndTemperature_Rvn1_rtsketch_jul21b" code.
```

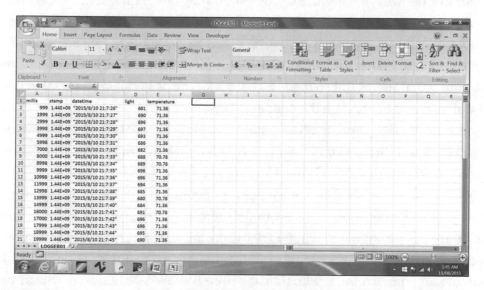

Figure 10-13. *Excel display of logged data from autonomous collection*

When first opened, the Excel spreadsheet is in a default configuration. The "millis" and "stamp" columns, which may be in the 5-to-10-digit range, are expressed as exponential notation until the column width is adjusted to accommodate the larger numbers of digits.

Data Logging with RPi

Data recording from the Sense HAT board is discussed in Chapter 6. Sense HAT boards are equipped with a programmable LED array for visual communication or alarming and provide both navigational and environmental sensor data through connection to the RPi GPIO array. The data logging is not stored on an SD card but the RPi Linux operating system's main storage drive. Timestamped data is stored in the comma-separated value format (CSV) compatible with most spreadsheet software programs. Complete tutorials are available from the GitHub repository for logging all or specific data streams from the Sense HAT board available from the Raspberry Pi Foundation and many suppliers.

Arduino microcontrollers, RTC, and SD data collection systems are completely compatible with the RPi/Python platform.

Networking

Networking is the basis on which supervisory control and data acquisition systems are built. Within a network, the individual computers may be of equal stature and exchange information such as text, graphics, or data in a client-server arrangement. One unit transmits while the second receives. Networks can be as simple as two computers connected to share information or involve multitudes of computing units connected in various configurations, all linked together by specific devices called *routers* that control the flow of information through the connected systems.

A common configuration involves several computers connected via a router that permits cabled and wireless connections between individual units. This allows the computers to communicate freely in a local area network (LAN).

LANs using a router in a wired or wireless configuration are subject to physical limitations. Cabled connections are assured if there is electrical power to the system and the cables are physically intact. Wireless network connections are dependent upon the sending and receiving stations having power, functioning transmission, and receiving equipment and uninterrupted radio transmissions. Wireless systems have the advantage of virtually unlimited localized mobility if radio contact is maintained. Often localized wireless systems must use repeaters to ensure that a strong radio signal is available throughout the desired operating area.

Homes, businesses, and various institutions use router connected LANs to interface a wide variety of fixed and mobile computing devices to process information. In addition to structuring the LAN, a router may be connected to the Internet to access resources available globally. A router controlling a LAN and providing a connection to the Internet is often called a *gateway*.

Cabled networks restrict the flow of information or network traffic to the system's workstations and LAN cables. Wireless connections broadcast network traffic to any receiving station within the LAN effective broadcast range. A security system is required for wireless connections to prevent unintended interference with control information flow between clients and servers.

SCADA systems were originally developed to operate at longer distances allowing a central location to monitor and control remote facilities such as power stations and public utilities. Continuing advances in micro-miniaturization have made remote control of both local and globally distant devices commonplace. When used over Internet connections, HMI and special computer communications involving hardware and software languages such as HyperText Markup Language (HTML) create local to global remote-control capabilities.

Communication consists of an information transfer between two entities. One entity transmits data while the other receives the information. Communicating integrated circuits use a low-level master-slave (I^2C) data transfer protocol involving bits. Networked computing devices use a higher-level language client-server protocols that exchange web pages of information. In an Internet client-server communication, a client requests information from a server, and the information exchange involves the exchange of whole or partial web pages.

An inexpensive, readily available Arduino microcontroller can be programmed to act as a web server component of an Internet connection that permits the two-way flow of data collection and supervisory control commands between a PC host and remote experiments.

This exercise in developing networking connections to experimental operations begins with integrating, and locating an Arduino microcontroller in a local area network (LAN). Once the microcontroller is integrated into the LAN, the connections are expanded to transmit data and control signals between a desktop unit and the microcontroller through an Internet connection with its global communication ability. As with all computing technology, the configuration development process is constantly tending to become more automated.

In-depth web page design, the scripting languages to implement client-server programming or interactions, and the additional security concerns required to prevent accidental interactions between broadcast radio signals in wireless systems are only being introduced in simple examples to maintain the introductory nature of this book. A summary of some of the terms and acronyms used in Internet access are listed next.

- Client-server model: Internet information is often stored and transferred in web pages. Servers are computers that store and dispense pages of information to client units that request access to the pages. An information transfer is initiated when a client asks for information from a server. A web server is constantly listening for a client to ask for information and, when asked, supplies the required information in the form of a whole or partial web page.

- DHCP: A dynamic host configuration protocol is a program that automatically assigns an Internet address to a device. A DHCP program resident in the Arduino Ethernet library locates and assigns an IP Address to the microcontroller when the device is integrated into a LAN.

- Forms: A web page for collecting user input that contains various visual display elements such as check boxes, radio buttons, text input boxes, slider bars, and other elements for inputting user information is called a *form*. Forms are displayed when a host's web browser program runs a passage of code written in HTML (example follows). Within the HTML, the start and finish of the form are defined by the <form> and </form> tags. The data movement between computing units is controlled by the GET and POST methods.

- GET/POST: Two methods for transferring information to and from remote servers are GET and POST. Universal Resource Locators (URL) that terminate with sequences such as /?s=arduino are GET requests in which the variable "s" is being set to the value "arduino". GET defines a series of variables that follow the ? in the URL. The functions of GET and POST represent two ways in which data can be moved between clients and servers.

- HTML: HyperText Markup Language is the standard "scripting" or "markup" language to create web pages. A web browser program reads HTML files and renders the code into web pages. HTML describes how to display the pages in a web site and is called a *markup language* rather than a programming language.

HTML code elements are the structuring details for all websites. HTML blends images and objects into page elements that can create interactive forms and provide methods for generating structured documents through text-based structural semantics describing headings, paragraphs, lists, links, quotes, and other items.

HTML elements consist of non-displayed *tags* enclosed in angle brackets (like</p>) that configure how the browser program displays the page content.

Numerous other HTML capabilities are available for web site creation. Refer to the World-Wide Consortium standards, which have presided over the creation, modification, and implementation of HTML since 1997.

- HTTP: HyperText Transfer Protocol is designed to enable communications between clients and servers and functions as a request-response protocol between the two. A web browser program, resident on any computing system may be the client that requests web page-based information from any other computing system running a web server program dispensing web pages of information as requested by the network connected client. In a typical Internet or LAN exchange example, a client (browser program) submits an HTTP request in a standardized format to the server that acknowledges the request before fulfilling the requested web page transaction.

- IP address: Locations on the Internet are identified by Internet Protocol addresses that consist of four grouped numerical values that vary from 0 to 255 (a byte, or 2^8).

- MAC addresses: A media access control address is a unique identifier for the network interface device connected to the Internet. In this exercise, it is the six hexadecimal paired numbers on the Arduino Ethernet Shield. (On my board, it is 90-A2-DA-0D-79-2A).

- Routers: Early networks were formed by connecting cabled computing units or workstations to a hub to form a LAN. Hubs with modified hardware were created to allow wireless and cabled connections of workstations to form a LAN, and the addition of logic circuitry formed routers that could then direct the flow of network messaging signals between the LAN members and the global Internet.

- URL: Uniform Resource Locator refers to the web address. The addresses consist of the uniform resource locator and the uniform resource name.

To use the following set of exercises that progressively increase the functionality imparted to an Arduino Internet connection, the complexity of the sketches written increases markedly. Rudimentary explanations of how the functionality is created may require the experimenter to learn or review the underlying technology of HTML, C, C++, web page creation, and advanced Arduino programming. (References are provided along with the sources from which the original code was derived.)

Connecting Arduino to a Network

An Ethernet shield is a circuit board that stacks on top of the Arduino with headers allowing access to all the microcontroller I/O pins and providing the circuitry required to connect the microcontroller with a LAN. The shield has an RJ-45 cable socket for a cabled connection. The Arduino USB connection gains access to the IDE on the host computer to create the required sketches. Once the sketches are loaded to the Arduino, the microcontroller can communicate through the Ethernet connection with any device on the LAN or Internet.

Figure 10-14 depicts an Ethernet shield in place on an Arduino UNO. USB and network cables are to the left of the image and are captioned as (2) and (1), respectively.

When configured to act as a web server, the code required to display a web page on the client browser can be provided by the Arduino sketch or stored on the SD card (3). The shield mounted card can also log data derived from Internet-connected experiments. A prototyped experiment can be assembled on and connected to the Arduino-Ethernet Shield stack through a prototype board (4) and the appropriate wiring. In Figure 10-14, an audio tone generator (5) and an RGB LED (6) on long leads are electronic components that can be monitored or controlled through data transfer over an Internet connection.

In Figure 10-14, the SD card (3) is loosely stored within its holder. When not in active use, the SD card should not be seated in the card reader as it may interfere with the intended operation of any sketch running that does not require access to the device.

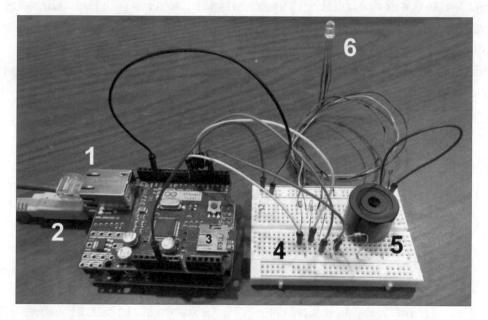

Figure 10-14. *An Arduino Ethernet Shield and prototyping breadboard*

The code, hardware, and techniques that follow are *extensible.* They can be used or easily modified to move information, data, and commands between an experimental process connected to the Arduino and an observer via the Internet. The compilation of programs that follow was collected from books, online tutorials, forums, or references and modified to demonstrate the techniques available for Internet monitoring and management.

Simple Web Pages

This exercise begins by creating a basic web page on the host PC to demonstrate a web browser's interpretation of HTML.

HTML is written in a simple text editor, such as Windows Accessories, WordPad, or RPi's text editor, and saved with the .htm extension to form a file able to be read by a browser program. HTML can also be written in an advanced featured text editor such as WordPad++ (D/L freeware).

Configuring a microprocessor to process characters moving through its serial port and providing the appropriate identification logic to act upon the character sequences is a robust technique that allows the device to function as required by the experimenter. A web server or client response can be invoked from the microprocessor when the Internet is connected to the device serial port. Sketches able to read the serial port characters can reassemble commands to manipulate the microcontrollers I/O pins or read and return the voltage levels present at selected pins.

The web pages examined in this exercise are "extended" from code and methods in the following sources.

- *Programming Arduino: Getting Started with Sketches* by Simon Monk (McGraw-Hill, 2011)

- *Programming Arduino: Next Steps Going Further with Sketches* by Simon Monk (McGraw-Hill, 2018)

- *Exploring Arduino* by Jeremy Blum (Wiley, 2013)

- *Raspberry Pi Cookbook* by Simon Monk (O'Reilly Media, 2019)

- `http://arduino.cc/en/reference/ethernet`

Internet technology and physical computing hardware are constantly evolving. The most current sources of information on the Arduino microcontroller are found on the Internet.

Experiment
Creating a Simple HTML Web Page

Any readily available text editing program, such as Windows Notepad, the RPi text editor, or the multifeatured text editor Notepad++ can be used to assemble an HTML document. All web pages have a bare minimum of code required to implement and display a web page in a browser.

Enter the following HTML code in a text editor.

```
<html>
<body>
<h1> Arduino Measurements in Science</h1>
<p>Physical Computing with Integrated Circuits for
the Experimental Sciences.</p>
</body>
</html>
```

Save the code with an appropriate title and the extension .html to an easily accessible storage location. After storing the file, launch a web browser such as Google Chrome. Press Ctrl+O on the keyboard and navigate to the stored file. Open it, and you should see the screen in Figure 10-15.

Figure 10-15. *A simple HTML file displayed in a web browser*

Separate HTML files and browser viewing of these files are used to develop web pages. Experimenters can use HTML files to create the user interface needed to control an Internet-connected microcontroller running an experiment. The HTML code required to display the experimenter's desired user interface can then be integrated into the microcontroller web page server sketch code for delivery to the host web browser during actual investigative networked operations.

HTML is composed of tags consisting of lowercase letters and symbols encased in the angle brackets or < and > markers. Tags used in pairs such as <p> and </p> start and end a display feature such as paragraphs. Web browser programs use tags to create visual page displays by interpreting a large number of tags available in HTML 5 created in 2012.

Network Device Locations

To locate devices on a network, locations must be identified. The Arduino Ethernet library provides a DHCP service that assigns the appropriate device locations. The following sketch located the IP address of the Arduino Ethernet Shield on my LAN, configured with a D-Link, DIR–615 wireless, and cable connection router. To use the code, the MAC for the individual Ethernet Shield must be entered in the MAC defining array line in hexadecimal format.

byte mac[] = { 0x90, 0xA2,0xDA, 0x0D, 0x79, 0x2A };

After verifying and loading the sketch code into the Arduino and activating the serial monitor, the Arduino Ethernet Shield's IP address should appear. My boards were assigned the 192.168.0.103 IP address used in Listings 10-3, 10-4, and 10-5).

This simple sketch uses the Ethernet library's commands to provide a serial monitor display of the address assigned to the Arduino server. The complete set of commands in the library is available from the referenced online Arduino website.

Reading Data from an Experiment Attached to an Arduino Server

You can establish two-way client-server IP communication links between the host computer and the remote devices connected to the microcontroller. Two-way client-server dialogs begins with the host computer browser sending a request for information to the web server microcontroller. The Arduino code is written to listen for the browser request and then transmit an acknowledgment when the request is heard. Code from the client request is read, and a page of the desired information is sent back to the host resident browser program.

HTML-based Internet communications are in fixed formats, and each line ends with a carriage return and new line feed indicated by the sequence of \r\n in the transmitted code. The transmission of a blank line signals an end to the transmission.

Within the Ethernet library are the EthernetServer and EthernetClient classes with all the functions and commands necessary to serve and receive web pages.

Listing 10-6 reads the first two analog input values from the Arduino's analog inputs. The Arduino sketch provides the host browser with the HTML necessary to create the web page in Figure 10-16, which displays the values of the two inputs at the time of code execution.

Figure 10-16 illustrates the simple, static web page produced by the HTML code sent to the web browser by the sketch on the Internet-connected Arduino.

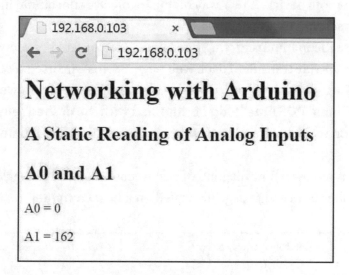

Figure 10-16. *Data read and page served by an Arduino web server*

Signal variations on the Arduino's analog inputs can be updated by periodically "refreshing" the page displayed by the browser or by installing a refresh button on the host displayed web page.

The addition of the comment and line of code after the empty line, signaling the end of the reply header, causes the voltage analog values on A0 and A1 to update in 5-second intervals.

```
// add a meta refresh tag for an auto page refresh
   client.println("<meta http-equiv=\"refresh\" content=\"5\">");
```

Meta elements are tags used in HTML headers that contain information about data. Numerous attributes must accompany the use of the metatag. The 5-second "refresh" option updates the data. A metatag refresh technique is a simple method that causes the web page to flicker noticeably. More sophisticated methods involving JavaScript programming can up-date only the varying data in a flicker-free display.

A second method for updating the data in a display is to use an image of a push button, radio buttons, or a checkbox on the browser displayed page. The use of host displayed buttons or checkboxes to activate the I/O on a remote Arduino connected to sensors or experiments now involves a two-way dialog between the client and the server.

Push buttons to activate a LED and update analog input readings are demonstrated in the following program. A table display of buttons on the host can control and monitor I/O pins on the remote device. A two-way dialog involves a substantial increase in the amount of code required to transfer data.

Web pages are the medium carrying information or content between client and server, and for a two-way transfer of data, web page "forms" are used. Forms can be configured in HTML with the <form> </form> tags, and the form is moved back and forth with the GET and POST methods. Forms filled with the desired sensor or control device information move back and forth when the user clicks the Update button in the page display.

Figure 10-17 is a typical flow diagram of the process required to toggle an output pin on a microcontroller from a web page displayed on a host computer.

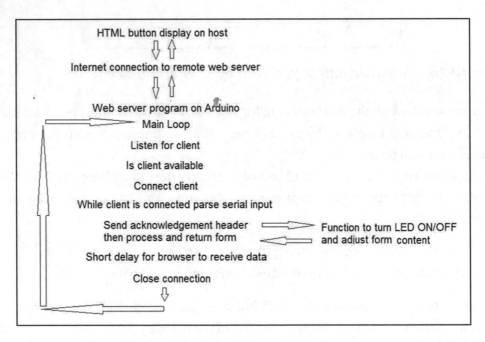

Figure 10-17. *A flow diagram for the process of activating microcontroller output*

The flow diagram is compact but unintentionally minimizes the code required to process and return the updated form. The HTML code that the microcontroller sketch must write to the host browser program to display the requested up-dated information can be substantial depending upon the complexity of the desired user interface.

Control elements such as buttons, variable sliding controls, and display box sensor readouts can monitor and activate the devices connected to a remote, Internet-accessible, Arduino microcontroller with the exchange of forms.

Two programs on the GitHub repository use simple, readily available components that demonstrate the Arduino web server's use as an Internet controller of remote experimental setups (see `github.com/simonmonk/programming_arduino/blob/master/sketch_10_02/sketch_10_02.ino` and `github.com/sciguy14/Exploring_Arduino_1st_Edition/tree/master/Chapter%2014`).

The first referenced program of 148 lines of code presents the experimenter with a screen similar to Figure 10-16. An Update button is at the bottom of the screen. The code allows the system operator to turn the LEDs on a prototyping board on and off from the control screen or web page. The Update button sends the pin settings to the Arduino for action implementation. The five pin buttons on the display screen can be toggled between on and off settings. When testing the system, I reduced the component count by altering the code and hardware to process only two LEDs.

Program 2 in the reference is 165 lines of code and has three buttons to control an RGB LED and an edit box to enter a frequency for the sound produced by a tone generator mounted on the prototyping board with the diode.

Both programs are documented but assume the code user is reasonably well acquainted with the Arduino and HTML structures and formats. If you do not have a background sufficient to reproduce the programs, the original literature in reference 2-1 (Practical Electronics for Inventors 3rd Edn. Sherz and Monk, McGraw Hill, ISBN 978-0-07-177133-7) and 2-3 (Exploring Arduino, Blum, Wiley, ISBN 978-1-118-54936-0) can be reviewed.

Discussion

Data logging applications can be used in several varied applications. This exercise collects humidity and temperature data inside a closed and sealed, small chamber to measure water activity in the materials under test. Data logging can be used in a food safety quality control system to validate system performance. Data records prove that insulated sheet metal enclosures or cooled, light-proof chambers with biologically sensitive materials returned to their desired temperature and darkened conditions within certain time limits after being opened to add or remove materials in storage. (See relative humidity determination in Chapter 7.) Using infrared motion sensors, data logging systems can record people or animals passing through a portal or passageway (see Chapter 6).

Initial development work on the data logging system presented consisted of assembling the desired hardware and uploading the Arduino code to the experimental setup to start the operation under development. For practical use in either a laboratory or some field experiments, such a coarse method for activating and deactivating data logging activities is acceptable. A typical RTC depends upon its own battery to power the timekeeping integrated circuit. The IC's power consumption determines the service life of the timestamping capability.

Recording data from the 3-second equilibrium relative humidity sensor takes approximately 3600 days to fill an 8 GB card. SD cards have read and write speeds of 10 and 30 megabits per second (MB/s), and newer devices suggest speeds up to 98 MB/s are possible. At the manufacturers' elevated usage speeds, a 1 GB SD card could be filled in 10 seconds. A typical two- to three-year RTC battery life is not a concern where high read/write data logging speeds are encountered in relatively short time frames of minutes, hours, days, or months but can be a concern for experiments collecting data in yearly time frames.

As with all complex projects, you should start with simple tutorials and experiments to gain a basic understanding of the system being evaluated. Once the fundamentals of a system are understood and mastered, the next more complex applications can be studied and tested. Networking and Internet expansion is one of the more rapidly changing facets of SCADA types of process management from both a hardware and software point of view. The investigator new to this technology should start with the simplest exercises before entering the more advanced cabled, wireless, or unattended autonomous experiment monitoring. New technology cannot be appreciated without a thorough understanding of the basics upon which the recent innovations are founded. A great deal of time and effort can go into monitoring remote or inaccessible experimentation. You must ensure that reliable data is harvested.

Code Listings

Listing 10-3. Data Logging

```
//Time stamped data logging onto SD Card storage media.
// Electrical connections to Arduino
// RTC BoB - SCL -> analog pin 4; SDA -> analog pin 5; +5v & gnd
// SD BoB - CLK -> DI/O pin 13, DO -> DI/O pin 12, D1 -> DI/O pin 11,
   CS -> DI/O pin 10
```

```
//
const int chipSelect = 10;
//The RTC Library needs Wire
#include <Wire.h>
#include "RTClib.h"
RTC_DS1307 rtc; // define the rtc time object
//The SD library needs SPI
#include <SPI.h>
#include "SD.h"
// LCD library
#include <LiquidCrystal.h>
// constant for rows and columns on LCD
const int numRows = 4;
const int numCols = 16;
// initialize the LCD lib. with the numbers of the interface pins
LiquidCrystal lcd(9,8,7,6,5,4);
//
//
// set up variables using the SD utility library functions:
File dataFile;
#define LOGFILE "datalog.txt"     // "DATALOG" will be the file name title
                                  on the SD card
//
//library to read the temp/humid sensor
#include "DHT.h"
#define DHTPIN 2      // Arduino to DHT connection
// DHT 22 is the sensor with the required sensitivity and resolution
// for water activity measurements.
#define DHTTYPE DHT22    // DHT 22  datatype definition
//
// Connect pin 1 (on the left) of the sensor to +5V, grille is front of device
// Connect pin 2 of the sensor to DHTPIN 2 (Arduino DI/O pin 2)
// Connect pin 4 (on the right) of the sensor to GROUND
// Connect a 10K resistor from pin 2 (data) to pin 1 (power) of the sensor
```

```
//
DHT dht(DHTPIN, DHTTYPE); // declare an instance of the DHT class
//
void setup() {
  Serial.begin(9600);
  lcd.begin(numCols, numRows);
  dht.begin();
  //
  lcd.print("Logging Water"); // print message to the LCD
  lcd.setCursor(0, 1);
  lcd.print("Activity Data");
  //
  //Initialize the Sensor
  Serial.println("Initializing datalogger with RTC version 1.0");
 //
  Serial.println("Starting Temp and Humidity Sensor");
  dht.begin();
 //
  Serial.println("Starting SDCard reader and card");
  pinMode(chipSelect, OUTPUT);
  pinMode(SS, OUTPUT);
  //
  if (!SD.begin(chipSelect)) {
    Serial.println("SD Card initialization failed!");
    return;
  }
 //
  Serial.println("Opening logfile for write.");
  // Open up the file in which to write the data to be recorded or logged.
  dataFile = SD.open(LOGFILE, FILE_WRITE);
  if (! dataFile) {
    Serial.println("error opening log file");
    // check connections and test card in reader.
    while (1) ;
  }
  //
```

```
  //
  Serial.println("Starting Real Time Clock");
  #ifdef AVR
    Wire.begin();
  #else
    Wire1.begin();
  #endif
  //
  rtc.begin();
  //rtc.adjust(DateTime(F(__DATE__), F(__TIME__)));
  //If the RTC in use has not been synchronized with the time zone desired
  //two options are available. the rtc.adjust function two lines above
  //can be un-commented and this program rebooted. When the RTC shows the
  //time of the host computer, re-apply the comment indicators and the RTC
  //will then keep track of the time.
  //
  if (! rtc.isrunning()) {
    Serial.println("RTC is NOT running!");
  // The second time setting option that sets the RTC to an explicit
  // temporal point of a date & time desired, uses the following code to
  // set the parameters for January 21, 2014 at 3 am, call this uncommented
  // code once, then comment it out when the rtc shows the time required by
  // the investigator.
  // rtc.adjust(DateTime(2014, 1, 21, 3, 0, 0));
  }
  DateTime now = rtc.now();
  Serial.print("Unixtime: ");
  Serial.println(now.unixtime());
}
//
void loop(){
  char temp[6]; //2 int, 2 dec, 1 point, and \0
  char hum[6];
  char msg[13];
```

```
  //
  //get the temperature and humidity floats into chars to format
  ftoa(temp, readTemp());
  ftoa(hum, readHumidity());
  //
  //Compile a comma delimited string to send to the log
  sprintf(msg, "%s, %s" ,temp, hum);
  logThis(msg);
  delay(3000);// the equilibration time interval required between readings
              on the DHT
}
//
void logThis(char* logmessage){
  char message[120];
  DateTime now = rtc.now();
  long epoch = now.unixtime();
  int Year = now.year();
  int Month = now.month();
  int Day = now.day();
  int Hour = now.hour();
  int Minute = now.minute();
  int Second = now.second();
  sprintf(message, "%ld,%d/%d/%d %02d:%02d:%02d,%s",epoch,Year,Month,Day,
  Hour,Minute,Second,logmessage );
  //Write the entry to the log file.
  dataFile.println(message);
  dataFile.flush();// note that the message is not actually written until
                   the buffer is flushed.
  // print to the serial port:
  Serial.println(message);
}
//
```

```
//
float readTemp(){
  // The actual temperature and humidity readings take 250 milliseconds but
  // the sensor is based on there being an equilibrium between the sensor
  // surface and the headspace atmosphere which may take seconds to settle.
  float t = dht.readTemperature();
  float tf = t * 1.8 +32;   //Convert from C to F if desired
  lcd.setCursor(0, 3);
  lcd.print("tf=");
  lcd.setCursor(3, 3);
  lcd.print(tf);
  return    tf;
}
//
float readHumidity(){
  float h = dht.readHumidity();
  lcd.setCursor(9, 3);
  lcd.print("h=");
  lcd.setCursor(11, 3);
  lcd.print(h);
  return h;
}
//
//
int ftoa(char *a, float f)   //translates floating point readings into strings
{
  int left=int(f);
  float decimal = f-left;
  int right = decimal *100; //2 decimal points
  if (right > 10) {   //if the decimal has two places already.
    sprintf(a, "%d. %d", left, right);
  } else {
    sprintf(a, "%d.0%d", left, right); //pad with a leading 0
  }
```

```
  // LCD display code
    {
      // set cursor
      lcd.setCursor(0,2);
      //print the number of seconds since reset
      lcd.print("ET(sec) = ");
      lcd.setCursor(10, 2);
      lcd.print(millis()/1000);     // division by 60,000 will give minutes
        }
}
```

Listing 10-4. Recording Data as a 10-Bit ADC Scaled Numerical Value

```
#include <SD.h>
#include <Wire.h>
#include "RTClib.h"
#include <SPI.h>
// A simple data logging sketch for recording Arduino analog pin data from
// a light dependent resistor and a solid state temperature sensor. (TMP 36
// or LM 35) Data is time stamped and recorded each second by setting the
// milliseconds value to 1000.
//
#define LOG_INTERVAL  1000 // adjust as required for application at hand.
//
#define STOR_INTERVAL 1000 // mills time interval between calls to close()
                           that actually writes
// data to the SD card
uint32_t storTime = 0; // time of last data write
//
#define ECHO_TO_SERIAL   1 // echo data to serial port
#define WAIT_TO_START    0 // Wait for serial input in setup()
//
// the digital pins that connect to the LEDs
#define redLEDpin 2
#define greenLEDpin 3
```

```
//
// The analog pins that connect to the sensors
#define photocellPin 0          // analog 0
#define tempPin 1               // analog 1
#define aref_voltage 3.3   //Aref is connected to 3.3 volt supply
//
RTC_DS1307 RTC; // define the Real Time Clock object
//
// for the data logging shield, we use digital pin 10 for the SD cs line
const int chipSelect = 10;
//
// the logging file
File logfile;
//
void error(char *str)
{
  Serial.print("error: ");
  Serial.println(str);
  //
  // red LED indicates error
  digitalWrite(redLEDpin, HIGH);
//
  while(1);
}
//
void setup(void)
{
  Serial.begin(9600);
  Serial.println();
  //
  // use debugging LEDs
  pinMode(redLEDpin, OUTPUT);
  pinMode(greenLEDpin, OUTPUT);
```

```
  //
#if WAIT_TO_START
  Serial.println("Type any character to start");
  while (!Serial.available());
#endif //WAIT_TO_START
  //
  // initialize the SD card
  Serial.print("Initializing SD card...");
  // ensure the default chip select pin is set to output, even if not used:
  pinMode(10, OUTPUT);
  //
  // check for card presence and initialize:
  if (!SD.begin(chipSelect)) {
    error("Card failed, or not present");
  }
  Serial.println("card initialized.");
  //
  // create a new file
  char filename[] = "LOGGER00.CSV"; //recall 8.3 FAT SD restriction on
                                     filenames
  for (uint8_t i = 0; i < 100; i++) {        // uniquely identify
                                                numerically each
    filename[6] = i/10 + '0';                // file of data stored on
                                                the SD card

    filename[7] = i%10 + '0';
    if (! SD.exists(filename)) {
      // only open a new file if it doesn't exist
      logfile = SD.open(filename, FILE_WRITE);
      break;  // leave the loop!
    }
  }
  //
  if (! logfile) {
    error("couldnt create file");
  }
```

```
  //
  Serial.print("Logging to: ");
  Serial.println(filename);
//
  // connect to RTC
  Wire.begin();
  if (!RTC.begin()) {
    logfile.println("RTC failed");
#if ECHO_TO_SERIAL
    Serial.println("RTC failed");
#endif  //ECHO_TO_SERIAL
  }
 //
  logfile.println("millis,stamp,datetime,light,temperature");
#if ECHO_TO_SERIAL
  Serial.println("millis,stamp,datetime,light,temperature");
#endif //ECHO_TO_SERIAL
 //
  // If you want to set the aref to something other than 5v
  analogReference(EXTERNAL);
}
//
void loop(void)
{
  DateTime now;    //declare an instance of the DateTime
//
  // delay for the amount of time we want between readings
  delay((LOG_INTERVAL -1) - (millis() % LOG_INTERVAL));
//
  digitalWrite(greenLEDpin, HIGH);
//
  // log milliseconds since starting
  uint32_t m = millis();
  logfile.print(m);     // milliseconds since start
  logfile.print(", ");
```

```
#if ECHO_TO_SERIAL
  Serial.print(m);      // milliseconds since start
  Serial.print(", ");
#endif

  // fetch the time
  now = RTC.now();
  // log time
  logfile.print(now.unixtime()); // seconds since 1/1/1970
  logfile.print(", ");
  logfile.print('"');
  logfile.print(now.year(), DEC);
  logfile.print("/");
  logfile.print(now.month(), DEC);
  logfile.print("/");
  logfile.print(now.day(), DEC);
  logfile.print(" ");
  logfile.print(now.hour(), DEC);
  logfile.print(":");
  logfile.print(now.minute(), DEC);
  logfile.print(":");
  logfile.print(now.second(), DEC);
  logfile.print('"');
#if ECHO_TO_SERIAL
  Serial.print(now.unixtime()); // seconds since 1/1/1970
  Serial.print(", ");
  Serial.print('"');
  Serial.print(now.year(), DEC);
  Serial.print("/");
  Serial.print(now.month(), DEC);
  Serial.print("/");
  Serial.print(now.day(), DEC);
  Serial.print(" ");
  Serial.print(now.hour(), DEC);
  Serial.print(":");
  Serial.print(now.minute(), DEC);
```

```
  Serial.print(":");
  Serial.print(now.second(), DEC);
  Serial.print('"');
#endif //ECHO_TO_SERIAL
//
  analogRead(photocellPin);
  delay(10);
  int photocellReading = analogRead(photocellPin);
  //
  analogRead(tempPin);
  delay(10);
  int tempReading = analogRead(tempPin);
  //
  // converting that reading to voltage, for 3.3v arduino use 3.3, for 5.0,
      use 5.0
  float voltage = tempReading * aref_voltage / 1024;
  float temperatureC = (voltage - 0.5) * 100 ;
  float temperatureF = (temperatureC * 9 / 5) + 32;
  //
  logfile.print(", ");
  logfile.print(photocellReading);
  logfile.print(", ");
  logfile.print(temperatureF);
#if ECHO_TO_SERIAL
  Serial.print(", ");
  Serial.print(photocellReading);
  Serial.print(", ");
  Serial.print(temperatureF);
#endif //ECHO_TO_SERIAL
//
  logfile.println();
#if ECHO_TO_SERIAL
  Serial.println();
#endif // ECHO_TO_SERIAL
//
```

```
  digitalWrite(greenLEDpin, LOW);
//
  // Now data is written to the card.
  if ((millis() - storTime) < STOR_INTERVAL) return;
  storTime = millis();
  //
  // blink LED to show we are writing data to the card & updating FAT!
  digitalWrite(redLEDpin, HIGH);
  logfile.flush();
  digitalWrite(redLEDpin, LOW);

}
```

Listing 10-5. IP Address of 192.168.0.103

```
//DHCP - Dynamic Host Configuration Protocol
#include<SPI.h>
#include<Ethernet.h>
//
byte mac[] = { 0x90, 0xA2,0xDA, 0x0D, 0x79, 0x2A };
//
void setup() {
  Serial.begin(9600);
  while (!Serial) {};  // for Leonardo compatibility
  //
  if (Ethernet.begin(mac))
  {
    Serial.println(Ethernet.localIP());
  }
  else
  {
    Serial.println("Could not connect to network");
   }
}
  void loop() {
}
```

Listing 10-6. Reading analog inputs

```
// A simple reading from an Arduino web server.
#include <SPI.h>    // the SPI library for Arduino shield communication
#include <Ethernet.h> // Ethernet communications
// MAC address from the Arduino ethernet shield
byte mac[] = { 0x90, 0xA2, 0xDA, 0x0D, 0x79, 0x2A };
// The LAN IP address for Arduino shield determined by library DHCP program
byte ip[] = { 192, 168, 0, 103 };
EthernetServer server(80);        // declare an instance of the server on
                                  port 80
void setup() {
  Ethernet.begin(mac, ip);        //start ethernet
  server.begin();                 // start server program
  Serial.begin(9600);             // start serial
}
void loop() {
  // listen for incoming clients
  EthernetClient client = server.available();
  if (client)                     // true when a client becomes available
  {
    while (client.connected())    // true as long as connection maintained
    {
      // acknowledge connection by sending a standard http response header
      client.println("HTTP/1.1 200 OK"); // 200 indicates a connection, 400
                                     is an error
      client.println("Content-Type: text/html");
      client.println();      // empty line for end of acknowledgement
                                transmission
      // send the body
      client.println("<html><body>");
      client.println("<h1>Analog Inputs</h1>");
      client.println("<h2>Read from an Arduino Server</h2>");
      client.print("<p>A0 = ");
      client.print(analogRead(0));
      client.println("</p>");
```

```
    client.print("<p>A1 = ");
    client.print(analogRead(1));
    client.println("</p>");
    client.println("</body></html>");
    client.stop();
  }
  delay(1);
  }
}
```

Summary

Experiments conducted over very long time frames or in environments that are not able to be accessed by SCADA systems for process or experiment control in real time must autonomously collect and store data for future review.

Battery powered microprocessors equipped with real time clocks and secure data storage cards can form a compact, mobile, autonomous data collection and storage module able to activate and control the outputs from process or environmental sensors carried by the isolated independent unit.

Providing a host resident SCADA system with an Internet connection allows access to a virtually world-wide communications facility.

In Chapter 11 many of the various means by which power can be supplied to processes and experiments either local to or remote from the SCADA system will be examined.

## CHAPTER 11

Powering Experiments

Experiments that are an essential part of the scientific method must often be mobile, conducted in remote locations or in conditions isolated from disturbing laboratory influences. Isolated experimentation must carry with it or harvest from its surroundings the energy needed to generate, collect, process, store, or transmit data.

In alphabetical order, the readily available, longer-term power sources are batteries, mechanically powered generators, photovoltaic cells, thermoelectric piles, and thermoelectric generators. Wind or water-powered generators that spin electromagnets can be a source of either direct current using brushes or alternating current electrical energy in brushless devices. Brushed systems produce pulsed DC, while brushless devices that can produce usable AC require a rectifier to generate DC power.

In this section, our discussion on power sources focuses on the simpler, portable technologies consisting of batteries, photovoltaic cells, and wind- or water-powered generators. Mechanical-electrical energy generators can be assembled from smaller motors for low-power DC energy or larger currents from automotive alternators to provide an alternating electrical current. The theory and use of thermoelectric systems were explained in the chapters on measuring voltage and thermal phenomena.

In many applications, the power generated by sporadic or random variations of environmental conditions is harvested and stored through recharging batteries.

Batteries

Batteries are power sources that convert chemical energy into electrical and can be classified into two categories consisting of single-use and rechargeable units. The two battery types are often referred to as primary and secondary cells.

In 1800, Alessandro Volta described the first practical battery consisting of stacked pairs of silver and zinc circular plates separated by brine-soaked layers of cloth. The silver and zinc disks separated by the brine-soaked clothes were called *cells*, the metals

© Richard J. Smythe 2022
R. J. Smythe, *Arduino Measurements in Science*, https://doi.org/10.1007/978-1-4842-6781-3_11

were called *electrodes*, and the brine became known as the *electrolyte*. Silver was later replaced by copper, and the ability to vary voltages and current created by the constructs that were named *voltaic piles* through placing multiple cells in series and parallel to form what became known as *batteries* was developed throughout the nineteenth century.

In the original zinc- and copper-based devices, electrical energy is produced at the zinc electrode by the spontaneous chemical reaction in which the zinc metal dissolves in the electrolyte and releases two electrons. Zinc metal atoms from the surface of the metal plate area in contact with the electrolyte dissolve in the liquid water-based solution to form Zn^{2+} ions and concurrently release two electrons to the electrical circuit connecting the zinc electrode to the copper electrode of the cell.

At the silver or copper electrode, two hydrogen ions of a single positive charge each accept the two electrons from the electrical circuit connecting the negative and positive electrodes to become neutral atoms that form hydrogen gas.

$$Zn \rightarrow Zn^{2+} + 2e^- \text{ (oxidation reaction)}$$

$$2H^+ + 2e^- \rightarrow H_2 \text{ (reduction reaction)}$$

The chemical reactions occurring at the two metal surfaces are called *oxidation* and *reduction*. In the oxidation, the metal atoms undergo a change of oxidation state from zero to plus two for the zinc in the voltaic pile. The total zinc metal mass decreases as the pile produces an electrical current. In the reduction reaction, the positively charged hydrogen atoms, called *protons*, accept electrons from the copper electrode to transition from a net atomic charge of plus one to zero forming neutral hydrogen atoms that quickly combine to form hydrogen gas (H_2).

Within the voltaic pile, the mass of the zinc electrode is transformed from the metallic state to the oxidized form while water is converted into its constituent elements of hydrogen and oxygen.

In a voltaic battery, the action of zinc oxidation to form an aqueous compound zinc oxide, consumes the metal electrode. Eventually, the cell runs out of the ability to supply energy because of several interferences caused by the chemical reactions providing the pile's electrical driving force.

All materials resist the flow of electric current. For a battery constructed from metals and electrolytes, there is an inherent internal resistance in the battery due to the materials of construction and the electrolyte's chemical conductivity. In the pile's life cycle, a new assembly has minimum internal resistance.

As oxidation products accumulate in the electrolyte and on the electrode surfaces, the internal resistance of the pile increases. Further discharging causes the electrolyte's properties to change as the loading of oxidation products continues to increase in the liquid phase and reduce conductivity. Eventually, the increased resistance and increasing difficulty for the reactants to move and contact one another for the needed electrochemical reactions to occur causes the pile to cease being a useful power source.

In the two chemical reactions for the voltaic pile, the reaction products must be free to diffuse in the electrolyte to the metal electrodes where chemical reactions occur. The diffusion of the chemical reactants and products from the cell chemical reactions within the electrolyte determines the rate at which the battery can supply electrical power.

The effective total internal resistance of a battery is the sum of the electrical resistance of the construction materials and the ionic resistance of the electrolyte. All the metallic components used to construct the battery have electrical resistance to current flow and present a relatively constant contribution to the cell's internal resistance. Accumulation of electrochemical reaction products that influence electrolyte conductivity, ion mobility, and the electrode surface area are major contributors to the battery's internal resistance. At the electrodes' surface where the liquid electrolyte and solid electrodes contact one another, there are two ionic double layers (see Figure 7-5) in Chapter 7) that represent two capacitor elements. The presence of the two capacitive elements represents an impedance that renders the measurement of a battery's resistance by the simple application of Ohm's law as an approximation. However, the apparent resistance increase as a battery is discharged can be a useful approximate measure of the energy left in the battery. Internal battery resistance can be calculated with Ohm's law by measuring, simultaneously, the current drawn and voltage drop observed as a battery is discharged through a known resistance load.

Battery capacity is the amount of electrical energy stored in the device. A C rate, also called *hourly rate*, is the value used to find the maximum continuous safe discharge or charge rate at which the battery can be cycled. Ampere hours are also used to measure a battery's ability to deliver current to a load expressed as its ability to produce a fixed current for a defined period of time.

Slow discharge rates allow chemical reaction products to diffuse through the electrolyte, thus extending the battery's performance under load.

A battery in which the chemical action creating the electrical energy is not a reversible chemical reaction is known as a *primary cell*. Batteries assembled from these cells can only be used or discharged once.

Batteries made to use reversible chemical reactions as their source of electrical energy are classified as secondary cells and are rechargeable. Rechargeable battery chemistry is well over a hundred years old. The first rechargeable battery was described in 1859 using lead sulfuric acid chemistry. The nickel-cadmium rechargeable battery chemistry was published in 1898. Rechargeable batteries use a chemical reaction in which the reaction products form an insoluble product that adheres to high surface area electrodes.

All batteries using chemical reactions to create electrical energy are limited in the number of times they can be discharged. Single-use cells are discharged only once, while nickel-cadmium cells can be discharged hundreds of times and lead-acid batteries occasionally, thousands of times. Ultimate battery failure can usually be traced back to mechanical failure, impurities in the materials used in fabricating the battery, and most frequently, overcharging.

Different battery chemistries create different battery characteristics. Battery type is best selected after considering the electrical service required and costs involved. Frequently cost, weight, and convenience in the form of ease of recharging and cell robustness are the main parameters that determine what type of battery is to be used in an experimental application.

Battery costs are minimized by mass production of standard sizes. Cylindrical AAA, AA, C, and D batteries and the rectangular 9 V battery are the most common units. There are many sizes and shapes of batteries in production that vary from lightweight, coin type cells used in watches or computer memory applications, rectangular, thin, flat prismatic cells for telephones to heavy, box-like, automotive and forklift truck batteries. The first four standard sizes are usually only single-cell chemistries with voltages from 1.2 V to 3.4 V, as tabulated in Table 11-1. The 9 volt is a battery made up of multiple, single-cell units of 1.5 V placed in series. Lead-acid 12 V batteries are also multicell systems made up of six 2-volts-per-cell units to produce the nominal, familiar 12 V entity.

12 V lead-acid batteries are manufactured in many different sizes or amperage capacities because of their robustness, ability to supply a high current, ease of recharging, and readily available materials of construction. Primary batteries and single-cell rechargeable versions of the standard sizes are available in most of the electrochemical systems in use today. Different chemistries produce different energy storage capabilities, as shown in Table 11-1. AA batteries with alkaline, nickel, or lithium-ion chemistries have different capacities for current storage at slightly different voltage levels.

Battery capacities are measured in terms of current production capability for an hour, expressed as ampere hours (Ah) or milliamp hours (mAh) for smaller systems. C often denotes the nominal charge or capacity of a battery and is frequently used in discussions of charging or discharging rates.

Although batteries produced through mass production have uniform properties, individual units differ in voltage produced and internal resistance (see Table 11-2). Individual battery variations are minor differences in single-use applications such as flashlights but become a problem when used in rechargeable battery packs assembled from several rechargeable cells. Multi secondary cell battery packs assembled from standard-sized commercially available single-cell units to provide voltage and current capabilities not available from single-cell entities should exhibit the same internal resistance.

When connected into an electrical circuit, multiple single-cell, rechargeable battery units configured in parallel to provide higher currents in a battery pack function as resistors in parallel. If the internal resistances of the individual batteries in a parallel configuration are not as evenly matched as possible, the lowest resistance valued member of the group will pass the most current, develop the most heat and fail first.

All batteries must have a cathode, anode, and electrolyte to deliver power to a load when connected to an electrical circuit. A potential difference must exist between the anode and cathode before the cell can produce electrical energy. Energy in the form of an electrical potential difference is created by the pairing of electrochemical oxidation and reduction reactions that occur at the cathodes and anodes of batteries.

For measuring the voltage generated by a single electrochemical reaction, the standard hydrogen electrode was developed. A platinum electrode immersed in an acidic aqueous solution saturated with hydrogen gas was selected as the zero (0) voltage reference point for electrochemical reaction comparisons. With a standard reference electrode defined at 0 V, it is possible to measure the potential difference or voltage generated by an individual electrochemical reaction when combined with the *standard hydrogen electrode* (SHE).

When a SHE is configured as half of an electrochemical cell with an electrochemical reaction, the voltage developed by a single half-cell reaction can be measured. When a measured EMF for a chemical reaction is combined with a second reaction EMF, both determined with respect to the SHE the total EMF of the cell formed by combining the two tested reactions can be calculated.

The standard hydrogen electrode creates the electromotive series, which is an ordered listing of the electromotive force generated by the oxidation and reduction reactions of various elements and compounds.[1]

As listed in the electrochemical reactions discussed next, half-cell potential differences for the various common battery types available are given with respect to the standard hydrogen electrode.

Alkaline

Alkaline cells were first offered commercially as a replacement for zinc-carbon in 1959. Alkaline cells have a higher energy density than the zinc-carbon, exhibit a lower internal resistance than zinc carbon batteries, and are less prone to corrosion. Equipment was often destroyed when the ammonium chloride electrolyte leaked from a zinc-carbon battery due to corrosion.

The alkaline negative half-reaction is

$$Zn_{(s)} + 2OH^-_{(aq)} \rightarrow ZnO_{(s)} + H_2O_{(l)} + 2e^- \quad [e° = 1.28 \text{ V}]$$

The positive half reaction is

$$2MnO_{2(s)} + H_2O_{(l)} + 2e^- \rightarrow Mn_2O_{3(s)} + 2OH^-_{(aq)} \quad [e° = +0.15 \text{ V}]$$

They can be combined to form the overall chemical reaction as

$$Zn_{(s)} + 2MnO_{2(s)} \rightleftharpoons ZnO_{(s)} + Mn_2O_{3(s)} \quad [e° = 1.43 \text{ V}]$$

Alkaline cells can be built in a rechargeable format but such cells are not robust in comparison with other secondary batteries.

Lead Acid

Lead-acid batteries are the oldest form of rechargeable systems initially described in 1859. The 12 V rectangular format, most often encountered in lead-acid batteries today, often consist of thin lead rectangular plates immersed in an inert polymer box

---

[1]*Handbook of Chemistry and Physics*, 101ˢᵗ Ed. by John Rumble (CRC Press, 2020)

containing an aqueous 35%/65% volume on volume (V/V) sulfuric acid/water solution or a gelled electrolyte. Lead-acid systems are inexpensive, robust, and can deliver very high currents. Liquid filled batteries are becoming less popular as sealed lead acid systems with maintenance-free service lives become less expensive to manufacture. The disadvantage to all lead-acid systems is their weight. The current generating capability of this type of battery chemistry is of such value and utility that these systems have been studied, refined, and extensively modified from their initial simpler configurations.

The anodic or positive plate reaction (oxidation) is

$$Pb(s) + HSO_4^-(aq) \rightarrow PbSO_4(s) + H^+(aq) + 2e^- \quad [e° = 1.685 \text{ V}]$$

The cathodic or negative plate reaction is

$$PbO_2(s) + HSO_4^-(aq) + 3H^+(aq) + 2e^- \rightarrow PbSO_4(s) + 2H_2O(l) \quad [e° = -0.356 \text{ V}]$$

The total reaction can be written as

$$Pb(s) + PbO_2(s) + 2H_2SO_4(aq) \rightarrow 2PbSO_4(s) + 2H_2O(l) \quad [e° = 2.041 \text{ V}]$$

Lead metal is oxidized from the neutral state to the +2 state as $PbSO_4$ is formed at the cathode releasing two electrons while the lead in lead dioxide, PbO_2, is reduced from the +4 state to the +2 state in the formation of $PbSO_4$. Discharging depletes the sulfuric acid in the electrolyte and hence in the winter, a low charge can result in the battery being destroyed by freezing. Charging lead acid batteries restores the sulfuric acid to the liquid and hence the density of the electrolyte is indicative of the state of charge of the battery.

In liquid systems, the electrolyte's water level and density are monitored to maintain the battery, while sealed lead-acid systems are maintenance-free. A 12 V potential in lead-acid batteries is achieved by placing six 2 V cells in series.

Lead-acid batteries are manufactured for service in two differing applications. Starting batteries (SLI: starting, lighting, and ignition) have more and thinner plates than "deep cycle" batteries. SLI batteries use thinner plates in larger numbers to provide for higher surface areas that lowers the internal resistance of the battery and allows more current to flow on initial demand. Starting units rapidly deliver a high current. Deep cycle units with fewer but thicker plates are designed for lift trucks, wheelchairs, and golf carts where moderate but longer constant current delivery is desired and the battery is discharged to a very low voltage before being recharged.

The traditional form of a lead-acid battery in which an accessible liquid sulfuric acid serves as the electrolyte are being replaced by the much safer sealed, service free systems. Although the sealed system encloses corrosive liquids and allows no access to the acidic electrolyte, the battery is not gas-tight. Adequate care must be exercised in battery installations to accommodate hydrogen gas seepage from the unit. Sealing of the battery case is possible only when provisions have been made for the recombination of the gases produced by the electrochemical actions within the battery.

A valve is required to regulate sealed lead-acid batteries (VRSLA) so that the evolved hydrogen and oxygen can be recombined to form water within the battery case. Low pressures with internal and external catalysts aid in the formation of water. The regulator valves vent any excess internal pressure resulting from overcharging.

Sealed system batteries are also available in gelled cell and absorbed glass mat (AGM) variations in which there is no free fluid liquid in the device. The sealed and gelled electrolyte batteries are easily recognized by the absence of filler caps on the battery case. Gelled cells are manufactured in two consisting of those in which the electrolyte is thickened with silica compounds and those in which a glass mat is used to absorb the acid. Sulfation is a much lesser concern with the immobilized electrolytes than in the liquid-based cells. The gelled cell batteries store well and do not self-discharge as quickly as flooded cells but can be up to twice the cost of wet cells.

There are differences between the gelled cell and absorbed glass mat technologies that determine the best type of battery to use in an application. Gelled cells contain a thickened electrolyte while absorbed glass mat systems have the electrolyte dispersed in the glass cloths separating the plates. There is more electrolyte volume in the gel cell than in an equivalent AGM battery, which renders the gel cell a better selection for deep cycle service. AGM batteries can be fabricated with lower internal resistance, making them the preferred system for SLI service applications.

Regardless of the type of lead-acid battery deployed for field service, the manufacturer's charging recommendations should be followed closely since overcharging is one of the main causes of premature battery failure. In liquid-filled systems, the electrolyte levels must be maintained. The battery level of charge must be kept above the manufacturer's minimum allowable values.

Lithium Batteries

Lithium is the lightest, smallest atom in the alkali metal series of elements and has the highest electrical potential of –3.045 V. (The metal atom under the correct environmental conditions exhibits a 3 V potential driving force to get rid of its outer shell electron.)

Batteries are manufactured from relatively expensive materials in both primary and secondary formats. The primary cells used in critical applications that require long and dependable service, as required in surgically implanted pacemaker applications and portable electronic devices requiring real-time clocks (see Chapter 10).

There are approximately two dozen different chemistries used in lithium-based primary cells in which lithium metal or compounds serve as the anode. In many lithium primary cells, the toxicity and reactivity of some of the materials used in battery construction limit their availability for consumer applications.

Lithium secondary cells store and release electrical charge by moving the tiny lithium-ion in an electrolyte, back and forth between anode and cathode. The chemical phenomena in which an atom or molecule is stored in a layered structure is called *intercalation* and is the mechanism on which lithium-ion batteries operate.

Lithium cells exhibit some of the highest energy storage densities available, as witnessed by the proliferation of manned and unmanned electrically powered flying vehicles.

Rechargeable Lithium-Ion Electrochemistry

Lithium-ion migration is the charge transfer process operative in lithium-ion cells.

The positive layered electrode half reaction is

$$LiCoO_2 \leftrightarrow Li_{1-x}CoO_2 + xLi^+ + xe^-$$

The negative intercalated graphite electrode half reaction is

$$xLi + xe^- + xC_6 \leftrightarrow xLiC_6$$

This chemistry was used in the first commercially available rechargeable Li-ion cells developed by Sony in 1990.

Electrolytes for lithium batteries are typically $LiPF_6$ (lithium hexafluorophosphate), $LiBF_4$ (lithium fluoroborate), or $LiClO_4$ (lithium perchlorate) dissolved in propylene carbonate or dimethoxymethane solvents. All lithium and lithium-ion batteries built using toxic complex inorganic salts and flammable, poisonous organic liquids as electrolytes require care in the design, construction, applications, and end of life cycle disposal. The higher voltages and currents characteristic of these types of batteries, together with the volatile flammable nature of the electrolytes, can cause some spectacular fires when mechanical failures occur in these powerful battery systems.

Batteries constructed with lithium, cobalt, fluorine, and perchlorate–based chemistries are expensive, poisonous, and potentially reactive. Research groups are constantly investigating methods to mitigate these undesirable properties of lithium-based batteries. Consequently, there are numerous lithium battery systems available, each with its own compromises and properties.

Lithium-Ion Cobalt

Lithium-ion batteries based on layered cobalt oxide cathodes with graphitic anodes charge and discharge when lithium ions move through the cell electrolyte and enter the micro-structure of layered electrodes. The lithium cobalt batteries have been available since 1991.

Lithium-Ion Manganese

A layered structure such as a spinel mineral and lithium manganese dioxide has been used as an electrode in lithium graphite ion batteries since 1999.

Lithium-Ion Nickel Manganese Cobalt

Nickel manganese cobalt oxide ($LiNi_xMn_yCo_2O_2$) is a mixed metal cathode used with a graphite anode to compromise between high current, high capacity, and lower cost, first made available in 2008.

Lithium-Ion Phosphate

The lithium-ion phosphate ($LiFePO_4$) battery (LFP) is a lithium-ion rechargeable battery using lithium iron phosphate as a cathode material. LFP batteries have somewhat lower energy storage capacity than the more common lithium-ion designs but can last longer, supply slightly higher discharge rates, and are safer. LFP batteries were commercially available in 1996.

Nickel Cadmium

Nickel-cadmium battery chemistry is an older, well-established technology. Nickel-cadmium rechargeable cells can provide long service lives, are good at lower temperatures, can provide high discharge rates and relatively constant voltages during discharge. In certain circumstances, the constant voltage discharge can cause problems for applications that use the voltage drop to measure the energy left in a battery pack.

Nickel-cadmium cells can deliver full-rated capacity at relatively high discharge rates. Nickel-cadmium batteries are more expensive than lead-acid and have a higher self-discharge rate of about 15% to 20% of charge per month. Nickel-cadmium cells have approximately double the energy density of lead-acid batteries.

When manufactured from finely powdered materials, nickel-cadmium cells have a high surface area. If the cells are overcharged and not periodically deeply discharged, the finely divided active materials crystallize into larger aggregates that decrease the active surface area and sometimes radically reduce the battery storage capacity. If an overcharging loss of capacity occurs, consult the manufacturer's literature for the recommended pulsed charging procedure to restore most of the battery capacity. Nickel-cadmium batteries are sealed systems, and overcharging can cause excessive gassing that may destroy the cell.

The chemical reactions during discharge are as follows at the cadmium electrode.

$$Cd + 2OH^- \rightarrow Cd(OH)_2 + 2e^- \quad [e^o = -0.88 \text{ v}]$$

The chemical reactions during discharge are as follows at the nickel electrode.

$$2NiO(OH) + 2H_2O + 2e^- \rightarrow 2Ni(OH)_2 + 2OH^- \quad [e^o = +0.52 \text{ v}]$$

The net reaction during discharge is

$$2NiO(OH) + Cd + 2H_2O \rightarrow 2Ni(OH)_2 + Cd(OH)_2 \ [\text{cell} = 1.2 \text{ v}]$$

During recharging, the reactions reverse and proceed from right to left. The alkaline electrolyte (commonly potassium hydroxide KOH) is not consumed in this reaction and therefore its density is not a measure of the battery state of charge.

Nickel Metal Hydride

Nickel metal hydride batteries (NiMH) to a large extent have replaced the older nickel-cadmium technology since the commercial hydride introduction in 1989. A positive electrode chemical reaction involving nickel oxyhydroxide as found in the nickel-cadmium cell chemistry was paired with a negative electrode hydrogen-absorbing alloy consisting of rare earth elements to create a battery with no cadmium and two to three times the energy storage capability of the nickel-cadmium system.

The negative electrode reaction occurring in a NiMH cell is

$$H_2O + M + e^- \rightleftharpoons OH^- + MH \quad [e^\circ = +0.52 \text{ v}]$$

The equilibrium represents the charge and discharge reactions. When current is applied to the cell, an added electron causes water in the presence of the mixed metal rare-earth electrode to split into the hydroxide anion and metal hydride. When discharged, the metal hydride hydrogen atom combines with the hydroxyl anion and releases an electron to the circuit connecting the battery electrodes.

The nickel oxyhydroxide, NiO(OH), is formed on the positive electrode.

$$Ni(OH)_2 + OH^- \rightleftharpoons NiO(OH) + H_2O + e^- \quad [e^\circ = +0.83 \text{ v}]$$

A cell usually produces a voltage of 1.25 V, and like the earlier NiCd batteries provide a relatively constant voltage throughout their discharge. Some manufacturers suggest that cells not be used in applications that drain their voltage to values below 1 volt before recharging. Recharging should be done by following the manufacturer's specifications, and as with all battery types, overcharging should be avoided.

Rechargeable batteries using Ni chemistry have some of the highest self-discharge rates known. In 2005, NiMH batteries were made available with self-discharge rates reduced by a factor of 10.

Research is constantly improving the NiMH cell chemistry, the materials of construction, and at the time of writing, battery performance is only surpassed by lithium systems.

Zinc Carbon

Zinc carbon cells were the first commercial, portable batteries produced and were used in the first flashlights sold in 1900. Zinc-carbon *dry cells* are the least expensive batteries in production today. Although called *zinc carbon*, the carbon does not play an active part in cell electrochemistry. Zinc metal is used as the battery case and serves as the negative battery terminal. Corrosion of the battery terminal can lead to leakage of the internal electrolyte, resulting in the battery compartment of the device being powered getting contaminated with liquid ammonium chloride electrolyte.

As in all zinc electrochemical energy production the metal is oxidized, as shown in the battery half cell reaction.

$$Zn(s) \rightarrow Zn^{2+}(aq) + 2\ e^- \ [E° = -0.7626\ V]$$

The positive terminal is a non-corroding graphite rod surrounded by a powder of manganese (IV) oxide and finely granulated carbon to increase the electrical conductivity. The half-reaction is as follows.

$$2MnO_2(s) + 2\ e^- + 2NH_4Cl(aq) \rightarrow Mn_2O_3(s) + 2NH_3(aq) + H_2O(l) + 2\ Cl^- \ [E° \approx +0.5\ V]$$

In the chemical equation, the ammonium chloride forms chloride anion, ammonia gas, and water, while the manganese is reduced from a charge of (+4) to (+3).

There are other possible side-reactions, but the overall chemistry in a zinc-carbon cell can be represented as

$$Zn(s) + 2MnO_2(s) + 2NH_4Cl(aq) \rightarrow Mn_2O_3(s) + Zn(NH_3)_2Cl_2\ (aq) + H_2O(l)$$

During the last century, numerous mechanical and chemical advances were made to improve the zinc-carbon system's performance, including zinc chloride as an electrolyte and plastic coatings to prevent leakage.

Zinc Manganese

Zinc manganese or alkaline batteries differ from the zinc-carbon cells in their use of potassium hydroxide rather than the corrosive acidic ammonium or zinc chloride electrolyte. These batteries were first commercialized in the late 1960s as primary cells. Although less prone to leakage, these batteries can still release caustic potassium hydroxide and should be stored separately from infrequently used equipment.

The voltage of an alkaline battery declines steadily during discharge.

Table 11-1 summarizes some of the features of readily available battery systems.

Table 11-1. *Properties of Readily Available Battery Types*

Battery Type Name	Battery Chemistry	Cell Voltage	Energy Wh/kg	Density Wh/L	Self Discharge	Recharge cycles
Alkaline	Zn/MnO_2	1.43	85-190	250-434	n/a	< 100 essentially not rechargable
Lead acid	$PbO_2/PbSO_4$	2.04	30-40	60-75	4-6%/mo	500
Lithium	$Li^+/graphite$	3.2 - 3.9	90 - 220	333 - 600	2-3%/mo	300 - 7000
nickel cadmium	NiCd	1.2	30	100	15 - 20%/mo	500
nickel metal hydride	NiMH	1.2	100	353	30%/mo and 2-3%/mo	300 - 1500

Recharging Secondary Cell Power Sources

To recharge secondary cell batteries, electrical energy must be supplied to reverse the chemical reaction that provides electric current during discharge. Since the energy production reactions are diffusion-controlled, the rate at which the battery can deliver and receive energy is also fixed. In addition to diffusion, the battery has its own internal resistance that regulates the current flow into the cell for a given charging voltage and can create heat with prolonged charging times.

Each manufacturer has a recommended recharging procedure that must be followed to achieve optimum performance from single-cell rechargeable batteries.

Although mass-produced, each individual cell has its own internal variation in variables, such as materials of construction, quantity and quality of chemicals used, dimensional variations, and other parameters that should result in each cell having a different charge storage capacity.

A high-resolution voltage measurement made on 6 AAA cells selected at random from a bulk 24-unit package displayed the values tabulated in Table 11-2.

Table 11-2. *Variation in AAA Cell Voltages*

cell	voltage	cell	voltage
1	1.609	4	1.607
2	1.611	5	1.609
3	1.606	6	1.609

The variations measured in the AAA cells that apply to all single-cell batteries can cause problems in recharging battery packs made from several individual cells wired in a series or parallel configuration. When designing a higher voltage or current battery pack using multiple single cells, using an appropriate battery cell holder that allows the removal of the individual cells for recharging is recommended for non-critical experiments.

When using a series of removable cells in a battery pack, you should selectively match the cells in the pack, so the internal resistance or capacity of the individual cells is as close together as is possible.

When a multiple cell rechargeable battery pack is to be used in a remote field or difficult to access experiment, a battery balancing charging/discharging system should be used. Individual cells have different voltages and charge storage capacities. A charge balancing system distributes charging and dispenses current to maintain each cell's state of charge (SoC) at the same level. The system actively minimizes the influence of the individual cells' different capacities during charging and discharging. A weak or low-capacity cell does not determine the battery pack's behavior and does not prematurely fail from overloading. Charge balancing circuitry can be implemented in either the charger or the battery pack.

Charge balancing is controlled by a microprocessor unit that avoids overcharging any one cell, balances the charging to all cells, and can monitor the temperature of the battery pack during charging and discharging cycles when equipped with a thermistor sensor.

Charge balancing allows the battery pack to accept and deliver the maximum energy possible while providing the maximum possible service life for the system.

Lithium-ion, nickel-metal hydride, and lead-acid batteries are probably the most often used sources of stored electrical power. Line voltage powered intelligent charging systems are the most common form of restoration of the energy in these devices.

Service life demands often dictate the type of battery used in an application, as with the two types of lead-acid battery used for starting or deep cycle power delivery. Recharging with programmable charging systems to adapt to the different cell chemistries and battery pack configurations is the best way to obtain the most power and longest service life from these power sources.

Figure 11-1 depicts a collection of rechargeable power supplies and batteries.

Figure 11-1. *Rechargeable power supplies and batteries*

Item A is a nickel-cadmium battery charger that can handle all formats of NiCd batteries as single or up to six serial connected cells for the AAA to D formats and single-cell 9 V batteries.

Items B, C, and D are 12 V lead-acid recharging power supply, sealed lead acid battery, and heavy current cables.

Item E is a microcontroller "smart" or balanced charging system. Two lithium phosphate battery packs of 4000 (blue) and 2600 (white) mAh capacity are immediately below the charger. Distributed around the charger are some of the connection cables (black and red) that connect the different battery types to the charger.

Virtually all types of consumer-available battery types and battery packs can be recharged with the balanced charger. Lithium batteries and battery packs require special control circuitry in both discharging and recharging. Lithium cells cannot be discharged completely and must not be overcharged. Each battery pack must have a battery management system (BMS) either as an internal or external circuit board that monitors the battery pack voltage drop and limits it to a safe level. The BMS must also monitor the charging process to limit any overcharging that destroy the lithium cells. The "smart" charger can function as a BMS for the lithium battery packs.

Item F is a one to four-cell nickel-metal hydride charger. Surrounding the NiMH charger are four-cell battery packs with cells whose internal resistance was determined and marked on their outer cases as they entered service several years ago. To maximize service life, the cells with similar internal resistances are grouped when used as rechargeable battery packs.

Four cell rechargeable battery packs, especially the AA formats, are exceptionally useful in developing bench or desktop prototype digital-analog circuitry.

Over the years of developing the projects in this book and creating novel physiochemical testing procedures for a civil forensic science practice, I have accumulated a large assortment of AA format cells, some of which are seen in Figure 11-1. Nickel-cadmium cells have been in use for a long time and are found in many older portable battery-powered electronics. Many of the nickel chemistry-based cells that I accumulated lost their capacity to hold a usable charge through "memory effect" and overcharging.

Some of the five sources in Figure 11-1 were unable to retain much charge when recharged with the NiCd and NiMH chargers A and F in Figure 11-1. Most of the nickel-based batteries exhibiting poor performance were restored to a usable state, and in some cases, a state comparable to new batteries after being cycled through charge and discharge cycles with the equipment depicted in Figure 11-2.

Items A and E in Figure 11-2 are inexpensive DMMs set to measure the open circuit voltage (OCV), voltage under load, and the current through the load to provide the data required to calculate the apparent internal resistance of the battery or battery pack. Item B is a load testing circuit with terminal boards to change resistance loads as required, switch resistance loads into and out of the voltage drop testing circuit with the requisite meter connections to monitor load current and voltage differential. The schematic for the circuit is depicted in Figure 11-12. Item C is a six AA NiMH cell battery pack, and D is an Imax B6 microprocessor-based "intelligent" battery charging and discharging system.

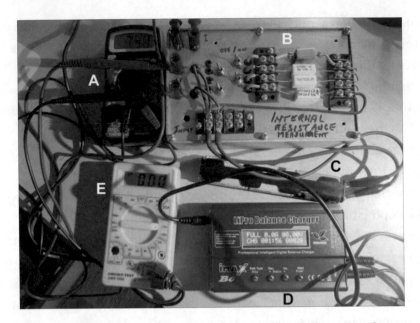

Figure 11-2.   *Rechargeable battery maintenance, monitoring and testing*
equipment

Discharged batteries are recharged by applying an electrical potential high enough
to overcome the EMF of the discharged cell and its internal resistance, and force a
current into the cell that reverses the original discharge reaction chemistry, thus storing
electric charge in a chemical format. Electrical energy input must be terminated as the
cell charge approaches its design level of capacity to prevent overcharging, the primary
cause of shortened battery service life.

Photovoltaic Cells

In moderate latitudes, sunlight can irradiate the earth with approximately a kilowatt of
power per square meter (93 watts/ft^2). Photovoltaic (PV) solar panels can recover 130
watts per square meter under optimum conditions.

A PV cell directly converts sunlight into electrical energy. Most PV cells are large
area PN junction diodes fabricated in the traditional method by adding low quantities of
elements that create holes and excess electrons in the host silicon crystal lattice's structure.

The PN junction exhibits a band gap that forms a ½ V potential difference across the
silicon photovoltaic cell. PV cells are made from semiconductors in which the incident
sunlight can raise electrons to an energy level sufficient to jump the PN band gap created

in the chemically altered semiconductor material. The number of electrons elevated in energy and crossing the band gap is proportional to sunlight falling on the cell. PV power is thus dependent on physical factors involving the geographic location of the solar array, angle with respect to the incident sun, time of day, and local weather at the time of power demand.

Like the electrochemical cells that assemble battery power packs, PV cells can be combined in series or parallel arrays to produce the desired voltage and current required for an experimental application. The lower voltage produced by PV diodes means that larger numbers of cells must be combined to generate the nominal 5 V, 6 V, 9 V, and 12 V standard systems common in battery power supplies.

To combine PV power sources in series and parallel to obtain additional voltage or current in the cellular array, sources must be of equal voltage to add currents and equal current ratings to be additive with respect to voltage.

Many solar energy collection systems replenish storage batteries or battery packs. Electrical loads that depend on a constant source of energy for continuous operation can then operate when darkness or inclement weather reduces or eliminates solar radiation. The electrical power generated by PV panels must be passed through a controller to recharge a depleted battery or battery pack but not harm the storage cells through overcharging.

When no current is drawn from an illuminated PV cell, the voltage across the cell is known as an *open circuit voltage* (OCV). Light intensity creates the cell current, and attempting to draw more current than the cell can supply causes the voltage to drop to zero, and the maximum current that can be drawn is called the *short circuit current* (SCC). When solar energy is used as a recharging source, an integrated circuit is needed to control the current draw by the battery charger to the point at which the maximum current drawn is just below the point at which the voltage is noticeably affected. Charge controllers are available from many manufacturers to manage both low and high-current PV panels.

Larger current PV panel controllers handling amperes of current use PWM or maximum power point tracking/transfer techniques (MPPT). PWM applies recharging power in proportion to how far below the normal operating voltage the cell in service has been discharged. As the cell or battery pack approaches its normal operating voltage, the pulse width narrows, and less current is applied, thus not overcharging the storage device.

MPPT or maximum power point tracking converts voltage to current and allows the PV charging system to operate at maximum efficiency all the time.

PWM and MPPT systems are only for high-current applications and are expensive, with PWM systems being half the cost of MPPT. The expensive nature of systems collecting and managing high-current electrical power is best selected after researching the techniques' applicability to the collector and storage devices at hand.

As depicted in Figure 11-3 illustration A, PV cells can be considered a diode when in the dark, and a voltage source able to power a load when illuminated. PV cells can be represented as a current source in parallel with a diode in Figure 11-3 illustration B and display the typical current-voltage curves found for semiconductor diodes as graphed in illustration C.

When exposed to sunlight, the photons absorbed by the photovoltaic cell cause the separation of charge by exciting electrons that jump across the PN junction. The holes and electrons can recombine when the current flows through an external circuit whose impedance matches the PV source. The PV array's internal impedance can be determined by measuring and recording the currents and voltages present in an electrical circuit that has varying values of total resistance within the current loop. Typically, PV cells have a higher internal resistance of approximately 1 Ω/cm^2.

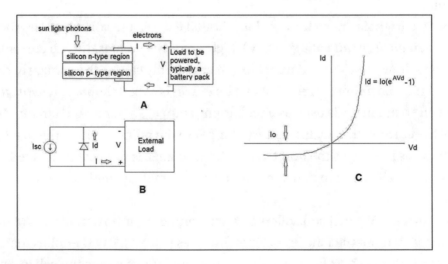

Figure 11-3. *Photovoltaic power*

PV array panels are available from many sources that cater to the camping, boating, and home improvement interests and electronics suppliers. Figure 11-4 depicts a nominal 12 V, 7 W panel of amorphous silicon solar cells, suitable for charging car, boat, and power sports vehicles 12 V batteries. The large panel is 16 in × 12 in × ¾ in (40 cm × 30 cm × 2 cm), weighing 4 lbs or 2 kg purchased from a large automotive supply store for $40 CDN. Typically, PV panels cost $4 to $5 USD per watt.

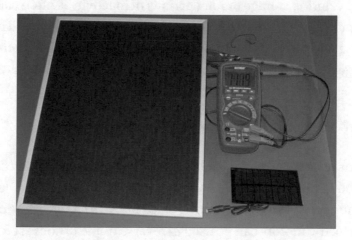

Figure 11-4. *Photovoltaic panels*

The larger panel in Figure 11-4 is connected to a multimeter that indicates a voltage output of 11.19 V solely from overhead fluorescent light illumination. In outdoor daylight, on a completely overcast day, the voltage rose to 20.5 V but only produced single-digit mA of current.

The smaller 12 cm × 7 cm (2¾ in × 4¾ in) panel is equipped with a barrel jack for use with an Arduino.

On a bright sunlit day, the panel delivers 200 mA at 5 V—sufficient to satisfy the auxiliary power supply requirements of the microcontroller. (Arduino has a built-in voltage regulator circuit to accommodate up to 12 V of unregulated input.)

The larger panel is equipped with two heavy-duty high-current battery clamps designed to furnish 7 W of power to a 12/24 V battery charger. The smaller panel was built specifically for supplying power to the Arduino's built-in auxiliary power supply-regulation circuitry.

Direct sunlight that provides the maximum amount of activity across the PN junction also heats the bulk mass of the collector array and decreases the efficiency. PV panels are evaluated at 25°C (77°F) and have a specified temperature coefficient that predicts the loss of efficiency per degree of temperature difference from the 25°C standard temperature. A typical value of a fifth of a percent per degree can make a substantial difference if panels heat to 50°C or 75°C on a hot, sunny, summer day or operate near-freezing temperatures.

Lead-acid battery charging can be divided into classifications involving replenishing charge depleted from heavy power draws on the battery and maintenance of charge to offset self-discharging effects during prolonged storage. Adding a small amount of charge to a battery during storage or long periods of inactivity is often called *trickle charging*. Distinguishing between the requirements of replenishing and maintenance or trickle charging are the two major reasons that a solar charging system must provide power to a storage device by way of properly designed charging circuitry.

Wind- and Water-Powered Generators

Electric motors have been in use for well over 125 years and commonly convert electricity into rotary motion. Continuous rotation electric motors can be built in various sizes to power the cooling fans on computer chips or drive streetcars. Virtually all the various sizes of electric motors can be used in reverse mode to convert rotary motion into electric current.

Electric motors (also known as *stepper motors*) are built to partially and fully rotate. Stepper motor rotation direction and speed can be controlled with microprocessors and integrated circuits manipulating the pulsed electrical power delivered to the windings of the motor. Stepper motors are built in many sizes and with several internal wiring and shaped coils for specific applications. Only the simpler forms of stepper motors are in this demonstration exercise for creating electrical power from wind or water motion.

The purpose of creating the smaller, simpler, stepper motor power source is to use readily available inexpensive components to familiarize the experimenter with the basic design process that can then be scaled up if necessary, for heavier field use as required.

Wind or moving water can turn a purpose-built generator or automotive alternator to produce alternating current electrical energy. The size of the coils inside the rotating device determines how much power can be generated. Automotive and light truck engine driven alternators typically produce 50 A to 70 A when driven by 100+ horsepower sources. Smaller stepper motors that fit into the hand, will produce correspondingly smaller electrical power outputs.

A stepper motor is built with numerous sets of connected and center tapped coils evenly spaced around the peripheral of its circular case. The wiring schematic for a typical six wire motor is depicted in Figure 11-5. The center-tapped six-wire configuration is called a *unipolar winding*. In a five-wire motor, the two common wires are combined into one. A bipolar motor has continuous coils and requires an H bridge to reverse the current through the coils to reverse rotation. Bipolar motors are usually bigger with more torque. The rotor of a stepper motor is built with permanent magnet segments or teeth magnetically attracted to the nearest energized electromagnet around the inside surface of the motor case. By controlling the sequence in which the outer coils are energized, the motor can be made to rotate in either direction with speeds varying from single "steps" to several hundred RPM.

A rotational force applied to a stepper motor converts the motor into a small multipole alternator/magneto that can generate power at relatively low rotational speeds, usually under several hundred RPM. The stepper motor's ability to produce electrical energy at relatively low rotational speeds makes it a good experimental development project. A hand crank can simulate the sporadic nature of wind or water flow to aid in the laboratory benchtop prototype development of stepper motor electrical generators. To investigate the power output as a function of rotational speed a second stepper motor driven from a mains-powered controller or a variable speed drill (see Figures 11-14 and 11-20) can spin the motor-generator to collect data and optimize system performance before field deployment.

To use a stepper motor as a DC power source, the alternating current pulses created as the rotor's segmented permanent magnets are spun past the inner coils a rectifier and capacitors can be used. A typical small stepper motor has 12 magnetic poles on its rotor (see Figure 11-13). Spinning a rotor with 12 magnets on the peripheral edge produces a complex pattern of electrical pulses to any load attached to the motor winding leads (see Figure 11-14).

The coils in stepper motors have a relatively large inductance. As the RPM increases, the output frequency rises, and the coil impedance tends to limit the current.

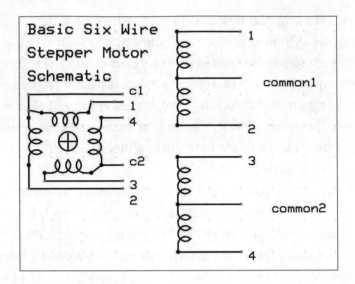

Figure 11-5. *A six-wire stepper motor schematic*

A simple schematic for creating a rippled DC output from a wind- or water-driven turbine is depicted in Figure 11-6.

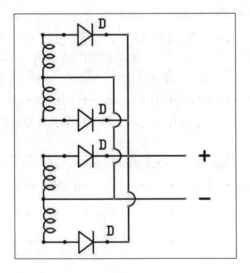

Figure 11-6. *A stepper motor rectifier*

Because the power production from an alternator or magneto spun by wind or water is in an AC format the voltage from the alternator can be increased using the multiplier circuits in Figure 11-7.

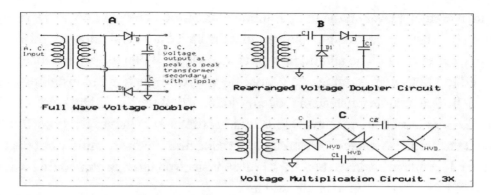

Figure 11-7. *Voltage multiplication circuits*

In the schematics in Figure 11-7, a transformer is depicted as the source of the AC that is to be manipulated by the following diode capacitor circuitry. For simple doubling or tripling of the low-level voltages produced by natural power sources turning a small stepper motor, the motor windings become the transformer's output windings and the desired diode capacitor circuits can be used. During the design of an amplification circuit, the laws of conservation of energy must be kept in mind. As the voltage doubles, the current available is halved. As the voltage increases, the diodes' and capacitors' voltage breakdown limitations must be adjusted accordingly.

To begin designing a stepper motor-based energy-harvesting project, a simple qualitative evaluation experiment can be performed with LEDs, the correct current limiting resistors, and a prototyping board. The stepper motor common wire or wires can be inserted into the ground or common strip on the board. The LEDs with the proper value of current limiting resistor can be connected in series with the diode and the colored wires of the motor coils.

When the diodes and resistors are connected and the motor shaft is rotated by hand, all the diodes flicker on and off in proportion to the rate at which the shaft is rotated. As the power being produced is AC, the experiment shows that the generator system lights the diodes, regardless of which way the shaft is rotated and regardless of which way the diodes are wired into the circuitry. With a Howard Industries, 12 V DC, 3.6° step, 1½ in (37 mm) square stepper motor, I generated 2 V AC by twisting the 3/16 in (5 mm) shaft between thumb and forefinger.

The system can be vastly improved by installing a set of four diodes as depicted in Figure 11-8 and placing a high-value electrolytic capacitor across the positive and negative output leads. The diodes provide a half-wave rectifier creating a varying DC voltage, and the storage capability of the capacitor smooths the output ripple and provides a measure of energy storage.

With a cranking lever on the shaft, rotation of the motor created a 4 V to 5 V charge across a 16 V 1000 µF electrolytic capacitor that displayed a several minute typical voltage decay curve with no additional input and no load. When the capacitance was increased to 11,000 µF by adding a 25 V large electrolytic capacitor and installing two full-wave bridge rectifiers instead of the four diodes, the system could be hand-cranked to store 6.75 V across the capacitor. Hand cranking the motor charges the capacitor in the expected fashion. The voltage measured on the capacitor increases rapidly but begins to slow as the voltage begins to build. A 47 µF 35 V electrolytic capacitor could be hand-cranked to 7.25 V with no load on the system.

By modifying the circuitry to that depicted in Figure 11-8, with two 1 µF 400 V electrolytic capacitors in the circuit, the hand-cranking could generate slightly over 24 V for brief periods of time with no load.

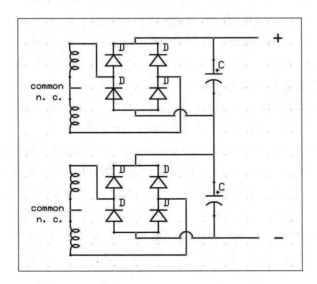

Figure 11-8. *A voltage doubler for stepper motor electricity*

Probably, the best strategy for using the power generated by the stepper motor is to rectify it, smooth as much of the ripple out of the current stream as possible, and use the DC formatted power with a voltage regulator to charge a battery.

Battery charging circuits can be assembled from voltage regulator ICs such as LM317, and the type of battery charging suggested by the battery manufacturer should be followed.

Thermoelectric Power

Experimental equipment operating near a readily available source of waste heat can use bismuth telluride solid-state systems to create DC electrical power. Bismuth telluride plates are mainly used to pump heat (see Chapter 3) and generate low-voltage electrical energy.

Thermoelectric power systems are similar to PV. Each power-generating element or array has a limited low-voltage energy supply in which the power developed is directly proportional to the temperature difference across the plate. As with the other electrochemical and PV power generation, the open circuit voltage, internal resistance, power generation variation, and load to be energized must be determined.

Thermoelectric generation (TEG) is not very efficient (i.e., 2%–3%) and can only be used where a significant temperature differential can be created across the generating plate (maximum temperature exposure of plate < 100°C). Bismuth telluride TEG plates have high internal resistance, and drawing current with a low impedance load causes the voltage to drop and increased heat to be developed inside the plate.

Maximum power transfer can only occur when the supply's impedance and load match. To use off-the-shelf TEG plates to supply optimal electricity to a load, the parallel/series combinations of the plates must be arranged so the internal resistance of the TEG array matches that of the load. Series voltage and parallel current connection additions apply to TEG plates as with PV and electrochemical sources. In practice, better system performance occurs when load resistance exceeds the internal resistance of the TEG array.

Thermopiles consisting of multiple thermocouples in series are most often encountered in pilot light safety circuits on gas-powered appliances. The thermopile is heated by a flame that serves as an ignition source for a main heating burner. The low-voltage signal from the thermopile is monitored by a circuit that controls the main power to a solenoid that controls the gas flow to the main burner. If the pilot light goes out, the solenoid closes, and gas cannot be supplied to the burner. To use a thermopile as a power source would require a heat source of hundreds of degrees to produce usable electric power.

Creation, Control, and Measurement of Higher Voltage, Low-Current Electricity

Introduction

Although low-current high-voltage electrical energy is a destructive force for the integrated circuitry used in computing and electronics, it has become a mainstay of life sciences. High-voltage potentials are used in numerous liquid-phase ionized biological structure separations. Chromatographic separations (first reported by Tswett at the turn of the nineteenth century) driven by gravity led to pressure-driven gas-phase separations developed by Martin and Singe in the mid-twentieth century. The need to increase separation capabilities progressed into high-pressure liquid chromatography and eventually to electric potential driven fractionation of charged species in liquid systems currently known as *electrophoresis*. High-voltage potentials are used in gas chromatographic flame ionization detectors to collect the ions from hydrogen flame combustion. High-voltage potentials serve as a driving force in gas phased ion mobility separations.

Electric potential driven chemical separations of both analytical and bulk quantities of biological materials have led to the development of the mathematical theory of separations in terms of the chemical engineering concept of distillation columns using internal refluxing plates. Chemical separation efficiency is mathematically defined in different terms for each of the various types of physiochemical separation methods in use, and all figures of merit are expressed as the *height equivalent to a theoretical plate* (HETP).

In high-voltage capillary electrophoresis, the separation efficiency of an experiment is given by N where

$$N = \mu V / 2D_m$$

μ is the apparent mobility in the separating medium. V is the applied voltage. D_m is the diffusion coefficient in the separating medium. In the separation equation, N, the separation efficiency, is directly proportional to the applied voltage.

Practical limitations restrict the applied electric field to several hundred volts/cm. The best resolution for a separation is often obtained at the point of maximum field strength for which joule heating is insignificant.

High-voltage potentials are required for ionization types of detectors, ion optics, and devices such as cloud chambers.

There are several different techniques to create high-voltage potentials. Van de Graff generators, Wimshurst machines, and devices such as the Dirod machine described by Prof. A. D. Moore generate high static voltage potentials most often used in classroom demonstrations.[2] For quantitative and qualitative experimentation, most high-voltage power supplies must be controlled and regulated. Controlled and regulated high-voltage supplies can be created from lower voltage sources using multiplier circuits such as those depicted in Figure 11-7.

A completely solid-state switch-mode DC to DC higher voltage converter without a transformer is the most efficient power converter known and used extensively in portable battery-powered devices. Switch mode systems use either inductors or capacitive storage media and require significant electrical engineering knowledge to design and implement.

An inexpensive, easier to understand and construct high-voltage supply based on a traditional method was developed by the MIT physics department. Fortunately, the high-voltage, low-current DC power supply described in the following text is compatible with researcher safety concerns producing very unpleasant shocks or minor but painful burns if you accidentally short-circuit the power supply output.

High-Voltage Power Supply Components

High-voltage, low-current, electrical energy can be created with compact, lightweight, wire wound, ferrite core transformers that are the physical opposite of the heavy, bulky units used to create high-current, low-voltage DC power sources for dry-well heaters and electric motor applications. High-voltage, low-current transformers operate at much higher AC frequencies than the common 60 Hz units used for low-voltage applications.

Transformers use electromagnetic induction to transfer energy between two mechanically and electrically isolated circuits. In schematic drawings like Figure 11-7, simple transformers are represented by a three-component symbol consisting of two oppositely facing spirals, separated by a series of parallel lines. The spiral on the left represents the input or primary coils of the device; the series of parallel lines represent the core of the transformer around which the coils are wound, while the spiral on the right represents the output or secondary coil of the component symbol (see Figure 11-7).

---

[2]*Electrostatics* by A. D. Moore, (Laplacian Press, 1997).

High voltages at a low current can be created from lower voltages at higher current using a transformer with a large difference in the number of turns of wire on the primary and secondary coil windings.

A transformer is a device that requires an alternating current to function. By using a variable, direct current source to power a higher frequency oscillator connected to the primary windings of a high-voltage transformer, a higher voltage, low-current signal is created in the secondary windings of the device. By using a different number of coiled conductors in the primary and secondary coils, the electromotive force (EMF) or voltage levels can be "stepped" up or down as desired.

To generate the higher voltages commonly encountered in experiments involving electrophoresis and high-voltage static accumulations, an adjustable output value power supply capable of generating kilovolt electric fields, at virtually no-load conditions, would be desirable.

In 2005, the MIT physics department published the plans for a laboratory assembled, adjustable high voltage power supply. The documents described how a controlled, high-voltage potential could be created using a variable, low-voltage, DC supply as the input power source.

Figure 11-9 is a block diagram illustrating the electronic components used to assemble an adjustable high-voltage source. Initially, a variable low-voltage, high-current electrical flow is used to power a high-frequency oscillator circuit in the primary windings of a radio frequency transformer. When current from the high-frequency oscillating circuit is passed through the primary windings of a specially wound transformer, in which the ratio of secondary to primary turns is large, a high-frequency, high-voltage electrical signal is created in the circuitry connected to the secondary windings.

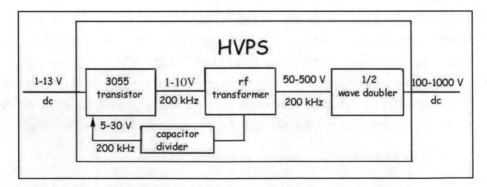

Figure 11-9. *MIT high-voltage power supply block diagram*

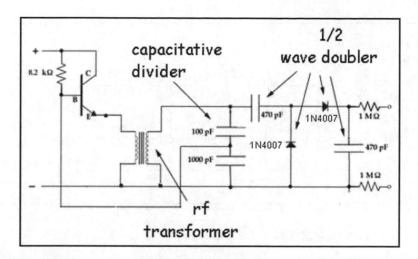

Figure 11-10. *MIT high-voltage power supply*

The MIT circuitry published in 2005 used a wire-wound 4 mH inductor that students wrapped with several turns of a heavier wire to serve as the primary windings of a high-voltage transformer in which the inductor then functioned as the secondary coil.

I modified the original MIT design by using a high-voltage transformer from Information Unlimited, part number 28K077, with a step-up ratio of 1:135. In addition to the new radio frequency (rf) transformer, 1N4007, 1 kV diodes were used in the secondary output that now provided a slightly higher output than the original circuitry.

The high-voltage supply in Figures 11-9 and 11-10 uses a low-voltage, adjustable output DC voltage of 1 to 13 V to power an oscillator using the 2N3055 power transistor and the primary windings of the rf transformer. The oscillator operates at a much higher frequency than the line voltage while driving current through the transformer's primary windings, so the output can be varied from a nominal 100 to a 1000 V at a safe current of less than a milliapmere. The secondary windings have a voltage divider that takes 1/ 11th of the output to feedback to the 2N3055 based oscillator at up to 30 V at 200 kHz. Usage of the new rf transformer increases the upper limit of the supply range to 1.3 kV.

The high-frequency oscillator circuit power in the primary windings of the high-voltage transformer is stepped up by the high-voltage windings to the 600 V range and applied to a half-wave voltage doubling circuit to provide the kilovolt output.

A typical circuit schematic for the adjustable low-voltage supply is depicted in Figure 11-11. The high-voltage supply could work with any low-voltage source able to produce an adjustable 2 to 12 V supply able to deliver up to 1 A of current.

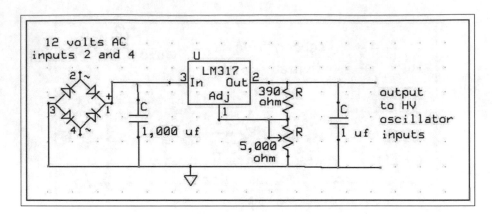

Figure 11-11. *Low-voltage oscillator supply*

Most of the high-voltage applications in scientific experimentation, such as for the polarizing voltage in ionization detectors, the accelerating voltage in ion optics, and cloud chambers, are used in situations of extremely high impedance, and virtually no current flow is expected.

Electrophoresis systems for separation of bioactive materials need the isolation of sufficient materials for further experimental work. They may operate with milliamps of current, thus requiring extra heavier components in the high-voltage supply and extra care to safely handle the possibly lethal voltage-current power levels created by high-voltage regulators.[3]

A simple application of the low-current high-voltage supply can be realized in the design and semi-quantitative calibration of classical electroscopes for electrostatic demonstrations. My high-voltage system was built in accordance with the circuits shown in Figures 11-10 and 11-11 to test the aluminized Mylar film electroscope (see item 1 in Figures 8-19 and 8-20 in Chapter 8).

A direct connection of the positive lead of the high voltage output to the aluminum collector plate on the electroscope was used to determine the applied DC voltage at which the metallized film began to diverge from the supporting plate that started at about 400 V. A low-power laser pointer reflected from the metal leaf could increase the sensitivity of the measurement and provide a calibration scale for semi-quantitative measurements.

---

[3] *The Art of Electronics* by Paul Horowitz (Cambridge University Press, 1989)

High-Voltage Measurement

Many handheld and benchtop DMM and VOMs can measure voltages between 600 V and 1000 V without damage. You should confirm the meters' specifications before attempting to test circuits. Voltages higher than the meters' capability can be attenuated with a voltage divider that divides the supply output into a range compatible with the meter's specifications. The resistors used in assembling the voltage division network should be as high a resistance value as possible and of an accurately known value to minimize the load current drawn from the supply while simultaneously minimizing resistance heating and providing a reasonably accurate division of the voltage tested. Resistance voltage divider circuits and the effects of load impedance are discussed in *The Art of Electronics*.

Test measurements should not be attempted on live high-voltage circuits. Test probes or voltage divider networks should always be connected to circuit components with the power off and the voltage test points grounded before connections are made.

Once the test probes' attachment to the circuit or the divider network is confirmed, and all connections are sound and short free, the power can be restored to the circuit and the readings taken from the meter. High voltages can be lethal.

Experiment

Determining the Internal Resistance of Power Sources

Battery Packs

As battery packs and batteries discharge oxidation products are generated and accumulate in the electrolyte increasing the solution resistance. The internal resistance of a discharging battery rises throughout its service life until it reaches the point at which no useful current flows through the load in the circuit. By measuring the internal resistance of a battery or battery pack, you should be able to gauge the charge or service life remaining in the power supply.

Batteries consist of two separated, dissimilar metal electrodes immersed in a liquid electrolyte (see Figure 7-5 in Chapter 7). Each electrode is surrounded by a liquid ionic "double layer" that forms two capacitors within the cell. The presence of the capacitor elements requires an impedance measurement technique to properly determine the internal resistance of a battery or battery pack.

Although the complex electrochemistry that occurs within the battery requires special techniques to determine the true internal resistances, two simpler techniques can gauge the apparent internal resistance of a battery or a battery pack.

A power supply driving a load constitutes a complete electrical circuit. Theoretical electronic calculations show that the optimum transfer of power from supply to load occurs when the load's impedance matches that of the supply. Ohm's law applies to the completed circuit of a supply driving a known load and can determine the power supply's apparent internal resistance through several methods.

Determinations of the open circuit voltage and the circuit voltage under a known load can calculate the power supply's internal resistance through the following reasoning. The source produces a maximum EMF when no current is drawn. When the load draws a current, the EMF drops as the load resistance and the source's internal resistances add to regulate the current flow in the circuit. With the current flowing in the circuit, the voltage drop across the circuit total resistance is defined by Ohm's law, represented as V_{cct}. Hence,

$$EMF = I(R_{cct} + r_{int}) \text{ or } EMF = IR_{cct} + Ir_{int}$$

$$\text{substituting for } IR_{cct} ; EMF = V_{cct} + Ir_{int} \text{ and } EMF - V_{cct} = Ir_{int}$$

$$\text{from which; } (EMF - V_{cct})/I = r_{int}$$

EMF is the open circuit or no-load voltage of the source. r_{int} is the internal resistance of the source. V_{cct} is the voltage drop across the circuit resistance. I is the current through the load resistor.

The testing circuit in Figure 11-12 can be used for any DC power supply, including electronically regulated laboratory devices, small plugin wall units, battery packs, and photovoltaic cells and panels. A voltmeter determines the voltage drop across a known series electrical resistor. The current flow through the circuit is measured by the ammeter.

In the circuit diagram in Figure 11-12, there are no values given for the resistors R1 to R4 because the actual values used are determined by the DUT's nominal voltage value and the ammeter's current-measuring capabilities.

In Figure 11-2, the load resistor array in item B consists of a selection of high-power, low-resistance devices selected for testing the nominal voltage of 3.3 V, 5 V, 6 V, 9 V, and 12 V power sources. The resistance values were 1Ω, 10Ω, 150Ω, and 1200Ω with 1% and 5% tolerance limits and 5 W power ratings to accommodate the anticipated low-voltage drops expected during actual testing.

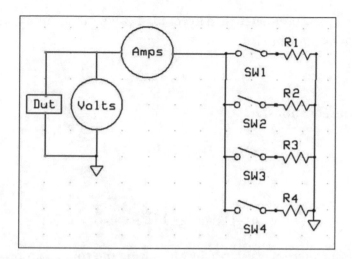

Figure 11-12. *Circuit for determination of internal resistance of power supplies*

The preceding formula is of limited utility with fully charged, large, high power lead-acid batteries or well-regulated power supplies. If the measured voltage change under load is not large enough to generate a reliably measurable value for the EMF – V_{cct} term, then a different load or technique may be necessary to measure the supply's internal resistance.

Care must be taken when using the circuitry in Figure 11-12 to avoid a damaging current flow at low load resistance in the ammeter.

A second method of measuring the internal resistance of a battery or battery pack that uses the resistor array in item B in Figure 11-2 does not measure the open circuit voltage.

Connecting a battery to a circuit (as depicted in Figure 11-12 with the closed topmost switch) establishes the well-known voltage, current, resistance relationship with load resistor 1 in the circuit, as follows.

$$V_{LR1} = V_{oc} - I_{LR1}r_{ir}$$

After recording the circuit's electrical parameters with load resistor 1 in place, the load control switch is opened, removing the resistor from the circuit. The next measurement is made by closing switch number 2 to place a second lower value load resistor into the circuit. When the voltage and current have stabilized, the values are recorded, and the load control switch is opened to minimize the power drain on the supply under test.

For the second measurement with a lower load value in the circuit, the current, voltage resistance relationship is

$$V_{LR2} = V_{oc} - I_{LR2}r_{ir}$$

Subtracting the equations,

$$V_{LR1} - V_{LR2} = r_{ir}(I_{LR2} - I_{LR1})$$

or

$$r_{ir} = (V_{LR1} - V_{LR2})/(I_{LR2} - I_{LR1})$$

Determining the internal resistance by measuring the voltage drop with increasing load current eliminates the need to measure the OCV of the DUT. Battery manufacturers use an automated version of the dual loading method in their quality-control operations.

Photovoltaic Panels and Arrays

To test PV panels or arrays for their internal resistance, a source of constant illumination must create a constant EMF and current supply.

PV cells and panels are best tested with varying resistance loads beginning with an open circuit EMF voltage measurement under no-load conditions. An incremental load resistance is added to the evaluation circuit, and the cell voltage and load current are recorded. If the load draws a current less than what the cell can supply, the voltage drop is minor, and the internal resistance is low. A second measurement can be made with a lower value load resistance to draw a higher load current and the panel or cell voltage and load current recorded. The process is repeated until an incremental current draw causes the source voltage to drop significantly. The current drawn at the point where the cell EMF is virtually non-existent is the SCC.

If required, the true internal resistance can be calculated from the tabulated current and voltage data immediately preceding the SCC point (see Figure 11-17).

Integrated circuits on breakout boards can regulate the load current drawn from the PV panel for battery charging to keep the photocell voltage level at the peak power transfer point. (See Microchip MCP73871 USB/AC Battery Charger with Power Path Management and Microchip Portable Power Conversion Design Guide at www. microchip.com/analog).

Power Generation from Mechanical Action

In addition to solar power, a large portion of the electrical energy made available today is derived from the additional renewable resources of wind and water. In 1831, Faraday demonstrated that passing an electrical conductor through a magnetic field causes a current to flow in the conductor. Faraday's laws of induction show that electrical energy and mechanical energy can be interconverted with motors and generators.

Figures 11-13a and 11-13b display a selection of various types of small motors collected from the repair and salvaged stock supplies in my laboratories. The two images show the shape and size variations seen in small motors used in computers, printers, scanners, robotics, and cooling/heating oven circulating fan applications.

The small size of the motors seen in the figures is indicative of the small power generation that can be expected from using some of these devices as electrical generators.

Items A, B, and C are three possible devices that might be adapted to producing small quantities of power for sensors. Items in the lower row are typical examples of the different types of brushless stepper motors recovered from obsolete equipment. Item E has a convenient connector board to make removal and installation of the motor for any required servicing easier.

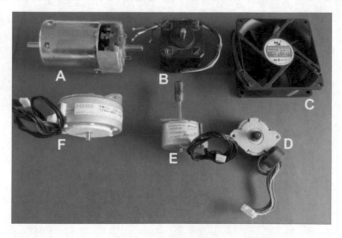

Figure 11-13a. *Motors able to generate electricity*

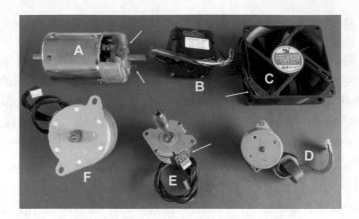

Figure 11-13b. *Motors able to generate electricity*

Item A in the dual figures is a brushed DC motor in which 12 V DC is applied to the copper terminals indicated by the white arrows. With a 375 mA current, the motor spins at 1200 rpm under no load. If the motor's rotor is spun at 600 rpm, a 1.93 V output can drive a 1.6 mA current through a 1200 Ω load (see Figure 11-20).

Item B is a Howard stepper motor that divides each revolution into 100 steps of 3.6° each. When fitted with a hand crank and rotated vigorously, the 12 V motor, configured with the circuitry in which the two rectifier bridges provided varying DC to a dual 1 μF 400 capacitor voltage doubling configuration could sporadically produce 20 V to 23 V.

To collect quantitative current and voltage data at different rotation speeds from the motor-generator, a second stepper motor driven from a motor speed controller and the mains was coupled to the Howard stepper motor "power generator" as depicted in Figure 11-14.

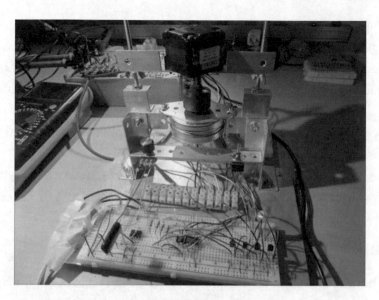

Figure 11-14. *Stepper motor magneto/generator powered by a controlled stepper motor*

Figure 11-15. *Stepper motor magneto/generator rectifier and voltage doubler*

To increase the rectification circuit's electrical storage capacity, the capacitor bank was increased by fitting a pair of 1000 µF 35 V electrolytic capacitors into the circuit in Figure 11-6.

Item C in Figure 11-13b is a simple two-wire 12 V brushless DC motor cooling fan. In normal usage power is applied to the motor to drive the fan and force cooling air over heated electronics. The compact electronically controllable brushless DC motor produces only a rectified 217 mV electrical output and virtually no measurable current when spun by a 9 m/s air stream.

Items D, E, and F are various sizes and shapes of stepper motors found in printers, scanners, and robotics applications.

To evaluate the power generation capability of motors like those in Figures 11-13a and 11-13b, a variable speed hand drill can rotate the shaft (see Figure 11-20).

Observations

Before testing battery and solar power sources for internal resistance, the low-voltage resistance box depicted as item B in Figure 11-2 with the circuit diagram in Figure 11-12 was tested on a 12 V 2 A wall mount power supply. Open circuit voltage drop and current measurement techniques indicated an internal resistance of 0.398 Ω while the voltage drop under dual loadings suggested an internal resistance of 0.170 Ω. The two different values illustrate the nature of these simplistic measurement techniques.

A series of internal resistance measurements were made on the supply of nickel-metal hydride (NiMH) and nickel-cadmium (NiCd) batteries in my possession, with the results tabulated in Table 11-3. The data was collected to assemble rechargeable battery in which each bank of four cells could be as closely matched in internal cell resistance as possible to minimize the stress on the lowest resistance cell when multiple cells were recharged in parallel.

The NiCd cell #12, with an internal resistance of 0.444 Ω, would not produce a stable voltage or current readings when loaded with the low resistance testing value after an initial charging to full capacity preceding internal resistance measurement. The cell was discharged through the 10 Ω resistance value until its voltage dropped into the millivolt range, at which point it was then placed back in the charger for second recharging. The deep cycling returned the cell to an open circuit voltage of 1.376 V. The cell performed as expected in the testing sequence exhibiting stable readings indicating an internal resistance of 0.444 Ω. Cell #7 responded to a similar refurbishment.

Table 11-3. *Internal Resistance of Typical in Service Nickel Rechargeable AA Cells Sept. 2016*

Rechargeable Cell Internal Resistance and Capacity				
AA Cells	NiCd	Capacity	NiMH	Capacity
1	0.496	900	0.246	2500
2	0.354	900	0.241	1400
3	0.496	900	0.122	2500
4	0.708	900	0.348	1400
5	0.600	700	0.232	600
6	0.882	600	0.115	600
7	3.670	1000	0.343	600
8	0.477	1000	0.232	600
9	0.595	900	0.227	2000
10	0.750	900	0.114	2000
11	0.896	600	0.121	2000
12	0.444	900	0.118	2000

Diffusion plays a significant part in the electrochemical reactions during charging and discharging cells and is also active during cell storage. Four AA cells of equal capacity electrical energy storage capability in both NiMH and NiCd chemistries were mounted in four place battery holders to measure the typical self-discharge rate for each battery type. The battery packs' open circuit voltage was measured over 60 days and plotted as depicted in Figure 11-16.

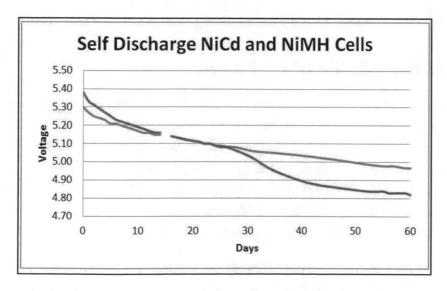

Figure 11-16. *Self-discharging NiCd (in blue) and NiMH (in red)*

During the creation of this book, several battery packs were assembled from new, salvaged, and refurbished NiCd and NiMH batteries from a wide variety of sources. The battery packs were all labeled in a somewhat arbitrary fashion as they were assembled, and several of the four cell units have been in use for five or more years. Table 11-4 is compiled from data collected during the preparation of this exercise to demonstrate the utility of measuring the internal resistance of battery packs and demonstrate the variation between the OCV depression and voltage difference by incremental loading techniques.

Table 11-4. *Assorted Battery Pack Internal Resistance Determination by Two Methods*

Bttry Pk	OCV	V_{load}	i_{Load}	Intrnl Rstnc	V_{load2}	i_{load2}	Intrnl Rstnc
1	5.6	5.57	5.74	5.23	5.39	49.8	4.09
2	5.42	5.41	5.58	1.79	5.35	49.6	1.36
3	5.2	5.19	5.35	1.87	5.13	47.4	1.43
4	5.41	5.4	5.57	1.80	5.36	49.6	0.91
5	10.5	10.44	10.77	5.57	8.65	80.3	25.74
6	7.81	6.48	6.7	198.51	6.25	57.8	4.50
6r	8.29	8.26	8.55	3.51	8.15	75.5	1.64
5r	11.1	11.02	11.46	6.98	10.58	98.3	5.07

Battery packs 1 and 2 are NiMH. Battery packs 3 and 4 are NiCd. Battery pack 5 is an eight-cell unit with 4 NiCd and 4 NiMH. Battery pack 6 is 6 NiCd cells. (Each "bank" of cells in pack 5 are charged separately.)

Internal Resistance of PV Panels

To evaluate the variation in power collection typically observed with a solar panel, and to measure the current-voltage relationships under load, the small 5 V 200 mA PV panel in Figure 11-4 was tested under the constant illumination of solid-state LED desk lamps placed close enough to the panel surface to produce an open circuit voltage (OCV) potential of 5.35 V. In the constant illumination condition, a sequence of known *resistance values* were placed in series with the panel. The resulting current and voltage values were measured. Figure 11-17 depicts the panel's I-V curve.

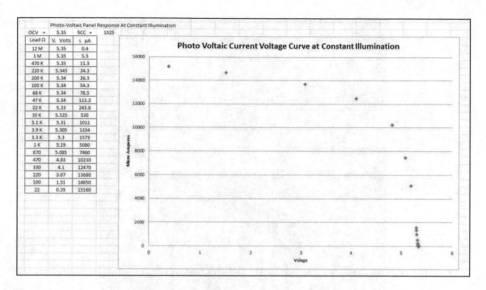

Figure 11-17. Current-voltage curve for 120 x 70 mm PV panel

On a partially overcast day in November, the large panel depicted in Figure 11-4 developed a 23.9 V potential difference. Although fluctuating because of cloud conditions, it still deliverws approximately a half-watt of power to a 1200 Ω load.

Internal Resistance of a Stepper Motor Magneto/Generator

Figure 11-18 depicts the voltage "ripple" created by the multiple poles of the stepper motor used as a magneto/generator source to generate electrical energy.

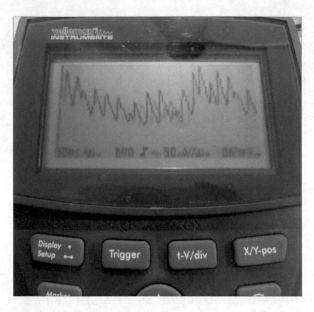

Figure 11-18. *Rectifier output waveform from stepper motor magneto/generator*

A series of test measurements made using the dual stepper motor driver-stepper motor-generator setup in Figures 11-14 and 11-15 produced the data tabulated in Table 11-5.

Table 11-5. *Stepper Motor-Generator Output*

RPM	OCV	V$_I$	I$_I$	Power
67	14.86	3.9-3.1	3.88 - 3.45	12.8
67	15.0 - 14.9	3.8 - 3.6	3.26 - 3.91	13.3
68	16.25	3.3 - 3.8	3.88 - 3.46	13
150	14.68 - 14.70	5.2 - 4.9	5.25	26.5
93	14.71 - 14.75	3.60 - 4.23	4.23 - 3.62	15.3
89	14.35	3.3 - 4.1	4.07 - 3.61	14.2
193	22.5	7.6 - 7.1	7.50 - 7.45	55.2
186	31.1	7.4 - 7.1	7.30 - 7.43	53.4
193	21.65	7.35	7.69 - 7.57	56.1

Discussion

Powering experiments becomes difficult when the apparatus is out of reach of the mains power supply or is disturbed by its presence. Batteries are often the most practical power source for remote field locations and in isolated environments. If battery longevity is necessary in a remote location, an electronic charging system could be constructed to harvest energy from the surroundings to replenish power.

Power derived from electrochemical reactions in batteries is virtually noise-free and often suitable for use in sensitive experiments such as those using electrometers.

Batteries

Single-use and rechargeable battery power supplies can be assembled from the standard formats commercially manufactured for consumer use. The majority of single-cell or grouped cell battery packs rely on electrochemical reactions to produce electricity in discharge mode, and in secondary cells, absorb charge during recharging.

Battery cell electrochemistry is, in many cases, a liquid-based reaction in which the rate at which ions can diffuse to and away from the electrode surfaces determines the rate at which power can be delivered to, or received from, the external circuit connected to the cell.

An electrochemical system in a battery cell generates electrons by oxidation/ reduction reactions. In a fresh, zinc-based chemistry battery, the preponderance of the chemicals is in the reduced metallic state and, when oxidized, releases electrons to do work in the external circuit. In primary cells, the oxidation proceeds until there is not enough metal left to sustain a usable electron flow. The transition from metal atoms to oxide-based compounds is accompanied by a corresponding rise in cell resistance. In many energy-production electrochemical cells, the internal resistance can gauge the state of charge in the system.

As is evident in Table 11-4, the two methods for measuring internal resistance produce figures of merit of similar magnitudes but consistently different numerical values. The two methods appear to differ by about 20% at low values of apparent internal resistance, with the dual current measurement being lower. When the measurement of the OCV is being made, the cell interior is in a static electrochemical environment because no oxidation/reduction is taking place. When the current flow is initiated, diffusion to and from the electrodes controls the rate of charge transfer to the external circuit. It could be argued that using Ohm's law in a static environment that changes to a dynamic system is biasing the technique to a higher apparent internal resistance than is calculated when the high OCV is eliminated.

Some support for the bias toward higher internal resistance values resulting from the use of the OCV is found in the values calculated for the mains powered wall mounted supply that contains no electrochemical cell.

Each of the two techniques is reasonably reproducible and can be a reasonable technique to estimate the relative state of charge of a battery. When working with one or more types of batteries, you should note the technique to measure the apparent internal resistance of any given cell and the value measured for primary cells or freshly charged for secondary cells. Use of the apparent internal resistance technique is a comparative exercise, and reference data must be available for the technique to be of any value.

A common feature in both of the mathematical techniques used to estimate the internal resistance of an electrochemical storage media is the elimination of the numerical values of loads in use. Although the load resistances' numerical values do not appear in the calculations, the values chosen for a testing circuit (see Figure 11-12) should be as high as practical. High load resistance values create low-current flows, and the ammeter must be able to accurately measure the lower currents.

Both internal resistance measurement techniques draw current from the storage media. If the battery being tested is a coin cell or an expensive lithium primary in a circuit troubleshooting exercise, the OCV technique only draws current once while the dual current technique does so twice. If the tested primary cell is to be returned to service, the OCV method is preferred.

Battery manufacturers use an automated voltage drop technique because it requires only current and voltage measurements at two different loads.

Precautions must be practiced when using the voltage drop technique.

- The resistors used as test loads must be scaled to accommodate the source's voltage with wattage ratings sufficient to handle the current draw.

- The meters to determine the source voltage and circuit current should be fuse protected on their inputs and must sustain and read with sufficient resolution the current and voltage parameters during testing.

– The current draws should be as short as possible to minimize heating of circuit components and discharge the batteries/source. Secondary cells can be replenished after testing but primary cells cannot. Excessive current draw should be avoided if the battery is to be placed into service after testing.

The leading cause of rechargeable battery failure is through overcharging. Overcharging causes overheating that can destroy many of the finely divided, high surface area materials and chemical compounds that allow the battery to function cyclically. Overcharging can be avoided by using a microprocessor-controlled recharger such as item E in Figure 11-1.

Programmable control of the recharging power applied to the different electrochemical reactions in the cells can reduce the power applied as the cell voltage rises from its discharge state back to its fully charged level. A microprocessor can limit the time of power application and measure the amount of charge accumulated by the battery to avoid overcharging. Energy can be restored to the cell with a host of different techniques such as recharging at either constant voltage or constant current and using PWM to reduce power application as the cell returns to its fully charged state.

A microprocessor can avoid overheating by pulsing the recharging power on and off, allowing the cell to cool between current inputs.

In addition to recharging, the microprocessor-controlled charger can also "recondition" certain types of rechargeable cells, especially the nickel-based units. Controlled discharging and recharging cyclically as described in charger operating manuals can often restore much of the original nickel battery capacity in deteriorated cells.

Before discarding NiCd or NiMH cells with a high internal resistance, the variable resistance apparatus in Figure 11-2 discharged these cells to less than one volt. The cells were then recharged with the dedicated NiMH charger seen as item F in Figure 11-1. By deep discharging and recharging, I successfully restored several cells to a useful state.

The microprocessor-controlled unit in Figure 11-1 can automatically refurbish nickel chemistry cells with precise discharging-recharging cycles.

Recharging can cause minor quantities of side reactions in battery electrochemistry that accumulate and eventually limit the number of times that a cell can be recharged.

A comprehensive summary of the electrochemistry and physical characteristics of batteries and chargers is at www.mpoweruk.com/index.htm.

Constant voltage charging applies a DC current at a voltage higher than the EMF of the cell being restored. Lead-acid and lithium-ion batteries use this simple and inexpensive method.

Constant current charging systems are often used with nickel chemistry batteries switching off when full charge is achieved.

Taper current is used for SLI batteries only. The charger current tapers off as the cell voltage rises to meet the fixed voltage of the charging source.

Pulsed charging applies current to the battery in modulated widths. PWM pulsing allows the chemical reactions at the electrode to proceed, diffusion to replenish chemicals at the electrode surface, excessive heat to dissipate and allow measurement of the OCV between pulses.

Battery charging or discharging rates are often quoted as the C-rate that measures the rate at which charging or discharging occurs relative to the battery's capacity. A battery rated at 250 mAh charging it with 25 mA current would be a C rate of one-tenth. Discharging it at a rate of 2500 mA would be a discharge rate of 10. Consult the battery manufacturer's literature for the allowable C rates on charge or discharge for the battery at hand.

Experiments that use secondary cell battery power sources benefit from acquiring a recharger using a programmable microcontroller to recharge the power packs in benchtop or lab use where line voltage power is available.

Photovoltaic Cells

Silicon photocells can generate 0.6 V of potential difference for each PN junction exposed to sunlight. The number of cells in series determines the maximum voltage that a panel can deliver. Current flow is dependent on the absorption of photons. The brighter the sun exposure, the larger the current flow for driving a managed load.

The two panels seen in Figure 11-4 are two readily available units that are purposely built for harvesting solar energy to supply a "downstream" voltage regulator or battery charger. The small 5 V panel is designed and built to plug directly into an Arduino's auxiliary supply to provide solar energy to the microcontroller. The large 24 V panel is sold primarily as a source of energy for a lead-acid battery charger to replenish large current draws from a battery bank and provide "trickle" charge maintenance during periods of inactivity.

The curve seen in Figure 11-17 is typical of solar panels. To use the maximum power available from these devices, the current draw must be controlled to keep the voltage below the "knee" portion of the I-V curve. The electrical power harvested from the PV panel must be channeled through a charging controller to keep the power transfer at its maximum and simultaneously avoid overcharging the battery bank.

There are many solar battery charging systems available from automotive, sporting goods, and home improvement suppliers for virtually all forms of rechargeable batteries used in vehicles, portable power tools, and electronics.

If required, solar power controllers for small systems able to handle fractional ampere currents in experimental setups can be obtained from several electronic kit suppliers such as Adafruit Industries and SparkFun Inc.

Mechanical Energy

Experiments conducted in locations near moving water or in locations devoid of sunlight but accessible to moving water or wind can also draw power from the environment through mechanical action. Water is 820 times as dense as air. Small amounts of moving water can provide a large amount of force to turn a turbine at a useful speed. Moving air requires a large amount of surface area to collect enough force to spin turbines at the same useful speed.

Speed of rotation determines the voltage that a motor can create when used as a generator. Using electromagnetic induction to create electricity by powering a motor to act as a generator is inefficient. An inefficient conversion process is offset by the readily available and virtually free nature of the driving force.

Because of their dual purpose of limited or full rotation design, stepper motors are not suitable for high-speed continuous rotation. They are mainly built for positional rotation in steps. Reversing the intent of the motor from a consumer of electrical energy pulses to the production of pulsed electrical energy, much like a magneto is limited in the amount of energy that can be created by the relatively low continuous rotation speed available with stepper motors.

Figure 11-18 illustrates the electrical output from a rotating Howard Industries 3.6° step motor. The multiple spike pattern is due to the large number of poles that a stepper motor uses to move in discrete rotational increments. A typical 7.5° stepper motor has 12 poles, so each rotation generates 12 electrical pulses.

A plotting of the data tabulated for RPM and power through a 1200 Ω load (tabulated in Table 11-5) is depicted in Figure 11-19.

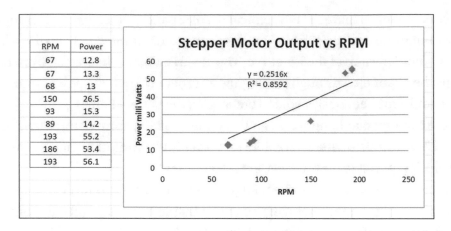

RPM	Power
67	12.8
67	13.3
68	13
150	26.5
93	15.3
89	14.2
193	55.2
186	53.4
193	56.1

Figure 11-19. *Stepper motor output power vs. RPM*

Figure 11-19 illustrates several considerations that must be addressed when using stepper motors to harvest energy from the experimental surroundings. Stepper motors usually have a mid-range "resonant" frequency at which their performance deteriorates, and excessive wear occurs. If a continuous rotation service is implemented, the rotational speed should be above or below the resonant frequency, which may be difficult in wind-driven operations but possible in moving water situations.

Using wind or water power to drive a brushed motor can produce a rippled DC current that can be smoothed with capacitors to supply a voltage regulator or battery charging circuit. To derive power from a larger brushless DC motor, you must add power to the source and measure the output with a rectifier to determine if a particular brushless motor is amenable to generator service. Figure 11-20 illustrates a method for testing high-speed motors for electrical generators.

Figure 11-20. *Testing high-speed motors as generators*

Ratcheting band clamps can fix a hand drill and a motor for testing into an aligned configuration on a benchtop for a rotational power generation test. In Figure 11-20, the motor is a brushed 1200 RPM 12 V DC unit (item A in Figures 11-13a and 11-13b).

At a rotational speed of 173 RPM, the motor power output was virtually undetectable. At 600 RPM (the maximum drill speed), the output rose to 1.93 V that could force a 1.60 mA current through a 1200 Ω load for a power level of 3.1 mW. A significantly higher RPM on the motor shaft is required to produce a larger power output.

Electrical energy production from generators created from new or used electric motors is inefficient. The low costs associated with the generator and driving force often warrant the development of these systems.

Summary

For sensitive or low-level measurements, the low-noise power available from the electrochemical reactions inside batteries is preferred.

Batteries are manufactured in rechargeable and single-use formats using one of six or so electrochemical processes in use today.

A battery's internal resistance is an important parameter that plays a large part in the rates at which the battery can deliver or receive electrical current and indicate the service life remaining in a specific device.

A microprocessor-controlled recharging station can avoid overcharging, the major cause of failure in rechargeable cells and battery packs.

Photovoltaic panels maintain the state of charge in batteries supplying power to experiments or processes in isolated or remote locations.

Wind and water-powered mechanical generators assembled from electric motors, although inefficient at power production, are driven by free sources of energy.

Many scientific measurements and experiments require high-voltage, low-current power sources that require care in handling, can be fabricated from low-voltage adjustable power supplies, high-frequency oscillators, high-voltage transformers, voltage doublers, and high-voltage rectifiers.

APPENDIX 1

List of Abbreviations and Acronyms

A/D	analog to digital
ADC	analog to digital converter
AGM	absorbed glass mat a form of lead acid battery
AMR	anisotropic magnetoresistance
API	application programming interface
ASCII	American Standard Code for Information Interchange
ASIC	application specific integrated circuits
AO	analog output
AWG	American wire gauge
BCD	binary coded decimal
BJT	a base junction transistor (NPN or a PNP)
BLDC	brushless direct current (a DC-powered motor)
BMS	battery management system
BoB	breakout board (adapter to use SMT IC with a prototyping board)
C4D	capacitively coupled contactless conductivity detection
C and C++	an efficient programming language and a variation for Windows applications
CCC	constant current charging
cGLP	current good laboratory practice (a QA/QC protocol)

(*continued*)

© Richard J. Smythe 2022
R. J. Smythe, *Arduino Measurements in Science*, https://doi.org/10.1007/978-1-4842-6781-3

CLR	current limiting resistor
CMOS	complementary metal oxide semiconductor
Ctrl	Control key
COM	serial communication port
cps	cycles per second
CPU	central or computer processing unit (main processor chip)
CPVC	chlorinated poly vinyl chloride
CR	carriage return in printer control code
CSA	Canadian Standards Association
CSM	current shunt monitor (ASIC for current measurement)
CSS	chip slave select (4 line SPI data transmission protocol)
CSV	comma-separated values a common file data storage format
CV	computer vision
DHCP	dynamic host configuration protocol
DI/O	digital input output
DIP	dual inline plastic (IC package description)
D/L	download
DMM	digital multimeter
DPM	digital panel meter
DSP	digital signal processing
DUT	device under test
DVM	digital voltmeter
EEPROM	electronic erasable programmable read-only memory
emf	electromotive force
EMI	electromagnetic interference
EPS	electric potential sensors

(*continued*)

ERH	equilibrium relative humidity
ESD	electrostatic discharge
FFT	fast Fourier transform or flicker fusion threshold
FOV	field of view
FID	flame ionization detector
FSD	full screen display or full-scale displacement
GND	ground
GPIO	general-purpose input/output
GPR	ground-penetrating radar
GPS	global positioning system
GPU	graphics processing unit
GUI	graphical user interface
HAT	hardware added on top (RPi add-on board)
HDMI	high-definition multimedia interface
HMI	human-machine interface
HTML	HyperText Markup Language
HTTP	HyperText Transfer Protocol
HTTPS	Secure HyperText Transfer Protocol
I^2C or I2C	inter-integrated circuit data transmission protocol
ICAP	inductively coupled argon plasma also ICP a spectroscopic source
ICFT	input capture feature of the timer (Atmega 328)
IDE	integrated development environment
IEPE	integrated electronics piezo-electric (vibration sensors)
IMS	ion mobility spectroscopy (plasma chromatography)
IMU	inertial measurement unit

(continued)

INS	inertial navigation systems
INU	inertial navigation unit
I/O or IO	input/output
IP	Internet protocol
IR	infrared
ISR	interrupt service routine (programming code)
ISRC	internal stray resistance and capacitance on a circuit board or IC chip
ITO	indium tin oxide
LAN	local area network
LCD	liquid crystal display
LDR	light dependent resistor
LED	light emitting diode
LF	line feed (printer control code)
LFP	lithium iron phosphate
LiMH	lithium metal hydride (a type of rechargeable battery)
LSB	least significant bit
MA	moving average (a form of DSP)
MAC	media access control
mAh	milliampere hours (sometimes mAh)
mcd	millicandela (measure of light intensity)
MEMS	microelectromechanical systems
MHz	megahertz (frequency of millions of cycles per second)
MISO	master in, slave out (4 line SPI data transmission protocol)
MOSFET	metal oxide semiconductor field effect transistor
MOS	metal oxide semiconductor
MOSI	master out, slave in (4 line SPI data transmission protocol)

(*continued*)

MPCLC	multiple plate capacitor load cell
MPPT	maximum power point transfer
MSB	most significant bit
NC	normally closed (relay or switch normal configuration)
NiMH	nickel metal hydride (rechargeable battery chemistry)
NIST	National Institute of Standards and Technology
NMR	nuclear magnetic resonance (a form of spectroscopy and the basis for medical imaging)
NO	normally open (relay or switch normal configuration)
NPN	a base junction transistor consisting of a P-type semiconductor between two N-types
NTC	negative temperature coefficient (used with thermistors)
OCV	open circuit voltage
OH-MPCLC	overhead multiple plate capacitor load cell
OS	operating system
PC	personal computer (IBM/Microsoft Windows OS)
PCB	printed circuit board
PDIP	plastic dual inline package
PE	polyethylene (a plastic)
PGA	programmable gain amplifier
PID	photoionization detector or proportional integral derivative (a control algorithm)
PIN	an intrinsic PN junction used in high sensitivity photodiodes, a thick light sensitive layer
PIR	passive infrared an infrared sensor
PLC	programmable logic controller
PM	permanent magnet
PNP	a base junction transistor consisting of a N-type of semiconductor between two P-types
PV	photovoltaic

(continued)

PVC	polyvinyl chloride (a plastic)
PVDF	polyvinylidene difluoride (an inert plastic polymer)
PWD	pulse width difference
PWM	pulse-width modulation
PZT	lead zirconium titanate
QA/QC	Quality Assurance/Quality Control
RMB-PUM	right mouse button pop-up menu
RC	resistor/capacitor (electronic circuit time constant elements) or radio controlled
RE	rare earth
REM	rare-earth magnet
rf	radio frequency
RFI	radio frequency interference
RGB	red, green, and blue (the three basic colors used in LED displays)
RH	relative humidity
rms	root mean square (a measurement form used with AC or sinusoidal power signals)
RPi	Raspberry Pi
RPM	revolutions per minute (a measure of rotation speed)
RTC	real-time clock
RTD	resistance temperature device
RTV	room-temperature vulcanization (describes a silicone sealant/adhesive)
SAR	successive approximation register (a type of ADC)
SBC	single-board computer
SC	specific conductivity
SCADA	supervisory control and data acquisition
SCC	short-circuit current
SCL(K)	the clock line designation in 4 line SPI data transmission protocol

(continued)

SCR	silicon controlled rectifier or strip chart recorder
SD	secure data (a plug-in digital data storage media/card)
SDA	I^2C serial protocol for slave data
SHE	standard hydrogen electrode
SLI	starting lighting ignition (a lead acid battery)
SOIC-8	small outline integrated circuit (8-pin SMT-defined package format)
SIP	single inline package (an IC with only a single row of power I/O pins)
SMBus	system management bus (one-wire serial communications protocol)
SMT	surface-mount technology
SoC	state of charge or system on a chip
SPAD	single photon avalanche diode
SPC	statistical process control
SPI	serial peripheral interface
SRAM	static random-access memory
SS	slave select
SSR	solid-state relay
TCR	temperature coefficient of resistance
TEC	thermoelectric conversion or converter
TEG	thermo electric generator
TIA	transimpedance amplifier
TIG	tungsten inert gas (a form of welding)
ToF	time of flight a form of distance measurement or mass spectrometry
tpi	threads per inch
TTL	transistor-transistor logic
UART	universal asynchronous receiver (transmitter serial data transmission protocol or IC)
UAV	unmanned aerial vehicle

(continued)

UI	user interface
URL	Uniform Resource Locator (an Internet address)
USB	Universal Serial Bus
UTC	universal time coordinates
VCO	voltage controlled oscillator
V_{cc}	the supply voltage for the circuit
Vdd	voltage drain (usually the positive supply)
VLS	visual light systems a communications technique
VOM	volt ohm meter
VRSLA	valve regulated sealed lead acid (a battery)
V_{ss}	voltage source supply (usually ground potential)
VVC	variable value component (a GUI screen numerical display of DAQFactory software)

APPENDIX 2

List of Suppliers

Chapter 2	AD8628	www.analog.com/media/en/technical-documentation/data-sheets/AD8628_8629_8630.pdf
	LMC6081	www.ti.com/lit/ds/symlink/lmc6081.pdf
	INA219	www.ti.com/lit/ds/symlink/ina219.pdf
	MCP3008	www.microchip.com/wwwproducts/en/MCP3008
Chapter 3	AD620	www.analog.com/media/en/technical-documentation/data-sheets/AD620.pdf
	SiC thermistors	www.adsem.com
	Melexis MLX90614	www.melexis.com/en/product/MLX90614/Digital-Plug-Play-Infrared-Thermometer-TO-Can
	MAX31855	www.maximintegrated.com/en/products/sensors/MAX31855.html
	AD595	www.analog.com/en/products/ad595.html
	AD594	www.analog.com/en/products/ad595.html
	FQP33N10	www.onsemi.com/products/discretes-drivers/mosfets/fqp33n10
	HC-501 PIR	www.mpja.com/download/31227sc.pdf
Chapter 4	OP505	www.mouser.com/datasheet/2/414/OP505A-42094.pdf
	OPT101.	www.ti.com/lit/ds/symlink/opt101.pdf
Chapter 5	A1326	www.allegromicro.com/en/Products/Sense/Linear-and-Angular-Position/Linear-Position-Sensor-ICs/A1324-5-6

(continued)

R. J. Smythe, *Arduino Measurements in Science*, https://doi.org/10.1007/978-1-4842-6781-3

	AA005	www.nve.com/Downloads/analog_catalog.pdf
	HMC1001	https://aerospace.honeywell.com/content/dam/aero/en-us/documents/learn/products/sensors/datasheet/N61-2056-000-000_MagneticSensors_HMC-ds.pdf
	LSM303DLHC	www.st.com/resource/en/datasheet/lsm303dlhc.pdf and www.adafruit.com/product/1120
Chapter 6	BMP180	www.adafruit.com/product/1603
	OP165A	www.ttelectronics.com/TTElectronics/media/ProductFiles/Optoelectronics/Datasheets/OP165-166.pdf
	BPV11F	www.vishay.com/docs/81505/bpv11f.pdf
	HC-SR04	https://learn.adafruit.com/ultrasonic-sonar-distance-sensors
	VL53L0X	www.pololu.com/product/2490
	LSM303DLHC	www.st.com/resource/en/datasheet/lsm303dlhc.pdf
	ADXL345	www.analog.com/media/en/technical-documentation/data-sheets/ADXL345.pdf
Chapter 7	LM317	www.ti.com/lit/ds/symlink/lm317.pdf
	TL074	www.ti.com/lit/ds/symlink/tl074.pdf
	TL084	www.ti.com/lit/ds/symlink/tl084.pdf
	DHT11	www.mouser.com/datasheet/2/758/DHT11-Technical-Data-Sheet-Translated-Version-1143054.pdf
	DHT22	www.sparkfun.com/datasheets/Sensors/Temperature/DHT22.pdf
Chapter 8	MFP102	www.onsemi.com/pub/Collateral/MPF102-D.PDF
	2N5116	www.mouser.ca/datasheet/2/68/2n5114-5116-42739.pdf
	2N3819	www.onsemi.com/pub/Collateral/2N3819-D.PDF

(continued)

	FQP27P06	www.onsemi.com/pub/Collateral/FQP27P06-D.PDF
	HFP730	www.huashan.com.cn/products%20catalog/english/MOS/HFP730_en.pdf
	2N7000	www.onsemi.com/pub/Collateral/2N7000-D.PDF
	RFP50N06	www.onsemi.com/pub/Collateral/RFP50N06-D.pdf
Chapter 9	FQP30N06L	see above
Chapter 10	DS1307	https://datasheets.maximintegrated.com/en/ds/DS1307.pdf
	HD44780	www.sparkfun.com/datasheets/LCD/HD44780.pdf
	TMP 36	www.analog.com/media/en/technical-documentation/data-sheets/TMP35_36_37.pdf
	LM 35	www.ti.com/lit/ds/symlink/lm35.pdf
Chapter 11	28K077	www.amazing1.com/content/download/28K077-28K074-28K089.pdf
	1N4007	www.vishay.com/docs/88503/1n4001.pdf
	2N3055	www.onsemi.com/pub/Collateral/2N3055-D.PDF

Index

A

Absorbed glass mat (AGM), 624

AD595/Arduino/RPi temperature
monitoring, 145

Alkaline cells, 622

Alternating current (AC), 87

Alternating current/direct current
(AC/DC) motors, 420

Alumel, 112

American Wire Gauge (AWG) system, 530

Ammeter, 46

Amperes, 45

Ampere's law, 269

Analog to digital converter (ADC),
179, 182, 451

Anions, 381

Anisotropic magnetoresistance (AMR), 272

Application program interface (API), 334

Application-specific integrated circuits
(ASIC), 114, 271, 377, 567

Aqueous conductivities, 391

Arduino-based conductivity
measurement systems, 405

Arduino microcontroller, 351

Arduino sensor data stream, 142

Arduino TEC testing system, 132

Artificial lighting, 171

asctime() function, 136

Astable oscillator, 9

Atmospheric pressure, 523, 524

Autoranging measurements, 18
calibration, 21
devices, 20
observations, 20
software code, 19

B

Batteries, 617
capacity, 619
chemistries, 620
manufacturers, 662
primary, 620
rechargeable, 620
recharge secondary cell, 630, 632–634
variations, 631

Battery cell electrochemistry, 661

Beer-Lambert law, 177, 217

Betalains, 177

Bifilar/two-wire pendulum, 329

Binary coded decimal (BCD), 567

Bourdon pressure gauges, 527

Breakout boards (BoB), 568, 574

Burden voltage, 46

C

Cadmium sulfide (CdS), 174, 181

Cadmium sulfide/selenide light-sensitive
resistor, 190

Capacitance, 1

© Richard J. Smythe 2022
R. J. Smythe, *Arduino Measurements in Science*, https://doi.org/10.1007/978-1-4842-6781-3

M

Q

R

Printed in the United States
by Baker & Taylor Publisher Services